The Memoirs of Cordell Hull

THE MACMILLAN COMPANY
NEW YORK · BOSTON · CHICAGO · DALLAS
ATLANTA · SAN FRANCISCO

MACMILLAN AND CO., LIMITED
LONDON · BOMBAY · CALCUTTA · MADRAS
MELBOURNE

THE MACMILLAN COMPANY
OF CANADA, LIMITED
TORONTO

The Memoirs of
Cordell Hull

IN TWO VOLUMES

VOLUME I

New York

THE MACMILLAN COMPANY

1948

History

First Printing

To My Wife
FRANCES

AUTHOR'S NOTE

In the preparation of this book I had throughout the assistance of

ANDREW BERDING

(Lt. Col., U. S. Army, Res.; M. A., Oxford)

Without him this book would not have been written. I owe to him a

lasting debt of gratitude.

Foreword

IN THE WRITING of these memoirs the advice of many of my old associates has been of inestimable value. I particularly want to acknowledge the contribution of Green H. Hackworth, Leo Pasvolsky, and Carlton Savage, who have counseled on this work from its inception. Dr. Allan Nevins provided helpful guidance from his profound historical learning.

Many others have been of great help by reading chapters, furnishing advice, or providing facilities in fields in which they played a part. They are:

Dean Acheson, Ambassador George V. Allen, Ray Atherton, Joseph W. Ballantine, Jacob D. Beam, William E. Beard, I. D. Beasley, Charles E. Bohlen, Ellis O. Briggs, William C. Bullitt, Hugh S. Cumming, James C. Dunn, Herbert Feis, Joseph C. Green, Harry Hawkins, Loy W. Henderson, John D. Hickerson, Stanley K. Hornbeck, Frederick Livesey, Breckinridge Long, H. Freeman Matthews, Harry McBride, Michael J. McDermott, H. B. McGinness, William D. Moreland, Jr., Harley Notter, Dr. Matthew W. Perry, William Phillips, Charles Rayner, James W. Riddleberger, the late Leo S. Rowe, Francis B. Sayre, E. Wilder Spaulding, C. W. Taussig, Frank C. Walker, John E. Walker, and Sam E. Woods.

Colonel Berding was assisted by a staff consisting of Louis E. Gates, Mrs. Virginia Fox Hartley, and Miss Marian L. Griffith, to whom I pay tribute for earnest, skillful, and impartial work.

I acknowledge gratefully the cooperation of the Department of State in making the records during my tenure in office available to us.

I acknowledge the kindness of the Brookings Institution and of the Carnegie Endowment for International Peace in making office space available.

I have quoted extensively from memoranda of conversations I had with representatives of other governments but I have attempted to give the main points of these conversations rather than the texts. In the same way, while drawing upon telegrams and other documents, I have sought to give their substance rather than to use them as texts. I have tried throughout to make these memoirs a narrative rather than a textual presentation.

Wherever possible, I have sought to simplify terminology—for instance, using the popular term "State Department" rather than the official title "Department of State," and "United Nations Declaration" rather than the official "Declaration by United Nations."

It has taken exactly two years to complete these memoirs. While they do not pretend to cover every item of our foreign relations during my nearly twelve years in office, I do not believe that any important development has been omitted. I have narrated events as I saw them and have drawn conclusions in the light of those events at the time. I have tried to be as frank, impartial, and accurate as is humanly possible.

CORDELL HULL.

Contents

VOLUME I

Part Four NEUTRALITY AND SELF-DEFENSE (1939–1941)

VOLUME II

Part Five THE YEAR OF WAR (1941)

Part Six DIPLOMACY IN WAR (1942–1943)

Part Seven THE LAST YEAR (1944)

Part Eight PEACE AND AFTER (1939–1945)

Part One

TENNESSEE AND CONGRESS

(1871–1933)

1: Cabin in the Hills

I WAS BORN October 2, 1871, in Overton County, Tennessee, on the ridge between the Wolf and Obed rivers, among the foothills of the Cumberland Mountains. A small log cabin rented by my father was my birthplace. This, somewhat enlarged by a lean-to, fronted immediately on the dirt road. From the porch behind it planks led to another log cabin containing the kitchen-dining-room. There was no porch then on the front of the house. Whether there were glass windows, I do not remember; but at that time many of the neighboring cabins lacked them. They had holes in the walls for windows, and shutters to keep out bad weather.

Our cabin stood about a mile from a small country store, the only store in the entire section. This was also the post office, called Olympus.

My father was farmer William Hull, one of the fourteen children of farmer Allen B. Hull and Serena Maynard Hull. Allen Hull had been a soldier in the Mexican War, which ended before he could reach Mexico. His ancestors came from Asheville, North Carolina, just prior to or immediately after the turn of the nineteenth century, and lived near the western border of east Tennessee, in Overton and Fentress counties. I have not attempted to trace them back to their old country, but it would seem my father had an English name. Though I have seen it stated he had Cherokee blood, this is not true. My forefathers on both sides were all poor, but law-abiding and honest. I never knew of any bad characters among them.

Father was thirty-one years old when I was born, having been born in 1840. He was of slightly less than medium stature and weighed one hundred and forty to one hundred and fifty pounds, but he was very powerful and could handle much larger men than he. He was of rather dark complexion and had black eyes.

During the Civil War a band of "Yankee guerrillas" shot Father, killing a man who was with him. The bullet entered between Father's right eye and nose and passed out at the back of his head. He fell to the ground near the house of a woman named Loveless. Mrs. Loveless threw her apron over his head and cried to the guerrillas: "Don't shoot again. He's dead!" They left him lying there.

Father's life was despaired of for a long time. His father knew something about medicine, though he did not practice it but helped out a

3

neighbor whenever required. It may be that this knowledge aided in saving Father's life. At the end of the war he had partly recovered, although the sight of his right eye was destroyed and the wound never healed, keeping him in constant misery. Having ascertained the name of the person —Stepp—responsible for the deadly attack, he pursued him through portions of two states, and finally ran him down, a considerable distance away in what is now known as Monroe County, Kentucky.

When Father came upon him, Stepp tried to be friendly and said, "Why, hello, Bill." Father went straight to him without ceremony and shot him dead. I do not know what was said first. My father was never any hand at talking about it. Now and then someone would draw him out and I would overhear a remark. After he came back home from Kentucky, nobody ever said anything against what he had done. No one ever thought of prosecuting.

Father, most grateful to Mrs. Loveless for saving his life, went to see her from time to time and gave her some financial aid. I have heard the story that some years later, when I was a judge, Mrs. Loveless came to me and asked for money at the same time that her son was reported to be charged before me for an offense. The story goes that I gave her one hundred dollars and then fined the son fifty dollars. This is fiction.

At the time of his marriage, Father was without means. His father worked a mountain farm near Clear Fork River in Fentress County. Father rented the small farm where I was born and, to work it, bought a horse on credit for fifty dollars. He possessed unusual common sense and remarkable energy. He rose at four o'clock in the morning the year round and was off to work before daylight. My earliest memories of Father are seeing him at various kinds of work about the farm, either plowing or clearing the land or hoeing or harvesting. He devoted his entire life to work or business, but he always took an interest in community affairs. After he had gotten on his feet in a business way, he became definitely interested in politics.

Soon after his marriage in 1867, Father for a short time had some connection with a little "one-gallus" still. He set this up, a mile or so from our house, in Buncomb Cave, a deep cavern whence flowed a creek. In later years stilling was naturally looked upon more critically, but in our section at that time it was not considered bad conduct to still. People had been accustomed, from the beginning of the Government, to the freest exercise of this practice and thought little or nothing about it. A number of people in the ridge country stilled whisky for their own use, but also sold and bartered some so as to have a few items of food and clothing. Until the Civil War there was no tax on making whisky. When the war came the Government put a tax on it because it needed revenue. Everyone in our section looked upon the tax as an outrage, an infringement of human rights, popular rights, and everything else.

My mother, who was thirty years old at my birth, was Elizabeth Riley Hull, daughter of Isaac Riley and Lucy Flowers Riley. Her great-grandfather, James Riley, from Virginia, fought in the Revolutionary War. Her people, who were of Irish origin, came from Fauquier County or thereabouts in Virginia soon after the Revolutionary War, and settled along the western base of the Cumberland Mountains, some on one side of the Tennessee-Kentucky line, some on the other.

Mother was of medium stature and weight, with fair complexion and brown eyes. Like Father she was exceedingly industrious. I vividly remember her spinning and weaving. She had to make clothes for seven persons, including herself.

Most of the people, young and old, in that section wore homespun. Every family able to do so had a loom and a spinning wheel. When you rode past a farmhouse you could hear the whirring of loom and wheel. We children wore coarse, homemade shoes of thick cattle hide called upper leather. The old coonskin cap was just going out when I came along, and you could still see a few scattered ones in the mountains. It was hard to get hats. Many of the store goods around the time of the Civil War came over the mountains from Baltimore.

Mother had to do her spinning and weaving between housework and farm work, which included part of the milking. We children helped in all chores. She continued all these labors until she became too afflicted with inflammatory rheumatism. For years she suffered terrifically, and at last was confined to a wheel chair. Even then she sewed until her hands stiffened in the joints.

With all her work, however, she taught us our A B C's and the first portion of Noah Webster's old blue-back speller, which was current for generations in all public schools. She required us children to read the Bible as much as possible, and she herself read it constantly.

I was the middle one of five brothers. We had no sisters. My older brothers were Orestes (called Ress by the neighbors) and Senadius Selwin (called Nade). The younger brothers were Wyoming and Roy. The first four of us were born between 1868 and 1875, and Roy in 1881. Ress was three and a half years old and Nade just two when I was born. I was named Cordell after County Judge John M. Cordell, a special friend of my father. He lived two counties away, on top of the Cumberland Mountains. I never did see him, for he died before I got that far away from home. My nickname was "Cord." I have never known why my brothers were given their unusual names.

The section where I was born and spent my earliest years was exactly on the border line between the North and the South during the Civil War. It was a backwoods country seventy-five miles from a railroad, and was called the "Mountain Section." The roads were almost impassable during rainy spells, especially in winter and spring. We had to cross mountains, hills, rivers and creeks on any trip of many miles. Mud was axle-deep. During bad weather it was one of the most difficult places in the world to travel.

The people who lived there were of pure Anglo-Saxon, Revolutionary War stock. Many spoke King Alfred language, as I call it, meaning the early Anglo-Saxon or Saxon tongue. It was a sort of home-grown English. During the migrations from east of the Alleghenies, some people stopped on the plateau of the Cumberland Mountains, others settled amid the foothills on the western slope, and still others tarried awhile and then went farther west. During my youth the younger and middle-aged folk steadily migrated from our section to the West where they could take up free lands.

There was only one negro in the section where I was born, and he was the only negro there when that part of Overton County became Pickett County in 1881.

People in our section were deeply imbued with the teachings of Andrew Jackson, John Sevier, and other great patriots and warriors. They were taught Jackson's favorite motto, "I love my country better than my life." As a result they sent adequate numbers of volunteers to all our wars from the Revolution on down to the present generation. While emigration kept the ridge area between the Wolf and Obed rivers somewhat denuded of population, many great minds in law, religion, and business rose from these primitive and poverty-filled surroundings. The public spirit of the people was such that, aided by policies of public works, they were later to bring their section abreast of other more favored areas, acquiring macadamized highways, networks of telephones and radios, and thoroughly modernized school systems.

For several years during the Civil War bands of guerrillas and bushwhackers operated back and forth across the borderline, pillaging, robbing, and killing. They stripped the entire area bare of livestock and other movable property. Only old persons incapable of military service, widows, and small children were left at their homes. To them life was a perfect hell.

Feeling in that border area was very bitter during and for some time after the Civil War. I remember old soldiers telling me that, at least in some localities, everybody of military capacity was expected to go to the war. It really did not make so much difference which side he fought on. He had the privilege of selecting his own side, but could not lie around in the community shirking and dodging. He had to go out and fight.

One man had come into the far end of Overton County from somewhere back East, and for some time after the war began he lingered in the neighborhood where he was living. He was warned frequently to go to war but failed to do so. In due course, an officer commanding some soldiers on a recruiting mission shot and killed him. The dead man had a sweetheart named Fannie Webb. Soon afterwards, the officer made another visit to the community. When Fannie Webb heard he was in the neighborhood she took her pistol, got on a horse, and went out to find him. She went from one house to another until she located him. She promptly dismounted to enter the house, but she saw him coming out toward the gate. She moved directly toward him, drew her pistol, and shot him dead. This was an illustration, the telling of which made a deep impression on us boys, of the type of feeling that actuated persons on the border during the Civil War.

To combat intolerable lawlessness Ku Klux Klan groups were formed, composed at first almost entirely of Confederate veterans in disguise. They had to take the law into their own hands. In the beginning their actions were beyond reproach. Then bad elements crept into the organization, the Confederate veterans left it, and it quickly fell into disrepute.

The people in that section, especially after the Civil War, held definite political views. Those of the Confederate persuasion adhered to a man to the Democratic Party, while those of the Union persuasion, with some scattering exceptions, adhered to the Republican Party. In Pickett County it was possible for a candidate for county office to forecast within two or three votes the vote he would receive in a forthcoming election. That seems incredible, but it occurred. Each person stood solidly by his politics and religion.

Father and all of his people were Democrats of the strictest sect from the Civil War on. On Mother's side there were two sets of children. One set were Confederates and the other set, reared with them as part of the family, were of the Union persuasion. After the war the Confederate group were 100 per cent Democrats, and the other group 100 per cent Republicans; and they so remained. Both groups came back to the section after the war was over.

The people of our section were mostly Primitive Baptists and Methodists. They stood by their religion, but this does not mean that all were churchgoers. I do not recall any Methodist church building in that area. We had to go between one and two miles to the Primitive Baptist church on Wolf River, though sometimes services were held in private homes. The preacher was generally a farmer who tried to make a living on a farm and also undertook to preach. He was known locally as "the preacher." Members of the church gave a little toward paying the preacher, but not much.

Sometimes they had a preacher come from a distance and then they held splendid meetings. People went to the church from far and near. They walked or rode horseback or in wagons and carts. There were no buggies in the ridge country at that time. Young men joined up with their girl friends and went together to church. The boys wore stiff-standing paper collars, which on hot days were pretty well wilted down by the time they got to church walking or riding. I shall never forget the solemnity and fervor with which those people sang the hymn, "How Firm a Foundation."

If a person was "skeptical," he was promptly discovered and branded as an infidel, which rendered him somewhat unpopular and at that time deprived him of the right to testify under oath. Such persons were few and far between.

The social life in the ridge country revolved largely around the church and around log-rolling, house-raising, and corn-husking for the men and quilting bees for the women. Neighbors would come together to help a farmer build his cabin by laying heavy timbers one upon another. The work done, they had feasts of good things to eat and some would drink.

The farmers who had located on the Obed or Wolf River bottoms were considered in fairly good circumstances, provided they kept out of debt. A few of them subscribed to weekly newspapers. In that area scarcely anyone saw a daily newspaper before he was full-grown. The people like us, who lived back in the sparsely settled ridge country between the rivers or on the mountain, did not have the same means of livelihood, and suffered many privations.

It was in this region and among these people that my father undertook to make a living and rear a family.

2: Work and Learning

WHEN I was about four years old we moved from the cabin where I was born. Father gave up the farm he was renting and bought a new place on credit down on the Obed River, three and a half miles southwest. He had been looking for some time toward moving to the richer river-bottom land. The small farm up on the ridge had given him and his family a bare livelihood and just a little more to make the part payment on the new farm. He figured he could do better than that down near the river.

The river-bottom farm, however, had no farmhouse, and we stopped for more than a year in a small log cabin a mile from our first house, until one could be built. Father hired a local carpenter to build it, but he himself secured the lumber. While the house was in construction he started to work the new farm. About this time he began to get into the business of cutting logs and rafting them down the river. And that was largely the way he paid for the farm, in small sums of ten dollars, twenty-five, or fifty.

For several years Father had very little competition in the timber business. In that region were almost unlimited growths of poplar, walnut, oak, ash, cedar, and hickory. When crops were laid by in early summer, Father cut logs, hoisted them onto strong wagons drawn by oxen, and hauled them to the river, sometimes as far as three miles away. Once at the river's edge, he put the logs, one by one, into rafts during late summer and fall. When the rivers rose in winter and spring, he took the rafts down the Obed River to the Cumberland River at Celina, and then down the Cumberland to Nashville.

We brothers had to do our share on the farm. As we grew old enough to work, we got up long before daybreak and, with Father, fed the livestock and milked the cows. Then, as we washed our hands and faces in the branch, Mother would call: "Come to breakfast and bring your chairs." This last acknowledged the fact that we did not have enough chairs for our few rooms and had to carry to the table those we had been using elsewhere. The moment breakfast was over we were on our way to the field or woods—still before the break of day.

I was too young at first to help with the logging, but the garden and truck patch had to be worked. As our years increased, our tasks grew too.

Until we were eight or nine we had chores to do about the house and truck patch. When we were ten we worked in the cornfields and on the farm in a light way. Likewise with the logging. When we were ten to twelve we helped haul logs down to the river's edge. We guided the oxen, walking alongside them. At this age we also helped assemble the logs into rafts. But we were not considered suitable hands at running rafts down the river until we were fifteen or sixteen.

Shortly after moving, Father hired a young man named Newton Staley to come out to our house and teach us during three and a half months of winter and early spring. He also let two or three neighbors send their children to this school. We all sat in the front room, and school went on throughout the day. Staley, and Hiram Craig, who succeeded him, did no work on the farm, for those were the months when little work could be done. Their job was to educate us, and they kept at it all day long. For two or three years they taught us the three R's, with some history and grammar. At night we studied by the light of tallow candles made at home.

In the summers, beginning at the age of six, I went to a free school at Harrison schoolhouse with my two older brothers, Ress and Nade. The school was about a mile and a half from the farm, and of course we had to walk. The term began between the first and middle of July and lasted until October 15th.

But life on the farm was not all work or school. We used to fish, and we hunted and trapped fur animals. Children in that section grew up close to nature. We knew the different trees and plants by name, and the animals, fish and fowl. Saturday afternoons and nights were the times for our hunting or trapping. We caught fox, coon, possum, and other fur-bearing animals. Taking the furs to the little country store, we often exchanged them for Christmas gifts for one another and for our parents.

I did not go to a county fair until I was fifteen years old. After that we would occasionally get together a wagonload of friends and go to one twenty miles away over very rough roads.

Occasionally I attended shooting matches, though my eyes kept me from being a good marksman myself. The matches were held in a field against targets at twenty-five paces for free shooting standing up, and forty paces for shooting from a prone position. Farmers taking part put up a beef as a prize, generally cut into five parts. The winner of the match took the best part, then on down the line to the least-favored section, which was hide and tallow. A remarkably good shot might, as we called it, "walk away with the beef on the hoof," meaning that he won all the cuts.

The logging had its interests too. We would hitch three or four yoke of oxen to a wagon and haul all-size hardwoods, generally from two and a half to four and a half feet in diameter and from ten to sixteen feet in length. We got them into the river one at a time and there put them in the form of rafts. We took hickory binding, called waling—these were hickory saplings split in half, between fifteen and twenty-five feet long— and bored holes through them and drove pegs through the holes into the logs to bind the logs into rafts. A raft would be fifty yards in length or less to run down a small river like the Obed.

Four or five years after buying his new place, Father built a small store on the farm, just to the side of a public road that wandered up and down the river and around the edge of the farm. There he ran a country store with the aid of clerks; he himself only supervised it. A post office was established in the store. Generally a post office was put in a store so that people could get their merchandise and mail at the same time and place. It was the custom in that section to call the post office after a local person. This one was named Hull.

I had to help about the store when I was not at school or at work on the farm. And when I was eleven or twelve I used to clerk alone in the store. Sometimes a customer would come in and ask for the man in charge. I would reply proudly, "I am the man in charge." The store had great fascination for us children because of its seemingly inexhaustible stock of tools, candies, toys, and other things that were marvels to a backwoods boy.

From the age of nine until twelve I was given a chore which tested whether such a boy would be afraid. It was my lot to take a turn—a bushel and a half—of corn or wheat on a horse or mule to a water mill four miles away. The journey lay through a thickly wooded and sparsely settled community. Often darkness overtook me. I had to find my way through heavy woods in the blackness, and returned home far up in the night.

The quiet woods are more filled at night with sound than a large city, and a low-hanging branch is as menacing as a robber band; but my recollection is that I was not scared. The journey, in the comforting companionship of horse or mule, was always completed.

One day when I was nine or ten, I was with one of my brothers on a bank of the Obed River when suddenly a man and a woman appeared in a buggy, in the back of which lay a small coffin. One of their children had died, and they were on their way to the family burial place. But the river was swollen, and they could not ford it. There were no ferryboats, much less bridges, in that locality. They besought my brother and me to help them, and we readily agreed. We had two canoes which were carved out of halves of poplar trees. These we placed parallel to each other a distance apart equal to the width of the buggy. We unhitched the span of horses and lowered the buggy down the bank until it rested in the canoes. Then we led the horses to the water and paddled the canoes across the swift running stream, with the horses swimming alongside us held by their bridles. The bereft parents were most grateful.

On one occasion I myself came perhaps near death when a team of horses I was driving ran away. Nade and I were each driving two-horse wagons, Nade being in the lead. The harness had a breast yoke with a ring that hooked over the tongue and was fastened there. This enabled the horses to hold back the wagon except where the hills were steep enough to require us to put rocks under the wheels or in cases where the wagon did not have brakes, which it did not always have. On this occasion we were driving down a slope or slant in the road. Suddenly, at the steepest point on the small hill, the breast yoke of my team got loose and automatically slid back on the tongue, with the result that the wagon leaped forward and bumped against the horses. They promptly jumped ahead and started racing down the slope. Holding the rope lines, I sprang from the wagon to the side of a steep bank. But the lines became entangled in my feet and jerked me back under the wagon. A hind wheel or wheels passed over me, and the lines dragged me along until the runaway horses ran into and somewhat up on Nade's wagon and came to a standstill. I found myself much messed up and bruised but fortunately not seriously hurt.

With what we boys grew and what we hunted and trapped, we had no great need for money. Two hundred and fifty dollars was a great sum. It was then a good year's salary.

Father's farming and especially logging and rafting now began to pay. After years of grinding work he at last could see profits.

In the spring of 1884, when I was twelve and a half years old, we moved again. Father had bought a bigger farm at Willow Grove, in Clay County, some eighteen miles below on the Obed River. The Willow Grove country was a somewhat larger farming section, although without any more facilities for ingress and egress than existed back in Overton County.

There Father continued his farming and above all his timber work. And my brothers and I had to do our share. He still did a good deal himself, but was able to hire men to help him, and he spent much of his time overseeing their work of farming and logging. Some time before this, Father got a hired girl to help Mother with the housework.

I briefly attended free school at Willow Grove, a little over two miles from the farm, and then was sent back with Ress to Byrdstown, the county seat. There I went to a subscription school under Professor John A. Capps for four months in the first part of 1885. We boarded part of the time in a private house and part in a little hotel. Our crude homemade clothes, including heavy white wool socks knitted by Mother, marked our origin, and some of the wealthier students held aloof from us. The same reception was to occur at later schools as well.

Byrdstown is most memorable to me because there I attended my first court session. This was a district circuit court which came periodically and tried all types of cases, both civil and criminal, right up to murder cases. I used to listen to the lawyers' arguments and examinations and the judges' charges, following raptly every word of what was said. It was then that I first thought to become a lawyer.

After the term at Byrdstown I returned to the farm and then, in July of 1885, again entered the free school at Willow Grove. The parents of the Willow Grove section were generally farmers, with very limited education, but they were deadly in earnest that their children should get the utmost from their schooling.

It was they who established a debating society at the schoolhouse so that their children could develop themselves in debate. They attended the debates and followed the arguments closely and seriously. They would not stand for levity. I remember that at one debate various parents rose and protested that some of us had not fully prepared our arguments. In my first effort to speak before this society I was so excited that I remained completely speechless and sat down without having uttered a word.

In one of the debates, in 1885, however, I not only made what was thought to be a really good showing, but started my career on its way. I was given the side of Washington in the question whether Washington did more for America by defending it or Columbus by discovering it. During the whole week I spent every minute of my spare time working on my argument. Wherever I was, I was working on my speech. I looked up every reference I could. I marshaled every point. I was determined to put it over if it were possible.

When the night of the debate came, the schoolhouse was crowded not only with parents and pupils but also with the schoolteachers of the entire county, who had been attending a convention at Willow Grove. I delivered my speech and handled my points in such form that I won the decision.

My father, who was present along with most of the parents of the region, was delighted. He thereupon decided that I should go away to the best school he could afford. Generally the children of the section were given only a few years of free schooling and then were put to work on the farms. Only a few who showed outstanding promise were offered a chance to go on.

This debate resulted in my being sent to Celina, county seat of Clay County, twelve miles away, where during the first five months of 1886 I attended Montvale Institute, at the edge of the town. Ress and Nade went with me. Ress was a good student, Nade was not of the same application.

Professor Joe S. McMillin was the principal teacher at Montvale and one of the chief inspirations of my early life. In my opinion no students ever made better progress in a five-month term under any teacher than we did under Professor McMillin. He was a brother of our own Congressman, Benton McMillin, who had already gained high rank in Congress. Benton had gone on the Ways and Means Committee, where for many years he fought against excessive tariffs and, during the last years, in favor of an income tax. Another brother, John H. McMillin, at Celina, was a brilliant lawyer and took the liveliest interest in public affairs.

Professor McMillin, comparatively a young man, was highly versed in public as well as in educational matters. He had taken part with old Confederate soldiers in discussions on government. Having a brother in Congress, he naturally developed valuable information about the national administration. Moreover, he himself had qualities of leadership that inspired his pupils. I have heard there was a motto on the wall of the Montvale school, "There is no excellence without labor," though I do not remember it. Labor there was indeed, but our real inspiration came from our great teacher, Professor McMillin.

At Montvale I studied algebra, geometry and trigonometry, a little surveying, advanced English, rhetoric, Latin, Greek, and German. The surveying was to come in handy in later years when, as a lawyer or judge, I had to handle or decide cases involving land boundaries. I found myself, as before, more attracted by mathematics, history, and literature than by languages and science. From before the age of twelve I could answer any question in the United States history textbook, footnotes and all, even such items as the names of the three Americans who captured Major André.

I reveled in biographies of the great philosophers, military commanders, teachers, statesmen, and orators of the ancient world. Some of us devoted most of our time to such reading, dwelling long on the epochal events of Egypt and Greece, Macedonia and Rome, coming on down to the Middle Ages with their Magna Carta, and then into the marvelous Renaissance. The Bible furnished us our early history, after which came Grote's "Greece" and Gibbon's "Rome." I vividly recall reading and rereading Aesop's Fables, which contain a fund of good, sound sense.

Like any enterprising young persons seeking knowledge, we managed in different ways, whether at school or at home, to get hold of some of the best known books, such as Shakespeare and "Pilgrim's Progress." We also had Milton; but he was too deep for most of us young people, though we got into some of his poetry and all of his prose. Pollok's "Course of Time" and Barnes' "History of the United States" and other histories were additional favorites.

Though I studied Latin and Greek, I found that my severest task was to learn good English. The language then spoken by most of the people of my section was not what would have been called the correct usage, though it has long since become up to date. I recognized good English in print, but had few occasions to use it in speech, for to do so gave a stilted impression and was quick to draw ridicule. This was a tremendous drawback in my learning to deliver stump speeches, and it took me many years to become fluent in extemporaneous speaking.

People who grew up in that section during the forty years' background of the Civil War, while suffering the terrific hardships and privations resulting from the war and Reconstruction, had a rare privilege—the benefit of the discussions of government and related questions between old soldiers congregated inside and outside the little country stores, on rainy days or on Saturday afternoons; and debates by the ablest men in public affairs. The big vital questions of government came under the liveliest discussion before, during, and for long years after the Civil War. Many of these old soldiers knew as much about government as high government officials and college instructors.

They infused the whole doctrine and spirit of individual liberty and freedom in the young people who were fortunate enough to listen to them

—and I was one. Partly as a result of absorbing the talk of these veterans, a few of us could answer virtually any question to be found in our political histories, and we knew the names and political records and doctrines of most of the Senators and leading Congressmen, the Cabinet and members of the state and county governments.

In these discussions, we boys learned to thrill to the military achievements of our State of Tennessee, to its constant readiness to respond to our country's call for whatsoever purpose, right from the very beginning. We knew how General John Sevier rallied the Tennesseans and, with the valuable aid of General Campbell and his Virginians, marched to King's Mountain and turned the tide of battle as well as the Revolution itself.

Tennesseans, in all subsequent wars, volunteered in larger numbers proportionately than the men of virtually any other State. This included the War of 1812, when General Andrew Jackson and his Tennesseans played their memorable part in the battle of New Orleans; and later, when former Tennesseans like General Sam Houston showed up in what was to be the Texas country and furnished a chief portion of the leadership in the struggle with Mexico for Texan independence. When the Mexican War came, all the States were asked to send volunteers in proportion to the number of their people. Tennessee's quota was 2,800. Actually 30,000 Tennesseans volunteered. This fact gave to Tennessee the name Volunteer State. This page of history was fervently preached to my generation by public speakers, teachers, and the old Confederate veterans.

Andrew Jackson stood out among all others as the hero of my youth —a great military commander and one who resigned more offices than were held by most Americans.

Here at Celina, amidst these new personal contacts and broader opportunities to secure information and ideas, I found increasing incentives to keep myself better informed about government and its affairs. At Celina I also continued the practice I had started at Byrdstown of visiting the courthouse when the district court held its periodical sessions. Whenever I had the chance I dropped in at the courthouse and listened with total absorption to the arguments of the lawyers and charges of the judges. Here I finally developed the definite purpose to become a lawyer. I was then fourteen.

It was at that age, and at Celina, that I saw my first daily newspaper. This was the Nashville *American*. In that year, 1886, a Senator from New

Hampshire, Henry W. Blair, introduced a bill for Federal aid to State education. That was the major issue in the 1886 campaign. I read about it avidly in the newspaper, and we discussed it among ourselves. The bill was considered to be an attempt to infringe on State rights and to give the Federal Government power to go down into the States and interfere with their educational systems. The amount of Federal aid the Senator proposed was only nominal at that time, but the incident is illustrative of how serious such issues could be in those days.

At Montvale I read a paper at commencement exercises entitled "Clothes Do Not Make the Man." Since then I have heard it said that I donned an old shirt to make the talk. Actually, I simply wore the one I always wore, called a hickory shirt because it was very hard-wearing. This was light blue, with white stripes, made out of cotton.

I also remember making a recitation, "Bingen on the Rhine," at an educational gathering. Years later I was traveling along the Rhine in a train with Mrs. Hull when suddenly I heard the porter call out "Bingen! Bingen!" There was the Bingen of my recitation, and seeing it "in the flesh" brought back my term at Montvale.

At Celina my brothers Ress and Nade, I and another student, Andrew J. Taylor—one of the neighbors' children who had attended school with us in our house on the Obed River—rented a two-room house in the residential part of the town. We did our own housekeeping, taking turn about at cooking. At the week end some of us brothers often walked the twelve miles to Father's house to spend Saturday afternoon and Sunday with him and Mother, and walked back again on Sunday evening.

To do so we had to cross the Obed River. Generally this was not too difficult if we could find a boat on the right side of the river. But sometimes there was not a boat on the right side and we would go hollering up and down the river until we found one. In the summertime one of us would just swim over and get a boat. That was a hard walk home because it was up and down many hills, including one very steep climb. When the rain came and the river was high, one of us would walk home, week end or not, because we knew Father might then be going down the river with a raft and Mother would need help at the house.

On September 1 of that year, 1886, I went with my brother Ress to the normal school at Bowling Green, Kentucky, for two terms until June, 1887. My trip to Bowling Green is memorable because I then saw my first train. Ress and I put a small trunk containing all our clothes in a covered wagon going to Nashville for a load of goods. This was at a time of the year when there was no river navigation. To catch the train we drove the seventy-five miles from Celina to Gallatin and slept in the wagon at night. When we got to Gallatin the second night we tied our horses up at the railroad station to await the train. A freight engine came along every fifteen minutes or so, and each time the horses jumped and snorted. We got no sleep.

We went to the Bowling Green school because we had learned about it from friends who had been there. Some very good teachers taught there, and we could learn wonderfully well. Also it was cheap. Father, who was then making more money, did not skimp us on expenses. He left the choice of school up to us, and he was getting along so well he would have put us into any school we might have selected. We chose schools, however, which did not cost too much. That was our idea of economy, which may have been a mistaken one.

At Bowling Green, Ress and I did our own housekeeping, or, as we called it, "kept batch." Our expenses for the ten months were $175 each, which included everything, train fare, board, lodging, and tuition. We took one meal per day at the dormitory of the school, which was called the "soup house."

In the summer of 1887 I worked on the farm; also at timbering and rafting. It was either in that summer or in the previous summer that an incident occurred which illustrates the constant care Father had for my improvement. Father, and Mother too, used every opportunity they had to give us instruction in morals and manners and to see that we got every other guidance possible. A noted educator had come out from Nashville and encamped for several days about eight miles from our house beyond Willow Grove. Father heard about his being there, rode eight miles there and eight miles back so as to see him and ask him to see me and talk with me. The educator consented, and accordingly I rode out and talked with him for three hours, asking many questions and getting as many instructive replies.

In the autumn of 1887 I read law for several months in John H. McMillin's office in Celina. Here the more active Democratic leaders throughout the county would congregate when in the county seat. I became acquainted with them and gathered much information and stimulus toward public affairs. But my health became impaired, and I returned to the farm.

About this time, at the age of sixteen, as a raft hand on a raft of Father's hardwood logs, I made my first trip down the Cumberland River to Nashville. I had already made several rafting trips down the Obed River to Celina, where the Obed meets the Cumberland, but never before down the two hundred and twenty miles from Celina to Nashville. On the Obed River our rafts would be fifty yards or less long, but when they reached Celina we more than doubled them up to go down the Cumberland. My first trip was with Father.

Ordinarily the trip to Nashville was some five days' run unless the pilot went by night as well. Many trained pilots, including my Father, could run as smoothly in the darkest night as in the daytime. The pilot stood on the stern of the raft. He had to keep watch for narrow turns and bends in the river and go around islands. At night he could see the bare outline of hills and mountains on the river, but from that outline he knew where he was and he could make the raft go where he wanted. He would call out to the raft hands on the bow which way they were to pull their long oars. Sometimes the rafts were so long the pilot could not make himself heard but had to signal with his arms. The pilot did not use an oar himself unless he got into a tight place.

On the raft we had an inverted **V**-shaped shanty, which served as a hut for pilot and raft hands. This we made of two forked posts on either end of a log. We ran a pole between the forks and let other poles taper down to the logs below. We placed rafters over them and covered these with coarse boards. At one end of the shanty we put a load of dirt so that we could build a fire without burning the log. We put straw in the shanty and there we slept, with our feet to the fire.

Our most dangerous moments arrived when the steamboat came along. Three steamboats weekly navigated the Cumberland from Nashville, and it was always risky to pass them. If the boat were rounding a point and put her stern wheel toward the raft in turning she threw high waves against it and might break it up. We would hear the boat whistle way down the river. We dreaded it, especially if we had to pass it in a perilous stretch of water.

On these rafting trips Father always paid me the same wages he paid the other raft hands—ten dollars per trip. Each of us also got a fixed amount of rations for the journey, generally a shoulder of hog meat, a sack of corn meal, a bag of Irish potatoes, a pound of coffee, and a gallon of sorghum. If we ran out of victuals we stopped the raft at one of the stores sparsely strung along the river and bought some more.

My first sight of Nashville—the first large city I ever saw—was from the raft. It was a sight to be treasured, one I shall always recall.

The buildings were more magnificent and the people more numerous than I could have imagined. Nashville was the metropolis of middle Tennessee, most of which was a bluegrass section. It was a large hardwood market as well as a market for livestock and farm commodities generally. It was then, as now, a noted educational city, sometimes called the Athens of the South. The city was calculated to impress, not to say overawe, the average young backwoodsman like myself who first visited it.

In Nashville I bought, secondhand, my first law books—Blackstone and Greenleaf, Stevens on pleadings, and others—paying for them out of my wages as a raft hand. These I later took with me to read in school and at nights and on Sundays, whenever I had a chance. On further rafting trips I also bought other books, such as sets of Gibbon's "Decline and Fall of the Roman Empire," Addison, Swift, and Grote's "History of Greece." I could never resist buying a good biography. These books absorbed much of the wages I received for rafting.

I came back from Nashville on the steamboat. We left at night, and the trip took two nights and a day. Later I made more rafting trips down the river to Nashville. I came to pilot a raft to Nashville well enough. I began to know every crook and turn in the river, every island, every towhead (small, half-submerged island), every "hard-pull," and every bad place. I also learned to pilot at night, taking turns with someone else.

In the summer of 1888 I made my first political speech. Though not yet seventeen years old, I had already listened to many political addresses. Now I was to make my own. The campaign between Cleveland and Harrison was engaged, the chief issue being the tariff, owing to Cleveland's tariff message of 1887. With an early bent for political matters, I took a sharp interest in the campaign and its issues.

I was asked to make my maiden speech by one Andrew Johnson, of that region, who later journeyed West. He and others had heard me make the winning debate address at Willow Grove over the question of Washington versus Columbus. They needed a speaker on the occasion of a combined picnic and public speechmaking in July or August at Willow Grove, and Mr. Johnson asked me to talk. The picnic was to have been a Fourth of July celebration but for some reason had been postponed. I remember to this day my opening sentence:

"The Fourth of July has already passed, and November will soon be here; then the American people will be called upon to go to the polls and decide on what policies this country shall be governed by during the next four and perhaps the next twenty-five years to come."

My speech must have been acceptable, because I spoke three or four more times during the campaign, including once at each of two county seats. Cleveland lost, but the campaign has its place in my story because I became even more impressed than before with the importance of the tariff question. I was later to devote much time and thought to the problem during my period in Congress and as Secretary of State.

I made my last political speech of the campaign at Jamestown, in Fentress County, while riding with Ress toward school in far-away Lebanon, Ohio. Father drove us in a wagon some eighty to ninety miles far back on the Cumberland plateau so that we could take a Cincinnati and New Orleans train to Cincinnati.

Up on the plateau we spent the night with Grandfather Allen Hull, the first and only time I recall seeing him. Traveling was so difficult in the mountain section that relatives only a few dozen miles apart went years without seeing one another. Grandfather Hull lived on a little farm on Clear Fork River. As I remember him, he was of comparatively small build, and, in conformity with the custom in that section, wore a full beard, then entirely gray. He spoke encouragingly about my education. He was to live to the age of ninety-one.

Next morning we drove on to the train, and in due course arrived at the National Normal University at Lebanon, Ohio, a few miles from Cincinnati. This, under Professor Holbrook, was the parent school of the one we had attended at Bowling Green, Kentucky. The normal schools founded by Professor Holbrook gave at that time splendid instruction. A boy could learn as much there as anywhere, within limitations. They did not have the curriculum of universities and colleges, but theirs was full enough.

I studied higher mathematics, including calculus, advanced rhetoric which covered all the best phases of literature, and some of the sciences. I also read the law books I carried with me. Both there and at Bowling Green I took part in the strenuous discussions held by the schools' debating societies. At Lebanon, for the first time in my career, girls took part in the debates.

In those years girls and social affairs were the least part of my life, which was filled with work and study. I had an ample number of girl friends, but there was nothing too serious, much less tragic, in any way in our encounters.

In attending this school I quickly realized the broader vision and understanding that one experiences who goes to an entirely new section of the country and is thrown with those who have different habits and ideas. It was wholesome and beneficial for a boy from the South to attend this school above the Ohio. The other students were from many states, both North and South, and a fine fellowship and comradeship sprang up among all alike.

Ress and I lived in the school dormitory. Our board cost us each $1.25 per week. We passed through Cincinnati on our way to and from the school, but did not visit the city.

Ress and I returned to Lebanon in September, 1889, but that winter I caught the grippe, in the first influenza epidemic noted in the United States. I went back to the hills of Tennessee to recover.

My literary schooling was now at an end. I have since regretted that my ardor for the law prevented completion of my academic education. In the following years I made efforts from time to time, largely through reading, to reach back into the past and fill the blank spaces of my education. But then I was eager for the law, the career of a lawyer, and the pursuit of politics that went with it. I could not wait. I was on the threshold of the next big step of my life.

3: Law, Legislature, and the Spanish War

WHEN THE 1890's began, my political career began too. Back on my father's farm among the Tennessee hills, I quickly recovered from the influenza I had contracted at Lebanon, and went on to Nashville for the remainder of the winter and until May to read law in the office of Pitts & Meeks. A schoolmate whose family lived in Nashville was a great admirer of this firm and had urged me to go there to study law with them and board with his family.

That summer of 1890 proved an important landmark in my life. I was then selected for an office that thrilled me more than any other since that time. Every two years the Democrats of Clay County met in the courthouse at Celina to reorganize the county committee. I was sitting there on one of the back benches when suddenly an old solid Democrat, John Hampton, a leading farmer and prominent ex-Confederate soldier, rose up at the proper moment and put me in nomination for chairman of the Democratic County Executive Committee. I was astounded. Mr. Hampton had seen me often about the county seat, particularly in John H. McMillin's law offices. Perhaps he had been thinking of me as chairman, but he had not talked to me about it. Before I could say a word I was elected. This was before I was nineteen years old, long before I was a voter.

Being chairman of the County Committee entailed innumerable tasks in organizing the rank and file of Democrats throughout the county. I rode horseback through all voting precincts during the campaign and talked to hundreds of well known Democrats and voters personally.

At about this time I began to build up what I called my political bible. I had heard an able man say, "A person can't ever amount to something unless he stands for something." I thereupon started to outline in my own mind what I stood for. In the course of my history studies, of which I was most fond, I had become greatly interested in Jefferson's philosophy and preachments. I took the basic principles of Jefferson and molded them into my own tenets of political thought and action. I learned from memory large extracts from the Declaration of Independence, Jefferson's first inaugural address, and the Bill of Rights in the Federal Constitution, modeled on the Virginia Bill of Rights.

I believed that the final achievement of the five hundred years' struggle for Anglo-Saxon liberty was written in these axioms and principles. They were to carry a strong appeal to me during my years in Congress and in the State Department. In speeches to the public, especially in many of my campaigns for office, I strove earnestly to impress on the minds of both young and old the incalculable value these precious rules and doctrines had for all persons aspiring to freedom or having the responsibility of maintaining freedom.

I suggested that these should be memorized by every schoolboy and girl, especially such living words as: "All men are created equal, . . . they are endowed by their Creator with certain unalienable Rights, . . . among these are Life, Liberty and the pursuit of Happiness . . . to secure these Rights, Governments are instituted among Men, deriving their just powers from the consent of the governed."

I believed that the sound principles of Jefferson's inaugural address were also worth memorizing, such as: "Equal and exact justice to all men, of whatever state or persuasion, religious or political; peace, commerce, and honest friendship with all nations . . . the diffusion of information and the arraignment of all abuses at the bar of public reason; freedom of religion; freedom of the press; freedom of person under the protection of the habeas corpus; and trial by juries impartially selected."

That same summer of 1890 I was named a delegate from Clay County to go to the State convention at Nashville to nominate a candidate for Governor. Another delegate and I drove seventy-five miles across country to Gallatin to get to Nashville.

For a young, passionate follower of politics like myself, the convention offered endless thrills all the way through. The contest was extremely sharp. Here occurred the first serious clash between the forces of the old-line regular Democrats and the Farmers Alliance, which was budding into what was later known as the Populist Party. During the several days of the convention I saw and followed exhibitions of every sort of parliamentary tactics and heard every brand of oratory.

The two leading candidates were Josiah Patterson, old-line Democrat, and John P. Buchanan, candidate of the Farmers Alliance. Buchanan gained the nomination. My delegation from Clay County supported Patterson in the convention, but gave wholehearted backing to Buchanan in the regular elections that followed. Buchanan won. This first convention is engraved in my mind today as sharply as the later conventions I attended right up to the 1924 National Democratic Convention, over which I presided temporarily until it was organized, and the 1932 convention that nominated Franklin D. Roosevelt.

After working on the farm the remainder of the summer, I read law that autumn and early winter in the office of John H. McMillin in Celina. The period in our district was one of great hardship; there was virtually no money in circulation, and the Farmers Alliance and Populism were rapidly taking root and spreading like wild honeysuckle over the country. I became so consumed with a desire for the fullest information obtainable regarding conditions in the nation and the operation of the governmental machinery at the national capital that when my Congressman, Benton McMillin, came through our section on his fall campaign for reelection I, by much effort, got hold of enough money to engage a span of horses and a buggy at a livery stable in Celina and drove him for seven days across the almost impassable sections of the Cumberland Mountains primarily to ask him questions. I defrayed the entire expenses of the trip. It was for me an opportunity to secure much valuable information that I greatly desired.

I learned many of my political lessons then and later at Benton McMillin's feet. Though not the greatest intellect, he was on the top level. He was one of the leaders in Congress and a splendid campaigner—a very fluent speaker, ready in debate and most attractive on the stump. He could recite facts and figures by the hour from memory. He was always in special demand in national campaigns. The Democratic Party sent him out all over the country, where he made excellent speeches.

While McMillin was in Congress I obtained from him a great deal of literature about Congress and the Government. I had found out how to write to Senators and Congressmen for their speeches. They always responded right away, for they liked to circulate their addresses. I read them with the keenest interest, whether I agreed with them or not.

In early January, 1891, I began my formal law education, entering the senior class of the Cumberland Law School at Lebanon, Tennessee. Since the roads were well-nigh impassable through the mountain country in the winter, I took a raft down the Cumberland to Carthage and caught a train to Lebanon.

The law course consisted of ten months, divided into two classes of five months each. One could enter the senior class directly by taking a very stiff entrance examination. This I did, and passed.

Cumberland Law School was a famous institution which had turned out many Senators and Congressmen—in fact, one of the greatest second-category schools in the country. There I enjoyed the teaching of three of the finest law instructors I have ever known at any institution of learning —Chancellor Nathan Green, Dr. Andrew B. Martin, and Judge Edward E. Beard. Young men came from many states to get the benefit of their instruction. When I went to Congress sixteen years later I found in Washington four or five Senators, one Justice of the Supreme Court and twelve to fifteen Congressmen who were graduates of Cumberland University.

At Cumberland I took the regular course in the prescribed textbooks. I participated in many mock court trials and in the lively discussions in the Philomathian Law Society. In June I passed the final examination and was graduated. According to custom, we members of the graduating class, the moment we received our diplomas, took them to the courthouse, where a district judge awaited us. He swore us in as members of the bar. I was not twenty years old. According to an Act of an early State Legislature, graduates of the Cumberland Law School could be admitted to the bar under the age of twenty-one—others could not.

I ran into my first law case on my way back from the law school— even before I reached my law office. While in school I had formed a law partnership with M. C. Sidwell, an older lawyer, at Celina; and I joined him at Willow Grove in trying this case, which had been brought some days before. The Justice of the Peace decided the suit in our favor. Then I went on to Celina, where I began practicing law with Mr. Sidwell. Our law office was located in a small frame building on the public square opposite the courthouse.

Since I was with an older lawyer, we had a very good practice right from the beginning. As clients came to me, I took their cases if they had an honest basis for contest. If the case was bad or seriously doubtful I so advised the client frankly. Rather than accept his case and take it to trial, I counseled him to compromise if he could. I remained in partnership with Mr. Sidwell one year and thereafter practiced alone while I lived in Celina.

In the summer of 1892, on some theory or other I conceived the idea of running for the State Legislature. I was still several months from being of age; the sitting member, Mr. Carlock, was popular; he lived in the one large county of the four comprising our district; and not one of my neighbors had urged me to run.

When I announced myself for the Legislature at a meeting of Democrats in the courthouse at Celina, I doubt that a single person there thought I could be nominated. After I made my announcement the meeting broke up, and the Democrats filtered down into the courthouse yard.

I approached several individuals and greeted each one, but no one said a word about my candidacy. They spoke about crops and everything else but. Instead of being discouraged, I dug my toes in and increased my determination to win.

At that time the selection of the nominee was made in a party, or delegated, convention; the primary system had not come into practice. I began to realize more fully my heavy disadvantage at a convention in being from a small county. Carlock, being from a large county, would have a far greater number of delegates pledged to him. I saw I stood a much better chance in a primary than in a convention.

I thereupon challenged Carlock to a public debate, which he accepted. Such debates were common in political campaigns in the nineteenth century. They aroused much interest among the voters and were well attended. I maneuvered to be able to speak first. This was not difficult because in such a debate each speaker generally wanted the second, or clinching, position.

In the course of my speech I drew from my pocket with some flourish a document I had carefully prepared in advance. I held it up to the full view of the audience and explained: "This is a draft agreement calling for the nomination of the Democratic candidate to be made at a primary election. If adopted, this means that all Democratic voters in the district will have a voice in the selection of the candidate, rather than a small number of delegates." Then, with another dramatic gesture, I proceeded to sign it in the presence of the audience. Finally I placed it on the table near my opponent and finished my speech by saying: "And now I invite Mr. Carlock to sign it too."

When Carlock rose to speak he began his regular set speech and did not refer to the paper lying before him in full sight of all. But as he approached his conclusion he began frequently to glance down at the document. He obviously was trying to make up his mind, and while doing so went right on talking. Every few sentences, another glance down at the agreement. This continued for many minutes and many sentences. Finally he announced he would give the proposal consideration later—and sat down. This ended the matter between us.

I then circulated the agreement among the members of the Democratic executive committees of the four counties. Three out of four signed it. In that way I took my opponent into the primary, and the campaign was on. I waged a vigorous fight. I bought a good bay horse from a neighboring boy, Bob Gilliland, and rode over the four counties seeing voters and making speeches. I did not know three people in Carlock's county; but I went over there, spoke over the county, and met many.

When the primary election came, I won, carrying each of the four counties. Carlock later became my loyal friend and supporter. I also won against the Republican candidate at the regular November election. I had become of age the month before.

Traveling down the Cumberland on a steamboat, I went to my first session of the Legislature in Nashville, the first week in January, 1893. I was dressed in a rather long, somewhat striped Prince Albert coat, and wore a large high-crowned broad-brimmed light hat. I recall this manner of dress because for a quarter of a century afterwards some of my friends did not allow me to forget it. I was at that time quite slender, nearly six feet tall and possibly a little gawky.

It so happened that one of the ablest members of the Legislature, with previous legislative experience, Ephraim Story of White County, had originally come from my section of the State. I promptly sought him out when I reached Nashville, with the result that he and I agreed to room together during the session. This association proved of much help to me. Story was chairman of the Judiciary Committee, of which I was a member. He brought home sheafs of bills each evening, and we went over these together until late at night.

When I entered the Legislature the State was still gradually recovering from the effects of the Civil War and Reconstruction, and there were no special developments in the political, economic, or social affairs of the people. My first session had no particularly outstanding matters of legislation on its program and passed without any unusual features.

I participated frequently in the discussions. I started in as chairman of the Committee on Enrolled Bills, but resigned because I preferred to be a member of the Committee of the Whole and of the Judiciary Committee and participate more in the debates. I declined any other committee chairmanships for the remainder of the session. When the Legislature was not in session I actively engaged in the practice of law in Celina and Nashville. About that time Father moved to Celina and bought a house.

The spring of 1893 is memorable to me because I then made my first trip to Washington, just after Grover Cleveland's second inauguration. I decided to visit Washington as many persons do, and also I sought to aid some of my friends who were applicants for positions in the new Administration.

In Washington, with Congressman McMillin, I called on President Cleveland, whose office in those days was upstairs in the Oval Room in the main White House building. Here was the first President in office I had seen. To a young man like myself, who had followed Cleveland's policies closely and had delivered political speeches for him at the age of seventeen, this personal meeting was one to be remembered long.

The President impressed me most favorably. He seemed very human and at the same time definite, clear, and positive in his conversation. He was democratic in demeanor. To me he had to his credit a number of outstanding achievements that gave him the deserved reputation of being on the limited list of exceptionally capable Presidents.

En route home from Washington the train stopped at Roanoke, Virginia. A friend and I got off to get breakfast, thinking we had twenty minutes to spare. Two blocks from the station we saw the train pulling out. We had to wait all day long for the next train and meantime had to send telegrams to locate our baggage which had gone on with the train.

At the end of the first session of the Legislature a friend and I bought a raft at Celina and took it down the Cumberland to Nashville to sell it. We expected to make a good profit, but unfortunately we were careless in navigation. One morning, when we were sitting in the shanty having breakfast, we heard a terrific crash. We scrambled out of the shanty. The river was well over its banks, in flood stage, and in coasting through an island chute we had banged into some trees. Before our dismayed eyes the raft broke up into good-sized blocks, which went floating away down the river. We remained standing on one.

A mad scramble followed. In a little bateau, or john boat, the only boat we possessed, we had to overtake the different blocks, one by one. We had to get them all together and land them at the same spot. We then had to bind them together with hickory bindings, or waling. It was not until two days later that we were able to get all the blocks assembled and bound together again into a regular raft. This delay and expense resulted in our getting just the same amount of money we had paid for the raft. We made no profit.

In 1894 I was renominated for the Legislature without opposition. During the campaign period I caught typhoid fever. I was laid up for some time and was not able to participate in the campaign except to make one speech at its close. I won the election, though this was a year of a Democratic slump and my majority was much cut down.

As the meeting of the Legislature approached, a very able and experienced member, John A. Tipton, became a candidate for Speaker of the House. I went to Nashville at his request to manage his campaign, and established a headquarters there. He and I and other friends finally succeeded in securing his election without opposition.

Having served on the Judiciary Committee among others in the preceding Legislature, my mind was set on the chairmanship of that committee. After Tipton's election, I soon discovered, to my surprise, that Samuel G. Heiskell, of Knoxville, another experienced legislator and an able lawyer, felt that he was entitled to the place, and that he had what he considered an implied commitment from Mr. Tipton. Heiskell had been urged by some for Speaker and would have made a formidable candidate, as Tipton well knew. I was much disappointed and displeased at this arrangement, made without my knowledge.

Tipton at once set about to reconcile the situation without strife or hard feelings among his friends. The result was an agreement that Heiskell would be made chairman of the Judiciary Committee, and that a resolution would be passed consolidating the important Corporations and Municipal Corporations committees and combining their functions, and I would be made chairman. In addition—and of great importance—I would be named ranking House member of the forthcoming Joint Legislative Committee on the election contest then pending between Governor Turney and H. Clay Evans, the Republican candidate. All these understandings, entirely satisfactory to me, were scrupulously carried out. I suggested nothing. The arrangements were suggested and offered to me.

Sharp bitterness arose in the contest for governor, which became overwhelmingly a party issue. Evans had received a few more votes than Turney, but Turney contended that many of Evans' votes were illegal in that they were cast by persons who had not paid the poll tax as required by the State Constitution and laws, or whose poll tax had been paid by the Republican Party. A small minority of Democrats, especially in east Tennessee, held that, since Evans, on the face of the returns, had a majority, he should be treated as duly elected. But the Democratic Party and its leaders generally gave their support strongly and enthusiastically to Governor Turney and his contention, which to a large extent was based on constitutional provision and a State law of some years standing to the effect that, as a prerequisite to voting, one must have paid a poll tax within a certain period prior to the election.

There yet remained in Tennessee many of the grievances and much of the bitterness and opposition growing out of the evils resulting from the Reconstruction policy. As late as the nineties, people still vividly recalled the time when all Confederate soldiers were disfranchised and troops were stationed at the polls to assure a majority vote by the densely ignorant elements of every kind, with no property interests. This balloting included the election of local officials who were notoriously incompetent and fell under the worst influences, with resulting maladministration destructive of the rights and interests of the better elements and property owners. It was under these circumstances that the Democrats, on securing control of the State government with the aid of a limited number of Republicans, wrote into the Constitution and laws a poll-tax qualification and provided that the proceeds should go into the common-school fund. It is sufficient for me at this writing, half-a-century later, to say that the conditions attending the adoption of this poll-tax Act have changed very greatly.

Any Democrat in the Legislature—except a few who were supporting Evans—would have given almost anything he had to secure the appointment as ranking member of the House committee on the election contest, which went to me. Certain bitter critics at the time circulated a report that no older and experienced member would have the appointment, on the ground that the contest was unpopular; that on account of my youth—I was then twenty-three—I did not know any better and allowed it to be put off onto me. This is absurd. The Democratic State and county organizations and virtually all the Democratic leaders and Press, as well as the party rank and file, stood overwhelmingly behind Governor Turney and his contentions.

The full Joint Committee decided to divide itself into subcommittees and assign them territories throughout the State to which to go and examine voters and election officials, taking proof of the ballots cast. I deliberately chose east Tennessee, where the real seat of the contest lay. There feeling ran high, and the area, being overwhelmingly Republican, was particularly antagonistic to our side.

We quickly encountered threatened clashes and threats of physical violence. From some counties such as Hawkins and Sevier, a few persons sent us warnings that if we went into those counties it would be just too bad for us. But we went just the same. We met demonstrations bordering on overt acts on the part of persons of known courage. In Sevier County early one night shots were fired in front of our hotel. But for six weeks we went on taking testimony, going from county to county and giving little open attention to the threats against us.

Accompanying us were John J. Vertrees, one of the great lawyers of the South, and Congressman Henry R. Gibson, leading counsel for Turney and Evans respectively. They became my lifelong friends.

It had been my function to introduce in the House the joint resolution authorizing the election contest. When we completed taking testimony in east Tennessee, it then became my duty to take the lead in carrying forward Governor Turney's side of the controversy in the House and in the House side of the joint proceedings. This I did as best I could, and made the opening speech. After much heated debate, the Senate and House voted. The successful outcome in favor of Governor Turney by a margin of votes easily calculated in advance has long since been history.

My experiences in this contest, especially during the month and a half I was out in east Tennessee taking testimony, were invaluable to me. I was brought into close contact with many Democratic leaders in the State and its subdivisions. I have always highly valued the standing it gave me then and during the years that followed. This is entirely contrary to the suggestions made by a few opponents that this experience was injurious to me.

I continued to practice law during my second term. Although offered a nomination for a third term, I declined because I desired to devote my time entirely to the practice of law.

During the campaign of 1896 I took the side of William Jennings Bryan in his famous split with Cleveland over the silver issue. Senator Harris of Tennessee, an unusually able man who belonged in the top group in the Upper House during the period after the Civil War, had gone with Bryan and the organized element in the party, as had also Benton McMillin, and the Democratic National Convention had sustained them. Hence I thought with Harris and McMillin for the reasons they gave on the silver issue, coupled with the fact that one can get nowhere outside an organized political party. I figured that, whatever the merits of the monetary question, it was wiser to keep with the party in its organized capacity, especially when the leaders in my area took the same view, and that we could accomplish nothing in the future if we split away from the party.

An abrupt interruption to my practice of the law came in the summer of 1898 with the Spanish-American War. I had followed with absorbing interest the events, such as the sinking of the *Maine,* which led to the conflict. Like many others in my district I was raring to do what I could to help the country. In those days, and earlier, if this country were seriously threatened by war, some young man or men in most localities proceeded to enroll companies of volunteers and to send word to the Capital that they were ready. This meant that, almost overnight, they would abandon their business affairs and leave with their command to be gone whatever length of time they might be needed.

I raised my company, H of the Fourth Regiment, Tennessee Volunteer Infantry, in Clay and adjoining counties in the spring of 1898, and was commissioned captain. We were wildly eager to leave at once, but waited and waited for the call. Wearing a heavy mustache that drooped at the sides, I drilled the one hundred and four members of the company throughout the summer of 1898. Meantime the First, Second, and Third Tennessee regiments were called up. We were in the second call, and finally it came.

I was in the courthouse trying a lawsuit when I received orders to report at Knoxville with my company. I sent messengers at once to the enrolled men scattered over several counties to muster at Celina two days later, and this they did. We were given a splendid reception and tearful send-off by the local people. We did not know how long we should be gone, and thought we should fight a real battle around Havana. I happened to be wearing a tie with stars on it. Someone took it off, cut it into pieces and distributed them to the people as souvenirs.

Some of my Republican friends in the regiment who kept close to the War Department at Washington assured me that our regiment was originally destined for the Philippines. All our officers and many of the men wanted to go to the Philippines. However, the First Tennessee Regiment was then stationed on the California coast, and its desire to go on to the Philippines could not be turned down. The result was that the First Tennessee did sail for the Philippines and we sailed from Savannah for Cuba later in the year. The war was already over.

We landed in the province of Santa Clara, forty-two years before my second visit to Cuba, when, in the midst of another and far greater war, I worked at the Havana Conference to help organize this hemisphere to protect itself against the aims of the Axis. We remained in Santa Clara on garrison duty for five months until May 1, 1899. I was in charge of the legal department of the Province, my task being to cooperate with the Cubans in getting a suitable local government restored and operating.

I quickly found that there were many practices ingrained in the old administration which I had to remove. For example, the registrar of written documents such as deeds and mortgages received his office from

the Spanish crown, and it went on down through the family from generation to generation. If a person carried an important instrument to him for
registration, the registrar would point to a great stack of documents he
always kept on hand, and say: "There are hundreds of documents ahead
of yours. It will take many days to get around to yours." If the applicant,
however, knowing what to do, replied: "Obviously you need more help.
Here is some money with which to hire it," the registrar would accept it
and say: "I'll see what I can do. Come back this afternoon." The applicant would accordingly return in the afternoon and find his instrument of
writing duly recorded.

On one occasion I took a four days' inspection trip on a pony across
the mountains through Jibacoa valley, a marvelously rich valley
through which a small river ran until it reached the coastal mountain,
where it went through a natural tunnel on to the plain and into the sea.
Great forests of mahogany and cedar stretched out there, while large
coffee plantations long neglected and abandoned because of the war could
be seen on the coastal side of the mountains.

I spent one night in the foothills with a family living under a shed
of bamboo bark. They had three or four children who had been born out-
doors amidst the hills while the family dodged and ran from Spanish
guerrillas. Large numbers of Cuban people in that area were in the lowest
stages of starvation, and many did starve.

While I was absent from my regiment working in the office of the
attorney general of the Province, some serious homesickness developed in
a few of our companies, fanned by several agitators. I discovered then
that a man does not reason when he is seriously homesick. The result was
that I had to give dishonorable discharge to a few in my company, but
generally the conduct was excellent. I lost three of my men through
sickness.

In Cuba I studied Spanish and learned to speak it a little, though in
later years it escaped my memory.

One of my frequent companions was the mascot of the regiment, a
little black dog called Nig, belonging to Lieutenant Clare Smith of my
company. He used to come into my tent while I was working and sit near
my feet and fall asleep. I would blow smoke from the cheroot I was
smoking into his face. He would wake up, give me a hard look, and then
walk in wounded dignity out of the tent, with one final glance of reproach
as he disappeared.

There have been published many accounts of poker playing among the officers and also among the men of my regiment while it had much time on its hands in Cuba. Ways of passing the time were at a premium, and many of us indulged in a social game of poker from time to time. I participated in my last game of poker the night before the Regiment was mustered out of the service in Savannah early in May, 1899. It is sufficient to say I had enough money left to buy my ticket home. I have not played the game since.

I owe a certain debt to the Spanish-American War. It brought me into contact with Latin America, the first of what were to become literally thousands of contacts. It gave me a better idea of the wider problems of relations to the world which would face the Republic from then on. Army life is so basic a change from civilian life that it afforded me a different outlook. Probably it increased my understanding of human nature. In any event, I was a broader man for that experience as I turned from the army back to civil life.

4: From Bench to Congress

WHEN I CAME HOME from the army, I felt I should widen the range of my law practice which had been twice interrupted, once by the Legislature, once by the war. My early career was indeed a struggle between law and politics. I had begun reading Blackstone before I was seventeen, but in the years that followed I proceeded to familiarize myself with the liberal political teachings of Coke, Milton and Locke, Pitt and Burke, and then Gladstone. Jefferson's teachings, sandwiched in between the teachings of other liberals, were proclaimed everywhere after the Civil War, especially in the 1890's, and I drank them in. Like many others, I carefully studied government from the Achaean League and the Athenian democracy down to the present. Each year I found increasing interest in such studies. I was prepared to participate in carrying forward the chief portion of William Jennings Bryan's preachments on domestic affairs, and later to give unstinted cooperation to President Wilson's progressive democracy. I considered myself a Gladstone liberal in the 1890's and moved forward with the Jeffersonians past the turn of the century.

All through the years when I was practicing law, I gave constant and serious attention to public affairs, and particularly their political aspects. I persuaded myself that I preferred law as a life profession; but I simultaneously took the liveliest interest in campaigns and elections. I did not take the initiative toward public office myself, however, with one exception. This was when I butted into the State legislative campaign and secured my first election to the Legislature. This was entirely on my own; no one had advised me to do so.

Nevertheless, right up to the time I went to Congress in 1907, I still had uppermost in mind the purpose to devote my life to the legal profession. Going to Congress meant the abandonment of law. But even then I kept in the "Congressional Directory," in my biography, the phrase: "is a lawyer by profession."

Pursuing my determination to broaden out, I left Celina at the beginning of 1901 and moved down the Cumberland River to Gainesboro, Jackson County. Colonel M. L. Gore, a personal friend, lived there. I entered into partnership with his lawyer son, John J. Gore, who was popular and possessed excellent native ability, a most agreeable personality, and a wide acquaintance. John Gore was a leading local Republican

37

who later became State senator and then made an excellent reputation as judge of the United States District Court of Middle Tennessee.

We began industriously, to say the least. Each night we worked until midnight or even two in the morning, and slept in the rear of our law office. We acquired a very good practice extending to a number of counties.

But once again my private practice was not to continue long. This time it was to be interrupted by the judiciary. In the spring of 1903, the presiding judge of the Fifth Judicial Circuit, W. T. Smith, one of the finest men I ever knew, came to me and very confidentially informed me he had decided to resign the judgeship and desired me to take his place on the bench.

I declined with profuse thanks. I was genuinely interested in my private practice, and besides I was not sure I was fully capable of handling large personal injury and other complicated cases in the railroad and mining section of the circuit. I had already had experience of being judge when, in 1898, during an illness of Judge Smith, the members of the bar, gathered at Livingston, elected me to occupy the bench until his return. I functioned for perhaps a week.

Judge Smith seemed disappointed at my reply but soon came back a second time and pressed the matter with unusual earnestness. I was in the act of declining again, but I observed that his feelings were being badly hurt, and as he was one of my most valued personal friends I finally accepted his offer with renewed expressions of gratitude.

The judicial circuit embraced ten counties. The bar of each county except one endorsed me with unanimity—and that one with virtual unanimity—to the governor, James B. Frazier, for appointment to fill the unexpired portion of Judge Smith's term. He thereupon made the appointment. I was a judge, and one of the youngest in the history of the State. I was thirty-one.

The task that confronted me was overwhelming. In each of my ten counties I had to hold one week-long—sometimes a two-week—term of court every four months. I had to travel by horse and buggy, and the roads through these upper Cumberland counties, several of which lay in the foothills of the Cumberland Mountains, were almost impassable during the winter and spring. In addition, most of the dockets were one to two years behind, despite the best efforts of Mr. Smith, a most efficient and able judge. When I went to Sparta, White County, to hold court for the first time, I found ten murder cases on the docket at the same time, all standing for trial. I had to work night and day to clear up the dockets. At times we would get into court in the summer as early as seven o'clock in the morning—never later than eight, summer or winter—and go on until late in the afternoon.

After court adjourned and I had had supper, I would go to the largest law office in town. When important cases were on hand, I remained there until far into the night, consulting the law books. The lawyers always extended me that courtesy, since I could not carry any books with me in traveling about by horse and buggy.

I doubled back on the circuit and held extraordinary sessions of court every time I had as much as a week to spare. As a result, the court for some time was in session virtually fifty-two weeks in the year. I never got home except when I arrived in my own county, Clay, to hold court.

I held my first court in White County where the docket listed a number of complicated cases. I was not very familiar with the personal injury law as applied to mining and railroad cases, since my law practice had been on the other side of the circuit, which was largely agricultural. And there in White County one of the first big civil cases I ran into was a hotly contested personal injury case involving many phases of mining law about which I knew little.

If either side had requested a continuance, I probably would have exhausted my discretion to grant the motion and thereby obtain time to study up the law. But to my disappointment both sides announced ready. In the course of the trial of several days I sat up two or three nights until chicken crow, running down the technical law to prepare my charge to the jury. The plaintiff won the lawsuit which was promptly appealed to the Supreme Court by the defendant. I was greatly pleased when my decision overruling a motion for a new trial was later affirmed.

I started out with a vigorous law-enforcement policy. I made short shrift of law violators, especially if they were chronic. This policy met with general approval except on the part of the lawless element. Sometimes I got reports of threats against me by criminals I had sentenced or who were under indictment, but I never gave them serious attention. I traveled by myself over that mountain country, covering long distances scores of times and at all hours of the night, but I never carried a pistol.

The story is told that one day a bumptious man appeared before me for some offense, and I fined him thirty dollars. He exclaimed facetiously: "O K , Judge, I've got it right here In my jeans." "And thirty days in jail," I went on. "Have you got that in your jeans too?" I do not recall the case in this form, but it is typical enough of some that appeared before me and the way I had to handle them.

Drunkenness was one of the worst problems I had to face. This seemed particularly true during court sessions. Court in session was a prime attraction to people of the county who came from miles around to witness the trials. And some of them would celebrate.

In one county seat of my circuit, when I adjourned the court at noon to go across the street for lunch, I could see a large number of men drunk in the public square. As soon as I returned to the courthouse, I called before me the grand jury which was in session in the courthouse at the time. "Go into the square," I ordered. "Keep your eyes open and observe who these drunken people are, and bring presentments against them." They did so at once. I had the sheriff arrest them all. Soon they were brought before me for trial and I duly fined them.

Drunkenness gradually decreased to a minimum in that and other counties of my circuit. Any lawyers addicted to drink took notice of my intentions at once. I myself probably shocked the circuit because I was then an inveterate smoker of cigars, and I took to smoking on the bench. I was the first to do so.

Some persons in the district had a habit of defacing government buildings such as the courthouse or post office by carving or writing on them. I was determined to wipe out the practice, and sternly punished any such offense. The story is told that on one occasion an old friend of mine was charged before me with defacing a government building. He counted on our friendship to obtain clemency, but I fined him the limit of the law —fifty dollars. After court adjourned, I loaned or gave him the fifty dollars with which to pay the fine. In truth, I no longer recall the event in exactly this way; but it is very likely, for I do remember that on several occasions old friends appeared before me charged with some offense or other. Whatever their expectations, they received the same justice I meted out to other persons.

On one occasion, so I am reminded, a defendant came up before me charged with gambling. He, too, was an old acquaintance.

He admitted the charge but pleaded: "Judge, you and I used to play cards together in the army."

"Yes," I replied, as I imposed the usual fine, "but I've quit and you've got to quit too."

An unanswerable excuse always sure to get a man out of serving on a jury in my circuit was that his wife was "expecting any minute." In those days doctors or midwives were not close at hand, and a husband was required to do what he could to assist.

One day, as the jury was being drawn for an interesting trial, a prospective juror made this plea. There was no argument. "Excused," I said.

Several hours later I looked up and saw him sitting at the back of the courtroom, following the proceedings. I interrupted the trial and called him to his feet.

"If you're not out of this courtroom in thirty seconds and on your way home," I said, "I'll have you pay a stiff fine."

He left in haste.

An important divorce case came up for trial when I first went on the bench. The couple, who had five children, were excellent people but incompatible. I learned later that both husband and wife were very much afraid to have me try the suit. They said: "He's a bachelor and a comparatively young man, and is liable to do just anything in disposing of our children." When I came to decide the case, I directed that the children who had reached the age of some degree of discretion should be permitted to choose between going with their father or their mother, while those of tender age should be placed in charge of the mother. Both sides were entirely pleased.

I shall never forget the first marriage ceremony I had to perform as a judge. I had forgotten that a judge has this function. One day I heard a commotion outside my office. I got up, the door opened, and in came three or four white men, friends of mine, with a group of colored folks. They pushed forward a colored man and woman and said: "These people want to get married—and get married now." My friends hoped to give me some embarrassment. They guessed—and rightly—that I had never thought about the marriage ceremony and what composed it. I recovered from my surprise and said to the colored couple: "Does each of you agree with the other to become man and wife?" Each one said, "Yes." Then I said. "Well, that's what you are." It was done!

At about that time a colored man appeared before me charged with a misdemeanor, and the defense attorney offered character witnesses in his favor.

One of the usual questions asked each witness was: "What is the character of the defendant as to truth and veracity?"

When one of the witnesses replied, "Good," the prosecutor cross-examined him and asked:

"What is meant by truth and veracity?"

To which the witness promptly replied: "Truth means telling the truth, and veracity means telling a lie."

Many great lawyers pleaded cases before me during my sessions. As in preceding generations, the more noted lawyers continued to travel this circuit, going about as I did, by buggy and on horseback, to practice their profession in several counties. I made it a point to visit them in their hotels after the sessions had adjourned, and they told me many interesting points of law and politics.

In the fall of 1903, my mother, who had long been an invalid, died. I was holding court in Macon County, forty miles distant, when I learned of her turn for the worse. I immediately drove home, where I found her in the very last stages of her illness. Her death was a terrible blow to me not only because she had been my mother in the fullest sense, but also because she had overexerted herself through the years to give us children exceptional attention and care and aid in our upbringing. Her teachings of morals and religion were invaluable to me. No one ever had a better or finer mother.

Having filled the unexpired term of Judge Smith, I then stood for election in 1904. I was elected unanimously. I went on with the grinding but highly interesting work of the circuit. In the course of many months I began to bring the dockets up to date. This work made such an impression on people in the circuit that many of them call me "Judge" to this day. It was the largest single factor in my getting to Congress.

In 1906 some political friends, and some disinterested Democrats as well, thought they saw an opportunity in the Fourth Congressional District situation, and they insisted I make the race for the nomination in the primary. Until seven years before, this seat had been filled for twenty years by my old friend Benton McMillin. After much consideration I agreed and made my formal announcement of candidacy.

A strong opponent, James T. Miller, residing in the big Democratic end of the district, was already an avowed candidate. Miller was somewhat of an orator, and I was not. Mutual friends, however, had satisfied me that the incumbent, M. G. Butler, had decided not to be a candidate for renomination. He lived in my own county, and we both lived in the small Democratic end of the district. Later, after my announcement for the nomination, Mr. Butler decided to become a candidate. This made the contest all the closer.

Then followed one of the hardest fights of my career. I traveled throughout the fourteen counties of the district, making speeches and seeing voters. My father's wide acquaintance in the upper Cumberland and mountain counties was of great assistance. He personally visited numerous counties and interviewed acquaintances and friends in my behalf. Up to that time I had lived in the part of Overton County later called Pickett and in Clay and Jackson counties; and I was to live in Smith County. I therefore had a personal following in each of the first three counties. Some of my opposition charged me with moving around on purpose to build up political support for use at some future time. I replied that I thought enough of the people in each county to move into their midst, be one of them and cast my lot with them, while my critics had not.

When the primary election arrived, I won by only fifteen votes. I received 6,298 votes; Mr. Miller, 6,283, and Mr. Butler, 3,103. The Democratic primary election organization, comprising a member from each of the fourteen counties, canvassed the returns and declared me duly nominated.

After a victory by so narrow a margin, there were inevitable threats of a contest by Mr. Miller. In the hope of quieting the controversy then and thereafter, I offered to pay the expenses of conducting any contest that might be instituted. There was no contest, and I later defeated the Republican candidate in the November elections. Mr. Miller chose again to seek the verdict of the voters in the district in the next Congressional primary two years later. I was able to win by twelve hundred votes in that contest and had no more opposition within the Democratic Party during the next twenty years.

The Congress to which I was elected in November, 1906, did not assemble until December, 1907, according to the law then existing. To all appearance, from the time a candidate was elected, more than a year passed before he assumed all his functions as a Congressman. He did not take his oath until the new Congress convened the following December 1. But in actual fact his term began on March 4 following the November election, and except for participating in the House proceedings he functioned just as if he had been sworn in.

My first move after my election was to go to Washington and secure the help of five or six agricultural and public highway experts. Returning with them, I accompanied them on a visit to each of the fourteen counties of my district, where we held meetings lasting several hours each. These were largely attended by the farmers and were very beneficial in educating and awakening the people to the need for greater progress in agriculture and highway development.

I also went on to Nashville and held a meeting there, attended by delegates from the various counties of the Cumberland Valley, to discuss the improvement of the Cumberland River. This was a project very dear to my heart. The Cumberland had played a vital part in the struggle of my father to get ahead, and its current had carried his rafts by the hundreds down to market at Nashville. I myself had repeatedly ridden on the Cumberland's back, by raft and by boat. The river ran right through the central part of my district for over two hundred miles, and through Carthage where I later lived. It was capable of yielding great navigational benefits to the people, but to secure them it was necessary to construct locks and dams. Toward this end I constantly spurred an organized movement of interested persons from one end of the river to the other to influence Congress to grant the necessary appropriations. We made real progress.

In 1907 the Mississippi Valley organization for the development of the Mississippi and its tributaries invited President Theodore Roosevelt and the Senators and Congressmen representing the valley and its tributary valleys to go to St. Louis and take a boat trip down the Mississippi to New Orleans to gather further first-hand information about the area. I accepted, made an altogether interesting and helpful trip, and became acquainted with all the other members of the party, most of whom I was later to see in Washington.

Then I turned my eyes to Washington and the national scene. I had finished my apprenticeship in local and State politics. I had my judgeship behind me. I was thirty-five years old and had already given much study to the problems of the country as a whole. I felt I had some ideas and convictions. Now I was eager to ring them on the anvil of the nation.

5: Novice in the House

EVEN PUTTING ASIDE the natural thrill I had in going to Washington as a Congressman for the first time, I had many other reasons to be interested in the national scene as the Sixtieth Congress convened in 1907. Theodore Roosevelt, a masterful politician, was President—with all the dynamic developments or threats of developments this fact brought with it. And a panic, the so-called Bankers' Panic, was raging, with eight thousand banks closed down.

I vaguely detected, from President Roosevelt's restlessness and denunciation of certain elements, that he had found dangerous conditions of a threatened split within his own Party which imperatively called for attention. I often heard him declaim against "swollen wealth" and the "criminal rich," and his utterances were actually accompanied by an attack on some of the great Republican bosses of the special privilege brand. I gradually concluded that the seeds of a revolutionary change, political, economic, and social, were sprouting all about.

Almost since the Civil War the United States had been dominated by what was termed the privileged groups. Extreme reactionary elements known as the standpatters were in charge of the Government. As a result, the nation had become stagnant on the most important public problems. Legislation affecting agriculture, labor, finance and taxation, legitimate business, and the general public was long overdue. Agriculture had been most depressed for many years, labor had received almost no recognition in its relations with capital, and the nation was hopelessly handicapped by great trusts and monopolies operating virtually without restraint. The great middle class—the backbone of any democracy—was borne down along with the working class under the weight of discriminatory government policies.

The necessity for reforms had become increasingly apparent from month to month. The evils of the single policy of nationalism and reaction had become well-nigh intolerable at times, so much so in fact that even the standpat element in control felt obliged to take a step at infrequent periods to appease the public. This included the Sherman Antitrust Act of 1890 to curb the vicious monopoly and trust expansion.

Involved in these controversies was the question of the virtual collapse of prices and values, with resultant panics such as those of 1883,

1893, and the Bankers' Panic of 1907. A violent outcropping of unsound monetary panaceas suddenly swept over the country in the Bankers' Panic. This was the signal for a broad national awakening and widespread agitation for relief, especially monetary, economic, and social. More and more of what were termed progressive ideas were spreading over the country. I could see signs on every hand that some sort of fundamental change was not far in the future.

When I got to Congress I soon discovered that there were two groups of Congressmen. One group, a small minority, were content merely to cultivate their respective districts and thereby continue themselves in office. At that time the distribution to one's constituents of garden seed, agricultural bulletins and yearbooks was still quite popular among the farmers. Congressmen representing agricultural constituencies did not overlook this fact.

The other and larger group pursued the policy of representing both their districts and the nation as a whole. I felt that any Congressman worth his salt should be able to furnish leadership to his district and at the same time perform a much broader duty to the nation as a whole. This duty manifestly devolved upon him and was in addition to that toward his immediate constituents.

I am glad that the distribution of garden seeds, once an important influence in keeping Congressmen in office, has disappeared, and that now a Congressman has greater incentive to extend his activities beyond the limits of his district. The need for a broad national and international attitude today is tremendously pressing, and I hope that more and more Congressmen will undertake to furnish leadership both at home and in the nation at large.

I myself decided early to pursue the broad national objective. Hence I made earnest search for the facts and truth on the major questions and conditions then current in the nation.

I had also been told by experienced leaders that unless a new Member specialized he would get nowhere in Congress, and if he did so he might or might not get somewhere. I decided to specialize in revenue, tariff, and other forms of taxation, economics, and finance. I noticed that there were few serious students of these subjects, whereas so-called dry statistics were as interesting to me as a "dime novel."

I studied innumerable books, reports, and brochures on these topics. While not subscribing to magazines, I did research to find magazine articles dealing with fiscal subjects, and read them thoroughly. When I was in Washington, during my twenty-four years in Congress, I doubt that half a dozen Sundays passed that did not find me in my office studying. Sundays were marvelous days of quiet when I could penetrate deeply into the intricacies of this field.

On arriving in Washington, I stayed at several different hotels until I settled for a long period at the Cochran Hotel on Fourteenth and K streets. I was influenced to reside at the Cochran by the large number of Senators and Representatives living there. During the evenings we Congressional people, preempting one side of the hotel lobby, sat there for one to two hours, discussing legislative questions or problems of government. This group constituted a good clearinghouse for gathering information quickly about what had occurred in important Senate and House committees during the day.

My first office was in my hotel room. The House Office Building had just been built when I arrived in Washington, but it was not ready for occupancy until some weeks later. As I entered Congress the new salary of $7,500 had just come into effect, having been raised in the preceding Congress from $5,000. We were now furnished offices, whereas previously this had not been the practice. I used to ride to the Capitol from my hotel on a streetcar.

I took to Washington with me as my secretary H. B. McGinness of Carthage, Tennessee, who became my adviser and both political and personal representative throughout all my years of Congressional service— and no one could have been more capable. He represented me in my district for Congressional and State political affairs and was also my chief representative in proceedings of a national political nature. He left my service in Washington in 1910 and returned to the practice of law in Tennessee where he soon became one of the outstanding lawyers of the State. He religiously looked after my political interests everywhere in the years following. When he resigned as my secretary, he was succeeded by Miss Will Harris, who loyally and capably worked for me throughout my remaining years in Congress and in the State Department.

In Washington I found numerous veterans of the Civil War, along with the early postwar group of statesmen, still lingering on the public stage. Many generals and other military ranks were listed among the Senators and Representatives. But a new generation was rapidly succeeding them as old age brought their disappearance.

My social life in Washington was most limited. I preferred to spend my evenings studying the issues before Congress or in discussions with other Congressmen at the Cochran Hotel rather than to go to the numerous dinners and receptions offered in the Capital. Throughout my entire stay in Washington as a Congressman, I went out socially only on rare occasions, and this practice I carried also into my career as Secretary of State.

Within three weeks of the opening session, I introduced on December 19, 1907, a comprehensive income-tax bill. This was in the face of the fact that almost all statesmen acquiesced in the view that income tax was probably dead legislatively since the United States Supreme Court decision in the Pollock case in 1895, declaring the income-tax law invalid. This view was based on the belief that income taxation could not be enacted except through Constitutional amendment. And with special privilege in supreme control of both Houses of Congress, there appeared to be no chance to secure the submission of an amendment by Congress, even if ratification by the requisite number of States proved possible— and this appeared quite doubtful at the time.

By introducing the bill I accepted a challenge. The Republican campaign book of 1894 had stated: "In this country an income tax of any sort is odious and will bring odium upon any party blind enough to impose it. Prepare for the funeral of the political party which imposes such a burden." I was willing to risk both the odium and the funeral.

I was vitally interested in the income tax, having studied it for nearly fifteen years. My public speeches, beginning with some of my earliest campaign addresses, rarely failed to contain some reference to it. I had examined income-tax law from the Civil War period on. I had closely followed the great debates of 1893 and 1894 leading to the enactment of the Wilson Tariff Act, of which the income-tax law was a part, and I had deeply pondered the adverse Supreme Court five-to-four decision and the opinions written on both sides.

I was greatly influenced by the fact that the political leader whose actions and ideas I had so closely observed—Congressman Benton McMillin—had embraced the income-tax theory and was the author of the income-tax provision in the Wilson Tariff Act which the Supreme Court declared unconstitutional. McMillin at that time had been in Congress about fifteen years and had been named to the Ways and Means Committee at the end of his second term. When Grover Cleveland was elected in 1892 for the second time, McMillin was the ranking Democrat on the Ways and Means Committee in line for the chairmanship. Some of the Eastern leaders, however, who were in with Cleveland—men of the David

B. Hill and William C. Whitney group—pointed to William L. Wilson of West Virginia, who had made a fine tariff speech on more than one occasion. They thought he was safer, more conservative, than McMillin, and they just heaved him up over McMillin.

My Congressman did not say anything, being a good soldier, but he could not dislodge this disappointment from his mind. When the Wilson Tariff Bill came on, McMillin did faithful work, but at that time the Farmers Alliance and others were preaching income tax, and McMillin made that his objective. He determined that, in return for Cleveland's keeping him out of the chairmanship, he would push the income tax over on the East. He did not stop until he did just that. He was chairman of the subcommittee that drafted the income-tax provision. Just as the two Houses were concluding consideration of the bill in conference, McMillin forced a caucus and got his provision adopted.

I was keenly impressed with the income-tax doctrine in the light of our lopsided tax condition in 1907, in which wealth was shirking its share of the tax burdens. Revenue for the expenses of the national Government was then obtained largely from customs duties on imports and excise taxes on such items as whisky and tobacco. Obviously this system was unfair to the poorer classes because they, with their small incomes, were paying the same taxes on such products as the rich, with their large incomes.

I felt so strongly that I was moved to attempt to revive the whole doctrine, notwithstanding that the Court had pronounced it dead. I felt hopeful because Justice Shiras was no longer on the Supreme bench and we had a reconstituted Court that might be more favorably disposed toward the principle. I also believed there was room for another construction of the Constitution, if the Court were willing to adopt it. It was inconceivable to me that we had a Constitution that would shelter the chief portion of the wealth of the country from the only effective method of reaching it for its fair share of taxes. President Theodore Roosevelt's denunciation of certain privileged elements created some sentiment that I felt might be fully aroused in support of income taxation, which I called taxing wealth under the rule of ability to pay.

But I must confess I got nowhere with income tax in the Sixtieth Congress. I went over the question in many speeches. I talked to any Member of either House of Congress who was willing to listen to me. I talked to outside leaders. I talked to some Congressmen so often they were no longer willing to listen. I well recall that House leaders such as

John Sharp Williams and Champ Clark, although strongly favoring an income tax, would turn and walk in another direction when they saw me approaching. Only a small number here and there joined in active support of the proposal, although many more favored it in principle but thought it impossible to get action.

I persisted. I believed it worth while that many Members of the House should be educated to the necessity for an income tax, even though my associates and I could not get Members to vote for it then. I began to acquaint myself with income-tax questions and conditions in foreign countries. I wrote the Secretary of State, Elihu Root, asking him to request our embassies and legations abroad to send information on the income-tax systems in those countries. I prepared a long, detailed questionnaire for him containing the type of information I needed.

I received a vast amount of information in return, a large portion of which I had inserted in the *Congressional Record,* hoping that other Members would read it. The information proved useful to me not only in developing our own income taxation but also in shedding light on international questions, particularly financial, economic, and social conditions abroad.

The House of Representatives I entered was under the absolute domination of the powerful machine of Speaker Joseph Cannon, then in full flower. Affectionately called "Uncle Joe" by his proud, faithful followers, who would fight for him as for themselves, he had the power to say which measures in Congress could become law and which could not. The machine of this rather small, thin, and wiry-appearing man who became prematurely gray under the crushed-in, cocked-looking hat he wore on the side of his head, was supreme even in the most minute ways. He himself appointed members of committees from both the majority and minority parties. Sometimes he listened to the suggestions of our minority leader, John Sharp Williams, with regard to appointment of Democratic members, but he was not obliged to do so under the rules.

Occasionally Cannon would pick up a Democratic Member of whom he could make use. He would give him positions and favors in return for his vote for the measures Cannon wanted. I personally knew of several such persons, including one from my own State. They would stick their heads off the reservation when Cannon said to; sometimes, if their actions looked too bad, they would come back. I witnessed what was in effect the treachery of the Tammany group of the Democratic Party in this same connection.

Cannon, who had a habit of being very profane, was coolly collected under attack and acted with almost painful deliberation on critical occasions where a decision was extremely important, for good or bad. He was a perfect model of the machine leader, exceedingly able, courageous, and well equipped to dominate the legislation of the two Houses of Congress, which he sometimes did in a ruthless way.

When Congress met and the oath was administered to the Members, the question of committee appointment immediately confronted the House. Most new Members sought to improve their chances for good committee appointments by bringing influences to bear on the Speaker, but I did not make or request any of my colleagues to offer any representations to the Speaker in my behalf.

When the appointments were announced, I discovered I had been placed at or near the bottom of two wholly unimportant committees, Reform in Civil Service, and Pensions. I decided to dismiss my attention to my two committees and to devote myself entirely to the broad aspects of our national affairs, with particular reference to the subjects in which I would specialize.

In pursuance of this plan, I undertook to prepare and deliver my maiden speech in March, 1908, less than four months after Congress met. I was determined to lift my initial address above a mere discussion of my district or local issues and to make it a real examination of the issues facing the nation. I felt that Congressmen too often refrained from discussing broad national questions, especially in their opening speeches. I knew, too, that a Member's maiden speech was quite often one of the most important of his career. Many of his colleagues listened attentively and judged his ability on the basis of it, and the impression he created might determine whether they would listen to his subsequent addresses or not. I spent all available time for many weeks in preparing my address. Here the information and views of sound statesmen with whom I conferred from time to time stood me in good stead. At last the fateful day, March 18, arrived.

To many Members their maiden speech is a real ordeal. Their friends usually have a quorum call of the House to bring in the largest possible audience, and their colleagues from their home State take a particular interest both before and during delivery. I had a good audience without a quorum call.

When the House convened, arrangements had already been made for the Speaker to recognize me at a given point in the proceedings. I recollect

I diverted my mind from the seriousness of the situation by conversing with colleagues sitting near me up to the last moment before the Speaker recognized me. At that instant I whirled around in my chair to face the Speaker, rose, and addressed him. Thus I avoided the stage fright that grips so many Members in their opening speeches.

I made a vigorous attack on the high tariff and the monopolies and trusts that had grown up behind it. "So long as no fountain can be purified while a contaminated stream flows into it," I said, "so long can no kind of effort to curb and suppress trust violators succeed unless such effort strikes at the main source of their constant creation—the protective tariff, . . . the king of evils, our present tariff, should be given a place near the center of the stage."

I came out strongly for a national income tax. I quoted the Republican campaign statement of 1894 on odium and political death, but advocated it just the same.

President Roosevelt came in for some of my sharpest comments. I attacked what I called his paternalism, saying: "The President is paternally and eternally advocating doctrines so extremely Federalistic and paternalistic as to cause the present generation to view his strange course with awe and amazement, and such as would have put to shame Alexander Hamilton himself."

President Roosevelt had obtained wide publicity from his antitrust activities, but I said: "Far more time and effort has been consumed in exploiting *proposed* and *threatened* prosecutions than has been devoted to *actual* prosecutions. Under the fostering and protecting wing of the Dingley Law a dozen trust violators spring into existence even while the President is effervescing and threatening to prosecute one. Yes, the President loudly inveighs against the trust evils—*the evils of the protective tariff which he champions*. The American people are merely experiencing an optical illusion due to the pyrotechnic display of the President."

Finally I pointed out the rich field of issues for the forthcoming Presidential campaign. "Suppression of lawless combinations and proper curbing of corporate wealth is an issue," I said. "So is the outrageous tariff, Executive usurpation, home rule and the guaranteed rights of the States, government by injunction, income tax, efficient railway rate regulation, steamship and other subsidies, extravagant appropriations, legislation securing to labor its just rights, a sound financial system, maladministration of government."

Today the language of my maiden speech appears more violent in a few instances than it would in those days when the tide of political acrimony ran high. Then partisan feeling at times was fierce and re- criminations extreme. This accounts for bitter verbal attacks and counter- attacks even between personal friends. Terrific passages occurred between President Roosevelt and William Jennings Bryan, each of whom, in several instances, was supporting the same progressive proposition.

When unduly vain Members made an important speech, they were sometimes accused of retiring directly to the cloakroom to receive con- gratulations. This I did not do. I had reason, however, to be more than gratified with the reaction to my address.

We new Congressmen often had an exaggerated notion about pub- licity. We assumed very unwisely that the metropolitan press would show us the same marked attention we received from our local press. This was especially true when we delivered a speech that we considered of serious importance, especially a maiden address. Many of us, after making such an oration, rose early the next morning to buy an armful of newspapers and read the anticipated front-page headlines paying high tribute to our expression. Generally nothing appeared on the front page. With but a slight dent in our enthusiasm, we turned to the second and third pages, but found nothing there. Then more rapidly, with dwindling ardor, we turned page after page, until finally we discovered two or three lines near the back page, stating that Congressman Blank also spoke.

Throughout that session President Roosevelt preached progressivism rather broadly, but for some reason, which might well have been the opposition of the powerful standpat element in his party, he did not secure progressive action except in a limited way such as the Railway Rate Regulation Act. Generally I regarded him, however, as one of the exceed- ingly able Presidents, who rendered valuable service. He was capably opposed by Mr. Bryan who did marvelous work in keeping public opinion informed and organized in support of progressive ideas. Bryan was the greatest political and moral evangel of his time, and a matchless orator.

As the campaign of 1908 approached, I found myself in the throes of a serious political fight for nomination to Congress for the second time, being opposed by Mr. Miller whom I had so narrowly defeated two years before. At about that time I introduced in the House a bill to establish a branch of the United States Court in the center of my district, at Cooke- ville, Tennessee. The bill was really meritorious because of the inaccessi- bility to the mountain people of Nashville, one hundred miles away, where they were obliged to go to attend Court. With the election coming on, the passage or defeat of the bill meant a great difference to me.

But the question was how to get the bill through the House, with Speaker Cannon dominating the entire legislative proceedings. In the House a Member could not secure recognition from the Speaker to call up a local bill without making satisfactory arrangements with him in advance. Even then, under the rules, the Member could not get his bill considered except by unanimous consent. But Cannon had from one to three of the ablest Republican Members always planted in the House to offer objections to unanimous consent save in instances where the Speaker was agreeable to the passage of the measure.

I simply had to get my bill through if humanly possible. I thereupon called on Speaker Cannon in his office. It was my first visit to him. He was sitting behind a table with a pencil and pad before him on which he recorded requests for recognition at the session scheduled to open a short time later. He looked up and said: "What do you want?"

"Mr. Speaker," I said, "I haven't bothered you any in the past. But now I have a little local bill to call up which is most important to me."

"What is it?"

I explained.

"Oh, hell!" he exclaimed. "That just means a public building, and Payne will object to consideration of the bill."

"No new building will be required," I said. "A new county courthouse has been built at Cookeville and the Federal Court can gladly have space in it." And I added: "The only way to find out for certain whether Payne will object is for me to be given recognition and to request unanimous consent for consideration."

Cannon said no more. He suddenly picked up a pencil and began to write on his pad. I guessed this meant he would recognize me and, without asking further, I said, "Thank you, Mr. Speaker," and walked out of his office.

I went quickly onto the floor of the House where the Members had begun to gather for the opening of the session within a few minutes. I had long observed that there were three Republican Congressmen who did most of the objecting to unanimous consent—Sereno Payne, James R. Mann, and Joseph W. Keifer. I went first to a Republican colleague from Tennessee, Nathan W. Hale, who sat near General Keifer. I told him of my bill and its merits and said: "If General Keifer should rise to object, I wish you would walk up to him and speak to him privately while he is on his feet and say that the bill is meritorious and you hope he will let it pass." Hale said he would.

I then made the same proposal to Congressman James M. Griggs of Georgia, whom I had seen at times in close fellowship with Congressman Mann. Griggs agreed. I next made the same arrangement with a third Congressional friend, who was also a friend of Payne.

After the session began, I rose and was duly recognized by the Speaker. But I had scarcely got the title of my bill out of my mouth when, sure enough, up rose General Keifer just across the aisle and started in vigorously to attack the bill. I saw Hale get up and hurry across to Keifer and whisper in his ear. Keifer finally subsided.

Thereupon up rose Congressman Mann and, in what seemed to me to be his usual perverse tone and demeanor, opposed the bill. At almost the same moment I saw Griggs quickly rise and move across the aisle and whisper to Mann. At length Mann sat down without making his objection.

But instantly Congressman Payne, rising, began to object. And my third Congressional friend approached him and began whispering fervently. I thought Payne never would cease his unfriendly remarks, but after much whispering he suddenly branched off to some other subject and let me alone.

Thereupon my motion was without objection, and the bill promptly passed the House.

This method of tackling Cannon's professional objectors by close-up personal contact while they were on their feet was something new. I have often wondered what Cannon afterwards said to his objectors about allowing this bill to slip through their fingers.

Cannon was eventually right, though, that the bill would call for another public building. The Federal Court began by using the Cookeville County Courthouse, but another building later became necessary. I introduced a bill for this purpose, and it was passed without difficulty.

During the campaign of 1908 I spent two months in my district successfully campaigning for renomination. Taft was elected; the Republicans retained control of Congress; I retained my seat. When the new Congress reconvened it called for the usual appointment of the committees by the Speaker. I addressed a letter to Speaker Cannon requesting that he transfer me from the two committees I was on. Presumably it was a clerk in his office who sent back a formal acknowledgment. At any rate, when the committees were soon announced, I was left on the same com

mittees as in the preceding Congress. This gave me even greater incentive
to go forward with the broader course I had planned in the beginning.

A couple of years later, during the transition period between Theodore Roosevelt and Wilson, I was to be close by when Cannon was completely floored in combat with Roosevelt. This was in Chicago, at the
end of a trip Roosevelt had made to the West while feeling between
progressive and reactionary factions of the Republican Party was at fever
heat. The Republican Club of Chicago, founded largely by another machine leader, Senator William Lorimer, had conceived the idea of giving
a great dinner in the Congress Hotel for Roosevelt. All plans were made
and the coming dinner was publicized far and wide as a great Republican
get-together. I was then in the same hotel attending a meeting of the
Democratic Congressional Committee.

When Roosevelt arrived within a few miles of Chicago, he suddenly
gave out a sensational statement denouncing Lorimer and stating he
would not attend the dinner that night if Lorimer were present. The turmoil that followed in the hotel was as if a hurricane had got in through
the open windows. Republican leaders, including Speaker Cannon, had
come from far and near to attend the dinner. They were doubly dismayed
because the dinner had been intended to be a harmony affair.

Senator Lorimer solved one difficulty by announcing he would remain away from the dinner. I talked to prominent Republicans before
they entered the banquet room, and they made sharp criminations. Later
they told me what happened. The banquet began without surface discord,
but the conversation at the tables was at times acrimonious. As the dinner
ended, the presiding officer introduced Roosevelt. The former President
proceeded to make a terrific attack on Cannon and his reactionary and
predatory policies.

When Roosevelt sat down, there were instant shouts for "Cannon!
Cannon!" For a moment it looked as if pandemonium would set in. Cannon, as usual, was very deliberate. On his speaking occasions in the House
he was slow-moving as he took the floor and went into action. On this
occasion, as the shouts of "Cannon! Cannon! Speech!" grew louder, he
sat with head lowered, apparently deciding what reply to make. Then, as
he showed signs of rising to reply, which he fully intended to do, Roosevelt quickly turned to the presiding officer and said: "You understand I
am to give a reception following this dinner and catch my train for Cincinnati immediately afterward." He had scarcely said this when he added,

"I think the time has come for the reception, if I am to make my train connection," and he showed signs of rising to his feet.

The presiding officer thereupon rose, accompanied by about half the diners, while the remaining half sat solidly, shouting for Cannon. For a few moments that seemed like minutes, the situation hung in the balance. Then the whole crowd gave way and followed Roosevelt out of the dining room to the reception. Cannon, in the very act of coming to his feet with one of his typical sledge-hammer replies undoubtedly on his lips, was left without an audience. Roosevelt got away with it by presence of mind and genuine strategy.

In March, 1909, I witnessed one of the most sensational revolutions in Congress, explosive and far-reaching: the toppling of "Uncle Joe" Cannon from his Speaker's dictatorship. One afternoon the House was droning along on a minor routine matter, with but a few Members in their seats and the galleries empty, when suddenly Congressman George W. Norris of Nebraska, standing near the well of the House and somewhat on the Democratic side, arose and said, "Mr. Speaker!" Whereupon Speaker Cannon inquired: "For what purpose does the gentleman rise?"

Norris said he rose to a question of the highest constitutional privilege and wished to offer a resolution. It was a resolution to attack and overthrow the Cannon rules—or Cannonism, as it was generally called. Cannon, with no alternative, bowed to this demand and recognized Norris.

Instantly the prosaic proceedings of the House changed as if a bolt of lightning had struck the Capitol. Everyone came to the highest alert. There was much rushing to and fro. Within a half-hour it seemed to me that every Member had rushed to the House floor; the galleries were jammed with spectators who knew the significance of this sudden explosion.

For nearly three days and two nights Cannon stood at bay while the constant attack went on. Most of the Members stayed on the floor or about the cloakrooms, where they took brief spells of sleeping on the divans. Cannon kept studying how to rule on Norris's resolution. Finally, on the third day, amid great tension, he ruled that it was in order. He knew that his ruling meant that, if the House adopted the resolution, he would be stripped of all the arbitrary powers and privileges vested in his purely autocratic system for governing the House.

The House promptly passed the resolution. Cannon was not removed from the Speakership but his little czardom was destroyed, and Congress largely enjoys to this day the freedom then restored to it. This episode, in my opinion, marks one of the most important epochs in the parliamentary history of our Government.

Later Champ Clark, our floor leader, told me some of the background of this significant fight. If the Democrats were to shatter Cannon's power they had to have the support of the progressive Republicans. For a number of years, as a new Congress was about to assemble, there was much talk among the progressive Republicans that they would join the Democrats in any move to overthrow Cannonism. But at the last moment they always weakened and went along with the Republican majority. They knew that such progressive Republicans as were suspected of lack of loyalty to the Cannon machine received severe punishment such as loss of committee rank. However, the sentiment of the country against Republican standpatism, as it was termed, became increasingly hostile. Finally, Albert S. Burleson, later Postmaster General, who had a natural disposition for intrigue and was always talking to the Progressives about the possibility of combining, reported to us that they had sworn they would stick and work with the Democrats.

Congressman Norris, Champ Clark told me, would not agree to lead the progressive Republicans in supporting the Democrats unless he were permitted himself to offer the resolution. Not unnaturally, the Democrats who had fought so long in a vain effort to destroy the Cannon rule at the opening of each new Congress were the rightful Members to offer the resolution. Clark, however, did not hesitate but readily gave Norris the privilege of assuming the lead. The progressive Republicans rallied round him, and the deed was done.

Not discouraged by the lack of success of my income-tax bill in the Sixtieth Congress, I immediately introduced the same bill on the first day of session of the Sixty-first Congress in March, 1909—and the fight was on again. A few weeks later, on March 29, I delivered a comprehensive speech in favor of the income tax. "I have no disposition to tax wealth unnecessarily or unjustly," I said, "but I do believe that the wealth of the country should bear its just share of the burden of taxation and that it should not be permitted to shirk that duty. Anyone at all familiar with the legislative history of the nation must admit that the chief burdens of government have long been borne by those least able to bear them, while accumulated wealth has enjoyed the protection and other blessings of the Government and thus far escaped most of its accompanying burdens."

There were two solutions to the income-tax impasse. One was to pass a bill that I believed the Supreme Court would uphold, even though it had to reverse itself. The other was to seek a constitutional amendment. I favored the former because, as I pointed out, an amendment would require the affirmative action of two-thirds of both Houses of Congress and three-fourths of the States, and statisticians figured that 3 per cent of the people in the States could prevent an amendment to the Constitution. One of the hardest tasks of my associates and myself was to overcome the reluctance of Congress to throw the question again onto the laps of the august Supreme Court.

"I agree," I argued, "that Members of Congress are under oath to support the Constitution, and that it is the duty of the Supreme Court, under proper circumstances, to construe and expound the instrument; but I submit that where, in the judgment of Members of Congress, a palpably erroneous decision has been rendered by the Supreme Court, stripping the coordinate legislative branch of the Government of one of its strong arms of power and duty . . . every Member of Congress owes to himself and to the country the duty of exhausting every reasonable and legitimate means to secure a review by the Court of the questions erroneously decided."

I made my speech in the course of a spirited debate on the Payne Tariff Bill of 1909, which I sharply denounced because, instead of lowering tariffs, it was raising them. I could not know it then, but this very bill was to open the door to the income tax.

A rift in the Republican Party, which flowered into the battle between the Taft Republicans and the Roosevelt Progressives in the 1912 election, was steadily becoming more serious. It revealed the Progressives clamoring, among other items, for tariff revisions downward. This, of course, was the general attitude of Democrats. The demand was an outcropping of the coming uprising against those long in control of the Government. To meet the demand it was felt necessary to insert a promise in the Republican platform of 1908 pledging the Party, if retained in power, to revise the tariff.

As a result of this promise the Payne Tariff Bill was introduced into the House when the new session opened. I and others of like mind opposed any upward revision of the tariff rates, but we lost all along the line. Interest in income taxation, however, gathered noticeably during the discussion of the Payne Bill in the House. The Republican Progressives in the Middle West were loud and emphatic in their declarations. A further response from Western sentiment came in statements by Senator Cummins of Iowa and Senator Borah, among others. Finally, when the bill came

to a final vote, I urged Champ Clark, our great minority leader, to insert
the income-tax proposal in his motion to recommit the bill. Mr. Clark
had always favored the income tax and favored it then. He introduced
the motion, but it was defeated. The Old Guard crowd, standing pat, was
able to carry the day and preserve the Payne Bill free from unfriendly
amendments.

When the bill reached the Senate, however, a powerful Republican
minority opposition greeted it with hostile cries. It so happened that, while
the Payne Bill was still under consideration in the House, I met Senator
Joseph W. Bailey of Texas on a train. Bailey had a legal mind scarcely
second to that of anyone else in our history. I recalled that he had been
a strong advocate of the income tax in 1893–1894 and I proceeded to
bring him up to date on all the later facts and developments on the
question. I could see he was becoming more and more interested. As we
parted he told me he would introduce an income-tax amendment to the
Payne Bill when it went over to the Senate a short time later and would
do everything possible to advance it. He fulfilled his promise. Senators
Borah and Cummins were also getting income-tax amendments ready.

The outcome was that the Old Guard crowd in charge of the Senate
under the leadership of Senator Aldrich saw there was a real chance of
the provision being approved. They decided they could give an appearance of acquiescing in income tax and at the same time kill it by sub-
stituting for the provision a proposed constitutional amendment. They
felt confident that the requisite number of States would never ratify an
income-tax amendment. They introduced and passed their amendment,
and the House also approved it. Four years later they were greatly surprised to see its ratification as the Sixteenth Amendment.

In the circumstances at the time, I would have preferred a simple
income-tax law rather than the constitutional amendment, but later developments strangely caused these two proposals to contribute to the
success of each other. Admittedly, the Democratic platform of 1908 demanded only the constitutional amendment. But if we had merely based
our fight for income tax on trying to secure an amendment, we would not
have gotten it through at all at that time for the reason that we had to
make a fight for the direct enactment of the tax in connection with the
Payne-Aldrich Bill, and endanger the passage of the bill unless it contained an income-tax measure, either the direct law or the Constitutional
amendment proposal. Senator Aldrich, seeing the bill in peril, chose the

amendment as the better compromise, believing this was actually the best means of defeating the income tax.

Unfortunately, the great battle that the giants had waged against the tariff rates in the Payne Bill, which then came to be known as the Payne-Aldrich Bill, dwindled off after the approval of the proposal submitting the constitutional amendment to the States. There was a letting down in the movement to defeat or weaken the bill, especially among the progressive Republicans. In the Senate the Aldrich machine built the tariff bill by pure and simple log-rolling. They placed the tariff schedules on the middle of the floor and said to each Senator, in effect: "We are starting in here to build up the tariff; we will subscribe to this. What particular tariff increase do you want? We will put it in if you will approve all the other tariff increases." If a Senator did not subscribe to the full bill, he could not get in what he wanted. I frequently went over to the Senate to listen to the debates.

Although the proposed constitutional amendment providing an income tax was now going the rounds of the States, I did not cease my struggle to get an income-tax law directly. No one could tell whether or when the States would ratify the amendment. On January 27, 1910, I delivered a speech which proved to be prophetic of the role the income tax was later to play in financing America's share in the First World War and the Second World War.

"The wonderful flexibility and certain productiveness of this tax," I said, "enables it to meet every requirement of peace or war emergencies, having thus proven in England, in the language of Gladstone, 'an engine of gigantic power.' During the great strain of national emergencies an income tax is absolutely without a rival as a relief measure. Many governments in time of war have invoked its prompt and certain aid. It enabled England to conquer Napoleon. It came to the relief of our depleted Treasury during the Civil War, when the customs revenues were at a low ebb, and saved the rapidly sinking credit of the nation. We cannot expect always to be at peace. If this nation were tomorrow plunged into a war with a great commercial country from which we now receive a large portion of our imports, our customs revenues would inevitably decline and we would be helpless to prosecute that war or any other war of great magnitude without taxing the wealth of the country in the form of incomes."

The war to lower tariffs and enact an income tax required the fighting of further battles. But our chance for victory was fast approaching.

6: Fruits of Victory

THE PROGRESSIVE and reform movement broke on the country with fury following the enactment of the Payne-Aldrich Bill. The new tariff became the spearpoint of the attacks of the progressive forces, both Democratic and Republican, against the many alleged evils calling for liberal remedies. The Payne-Aldrich Act did not at all satisfy the country. Many vital rates had unquestionably been revised upward, a fact that President Taft, unfortunately for himself, misunderstood as he vainly endeavored to quell the rising tide of progressivism.

In the Congressional campaign of 1910 the tariff came more and more acutely into controversy between the two parties. The Payne-Aldrich Act had left wood pulp and print paper subject to a heavy tariff rate, and this incensed the press generally. As the election approached, it became clear that progressive ideas were greatly undermining the conservative portion of the Republican Party in control of the Government. The election result was as we predicted. The Democrats carried the House of Representatives by a suitable majority. Now at long last we had power, and with it a chance to put into effect some of the ideas we cherished.

Our first task was that of organizing the Democratic side of the House so as to administer and conduct its legislative activities. The powers of the Speaker had been sharply clipped, but we were now to go still further and propose that the faculty of appointing members of committees be taken entirely from his hands. We did not want even a Democratic Speaker to have the authority Cannon had exercised. At the right moment three prominent Democratic Members of the House—James Hay of Virginia, Dorsey Shackleford of Missouri, and William Hughes of New Jersey—formed themselves into the nucleus of an organization, very secret at the beginning, to propose to the Democratic membership a carefully thought out plan of operation.

To my surprise these three gentlemen approached me, among the first Members, and invited me to join their movement. I accepted gladly. We proposed that the power to appoint committees be taken from the Speaker and placed in the hands of the Ways and Means Committee, which would be appointed by party caucus. This committee would select and nominate the membership of all other committees of the House, subject of course to the approval of the House caucus. The caucus would be expected to ratify without change the list of committees as proposed by the Ways and Means Committee—as later always proved to be the case —and the Ways and Means Committee would become, in fact, the steering committee of the House.

Our plan was not opposed by the forthcoming Democratic House leaders, Champ Clark and Oscar Underwood, and it became an established procedure, lasting to this day. One result of this procedure was the privilege given the minority party to select its own minority membership on the various committees and submit it to the majority for approval. Such approval was always given.

We then went to work—night and day and Sunday—with enthusiasm. Our first task was to make up the full Ways and Means Committee of fourteen Democrats and seven Republicans, subject to caucus ratification. I became one of these members. Our next task was to constitute the other committees. We were determined to strip each committee of every possible vestige of special privilege and so to mold such committees as those on Agriculture, Labor, and the Judiciary that they would join in securing maximum recognition by legislative action for classes of American citizens who had been long neglected or discriminated against by numerous policies of the Government.

If we had the least doubt about a prospective Member's attitude we sent for him beforehand, cross-examined him and pledged him unequivocally to do teamwork. We turned down William Sulzer as chairman of the Military Affairs Committee because he was extravagant. Edward Pou of North Carolina was removed from the Ways and Means Committee and Claude Kitchin, from the same State, substituted for the reason that Pou had once voted for a tariff on lumber. All this was a tremendous job, but we accomplished it in good time, and thus made up the committees of the House. The result was an effectively working organization along progressive lines.

To me the most fruitful period of my Congressional career had arrived. It was my function and duty to participate actively in the high Party councils during this vital Congress. The steering—Ways and Means —committee had the responsibility of initiating Party policy. I felt I had been lucky to move from the bottom committees of the House to this commanding position of sharing in Party leadership.

When I went on the committee I was the third youngest member of my State delegation, being thirty-nine years old. The older Members all stood in line for high committee recognition under a Democratic regime, and all were able men. The Tennessee delegation was a strong one, with long experience. Congressman Byrns was to be Speaker of the House and die in that office; Moon was to be chairman of the Post Office Committee; Padgett, chairman of Naval Affairs; Sims, chairman of Interstate and Foreign Commerce, and Houston, chairman of the Committee on Territories, while Garrett was to go on the Committee on Rules and move straight toward the floor leadership. The Democratic members of the Ways and Means Committee were ranked according to length of service. This placed me some distance down the list.

When we took charge of the Sixty-second Congress, Champ Clark, one of the finest and ablest men I ever knew and a lifelong champion of human rights and liberties, had become Speaker of the House. Oscar Underwood, our floor leader and chairman of the Ways and Means Committee, was universally conceded to be a splendid statesman and the most capable floor leader within anyone's memory. He never lost his temper. He was able, though not brilliant, possessed common sense and was always on the alert. By his personality he kept everyone united and in good humor. He exercised superb leadership in our fight for tariff reform.

The House proceeded to enact a long list of legislative measures dealing with the political, economic, and social matters calling so loudly for remedy. Some of us on the steering committee, who were deeply interested in the passage of necessary financial and related legislation, began by selecting for the appropriate committees suitable persons pledged to support the financial and economic plans we had in mind.

Our committee decided to pass through the House a number of tariff-reduction bills dealing with individual schedules and selected items rather than the entire fourteen schedules of tariff rates. We called these "popgun bills" because they dealt with single tariff schedules and items rather than with the whole tariff. We decided to put the high-tariff Republicans wholly on the defensive by striking them at the tenderest points. We early dealt with Schedule K—the wool schedule—which for many years had been more severely attacked than any other. Then came the iron and steel and the cotton schedules; and a select list of farmers' utensils and other articles needed by the farmer were assembled under the name of Farmers' Free List Bill and passed through the House.

It fell largely to my lot to prepare the first drafts of the iron and steel and the cotton bills and do much of the work on the Farmers' Free List Bill. My associates and I were ably assisted by two really remarkable clerks, one or both of whom served the committee during the entire war period—Daniel C. Roper and John E. Walker. Roper later held many high appointive offices, including those of Commissioner of Internal Revenue, Assistant Postmaster General, and Secretary of Commerce. When he left the committee, Walker succeeded him as clerk and continued his outstanding work as a revenue expert.

When the popgun bills went over to the Senate, they created serious embarrassment to the standpat element among the Republicans. Driven through the Senate over the opposition of proponents of the high tariff, they went on to President Taft who felt obliged to veto them all. These popgun bills proved, however, to be a high stroke of strategy to arouse favorable public support for the coming Underwood Tariff Bill in the next Congress and to demoralize the opposition and put it on the run even before then.

President Taft was extremely able and always patriotic. He possessed the judicial temperament, however, above all else. His disastrous experience in many instances showed he was not a politician in the fullest sense.

Taft called a special session to meet in April, 1911, primarily to consider a tariff reciprocity agreement with Canada. He had been hurt by the resentment among press and publishers owing to the high tariff on wood pulp and print paper retained in the Payne-Aldrich Act, and he was reported to have sought to placate this opposition by putting Canadian wood pulp and print paper on the free list. Since the Republicans were split and the Democrats had the majority in the House, it was necessary for Taft to send for Underwood and request him to take charge of the Canadian legislation. This being water on the Democratic economic wheel, Underwood accepted with alacrity.

We proceeded in rather short order to pass the measure through the House. It rent the Republican Party both in and out of Congress, but finally bumped its way through the Senate and went on to Canada. There it was rejected and the Laurier Government went out of power, not to return. The Canadian agreement embodied the Democratic doctrine of freer—not free, but freer—trade, in contrast to the straight-jacket condition under existing high tariffs, many of which were of an embargo nature. The objectives we sought in supporting the Canadian bill were similar to those some of us later sought in the expansion of trade on a world-wide basis.

In 1911 I became impressed with the significance of what was called the corporation-excise tax enacted in connection with the Payne-Aldrich Act in order to secure greater revenue. This was a tax on the "doing of business" by corporations, measured by their net income. In this tweedle-dum and tweedledee fashion the majority in charge sought to evade the 1895 Pollock decision holding income tax invalid. The Supreme Court in fact did proceed to hold that under this latter act the tax prescribed was on the "doing of business" instead of on the net income. I concluded that, if it was legally valid to impose such a tax on the "doing of business" by corporations, there was no reason why the same tax should not be extended to the "doing of business" by individuals.

I accordingly introduced a bill to extend the excise tax from corporations to individuals. It was at least embarrassing to House Republicans who had stood for the corporation-excise tax and it must have been embarrassing to the Senate Republicans too. The idea was new and provoked some controversy, but the bill passed the House without difficulty. When opponents of the income-tax amendment observed that we would have virtually the equivalent of an income tax in any event, they weakened their opposition to the ratification of the income-tax amendment.

It was the general opinion among those of the Democratic and Progressive persuasion that this Sixty-second Congress brought more beneficial results to more people than any other long session of any previous minority Congress. The House passed bills, among others, establishing an eight-hour day; creating the Department of Labor; reducing tariffs; providing for an excise tax on individuals; preventing abuse of the writ of injunction; calling on the President to abrogate the Treaty of 1832 with Russia because of Russian persecution of the Jews; creating a Legislature for Alaska; providing large-scale supply funds so as to lessen waste in Government expenditures; founding agricultural extension departments; requiring publicity for campaign expenses and fixing a limit on the campaign expenses of United States Senators and Representatives; and proposing an amendment to the Constitution to elect United States Senators by direct popular vote. The Sixty-second was truly a reform Congress.

The subject of direct election of Senators was of particular interest to me. I had known of many scandals in State Legislatures growing out of the election of United States Senators by Legislatures. And I also knew of the complete obstruction of wholesome and desirable legislation by Senators whose election was dictated by special interests. Hence I felt very strongly that the election of Senators should be transferred to the people themselves. As one member of the steering committee I was as active as possible in helping to push this idea, which later became the Seventeenth Amendment to the Constitution.

The foundations could not have been better laid or the way better paved for the incoming of the Wilson Administration than by the historic record of service of this Congress. The public sentiment against the stand-pat reactionary elements in charge of the government had tremendously increased as a result of these Congressional achievements, while the split among the Republicans had become wide. It was not too difficult to foresee political developments.

With the Republican Party under Taft torn asunder and with Roosevelt's strong personal following rallying around him, we beheld two rival Republican candidates for President in the general election. Their differences were bitterly accentuated in the Republican convention at Chicago. Roosevelt organized a third party which he called "Progressive."

In the Democratic Party, Speaker Champ Clark, Floor Leader Underwood, Judson Harmon of Ohio, and Woodrow Wilson of New Jersey, were the strong favorites, along with the newspaper publisher, William Randolph Hearst, and Joseph W. Folk of Missouri. I myself had mixed feelings. I had been working arm in arm with Underwood and Clark for several years and was on intimate personal relations with them. Both were fascinating persons. Clark had been the Democratic wheel horse for fifteen years or more. William Jennings Bryan had made some mistakes of judgment in his leadership, but Clark had always supported Bryan in so far as his progressivism was concerned. Underwood was recognized as a conservative. Clark and Underwood were good friends, and the struggle in 1912 did not estrange them.

As the fight in 1912 came on I took no part in it. Tennessee went for Clark, some of my chief friends in the State leading the campaign in his behalf. I felt that, between Clark and Underwood, Clark was the proper one to receive the nomination, although I was not active toward that end.

Woodrow Wilson was just coming out of the woods himself in so far as his policies were concerned. People were not sure whether he had the genuine doctrine of progressivism or not until after he broke with Henry Watterson and George Harvey, after having broken with Senator James Smith, political boss of New Jersey. Then Bryan wrote an identical letter to Clark and Wilson propounding certain interrogatories as to their position on the whole progressive situation. Wilson immediately seized the opportunity to embrace Bryan and his ideas, while Clark declined to answer.

Clark had got himself completely involved with reactionary leaders and bosses, with Senator Jim Reed of Missouri at their head. They were intimate associates of the political bosses and worked together at the conventions. Being from Clark's state of Missouri, Reed and associates were managing his campaign.

I had been studying Wilson's speeches and policies, and I was also learning something of him from his brother, Joseph R. Wilson, a member of the staff of the Nashville *Banner*, who used to talk about his brother and give me magazine articles the latter had written.

I attended the big banquet given in Washington for the Democratic candidates for the 1912 nomination. They were there—Wilson, Clark, Underwood, Harmon, Folk, and Hearst—and I was sitting not far from them. Wilson rose to speak among the last. Turning toward and facing Bryan, he seemed to take a step or two toward him, and then, in a long, unreserved speech embracing Bryan and Bryanism, he nailed down the issue. Consequently Bryan, although he wanted the nomination very much himself, did not feel he should be a candidate. He went over to Wilson, being convinced of his loyalty to progressive ideas.

Having gone from Washington to the Baltimore convention every day to observe developments there, I was present when Bryan rushed up the aisle to get recognition to change his vote from Champ Clark to Wilson, and I watched and heard the pandemonium that broke out at once. It was not generally known, but the truth is that Bryan felt that he himself was entitled to the nomination. I learned that very definitely later on. Bryan had made a speech in which he said that those who had borne the brunt of the fight during the long years of Republican rule, had the right, now that success was in sight, to sing the song of victory—not an outsider who had not contributed. It was not unnatural, considering Bryan's unremitting work on the Democratic side, that, when he saw the triumph looming up, he should want it.

I was told that, when Bryan went over to Wilson, Clark rushed over to Baltimore from Washington determined to mount the rostrum and denounce Bryan for treachery, saying that a man who had been a traitor to a friend and to his instructions would be a traitor to anybody else. Some persons who were looking out for the progressive cause ahead of any individual prevailed on Clark to desist, saying that his action would tear the Party to pieces. But Clark never forgave Bryan.

So far as I was concerned, I was quite content that Wilson had been nominated, although he had been on trial, and although Clark had been the packhorse for the Democratic Party and was a very fine man. There was no doubt that Wilson's principles were mine.

Wilson's election in November, 1912, was a foregone conclusion, and there was not much occasion for me to give close attention to the Presidential campaign. We felt more concern over the question of carrying Congress.

Woodrow Wilson's victory was for me the opening of a new era. I had never met him; I did not see him during the campaign, for I was then in my own district; but I had long observed his career and studied his ideas. There was great rejoicing among the progressive forces at the defeat of the powerful reactionary phalanx that had ruled the nation as with a rod of iron for sixteen years. To the victors the great day had come when they were to garner the fruits of patient, toilsome effort. My years of study of economic and financial questions were to be of greatest help to me in the tremendous legislative work ahead. We Democrats on the Ways and Means Committee, who had striven hard to meet our responsibilities of leadership and Party policy, were delighted to lay our work at the feet of Woodrow Wilson, enthusiastically cooperate with him and follow his leadership.

After Wilson's election we Democrats of the House, headed by Speaker Champ Clark, went to Seagirt, the summer residence of the Governor of New Jersey, and called upon the President-Elect. Clark introduced the entire delegation, one member at a time. Governor Wilson, by his affability and democratic demeanor, made a favorable impression on us all. He later held numerous conferences with many Democrats in Congress on the framing and passage through Congress of such vitally important measures as those on the tariff and the monetary problem.

On inauguration day I sat for five whole hours in the sun on the veranda of the Capitol building, watching the crowds and the parade. To me it was a new day dawning, and I could not leave the spectacle.

As the new President came into office, we had no acute issues or controversies pending with any other country, though trouble with Mexico lay just a few furrows away. Apparently there was no premonition of the World War coming seventeen months later. Both the Democratic and the Republican platforms of 1912 entirely omitted foreign policies except for one paragraph of five or six lines approving the abrogation of the treaty with Russia relative to the right of expatriation, primarily of Jews.

We had dabbled to a limited extent in international waters, following the Spanish American War, both in the Pacific and in Cuba and

Panama. The Spanish-American War was a venture in imperialism which caused a flurry of opposition in American politics, but this very soon became dormant except in Democratic platforms, and the country lapsed back into its traditional policy of isolation.

President Roosevelt had taken an active part at times, such as when he mediated the Russo-Japanese War and shot off skyrockets at the Kaiser. He had something to say first to one country and then to another in connection with problems pending between other nations. In fact, he was talking almost all the time.

Nevertheless, there was no general conception of the increasing rivalries and animosities boiling just beneath the surface among the nations of Europe. And no international issues existed with respect to external developments.

Shortly after his inauguration President Wilson departed from a more than century-old precedent by delivering his first message to Congress in person. Every inch of space in the hall of the House and in the galleries was occupied. The appearance of the President on the floor resulted in an exceedingly dramatic scene. Long-continued acclamation greeted his arrival, while applause punctuated his address throughout. He was perfectly composed and read his message and otherwise demeaned himself without any attempt at or appearance of dramatics.

A month before Wilson's inauguration occurred an event of fundamental importance to me. On February 3, 1913, the constitutional amendment on income tax was ratified. What Senator Aldrich and his standpat colleagues in the Senate believed impossible, when they sought to suffocate the income tax by wrapping it up in a proposed constitutional amendment, had become a fact. Here at last was fruition to my work and study of twenty years.

When the Ways and Means Committee met in 1913 and took up the drafting of the Underwood Tariff Bill, Chairman Underwood requested me to prepare the draft of desirable income-tax legislation. He designated himself, A. Mitchell Palmer and Andrew Peters as a subcommittee to review my draft. They made only one suggestion of consequence, which would have allowed the President, by proclamation, to raise or lower the income-tax rates each year as he deemed advisable. I definitely opposed this, and when we laid the bill, with this proposal along with it, before the full Ways and Means Committee, the committee overwhelmingly supported me and threw it out.

After I had written the final draft it went before the House practically as I wrote it. It fell to my lot to handle the income-tax provision on the floor of the House. We made some minor amendments to meet objections as the bill journeyed through the House. The measure was at no time in danger. I collaborated and sat in conference with members of the Senate Finance Committee when the bill reached the Senate. This is not infrequently done.

The provision became law as part of the Underwood Tariff Act on October 3, 1913. The United States now had a regular income tax as a permanent part of our fiscal system. No time was lost in applying it. It was forthwith made applicable to incomes received during the remainder of 1913.

When the income tax became law I received many communications describing in strong terms what the writers considered the enormous importance of this new tax policy. I myself felt that if I should live two lifetimes I probably would not be able to render public service equal to my part in the long fight for enactment of our income-tax system. This new tax was wholly indispensable in time of war while, by lifting vast tax burdens in consumption taxes from the backs of the poor and the masses generally, it became the one great equalizer of the tax burden and therefore a tremendous agency for the improvement of social conditions. Today the principle is so widely accepted that it seems difficult to visualize the need for the immense struggles that occurred before its adoption.

In addition to my labors on the income-tax section of the Underwood Act, I found an enormous amount of work given me in framing the tariff sections in the committee. Generally 90 per cent of work on legislation is done in committee. I worked closely with Underwood.

William Jennings Bryan came to Washington at this point and took an active part in drafting the measure. Then occurred his notable break with Underwood over the question of whether wool should be placed on the free list, as Bryan contended, or be given a 15 per cent duty, as Underwood urged. Strongly as I was for tariff revision downward, and friendly as I was toward Bryan, I stood with Underwood in the controversy. This was because of the belief I later practiced with trade agreements that, instead of jumping off the top of the building, it was safer to come down on the elevator.

We held tariff hearings which passed without special incident except for the tariff lobbyists. For the first time in many years the beneficiaries of high-tariff privilege found themselves confronting an unfriendly committee which would not permit them virtually to write their own rates.

This seemed very disconcerting to many of their representatives who appeared before the committee. The lobbyists, as usual, frequented most of the vacant space in the hotels and about the Capitol. Many of them called on all of us who were engaged in preparing the bill. We would receive and hear them courteously, but after that our courses diverged.

When the lobbyists became really pestiferous, we urged President Wilson to expose their activities. He promptly issued a blast against them in the form of a public statement urging them to leave Washington and give Congress a chance to proceed in an orderly way with its great legislative task. From then on the majority of them remained away from the city. Those who stayed on became less pestiferous when they discovered just what our policy was and saw they could not influence us.

We proceeded to consider the many items of the whole measure from the viewpoint of what Underwood proclaimed as a competitive rate level. We completed drafting the bill well under the early schedule previously planned.

Some of us who strove to be most active on the steering committee kept close contact with legislative measures of major importance in addition to the tariff and income-tax questions, such as the Federal Reserve, antitrust, farm-loan, and labor measures. We gave all possible aid to the committees immediately in charge until these important bills passed the two Houses and went to President Wilson for signature.

We pressed hard for the measure for the Federal Reserve System. Our Ways and Means Committee appointed a great statesman, Carter Glass, chairman of the Banking and Currency Committee, to assure a final and constructive solution of what had been the insoluble money and currency problem. Glass and I were very intimate for many years, calling each other by our first names like double cousins. We were thrown together all through the Wilson Administration in matters of different kinds, particularly in the House, until Glass went over to the Senate. Glass shifted over to the conservative side because of his fight with the Martin-Swanson machine in Virginia, but he swung in behind Wilson and was for Wilson's measures, so much so that the President made him Secretary of the Treasury. Glass was very taciturn, quiet, and reserved.

My associates and I on the Ways and Means Committee gave the Federal Reserve measure our special support at every stage, particularly on the crucial issues such as whether bankers should be on the Federal Reserve Board. We participated in many conferences with House Members or groups of Members in efforts to facilitate its progress through the two Houses of Congress. When some Members rebelled against the measure, President Wilson got Bryan to send a statement to the House that pulled the rug out from under them. Congressman Robert L. Owen of Oklahoma, a good friend of mine, rendered efficient assistance and later always claimed some of the credit that Glass and his friends claimed for the Federal Reserve Act. I always felt that Owen rendered valuable service but that the Wilson Administration built the measure around Glass and his committee. Glass's committee functioned wonderfully well, and the Federal Reserve Bill, passed through the House and Senate, became law with President Wilson's signature on December 23, 1913.

I was strongly in favor of antitrust legislation, having long opposed the trusts. We of the Ways and Means Committee made Henry Clayton of Alabama, a very able lawyer, chairman of the Judiciary Committee, and this committee secured the passage of the Clayton Antitrust Act.

My interest was also strong in favor of the Federal Trade Commission bill. We on the steering committee kept fully alive to the steps leading up to the passage of this important measure designed to bring order and fairness into American business.

President Wilson himself kept in intimate touch with legislation. He continued the practice he had started following his election of conferring with many Members of the House and Senate. On our side some of us members of the Ways and Means Committee, especially with Chairman Underwood acting as spokesman, kept in close contact with the White House and some other heads of the executive departments. This promoted the fullest teamwork between the Executive and the House of Representatives, and at times proved of special value. On occasion we would ask the President to call up or send a message to a Member who was wavering on an issue. We sought to know exactly where this approach was needed and to see to it that it was taken.

In February, 1914, with the income tax already operating, I invaded the territory of greatest opposition to the tax in order to explain it, and delivered an address in New York City before the State Bar Association. New York, being the headquarters of great wealth, had strenuously fought the enactment of the income tax, and it was my task to win them to support it. "I am well aware," I said, "that in the past the greatest opposition to an income tax in the United States has come from the eastern section of the country upon the theory that it would unjustly contribute more taxes than any other section."

But I went on to say: "From this view I respectfully dissent for the reason that New York, for example, is the great center of commerce of the nation. It is a great distributing center. Hundreds of thousands of citizens of other States come here to reside. Her great incomes are drawn from all sections of the country. These concentrated profits are chiefly the product of the great industries throughout the nation. I deny the right of wealth anywhere to segregate itself and then upon the plea of segregation to exempt itself from its fair share of taxes."

Later that year I was delighted to receive from William G. McAdoo, Secretary of the Treasury, "just a line to congratulate you on the results of the income-tax law for the fiscal year ended June 30, 1914." Mr. McAdoo, in his letter dated July 8, 1914, wrote: "I am sure that you are as much gratified as I am with the showing. The law is new and, although unpopular in some quarters, it is not one-tenth as unpopular as partisan papers represent it and certainly not near so unpopular as the average men expected it to be. On the whole there is every reason to feel gratified with its success thus far." McAdoo never hesitated to characterize me as the author of the income-tax law.

In 1914 I was entrusted with further national Party responsibility by election as a member of the Democratic National Committee to fill a vacancy caused by the death of a most able and eminent Tennessean, R. E. L. Mountcastle. I served in this capacity without opposition during the next fourteen years and then retired voluntarily.

How different the first half of 1914 from the latter half! The former saw us working every possible hour, putting into effect the measures for which we long had fought. We were observing and studying the lower tariffs and the income tax in operation. We were preparing further legislation and steadily enacting a long list of wholesome measures. We Democrats in the House of Representatives, under the leadership of the steering committee and the Speaker, had full and constant teamwork, and the same relationship existed between us and the White House.

And then in June a shot rang out at Sarajevo!

7: War and Trade

A MONTH AND MORE passed from the shot at Sarajevo until the cannon started booming on the Eastern and Western Fronts, but this was insufficient time for people over here to visualize what waves of repercussion would roll over them. It was not until the New York Stock Exchange closed, following the closing of the London and Paris exchanges, and our foreign trade collapsed that our people came to see that the war in Europe would not leave them untouched.

The First World War was a culmination of years of intense, bitter rivalry among a number of daring and desperate powers seeking territory, trade advantage, raw materials, control of trade routes, and political, economic, or military domination of small and helpless peoples. This strife, much of it just below the surface, had been steadily growing more bitter and dangerous. Some of Europe's rulers more than once had resorted to tactics of threatening and bluffing and engaging in dangerous acts on the very verge of war. Underlying conditions of hostility, readiness for military conflict, and determination to seek certain objectives were ripe for a surface occurrence, such as the assassination of Archduke Ferdinand, to touch off a great war.

This country was generally opposed to involvement in the war. President Wilson and leaders of all political parties echoed this sentiment. Leaders of public thought and advocates of peace for this nation who had contacts with the Allies or the Central Powers sought vainly to encourage some means of ending the war and establishing a sound basis for future peace. Various kinds of world organizations were soon proposed by different groups of peace advocates and by individuals in this country, such as an association of nations to function after the war.

To me, the war, disastrous as it was in all aspects, offered both tragedy and a springboard for constructive legislation.

The conflict would unquestionably be long and sanguinary. Respect for treaties was already in the discard. Commerce would be overthrown and industry distorted. A harvest of hatred and revenge was being sown, the evil fruits of which a quarter of a century later were to strew my path in the State Department.

As an immediate result, the war hopelessly impeded the natural operation of the Underwood Tariff Law from which we had predicted great economic and trade benefits. With both imports and exports drastically transformed and demoralized as some sections of the world became closed to our commerce and other sections changed the nature of their trade, the Law had little opportunity to produce the results we expected.

On the other hand the conflict forced the further development of the income-tax principle. Aiming, as it did, at the one great untaxed source of revenue, the income-tax law had been enacted in the nick of time for the demands of the war. And the conflict also assisted the enactment of other great measures such as the Federal estate and inheritance tax and the putting into effect of the Federal Reserve System, likewise in the nick of time.

Opponents of lower tariffs savagely attacked the Underwood Act, as if it were responsible for the diminished revenues then coming in through customs receipts. I hurried to the defense on September 25, 1914, less than two months after the outbreak of war, and called attention to "the almost complete standstill to which not only the interstate but the international commerce of the entire world has come." As for the opponents of the Underwood Act, I said: "Now we know—a blind man or a driveling idiot knows—that when this war broke out and our $700,000,000 commerce with Germany, Belgium, Austria, and European Russia suddenly went out of existence, when our international exchange broke down, when our exports of $650,000,000 of cotton and $50,000,000 of tobacco ceased, when every class of international business came to a standstill, the Treasury suffered losses at the customhouse."

While I could not see any immediate end of the war, I could indeed see growing effects upon the United States. "Our imports from Europe," I said, "must naturally fall off as long as the war continues, and no one can prophesy that it will end within any short time. While we are not actually at war, we are actually facing war conditions as much as or more than, in some respects, if we were at war."

Several months passed; the war increased in fury and its effects on this country intensified, but still I felt that Americans did not adequately appreciate its meaning and especially its danger. On February 26, 1915, I opened a long address in the House by saying:

"Mr. Speaker, one of the surprising facts relating to the existing European war is the entire failure of so many intelligent citizens of the United States to realize and appreciate its tremendous effects upon finance, commerce and industry throughout the world; indeed, they do not grasp the real scope and extent of the war itself. Little do many people, especially in the peace countries, realize that we are passing through the most momentous epoch in the history of the human race."

Neither the Federal Government nor the States had made any serious effort to reach vast estates and inheritances for taxation prior to the enactment of our new income-tax law. I and many others had stood also for the State development of estate and inheritance taxation, but up to this time most of the States had shown little interest and had done little or nothing in this direction. I urged that $300,000,000 to $400,000,000 of revenue could be raised by this tax either by the Federal Government or by the States, and therefore the Federal Government should proceed until the States might decide to develop it to the same extent.

During 1915 I proceeded to make the necessary studies and to formulate a Federal estate and inheritance-tax proposal. As in the case of my investigations of income-tax problems, I procured the estate and inheritance and related laws of all the important nations of the world. After full examination, I stripped out the provisions I considered most practical for this country. I also began to prepare a revision of the income-tax law of 1913.

When Congress adjourned in March, 1915, I found myself thrown into a bitter political fight in Tennessee. Since going to Congress eight years before, I had taken no part in State politics. By 1915 the senior United States Senator from Tennessee, Luke Lea, had made himself head of an arbitrary and powerful Democratic political machine in my home State. Lea was brilliant; he had been elected to the Senate when he was scarcely beyond the constitutional age of thirty; he owned one of the leading newspapers in the State and was connected with many of the most influential families in Tennessee. Scarcely anyone entering the Senate had a finer opportunity to succeed.

Lea, however, had an overweening ambition to dominate all political affairs within his range. To accomplish this purpose he, like many politicians, fell into practices of so arbitrary or unfair a nature as to arouse much opposition. I felt that Lea was gradually developing a reign of terror in Tennessee Democratic politics, which were just emerging from the chaos of the Governor Patterson regime. Governor Tom Rye was his friend, and Lea was able to offer patronage to opposing or wavering members of the State Democratic Committee in his effort to line them up. Congressmen from the State were being intimidated and improperly interfered with by his machine. I felt his pressure in many ways.

I became convinced that State politics, and also those Federal

politics tied in with Tennessee, would soon again reach a state of anarchy
under the Lea organization. Therefore, without consulting Lea's top assistants or those opposed to him, I decided to do what I could to destroy his
machine. I determined to establish close contact, personally and through
my most influential friends, with members of the Democratic State Executive Committee, over which Lea was struggling desperately to win absolute control.

When Congress adjourned I went to my home in Carthage. From
there I quietly journeyed every Friday to Nashville and, without the least
publicity, established myself in a hotel. During the week ends I and two
or three friends, whom I called in for each visit, talked personally or by
telephone to suitable members of the committee throughout the State. We
were likewise in touch with the friends of such committeemen. To each
committeeman in the least doubt as to his attitude, our plea was that he
withhold any thought of allying himself with the members of the committee already threatened with Lea's domination. I went to the friends of
Governor Rye and told them we were for him for Governor; but I suggested he run his own race for Governor since we would not want to see
him get into the Lea fight. Of great assistance to me was Major James
Stahlman, the notable publisher of the Nashville *Banner*, a great civic
leader and always a power in the public affairs of Tennessee.

For a time our efforts seemed to meet with success. But as March,
April, and May passed by, I perceived that Lea, with the use or promise
of patronage, was gradually making progress toward securing control of
the supreme Party agency in Tennessee. I thereupon decided upon a new
strategy. Lea was to come up for election in 1916. The primary election
would ordinarily be called for 1916, to nominate Lea's successor.

I approached my Democratic associates and suggested that the Senatorial primary be called one year earlier. My reason was that it would
deprive Lea of the time he needed for organizing his machine so as to
obtain control of the State Committee. Some of the friends who had been
helping me immediately objected that this would be likely to cause a
reaction in Lea's favor, on the ground that he was being placed at a
disadvantage.

I replied that, in ordinary circumstances, a candidate could raise
that cry with some effect. However, Lea was being heralded over the
State by his supporters as supreme and unassailable by reason of his
great strength and his arbitrary control over the Party machine and
patronage. Therefore, if Lea should charge that he was being placed at

a disadvantage, the people would be disposed to laugh at rather than to sympathize with him.

Finally, after much discussion, our whole group agreed to follow this strategy. We concentrated on persuading members of the State Committee to adopt our plan. The committee was called to meet in special session on August 4 to consider issuing a call for a State-wide primary election to nominate a candidate for the United States Senate.

Naturally Lea and his machine reacted violently. They exhausted every imaginable effort to prevent the committee from calling the primary. The pulling and hauling by both sides as the committee meeting approached was terrific. We of the opposition called in a number of important Democratic leaders who had not been active in the contest, among them Congressmen Finis Garrett, T. W. Sims and Kenneth McKellar.

The State Committee duly met amid sharp tension and wide publicity. After full debate, the committee decided to call the primary for 1915, as we proposed. Lea's Nashville newspaper next morning said: "The Senatorial trust headed by Cordell Hull, with the aid of . . . other very doughty warriors, are entitled to all of the discredit for the plan."

Immediately former Governor Patterson and Congressmen Sims and McKellar announced their candidacies for the United States Senate against Lea. Many friends urged me also to announce my candidacy. I had told many Democratic leaders, however, that my fight against the Lea machine was not a personal matter from which I expected to profit but was a sincere effort to rid the State of an organization that was rapidly disrupting the party. I received many encouraging assurances of support if I should run, and I believe I could have won—but I said No.

Moreover, the position I occupied in the House had its own importance. As a member of the Ways and Means Committee, I shared in jurisdiction over revenue, tariff and tax measures, all of which constitutionally had to originate in the House of Representatives. In the circumstances the Senatorship was not so tempting to me as it was to some of my associates.

The primary election that followed resulted in the nomination of McKellar and marked the end of the Lea regime for many years. From then on I had nothing further to do with State politics. But fourteen years later, when I announced my candidacy for the Senate, I was to come head on against Lea, who meantime had again built up a powerful State machine and become its chief.

I now turned again to national affairs, as we found it necessary to pass more revenue legislation in 1916. In that year the leaders of the House again let me handle the income tax. I redrafted the income-tax bill to put on somewhat heavier rates. But some of the people in the East who were afraid of income tax prevailed on President Wilson not to let us take the existing Act and put real rates into it. Wilson sent for me and several others, and asked us to defer the stiffer rates for the immediate present.

This was purely temporary, however, and I continued my work on a revised income-tax law and also on an estate-tax bill. I assembled all the inheritance-tax and estate-tax laws from other nations, and made use of certain provisions that I wrote into the Estate Tax Act of 1916, drawing mainly on the experience of Great Britain. I presented this and the draft of a revised income-tax law to the Ways and Means Committee for its approval, which it gave without material change.

We also prepared a good-sized excise-tax bill. I had been working on such tax questions day and night; the other Members had not been following them so closely; hence I had the opportunity to do much more work on these measures than would otherwise have been the case.

I had also made an exhaustive study of the sales tax, in view of the fact that many other Members were running pell-mell for it. I reported sharply against it when my opinion was asked, in view of my belief that it fell on the poor man, and I and others who thought as I did were able to beat it off.

At this point I introduced an innovation into the Ways and Means Committee—the use of expert draftsmen to draft bills. Columbia University had sent down two such experts to let Congress see what they could do toward rendering aid of value. I secured the services of these two gentlemen, one of whom, Mr. Middleton Beaman, still continues in that service, to take my draft of the estate-tax measures and give me and the committee such suggestions, especially technical, as they might be capable of.

The leaders of the Ways and Means Committee were much opposed to allowing these expert draftsmen to come into the private sessions of the committee in order to aid it. They adhered to the old theory that a Congressman was highly capable of doing his own drafting. The contest for their admission went on for weeks before I got them in. This drafting service soon became universally popular and highly useful in both Houses of Congress.

When the revised income-tax measure and the estate-tax measure were completed, they were duly reported to the House by the Ways and

Means Committee. I again undertook to do my full part in looking after them on the floor when they came up for debate. When they reached the Senate the Finance Committee referred them to a subcommittee composed of Senators John Sharp Williams, Ollie M. James, and Thomas P. Gore. On their invitation I sat with them for some weeks offering such assistance as I could. This included my passing on a vast number of technical amendments that were naturally being presented by interested persons over the country.

The bills were passed in due course and became law with President Wilson's signature September 8, 1916. The principle of income tax was now permanently established. It afforded the basis for the excess-profits tax, in effect a graduated corporations tax, which became law March 3, 1917. And above all it laid the cornerstone for the structure of Government financing during the First World War, the peace period following, and the Second World War. It then brought in tens of billions of taxes that could not have been otherwise raised in any practical manner and avoided the alternative of issuing bonds in unlimited amounts.

The year 1916 is a milestone in my political thinking. Then for the first time openly I enlarged my views on trade and tariffs from the national to the international theater. Hitherto I had fought hard for lower tariffs, largely because of their immediate domestic effect. I believed that high tariffs meant a higher cost of living for American citizens. They assisted in building up monopolies and trusts. By cutting down the sales by other countries to us, they also cut down the purchases by other countries from us.

But toward 1916 I embraced the philosophy I carried throughout my twelve years as Secretary of State, into the Trade Agreements, into numerous speeches and statements addressed to this country and to the world. From then on, to me, unhampered trade dovetailed with peace; high tariffs, trade barriers, and unfair economic competition, with war. Though realizing that many other factors were involved, I reasoned that, if we could get a freer flow of trade—freer in the sense of fewer discriminations and obstructions—so that one country would not be deadly jealous of another and the living standards of all countries might rise, thereby eliminating the economic dissatisfaction that breeds war, we might have a reasonable chance for lasting peace.

On July 8, 1916, speaking of high tariffs, I told the House of Representatives: "Apart from its essential injustice to the people, this system has become a positive menace to the peace of all trade countries. It is naturally utilized for purposes of rank discrimination, practical boycotting, undue preferences, and other irritating practices. . . . It is a matter of common knowledge that the operation of the many unfair, injurious, and trouble-making trade practices and the strenuous trade conquests pursued under these systems chiefly contributed to the outbreak of the present European war."

And then in that speech I made a suggestion:

"If I were President of the United States," I said, "I should, at a later and suitable date, propose to the governments of all commercial nations that at the close of the present European war an international trade conference be held in the city of Washington for the purpose of establishing a permanent international trade congress." The function and duty of such a congress, I said, would be to consider "all international trade methods, practices, and policies which in their effects are calculated to create destructive commercial controversies or bitter economic wars, and to formulate agreements with respect thereto, designed to eliminate and avoid the injurious results and dangerous possibilities of economic warfare, and to promote fair and friendly trade relations among all the nations of the world."

I had hoped to be able to do more than make a suggestion. In February of 1916 I had prepared a resolution calling for this world-trade conference after the war, and intended introducing it in Congress. Before doing so, however, I addressed a letter to Secretary of State Lansing, explaining the entire proposal and enclosing a copy of the proposed resolution. In a spirit of teamwork I requested his opinion as to whether he had any objection to my offering the resolution.

He replied that some features of it might produce friction with some other countries, and asked me to defer its introduction for the time being. Mr. Lansing did not have the broad international economic view. Accordingly I postponed introducing it until April, 1917. Then, I believe, it became the forerunner of Point Three of Wilson's Fourteen Points, for I had discussed tariff and commercial policy with the President, though I had no commitment from him. Point Three called for elimination of international trade barriers.

My thought and hope was that the proposal contained in my resolution could be communicated to the other nations even in the midst of war, so that when the war ended we would have something ready for discussion, something which, if agreed to, might have rendered another war less likely. But, as a Congressman, I was not able to do what I succeeded in doing as Secretary of State before and during the Second World War.

The transformation of my ideas on tariff and trade from the national to the international sphere was a long development. I became a tariff student in 1888 when the Mills bill was pending in Congress. In the 1890's I read the debates on the Mills, McKinley, Wilson, and Dingley bills. In those earlier years I breathed in the fire of great tariff battles—but they were battles fought on the home grounds that high tariffs or low tariffs were good or bad for the United States as a purely domestic matter. There was little or no thought of their effect on other countries, little or no thought of their effect on world peace.

Blaine, Cleveland, Harrison, and other great leaders in the past had therefore conducted strenuous national campaigns virtually on whether tariff rates should be somewhat raised or somewhat lowered. They had no permanent policies to deal with the international economic situation and its relation to tariffs. True, Mr. Blaine made a serious effort to initiate in a limited way the policy that domestic and international trade and economics were interlocked. But he was hopelessly overridden by the high-tariff interests in Congress; only a few feeble international trade gestures were inserted in the McKinley and Dingley Acts; and nothing of consequence came of them.

When I went to live at the Cochran Hotel, I found there a Congressman of unusual ability, the best informed man in Congress on tariffs, trade, and related questions—E. J. Hill of Connecticut. He was too modest and retiring to jump forward too many times; otherwise he would have been one of the best known men in the United States. A genius for facts and figures, he hid his light under a bushel. For years he carried a small black-backed notebook in his inside pocket, and when he and others were arguing almost any question on the floor of Congress, he would draw out his little book and recite some of its contents, thereby almost invariably administering a knockout to his competitors.

From 1907 forward Mr. Hill, a Republican, and I sat for hours at a time of Sundays and evenings discussing tariff, trade, and other business conditions. Sometime between 1907 and 1910 he had taken a trip around the world to investigate tariff and general economic conditions, and had visited practically everywhere. When he came back he was filled with reports of conditions overseas. I owe much to him for the inspiration that drove me to study the interrelation of trade throughout the world.

My work in connection with the Payne Tariff Bill also required me to study tariff and trade questions abroad. Later, the Underwood Bill called for extensive studies of overseas conditions so that I could answer criticisms on the floor from adherents of high tariff. My speeches to the House began to be liberally interlarded with references to tariff developments in other countries.

When the war came in 1914, I was very soon impressed with two points. The first was its terrific commercial impact on the United States. I saw that you could not separate the idea of commerce from the idea of war and peace. You could not have serious war anywhere in the world and expect commerce to go on as before. And the second was that wars were often largely caused by economic rivalry conducted unfairly.

I thereupon came to believe that if we could eliminate this bitter economic rivalry, if we could increase commercial exchanges among nations over lowered trade and tariff barriers and remove unnatural obstructions to trade, we would go a long way toward eliminating war itself.

After long and careful deliberation, I decided to announce and work for the broad policy of removing or lowering all excessive barriers to international trade, exchange and finance of whatsoever kind, and to adopt commercial policies that would make possible the development of vastly increased trade among the nations. This part of my proposal was based on a conviction that such liberal commercial policies and such development of the volume of commerce would constitute an essential foundation of any peace structure the civilized nations might erect following the war. This was the only means of providing wider access to raw materials, increased production, increased facilities for transportation and distribution, increased consumption and increased employment of labor throughout the world. It was calculated greatly to augment understanding and friendliness among peoples and nations.

In my letter to Lansing I suggested subjects for the international trade-treaty conference I proposed. One was the universal adoption of the principle of unconditional most-favored-nation treatment. The United States did not then embrace this principle, which meant simply that a nation would apply the same tariff rates and commercial regulations to all other nations without discrimination, provided the other nations dealt with it on the same basis.

I also suggested discontinuance of trade retaliation and undue discrimination; an understanding on maritime rights of noncontraband commerce; suitable action against unfair procurement of trade routes or unfair interference with trade routes, and against a powerful nation forcing trade upon a weak one; an agreement against subsidizing or aiding a domestic industry so as to enable it to undersell its rivals in other countries or destroy them by unfair methods; prohibiting boycotting of one nation by another; and the equal application of export duties and of the right of entry to the ports of other countries.

I opposed the well known colonial or empire system and asked for the discontinuance or a virtually nominal operation of preferential tariffs and other differential treatment as between a mother country and colonies. (Exactly a quarter of a century later President Franklin D. Roosevelt and I were to have strong exchanges with Prime Minister Winston Churchill on this subject.) I counseled the adoption of a reasonable system of commercial arbitration covering dealings between traders of different countries.

This, therefore, had become a large part of my philosophy for peace. From that day on I never ceased to urge it whether as Congressman, as Senator, as Secretary of State or as an American citizen. I carried it to the London Economic Conference in 1933 and to the Montevideo Conference later that year. And when I came back from South America I pressed it on Congress and saw the enactment of the Trade Agreements Act in 1934.

And I continue to urge it today with the same fervor as the day I first prepared the resolution, with Europe at war, or the day I presented it in Congress, with the United States drawn into the conflict. My only regret is that the United States and other nations did not see fit to embrace these ideas earlier and that I had to wait until after becoming Secretary of State to see the beginning of their adoption.

While I was evolving the proposal of 1916 for building a sound economic foundation of enduring peace, I had also been struck for some years by the fact that this great, young, undeveloped country, with no planning for broader objectives extending to the world and the future, was perfectly content to float along and produce immense surpluses in a steadily increasing number of industries, with no plan or preparation for their sale abroad. These were cotton, tobacco, numerous other agricultural products, many iron and steel products, agricultural implements and a long list of specialties, such as typewriters.

We permitted Britain and other countries to furnish most of our merchant shipping, to provide the insurance on our surpluses shipped abroad, and to handle the exchange and other financing in payment. Britain, Belgium, Germany, and other commercial countries, acting as our broker, came here, purchased and took our surpluses abroad and sold them, pocketing their profit or commission.

I felt that no country could get anywhere or make real progress with this sort of system fastened on its economic fabric. The proposal I offered in 1916 implied our own merchant marine and our own selling and buying in international markets, saving to ourselves the insurance, profits, and commissions on which other nations had been feasting for generations.

In 1916, as well as in the previous year, I closely followed the thinking and speaking being done by different groups, like William Howard Taft's League to Enforce Peace, and by individuals such as Theodore Roosevelt, Senator Henry Cabot Lodge, and President Lowell of Harvard, all of whom were driving toward some kind of association of nations to follow the war. I strongly believed in the idea from the beginning. During my study of the prewar economic situation in Europe, I had formed the firm conclusion that balance of power had to be replaced by an association of nations. Federations of nations had been organized in Europe ostensibly to protect themselves against other federations, but in reality, in the case of Germany, to advance their military principles of aggression. I felt that these federations, otherwise known as alliances, and their basic idea of balance of power had to give way in favor of a confederation of nations that would maintain the peace.

During the 1916 Presidential campaign between Wilson and Charles Evans Hughes, I spent some months working in the New York Democratic headquarters, aiding the Division on National Organization. I also delivered a number of speeches in support of our ticket, both inside and outside my district. So far as I could judge, the campaign of 1916 seemed well conducted from the Democratic side, even though all the reaction that had accumulated during Wilson's first term was being brought to bear against him. During the campaign I saw a great deal of Vance McCormick, chairman of the Democratic National Committee, and A. Mitchell Palmer. McCormick soon appointed me a member of the Executive Committee of the Democratic National Committee, which was the group that conducted the important affairs of the entire organization.

The Executive Committee met regularly and gave attention to the varied responsibilities imposed on it by President Wilson, most of which were of a nonpolitical nature. We kept a close relationship with many of the chief activities of the executive branch. Fairly often we voluntarily expressed our views on important questions to the executive branch either in person or through Chairman McCormick, when we felt we could possibly do so.

Following Wilson's victory in the election, I remained in Washington throughout the Christmas holidays and endeavored to aid the Democratic candidacies of Speaker and other elective Members of the House. This called for constant and delicate attention because of the virtually equal number of Democrats and Republicans who had been elected to the House. If anything, the Republicans, counting two or three Congressmen of loose political alignment, actually had a slight advantage. The problem was to nurse this whole situation in the light of the increasing disposition of Republican leaders not to assume the responsibility of controlling the House during the two years to follow, which they correctly believed would be filled with war and war's problems. As a result of this decision, the Democratic House organization was continued in power.

As 1917 began, the Germans were clearly creating a reign of terror on the high seas. Defiantly and contrary to all laws of right, justice, and humanity, they were sinking a growing number of American vessels with increasing loss of life and property. Ordinary diligence required this country to strengthen its army and navy and fortifications and other defensive agencies. My studies accordingly became directed toward finding added revenues to meet these added expenses. While some of us were sure President Wilson was doing everything within his power to keep this country out of war, we became increasingly doubtful how long he would be able to succeed. The Germans' reckless and lawless actions were pushing countries like ours to the very brink of war. It was inevitable that the United States would be forced in.

I felt that no other course was offered us, in justice to our own rights, interests, and self-respect. Here was another case when a ruling dictator decided to play the role of international desperado and conqueror, first of Europe and then of the world. This country moved rapidly toward the Herculean task of self-defense against the war which the Central Powers were precipitating.

I supported all Wilson's prewar bills, including the arming of merchant ships. I approved his policy toward Germany without exception. I could not go along with Bryan's attitude of opposition, which had led to his resignation in 1915. Bryan was a pacifist and, while he was truly wonderful in many ways, I found that now and then his judgment would fail him.

When it was clear that the die was cast, President Wilson came over to Congress with a proposal for a formal declaration of war against Germany. Every inch of space in the hall of the House was occupied; people came from far and near, and fabulous prices were offered for a ticket of admission to hear the President's war message. Amid high tension and great suppressed excitement, the applause as Wilson revealed his proposals was deafening and long continued. The occasion, which will be ever memorable in the history of the country, passed without untoward incident. Immediately a suitable resolution declaring a state of war between this country and Germany was prepared and offered for passage. The vote in support of it, including my own, was literally overwhelming. The United States was at war. We had authorized the President to proceed toward victory with "the entire naval and military forces of the United States and the resources of the Government."

8: Paying the War Bill

RIGHT AFTER our declaration of a state of war against Germany, I wrote the War Department tendering my services in the armed forces in any capacity in which I could be useful. My offer came to naught, however, because President Wilson shortly issued a statement that Congressmen should remain on duty in Congress and not enter the army or navy.

At the outset I favored a volunteer bill rather than the Selective Service bill. Coming from the "Volunteer State," and steeped in the tradition of our area that all able-bodied men who were alive to the nation's interests should volunteer for service the moment they saw large headlines in a newspaper indicating that the country was in danger, I preferred this historic system. Nevertheless, I also recognized that the conflict would go on and expand, and I therefore adopted the view that we should start in with volunteering and then adopt the Selective Service system at any time we needed it.

I decided from the beginning to concentrate on methods of financing the war. I had devoted my life to a close study of tariffs, revenue, finance, and economics. My job therefore was to aid in financing the war on the soundest possible basis. I had already worked unceasingly during many years for the passage of measures that were to prove of incalculable help. By that fateful April 6, the income-tax law of 1913 had been amended and strengthened, the estate tax was in effect, and the Federal Reserve System was operating. Even before we got into the war, the effects of the conflict, along with our expenses in the campaign in Mexico, had demanded additional financing on our part.

From the outbreak of the war in Europe in 1914, I, like many others, had become tremendously concerned about its future course and possible effects on our own country. I closely observed and analyzed every relevant fact, circumstance or development from day to day—particularly those of an economic nature—that might shed light on this momentous question. I therefore had at my finger tips most pertinent facts and statistics even to many of the minute details concerning methods of financing the war by other belligerent nations. I had studied all their important financial, revenue, and economic policies and enactments to see how they could apply here. In numerous speeches through and following the war I was able to offer for our domestic legislation analyses of all these precedents and effects of the war on the people of each major country concerned.

I again and again outlined to Congress the war financing experiences of other countries, going into great detail so that Congressmen could compare our methods with those of our Allies and the enemy countries, and the neutrals too. I reported on the systems in use in England, France, Germany, Austria, Russia, Italy, Belgium, Sweden, Switzerland, Denmark, and Norway, among others. Questions were put to me again and again by other Members seeking items of information on the methods of other nations.

On April 17 I delivered an address in the House, pointing out that what our Allies most needed at the moment was credit. "Almost a year will be required in which to raise, train and equip an army of sufficient size and strength to play an important part in the present military operations against Germany," I said. "The most powerful blow the United States can strike at this early stage would be to arrange suitable credits for the Allies to the end that their armies on the various battle fronts may be clothed, fed, and otherwise supplied with all the necessary equipments and munitions which will enable them constantly to prosecute their present military operations against the common enemy."

I had very definite ideas on financing the war. I pleaded that the war should be financed on sound lines right from the beginning, saying that this problem "cannot receive too serious consideration, for the reason that the wisdom and soundness of its solution would be calculated materially to affect the economic affairs of the country both during and after the war."

My speech was on the occasion of a war-bond issue for $7,000,-000,000, but I then emphatically stated a principle I stoutly adhered to throughout the war. This was that the war should be paid for as largely as possible by taxation, with bonds and other loans accounting for the remainder. I felt that we should undertake to defray as much as 50 per cent of the war expenses by taxes, and this in fact became the goal of the fiscal authorities of the Government.

"Suggestions," I said, "are always offered to the effect that future generations should bear a share of emergency indebtedness incurred in fighting a great war. These suggestions overlook the fact that the same future generations are generally called upon to bear contemporaneous war or other emergency taxes in large amounts."

I stated this principle further on September 13, 1917: "The best policy is to levy the largest amount of taxes that can be imposed without actual and serious impairment or disruption of the normal business of the taxpayers, making increases in such tax levies as the war progresses and expenditures swell, and as business adjusts itself to the new conditions which such tax levies create. The remainder of the expenses should be met by the issuance of bonds."

I likewise stated another principle in my April 17 address; namely, "The experience of this and other nations in financing wars has taught the sound lesson that a nation should undertake to liquidate its indebtedness incurred in war or on account of other extraordinary causes as soon as possible, or at least within a period not exceeding twenty or thirty years."

Yet a further principle I advocated, which was later to prove of vital importance, was that the Liberty and other loans should not be tax free, lest the wealthy classes put their money into them and thus avoid taxation. "At the best," I said on September 13, "the amount of the world's capital which will be found to be exempt from taxation at the close of the war for a generation will be appalling. With the right to tax reserved, the curse of a bonded aristocracy can be avoided." Otherwise, I said, there would be "one class of idle and wealthy bondholders owing no financial obligations to the Federal, State, or local governments, and another class composed of the masses subject in their privations to enormous taxes to pay both the interest and the principal of such bonds and other expenses of the Government. Such condition would greatly conduce to socialism."

I also proposed the creation of a stabilization fund to prevent depreciation in the market prices of Government bonds, pointing out the constant efforts made by persons and groups of persons in other countries to create artificial fluctuations in the value of such bonds.

I favored a double system of bookkeeping, so as to keep in separate columns the extraordinary expenses of war and the ordinary expenses of the Government. This was embodied in the Revenue Act of March 3, 1917. Before we entered the war there was vicious, carping criticism by the old supporters of high tariff who most unfairly charged the loss of revenues under the Underwood Tariff Act to the Act itself and not to the slump in dutiable imports as a result of the war in Europe—which was the whole truth, a fact confirmed by the experience of other important countries.

My suggestion for the double system of bookkeeping had been

primarily to take care of the unfair criticism of the opposition. I figured that the general public could thereby see much more clearly what the extraordinary expenditures were and could account for them accordingly. With our own entry into the war, this system of bookkeeping naturally became more difficult but was still important.

In general, I insisted that every possible ounce of American resources be cast into the scales. "Now that the United States is at war," I said on April 17, "it will be worse than folly from every viewpoint to prosecute that war on a small or insignificant scale or in a seemingly weak or half-hearted manner. Every consideration of safety and self-respect now and in the future requires that the entire weight of this great country should unreservedly be thrown into the war."

After we entered the war we proceeded to prepare and pass through Congress the measure known as the Revenue Act of October 3, 1917. This was frankly an Act to defray war expenses. It was not as far-reaching by any means as some of us desired. We were turning principally to such new tax methods as the income and excess-profits. The largest amount of revenue that could be hoped for amidst unsettled and demoralized war conditions was entirely inadequate for the huge demands that would inevitably be made on the Treasury. The estimates of yield from the Act were only two billion dollars.

The Ways and Means Committee was now under the chairmanship of Claude Kitchin, since Oscar Underwood had been elected to the Senate. Mr. Kitchin possessed a delightful personality. He was very able and intensely patriotic. He rendered highly efficient service as chairman of the committee during the war period. Conscientiously opposed to entering the war, he voted against it, but resolutely supported all measures for its prosecution.

From the outbreak of the war on, I kept in close contact with the Treasury to facilitate the operation of revenue acts we had enacted in Congress. Among those I frequently saw were Secretary of the Treasury McAdoo, whose record was unexcelled; Assistant Secretary Leffingwell, extremely able and competent; and Daniel C. Roper, our old clerk of the Ways and Means Committee, who had meantime become Commissioner of Internal Revenue. Roper directed an important portion of the entire Treasury operations by reason of the rapidly accumulating internal revenue taxes constantly being levied during the war.

In the autumn of 1917 Congress had to face serious difficulties with its brand-new excess-profits-tax method. Owing to the many conflicting opinions in the committee and the complicated and artificial nature of our business structure, the law passed was considered almost impossible of administration. At the request of the Treasury I presided for the six weeks of the Christmas holidays over the Board of Excess Profits Tax Advisers at the Treasury. This had been created, at my suggestion, to write regulations that would make the new law workable, and no more capable group could have been selected to meet this complicated situation.

We labored day and night. We wrote much actual new law in the form of regulations, something the Treasury really had no authority to do. So sound and practical, however, were most of these regulations that Congress in its great Revenue Act of 1918 enacted them to a large extent as part of the Act.

It was while I was presiding over the Board of Excess Profits Tax Advisers, in the midst of this unprecedented emergency situation, that an important change occurred in my personal life. I got married.

Some years before, I had met in Washington my future wife, Frances Witz, of Staunton, Virginia. Her father was a banker and industrialist and had been a soldier under Stonewall Jackson. She had attended Mary Baldwin College.

We had known each other well for several years, and for some time we had planned soon to be wedded. As each month came and went with almost lightning rapidity, and demands on my time became more nearly impossible, we finally decided we would quietly get married after my Board of Advisers adjourned its day's work.

We were married in Washington on a Saturday night, November 24, dropped over to Baltimore for the night and Sunday, and returned Monday morning in time for me to be at the opening session of the board. That was our honeymoon. It was wartime, and there was work to be done. The real honeymoon did not come until eight years later, when we made a trip to Europe.

We made no advance announcement of our wedding to anyone. When we got back to Washington I proceeded to tell my associates, who expressed much surprise that I had not taken more time off. The announcement astonished our mutual friends everywhere.

The thirty years that have passed have convinced me that I am the most fortunate of men. Mrs. Hull has given me every help in my public life as well as deep contentment at home. From the time we were married she subordinated her own interests in every way to the task of giving me every possible support as I carried forward my official career. She abandoned all social and other opportunities for personal enjoyment and devoted her best efforts to the work of looking after all phases of my affairs where she could be helpful. She was so well equipped for all her varied responsibilities that she never faltered where the least opportunity was offered to assist me.

Whether I was campaigning through the mountains for Congress or dealing in foreign capitals with the highest officials of other governments on the most delicate questions, she was equally at home. She always accompanied me in political campaigns and proved a far more successful mixer with the crowds than I was. She plowed in when we got to a meeting place, shook hands right and left, and then took a seat back on the floor with several of the ladies while I made my speech.

We are members of the same church—St. Margaret's Episcopal Church, Washington.

During this Wilson period I came in contact from time to time with a comparatively young man of pleasing personality and strong convictions who was very active and aggressive as Assistant Secretary of the Navy. Our official positions then did not require any direct contact between us, but I was to work in increasingly closer relationship with him in the years to come, and to see him, by his service to the nation and the world, achieve great renown. He was Franklin D. Roosevelt.

As we moved into 1918 the financial needs of the Government to meet the demands of war increased and required constant attention on the part of the Treasury and certain of us on the Ways and Means Committee. New methods were constantly called for. "Most economists," I said in a speech on March 30, "were of the fixed opinion that it would be utterly impossible for even the most important commercial nations to finance a war of the present magnitude for but a very brief time. Yet, despite this general prediction, the war has progressed through a period of nearly four years, entailing expenditures aggregating far in excess of $100,000,000,000—a cost to every man, woman, and child on the globe of more than $60 each."

Two weeks previously, supporting in the House the creation of a War Finance Corporation to finance industries necessitated by the war, I said: "It is a matter of great pride to note that the financial center of the world which was first at Tyre, then at Carthage, then at Rome, then at Venice, then at Amsterdam, then at London, is now in New York. We are the leading banking power of the world."

In the spring of 1918 Congress, having been in session most of the time since the extra session in 1911, began to make a definite effort to wind up and adjourn, although the war was still going on. Members of both Houses manifested a strong desire to secure some rest. The press quoted the leaders of both Houses to the effect that Congress had performed all possible duties pertaining to the prosecution of the war, that no other urgent legislation lay immediately ahead, and that Congress therefore should—and they thought would—adjourn very soon. Personal contacts in the House and Senate gave me the same definite impression. On one day—May 11, 1918—the New York *Times* carried statements by Chairman Kitchin of the Ways and Means Committee, Senator Simmons of the Senate Finance Committee, and Representatives Fordney and McCormick, all supporting adjournment and a special session to be called in November.

I felt deeply concerned. I argued with my colleagues that it would be a mistake of the first magnitude for Congress to adjourn with no revenue laws enacted which would seriously tax the huge mass of war profits then piling up and certain to increase to colossal proportions during that year and probably the year to follow. I emphasized that when Congress reassembled late in the year it would be too late to enact a revenue law to reach war profits for 1918 without what the opposition would call retroactive legislation. Consequently, I argued, a vast amount of bonds would have to be floated wholly out of proportion to the amount of tax revenue raised to finance the war.

But my arguments and pleading were of no avail. Congress seemed determined to adjourn. I also discussed the question with Treasury officials. They agreed with the views I entertained so strongly, but said that little so far was being said or done about it.

In these circumstances I prepared an elaborate analysis of the whole financial and revenue situation, present and prospective, and sent it on May 15 to President Wilson. Throughout the war I had made it a habit to send him a memorandum direct whenever I thought it might be of special aid to him. He always replied in person. I stated to him the same arguments I had expressed to my fellow Congressmen. I strongly contended that Congress should not adjourn but should remain and proceed at once to enact a large war-tax measure that would impose real taxes, especially on war profits.

"A prompt dealing with the problem," I said, "and a consequent readiness to meet the great responsibility involved would be approved

by the people generally. When the full facts as to the necessities of the
government are presented to the American people, they will be ready
in a patriotic spirit, just as the people in other countries at war, to meet
without complaint such further burdens as an additional tax levy may
impose."

Since it was the function of the House of Representatives to initiate
revenue legislation and since my Committee on Ways and Means was
entrusted with this duty, I felt all the more justified in opposing the
leaders of the House and Senate who favored adjournment and in bringing the matter directly to the President's attention as strongly as the
facts warranted.

The next day I received the following letter from the President:

"Your letter of yesterday, which I have just read, embodies a very
weighty argument indeed for immediate action upon taxation. I am
waiting for the release of the Secretary of the Treasury from the sick
room to which he has been confined since his return from his Liberty Loan
campaign, and am very glad indeed to have my mind furnished with the
considerations which you urge with so much clearness and so much force."

The same day rumors concerning my letter filtered out from the
White House. Thereupon a group of newspapermen from the White
House came suddenly into my office at the House Office Building, taking
me by surprise. They asked at once: "What was the communication you
sent to the White House that aroused such interest and loud discussion
over there?"

I replied that I had nothing to say and parried each successive
inquiry by the same answer. I had the best of relations with the leaders
in the House and Senate, and I knew the great handicap it would be
to me in the future if I had a serious breach with them over the adjournment. I therefore kept absolutely quiet and refrained from claiming the
slightest credit publicly for the part I played in this vitally important
occurrence which had far-reaching effects.

The New York *Times,* on May 17, 1918, published a dispatch from
Washington that "Representative Cordell Hull of Tennessee, recognized
as an authority on taxation, today in a letter to President Wilson supported the argument advanced by Secretary McAdoo for an additional
tax levy at this session of Congress. Thus Mr. Hull comes into conflict
with the majority members of the Ways and Means Committee, including Mr. Kitchin.

"This action has caused uneasiness among members who have been looking forward to an adjournment in July. The fact that the news of the receipt of the letter was given out at the White House caused the conclusion among many that President Wilson favors another revenue bill. . . . Mr. Hull's letter on reaching the White House was sent immediately to President Wilson."

I would not assume too much as to the extent to which my views were a factor in the decision the President reached. I would prefer to assume too little. In any event, the President made an almost unexpected personal visit to Congress on May 28. He presented a statement of the present and prospective fiscal situation and earnestly urged Congress to abandon the idea of adjournment and to proceed instead to prepare a sweeping war-revenue measure that would reach war profits and other desirable items before they escaped through lapse of time.

Congress acquiesced and went into the huge task of hearings and the drafting of an enormous war-tax measure. The House imposed the very maximum of income and excess-profits taxes together with numerous miscellaneous taxes. The maximum rates were as high as 80 per cent, and the bill was estimated to raise eight billion dollars. If Congress had adjourned, as it wanted, until November, it would then have met after the Armistice and it would have found it virtually impossible to enact a comprehensive, heavy war-tax measure for any of the future years, much less a retroactive one for 1918.

Speaking in favor of the bill in an address to the House on September 10, 1918, I said: "Next to fighting in the front lines, there is no better test of patriotism than the willingness of the citizen cheerfully to pay the maximum amount of taxes for the support of the Government in its prosecution of the war. On the other hand, the lack, or the degrees, of patriotism can no more quickly be detected than in the person who complains of, or resents, the payment of his fair share of an imperatively high war-tax levy."

The German Government had made its first overtures for peace to President Wilson a few days before, but I said: "The most ignorant person is now familiar with the uncivilized, savage, and barbarous methods employed by the German Government in waging this unholy, outrageous, and unspeakable war of conquest. . . . Talk about 'peace by negotiation'! How can you negotiate any question with scoundrels and villains, with assassins and freebooters, with highwaymen and desperadoes! They must first either be killed or disarmed, and then let honorable men speak and act for their nation at the peace table." We did not follow

this unconditional-surrender policy in the First World War; we did follow
it in World War II.

Just before the revenue bill passed the House, the Armistice occurred and the fighting part of the war ended. Thereupon the Secretary
of the Treasury joined with the House Ways and Means Committee
in agreeing to a reduction of some of the most extreme rates so as to
bring the revenue down to an estimated six billion dollars. The Senate
passed the bill and it became law in 1919, being known as the Revenue
Act of 1918. Time and developments clearly demonstrated the timeliness
and soundness of this huge tax levy.

As the general election of 1918 approached, crimination and recrimination growing out of the war and politics and racial and almost every
other imaginable point of controversy were becoming louder and more
bitter from month to month. A few of the most outstanding leaders of
the Party then in the minority were unusually vindictive in denouncing
President Wilson in unmeasured terms. They sought to block almost
every important step he undertook in prosecuting the war and preparing
for peace then and in the postwar period.

On the other hand, there were plenty of able Republican leaders
who were not pursuing this bitter, personal, factional and very narrow
partisan course. The rank and file of the minority Party was, of course,
entirely patriotic and disposed to cooperate with the Government, except
for those elements willing to listen to their extreme and recalcitrant
leaders and follow them in their bitter hostility to most things the Government was attempting to do.

The Sixty-fifth Congress then sitting was almost exactly divided
politically, and the Republicans were waging a terrific fight for control
of the next Congress. Late in the campaign I was informed that a draft
of an appeal by President Wilson to the voters to elect a Democratic
Congress had been prepared and was being circulated among his advisers
for their comment. I at once called on Wilson's secretary, Joseph Tumulty,
and told him what I had heard. I expressed my opinion that that sort of
move was filled with dynamite and that the proposed letter or statement
of President Wilson should receive all possible study and scrutiny before
its release.

Mr. Tumulty indicated his favorable reception of my view by picking
up the telephone at once and calling Homer Cummings, vice chairman
of the Democratic National Committee. He repeated to Cummings the
substance of what I had said and urged him to see that I was given a

chance to examine the Wilson proposal. This meant that it was in Cummings's hands at that moment for study and comment.

I went directly from Tumulty's office to the office of a cabinet member who I knew was one of the President's chief political advisers. I repeated to him the opinion I had expressed to Tumulty. I had scarcely concluded before he proceeded to say in a tone of finality that President Wilson had drafted a statement for the general public such as I had referred to and that it was thoroughly suitable, appropriate, and effective.

I thereupon abandoned any further pursuit of the matter, and the next I knew the Wilson statement was published. It contained some passages with which I would have found ready fault. The letter would have been better had it confined itself to exposing and condemning certain ringleaders, who happened to be among the very top Republicans of that time and were opposing the President and his administration mainly through personal hate, and to pointing out the complete unwisdom of voters or Congressmen following their leadership instead of that of more temperate Republican leaders. In that case the counterattack on the letter on the charge that it impugned the motives of the Republican rank and file as well as the leaders could not have been made.

Partly as a result of the sharp reaction to the letter, the Republicans gained a majority in the House of Representatives in the November elections, and President Wilson became confronted with a House in which his own Party was outnumbered.

With the fighting part of the war at an end, I began to urge at once that the Government adopt an adequate sinking-fund plan, before the present Congress expired on March 4, 1919, to reduce the national debt incurred during the conflict. On November 14, 1918, I wrote directly to the President urging this step. "Such action," I said, "would include desirable sinking-fund arrangements, authority to refund into lower rates of interest as the opportunity arises, and also authority to purchase bonds from any surplus in the Treasury and their cancellation. These steps, in my opinion, should be taken to as full extent as possible at this stage."

I recalled to Mr. Wilson that, during the Civil War, Congress enacted the first sinking-fund provision for handling the Civil War debt as early as February, 1862. "It would be both wise and timely to take such comprehensive action as may be possible at this time," I concluded, "and such course would undoubtedly meet the hearty approval of the country."

The President replied two days later: "I have read your letter of November 14th with a great deal of interest and am inclined to agree with its conclusions, though I must admit that my mind has been so much engrossed in other directions that I have not given any study to the matter. I am going to take the liberty of sending your letter to the Secretary of the Treasury in the hope that he may think it wise to suggest definite legislation along the lines you indicate."

In due course sinking-fund legislation was prepared and passed.

I summed up the financing of the war in a comprehensive speech in the House on February 26, 1919. I pointed out that, between April 6, 1917, the beginning of the war, and June 30, 1919, "our total ordinary and war receipts, exclusive of those from loans, are about 33⅓ per cent of our combined ordinary and war expenditure." (Deducting loans to the Allies from expenditures, the tax receipts amounted to 44 per cent of our own expenditures.) "Therefore we have paid one-third of our expenses with taxes. In other words, the ratio of loans to taxes was only 2 to 1." I compared this with Civil War financing when, in 1862, the ratio of loans to taxes was 8½ to 1, and in 1863 was 5½ to 1. In other respects as well, we had financed the First World War on a sounder basis than had occurred in the Civil War.

Comparing our financing of the war with both the financing of the Civil War and the financing of the First World War by other Governments, I said: "Such comparison makes a wonderful showing of wise and sound financial achievement by the Federal Treasury which far surpassed that of our own Government during the Civil War or of any foreign government during the present war." And that is my view today as well.

I strongly urged the paying off of the net total Government debt, estimated at not less than $18,000,000,000 after deducting the loans to the Allies, as soon as possible. I suggested that Congress allot certain specific taxes to the sinking fund for the repayment of the debt. But above all I argued for economy as the best means of retiring the debt, saying: "Economy furnishes the most desirable sinking fund." Throughout the war I had kept a keen eye on all bills for appropriations, and had not hesitated to oppose those I felt were unnecessary at the time, however meritorious they might have been in general.

Within a week I delivered two of the most comprehensive speeches of my Congressional career. One I have just dealt with, and the other, given on February 21, pleaded for a removal of economic barriers in international finance and commerce, in line with my new philosophy, first announced in 1916, that freer commerce made for peace and unfair trade made for war. With the war at an end and nations giving thought to a revival of commerce, it seemed to me that the moment had arrived for the world to take the right course at last, before tariff wars began anew.

Arguing emphatically against economic isolation, I said: "If a real economic peace can now be effected, it will afford the greatest possible assurance of permanent world peace. The accomplishment of this is most desirable and would in no wise conflict with any suitable plan for a League of Nations that may be devised, but on the contrary, would supplement, strengthen, and make easier its operations, in that there would be far fewer commercial and trade controversies for settlement."

After enumerating a long list of wars that had been caused by economic rivalry, I said: "It is undoubtedly true that trade relations will bring nations closer together or drive them further apart than any other, accordingly as those trade relations are fair or unfair."

Among the practices against which I inveighed, in addition to high tariffs, were the nonapplication of the unconditional most-favored-nation principle; economic alliances, subsidies, bonuses, rebates, dumping; discriminations in shipping, other transportation and trade routes; appropriation of trade-marks, trade brands, and patents; economic concessions obtained by loans; seizure of land for commercial development; colonial preferences, and the like.

I suggested the establishment of a permanent international organization to investigate and decide when certain practices were violations of fair trade, or an efficient arbitration tribunal.

I was to plead again and again for these principles of freer trade throughout the 1920's and into the 1930's, and then in my years as Secretary of State.

The attention of the public, however, was becoming far more absorbed with the political than with the economic aftermath of the war. The stage was being set for the Paris Peace Conference, and the eyes of the world were turning there. When President Wilson and his immediate advisers were considering whether he himself should go to Paris to attend the Conference I was asked by Tumulty what I thought about it. I promptly replied I thought it would be a mistake.

I felt, whether correctly or not, that notwithstanding certain advantages of the President's being on the ground in Paris, there were more than offsetting advantages in directing the course of the Peace Conference from Washington, such as preventing the domestic political situation from getting out of control.

I said I thought the President should stay here and send to Paris the best delegation he could possibly select. I also said the delegation might well have suitable Republican representation in persons of the type of former President Taft and Elihu Root. They at no time had belonged to the group of Party leaders who were playing a role of purely personal jealousy, hate, hostility, and narrow factionalism. There will perhaps always exist honest differences of opinion on this question.

As the Conference proceeded, factionalism and preachers of dissension were splitting the country. One division was ready to follow President Wilson and support his ideas wholeheartedly, while the other was bitterly opposed to anything he stood for. Senators Lodge, Reed, Brandegee, and Fall were among the ringleaders of the latter group. They violently opposed the League of Nations sponsored by President Wilson and held out the idea of an association of nations in lieu of it. The fight raged throughout the remainder of 1919 and in 1920 until the November elections. The hate and bitterness engendered by the wildest propaganda were terrific.

Senator Lodge, in the years just before and after our entrance into the war, had been strongly in favor of an association of nations. Nevertheless, he and others of his group maneuvered to edge gradually out of the movement for a League of Nations such as this and other Governments had in mind. They quietly slowed down and then, at the proper time later, found an opportunity to break with Wilson overtly, actively, and permanently. Actually, in my opinion, their break with his ideas came before the Paris Conference, but they used the Conference as their reason and excuse for the cleavage.

If Lodge and his group had been in earnest there would have been no trouble in settling the League question. The situation, as I saw it, was this: Lodge himself was the floor leader, brilliant but not broad-gauged. He could hate as well as Wilson could hate, and their personal relation was impossible. None the less, other men rather than Lodge were really taking the lead—men like Senators Reed and Brandegee. They created a veritable organization to fight Wilson by fighting the League. They planned the campaign, selected speakers to oppose Wilson's League, and told them what to say. Senator Borah, not a practical politician but a great orator, was one of their principal mouthpieces. On one occasion they had a blunderbuss sort of Senator from Illinois, Lawrence Y. Sherman, make a speech on racial questions and bring racial charges against the League, and they sent out 3,000,000 copies of it throughout the country.

As this group advanced, step by step, Lodge would run around in front and move up with them. Lodge kept his position as the ostensible leader, but it was the group behind him who were Wilson's real opponents. Lodge was irreconcilable, but the others were the true leaders of the movement that is generally entitled by his name, and his chief activity was to keep in their forefront.

I believe very strongly that if Wilson had undertaken to accept their purported offer of acceptance of the League with some reservations, the next morning we would have found that the Republicans, under the leadership of Reed and the others, with Lodge standing out in front, would have made more demands. They were determined to defeat the League at any cost and thereby defeat Wilson.

In April, 1920, I spoke against the joint resolution of the "bitter-enders" to declare peace with Germany, following the Senate's rejection of the Versailles Treaty. Here was a curious situation. The Constitution had given the President the power to negotiate treaties, and the Senate the power to give or deny its consent to such treaties. The House dealt with treaties only inasmuch as its legislation was necessary to implement them, as through appropriations. But when the Treaty of Versailles failed of ratification because of the fight against the League of Nations, the majority Party introduced a joint resolution to make peace with Germany, and the House was asked to pass it.

"I can scarcely conceive of a more dishonorable attitude before the world," I said, "than that in which this resolution would place the United States Government and the American people. It places us in an attitude of rejecting the treaty negotiated at Versailles and signed by Germany and all our Allied Governments, but at the same time demanding of the German Government that it shall comply with the terms of the treaty in so far as they bestow benefits upon the United States and its citizens. It would be impossible to express or to imagine the amazement, hatred, contempt, and ridicule with which the Allied Governments and enlightened nations the world over would view our Government and our people if this resolution should be passed over the President's veto by two-thirds of both Houses of Congress and seriously transmitted to Germany by a House or Senate messenger."

I still argued for acceptance of the Treaty of Versailles by the Senate, saying: "In my judgment, if all the politics contained in both ends of the Capitol Building could have been segregated and confined to the House end for as much as three hours of any day during the past eight months, the Treaty of Versailles would have been ratified without destructive reservations, and peace in the fullest sense and with all its blessings and advantages would have come to the people of this and other countries long since."

But our fight was in vain. President Wilson had returned from Paris and, recognizing the hostility against the League, delivered a series of speeches across the country in an effort to stem the opposition. Stricken at Pueblo, Colorado, he returned to the Capital a broken man and was unable to participate further in the contest. I did not see Mr. Wilson again until after the election of Harding and a strong Republican Congress and my election as chairman of the Democratic National Committee November 1, 1921.

I attended the San Francisco Democratic convention in 1920 which nominated James M. Cox for the Presidency. Cox was a splendid statesman and a strong supporter of the Wilson League of Nations. No one was more capable or patriotic. He was wonderfully gifted with common sense and stood for sound policy.

I was informed by a thoroughly reliable Democratic leader that President Wilson had sent to one of the chief leaders at the convention three suggestions for the Vice Presidency—Champ Clark, Judson Harmon, and myself. In view of the discouraging political outlook, I was not interested in getting on the ticket. Franklin D. Roosevelt, who was also at the Conference, secured the nomination.

The Harding forces not only overwhelmed the Wilsonian League but also the broader policies of political and economic cooperation to promote and maintain peace and economic well-being among the nations of the world. Immediately after the election it was made clear to the country that there would be no further steps to secure our participation in the League of Nations. The country moved straight back to the most extreme form of isolation—political, economic, social, and moral; and other countries did likewise.

And I, caught under the Republican landslide, was swept from Congress.

9: Again in the Opposition

POLITICAL CHAOS had arrived as the campaign of 1920 approached its climax. The antagonism to President Wilson and his Administration ran almost wild and out of self-control. Every imaginable means of influencing an election was brought to bear. Racial, religious, and foreign-extraction minorities were appealed to by specially prepared speeches and propaganda, and other approaches were used, including money. Supposed interest, prejudice, and bias of every possible description were aroused against Wilson. Not only was a good majority of voters moved to go to the polls and vote against the Democratic candidate, James M. Cox, but many Democrats who would not think of voting against the Party candidate were made lukewarm by floods of propaganda and deliberately remained at home on Election Day.

It was in these circumstances that I faced a constituency rather closely divided politically even in normal times. It had more than once given a Democratic majority of only 1,500 to 2,000. Ten days before Election Day I was called on the telephone from New York by a trusted friend who was keeping in close touch with political developments. He said he had reliable information that the Republican National Committee was sending a substantial amount of money to three Congressional districts in Tennessee to employ automobiles and other vehicles to bring out the full vote. Republican officials, he added, were confident they had my district won.

Although engrossed with the national problems growing out of the war, I had been mindful of the rising danger in my own district. When I started canvassing several counties in the district I discovered that many Democrats were planning to stay at home on Election Day, and that no appeal of mine could dissuade them. On receiving from New York the warning of serious danger I exerted myself to the fullest.

Try ever so hard, however, I found it was just impossible to prevail on the proposed stay-at-home Democrats to change their minds. Some of my best friends, ordinarily active in elections, were lukewarm toward the Wilson Administration; also, they just would not make any extra effort to get out the vote because they were cocksure that enough voters would come out and I would win anyway. My competitor, Wynne Clouse, thought so too until late on Election night. But, when the returns came in, although I ran some thousands of votes ahead of the remainder of the ticket, I failed by 200 to 300 votes to get the requisite number to win. I had suffered my first, and only, electoral defeat.

An ironical feature of the campaign was that my former law partner, John J. Gore, was chairman of the State Republican Committee, and therefore in charge of the fight against me. He was in a difficult situation, because at heart he wanted to see me win, but he was simply carrying out my advice given several times when we were partners:

"In regular elections where I am a candidate, with a Republican opponent, it is only fair that you should vote the Party ticket. Otherwise you might be in for serious attack in the event that you should seek political honors yourself in the future."

He never did tell me how he voted, and I never asked him.

Just as the 1920 election was about to come off, he remarked to me:

"I have no idea that you will be defeated, but some of the boys in the campaign think there's a chance."

Some years later I endorsed him for appointment as Federal judge, which he received. I chose to retain our friendly relations rather than break them on account of what he might or might not have done against me in the 1920 election.

I returned to Washington for the last session of the Sixty-sixth Congress, for I was still a Member until the following March 4th. On December 22 I sharply attacked a high-tariff bill introduced by the majority, called the farmers' tariff bill, showing that it was against the farmers' interests. I pointed out the absurdity of expecting European nations to pay their debts of $16,000,000,000 to the United States while at the same time increasing our tariff rates on their exports to us. This was ten years before the Hoover moratorium.

I pointed out that America now stood at the crossroads. One alternative: ". . . maintain our present supreme position in world finance, commerce, and industry, going forward with the development of our foreign trade, keeping alive and expanding our great merchant marine, making sound and permanent investments of surplus capital abroad, affording labor increased employment at home, negotiating wise reciprocal commercial treaties, cooperating with other nations in the elimination of unfair, hurtful, and dangerous trade practices so as to promote fair and friendly trade relations, prescribing a tariff for revenue only, and doing in other essential respects big things in a big way as sound, enlightened, and progressive policy would suggest."

And the other alternative: high protective tariffs. "This policy," I said, "so backward, antiquated, and utterly provincial for a full-grown country, would mean the deathknell to our present $13,000,000,000 of international commerce, and along with it our dominant position in the financial and commercial affairs of the world. It would then be entirely appropriate to remit our foreign debt and let the gift become a monument to our economic stupidity and our future national decadence."

For the next dozen years the Government chose the second alternative.

When I retired from Congress in March, 1921, my familiarity with the statutes on income and excess profits taxation, in fact with the origin of every term of law and its interpretation in that connection, brought me many offers of employment. These came from chains of textile companies, mining companies, and other groups with vast amounts of taxes in 1918 and 1919 still to be adjusted. The offers embraced enormous remuneration. Sums were specified which to me were fabulous.

I had thus far devoted my life to the public service, however; I had emerged from the war with the widest experience in dealing with all aspects of our war and postwar fiscal and other policies; and I had enjoyed close observation of all essential developments on the international and national stages. I decided I would turn away from the idea of making considerable amounts of money and devote myself still further to public service. This I undertook to do. Twenty-two years of such service were still to follow.

President Wilson made me another kind of offer. He proposed to send to the Senate my nomination to be Chief Justice of the Court of Customs. I declined. I greatly appreciated his friendly attitude and his disposition to recognize me, but I clung steadfastly to my purpose to return to a branch of public service where I could have a chance to accomplish far more than in a judgeship.

Leaving Congress then after fourteen years in the House, I could look back and appraise it from a distance. Then, as later, I believed the House to comprise the ablest group of its size to be found in any parliamentary body. A visitor who looked down upon the Members from the gallery once remarked frankly to me that he was not greatly impressed with the appearance of several of them. I replied: "You can be certain that if and when you attack any Member of the House, you will know for sure you have had a fight before you get through no matter how unprepossessing he may look. Each Congressman has sufficient superior equipment to give him the leadership in his district."

A Member of the House soon learned that discussions on the floor offered no safety zone for a novice. Once when two able Members of my acquaintance engaged in a verbal altercation, one asked the other a question and received an involved reply. The questioner said he could not quite understand the reply, whereupon the speaker said sarcastically: "It's not my fault that the gentleman can't understand me." Thereupon the questioner instantly shouted back: "No, it's not the fault of the gentleman that he doesn't make himself understood, it's the fault of God Almighty who made him."

I believed, and still do, that the Senate is the greatest deliberative body in the world. And the giants who adorned that body during the earlier generations of the Republic had worthy successors in the period when I was in Congress. Some of us Members of the House made it a rule, whenever we could, to go over to the sister chamber and listen to outstanding speeches by leading Senators. In those days a Senator would rise and announce that at a certain hour on a certain day he would deliver remarks on a given subject. If the Senator was a Bailey or a Borah he would have a packed gallery when the appointed hour came. This practice later ceased.

To me John Sharp Williams was the greatest debater I ever knew, Bourke Cockran the greatest forensic orator, Jonathan Dolliver the greatest combined orator and debater—a veritable cyclone when he was going well—and Oscar Underwood the greatest floor leader. Robert M. La Follette was a fine representative, but his speeches were five or six hours long and wore out his listeners. I knew his philosophy of progressivism thoroughly, and agreed with it throughout. Albert J. Beveridge was a brilliant man, but noted for his vanity. I once enjoyed listening to a forty-five-minute speech by Senator Pettus of Alabama perfectly imitating Beveridge's rather conceited airs and gestures.

James R. Mann, Republican of Illinois, had the ability to be a great parliamentary leader, but unfortunately frittered away his opportunities by giving attention to all the most minor details of legislation that came up in the House. He exhausted himself in keeping informed in regard to all of this chicken feed, as we called such details, and so destroyed the really great opportunities open to him. He was an exceedingly able Congressman, though utterly lacking in courtesy.

The Speakers of the House who followed Uncle Joe Cannon during my tenure in that chamber were capable men who preserved the best traditions of the office, being thoroughly imbued with the spirit and doctrine of popular institutions. I refer to Champ Clark, Frederick H. Gillett, Nicholas Longworth, Henry T. Rainey, Joseph W. Byrns, and William B. Bankhead. Nicholas Longworth, with character and excellent ability, made a, universally acceptable Speaker. He and I had served together on the Ways and Means Committee during numerous tariff fights. He possessed rather broad views and, although a Republican, he and I could have agreed personally on a tariff bill had he not been subject to the demands of his Party. Tennessee furnished Joseph W. Byrns, a thoroughly experienced and able Speaker, who rendered distinguished service to his country in many ways both as Congressman and as Speaker.

Later, during most of my tenure at the State Department, a great Speaker presided over the House, who possessed a high order of capacity, statesmanship, parliamentary skill, and intense patriotism, and never failed to offer all possible teamwork to other branches and the departments in support of every wholesome measure; the name of Sam Rayburn will always stand high in the list of Speakers.

In my early years in Congress I began a practice that some might consider a serious mistake. I frequently handed my legislative associates dozens of ideas and a mass of information, especially on questions of the moment. Some of these friends—particularly those who did not devote themselves night and day and Sundays to work and study—could find opportunity to exploit my ideas or data with almost unthinkable speed.

During the First World War a committee of Senators and Congressmen from tobacco states, including myself, met one morning with leading tobacco constituents to discuss Great Britain's blocking of our shipments of tobacco to Holland and certain other countries. We had just passed a revenue measure through the House providing a severe penalty against certain objectionable acts of other governments, and it was then pending in the Senate.

Within one minute before the meeting was called to order I hurriedly stated to an associate: "This virtually automatic penalty can be applied to Great Britain in connection with the blockading of our tobacco." As the committee was being called to order, and before I had quite concluded, my friend was coming to his feet to announce, "I have a complete remedy for this serious problem." He then stated my point in a somewhat disjointed and partial manner, but he got over the general idea. After he sat down I good naturedly came to his assistance by stating accurately and fully the exact proposition. The meeting promptly accepted it. For weeks the press in his State was filled with his achievement.

Another like incident occurred during the House tariff hearings on the Underwood Bill. Among my other studies for the hearings, I had assembled detailed data for an exhaustive cross-examination of the iron and steel, and especially the aluminum, tariff beneficiaries. Just as we were about to proceed with the examination, a colleague, who was not prepared, approached me most earnestly. "You must let me have your data and allow me to conduct the cross-examination," he begged. "In my State the Democratic fight against the Republicans is in a serious, not to say precarious, situation. If I can conduct this cross-examination, especially of the chief steel tariff beneficiaries, it will mean a great deal to the party situation in my State. And frankly, it will mean something to my individual standing there too." On this appeal, based largely on Party grounds, I obliged him. He conducted a splendid cross-examination, chiefly with my material—and, I trust, obtained the benefits he expected.

These examples were two among dozens during my Congressional years. That was the way I functioned, and I was perfectly satisfied to do so. In my long years in Congress I was slow and always reluctant to move toward the limelight. I did not leap out on every occasion with flashing statements. When I spoke it was only after the most careful preparation, and it was not always headline material.

Never having a strong voice, I was not a fluent speaker. I sought always to say something worth while, but it contained nothing of an oratorical nature. Dealing with the entire revenue and economic policies of a great nation like ours necessarily requires the joint work of a number of Members on committees or subcommittees. While a Member need not become submerged in this work, he does not have much opportunity to ride out in front.

I myself benefited innumerable times, of course, from my years of study. On one occasion, when a serious controversy over a general sales tax stirred Congress and the country, I was requested by the chairman of the Ways and Means Committee to investigate and make a report on the merits of such a tax in contrast to the excess profits and other taxes which many persons were objecting to. I had so much material in mind and at finger tips that I was able to prepare offhand an exhaustive report containing the pro and con viewpoints and data and bring it to the committee without delay. Ordinarily such a report would have required detailed investigation, perhaps by several men.

Generally, I never opposed any measure merely because it was new or drastic. My only inquiry in such circumstances was, "Will it uproot a deep-seated evil or prevent one from taking root?"

If I opposed any other Member of Congress or anyone in public life, I based my antagonism on principles or issues. I carefully refrained from personal attacks on other men, or "cussin' matches." A man in politics who does otherwise finds his path strewn with enmities which, as he moves forward, rise in ever greater number to plague him. I never hesitated to stand my ground, however, and I never took insulting or offensive talk from anyone, but stood solid in my tracks and called the other fellow down. I did not go out of my way, however, to seek such occasions.

Being an inveterate smoker, I found my pleasure and work in the House at odds, because smoking was not allowed on the floor. I thereupon took to standing in the door between the House and the Democratic cloakroom, where I could smoke and follow all the proceedings at the same time. Speaker Champ Clark, occasionally passing by, remarked: "I'm not sure whether you're violating the rules or not." But he did not interfere with my habit.

In my relations with the executive departments, I made it a practice to see the minor official handling the specific matter in which I was interested. I did not go to see the Secretary or the Assistant Secretaries. Once I got my ideas across to the minor official, and he made the appropriate recommendation, I could count on better action than if I had seen the top man.

Some of my most enjoyable memories of those years center on the courthouse lawn at Carthage, Tennessee. I had moved to Carthage in 1916. Father had moved there a short time before, and later I became the owner and occupant of the house he had bought. Virtually every year in that period and later I left Washington to spend some weeks at Carthage. My office was just over the drugstore facing the courthouse.

When the day was pleasant, I used to move a chair out onto the courthouse lawn and sit there. Before a couple of minutes had passed, an old friend would bring out a chair and sit beside me. Then others would come with their chairs from across the street. In a very short time I had around me a little circle of friends old and new, from elderly men to youths in their teens, some sitting, some standing behind them. They were avid for information, eager to get my views.

"Can Wilson save the League? What do you think of Lodge?"

"Are Senators better after direct primaries?"

"How is the war going? Will we stay in Europe after it's over?"

"Are taxes going up or down?"

"Do you ever see Teddy Roosevelt?"

"Is there any hope for the party?"

In some of the young faces staring at me so intently, I could see myself thirty years before when Benton McMillin and men like him came fresh from the Capital. I was being asked the same kind of questions I used to ask Benton. Now I was on the giving rather than the receiving end, and it was thrilling to see, in my section at least, some of the same interest in government I had noted so vividly at the close of the previous century.

After serving for fourteen years in Congress, I could now look back and realize how valuable had been the experience I acquired in different levels of life. Starting amid the hardships of the Tennessee ridge country; then moving to the slightly better river-bottom country; then to the school opportunities of the Bluegrass region and Ohio; reading law; serving in the State Legislature; army duty in Cuba; riding the circuit as a judge; and then serving in the national legislature at Washington—each gradation had brought its own trials, but above all its own lessons. All in all, it had been a strenuous period; it involved sacrifices and work; but I could not help believing that it gave me an equipment that would be invaluable in performing further public duties of greater importance in the years to come.

When I departed from Washington in March, 1921, I did not depart from my studies. The bitter and successful fight against Wilson's League of Nations was based on a policy of isolation, both political and economic. I profoundly believed that to head the country on such a permanent course would mean certain disaster within a few years. I sought by every means to continue the closest observation of both national and international affairs.

I prepared an article on the injurious economic effects of the defeat of the Treaty of Versailles. Some of its ideas occurred again in phrases I used as Secretary of State. I inveighed most sharply against isolation, employing the word a number of times. The Administration, I said, was following the idea that "America should live in prosperity unto and within herself and have no sort of relations with the balance of the world." This, I maintained, was impossible. Furthermore, it was in contradiction to the Administration's claim that the panic of 1921 over here was due to "world causes."

America's failure to ratify the Treaty of Versailles, I pointed out, delayed reparations by two years and prevented our extending even sound credits to European nations. Now, I said, "there is—three years after the Armistice—still no disarmament, no reduction of war taxes, no treaty of peace with Germany, and no conditions of real peace in Europe." "Yet," I said further, "the League of Nations, or a league, or an association of nations, or an association with nations, whichever the dodging, insincere politician prefers—like Banquo's ghost—will not down."

I made my headquarters at my home in Carthage. During the next few months I practiced law and delivered a number of speeches.

In early November I went to St. Louis to attend the meeting of the Democratic National Committee, called partly to fill the expected vacant position of national chairman. The committee, shaken by the heavy defeat of the previous November, was divided into two antagonistic factions. Both factions, however, without any solicitation on my part, looked to me to fill the position. I fully realized the almost impossible task ahead for whoever might be selected chairman. Having been on the Executive Committee for many years, I knew in detail the inside condition of the Democratic Party, both political and financial. From what I knew I did not in the least hanker for the new chairmanship. Nevertheless I was elected.

With the Party out of power and in the minority in both Houses of Congress, whoever occupied the office of chairman of the National Committee was in the highest position of Democratic Party leadership in the nation. This post, which at all times ranks near the top in a Party hierarchy, is at the very top when a Party is in the minority.

I took charge of the Democratic Party when it was at its lowest ebb, and its treasury bankrupt. Many persons had predicted it would not recover from the terrific blow dealt by the Republican 1920 landslide. The Party was heavily in debt. It was my task to awaken it, infuse new hope in it, stimulate its ideas, help formulate its program, and pay off its debt.

I traveled throughout the country, from State to State, with the exception of a few old-stand-by Southern States. I now had the opportunity to establish close relations with the State chairmen and other Democratic leaders. I held State meetings to wake up Democrats and improve their organization. I knocked at the doors of all prominent Democrats, asking for their help in reviving the Party and liquidating its debt.

As to the debt, I was received in most instances almost as if I had the smallpox. A respectable number of the more intense Democrats visited national headquarters with reasonable frequency. But there were others of known wealth, well aware of my strenuous efforts to raise money to pay off the pressing debts and to keep the headquarters door open, whose visits were noticeably rare. William Jennings Bryan, Bernard M. Baruch, Thomas L. Chadbourne, and a few others were shining exceptions. Barney Baruch was destined to become outstanding in both national and international affairs, and to render services of the most vital and lasting nature.

I next formed Victory clubs in each political subdivision throughout the country. Each club consisted of ten or more persons, who paid five dollars each into the Party treasury. They were to work for a Democratic victory in 1922.

At the request of the chairman of the Democratic Congressional Committee, I conducted the combined campaign of the National and Congressional committees. I considered it the best strategy to attack the political opposition wherever it was most vulnerable, and where major issues could be presented. Although I was not in Congress when the Fordney-McCumber Tariff Act was pending, I directed the campaign on the issue of that high tariff and the economic policy it embodied. We made another major issue of the scandals and maladministration under Harding. We were aided, too, by the panic of 1921-1922 growing out of war conditions and narrow nationalistic economic policies.

The election of 1920, I believed, had, in effect, turned the nation over to the worst elements in the Republican leadership. Naturally they ruled in the name of the entire Republican Party, and it was necessary to attack the whole regime in order to reach the malcontents among the Republican leaders. It was clear in my mind that they were heading this nation and, so far as their leadership had influence, other nations straight backward on the utterly disastrous course of extreme isolation, economic, political, and social. While utterly helpless to change this suicidal course which meant certain economic disaster, we struggled to keep alive the basic ideas and objectives of international cooperation.

In 1922 I closely followed the Teapot Dome investigation conducted by Senator Thomas Walsh of Montana, which, through exposing Harding's Secretary of the Interior Fall, turned out to be a windfall for the Democratic Party. As chairman of the Democratic National Committee I came into possession, from time to time, of items of information bearing on the investigation and turned them over to Walsh. The happiest man I have ever seen was Walsh when, after holding on with the utmost tenacity, he completely unraveled the case. Walsh was a great lawyer.

When the 1922 election arrived it brought an almost miraculous swing in our favor. We captured seventy-five new seats in the House of Representatives. The Party that seemed so dead in 1920 had become very much alive only two years later.

Meantime I had announced my own candidacy for Congress in my old Fourth District and received the nomination without opposition. I continued my national work until just before the election, when I went home to make a brief, hurried trip about the district. In 1920 I had noted the fact that the Republicans got out their womenfolk to vote, whereas the Democratic women in the South, not favorably enough impressed with the new policy of Women's Suffrage, had refused to a great extent to go to the polls. That may well have accounted for my defeat at that time. In 1922 I urged Democratic women throughout the country to go to the polls, and I similarly urged them to do so in my district. I was elected by seven thousand majority, part of which was due to women's votes, and returned to Congress on March 4, 1923.

In the early part of 1923 I lost my best lifelong friend. My father had been in failing health for a number of years. I induced him to spend his winters in Florida, and this probably prolonged his life. I had visited him in Florida and in Tennessee reasonably often. I had frequently invited him to visit me in Washington, but he was head-over-heels in work and never made the trip.

From the doctor who accompanied him to Florida I received notice of his last illness in sufficient time to reach his bedside while he was still entirely rational. I sat with him as he gradually approached his last moments on earth. I then accompanied his body back to our former home at Celina, Tennessee, and buried him by the side of my mother.

No father could have given more encouragement and cooperation to a son than did my father, especially during the years of my early youth. Nor did he neglect the other children. He was always an upright and God-fearing man. I render all honor to his memory.

Father, in his will, left his entire estate to me, believing that I had better business capacity than my brothers and knowing that I would look after them. The estate, including advances to us children, was worth nearly $300,000, a solid tribute to Father's industry and ability, for he had started with nothing. I carried out to the letter and in the fairest manner his wish that I should care for my brothers. Nade received even more from Father's advances and from me than what his share of the estate would have been. All were entirely satisfied.

Before and after Father's death my work kept me so constantly in Washington that I saw little of my brothers. None of them was ever able to visit me in the Capital. My eldest brother, Ress, who became a doctor with exceedingly bright prospects, had died from one of the early appendicitis operations. One of my younger brothers, Roy, spent his life in the army. The other two, Nade and Wyoming, remained throughout their lives at Father's home and farm, Nade specializing in timber work.

Although I was back in Congress, I continued as chairman of the Democratic National Committee until 1924, when I retired on my own initiative. Gradually I was able to liquidate the Party debt. On more than one occasion our fortunes were so low we could not pay the salaries of our employees. When the treasurer of the committee came to me with this information, I put up between ten and fifteen thousand dollars' worth of Liberty bonds I personally owned, and, with this collateral, we borrowed enough money to pay the salaries.

When I left the chairmanship, we had paid off the debt of about $300,000—equivalent to a million in later years—and had a surplus of $30,000 in the treasury. This achievement was not equaled again until the time of James A. Farley. As I was about to retire, the treasurer was able to pay off the loan we had made to pay employees' salaries and returned my Liberty bonds to me, somewhat to my surprise. After I retired from the chairmanship, my successor allowed the Victory clubs I had started to die out, which I considered a sad mistake.

My position as chairman required me to keep an intimate knowledge of both national and international affairs. At that time and for some years following, both the Democratic and the Republican leaders favored a general policy of peace with disarmament. But the agreements reached at the 1921-1922 Washington Disarmament Conference disturbed me in certain respects—and I stated so publicly at the time. I recognized the sincerity, and what appeared to be the justification, in the minds of Secretary of State Hughes and others when they sponsored the conference. But I found difficulty in bringing myself to the conclusion that we should spurn a world organization for peace and disarmament and substitute for it a more or less related regional arrangement. Wilson's idea had been to achieve this ideal on a universal basis, within the League. Hughes, extremely able, for whom I had much respect, attempted it on a regional basis, embracing a few nations.

I said at the time that, to the relatively small extent that disarmament was agreed upon, the work of the conference was good provided the agreements were carried out in good faith. Also, the work was good to the extent that international consultation and better understanding among nations were developed and conditions of peace in the Pacific were established.

However, I also felt that the achievements of the conference were very partial, and that the United States paid a heavy price compared with other countries and adopted some dangerous and unwise international policies. The disarmament agreed upon was in battleships and aircraft carriers and not in cruisers, submarines, and other means of combat. To my mind the destruction of such vessels was far greater on the part of the United States than in any other country. I pointed out that Japan was even then greatly strengthening herself in naval vessels other than battleships, and was now much stronger, relatively, than before.

I had no rosy illusions about Japan. "She is busy consolidating her influence in China," I said, "with the object of attaining a complete hold over the richest areas to the end that their entire resources and foodstuffs, coal, iron, and other products will be at the disposal of Japan in the future." The Open Door policy had been reiterated in the Washington agreements, but I said this "will amount to practically nothing in practice in the light of all past experience. Japan, as she has done for thirty years, will agree on paper and then proceed with her fixed policy of economic penetration of China, Siberia, Manchuria, and other portions of the Far East. England and America will, in the meantime, find that they are obliged gradually to abandon most of their great trade and commercial interests in that part of the world in favor of Japan." This was ten years before the Sino-Japanese War of 1931-1932 and almost exactly twenty years before Japanese airplanes bombed Pearl Harbor.

As I was writing this statement, William Jennings Bryan came to Democratic headquarters and said, "Hull, I wouldn't be surprised if the Democratic Party would have to forgo victory for some years to come because Hughes' Conference is sweeping the country." I replied, "I'm sorry, Mr. Bryan, but I can't agree with you." We had a long discussion, but nevertheless I continued with my statement that the conference's agreement would cripple us in the Pacific.

Being chairman of the National Committee brought me in close touch with Woodrow Wilson until his death in February, 1924. He requested me to call on him every ten to twenty or thirty days at his home and give him such information as I had up to date on both the national and the international situations. He invariably manifested an interest as keen, if possible, as he had exhibited while he was in health and active in public affairs. He asked me a surprising number of questions about a surprising number of developments.

His comments on men and measures, past and present, were highly interesting. He was unsparing in his criticism of the leaders who had opposed the League of Nations. (We had retained the League in the 1924 platform.) He believed they were actuated by personal jealousy, hatred, and malice. In all his utterances he expressed sublime faith in the ultimate triumph of the League or its equivalent. Once he remarked to me: "The world has been made safe for Democracy. The serious question, however, is whether Democracy will be able to sustain itself." Later on, as nations plowed their way through the depths of isolation, while dictators and desperadoes feverishly sought to conquer them, I often thought of his observation.

Mr. Wilson's emphasis, in all our conversations, was on international affairs. I kept myself specially informed on foreign events so as to be able to talk with him. The stimulus I received in these numerous conferences was reflected to the best of my ability in my movement to revitalize and rehabilitate the Democratic Party as well as all supporters of a practical program of world peace. Naturally, too, my interest in and knowledge of foreign affairs were greatly accentuated by these talks.

I made frequent written reports to Mr. Wilson on my efforts to rebuild the Democratic Party. He often replied with long letters, which he himself wrote on the typewriter, giving me comments and suggestions. These letters evinced his continuing, strong interest in national politics. He always addressed me as "My dear Mr. Chairman."

The ideals he entertained for the Party shone in these notes. On May 25, 1922, he wrote me:

"I think that we ought, in advising our friends about the choice of candidates for this autumn, to dwell upon the necessity of disregarding all the ordinary considerations of 'availability' and of considering only ability and suitability. North of Mason and Dickson's [sic] line particularly the Republicans have been able to build up the fiction that citizens of the first class in every community are the natural supporters of their party; in brief, that high social standing, moral elevation and wide practical influence belong chiefly if not only to men and women who vote the Republican ticket. We must break down that impression and this is the time to do it, because it is just people of that sort who are now everywhere turning to us. . . . We must fill our seats with gentlemen and men of honor and let the politicians get used to good company.

"I do not think that these considerations can be too earnestly or too imperatively pressed upon our party men everywhere. I am not afraid of making ours a 'high brow' party, for high brows at least think and comprehend the standards of high conduct."

Just four days later he wrote me again on the same subject:

"I can see that you are pushing,—and will continue to push,—the policy I took the liberty of suggesting in regard to candidates, and I believe that policy—if carried out—will alter the whole aspect of national politics for us.

"Perhaps a useful line of comment would be this: There are many signs from every part of the country that the class of people,—professional and business men and the leaders of social effort of every kind upon whom the Republicans used to count for cooperation,—are turning to us. It is manifestly good politics, therefore, to meet them half way and to choose our candidates from their ranks so as to bring over to our forces the social leaders (in the wide sense of that term) in every community. Even men of hitherto limited experience and narrow impulse ought to be able to see the practical expediency of such a course."

He frequently counseled for or against certain candidates. Of a nominee for the Senate he wrote on September 12, 1922: "I deem it my conscientious duty to write you a line of respectful warning (respectful to you,—not to him) about him. I have known him since he was a young man and feel it my duty to say that it would not be wise to admit him in any way to intimate party counsel. He is incapable of loyalty in any manner which he does not think likely to directly advance his own personal interests. He is by nature envious and intensely jealous, and cannot take part in disinterested service of any kind."

He sent me clippings with accompanying letters like that of August 28, 1922: "You may probably smile to think that I should have thought it possible that you had not got hold of what the enclosed clipping contains, but I have found this a wise rule of action: Make sure of each thing in turn; take nothing for granted. In order to avoid any mischance, therefore, I am sending this, which I found in The Baltimore Sun this morning."

On October 13, 1922, he wrote me: "If it is true . . . that the women of the country are taking an active and unusual interest in the present campaign, surely that should be greatly to our advantage since our ideals are assuredly nearer their standard than are the ideals (if there are any such) of the Republicans. . . . I shall be very much disappointed in them if they do not and think that they have forgotten that they are chiefly indebted to me for the suffrage."

Sending me on December 14, 1922, a copy of an address by Norman H. Davis, he suggested this be put into the hands of all Democratic campaign speakers in 1924, and added: "I am trying to help to get everything in shape at an early date for the most effective possible campaign."

He was overly optimistic as to the 1922 elections in writing on June 27, 1922: "Every indication that reaches me of what is coming increases my confidence that our party will be presently returned to power and will have the greatest opportunity for service that has ever been accorded it." But on November 9 he sent me fervent congratulations on the actual returns.

He was ever diplomatic in offering his suggestions, as when he wrote me on May 6, 1922, concerning a report that a resolution had been sent me calling for a Party conference to shape a program for the coming election: "May I volunteer the opinion, which I daresay is also your own, that such a conference would lead to nothing but talk and outside rumors about it which would be misleading and hurtful to the party. My knowledge of you convinces me that you are not in need of comment of that sort."

In my opinion, Wilson never ceased fighting for human rights, individual liberty, peace, and humanitarianism. As a statesman and patriot he was unexcelled in his generation, and as a peace advocate and peace leader he was unequaled. From his early youth he was serious-minded, studious, and broad-gauged in his views. Although serious, he had a sense of humor and greatly enjoyed jokes and limericks.

I always found him to be thoroughly receptive, agreeable, and considerate in conversation. He would listen closely while a person presented his views. After the presentation had been fully made, he would then proceed to apply to the problem all the reason and logic required, and finally, after careful deliberation, he would reach his decision. Thereafter it was difficult to prevail upon him to modify that decision. He was equally frank to praise or condemn individuals. On one occasion I remember, the name of one of his classmates was mentioned, whereupon he exclaimed emphatically, "That man is the most selfish person I have ever known!"

In physical appearance and demeanor during his last months, Wilson was very remindful of Andrew Jackson. His determination was visible in every feature. Three and a half weeks before his death, when the Democratic National Committee was in session, he sent me word to bring the members out to his house, which I did. He was insistent on seeing, greeting, and inspiring them even in that very last stage of his illness. Many affecting scenes occurred as old friends and supporters of former days when he was exercising his powerful leadership for the public good broke down and wept.

Wilson's secretary, Joseph Tumulty, was one of the most faithful and active lieutenants both in the official and in the political field that any President ever had. I had occasion to work with him a great deal in my relations with the White House.

During the period from 1921 to 1924, William Jennings Bryan was accustomed to stopping at my hotel, the Lafayette, when he came in from a trip across the country every two or three weeks. Almost invariably he would telephone me to join him at breakfast. We would then have long conversations similar in many ways to those I was having with Wilson. Bryan and I discussed both domestic and foreign affairs.

At one breakfast conversation the Party outlook appeared absolutely blue. I remarked, "Now, don't you get discouraged even among such utterly discouraging conditions as these!" Bryan said without hesitating: "No, it takes time in the life of a nation to measure the progress of movements being advanced for the public good. A period of some twenty-five years is necessary to determine the progress or lack of progress of great national movements. I recall the fight begun a quarter of a century ago for such great reform measures as the income tax, the estate tax, agricultural and labor legislation, election of Senators by the people, and other such progressive proposals." And then he concluded: "And now these wholesome measures are law." Bryan had been one of the early unfailing supporters of the income tax, although he and others were unable to get it into the Democratic platform in 1904.

To me Bryan was a magnificent orator. It was simply incredible how he could sway audiences. But he lacked judgment at times. Now and then he would make decisions that seemed entirely untenable on their face.

In those and later years I used frequently to see Colonel Edward House, who had been Wilson's ambassador at large and had exerted vast influence on our foreign relations. When I was in New York City I always called on him, and we went over the world situation. In the several years prior to 1932 he wanted me to become the Democratic nominee for the Presidency and promised me his support; but I discouraged the idea.

When the Democratic National Convention met in New York in 1924 to nominate a candidate for the Presidency, I opened it as temporary chairman and put the machinery of the organization into motion. According to many predictions, the convention would have nominated Governor Samuel M. Ralston of Indiana; but unfortunately he was fatally afflicted and sent word through his friends that he could not allow his name to be used. He was able and was a fine friend of the people. After three weeks of deadlock between McAdoo and Governor Alfred E. Smith brought about the retirement of both from the contest, Governor Austin Peay, head of the Tennessee delegation, came hurriedly to me under some excitement just before the end of the convention. "The inside leaders are in conference," he said, "to determine whom to nominate. I am directly informed that they will decide either on John W. Davis or you." Other persons on the inside confirmed this to me. I did not consider this possibility favorably. For one thing I knew that the Democratic Party had inflicted a serious wound on itself during the three weeks' convention. Mr. Davis, probably America's greatest lawyer and a statesman of wide experience, was nominated.

By that time I was tired out from the work of the Democratic National Committee. Without waiting to know whether Mr. Davis, who had been a close friend and associate of mine in Congress, would offer me a further appointment to conduct the campaign, I sent him word that, in any event, I must retire as chairman.

Just before that word spread that I had had a breakdown from overwork. I was in my hotel room having dinner when I was told that several newspapermen had asked for a story about it. "Send them up," I said. They appeared within a few minutes. They saw me sitting at a table eating a thick beefsteak—and that was the end of the story.

I received at about that time a letter from Hyde Park, Dutchess County, New York, saying: "Please let me thank you for your letter of July 22nd in regard to the old note of the National Committee. I am of course delighted that the obligation is safely out of the way, and I want at the same time to tell you that I consider your initiative and ability wholly responsible for the splendid state in which you have left the finances of the National Committee. . . . Every Democrat will count on your assistance during the campaign." It was signed, Franklin D. Roosevelt. He had been one of the endorsers of the note.

Within a few days Mr. Davis very earnestly requested me to accompany him as an adviser on his campaign across the country. This I did during the first portion of his campaign. Davis lost to President Coolidge, and I was to struggle along for eight more years in opposition, vainly striving to hammer some headway with my ideas on lower tariffs, equitable taxation, and international economic and political cooperation. Isolation was in the saddle, the League of Nations almost a byword for ridicule with many millions, and the stock market a panacea and a promise for all time to come. I and others prophesied, but few heeded; we worked hard, but the fruits of labor lay always beyond reach.

10: Disappointments of Opposition

THE TWENTIES WERE a crucial period. This country had gone wildly in favor of isolation, nationalism, and peace at any price. The public ran roughshod over the internationalist supporters of Wilson and of the League of Nations, center of Wilson's policies. Hence it was not remotely possible to carry through Congress or through an election any proposition involving international cooperation.

We never ceased pushing for more cooperation with the world, but we had to do so with limited objectives on which we could win the country. Only then could we promote the more fundamental peace objectives we had in mind through which to lift people up to higher levels. Continued championing, as a paramount election issue, of something so specific as American participation in the League of Nations would have jeopardized our chances at the polls and rendered it impossible for us to put our policies and ideals into practice. We did keep the League issue alive in our platforms and individual utterances.

My Congressional career in the twenties following my return to the House is in contrast to my Congressional career in the previous decade in two respects. In the first place, I had become one of the voices whose notes, pleading for lower tariffs, international cooperation, and better national financing, shattered against a stone wall. From 1911 until 1919 we had a Democratic Congress in which some of my ideas could leave the paper stage and assume shape and momentum. From 1925 on I got nowhere; my bills and resolutions failed to receive adequate or favorable consideration; and I became progressively more discouraged until in 1929 I had almost decided to retire from Congress.

In the second place, my interests and studies turned much more to the world sphere during my later years in Congress. The First World War and the inspiration of Wilson inclined my thoughts toward the foreign field, although my emphasis still remained on the economic side of international relations.

On February 7, 1925, I made probably the longest speech of my career in reviewing in the House of Representatives the Government's financing from 1913 to 1925, with special reference to the World War. As printed, it was forty-two pages long, and embraced many days of work. Carter Glass told me he sat up all night reading and studying it.

Of war debts I said: "Unless the heads of the various governments involved shall exercise patience and forbearance, the settlement and extinction of these debts is calculated to create constant feeling, broils, and bitter international strife for two generations. Experience has already shown that, had the United States, instead of assuming and maintaining an attitude of almost entire aloofness during the four years following the war, pursued the policy of practical cooperation, at least morally and economically, our debtor governments in Europe would have been in a far better financial situation and in a better humor with respect to payment of these debts in full, and the debts would probably have been long since funded at or near the full principal."

I pointed out, as I had done before, that the record of our financing during the World War was better than that of any foreign government engaged in the World War and of any American Government during previous wars. Replying to the charge that expenditures were excessive, I said: "Waste of money and of property there inevitably was, but no jackal has ever dared to charge the Wilson Administration, entrusted with American leadership during the war, with waste of human life. History now shows that the swiftness with which America threw her men, money, and materials into the war prevented its continuance into 1919, which would have cost countless lives and additional billions of money." I praised the operation of the sinking fund provided for in the Victory Bond Act of March 3, 1919, and demanded that officials keep their hands off it during the life of our World War debt.

In line with my steadfast interest in the international situation from the viewpoints of economics and peace, I accepted an appointment as a delegate to the World Congress of the International Chamber of Commerce at Brussels, Belgium, about the middle of 1925. I wanted to render any possible aid in keeping alive and advancing the peace-through-economics doctrine I had been urging in this country since 1916. The conference overwhelmingly supported all phases of the economic policies in which so many of us were interested.

Accompanied by Mrs. Hull, I also made the trip to Brussels the occasion for a journey through most of Europe to observe political and economic developments and conditions. Before and after the Congress we proceeded leisurely through Belgium, France, Italy, Germany, the Netherlands, England, Ireland, and Scotland. Since most of their parliaments were sitting at the time, I attended the sessions. The information gathered was a fruitful addition to the stock of knowledge I had acquired during many years through studying political, economic, and financial conditions in Europe.

Back in America again, I refought an old battle by introducing in the House on December 19, 1925, a resolution calling for a permanent international trade agreement organization to reduce trade barriers. One sentence of the resolution declared it to be the sense of Congress that the existing high tariff rates should be immediately revised downward, and of course this doomed it.

We were then more than three years from the outbreak of the worst panic in history, which began in October, 1929; but in a speech of April 14, 1926, I stated that America's prosperity could not endure behind high walls of protection. "Our foreign markets," I said, "depend both on the efficiency of our production and the tariffs of countries in which we would sell. Our own tariffs are an important factor in each. They injure the former and invite the latter."

The advocates of high tariffs, I believed, "had deliberately planned to junk our foreign governmental debts, for fear that their payment might force more liberal tariff and trade policies." My point was that the debts could have been paid if, right from the end of the war, we had reduced our tariffs and permitted other nations to sell us a portion of their goods, thereby obtaining dollars with which to pay the debts. I also said: "America is no weakling, but an economic giant, standing at the head of the column of nations in finance and industrial efficiency and capacity, and she cannot maintain a healthy growth in an industrial hothouse. Why wait for a crisis or a panic before correcting unsound policies?"

One of my bitterest disappointments in those years was to see the mounting spiral of higher and higher tariffs. Nothing seemed to stop it. Nations seemed to spend much of their time figuring how to place a few more stones on the high tariff wall. And we Americans, I felt, were originally at fault. Instead of accepting the wonderful opportunity which the end of the First World War gave us for economic cooperation throughout the world, we reversed the trend toward lower tariffs begun by the Underwood Act and started the upward spiral whirling with the Farmers Tariff Act of 1921 and the Fordney-McCumber Act of 1922. "Under the high-tariff leadership of America," I told the House on May 10, 1926, "more than fifty countries have constructed every sort of tariff and trade barrier, which tremendously handicaps and reduces the volume of trade among nations." Tariffs begat tariffs.

Of equal regret to me was our inability to promote international cooperation in general. The individualist and isolationist policy, initiated when the United States disavowed the Treaty of Versailles, continued under Harding and Coolidge.

Harding I had known very well in Congress, though I had no occasion to confer with him as President. He was one of the most charming persons in a social way one would ordinarily meet.

Coolidge was generally commented on for his extreme reserve in conversation and for the paucity of his words and abbreviation of his language. My own experience in official conversation with him at the White House was not in harmony with this estimate. Our conversations proved to be entirely normal. He talked freely and easily from the beginning to the end of a conversation, and was as affable as I could have wished.

On Woodrow Wilson's birthday on December 28, 1926, I made a speech at York, Pennsylvania, which was partly devoted to foreign affairs. "No person during the postwar period," I said, "more keenly realized than President Wilson the fact that the supreme question was whether democracy would be able to justify and sustain itself. It means rule by the people. If the world is to progress, the standard of world democracy which Wilson so ably carried must be upheld to the uttermost in the future. The alternative will be the lapse of the world back to the control of hereditary and arbitrary kings, dictators, and other autocrats, with every prospect of recurring wars and of government alone by hereditary or similar autocracies or aristocracies. The voice of the people will again be stifled."

This was about six years before Hitler came to power. America, I said at York, was never in such great need of a moral and spiritual leadership of the kind provided by Wilson, because standards of political morality and public virtue had been degraded during recent years to the lowest level in American history. "Another Wilson," I urged, "is needed to appeal to the public conscience for a restoration of these standards and for the dislodgment from power in high places of those who are corruptly exercising the power of government by the use of money."

It seemed to me we were drifting along without any foreign policy, and that our influence among the nations was in rags. Our decision to go it alone internationally was unfortunately coupled with domestic scandals like the Fall and Daugherty cases. Month by month you could almost see the strong world influence we held at the end of the war flowing through our open fingers.

"Six years ago," I said on April 13, 1927, at Woodward, Oklahoma, "America was the greatest moral force of any nation in the world or in history. . . . Six years ago the attitude of other nations toward the United States was never better; today it was never worse. The lack of vision, practical knowledge and morality in our foreign policies has been disastrous in the extreme. We have reaped a world harvest of economic and trade losses and of suspicion, contempt, and ill will. . . .

"The statement has become universal that for six years our Government has had no definite or adequate foreign policy. Under our slipshod and piecemeal policies we have drifted and muddled along until our moral influence has vanished utterly. Unless our interests are still more to suffer, this nation must speedily adopt a constructive foreign policy embracing intelligent, practical, and systematic cooperation. There are many ways of sane cooperation to promote better understanding, friendship, good will, peace, and justice consistent with our Constitution and traditions."

The little policy that we had, seemed to me entirely materialistic, based on high tariffs and such nationalistic considerations. "This is the coarse and sordid doctrine of materialism," I said, "which is rooted in selfishness and repugnant to the original ideals on which the Government was founded. Human rights, human welfare, national character, high ideals, morals, and Christian vitality, on which freedom and civilization must continue to rest if they are to endure, are matters of secondary consideration under our present purely materialistic Government since 1920."

This speech of April, 1927, was one of my most important addresses. It contained the broad, basic principles I felt necessary to keep alive and to preach—the same principles I carried with me later into the State Department. At the Democratic National Convention at Houston, Texas, the following year, Claude Bowers, temporary chairman, said to me and others that he had based his speech to the delegates on my Woodward address.

When the Kellogg-Briand Pact was signed in Paris in August, 1928, I, like every peace-minded person, was for it. But I knew it was more a matter of moral suasion than anything that purported to offer an agency for peace. After I became Secretary of State I brought it out and emphasized it but never depended on it too much because I felt that the ambitious Axis leaders were not to be stopped by moral suasion.

Speaking in the House on December 16, 1927, I examined our hold-off attitude toward the Reparations Commission and our awkward attempt to collect direct from Germany the costs of our army of occupation. "When twenty-five creditors adopt a plan dealing with the assets of a debtor," I said, "it is doubtful whether a twenty-sixth creditor may later proceed to deal with the assets as though the twenty-five creditors and their previous arrangement were not in existence. Some sort of concert is naturally necessary and logical."

About 1927 I underwent a tonsillectomy. When I went to the hospital I had two good cigars in my pocket. I had been smoking fifteen cigars a day for thirty-five years. On the second day after the operation I lighted one and began to smoke it. It tasted horrible—like a cigar made of old leaves rolled in a piece of newspaper. I had to put it away. Then, as I lay in the hospital bed, I began thinking whether smoking was necessary to me or not. I reflected that it had really been a nuisance and an expense, that the ashes got on my clothes and the smoke in my eyes. I decided to stop smoking entirely. As easily as that, I gave it up, and have never smoked since.

As the 1928 campaign approached, the Democratic members from Tennessee in both branches of Congress endorsed me for the Presidency. On January 20, 1928, they issued a statement recalling my twenty years' service in Congress, the fact that Wilson and other party leaders sought my counsel, and my achievements as chairman of the Democratic National Committee.

The movement for my nomination expanded as the Houston convention drew near. The Democrats of Tennessee were naturally friendly and favorable. Senator Furnifold M. Simmons and other leaders in North Carolina pushed me into the Democratic primary there and carried the State over Al Smith. Simmons, a very able and agreeable person, and I differed somewhat in our views, he being a conservative tinctured with tariffs and sometimes special privileges, but he had never ventured out too far and had worked well with Wilson and had been thoroughly in line on the big Revenue Act of 1919.

Such support as was generously given me, however, came entirely voluntarily and despite my frank statement that I was not attempting to secure the nomination. I refused to encourage movements in any state. Offers of support were made to me from many sections of the country, but I actually discouraged rather than encouraged organized movements, much less a nation wide movement.

I was not an active candidate for the Presidential nomination at

Houston. In fact, I have never been an active candidate for a Presidential nomination, although at several conventions beginning with the New York convention in 1924 friends and other Democrats saw fit to discuss my name in that connection.

At Houston I, in common with many Democrats, knew that under all the rules of calculation the nomination would go to Governor Alfred E. Smith. Numerous other names, including mine, were placed in nomination, but with the knowledge that Governor Smith would receive the requisite number of votes to nominate on the first ballot. We others could not refuse to allow our names to be presented by the State delegations that wished to vote for us, though we had not organized any campaigns. But we agreed in advance that our names would be withdrawn once the first ballot had been cast, and before it was announced. The ballot results would then be released in the light of that withdrawal. I think there was much favorable sentiment very generally over the country for other candidates; but Governor Smith's carefully organized preconvention campaign, set on foot throughout the nation at an early stage, was calculated to get affirmative results.

When the convention met it was evident to me that Governor Smith and his advisers were bent on heading the party in a high-tariff direction. I resisted this as best I could in numerous conferences with leading Democrats, including Governor Smith's manager, Judge Joseph M. Proskauer, but to no avail. It culminated in what I considered in many respects a typical old-time high-tariff speech by Governor Smith at Louisville, Kentucky, during the campaign.

Smith said: "I believe in the Democratic platform which recognizes that the high wages and constructive policies established by Woodrow Wilson and the business prosperity resulting from them in America, coupled with the economic ruin of the rest of the world, brought about a new condition that committed the Democratic Party to a stand in favor of such tariff schedules as will to the very limit protect legitimate business enterprise as well as American labor from ruinous competition of foreign-made goods produced under conditions far below the American standard."

The basic thought here was high tariffs, certainly not liberalization of trade. The tariff ideas of Smith and his advisers were accompanied by the usual professions of high-tariff Democrats—namely, generalities purporting to oppose high-tariff protection—but there was no serious doubt that their real thoughts and actions led toward higher tariffs.

Into the Democratic platform of 1928 Smith's official group wrote this plank: "Specifically the Democratic Party does not advocate tariffs higher than would equalize the difference between costs of production abroad and at home." This could have been lifted bodily from the Republican platform of 1904, which stated: "The measure of protection should always at least equal the difference in the cost of production at home and abroad."

What both Smith and the Republican Party failed to see was that such a policy actually meant an embargo on imports. If our tariffs were to make up the difference between cost of manufacture abroad and the cost of manufacture at home, no manufactured products could ever come into the United States over such walls, because the importers would still have to pay the cost of transportation, insurance, currency exchange, and the like.

I stated and restated that "the true and logical Democratic policy today should be tariff revision downward to a level of moderate rates reasonably competitive, coupled with liberal commercial policies calculated constantly to increase our export trade." I also said. "It was possible for a Democrat to subscribe to the method and program for dealing with the tariff as outlined in Governor Smith's Louisville speech. It was neither necessary nor possible, however, that in so doing a Democrat should concur in his expressed view that the tariff could be taken out of politics, or in other individual and abstract views he suggested relative to the merits or demerits of tariff protection." As for myself, I could not support his basic tariff opinions.

I, of course, backed the Democratic ticket in every feasible way, but we were again doomed to serious defeat. Following the election of Herbert Hoover, I proceeded as actively and energetically as I could during the next four years to conduct a quiet campaign among members of the Democratic National Committee and other Party leaders to reverse before 1932 what I considered a most unfortunate tariff position assumed under the leadership of Governor Smith.

"I admit that, as always," I said in a statement in April, 1929, "there are some Democrats who are undertaking to effect arrangements for the unconditional surrender of the Democratic Party to the forces of high-tariff greed and privilege, and they may think that such surrender is now assured. I predict, however, that in this they will find themselves as badly mistaken as was Benedict Arnold when he felt cocksure that he had arranged for the certain surrender of West Point to the opposition."

From then on, my conferences with Franklin D. Roosevelt intensified. Before and after he became Governor of New York, Mr. Roosevelt used to stop off at a hotel near the depot in Washington on his trips back and forth between New York and Warm Springs, Georgia. He always requested Senator Thomas J. Walsh, Congressmen Henry T. Rainey and William Ayres, and me to call at his hotel and confer with him on present and prospective political conditions. He entertained the same tariff and general economic views as myself. These conferences continued until the time arrived to organize in support of his candidacy for President in 1932. Louis Howe, his secretary, frequently visited my office for similar conferences, and I was in constant correspondence with him.

In 1928 I declined to stand for reelection as a member of the Democratic National Committee. I was worn out from my combined work on the committee and in Congress.

The year 1929 was perhaps the nadir of my Congressional career. We had again lost the national elections; I was disturbed by those Democrats who had swung toward high-tariff ideas; my fight of two decades to reduce tariffs was failing even to keep them at their existing level, because a new movement to boost them still higher was successfully under way in Congress, resulting in the Smoot-Hawley Act of 1930; and my health was not too good.

My battle against the Smoot-Hawley bill became almost an individual effort. In speeches both in and out of Congress I sought as an individual to contribute toward spreading wide notice to the public of the coming economic doom. I made it a point vigorously to cross-examine the beneficiaries of high tariffs when they came before the House committee conducting hearings on the bill. Scarcely anyone among the Democrats seemed to have kept up with this field, and the task of cross-examination rested with me. Although the Republicans allowed only several minutes for cross-examination, and an appeal from this decision to the committee chairman was always gaveled down, I got in all the opposition to higher tariffs I could.

There was a great deal of log-rolling in the Smoot-Hawley Bill. I saw many instances of it myself. Senator Grundy of Pennsylvania, on the Republican side, was open and avowed in his methods, stating in effect that the interests which put up the money for campaigns should be compensated in this way by high tariffs.

When the bill was reported by the committee to the House, I felt constrained to write a minority report on it. I signed it alone because, amid this atmosphere of greed and privilege, I feared the Democrats would split so widely that it would be better not to seek other signers. There were many in the party willing to go along with the idea of higher tariffs.

This report was dated May 11, 1929, or five months before the great panic burst upon the country. "It is safe to say," I said, "that our productive capacity today is 25 per cent in excess of our ability to consume. High tariffs cannot save us from growing surpluses. Some of the serious results already are the doubling and trebling of distribution costs in frenzied efforts to dispose of increasing surpluses at home; much idle labor and vast aggregations of idle capital, billions of which have gone into stock brokers' loans for gambling purposes, thereby seriously affecting the stability of both our money and trade structure; many loans abroad made more hastily than prudence and good investment policy would justify. . . . If American plants today were unloosed at full production capacity, they would flood all domestic markets within ninety days, and many artificial parts of our economic structure would topple and fall.

"It is my individual view that these glaring facts and conditions soon will compel America to recognize that these ever-increasing surpluses are her key economic problems, and that our neglect to develop foreign markets for surpluses is the one outstanding cause of unemployment."

As the House brought the Smoot-Hawley Bill to the point of vote on its final passage, Democratic Leader John N. Garner, later to be Vice President, exercised his right under the rules to make a motion to recommit the bill. His motion, however, contained numerous statements and theories relating to tariff revision with which I was not in agreement.

Garner and I had served together in Congress from 1907, he having preceded me by four years. I always entertained a high regard for him. He was frank, dependable, and, whether dealing with large or with small matters, he invariably stood foursquare towards all concerned. There was no equivocation or pretense about him. Like myself, he did not have many diplomas, if any, from colleges; but he possessed wonderful common sense and wide intelligence. We had our different situations to look after, especially on tariffs, which operated somewhat as a difference of views between us, but never to the extent of interfering with our friendly relations. Garner, whose district was filled with sheep and goats, had always been at heart as much a high-tariff man as Smoot or Hawley. But he kept quiet and never undertook to make arguments. This was one reason why I rather than Garner, who was the ranking Democrat on the Ways and

Means Committee, had to cross-examine witnesses supporting higher tariffs.

On May 28, 1929, I addressed the House to say that I disagreed with many of Garner's views on tariffs but supported his motion to recommit because of my deep opposition to the bill, which I felt would bring disaster to the country. The motion, of course, lost.

I, the Cassandra of Congress, saw that my prophecies were having no more effect than those of the prophetess of the ancients. I was becoming more and more discouraged. I wondered whether it was worth while going on. Could anything be achieved by staying in Congress? Was there any hope in continuing to raise a voice that had been heard so often and heeded so seldom? Was it not better to resign and return to practicing law?

Then in September, 1929, the door suddenly opened on the Senatorship from Tennessee with the death of Senator Lawrence D. Tyson and Governor Horton's appointment of William E. Brock to succeed him. I debated what action to take. Having been a Congressman for twenty years, I naturally had thought from time to time of the possibility of becoming a Senator. Brock would fill Tyson's position until November, 1930, and would then have to stand for election to the short term lasting until March 4, 1931. Voters in November, 1930, would also be called upon to elect a Senator for the six-year term beginning March 4, 1931.

The decision I arrived at was based on three factors. First, at Washington the overwhelming Republican rule was sending the country straight over the precipice of extreme political and economic isolation. Secondly, the Democratic organization was badly split on the whole question of international cooperation and its related domestic questions such as high tariffs. Finally, a powerful Democratic machine organization was dominant in Tennessee and was known to prefer one of its own members for the Senatorial vacancy.

I felt so profoundly the suicidal course of events generally that I decided to make one more effort to be of service in helping to steer the national and international course in an entirely different and sound direction. I first consulted my doctor to see whether my rather uncertain state of health that year would permit. He said, "Yes." I thereupon reconsidered my strong inclination to retire from public service, and, without conferring with any political groups in Tennessee, I announced my candidacy from my home in Carthage, on the same night that Brock was appointed to fill the unexpired term of Senator Tyson. I made it clear I was not a candidate for the short term but only for the six-year term beginning March 4, 1931. I rested my candidacy on my long service in the House and on the support both of personal friends and of a considerable element of Democrats more interested in the welfare of the Party and country than in any faction or individual.

I did not overlook the fact that I had a powerful Democratic State machine to fight. Former United States Senator Luke Lea, whose renomination for the Senate I had defeated, and whose organization I had wrecked in 1915, had re-created his machine by 1929. In the Memphis district was another strong machine, headed by Ed Crump, which then cooperated with Lea. I could expect nothing from either boss except enmity. It was not likely that Lea had forgotten the events of 1915. I did not consult either Lea or Crump before announcing my candidacy.

As I expected, the organized machine put out its own candidate in the person of Mr. A. L. Todd, and a little later Congressman Joseph W. Byrns. The latter, however, withdrew within a very few days after issuing a statement that he was retiring because of illness. I made many hurried trips from Washington to Tennessee during the months leading up to the Democratic primary early in August, 1930. In this way I was gradually able to cover the State in a very hasty manner and to reach a considerable portion of the more active Democrats.

Mr. Todd decided, notwithstanding I had been renominated to Congress for twenty years without opposition, he would cover me up with charges of every imaginable description. Although top officials of the national soldiers', farm, labor, and rural carrier and postal organizations had all given testimony to my uniform friendship and support of their respective groups, my opponent made charges to the contrary in each instance. I most emphatically condemned these allegations as absolutely untrue.

To meet them I not only cited my record, but, in the course of speeches, said my opponent's tactics reminded me of a certain gentleman who went on a hunting expedition in Arkansas. At that time the law of the State prohibited the killing of deer. However, when the hunter returned to the village hotel after his first day's hunting he talked rather loudly in the lobby about his fine luck in having bagged the choicest deer. At the height of his boasting a stranger in the group around him suddenly said, "Do you know whom you are talking to?" The hunter, in a quieter tone, admitted he did not. The stranger replied, "I am the game warden of this county." The hunter was much taken aback, but rallied in a second or so and said, "Do you know whom you are talking to?" The game warden said, "No." The hunter, in a louder tone, declared, "You are talking to the damnedest liar in the State of Arkansas."

My opponents picked up every conceivable chance to make political capital against me. They made much of the fact that my automobile carried a District of Columbia license rather than a Tennessee one. Mrs. Hull overcame this by going to the nearest courthouse, registering the car, paying a fee, and obtaining a Tennessee license, which she had the driver put on the vehicle.

We had brought a driver with us from Washington. This fact, too, proved a boon to my opponents, who used it to belabor me with the charge that I considered Tennessee drivers not good enough for me. We sent our regular driver back to Washington and hired local talent, who gave us several hairbreadth escapes.

I opened my campaign with a speech at Cookeville, the center of my old Congressional district, on June 17, 1930. A vast concourse of people from twenty to thirty counties participated in the meeting, and it was in every way a successful opening.

I devoted part of my address to a subject that worried me throughout the twenties. It seemed to me there had everywhere been a slump in democracy, or rule by the people. There was less sound political thinking than I had ever known. Some people were losing faith in the old maxims of liberty and democracy. The spirit of our national life seemed to be changing. From the two-party system of government, which I believed so necessary in a democratic republic, we were rapidly degenerating into the chaotic system of government by blocs as in Europe. The people, I thought, could speak effectively to their government only through political parties.

"The spirit of paternalism, bureaucracy, centralization, and materialism is abroad in the land," I said. "Human rights, human welfare, national character, morals, high ideals, and Christian vitality, on which freedom and civilization must rest if permanently to endure, are matters of secondary consideration to an amazing number of the American people. The cold, selfish, mercenary appeal of materialism alone is held out as the governing consideration for the American voter, with the result that no issue or condition, unless it be a panic, will arouse and move the people to change their government. Any sort of corruption or public immorality goes almost unchallenged by those in power, and creates not a ripple.

History teaches that a democracy, when once corrupted, has never been reformed. It has invariably perished."

I told my audience that we needed more plain living and high thinking in America. A surprising portion of the population had scarcely had a serious thought since the war except to secure a dollar in the easiest way and to spend it for amusement or pleasure or luxury. "The social life of the nation," I said, "has virtually been transferred from the parlor to the Ford car."

In my opinion, two of the greatest legacies bequeathed to us were the town or precinct meeting and the free school system. Those who presided at the birth of our government and watched over it during its earlier years, induced the people to utilize the free school and the town or precinct meetings to educate each generation in the fundamentals of popular government. The result was thoroughly intelligent leadership in every ward, precinct, and community in America.

"This period," I said, "constituted the golden age of representative government in world history. Can we not restore that fine, alert, and intelligent community leadership which, together with the American home, constitutes the chief foundation on which our free institutions have rested? The people are as patriotic as ever, but they are unconsciously and woefully neglecting a serious side of our political, moral, and economic problems."

Political parties, it seemed to me, had become weary and debilitated. They no longer functioned as united national entities behind definite programs that really meant something to the American people. There were vastly too many opportunists in high places, almost wholly concerned in holding their jobs. There was too much shadow boxing and sham fighting in both parties.

I admitted that government could not cure or prevent all the ills that overtake the people, but nevertheless it was true that the blessings of popular government, when wisely and soundly conducted, were more indispensable to the common man than to others. "The study of government is only second in importance to the study of the Bible itself," I said. "The present is the time for vigorous and searching inquiry into the manner in which representative government is functioning in the United States. During the past ten years the people have never been so inattentive to their governmental duties and tasks. The republic is no better than a monarchy unless the citizens meet their duties and responsibilities.

While we have government by the people in theory today, individuals and small minority groups in reality control."

I appealed to my own party to take the lead in a revival of sound interest in government. "The Democratic Party," I said, "will be recreant to its high mission unless it unifies itself behind a definite constructive liberal program, and proceeds during 1930–1932 to educate, organize, and bring about a civil revolution and political reformation as did Jefferson in 1800, Jackson in 1828, and Wilson in 1912."

I have gone at length into this philosophy for three reasons. First, it represented a great deal of thinking I had been doing for many years. Secondly, it echoes my thoughts today. And thirdly, it will be applicable again and again in American history. I was later to use these principles when I came to the State Department and found that almost all morals had disappeared from international relations, and that treaties once more were abused as scraps of paper.

The campaign that followed was restricted mainly to domestic affairs, although in many speeches over the State I urged the policy of international cooperation and my original proposal of international trade as a basis for peace and economic well-being.

Two days before the primary election, Crump released his machine to vote as they wished. Lea supported Todd to the end but was not extremely active, because I had many friends and supporters within his organization. The result of the primary election for a small State like Tennessee was an overwhelming victory for me. The soldier, farmer, labor, and postal employee groups Mr. Todd had appealed to sustained my record and repudiated his charges by voting for me in a landslide. My majority was 61,000.

Shortly before the November election, I was scheduled to speak in Chattanooga. Some of the machine Democrats unfriendly to me were in charge of hiring the hall in which I was to speak. That afternoon some of my friends informed me: "These fellows, who are not especially enamoured of you, went out and hired the biggest hall they could find. They don't believe the voters are coming out in large numbers for any-body, and they expect you will have the front-row seats taken and from then on there will be a great vacuum in the hall and galleries." But when I went down that night and walked onto the stage, I faced a crowded house, both main hall and gallery.

There was no real race in the general November election. While a Republican was nominally a candidate, it was universally recognized that the State leaned heavily Democratic that year. I received a majority of more than 100,000.

But Mr. Todd was not yet content. He demanded a United States Senate investigation of the primary campaign expenditures. Senators Nye and Wagner came down to Tennessee to investigate, and held formal hearings. I presented a detailed list of every dollar expended on my behalf. I had received many offers of contributions from friends, but had not accepted them. The Senate committee made its report that there had been no corrupt expenditures on my part. They then called on Todd to submit his expenditures. He refused to testify or to give any account.

There was now no opposition to my entrance into what I considered the most august legislative body in the world.

11: Steering the Party Toward Roosevelt

A CRISIS of the greatest gravity rose within the Democratic Party, I believed, at the beginning of 1931, and I prepared for one of the sternest fights of my career. Governor Al Smith and John J. Raskob, chairman of the Democratic National Committee, were in control of the Party organization. Their swing in 1928 toward high tariffs—in contrast to the traditional Democratic policy and my own heartfelt beliefs—continued in the years following the campaign of that year. They seemed to me determined to commit the Party to a 1932 platform of high tariffs and anti-Prohibition.

The Democratic convention to choose the next Presidential nominee was less than a year and a half away. The Party appeared to have an unusual opportunity because, with the economic crisis intensifying, the country was becoming more and more dissatisfied with the Hoover regime. And I believed that a desperate effort should be made to get the official control of the Party out of the Smith-Raskob hands and into the hands of others who entertained the ideas, especially on the tariff and international cooperation, for which I and many others actively stood.

I had not hesitated to speak my mind on the Smith-Raskob tariff defection. Personally, I had the highest regard for Smith and Raskob; but, as I viewed it, we differed basically on several questions, especially tariff and commercial policy. I had made a feeble effort in a Party exigency to defend Governor Smith's tariff-making methods outlined in his Louisville speech, in which he had virtually committed the Democratic Party to the Republican high-tariff policy; but it was not possible to do so on the basic doctrine. Smith and Raskob professedly spoke for international cooperation, but their utterances were negated by their support of high tariffs and the economic isolation that went with it.

On Prohibition, I maintained that this should not be a national partisan issue, but should be settled by the States individually. I had represented a district in Congress which was overwhelmingly for Federal Prohibition, and I always reflected their rather determined attitude by my vote in Congress. I had never spoken publicly on the issue, but I felt that the country might do as it pleased with the problem by any kind of nonpartisan action.

In the years following 1928 I strove hard but without particular publicity to organize members of the Democratic National Committee, and important Democratic leaders generally, against control of the Democratic Party by Governor Smith and his associates in 1932. I called on almost every National Committee member who came to Washington, and urged my views upon him. I wrote numerous letters and delivered a number of speeches. I antagonized the Smith group, of course, but I set forth my views to the country on both national and international policies.

During the conversations I constantly had with Franklin D. Roosevelt when he passed through Washington, we covered the most important domestic and international points. I made clear to him my fight against the ideas of Governor Smith and his Democratic chairman. Mr. Roosevelt expressed himself as being at one with me on the necessity for lower tariffs and full cooperation with other nations. He seemed to me to be alert, serious, and aggressive. But, since he continued to be associated, with the Smith organization, we did not discuss the plans I was formulating for a strong challenge to the Smith-Raskob leadership.

Early in 1931 the Smith-Raskob management decided to call a full meeting of the Democratic National Committee at Washington on March 5, the day after Congress adjourned, and to promulgate through the committee what appeared to be a full set of Party policies of their own selection. This would probably include high-tariff doctrines and also make Prohibition a political issue. Since there had been criticism of Governor Smith's personal selection of Mr. Raskob for the chairmanship of the Democratic National Committee in 1928, it was also reported that the meeting would strengthen the title and prestige of Mr. Raskob, who had always been a registered Republican prior to his selection as chairman. This would be done by his tendering his resignation to the committee in open session, with the expectation—if not the understanding—that the committee would then and there refuse to accept it and thus give the seal of its approval to his title as chairman.

The showdown was now at hand. I invited a few National Committee members, including Senator Harry Byrd of Virginia and Senator Cohen of Georgia, to join me in Washington two or three days in advance of the meeting and aid in resisting the Smith-Raskob plans. They agreed and rendered fine service. I also asked some of the other Senators, including Joseph T. Robinson and Claude Swanson, to help, and they joined heartily in our efforts at resistance,

Meantime I issued a series of public statements combating the whole course proposed by Smith and Raskob. I directly challenged any authority whatever of the Democratic National Committee to enunciate and proclaim any platform of principles. This, I maintained, was the task solely of the Democratic National Convention, which would meet in June, 1932. Basically, I wanted the Democratic fight in 1932 to be waged on economic issues, including low tariffs and commercial policy, and I did not want to see the Party splitting on any extraneous issues such as Prohibition.

"There must be more than mere hairsplitting differences between the two political parties on tariff and commercial policy," I said in a statement on February 15. "They must be fundamental. . . . If the two old political parties are to be merged with respect to this, the major and most powerful special-privilege group, then they should be merged as to all the minor forces of special privilege. There should be no sham fighting in either instance."

One of Al Smith's thoughts had been to "take the tariff out of politics." I attacked this on February 22, saying: "The Democratic and Republican parties must not be merged on economic policies, including high tariffs, under the false but attractive plea to 'take the tariff out of politics.' It is contrary to human nature for President or Congresses or tariff commissions belonging to the school of high-tariff philosophy to 'take the tariff out of politics' to any greater extent than to stabilize it in the same range or neighborhood of the high level favored by the chief beneficiaries."

Finally, on March 1, I issued my last and direct challenge to the Democratic National Committee under the Smith-Raskob leadership. I said the committee "has no authority, express or implied, to prescribe issues for the Democratic rank and file of the Nation. To assert this authority would constitute a broader assumption of power by the committee than that of selecting Party candidates for the Presidency and Vice Presidency."

Naturally, the Smith-Raskob organization were not idle. They, too, were lining up their associates for the meeting of March 5th. They planned to have the two former Democratic nominees for President, James M. Cox and John W. Davis, present at the meeting to speak on their behalf. This move failed in that Mr. Davis did not appear, and Mr. Cox delivered a harmony speech. Feeling was rapidly rising, and the attention of the whole Party and a large part of the country was centering on the forthcoming session.

On the night of March 3, as my wife and I were sitting after dinner in our apartment at the Lafayette Hotel, the telephone rang. I picked up the receiver and found Governor Franklin D. Roosevelt at the other end of the line at Albany. "I just called to say that I want to get in and help you to make that fight down there," he said. "The two National Committee members from New York will support you, and I will send Jim Farley [chairman of the New York State Democratic Committee] along with them to cooperate in every way."

I was really astonished to get this welcome news—but delighted. The powerful influence of Governor Smith's own State, New York, would be splendid support at the meeting. No doubt was left in my mind that a complete separation between the Smith and Roosevelt forces had thereby occurred. The reaction in the Smith camp next day was swift and bitter.

Some years later, when Mr. Roosevelt had become President, I asked him, during a luncheon we were having alone at the White House, how he had come to break with Al Smith. I recalled to him that at one time they had been very close, and that, during the 1924 convention, he had been Smith's floor manager. "Well," he replied, "Smith and his friends never took me into their counsel. I could work hard for him, as I did at the New York convention—but I was always on the outside, never on the inside, with him."

The two New York committee members came on, accompanied by James A. Farley. By their request Mr. Farley sat beside me at the meeting, as conclusive evidence of the genuineness of the Roosevelt movement away from Smith. I was to know a great deal more about him and to work with him through many years of the coming Roosevelt Administration. He was the highest type of individual, citizen, and official. His many fine qualities, including ability, truth, candor, loyalty, and absolute trustworthiness, endeared him to all who knew him and aroused their genuine admiration. I never knew a greater and more successful political manager or a finer man.

On the morning of the meeting, a short time before the session was to assemble, I ran into Raskob near an elevator in the Mayflower Hotel. I engaged him in conversation, especially with regard to the two main issues likely to come before the meeting—one, whether the committee would promulgate policies for the Party, and the other, whether he would tender his resignation in order to have it refused. We had a very vigorous but friendly conversation, which continued as I walked with him to his hotel room. There we ran into Jouett Shouse, an outstanding adviser and supporter of Governor Smith. In Shouse's presence I pressed with increasing vigor my opposition to Raskob's proposed political play involving his resignation. When I concluded, Raskob turned to Shouse and requested his opinion. Shouse supported my view. In the end Raskob abandoned his plan and said nothing about his resignation during the meeting.

Personally, I had high regard for Shouse, and he and I ordinarily agreed on economic ideas. I also highly regarded Charles Michelson, the able publicity director of the Democratic National Committee. But I strongly believed that, when the showdown came, Shouse would not have his way. This had been the case when Smith delivered his Louisville speech. I believed it would also be the case during the National Committee meeting if Smith's and Raskob's economic supporters left the door open for the restoration of the McKinley high-tariff principles contained in the Louisville address.

Raskob called the meeting to order and made a speech embracing Jeffersonian ideas, and also general policies, some of which were not objectionable to any Democrat, and some otherwise. He expressed his views on the controversial points such as tariffs and Prohibition, but did not make an effort to induce the committee to adopt them as a Party platform. My point, therefore, was won.

I spoke first for the opposing group. I stated my views very briefly on tariffs and Prohibition, but generally my speech was a harmony one. A great opportunity was coming to the Democratic Party in 1932, I firmly believed, and it must not be frittered away by internal quarreling. I concluded my address, which was made without notes, by calling attention to the danger of autocracy and dictatorship which even then, in 1931, I saw rising abroad.

"Let us go back to the origins, to the foundations, to the fundamentals," I said, "and then you will see this condition of autocracy that is springing up in South America and throughout Europe, and even in the Orient—you will see those great controversies that are now raging between despotism and democracies checked. And under our leadership there will be a revival that will bring this nation, and bring the civilized nations of the world, back to a keener realization of what government really means. And then you will see some steps taken to promote more satisfactory conditions of permanent peace."

The meeting over, we opponents of the Smith-Raskob program felt content that we had maintained our position denying the National Committee any authority to promulgate Party policies. Nor had the committee taken any action on the Prohibition controversy or in favor of any high-tariff doctrine. The Smith-Raskob group professed a measure of satisfaction in that Raskob and his associates had expressed their individual views, and that harmony speeches had been made by Governor Cox and other Democrats.

Impartial observers indicated very definitely that the prestige of the Smith-Raskob element in the Party had received a severe setback by the checkmating of their plans. This definite reverse, it seemed to me, was considerably accentuated by the loss in the committee of Smith's own State to Governor Roosevelt. Until this meeting, all the Prohibition population of the country, including those who did not desire to make Prohibition a partisan issue, had been clearly against the Smith-Raskob group. From this date on, these forces looked with either favor or much less disfavor on Governor Roosevelt and other Democratic leaders who fought the Smith-Raskob program. This attitude greatly redounded to Roosevelt's advantage as the Presidential race developed.

After Roosevelt's withdrawal from the Smith organization and his assertion of an independent political course, emphasized at this meeting, all or most of those opposed to the Smith movement were gradually and ultimately to turn to Roosevelt as the most effective way of killing off Smith. Roosevelt had a respectable following to begin with. While he had not made in the Governorship so spectacular a record as he later made in the Presidency, he had been a good Governor. Hence he became, after the March 5 meeting, a rallying point for a steadily increasing number of the Smith opposition.

There may be differences of opinion as to the effect of the meeting on the Presidential nomination in the year following, but it is my considered judgment that it was the most important turning point which ultimately resulted in the defeat of Smith and the nomination of Roosevelt for President. I feel that, if my associates and I had not been in there making this three-year fight, Raskob and Smith would have had control of the Party and its doctrines, and Roosevelt would have been in an extremely difficult situation.

The Smith-Raskob group, of course, did not abandon their fight for their policies, which they intended to carry into the 1932 convention. During the fifteen months until the convention opened, there was constant activity in the embattled Smith and anti-Smith camps. There was much debate in the press and over the radio by members of each camp. I sought on numerous occasions, by statements and addresses in and out of the Senate, to maintain the political and economic policies for which I had stood for years, and to oppose the objectionable portions of the Smith-Raskob preachments and plans.

Although I had now achieved my goal of being in the United States Senate, my role in that body was less important than my efforts toward steering the Democratic Party in the direction I thought it should follow in 1932. The first session of the Senate to which I was eligible did not meet until December, 1931, virtually at the gate of the election year. When I entered the Senate I did not feel myself a stranger there. Many of the Senators had been my colleagues and friends in the House, and I felt at home among them. During my twenty-two years in the House I had gone to the Senate on innumerable occasions to listen to addresses, at times to act as adviser to committees, and I was thoroughly familiar with its customs and procedure. As I entered the Senate I found a number of exceedingly able men there, among them George Norris of Nebraska; but there were not so many of this caliber as there had been before, for instance during the Wilson period. In any event, my major attention continued to be concentrated on the opportunity looming before the Party in 1932, which I felt should not be shattered by internal dissension or discolored by straying away from the traditional principles of the Party.

In a speech in the Senate on February 5, 1932, I said: "There is no disguising the fact that powerful influences are at work, either to commit the Democratic Party to high tariffs and trade isolation, or so to chloroform it that in practical effect it will be handicapped in its efforts to fight for the economic policies in which its overwhelming rank and file believe. The two old political parties must not be merged on economic policies."

In the same speech I advocated a three-point program to restore the American market abroad and help pull the country from depression: first, the President to call a permanent world economic congress; second, the President to be authorized to negotiate trade agreements based on mutual tariff concessions and unconditional most-favored-nation treatment; third, Congress to proceed toward careful and gradual readjustment downward of existing excessive tariffs.

I strongly opposed the "plow-under doctrine" then being preached, which was later adopted by a portion of the New Deal under President Roosevelt. "If we are to keep all American labor employed at good wages," I said, "we must prepare to sell our surplus. . . . Already we hear suggestions on every hand that this giant nation should again become as a little child and institute every artificial device possible to restrict output, to valorize, pool, and peg prices. These provincial notions include some recent instructions from Washington to plow up every third row of cotton, to kill one cow out of every ten, and similar freakish extremes to which we are surely headed if we continue, as we have since 1920, to isolate ourselves economically."

In an address to the Senate the following month I attacked the theory under which President Hoover had silently acquiesced in Congress's log-rolling of higher and higher tariff rates which resulted in the Smoot-Hawley Act, believing that his Tariff Commission could repair the damage caused by the Act. I quoted a bit of doggerel once recited by a British Member of Parliament:

> I hear a lion in the lobby roar;
> Say, Mr. Speaker, shall we shut the door
> And keep him there?
> Or shall we let him in
> In order to see whether
> We can put him out ag'in?

Hoover had let in the lion of high tariffs, and the Tariff Commission could not tame him. Some persons may have thought that Hoover would veto the Smoot-Hawley Tariff Bill. I never had any such illusions. Hoover had nailed himself fast to the Harding and Coolidge Administrations. Although he knew that the Smoot-Hawley Bill was generally unpopular, he also knew that the Republican machine was all-powerful and, if he was going to remain in good standing with the Republican Party leadership, he had to go along.

I pointed out that Hoover's temporary emergency relief measures "could only bring about very partial, unbalanced, and temporary prosperity in this country alone, leaving the balance of the world in its present prostrate condition, while the Administration's wild pursuit of the mad policy of economic nationalism will, instead of really curing, seriously aggravate both domestic and world business conditions."

In the same speech I quoted a phrase—"the forgotten man"—which was later frequently used by President Roosevelt. The quotation was from an article written fifty years before by the economist, Professor William G. Sumner, whose economic treatises I had read back in my school days. In criticising Government paternalism, Sumner asked who was to pay for it all. "Go and find him," he wrote, "and you will have once more before you the forgotten man. You will find him hard at work, because he has a great many to support. . . . He has to get out of the soil enough to pay all his taxes, and that means the cost of all the jobs and the fund for all the plunder. The forgotten man is delving away in patient industry . . . but he is the only one for whom there is no provision in the great scramble and the big divide." I had not previously seen the phrase—"the forgotten man"—used. I suppose Mr. Roosevelt got it from my speech, although he might also have taken it directly from Sumner's work.

I occasionally saw President Hoover on official business. He was more forbidding and less approachable in office than he was to be after his defeat in 1932. In this respect he resembled Charles Evans Hughes, who proved more affable following his defeat in 1916 than as Governor of New York. Hoover, however, was entirely agreeable in conversation and attitude. He did not indulge in humor, though I think he appreciated it moderately. He had excellent ability and a wide knowledge of business affairs, national and international. He had been out of the United States for many years until he became connected with the Wilson Administration. I thought he supported Wilson's doctrines, and as late as 1920, when the Presidential conventions approached, the New York *World* placed Hoover's name at its masthead for the Democratic nomination for President. Hoover, however, decided almost at the same time to go with the Republicans, who were strongly isolationist, avid for extreme high tariffs and against other policies he seemingly had been supporting during the Wilson period. He was handicapped in carrying out his earlier ideas by the overwhelming opposition of his newly adopted political party and by the fact that he himself seemed to have espoused them so recently. Hoover's main trouble was that he was working against his own ideas for a decade, and was highly irritated when they did not work out.

I rawhided Hoover when he was President, because of his economic views. On one occasion he remarked that other persons had no vision. I replied that one thing could be said about Hoover—he was a person of great vision; he could see a mare's nest farther than any other living politician. Later, when I entered the State Department, we were to come into frequent and cordial contact.

The nation was then wilting under the tragedy of a great economic crisis. The fact that I had foreseen its advent did not lessen one whit to me the force of its impact. My constant studies for many years having been largely in the field of economics, I could not see the crisis spreading its foul tentacles ever farther without scrutinizing every possible plan to overcome it. But it seemed to me that only through a change in Administration and a rebirth of confidence could it be met.

Hoover's Secretary of the Treasury, Andrew Mellon, had been just floating along for many years, in my opinion, knowing nothing about taxes and acting as the political banker of the Republican Party. Being intensely interested in national fiscal questions, I closely followed his policies and methods. That was a time when the special interests in the nation worked together in dominating the Government, with everyone taking orders from higher-ups in a fashion reminiscent of German discipline. When Mellon heard these leaders give the orders he let them dominate him.

As the Democratic National Convention at Chicago approached, there were Democrats over the country who were partial enough to suggest my name for the Presidential nomination. But I discouraged them and declined to allow any organized movement to be made. I continued in close, frequent correspondence with Roosevelt and Howe. Some time before the convention, Howe often came to Washington and made my office his headquarters.

Not being a candidate myself, I could work all the more enthusiastically for Party unity. Unable to forget the tragic cleavages at the San Francisco convention in 1920, the New York convention in 1924, and the Houston convention in 1928, I was determined to do all I could to prevent another at the Chicago convention in 1932. Harmony within the Party had always been one of my tight-held tenets.

Throughout my period as chairman of the National Committee from 1921 to 1924, I had sought constantly to organize and unify the Democratic forces and those in sympathy with them. The four years of the Harding-Coolidge Administration had witnessed sharp divisions in the Democratic Party, despite every effort to adjust and reconcile discordant views and ambitions. As the convention of 1924 approached, I had maintained an attitude of neutrality between McAdoo and Smith. I adjourned the Executive Committee a time or two in order to secure unanimity in the selection of the temporary chairman and the entire temporary organization. My reasons for neutrality were twofold: first, the National Committee must not favor one individual Democrat as against another; and, secondly, it was evident that, despite every precaution, the convention was likely to result in a deep, wide split, prejudicing or destroying chances of a Democratic success in the ensuing elections.

In the years that followed I continued the spirit of harmony, in speeches, statements, and personal conversations. My address to the Democratic National Committee at its celebrated meeting of March 5,

1931, was in that spirit. I continued to base my harmony appeal on the critical condition of the nation and of the world as a whole. My experience showed that I could not approach the ringleaders of opposing factions with much success, but I could make some impression on leading Democrats of each faction who were the immediate followers of the opposing chieftains.

At the beginning of 1932 I had one disappointment—Franklin D. Roosevelt's Albany speech of February 2, in which he said he did not favor United States participation in the League of Nations. He indicated that such participation would not serve to prevent war and settle international disputes in accordance with fundamental American ideals. William Randolph Hearst, the newspaper publisher, had prompted him to make this statement. The first I knew of it was when I saw it in the newspapers. In common with others having the international viewpoint, I was opposed to it.

In the spring of 1932 former Attorney General A. Mitchell Palmer came to me in Washington and earnestly asked me to work with him in preparing a draft for the Democratic national platform. He had been out of politics for some years, having been ruined politically by a labor injunction in Indiana he had requested as Attorney General. He was drifting about in Washington in the last stages of heart trouble, not knowing what day would be his last. Few of the active politicians paid him any attention, some being afraid to have him about because of the Indiana injunction. The fact was, however, that no one had rendered more valuable service to labor than Palmer when he was on the Ways and Means Committee. Later he had selected Vance McCormick for Wilson as chairman of the Democratic National Committee; and he had Wilson's fullest confidence. In some way he had got jockeyed into the labor injunction. Although political ruin followed, this had not affected his friendship for democratic ideas and for labor especially. Now he wanted to render one last service to the Party before he died, by helping to write the Party platform.

Palmer I knew to be intelligent and inherently honest, with a knowledge of politics running back many years. When he came to me with his proposition, I agreed. I had been developing ideas for platforms all through the 1920's. He and I both had notes, sketches, and outlines of platform material. We sat down together, molded our ideas together and prepared a draft, with Palmer doing most of the writing in language mutually agreed upon. I then called a number of meetings at my hotel, the

Lafayette, with Daniel C. Roper—who knew the Democratic doctrine from A to Z, was 1,000 per cent loyal and was a special champion of labor and agriculture—with a very capable Congressman, William Ayres, a modest, retiring man who otherwise would have traveled quite a distance; with Congressman Henry Rainey and others. Palmer, unable to get about much, did not attend these meetings. Later I had conferences with farm leaders on the agricultural plank, and with labor leaders on the labor plank, and no differences developed between us. We kept open the Federal Reserve plank for Carter Glass to write, and it went in as he prepared it.

Our draft was later to prove almost entirely acceptable to the Committee on Platform and Resolutions—barring, of course, their rejection of our plank recommending that the decision on Prohibition be referred to the States.

Several weeks prior to the convention, a number of intimate friends and earnest followers of Franklin D. Roosevelt, including myself, took to visiting him on Sundays at Hyde Park. There we conferred with him on all aspects of preconvention conditions and problems. We undertook to do all planning necessary to meet situations calling for his serious attention. At nearly our last conference at Hyde Park Mr. Roosevelt said he wanted me to be chairman of the Committee on Platform and Resolutions at the convention. I thanked him but said that, while this was a high honor, I could be of more service by being footloose and remaining on the floor, where I could defend all provisions of the platform draft against attack. I knew there was a terrific fight brewing among the high-tariff people, including many Democrats, several of whom would be on the committee, and that the tariff planks would need defending on the floor. At the convention, in fact, I had to handle a number of attacks against the platform. If I had been tied down in the chair I am not sure what might have happened, since I had been working with these issues for many years.

I recommended Senator Hitchcock of Nebraska for chairman and assured Mr. Roosevelt I would be constantly on watch as a member of the committee and would strive to take care of any or all questions arising that any one person could handle. I told him Palmer and I already had a draft of a platform which I felt was in the main adequate. Roosevelt acquiesced in my course and adopted my suggestion on Hitchcock. He later approved our platform draft, which Palmer read to him over the telephone.

Prior to the convention I reached what I thought was a valid agreement among a requisite number of Wet and Dry leaders not to make Prohibition a strict Party question but to leave it to the people to deal with as they saw fit. This agreement seemed to be generally acceptable until about the time the convention opened. Then suddenly the Wet forces from the big cities started a movement to write a plank in the platform making Prohibition a Party question. Wet leaders with whom I had reached my agreement proceeded to forget about it and joined the rapid procession toward an anti-Prohibition plank. The Committee on Resolutions adopted their view and wrote a plank I heartily opposed.

When the question reached the floor of the convention, I felt I should make a statement setting out the minority views and the record of what had happened, although it was then manifest that a Wet plank would be adopted. The Wet forces had packed the galleries, and they engaged in wild, unruly demonstrations seeking to shout me down by every kind of noise. But I had been in too many public gatherings to be disturbed by this gallery maneuver and racket.

Governor Smith followed me on the speaker's platform, and I was not a little surprised to see him engage in both demagogy and discourtesy at my expense. Possibly he was stimulated by the wild shouts of the packed-to-order galleries. I had cited his position on Prohibition four years before, which was the same as I was now presenting. He indulged in a tirade against me in order somewhat awkwardly to cloak the fact that he had reversed himself. No doubt he was also smarting under my four years' constant, active opposition to his organization.

Although I lost on Prohibition as a political issue, I won on tariffs, while general acceptance of other planks, including foreign affairs, was most gratifying. The Committee on Resolutions adopted my economic and tariff planks in their entirety. There was some debate in the committee on the subject, but the Smith group made only feeble resistance there and none at the convention, realizing beforehand that their fight was lost.

The convention adopted the platform without difficulty, although one ironic episode occurred. Senator Hitchcock had finished reading the platform, and the permanent chairman of the convention, Senator Thomas J. Walsh, had recognized me to make the minority report on Prohibition. At that moment Senator Hitchcock spoke up again. "I find that I turned over two pages as one," he explained, "and omitted one condemnation." And this, of all things, was our plank, which I had written, denouncing the Hawley-Smoot Tariff Law! Hitchcock then proceeded to read it.

The convention's adoption of the tariff and economic planks delighted my heart. I was gratified to see the Party swing back from the Smith-Raskob ideas to a fixed policy of sound economics. The way was paved for the trade-agreements legislation in 1934.

I was also pleased with the foreign policy plank, which read:

"We advocate a firm foreign policy, including peace with all the world and the settlement of international disputes by arbitration; no interference in the internal affairs of other nations; the sanctity of treaties and the maintenance of good faith and of good will in financial obligations; adherence to the World Court with appending reservations; the Pact of Paris abolishing war as an instrument of national policy, to be made effective by provisions for consultation and conference in case of threatened violations of treaties.

"International agreements for reduction of armaments, and cooperation with nations of the Western Hemisphere to maintain the spirit of the Monroe Doctrine.

"We oppose cancellation of the debts owing to the United States by foreign nations."

Palmer and I, in the light of the extreme state of isolation and pacifism then reigning, had not put fully into our draft all that we both or either of us personally desired in every instance. This was but natural and logical. We inserted as many basic peace and international cooperation objectives in the foreign policy plank as we felt could be gotten through the convention. The plank, so far as it went, met with my approval. The great panic, however, was raging and pulling the close attention of statesmen as well as the public away from foreign affairs.

As the convention began I engaged in every possible activity in aid of the Roosevelt cause. At one stage the situation became dangerous. On the third ballot Roosevelt had a clear majority, with 682.79 votes against Smith's 190.25, but he did not have the required two-thirds of the total vote. There was always a possibility of a long deadlock, which might throw the vote to a "dark horse."

Remindful of the three weeks' disastrous impasse in 1924, and after ascertaining through Howe that Roosevelt approved, I went with Daniel C. Roper to confer with our personal friend, William G. McAdoo, chief of the California delegation. California had been casting its 44 votes solidly for John Garner. We felt that if we could win California's support for Roosevelt the victory would be gained. We, in conjunction with other leaders, prevailed upon McAdoo to cast California's vote for Roosevelt in exchange for an arrangement to nominate Garner for Vice President. I do not know what other persons, save Farley and Howe, undertook to figure in this arrangement. I do know that Roper and I had been closely associated with McAdoo during the Wilson Administration and were among his special friends since then. We were vain enough to feel satisfied that this conference with him, which threshed out all phases of the California and Texas voting situation, played its full part in the favorable understanding reached.

At almost the same time, Representative Sam Rayburn, Carl Crowley, a Texas delegate, former Tennessean, and long-time friend, and I met with a large group of the Texas delegation, many of whom were my old friends and acquaintances. Texas had been casting its 46 votes compactly for Garner. I found considerable opposition in the delegation to Roosevelt, but we argued forcefully for our candidate. The pro-Roosevelt delegates, under Rayburn's leadership, won out, and Texas moved into the Roosevelt camp.

Roosevelt's situation greatly improved at once. The fight was really over. About this time, as Governor Smith stepped into an elevator, someone asked him how he felt, and I heard him promptly reply, "Not so hot!" He was evidently watching the convention barometer closely.

Governor Roosevelt flew to Chicago from Albany to deliver his speech of acceptance, thus reversing the old precedent whereby the nominee waited some weeks for the formal notification. We received him with tumultuous acclaim and listened to his exceedingly timely address.

During the campaign, after some weeks at national Democratic headquarters in New York, I delivered a number of speeches, principally in Tennessee. No one had any uneasiness about the outcome of the election. It was a foregone conclusion. At long last, my party was back in power, and I felt confident that a fruitful period of work and accomplishment lay before me and those of similar views.

12: I Am Named Secretary of State

RETURNING to my office in the Senate soon after the election, I resumed my efforts further to advance the economic and peace proposals I had long since made. It was obviously too soon to obtain action in this "lame-duck session," and nothing could really be achieved until the new President was inaugurated, but I did not hesitate to emphasize the remedial action I thought should be taken.

Economic disarmament and military disarmament seemed to me the two most vital and outstanding factors for peace and business recovery. I proposed two temporary solutions, in a statement on December 4. One was a truce on further increases in tariffs and similar trade obstructions; the second was a horizontal reduction of 10 per cent in all permanent tariff rates of all countries—both proposals to be made by our Government. I did not consider these proposals as a sound or permanent policy, however. Rather I regarded them as crude rule-of-thumb preliminary steps. I myself adhered to the principle of a reduction of trade barriers gradually and cautiously through reciprocal agreements based on unconditional most-favored-nation treatment.

"The war debts," I said in a statement on November 20, "were not a major cause of the panic, nor are they a major remedy." Suspending war debts, I pointed out, did not lower by one inch the skyscraping tariff barriers which, under American leadership, had been carried to the wildest extreme in every part of the world.

In the December 4 statement I suggested that war debtors, before pressing their claims for further reduction, should indicate their attitude toward the broader and more fundamental program of reducing trade barriers. "This Government, individually," I said, "could then hear and consider the applications of our debtor governments for further debt readjustment. This it should do entirely separately from but simultaneously with or following the proceedings of a world economic conference dealing with and acting on tariff policy—not tariff rates—and monetary stability and rehabilitation, credit policy, and economic disarmament generally."

I felt sure that the Democratic Administration, on March 4, would have ready a constructive program soundly interpreting postwar economic conditions. I knew that Congress would be willing to sit in extra sessions at any and all times the public welfare might require. And I was ready to take my appropriate part in such work.

I collaborated with Senator E. P. Costigan, of Colorado, on a resolution he introduced in January, 1933, requesting the Tariff Commission and other agencies to assemble information that would assist the incoming Administration to negotiate trade agreements. Senator Costigan had been a personal friend and co-worker since his membership on the Tariff Commission, and we had kept in constant conference in the Senate in support of all movements for liberal commercial policies.

In January I accompanied the President-elect down to the Tennessee Valley Authority area. During the earlier movements to develop the water power in the Tennessee River Valley, we Tennessee members of Congress had been in general agreement that the State of Tennessee had title to this power within the State. Opposed to trusts and monopolies, we favored any proposition that appeared feasible and free from monopoly. The Alabama delegation worked along with us. Congressman Sam McReynolds, of the Chattanooga district, accurately and succinctly stated the attitude of most of the members of both delegations at the time.

No governmental or other agency to develop this power was forthcoming in a serious way until Roosevelt became President. Just as soon as a real, worth-while plan to develop the Tennessee Valley water power on the broadest scale was presented, the entire Tennessee delegation quickly abandoned the partial and wholly inadequate methods that had been proposed by different Members of Congress, and gave its support to the Norris plan.

At that moment I was to experience a great surprise. Mr. Roosevelt stopped over in Washington in January on his way to Warm Springs, Georgia, and sent for me to call on him at the Mayflower Hotel. Then and there, without much introduction, he offered me the Secretaryship of State.

I was really almost thunderstruck. Previously, I had not conferred with him a minute about Cabinet appointments, and I did not have them in mind. No one had informed me I was under consideration for such an appointment. I had been looking forward to what I persuaded myself to believe might well prove a long career in the Senate. The people of Tennessee were overwhelmingly behind me and the ideas for which I stood. I believed I could do effective work in the Senate to put these ideas in motion.

Recovering from my astonishment, I first thanked the President-elect. I then said that, with great respect to him, I would have to take his offer under consideration. I told him frankly: "The post of Secretary of State has not been any part of my personal planning for the future, even though in the long course of my legislative work I've become more and more tied in with international conditions and problems." In any event, I definitely hesitated to give him a reply without much fuller consideration. He agreed to wait.

During the next thirty days or so I pondered all aspects of my situation. I went to Warm Springs about February 1 to discuss various problems with Mr. Roosevelt. He urged me to accept the appointment he had offered me, but I withheld any commitment and kept it under consideration. Finally, my thinking resolved itself down to this: In which position could I best promote the ideas for international economic peace and therefore political peace which I maintained? I felt deeply that the greatest blunder of all time had been made by killing off all plans and arrangements to prevent future war. The granite rock of isolation and narrow nationalism still stood in the middle of the road to the necessary international cooperation for a future world of peace and economic well-being. Only by the most desperate grappling with these terrific obstacles could this country and other peaceful democracies arm against danger and strive on to the ultimate goal.

I had devoted much of my time for many years, especially since the First World War and the League of Nations fight, to international affairs, particularly the economic side. I felt that my work in the Senate would be mainly on the domestic impact of foreign affairs, whereas in the State Department I should be dealing with foreign affairs directly. Also many Senators would be undertaking to deal with the same problems, with different approaches, whereas in the State Department my work would be more concentrated in the directions I intended. Finally I decided I could advance sound international views more effectively as head of the State Department than I could in the Senate.

At about this time I met Norman Davis, back from Geneva on a trip. I had known him from the Wilson days during the First World War when he came to Washington and worked in the Treasury, and we were the closest friends. He remarked, "Your name has been mentioned for the post of Secretary of State." I said, "If you want the position and think you can get it, I will not be in your way." He promptly, emphatically replied, "I want you to take it if it is offered to you."

In February, Mr. Roosevelt telegraphed from Warm Springs, asking me to meet him at Richmond as he came north, and ride on the train with him to Washington. This I did. We started off with a very agreeable general conversation on personal and official lines. He spoke with deep feeling of the wounding (later fatal) of Mayor Cermak of Chicago, his companion at Miami, Florida, the day before, although he seemed to feel toward it as a military commander might feel toward an important casualty in a military campaign. He made no reference to the assassin's attempt on himself, and the danger he had narrowly escaped. Then he brought up his Cabinet offer and asked for my answer. I did not say "Yes" right off, but held out to the extent that I first wanted to clarify the very important matter of our future personal and official working relations.

I said, "I need to know how well we can and will work in complete cooperation." Also, how the President, while performing his full functions as head of the Executive Branch charged with the conduct of foreign affairs through the State Department, would function within his province. And how free I should be to function in the most effective support of him and within my province as Secretary of State and head of the State Department. I said, "A clear understanding on these points is all-important for a successful administration of foreign affairs."

I explained to him, "If I accept the Secretaryship of State, I do not have in mind the mere carrying on of correspondence with foreign governments." What I did have in mind was that it would be my duty to aid the President in every possible way in the formulation and conduct of foreign policy. In this I would make use of the State Department's life-long experts on each important question of foreign policy covering every country in the world. I would constantly keep in closest touch with the experienced and best informed experts in the department from top to bottom. I would foresee and appraise to the fullest possible extent questions and problems arising or about to arise and would formulate my own ideas of policy, in conference with my associates where necessary. I would then recommend such policy to the President for his approval or disapproval and suggest the necessary action. The President himself would, of course, suggest a policy on a given situation at any time he might see fit, and I would develop all facts in relation to it and then, if he adopted it, carry it out through the State Department.

Mr. Roosevelt listened intently, and then emphatically expressed his approval and assured me, "We shall each function in the manner you've stated." I thereupon accepted his offer, and we shook hands.

We did not discuss foreign affairs to see whether we agreed in our attitudes toward them. Neither of us felt the need to do so. We had discussed foreign relations so many times in the past, especially during the later twenties when I used to meet him as he came through Washington, that we thoroughly knew each other's views in the main.

The President-elect made a formal announcement of my appointment on February 21. Three days later I made my first public statement outlining in a general way my thoughts on foreign affairs.

Although I said I could not discuss policies at that stage, I pointed out that demoralization and chaos, including the complete dislocation of the economic relationships of nations, characterized political and economic affairs. "There has been, too, a general letting down since the war of moral and political standards by both peoples and governments," I stated. "There should be no laxity on the part of this or any other nation in the observance of both the letter and spirit of treaties and of international good faith."

I added: "There should be sane and realistic international cooperation, keeping in mind our traditions and our Constitution, to aid in preserving the peace of the world. This policy is vital. This nation henceforth must play its full part in effecting the normal restoration of national economic relationships and in world commercial rehabilitation, from which alone business recovery in satisfactory measure can be hoped for. That the war debts owed our government are but one factor, will not be controverted. The policy of international readjustment assumes that all fundamental domestic remedies for trade improvement also will be pursued."

And, finally: "The success of the principal foreign policies of the incoming administration, therefore, will be determined by the extent of its aid in restoring world commerce, which would include our commerce at home; and its aid in maintaining world peace under the fundamental policy of right and justice. This great young country of ours possesses resources and wealth unequaled in all the past, and, under a sound and suitable program of fiscal and economic policies such as will be proposed, there can be no reasonable doubt about early revival."

In this statement I was reiterating the doctrines and policies contained in previous addresses and statements of mine. When I came to the State Department, I believed they offered much of the foundation for the most mutually desirable relationship among the nations of the world.

In the period between the public announcement of my appointment and the inauguration I busied myself with preliminary preparations for the weighty task before me. I had elaborate talks with outgoing Secretary Henry L. Stimson, who was most obliging in giving me the fullest pertinent information. I had first got acquainted with Stimson when he was Secretary of War under Taft. I knew him as a follower of Theodore Roosevelt who preached Teddy's doctrines generally, but I did not know how far he went in his views until the years unfolded and gradually I discovered that he was a man of sound ideas to which he held with the greatest imaginable tenacity and real courage. I knew he had had a difficult time getting President Hoover to agree to his policies on Manchuria. In our talks I found him to measure up to his reputation as a very able, broad-gauged, patriotic statesman.

At one of these conferences, Stimson laid before me an invitation from the League of Nations to our Government to associate itself with the League in its condemnation of Japan's invasion of Manchuria, and also his reply accepting in principle the League's findings. Being fairly familiar with the whole Manchurian incident, and entertaining like views, I readily assented to his position.

I saw William C. Bullitt, who acquainted me with the results of his trip to Europe for the President-elect, which were interesting and useful. I conferred in a tentative way with British Ambassador Sir Ronald Lindsay and French Ambassador Paul Claudel. Mr. Roosevelt had already stated his willingness to receive a representative of the British Government to discuss war debts early in March. But he had refused President Hoover's suggestion for a committee of Republicans and Democrats to consider war debts, armaments, and the proposed economic conference. He did not wish to commit his Administration in advance, since he did not yet have power to carry out commitments.

I also made it a point to meet and become acquainted with the key men throughout the State Department, whom I found in most cases to be capable and well informed. About a week before I formally took office I started spending most of every day at the Department, becoming familiar with its mechanics of operation.

As I was about to assume my new post, Mr. Roosevelt brought up the name of William Phillips for Under Secretary of State and asked me what I thought. I had known Phillips fairly well and very favorably while he was Assistant Secretary of State during the Wilson Administration. I immediately agreed. Phillips possessed splendid capacity and character and was loyal to friends and to principles. In whatever position he served he was unusually efficient.

Mr. Roosevelt, without much ceremony, appointed Raymond Moley as one of my Assistant Secretaries of State. Moley had been in my office in the Senate on more than one occasion for conferences on the general situation. I knew something of him and his leadership among the so-called brain trusters, and I felt that he lacked information on international affairs, and that his equipment would not be of any great aid in conducting foreign policy. I therefore readily concluded that Mr. Roosevelt was placing him in this position, not to render regular service as Assistant Secretary of State, but to continue to stay close around the President, be his chief utility man, and handle any questions arising anywhere in the Government to which Mr. Roosevelt might assign him. In any event, I was not at all enthusiastic about this sort of appointment, and I grew less enthusiastic until the London Economic Conference was over and Moley retired from the State Department.

The President-elect wanted an old friend of his, Wilbur J. Carr, to be retained as Assistant Secretary, to which I agreed. I knew Carr well and had a good opinion of him. In the face of the terribly complicated international situation, I wished to keep most persons in key positions who had experience and practical judgment and were loyal to the Government. Such periods of extreme diplomatic difficulties, I felt, were never the time for sweeping reorganizations of the State Department with "new blood" unless those at the head of the Government were prepared for disastrous results in the conduct of foreign policy. It matters not how brilliant an appointee may be, he is helpless when deep-seated questions arise in rapid succession about whose background he knows little or nothing.

Mr. Roosevelt was now laboring in transition from his station as a good governor of New York in peacetime to the position of President where he was destined to render vast and lasting service to the nation and the world and to take his place among our great Presidents. The terrific panic which had utterly prostrated all lines of endeavor in this country as never before had visited all the important countries in the world. I myself sought to deal with its effects in the international situation, but not with the purely domestic questions which at the time presented almost insurmountable problems to Mr. Roosevelt.

As the inauguration approached, I failed to detect signs of what I deemed sufficient progressiveness on the part of the President-elect. But this proved to be a joke on some of us. As an old Wilsonian progressive, I had a discussion with Daniel Roper on this point just before or just after the inauguration. He seemed to have reached the same conclusion. I urged that we persuade Josephus Daniels, former Secretary of the Navy, to have a conference with Mr. Roosevelt and induce him to become more outspokenly progressive. Daniels agreed to approach the President-elect. Mr. Roosevelt replied in reassuring terms, saying that he would make hard-boiled reactionism "pop like a new saddle." He implied something more than the progressivism we had been standing for since the Wilson period.

All preliminaries out of the way, I tendered my resignation as Senator and was ready to undertake my new work. I had not been in the diplomatic service, and I had not had much social contact with diplomats; but the background on foreign affairs I carried with me to the State Department was far greater than was generally known.

Even from boyhood I had kept reasonably familiar with important international developments, simply because they interested me. This I did by reading newspapers and other available periodicals and by listening to public speakers. I remember closely following Cleveland's controversy with Great Britain over Venezuela and his outspoken message, and Theodore Roosevelt's negotiations and actions concerning the Panama Canal. I do not want anyone to think I was an expert on foreign affairs in those days, but at any rate they engaged my attention.

From 1888 to 1933 I had made a thorough study of tariffs. In so doing I had had to examine the tariffs and trading arrangements and principles of all major commercial nations. That meant that I learned much of their whole social and economic structure. My knowledge of their economics deepened as I studied their income tax, inheritance tax, and excess-profits tax systems, and their methods of financing the First World War. And you could not have studied in detail the economics of a country without knowing something of its political problems, both domestic and foreign.

I had followed foreign affairs very closely during the First World War and immediately thereafter during Wilson's fight for the League of Nations. I had to keep in intimate touch with international events during my period as chairman of the Democratic National Committee, 1921 to 1924. My long and frequent talks with Wilson and Bryan were greatly revealing on foreign affairs. I had made an extensive tour of Europe in 1925, when I visited nine countries. I knew a little of the Latin Americans from my five months in Cuba during the Spanish-American War. I was an assiduous reader of articles and books on foreign subjects. I had made speeches on foreign policy. It is not too much to say that from the First World War on I devoted more time to a study and investigation of foreign and related domestic questions and conditions than to purely domestic developments.

I was vain enough to believe I was not a novice in foreign affairs when I entered the State Department. I had some definite ideas on what our foreign policy should be in the vital fields. I believed I had in mind the methods to make these ideas work.

Part Two

FIRST TWO YEARS AS SECRETARY OF STATE

(1933–1935)

13: I Begin My Major Work

PRAYER—WE NEEDED IT—opened the ceremonies on Inauguration Day, March 4, 1933. The members-designate of the Cabinet accompanied the President-elect to St. John's Episcopal Church on Sixteenth Street opposite the White House, where Dr. Peabody prayed to the Almighty to help the new President.

Shortly before noon we appeared with Mr. Roosevelt on the grandstand at the Capitol and witnessed the administration of the oath and heard his inaugural address. Chief Justice Hughes administered the oath in his usual clear, resonant voice. I have seen numerous Presidents inaugurated, but no one took the oath in a firmer tone and with a more solemn demeanor than Franklin D. Roosevelt.

The President in his inaugural address resolutely attacked the terrific problems of the domestic situation, which could scarcely have been worse. Then and thereafter he was to handle almost impossible conditions with masterly skill and power of analysis. He was to prosecute far-reaching, drastic domestic reforms during the first four years of his Administration, almost entirely to the exclusion of foreign policy. In his inaugural address he devoted just one short paragraph to foreign policy, when he eloquently proclaimed the everlasting doctrine of the Good Neighbor—a doctrine that applied alike to every part of the world.

He made a reference to international trade relations which was to have a decided effect on my actions during the coming months. Although he said he would make every effort to reduce trade barriers, domestic economic questions would have to have first place, and, "I favor as a practical policy the putting of first things first."

We went to the reviewing stand in front of the White House—constructed as a replica of Andrew Jackson's Hermitage near Nashville—where, with the President, we saw the inaugural parade. Late in the afternoon the President and the members-designate of the Cabinet, on his invitation, repaired to the Oval Room of the White House. There, in the presence of our families and friends, Associate Justice Cardozo administered to us the oath whereby we swore to uphold the Constitution of the United States. Never before had all the members of the Cabinet been sworn in at the same time by the same official, and never before had the ceremony taken place in the White House. Mr. Roosevelt, remarking that this was a new precedent, called it a "little family party," and handed each of us the commission of office which he had signed. We then went to our offices in our respective departments, to take up the grinding work that for some of us was to continue for many years.

The office in which I was to sit for twelve years was one of the most interesting in Washington. It was a large rectangular room on the second floor of the State Department. Well lighted by ample windows, it looked south across the Mall to the Washington Monument. In the center of the room stood my huge mahogany desk. I do not know how successful my predecessors were in keeping it clear, but for me it was always stacked with a mass of papers, reports, dispatches, diplomatic notes, memoranda—especially economic data—and the like.

I sat at the desk with my back to the windows so that the light streamed over my shoulders. To my left were two telephones, one a private line to the White House. On my right was a telephone direct to my secretary and a little interoffice communications box linking me with the principal officials of the Department.

My desk was flanked on the left by a solid, leather-covered chair in which a visitor might sit. Farther to the left, beside the vast fireplace, was a small "treaty table" on which I signed treaties with foreign countries.

If I looked straight up from my desk to the north wall, I could see portraits and engravings of Abraham Lincoln, Ulysses S. Grant, and William Henry Harrison. Below them hung a wide map case containing a dozen maps on rollers. Beneath the maps was a bookcase extending almost the whole length of the wall, filled and also topped by books.

A heavy door stood at each end of the wall. Through the one to the right entered Ambassadors and Ministers from the diplomatic waiting room across the hall. The one to the left opened on a large private washroom. On a table in the washroom were two more telephones.

To my left, the stone-faced fireplace was surmounted by a huge mirror outlined in redwood with the coat of arms of the United States crowning it. On the mantel was a bronze statue of Andrew Jackson on a rearing horse, tipping a cocked hat. To the left of the fireplace, over the treaty table, hung a portrait of Jackson. A door beside the fireplace admitted visitors in general. Open, it revealed a small anteroom, where two more telephones reposed on a table. This room was decorated with two paintings of my native section, one showing the Cumberland and Caney Fork rivers and the other a river and road scene near Carthage.

When I looked up from my desk to the right, I saw a well populated side of the room. Between me and the wall were a black leather divan and two chairs. On the right wall hung the engraved portraits of James Monroe seated, George Washington standing and declaiming, Thomas Jefferson standing and making an address, and John Quincy Adams seated. They looked down on a wide-stretched bookcase on which stood a marble bust of Washington. To their left was a dictionary on a stand, and farther to the left a big door leading to the office of the Under Secretary of State. We could thereby communicate with each other without going through the corridor. Just to the right of this door was a tall, loud-ticking grandfather's clock, with an expansive face. At the extreme right was a huge green safe, where I kept secret papers.

The south wall, at my back, seemed the most occupied of all, probably because its objects of ornamentation had to be fitted into the spaces between the three large windows. An opening to the left was taken by a marble plaque of James Madison, done in 1792, supposedly the most valuable piece of art in the State Department. To the right a floor standard held aloft an American flag and the flag of the Secretary of State. This latter bore, on a white background, a star in each corner, and in the middle the seal of the United States of which I, in my new position, was the keeper. To the right of the flags was a little rubber plant which during my service shot up to twelve feet.

The original State, War, and Navy Building was becoming old when I entered it. Its interior was impressive by reason of its simplicity and great tradition, but it contained too many exterior frills and furbelows to be as striking as it deserved to be in the light of the historic events that had taken place within its walls.

I myself gathered both stimulus and inspiration from the constant reminders around me of the great statesmen who had adorned the office of Secretary of State in preceding generations. The first Secretary of State, Thomas Jefferson, was in my mind a marvelous philosopher, patriot, and statesman. He launched the functions and standards of the department on the highest plane, but there were other able Secretaries, such as Madison, Monroe, John Quincy Adams, Clay, Webster, Hay, Root, Hughes, and Stimson.

If my desk was piled high with papers, there was a reason for it. It is doubtful if any previous Secretary of State was confronted by so many world problems of first magnitude in the first month of his tenure.

It is remarkable how so many of the stupendous developments of the next dozen years cast their shadows into that month of March, 1933.

The very day after I entered office, Germany held her parliamentary elections, and Hitler's Nazis and the allied Nationalist Party obtained between them a 52 per cent majority, thus consolidating Hitler in power. That same month outbreaks against the Jews occurred in Germany, resolutions were introduced in Congress requesting a formal protest by our Government, and we sent a cable to our Embassy in Berlin asking for a report on these events. The German Government denied that it was sanctioning race persecution.

Here was the first of many diplomatic steps we took in later years on the ground of race persecution, culminating in the recall of American Ambassador Hugh Wilson from Berlin in 1938. I had long been studying the purposes and effects of Nazism. In speeches back in 1930 and 1931 I had called attention to the growth of dictator movements abroad and the danger they offered to a peaceful world. There was little doubt in my mind in March, 1933, that Germany would provide one of my biggest problems in the years to come.

In the Far East, Japan had invaded and occupied Manchuria. The day I entered the State Department the Japanese occupied Jehol City, capital of Jehol, one of China's provinces. The prediction I made at the time of the 1921-1922 Washington Disarmament Conference—that Japan, regardless of her signature of treaties, meant to continue her expansion— had unfortunately come true. At Geneva the League of Nations condemned Japan's action and Japan, some three weeks after I became Secretary of State, formally withdrew from the League. There was no doubt that here, too, was a fertile source of future problems and trouble.

In Latin America the bitter Chaco War between Bolivia and Paraguay was raging, and another, between Colombia and Peru, over the Leticia frontier, was in the skirmish stage. Mexican newspapers were protesting the appointment of my friend, Josephus Daniels, as Ambassador because he had been Wilson's Secretary of the Navy when Vera Cruz was shelled in 1913. Cuba was in a state of growing ferment, the same ferment out of which revolutions had sprung in the past. Haiti, extremely restless, was complaining loudly about the presence of United States troops on the island for some twenty years and of a United States financial administration within the Haitian Government.

The League of Nations Council, on March 18, undertook conciliation of the Leticia dispute, and thus, for the first time in its history, began to be active in a territorial question in the Western Hemisphere. Two days later we instructed the American Minister to Switzerland, Hugh Wilson, to work with the League's advisory committee handling the dispute.

In March the Disarmament Conference at Geneva was still in session, and we were faced with the problem of keeping it alive and helping it achieve results. Peace with disarmament, prior to and during the 1930's, was always one of the urgent questions up for solution by the nations. Much was said about disarmament, by spokesmen of numerous countries, but I could not help noting that the final upshot of all meetings and conversations from 1921 on was that very little of lasting value was accomplished. On March 16, Prime Minister MacDonald presented a new, comprehensive British plan of disarmament to the Geneva Conference. Two days later he was in Rome and received from Mussolini the plan for a Four-Power Pact—Britain, Germany, France, and Italy.

Over the nations, like a pall, hung the enormous war debts, mainly due to the United States. The debtor nations, it seemed to me, spent more time finding ways to avoid or postpone payment than in efforts to make payment at least to the extent of their ability. Their actions raised the question in my mind, by the 1930's, as to whether, with the world panic on, most of the debtor countries were gradually adopting the attitude that they could not pay and would not seriously undertake to do so. This Government, on the other hand, with the Treasury more than the State Department having the leadership, treated the debts seriously and strove accordingly to make collections. The President, even before assuming office, had expressed his willingness to discuss the question with some of the debtor nations after March 4. The next payment was due June 15, only three months later. It was obvious that war debts would demand much study in the months to come.

Even more work confronted us in connection with the forthcoming Economic Conference, to be held in London under the auspices of the League of Nations. The Hoover Administration had committed the United States to participation in the Conference. A preparatory commission at Geneva, in which American representatives took part, had prepared an exceedingly interesting and elaborate agenda. It embraced a broad, practical program of tariff, trade, financial, and general economic readjustment with a view to reducing or eliminating excessive obstructions in international commerce and financing. This program in principle was in harmony with the economics and peace proposal I first offered in 1916.

I now had the hope that, under the new Administration, my long tilling in the field of lower tariffs and world trade might raise an additional crop. I was prepared to work for legislation authorizing the State Department to negotiate reciprocal trade agreements based on the unconditional most-favored-nation clause and permitting substantial tariff reductions.

In March I began to receive petitions asking that our Government recognize Soviet Russia, with whom relations had been non-existent for sixteen years.

Thus the very month in which I entered my new office was shadowed by most of the questions in the foreign field that were to confront us later. When the new Administration assumed charge of the executive and legislative branches of the Federal Government, it faced colossal problems in the domestic as well as the international field. Whichever way one's eyes turned, obstacles and dangers were in evidence. With their threats of early chaos, political, economic, and social, they presented the Government with tasks and responsibilities scarcely equaled in all the past history of the nation. In the domestic field, the unparalleled panic had brought utter collapse to our financial, industrial, agricultural, and general economic structure. Most of the vital processes of our very domestic existence had well-nigh ceased to function.

Such conditions were common to most other countries. All together, they seriously handicapped the conduct of foreign relations on anything approaching a high level. It was easy to observe a widespread decline of most standards of international conduct, both individual and official. The truth was that the whole international structure in many parts of the world had slipped down to the lowest level. Treaty observance was flouted by many nations. Truth, candor, law, and fair dealing had been banished from many chancelleries. There seemed to be no such thing as the peaceful settlement of disputes among nations. The movement for peace through disarmament was gradually failing. The world, in fact, never more nearly approached economic and financial catastrophe domestically, and anarchy internationally.

In my first speech as Secretary of State, delivered April 27, 1933, to the American Foreign Service Association, I said: "Today nearly all the nations of the world, including our own, have no fundamentals, either political, moral, or economic. The nations and their peoples everywhere are in a large sense prostrate without a definite program of ideas and ideals for the rehabilitation of their political, economic, and other affairs.

The wonderful spirit that moved and animated those who had prominent places in the statesmanship and leadership of the past, in large measure became dormant during this postwar period."

I therefore felt that, while it was necessary for our nation and others to conserve and offer sound policies and to rebuild domestic political and economic structures from the ground up, the task was even more complex in the international field than at home. Here on this side we could take measures on our own initiative. Abroad our actions depended partly on the actions and reactions of other nations.

Throughout the years from early youth I had preached the doctrines of Thomas Jefferson that were apt for quotation. In my speeches and public statements during this long period I had advocated what Lincoln termed the axioms of free society and also the political truths applicable to free institutions and the spirit of individual liberty. I put particular emphasis on these principles in my peace and economics addresses to Congress in 1916 and 1919, in speeches on a number of revenue and loan measures, my foreign affairs address of 1927, and my opening address in the Senatorial campaign in Tennessee in 1930. I felt that these principles were extremely important in the domestic life of nations everywhere, because they raised peoples to higher levels and made them all the stronger in their support of peace and of organizations to preserve the peace. I was determined to preach a revival and restoration of all these axioms of organized domestic and international society, not only to our own people but also to the Governments and peoples of other countries.

As I faced the stupendous problems to be dealt with abroad, it gave me some relief and greater confidence to feel that I was strongly grounded on the fundamental propositions that should govern relations among nations. I proceeded to assemble and classify these principles, all of which the President, too, believed in strongly, and to make practical application of them at appropriate times.

To begin with, I felt the urgent need of an awakening and revival in the people's minds and hearts of the doctrines, in both letter and spirit, of human rights, individual liberty, and freedom. There had to be a revitalization and restoration of higher levels of morals, truth, respect, and trust among nations, all official standards of conduct having greatly deteriorated in international relations.

Furthermore, I felt that all nations should be urged to make their chief rallying point the establishment of a state of world order under law, so as to maintain conditions of permanent peace. This would include justice, equality, fair dealing, observance of treaties, peaceful settlement of disputes, and nonintervention in the internal affairs of other nations.

All nations, especially the large commercial countries, I believed, should combine in working out plans and programs for the full world development of freer commerce. The expected result would be an increase of production, employment, and consumption, and the firm establishment of a basis of friendship and confidence on which permanent peace could be built.

The peoples everywhere—especially in all countries where they have a voice in government—had to be kept educated, organized, and alert with respect to international problems, conditions, and methods of cooperating to preserve the peace and general welfare.

Foreign affairs had to be kept out of domestic politics. As Secretary of State, I adopted this policy from the outset. I pursued it religiously during my twelve years in office. During the campaign of 1944, my desire to keep the future organization for peace out of politics was agreed to unqualifiedly and after lengthy negotiations between myself, representing the Democrats and other sympathetic groups, and John Foster Dulles, representing Governor Thomas E. Dewey, the Republican Presidential candidate. I was not to make a serious political speech during my stay at the State Department, with the exception of two last-minute addresses in 1940. I was therefore severely criticized during political campaigns by some of the Democratic leaders; but I held fast to this policy, which time and experience have demonstrated to be the only sound course in the conduct of foreign affairs.

The President and I proceeded, either jointly or with each other's knowledge, to apply these policies and to develop further policies and apply them as occasion required.

On my part, I urged these basic ideas and objectives on the United States and other countries in more than one hundred speeches, statements, and important letters for publication during the dozen years that followed.

In my address to the Foreign Service officers in April, 1933, I said: "We have the tremendous undertaking today of rebuilding more securely, along political and economic lines, our relationships with the other nations. I think we ought to build upon the solid and broad foundations of justice, equality, and friendship. I think, too, that the more we visualize those broader relationships, both political and economic, that should be restored, keeping at all times within the limitations of our traditions and our Constitution, the greater service we will render to ourselves and to other peoples."

I firmly believed that we should continue, from year to year, to be a trading nation on an ever-increasing scale. My mind harked back to the Phoenicians who fashioned little vessels on the shores of the Mediterranean and began to trade. For many generations they carried their commerce to every known people and clime, gathering together all the valuable customs, manners, learning, and culture of every locality in the Western world, with the result that they built up a great civilization far above and beyond those who were not trading peoples.

Underneath all these objectives lay the most basic of all—the constant pursuit of human liberties. I said to the Foreign Service officers: "I sometimes think that I would have given all the wealth of this great Hemisphere—and I am no more patriotic than any of you folk—if I could have been one of that little band that went out to the field of Runnymede in 1215 and extracted from King John that wonderful collection of human liberties known as Magna Carta. After liberty had been banished from the world for a thousand years, I repeat, if I could have had the wonderful privilege of being one of that band that thus took the first step back toward human freedom—the first step in that five-hundred-year struggle for Anglo-Saxon liberty—I would have parted with all the wealth of this Western Hemisphere. And I want to see some of that same spirit that finally culminated in our own country in the Revolution and the structure of our free government revived."

Better international relations, establishing a solid foundation for peace and well-being, would result in greater recognition, I hoped, of basic human rights everywhere. To me as a lawyer it was, as I said in an address to the American Society of International Law on April 29, 1933, "an amazing commentary on the human race that international law was virtually unknown during the first three thousand years of history." It was only at the end of the Thirty Years' War, with its indescribable brutalities and savagery, that the great Dutch jurist Grotius really founded this system of law. "Persistent effort through succeeding centuries," I said, "was necessary to extend it to the preservation of peace as well as the regulation of warfare. This phase, however, is not so surprising when we recall that the term 'human rights' was scarcely conceived until within the last eight hundred years, and that the common lot of 90 per cent to 95 per cent of the human race, until within the last two hundred years, was that of slavery, serfdom, or enforced war service, mainly to gratify the ambition of rulers."

Of one thing I felt dead sure: namely, that in the chaotic international situation existing when I took office, if the United States did not take the lead toward sanity, no other nation would. The United States had frittered away its chance for leadership once before, when Wilson's ideas were rejected, and I felt that we now had a double responsibility.

"The awful plight of all countries," I said to the international lawyers, "offers proof conclusive of the breakdown of leadership and the bankruptcy of statesmanship in every part of the world. Governments have been more responsible for the present world economic dislocations than for any similar conditions in the past. In my judgment, the destiny of history points to the United States for leadership in the existing grave crisis. Present-day statesmen in charge of governments of the various nations, in my opinion, must immediately realize that the people of each country alike are living in a new age, with new and transformed economic conditions, calling for more modernized policies."

In addition to these long-range objectives, I had an immediate objective—the establishment, on our part at least, of a permanent policy of absolute candor and trust in our relations with other countries. I hoped that other nations would adopt a similar policy of candor and trust toward us and one another. Perhaps they might thereby gradually establish confidence and genuine friendliness between themselves and us and other nations. On March 9, 1933, I received at the State Department the initial visit of sixty ambassadors and ministers comprising the entire diplomatic corps; and thereafter I began seeing them individually. In each of these first conversations I told the ambassador or minister, "I intend to be completely frank with you in all our conversations. I intend to tell you the exact truth. You will see that it is the truth." I also required all my subordinates to practice this policy religiously in their dealings with foreign representatives.

Our mountain of problems was hopelessly complicated by deep-seated convictions among the people on both political and economic isolation. Our policy of international cooperation faced almost overwhelming isolationist opposition during the years 1933-1941. It is due to say that those Americans who believed in isolation were well-meaning, patriotic citizens and thought they were pursuing this country's more or less traditional policies. This attitude of good faith by most of the isolationists made it all the more difficult to prevail on them to take note of external danger, however imminent and inevitable it might be. They failed to realize that a policy of isolation would make us as lonely in the family of nations as a martin on a fodder pole.

Hence, while advocating international cooperation at all times, we were faced with the extremely delicate task of being careful not to present and urge measures in such numbers as to alarm the people and precipitate isolation as an acute political issue in the nation. Had we done so, the Roosevelt Administration would have been thrown out of power bodily as soon as the American public had a chance to go to the polls, and the nation would have been thrown back still farther to the extreme isolationist period following the Senate's rejection of Wilson's League of Nations.

Our only alternative, therefore, was constantly to urge upon the country a general policy of international cooperation in every way we could, and from time to time present for Congressional approval such proposals as an arms embargo applied against an aggressor, peace through disarmament, American participation in the World Court and in the International Labor Organization, the Trade Agreements policy, and more flexible Neutrality legislation. These on their very face contravened nationalistic policies.

This was the only course under which we could hope to convince Americans that the United States was an integral part of world cooperation. Wherever the matter before Congress seemed about to become a serious national isolation issue, we did not press it to the point of a national campaign.

With all these problems facing me, I had to make one decision right at the start. This was the social question, which in itself was highly important depending on how one dealt with it. Immemorial custom required the Secretary of State to go out almost daily to luncheon or dinner, especially dinner. Whatever the beneficial effects of this practice, there was no doubt that it absorbed much time and more energy. I did not hesitate to make my decision. I said to the members of the diplomatic corps:

"I can go out almost daily to luncheons and dinners with you, with the result that I'll be unable to see and confer with you except to a limited extent and you'll have to see my Assistant Secretaries of State instead. Or I can refuse to go out to luncheons and dinners with you, with the result that I'll be able to see and confer with you myself at greater length. I prefer the latter."

This met with general approval, and I think it worked much to the advantage of all concerned. My evenings were freer for the study of documents and papers I took home to read. My days were freer for discussions with ambassadors and ministers and members of the department. During the twelve years to follow I carried out this policy with only such infrequent exceptions as official and diplomatic situations seriously called for.

I did go occasionally, however, to the Senate and House and drop in on Members to say hello and pay my respects and possibly to have luncheon with them. This was in addition to my regular appearances before the Senate and House committees. These visits were prompted both by my feeling of comradeship for my old associates and by a desire to achieve cooperation and teamwork between Congress and the State Department. I enjoyed them, and they appeared to be welcomed as well by my old colleagues in the two Houses.

Mrs. Hull proved invaluable in assuming the burden of what social life remained. She took personal charge of the arrangements for the dinners I had to give to visiting statesmen, and the annual Cabinet dinner to the President. When I attended conferences abroad, she made social calls on the wives of the delegates such as I was not able to make on the delegates themselves.

Some public men, often by mutual understanding, refrain from disclosing the secrets of their political and public affairs to their wives, who remain content to pursue their own courses relating to society and to the duties of rearing a family. I kept Mrs. Hull constantly informed, however, regarding any and all questions and persons having any importance to me. She scrupulously guarded every secret. I never knew her to make a single mistake in conversations with diplomats and statesmen abroad or at home.

She read the newspapers thoroughly and kept herself generally informed and in touch with public affairs from day to day. She was able to give me many timely, valuable suggestions, whether I was at home dealing with official affairs through the State Department, or away attending international conferences. Her judgment never went wrong in any important instance. She was frequently picking up dropped stitches, so to speak, or pointing out omissions or commissions that required attention. Throughout my career in Congress and in the State Department she was thoroughly at home whether in company with a Queen or with the wife of a hod carrier; and she knew and understood human nature and human viewpoints from the top to the bottom strata of society.

Although I eschewed social activities whenever possible, I allowed myself one diversion that proved of great benefit to me in body and spirit. Late of an afternoon once or twice a week in good weather, to clear my thoughts and get a little relaxation in preparation for the tasks I knew lay ahead, I would take three of my associates with me for a game of croquet on the lawn of "Woodley"—Henry L. Stimson's home. Croquet became my only sport, and, in the eyes of friends who had not so much occasion to play it, I grew to be something of an expert.

To some, croquet may seem namby-pamby; but it is really a very scientific game. A player must give it his full attention, or he has no success. Four or five times a season I could go completely around the croquet ground without stopping. I let two or three of the other players begin first. Then I started off from the first pole and began to contact them and take them with me so as to play off them.

On one occasion Harry McBride, formerly my assistant in my office and later administrator of the National Art Gallery in Washington, brought in a "ringer," introducing him to me as an old friend. It later developed he was the champion croquet player of a certain section of the United States. Nevertheless, I won, probably because of the champion's unfamiliarity with the grounds.

It was not often that I could play a game through without interruption. Sometimes Stimson came out to talk to me. At other times I received urgent telephone calls from the Department, even from the President. And frequently officers of the Department arrived with papers for me to go over and sign before they left their offices for the evening.

Croquet proved highly satisfactory to me because it took my mind off my work at times and induced me to go out into the open air and sun. But in my last several years at the State Department, as the work taxed my strength more and more, my doctor required me to taper off on the game, which probably proves it is more strenuous than most people think.

When I entered the State Department I quickly determined upon an innovation relating to the Department personnel. Some persons insisted that I make sweeping changes in order to give place to personal favorites and Democratic politicians. Others suggested, as they always seem to do when a change occurs, that there should be all new blood in lieu of what they called "antiquated, obsolete-minded" officials.

I could not but remember the long lines of suitcases stretching along the corridor wall outside William Jennings Bryan's office when he became Wilson's Secretary of State. They belonged seemingly to every Tom, Dick, and Harry from the "sticks" who had been his friends and had done Democratic service. These men came straight from the railroad station to his office, without even going to a hotel, feeling sure that he would instantly create jobs for them. ·

I had long believed, however, that our foreign affairs should not be the football of domestic politics.· I felt that domestic politics, when wisely and soundly conducted, had no place in our international affairs, except in rare instances. I carefully investigated the character and fitness of officers of the Department, especially those in key positions. Although I weeded out an official here and there who for one cause or another was not equipped to perform the most efficient service, I retained the seasoned, experienced persons in key positions. I did not bring to the Department a single important person from my home State.

When I was chairman of the Democratic National Committee, I was accustomed to making a speech to the State organizations in which I lauded the county chairmen. These men, I said, were the mainstay of the Party, because they, and not the higher officials, were the ones who came in close touch with the people. In the same way, I felt that the head of a geographic division and certain others like the economic adviser, historical adviser, legal adviser, and heads of the passport and visa divisions, were mainstays of the State Department because they were the ones in immediate touch with conditions and developments throughout the world.

With the personnel of the State Department thus established on a nonpartisan basis, I never knew the politics of a dozen persons in the Department. Outstanding individuals with knowledge and experience such as former officials of the Department or Government, leading editors and writers and other leaders of thought were accustomed to coming to my office and any other office in the Department, seeking or offering counsel with no thought on the part of any one of the political persuasion of the visitor or the official.

In formulating a foreign policy, I found no factor more indispensable as a rule than the long-experienced and patiently toiling, intelligent members of the geographic divisions of the State Department—those dealing with European, Far Eastern, Near Eastern, and Latin-American affairs. The desk man in each division—meaning an officer specializing in the affairs of one nation or group of nations—is the first person to make a constructive appraisal of the mass of facts, circumstances, and developments on which the higher officials, from the President down, must base any new policy.

This desk man has previously been stationed in certain countries abroad where he devoted long years of toil and investigation to their internal and external problems. Back in the Department, he has at his command nearly every important fact concerning the country in question. I desire to pay strong tribute to the efficiency, loyalty, and uniformly fine service these officers of the geographic divisions rendered during my years in the State Department. On important questions involving policy I called in every subordinate who could make a material contribution to the subject under consideration—always including the desk man. Other high officials and I would have been seriously handicapped in determining a sound policy without the aid of these men.

I believe I am reasonably accurate in saying that I have not known during my time a more capable, experienced, and sound group of associates than those in the State Department during my twelve years as its head. They were unassuming, and with very few exceptions were loyal, genuinely cooperative, and always on hand, especially when emergency tasks arose.

Among the important and capable, experienced and dependable officials I found in high position in the State Department were: Green H. Hackworth, Legal Adviser; Herbert Feis, Economic Adviser; Stanley K. Hornbeck, Division of Far Eastern Affairs; Edwin C. Wilson, Division of Latin American Affairs; Jay Pierrepont Moffat, Division of Western European Affairs; Wallace Murray, Division of Near Eastern Affairs; Herschel V. Johnson, Division of Mexican Affairs; Robert F. Kelley, Division of Eastern European Affairs; James C. Dunn, Division of Protocol and Conferences; Michael J. McDermott, Division of Current Information; Hunter Miller, Historical Adviser; Mrs. Ruth B. Shipley, Passport Division; Margaret M. Hanna, Office of Coordination and Review; Clinton E. MacEachran, Chief Clerk and Administrative Assistant; and John Farr Simmons, Visa Office.

After Mr. Roosevelt's first inauguration he appointed a number of new ambassadors and ministers. The policy I recommended to the President was to divide these appointments about 50–50 between career men in the Foreign Service and men outside the service, including political and other appointees. Among the capable ambassadors appointed during the first year were Alexander W. Weddell, to Argentina; Hugh S. Gibson, to Brazil; Robert W. Bingham, to Great Britain; Breckinridge Long, to Italy; Josephus Daniels, to Mexico; Claude G. Bowers, to Spain; Robert P. Skinner, to Turkey; and William C. Bullitt, to Russia.

Daniel C. Roper and I had been interested in Bingham in view of his fine career generally and his great support of Roosevelt. I never knew whether our recommendation was the influence that tipped the scales for Bingham's appointment to London, or whether Mr. Roosevelt had made the decision on his own at the same time.

Daniels had appeared in public life as early as the Bryan campaign of 1896, and had been going strong ever since. He was a little too radical at times to suit me, but we agreed in general and became warm personal friends. Always active, he kept his eye on what he considered the public welfare and the most effective agency for securing and preserving it. He had made and continued to make a much-above-the-average showing in whatever post he filled. Daniels came to Mr. Roosevelt and to me and told us what he wanted, the appointment to Mexico, and that settled it.

The appointment of William E. Dodd as Ambassador to Berlin was an outside one. I had known Dodd well as an enthusiastic supporter of the League of Nations when I was chairman of the Democratic National Committee. He had come to my office frequently while he was teaching at the University of Chicago. He became a close friend of Daniel C. Roper, and Roper and his friends chiefly brought about Dodd's appointment to Berlin. I was agreeable to the appointment in the sense that I was exceedingly fond of Dodd and was his personal friend. I had already discovered, however, that he would get out of bounds in his excess of enthusiasm and impetuosity and run off on tangents every now and then, like our friend William Jennings Bryan. Hence I had some reservations about sending a good friend, able and intelligent though he was, to a ticklish spot such as I knew Berlin was and would continue to be.

Hugh Wilson I kept on, with the President's concurrence, as Minister to Switzerland, although he was a Republican. I formed a high opinion of him then and in later years as an experienced and capable, though not necessarily a model, diplomat. We were able to use his capacities in numerous instances as an observer in specific deliberations or undertakings of the League of Nations. Since our relations with the League were microscopically scrutinized by the isolationists at home, we could function better through Wilson who had good standing with the general public and was a Republican. We later made him an Assistant Secretary of State and then Ambassador to Germany.

Hugh Gibson was another Republican whom I kept on as long as I could, because of his outstanding ability. But eventually the President wanted him out—Gibson was a close friend of Herbert Hoover, and there was bitter feeling between Hoover and the President.

In later years we enjoyed the services of two women as American Ministers, Mrs. Ruth Bryan Owen (daughter of my old friend William Jennings Bryan) to Denmark, and Mrs. J. Borden Harriman to Norway —the first time in our history that women had been named to head diplomatic missions. They both proved competent, and made excellent records.

The State Department under me started out with the disadvantage of overly rigid economy. The President, in keeping with the economy pledges in the 1932 platform, began his Administration by demanding reduction of expenses, although the New Deal group about him soon talked him into exactly the opposite direction. The first telegram I sent to the Foreign Service personnel abroad was one regretting that we were cutting down our staff to save money.

Wilbur Carr, the Assistant Secretary in charge of our budget, continued the policy of economy in the Department and kept asking Congress for just enough when other departments were asking for more than enough. The Appropriations committees became accustomed to slicing down the estimates of other departments and treated us in the same way, unfortunately forgetting that we were requesting only what we really needed. In the face of greatly expanded demands for State Department services here and abroad as world conditions descended toward chaos, the Department was to struggle along desperately with inadequate funds. The appropriations for our Department of Peace were less than 1 per cent of the appropriations for War and Navy.

Any typical day of my virtually twelve years at the State Department could be called hectic, being hopelessly crowded with emergency problems calling for feverish activity on the part of my associates and myself. My entire tenure could literally be termed an emergency period. Every aspect of human nature and conduct in all parts of the world passed before us as we strove to deal adequately with each vital question. So rapidly did foreign affairs crowd in on us for imperative attention that days, nights, and Sundays seemed blended in our close confinement within the heavy walls of the State Department building. We tried to maintain a regular schedule of engagements and tasks for the day, but more often than not the schedule would be thrown out of kelter by unexpected developments.

I always tried to reach my office between 9:00 and 9:10 in the morning, frequently walking from my hotel to the Department. I saw my chief secretary first. During the early years this was Harry McBride, who was invaluable to me because of his experience, judgment, ability, and diplomacy in dealing with people inside and outside the Department. He was later followed by Cecil W. Gray, a marvel of vigilance, efficiency, loyalty, and all equipment for sound service.

McBride or Gray brought in to me a large assortment of cables and other communications from all over the world, giving me analyses and estimates by our ambassadors, ministers, and consuls of developments and situations in the countries where they were stationed. He then gave me, in strict confidence, an account of any particular happenings throughout the Department during the preceding day, with suitable suggestions. He next laid before me a list of engagements for the day. A typical list embraced two ambassadors, three ministers, a Senator, two Representatives, another cabinet member or his representative, a Foreign Service officer returned from abroad, four or five officials in the Department, and an editor or correspondent.

As I went through the stack of papers, telegrams, and documents laid before me, I made decisions on them wherever possible, without further conference or investigation, and simultaneously sent instructions to appropriate officials in the Department for carrying them out. I had to decide which were important enough to show the President for his information or decision.

I then called in the Under Secretary of State—first William Phillips, then Sumner Welles, and finally Edward R. Stettinius, Jr.—and gave him all information that would be useful to him in performing his functions. Next came the Assistant Secretaries of State and other key officials of the Department for discussions of particular questions coming within their jurisdiction. Some of the problems laid before me required consultation with the Legal Adviser or the Economic Adviser; others needed the opinions of the heads of the geographic divisions, specializing in different sections of the world; others demanded the advice or concurrence of other Executive departments.

Always it was necessary to see that each division of the Department possessed reasonable knowledge of what we were doing everywhere, so that we should not be taking one stand in one field and another stand in another field. The world-wide interconnection of major events made this doubly essential. A move we took in Europe might well have repercussions on our policy in the Far East or in South America. Teamwork throughout the Department was required to keep consistency of policy and avoid mistakes.

During the day requests nearly always came in for emergency conferences in my office. As each succeeding year of world unrest amplified our difficulties, I held more and more meetings with the key men in the Department. Whenever a grave question arose, I called in every person in the Department, from the top right on down the line, who could make a contribution to any aspect of it, and gave him an opportunity to state his views. Then, after the fullest conference and research, I always preferred to sit down and make my own final decision.

When the discussions involved questions of new policy, which often would have far-reaching effects according to the type of decision made, I proceeded on the theory that such matters could not receive too much consideration, and that I could not consult too many qualified persons, even though I might feel reasonably sure of my own position at the outset. I laid down this standing instruction to those assisting me in preparing state papers either for the President or for the Department and myself: "An important document is never completed until it's delivered." This practice safeguarded us against hasty or ill considered decisions and assured the fullest possible consideration.

Occasionally a quick-acting person would charge me with being too deliberate—meaning too slow. The manifest answer to this criticism is that most of the mistakes arising in the conduct of our public affairs during the Roosevelt Administration were due to haste and lack of deliberation, whereas my policy of being deliberate, while also being on time, resulted in a record containing less of error than would otherwise have been the case. The President, so far as I knew, entertained the view that I never led him into serious trouble either when he was at home or when he was absent from the Capital. Actually we dealt with international problems either very deliberately or with more rapid decision according to their seriousness and the complications requiring solution.

My favorite writing instrument in outlining or going through documents was a red pencil. I used to keep four or five of these in my shirt pocket, to the horror of Mrs. Hull, who insisted they made marks on the shirt which were hard to get out.

Not infrequently, to induce my younger assistants to step out with their views, I would pull their legs a little. One official frequently prefaced his opinions by saying, "Although I don't profess to know anything about domestic politics, I think this or that." One day, when he was commenting on the possible effects in and out of Congress of a certain trade agreement, and had used this waiver, I commented: "I've frequently heard you use the phrase that you didn't profess to know anything about domestic politics. I used to think, when I heard it, that you really knew a lot about domestic politics. But today I've come to the conclusion that yours was purely an objective statement of fact."

At other times, to make them careful of the opinions they expressed, I sought to get them to commit themselves by saying something like, "Now you don't think that would have any adverse effect here, do you?" One official unwarily let himself be committed like that on a trade agreement. Later, as a flood of protesting letters and telegrams cascaded in, I used to send them to him, a batch at a time, with a note: "Apropos of your statement that there would be no adverse reaction to the trade agreement in question, I send you herewith some correspondence."

One day an official of the Department came to me to object to attending a meeting in the office of another official who was inferior to him in rank. I said to him: "If the porter out there in the hall had anything useful to offer in connection with any problem I was interested in, I'd be glad to go out to his desk in the corridor and talk to him about it."

When I had anything of a secret nature to impart to any of my assistants, I sometimes said to him: "I am telling you this confidentially —and that does not mean to tell it confidentially to the first person you meet."

On Monday mornings at eleven o'clock I held a departmental meeting in my office, consisting of the Under Secretary, the Assistant Secretaries, the Political Advisers for Europe, the Far East, and the American Republics, the Legal Adviser, the Economic Adviser, and one or two others. The attendance varied as time went on, and additional officials were called in. At these meetings we checked important policies and developments, brought our minds up to date, and planned ahead in connection with any given task.

The coordination upon which I insisted inside the State Department I also extended to relations with other departments and agencies of the Government. Foreign policy had varying reactions on other departments, such as Treasury, War, Navy, Commerce, Agriculture, and Interior, and

I required my associates to keep in closest contact with other interested sections of the Government as we went forward with any policy.

In receiving foreign ambassadors or ministers, I early adopted a practice of friendly informality. If my main office happened to be crowded with an important conference, I received the diplomat in a small, narrow room leading out of my office to the office of the secretaries. Later on I was to conduct, with British Ambassador Lord Lothian, in this tiny room with its almost primitive furnishings, the negotiations on the exchange of American destroyers for British bases. Thereafter, if a diplomat showed the slightest signs of disappointment in being received in this unimposing cell, I would at once recall to him the cheerful manner in which the British Ambassador and others of the highest diplomatic rank had sat down with me there for the most important conferences.

I sought to receive a foreign diplomat in the cordial, unassuming manner with which I would greet any other visitor. I treated him as I had treated Americans with whom I came into contact during my long political career. Generally I did not feel justified in giving an ambassador personal credit for the virtues of his Government or holding him responsible for its sins. There were exceptions when another Government had acted outrageously or offensively. Then, from the instant of the appearance of the diplomat in my office doorway, I found numerous ways of receiving him with the utmost coldness and going almost to the limit in showing my resentment and that of my Government. These exceptions principally concerned the Japanese Ambassador in later years.

As my work grew with the growth of tension in Europe and Asia, I established a practice of having the Under Secretary, and, in many cases, an Assistant Secretary, see diplomats on matters of lesser importance. I delegated to the Under Secretary, after the first few years, the duty of supervising the administrative side of the State Department, and relied on the Assistant Secretaries and other top officials to perform other important functions so that I could concentrate more fully on our foreign policy and methods of bringing it into play.

Diplomats usually came to me with some specific problem; but I seldom let them retire until I had talked to them, briefly or at length, about the existing dangers in the international situation, the feverish armament by dictator-aggressors, the corresponding need for the greatest vigilance on the part of peaceful nations, cooperative methods for preserving the peace and promoting liberal trade, and some of the major difficulties I was encountering, such as isolationism. I never failed to pound into them the eternal doctrines of peace, freedom, law, morals, and human welfare.

I made two rules, among others, in dealing with foreign ambassadors. One was to utter no threat unless we had the force and will to back it up. A threat without a backing of force was a bluff, and a bluff could be called with embarrassing results.

The other rule was to make no promise that was not certain of fulfillment. I used to tell my associates the story of the man who ran a small store in a town in Tennessee near a lake. One day he got in touch with a food company and offered to sell it a carload of frog legs. In due course a representative of the company arrived, and they signed a contract. The frog legs were not delivered, and after some months the same representative returned. He found only a couple of frog legs in the store and asked the storekeeper why he had not lived up to his promise. "Well," the man said, "the frogs around the lake were making so much noise I thought there must be at least a carload of them."

The moment an ambassador or minister left my office, one of my stenographers would enter automatically, by another door. I at once dictated to her an adequate account of the discussion, putting down as accurately as I could what he had said to me and I to him, and appending any written notes handed by one of us to the other. We cabled the substance of this memorandum to our ambassador or minister in the capital of the diplomat who had just called upon me, so that he could be kept fully informed of developments on this side; and other telegrams went out to our representatives in other capitals that might also be concerned.

This was only one of the many aspects of the close relationship I sought to maintain at all times between the State Department and our representatives in about three hundred and fifty posts throughout the world. For our foreign policy to work effectively there had to be an intimate partnership between the staff at home and the staff abroad. The Department determined policy and issued instructions. The Foreign Service carried out the instructions, but at the same time supplied much of the first-hand information on which we formulated policy and telegraphed instructions.

As I saw it, our representatives abroad had four main tasks. The first was to keep us informed, speedily, accurately, and with absolute impartiality. I insisted that our Foreign Service officers avoid undue sympathy with or prejudice against the country where they were stationed, and give us the facts, absolutely uncolored, with a fair interpretation of what the facts meant to them. I welcomed their advice given on the spot.

Their second task was to represent us abroad, interpret our ideals, explain our policies, make friends, and facilitate, through friendly, informal contact, the transaction of our Government's business.

Their third task was to carry out the Department's instructions and conduct any negotiations entrusted to them. Such negotiations were often highly technical, ranging from sanitation to aviation, and required detailed study.

Their fourth task, by no means last in importance, was to protect the lives and property of Americans in foreign countries. Americans abroad are subject to the laws of the country they happen to be in, and sometimes, knowingly or unknowingly, they become involved with the authorities and require our diplomatic help. This is particularly true during time of war, commotion, and civil strife. During my tenure, our diplomats performed outstandingly in protecting Americans throughout the Spanish Civil War, the Japanese invasion of China, and the Second World War.

With extremely rare exceptions, I found that our diplomats and consuls abroad brought to bear, in trying situations, all the efficiency, integrity, and zeal we could have asked of them. Our diplomacy was no longer synonymous with a pleasant, easy-going existence. Now it meant hard work, long hours, technical knowledge in a variety of fields, objectivity, skill in negotiations, and, on occasion, exposure to physical danger.

I was always glad to receive these Foreign Service officers when they came to Washington on leave or en route to another post. Their conversation brought me up to date on conditions in the countries where they had been stationed, and was always instructive. Similarly, I was delighted to receive American correspondents or other intelligent persons who had spent some time abroad and acquired a certain knowledge of foreign countries.

When the work day ended at the State Department it did not end for me. Each night I used to take to my apartment in the Carlton Hotel and later the Wardman Park Hotel a mass of papers and documents to study over during the more peaceful nocturnal hours. Fairly often the peace of these hours was broken, however, by a visit from an ambassador. If an emergency matter of real importance developed, the ambassador telephoned me at my apartment, and then came over to see me.

I early discovered that the press of work required me to go to the

Department on Sunday mornings. Mine was an aggravated case of the ox in the ditch on the Sabbath. At first I went primarily to go through documents and telegrams undisturbed while the Department observed the holiday. Then I often had occasion to request one or more of my associates to join me there. Soon word got around that Sunday mornings would find me in my office the same as on other days. Gradually a regular Sunday attendance of six to ten of my most important key men became a custom. Our discussion was always kept informal. Any subject could come up and be talked over; decisions were not demanded, notes were not taken; and many useful ideas came to the surface. When high noon had come and gone I walked back to my hotel and listened to Mrs. Hull's gentle remonstrance, "Sunday is a day of rest."

14: President and Secretary of State

NEVER AN UNFRIENDLY WORD passed between the President and me during my twelve years in the State Department. Naturally a few emphatic differences rose between us, which we threshed out earnestly and bluntly but in friendly spirit. Our association in general was very agreeable. The President respected the proviso I made in accepting his offer to become Secretary of State; namely, that I would not be a mere transmitter and receiver of messages to and from foreign Governments, that I would have my full share in formulating and carrying out foreign policy. He and I entertained in most respects the same philosophy in international relations. In case of sudden developments when we were separated, either of us could usually know what the other's action would be. This like-mindedness in foreign policy was a major factor in our effective working relations.

We thoroughly agreed on the general policy of international cooperation. We had both been preaching this since Wilson's time. We agreed on the Far Eastern policy, the steps toward disarmament, Latin America, the Italo-Abyssinian War, the Spanish Civil War, Germany, Italy, Vichy France, and peace plans and programs. We agreed most of the time on the principle of liberal commercial policy, but not always on the time and method of its adoption and expansion, which on occasion was vital. We disagreed in a few important instances, and I shall deal with these as I come to them.

In these memoirs I shall write primarily about the conduct of foreign affairs by this Government. I shall not include any account of the domestic achievements of the Roosevelt Administration, of which the President was the chief architect. The record of the panic to which Roosevelt's Administration fell heir and of the remedies prescribed under his leadership, vast reforms without precedent in magnitude and importance, will alone give him a high and lasting place in the history of our domestic affairs. Nor shall I undertake to write about the President's achievements as commander-in-chief of our armed forces during the recent World War except in those instances wherein there was a combined foreign and military policy. Here again his outstanding accomplishments mark him as one of the ablest commanders-in-chief in our history. All in all he was a truly great President.

During my tenure in the State Department I found that in the majority of cases I had to make my own decisions. Although a Secretary of State confers with the President on important matters of policy and is the President's agent in the field of foreign relations, in practice he acts largely on his own initiative and responsibility. I could issue instructions to American representatives abroad, demand explanations from foreign representatives here, dispatch diplomatic notes to foreign governments, and negotiate treaties with such governments.

Frequently a Secretary of State negotiates a treaty without having previously consulted the President. He does, of course, obtain full power from the President to sign. If the treaty is of a high political character, the Secretary may think desirable to discuss it with the President prior to and during the negotiations. He negotiates innumerable treaties and conventions relating to trade, commerce, and kindred subjects, however, and prepares them for signature before the President is aware of the negotiations. Usually he submits treaties to the President with explanatory reports and with communications, to be signed by the President if he approves, transmitting them to the Senate.

I naturally conducted the affairs of the State Department without bringing to the President's attention great masses of details and minor operations. Under the law certain duties are assigned specifically to the Secretary of State. Visas are issued by consuls; passports are issued by the Department; embassy, legation, and consular buildings are leased, bought, or sold; criminals are extradited; American citizens abroad are protected; claims by and against foreign governments are adjusted; good offices are employed in the settlement of international differences; the Foreign Service is administered—all this by or under the authority of the Secretary of State.

I had to use my own judgment as to whether given policies or developments were important enough to bring to the President's notice. Sometimes I would lay before him, with suitable recommendations, a question involving new policy. At other times a question of policy was not important enough to be brought to his attention, or it fell sufficiently within the lines of a general policy or a well defined philosophy on which he already entertained a favorable attitude.

To illustrate, I recommended the moral embargo during the Italo-Ethiopian War, having Italy particularly in mind. The President was then on a cruiser off the Mexican coast. I told him we proposed to announce the embargo in his name, if agreeable to him, and he readily consented.

Another illustration is the effort we made at the Montevideo Pan American Conference to settle the Chaco War. I treated this as a part of the conference's proceedings to promote peace, and took the appropriate decisions. I kept the President informed in a general way of what we were doing.

Still another instance is my conduct of the negotiations with Great Britain for the lease of British bases, from Newfoundland to British Guiana, in exchange for fifty American over-age destroyers. The President and I talked this over and reached a general understanding. He then turned over to me the task of conducting the negotiations with Britain. This I did for ten solid days, keeping the President informed from time to time as to the status of our discussions. When they were concluded, I was to assume the responsibility of signing my name for our Government. This also included responsibility for an exchange of cables with Winston Churchill in which he made an official pledge that the British Navy would not in any circumstances be allowed to fall into German hands or be scuttled.

A final example, among many others, is the negotiations with the Japanese Ambassador in the nine months before Pearl Harbor. I conducted some forty to fifty conferences with the Ambassador, mainly at my hotel apartment. I kept the President informed as to the general tenor of the discussions, and at the same time prepared the data for conferences between the President and the Ambassador, which I arranged.

The fact is not generally known that the State Department makes public, in the name of the President himself, an immense portion of its major work, including new policies which the President has approved. Records on file in the State Department include numerous recommendations of policy from me to President Roosevelt; recommendations regarding important steps to be taken; outlines with elaborate data for the foreign affairs portions of the President's public statements and addresses; drafts of the President's personal communications to heads of other governments and of messages to Congress; written suggestions for the President to follow in talking with diplomats and leaders of other governments; and a vast number of instances where important acts initiated and carried out by the State Department were given to the public in the President's name.

It is well for the public to know how greatly our volume of foreign relations has grown, and how our foreign policy is conducted. Owing to the vast expansion and the ramifications of our international affairs, the State Department of President Washington's time is obviously not comparable to the State Department of today.

In summary, with the present immense network and mass of details involved in conducting our foreign relations, the President finds it impossible to keep familiar with more than the principal acts of the State Department. The Secretary of State must do the rest. The President, because he is the leader and the official head of the Government, and because he furnishes the authority and has the ultimate responsibility, is entitled to credit for the combined achievements of his Administration, including the departments, divisions, groups, and individual officials and employees of the Government under his direction. At the same time, all officials and employees, from the President down to the lowest, are entitled to credit for any achievements accomplished through operations they have personally conducted.

The President and the Secretary of State should be as nearly one person as possible. This is particularly true in this modern era when so many complicated and different affairs arise to be dealt with.

Neither the President nor I had had any too much experience in handling the technical side of foreign affairs. We gathered this experience quickly because of the multitude of problems that faced us at once. The great task largely devolving upon me, of implementing our policies and applying fundamental principles to the hopelessly complicated situations abroad, was rendered all the heavier in the early years by the indescribable chaos in the domestic situation which required the President's daily attention.

During his first term in office President Roosevelt was so immersed in an avalanche of domestic questions that he left me in almost full charge of foreign affairs. I kept him thoroughly informed on all major developments, but he expected me to furnish the initiative in policy and action. His own speeches on foreign topics were few and short in the early years, and it was not until the beginning of 1936 that he made a major address on foreign affairs, this being his message to Congress on January 3. His interest in foreign affairs was keen, but his time was too heavily mortgaged by domestic issues to give it expression. Beginning with his second term, his interest and participation in foreign affairs greatly increased.

Mr. Roosevelt's knowledge about the world abroad was extensive. No President since Jefferson and the Adamses had a wider knowledge of peoples and conditions abroad. Though he sometimes tended to commit us too far in his direct approaches to the heads of other governments, and to forget the diplomatic implications of his military decisions, his viewpoint toward the world was progressive and forward-looking.

He was a man of great personal charm who could always make himself agreeable and attractive in conversation, and this was helpful to us in dealing with statesmen and diplomatic representatives of foreign Governments. He was a rare judge of psychology and always able to get over to the public most effectively any message or appeal. In this respect he had, in my opinion, no equal among his predecessors except Theodore Roosevelt. He was at his best in proclaiming to the world in highly dramatized form great slogans and principles such as the Four Freedoms. His wide knowledge of persons, together with his energy and good judgment as a rule, highly equipped him for leadership.

The President, with rare exceptions, could scarcely have been more considerate toward me as Secretary of State throughout my twelve years in that office. He almost invariably approved my recommendations or suggestions, which often included important foreign policy. With the exception of his conferences with Mr. Churchill and Marshal Stalin, which he regarded as being primarily military, he virtually always sought my advice or concurrence before taking an important step in foreign relations. He looked to me on innumerable occasions to provide the substance of his addresses on foreign affairs or to compose his messages and replies to Churchill, Stalin, and other heads of governments.

Harry Hopkins remarked to me on one occasion that a person might serve President Roosevelt for almost any length of time, and the President would never thank him. But Hopkins continued that Mr. Roosevelt was, in fact, grateful for all that such persons had done for him. I replied that my relations with him had always been free from personalities and without a short word, and I added that frequently he had spoken with entire appreciation in referring to given phases of my work.

Almost invariably, when either the President or I returned from a trip, as well as often between times, he invited me to his office for luncheon, so that we could talk over questions and conditions undisturbed.

If it were at all warm he said, "Let's make ourselves comfortable." He took off his coat, rolled up his sleeves, unbuttoned and opened his collar. I did the same.

Luncheon was brought in (no drinks were served) and placed on his great desk in the oval office that already had so many associations for me.

It was in that room that I had first seen President Wilson, and Presidents Coolidge and Hoover.

Our conversation was informal. The President usually had a good story to tell that he had just heard. Then, for about an hour, we could talk over the problems that faced us. Invariably we were alone. Interruptions were infrequent, although occasionally the President would answer the telephone if an important caller were on the line.

In conversation he was always considerate. When we sometimes differed on important questions, he never showed impatience as I argued the opposite side. He listened attentively through to the end, without interrupting. Each of us in due time learned to omit elaborate argument where one of us knew that the other, after full opportunity for consideration, entertained definite convictions.

Once in a while, when I went to the White House with a recommendation on foreign policy, President Roosevelt would open the conversation with a statement at variance with the Department's ideas. Refraining from countering him directly, I generally would say something like, "Yes, and I'd like to add a little to that." I then "added" the ideas of my associates and myself, and in the course of the conversation the President would most likely agree that the "addition" should be our policy.

Our conversation dealt almost entirely with foreign affairs, but I did not hesitate from time to time to express myself in a general way on domestic affairs as well. On several occasions I spoke something like this:

"From my youth on I've studied liberal teachers such as Locke, Milton, Pitt, Burke, Gladstone, and the Lloyd George school. I 'followed through' under the liberal leadership of Woodrow Wilson. In Congress I had a labor record between 90 and 100 per cent, chiefly on progressive legislation. Still I can't help feeling that you're going too fast and too far with certain of your domestic reforms. There hasn't been sufficient time to adjust them to conditions in the country. The people haven't had time to digest them. I think that periodically the country needs time to accustom itself to some of these drastic, new policies. And, in a few instances, the policies themselves seem too drastic."

I also made it clear to him that I was not in harmony with a permanent policy of government spending, having always stood for balanced budgets based on progressive and practical policies.

The President always heard me through with entire respect. Then he continued eating or smoking, without saying anything. After a few seconds of silence he or I mentioned something else, and the conversation veered in another direction.

I knew that Mr. Roosevelt was acquainted with my labor record, without my having mentioned it. Before deciding upon me for Secretary of State, he had had some one look it up. A representative of the American Federation of Labor at the Capitol had made a record of all Senators and Representatives. He had given me an average of more than 90 per cent. Mr. Roosevelt was surprised when he saw it, although he had known that generally I was all right in this respect. He had emphasized this record to labor leaders.

I felt that President Roosevelt went a little too far in such instances as the sit-down strikes and the Supreme Court issue. I had seen the predatory group of financiers and big-business men, from the Civil War on to the Wilson Administration, run away with Federal rule, labor having nothing when the Democratic Party came in, in 1913. Hence I often said to Mr. Roosevelt that, while I was 1,000 per cent with him in all needed reforms and social welfare legislation such as we had inaugurated in the Sixty-second Congress, there was a risk that when the opposite extreme got into the saddle, they, as was natural, would want to plant themselves there, just as the capitalists had done when they were in power. One kind of special privilege might thereupon supplant another.

Fundamentally and traditionally I was opposed to paternalism in government, but I realized that the terrific conditions confronting the Roosevelt Administration called for a broader interpretation. I had grown up in the antipaternalism background flourishing in Tennessee during the forty to fifty years following the Civil War. Old Confederate soldiers talked of little but popular rights as opposed to centralization of power in government. They were poisoned against the whole doctrine of concentration and paternalism. The Congressional campaign in Tennessee in 1886 was fought largely around the bill of Senator Blair from New Hampshire to appropriate less than $100,000 for Federal aid to education. My friends and I at all times followed and preached Jefferson's doctrine opposing centralization in government. Tennessee's representatives in Congress adhered fairly well to this view. In my maiden address in Congress I inveighed against the paternalism of Theodore Roosevelt. Democrats who were not sound on this theory were known far and wide as not being really dependable members of the Party.

This feeling went on among us until the First World War. Then, as we plunged into internationalism, it was discussed less prominently. I began to embrace the theory, as I expressed it in 1916, that there existed a much closer and richer relationship between the national and international economies than had been the case before. Consequently I felt that it would be necessary to give a broader interpretation to some of our doctrines of government in order to meet this fact.

I approved of the welfare legislation under Wilson. Sometimes Wilson, I felt, went a little too far, as in a few undesirable appointments, but as a rule I could go along with him in almost all ways. When Franklin D. Roosevelt came to the White House in 1933, the crisis was extraordinary and called for extraordinary remedies. I was therefore willing to see a broader interpretation of the principle of no paternalism at least for the period of the emergency, although I did not hesitate to call to the President's attention my belief that at times he was adopting cures too sweeping for the disease—cures that might bring on other ailments.

Once during my first few months at the State Department I was invited to a conference at the White House on domestic matters. The principal topic was Professor George Warren's theory that prices could be regulated promptly and effectively by changing the gold content of the dollar. I sat at the meeting and listened to all the discussion. As the end of the session approached, I was asked to offer any comment I might have in mind. "If Professor Warren's doctrine is effective," I replied, "it seems to me that, since all of the nations of the world are in the same financial and economic prostration as our country, some one or more of those nations would have discovered this doctrine and its beneficial effects and placed it in operation before now." That was the last White House conference on domestic economic matters to which I was ever invited.

Only one instance do I recall in which the President projected me into a purely domestic situation. This was a disastrous general strike in San Francisco, which broke out in July, 1934, when he was on his way to Hawaii. Mr. Roosevelt sent me a hurried dispatch requesting me to confer with Attorney General Homer Cummings and see whether there was something the Federal Government could do to compose the dispute which was seriously threatening the economic life of San Francisco and adjacent areas. I conferred with Cummings, and also with Secretary of Labor Frances Perkins. Cummings and I agreed that the Federal Government should not take direct action, but we prepared a possible statement for the President and wirelessed it to him for use if he wished. It appealed earnestly to both sides of the controversy to find ways of settlement without delay, thereby avoiding far-reaching injury to the people of San Francisco. This ended my part in the incident. The President, after a few days, abandoned the idea of giving out our proposed statement, because the Governor of California had taken charge of the situation and conditions were definitely improving.

In general, I did not participate in domestic affairs unless they dovetailed into our international policies and problems.

I often had occasion to see the President in the early morning, when he was still in bed. Usually he had already been up, eaten breakfast, and returned to bed to conduct the first business of the day. I found his bed strewn with newspapers, documents, letters, and telegrams. I pulled up a chair near by, and we began to discuss the question at hand. This practice continued throughout the years I was at the State Department.

In general, I was not a social intimate of the President. I was not invited to White House dinners except on official occasions, or to weekend excursions on Mr. Roosevelt's yacht or visits to Hyde Park. Mr. Roosevelt respected my determination not to dissipate my energies in social affairs but to conserve them for the events of my office. Moreover, I was frankly glad not to be invited into the White House groups where so often the "liberal" game was played on an extreme basis. I was known not to be an extreme liberal or semiradical, as were some of those who were close about the President, and my presence in their gatherings would have been as embarrassing to me as to them.

Of far more importance to me were the pleasant, quiet luncheons I had alone with the President on scores of occasions, when for an hour at least we could exchange shirtsleeve opinions without guarding every word and watching every comma.

My relations with the President's mother, Mrs. Sara Delano Roosevelt, were most cordial. In my opinion she was a remarkable woman, who had consecrated her all to her son and her country. I first learned to know of her through the information brought to me that she was frequently supporting me and my public views. She became my warm personal friend, and in our conversations exhibited at all times a wide intelligence and excellent understanding of international questions and conditions.

Mrs. Franklin D. Roosevelt was further to the left than I was, and my contacts with her were very limited, though sufficient to enable me to appreciate her ability. She was a valiant fighter for the organization of peace and developed a wide influence in the United States and other countries for peace and other humanitarian causes.

I am convinced that the President was completely frank with me. Although I did not attend his purely military conferences—unless the question was also one involving foreign affairs—or domestic conferences, I never asked him a question about the most secret military or domestic situation that he did not instantly and unreservedly respond with full information. Several of our ambassadors, particularly Bullitt in Moscow and later Paris, Kennedy in London, and Davies in Moscow and later Brussels, who were old friends of his, had the habit of writing to him direct, over my head. While it is always inadvisable for ambassadors and ministers to carry on a correspondence with the President which includes discussion of important questions of policy—a fact I deprecated in my talks with Mr. Roosevelt—I do not recall any instance of any consequence in which the views and course of the State Department were seriously interfered with by this practice. As a precaution against confusion and cross-purposes arising from such correspondence, I made it a point to coordinate with the President the instructions I sent to the ambassadors engaging in it, so that the President and I would be in agreement in our exchanges with our envoys. Mr. Roosevelt never sought, so far as I am aware, to push upon me the views stated in their personal letters, save in some rare instances such as Bullitt's desire to remain in Paris when the French forces were evacuating it in 1940. Usually the President passed these letters on to me and also told me of any oral conversations he might have had with the ambassadors. Then, if I asked him a question, he was quick to respond on any point he had overlooked or possibly reserved.

The President pursued one practice that was frequently disturbing to the Department—that of sending special envoys abroad as his personal representatives to talk with the heads of foreign governments or to perform certain missions. Among them Harry Hopkins, Henry Wallace, W. Averell Harriman, Patrick J. Hurley, William J. Donovan, and Joseph E. Davies, all went on one or more missions. Sending these special envoys tended in many instances to create havoc with our ambassadors or ministers in the capitals they visited, even though the envoys themselves had no such intention. Nevertheless their missions rarely interfered with the strictly diplomatic efforts of the Government.

The President and I conferred with regard to the appointment of my immediate assistants in the State Department and of our ambassadors and ministers abroad. As time went on, the President made a number of suggestions for such appointments; but in a good majority of instances the State Department made recommendations to him, and in due course he acted upon them favorably, with some exceptions.

His own suggestions came to me in laconic, penciled or penned notes on small sheets of White House stationery. Undated, they would read like this:

> Smith to Chungking
> Jones to Paris
> Bring Brown home
> ?

After Turkey moved her capital from Istanbul to Ankara, I got this penned note from him:

C. H.

Why shouldn't we move our Embassy from Istanbul to Ankara? "Everyone's doin' it."   F. D. R.

On the bottom I red-penciled:

A good answer.   C. H.

Occasionally a memorandum came from the White House with this note:

Memo for the Secretary of State: For your eyes only.   F. D. R.

With the use of a couple of words Mr. Roosevelt indicated the tone of friendship or formality he wanted in letters or other communications we prepared for him. He sent me a letter from Ambassador William D. Leahy at Vichy, France, with this note:

Will you read the enclosed from Admiral Leahy and prepare a reply for my signature—Dear Bill?

The President's personal notes were always cordial and often whimsical. Typical was a note of February 7, 1934:

DEAR CORDELL:
That birthday letter which you sent me made me very happy.
When I look around and see my old friends working so loyally with me, I feel that I must soon awaken. But we seem to be accomplishing things. Thank you again.   F. D. R.

Before Mr. Roosevelt became President, I always called him "Franklin." Afterwards I called him "Mr. President," because, for one reason, when I saw him he was so often with other people. But even when we were alone I addressed him as "Mr. President," although we had few occasions to use titles. He always called me "Cordell" both before and after becoming President.

The President visited the State Department only once. He came to the Department after hours to look over offices on an upper floor to be used by some of his "anonymous assistants."

More than once I suggested to the President that he call in former President Hoover for conference on certain subjects such as the food situation abroad. I myself had no hesitation in conferring with my predecessor, Mr. Stimson, and I received valuable assistance from him, particularly in connection with Trade Agreements legislation. But the President's and Hoover's relations had become embittered, with the result that the former never invited the latter to the White House.

I myself conferred with Hoover informally a number of times, though not officially at the State Department. Our conversations took place, on Hoover's suggestion, at the home of former Under Secretary of State William Castle, and I reported on them to the President. Hoover manifested the liveliest interest in public affairs. As to whether his extreme hostility toward Roosevelt gave a more bitter tinge to his partisanship I could not say. At any rate, it was a two-way hostility.

Among the innovations I early adopted was that, when I was seriously engaged, I would send the Under Secretary of State or one of the Assistant Secretaries of State to see the President in my stead. These visits were usually on matters of a comparatively technical nature, and I would point out the information to be given to the President and possibly send a note along. I had two thoughts in mind in permitting these assistants to go directly to the President: one, to delegate some of my work, thus saving myself in emergencies; the other, to give them more prestige and practice and thus encourage them in their departmental work.

This practice worked very well in most instances. Later on, however, instances occurred where an assistant badly abused his trust by going over my head to see the President without instructions from me and undertaking in one way or another virtually to act as Secretary of State. Sumner Welles was the principal offender.

Some of the extreme left-fringe people kept the President stirred up from time to time about the State Department. It was not Mr. Roosevelt himself who had difficulty with the State Department; it was a few of the left fringe who got to him and protested at times because I did not take orders from them. Apart from complaining now and then about a "leak" in the Department, he never made a remark to me about "hating" the

State Department, as one or two persons have later alleged. He knew that I and the officers of the department initiated the preparation of, or fulfilled his requests for, the first drafts of most of his speeches, statements, and letters on foreign policy, and he was content for us to do so.

On December 31, 1943, nearly eleven years after I entered the State Department, he sent me a note which is worth quoting:

> I am sending you herewith a copy of a memorandum I sent to Churchill. Thank the Lord I don't have the same trouble with the State Department that he has with his Foreign Office!   F. D. R.

This accompanied a memorandum I had sent to the President about the Free French Committee in relation to Italy.

The President's Cabinet filled, in general, a very minor role in the formulation of foreign policy. I did not find as much discussion of foreign relations at Cabinet meetings as might be supposed, except in certain instances where a given question was very acute and was being highly publicized, as in the later case of embargoes against Japan. The tremendous increase in the duties and problems of the various branches of the Government made it difficult, if not well-nigh impossible, for each Cabinet member to keep up with all the important questions arising in the entire field of Government so as to render prompt opinions, outside the affairs of his own department.

No decisions on foreign policy were taken by Cabinet voting during my tenure. The nearest the Cabinet came to formal voting on matters submitted to it by the President or any members was in the meeting of November 7, 1941, when I made a full report on the imminent danger of attack by Japan and Mr. Roosevelt asked each member his opinion on the gravity of the situation. Ordinarily the Cabinet did not take up a regular agenda of questions, debate them out, and at the end of the discussion have a show of hands or make any definite decision except to the extent that the comments of the members might indicate the trend of their opinion. Our cabinet is more a consultative body than the British Cabinet, which is the Government. This tends to be more and more the case because of the complexity of the matters discussed.

Our meetings were held in the Cabinet room behind the President's office. During the first part of the Roosevelt Administration we sat around a large oval table. The President sat at its head, and, as the Secretary of State had done from the beginning of the Government, I sat at his right. The Secretary of the Treasury was at his left, and the other Cabinet members occupied seats extending out around the table from the President's chair, according to their rank.

When Jesse Jones came into the Cabinet as Secretary of Commerce, he had a newly designed table constructed and presented it to the President for Cabinet use. Because of the table's lines, the President, as was more logical and appropriate, sat at the center, with the Vice President opposite him, I still at his right and the Secretary of the Treasury still at his left. According to custom, the Cabinet chair I occupied for virtually twelve years was presented to me when I resigned. This, along with the chair at my desk in the State Department, likewise presented to me, I sent to the State Library at Nashville, Tennessee, where they are today.

The President started out with a schedule of two Cabinet meetings each week, Tuesday and Friday. As time went on he almost abandoned the Tuesday meetings and, save in emergencies, continued only the one meeting on Fridays.

He usually opened the Cabinet meetings by referring to some important pending question. He would then begin with me and call for anything essential I might have to bring up with the Cabinet. From time to time I indicated to the President that, instead of first calling on me to make a full statement with regard to any unusual development in foreign affairs, he himself should lead off when he felt so inclined. I could then come along with a fuller exposition, including the major details. This the President did at times, leaving me free to make any further or fuller statement I might deem advisable.

I was often reticent about disclosing important secrets to the Cabinet because there were leaks of such information to favorite news writers or broadcasters. Such leaks were restricted to a very few Cabinet members, according to my best information.

Certain Cabinet members undertook from time to time to infringe on the jurisdiction and functions of another or other members. This became very disagreeable to me on several later occasions, as when an embargo on exports to Japan was under discussion, and when Henry Wallace's Board of Economic Warfare sought to appropriate the chief economic war functions of the State Department and other agencies.

Under my policy of keeping foreign affairs out of domestic politics, and under the President's policy of dealing himself with both domestic and purely military affairs, it was but natural that I would not become so intimately associated with him as several Cabinet members engaged in the field of domestic affairs who were in constant conference with him on the almost innumerable questions arising. It was also natural that there should develop an inside, "kitchen" cabinet composed of a few persons. These did not seem to receive a call-down from the President when they sought to interfere, in his name or otherwise, with the work of other departments. Paradoxically, two or three Cabinet members, along with certain White House attachés, would sometimes attack a policy of the State Department, always in the name of the President, while at that very time he and I were working closely together in harmony. This was one of the disagreeable experiences some of us Cabinet members had to undergo.

Although Harry Hopkins was nominally a member of this inside group at the beginning, he became more conscious of his responsibility to the President, grew more detached in his attitude, and began to disagree with some of the other members of the group.

The President was delightful and interesting in these Cabinet meetings. His pleasing personality made itself felt in full. He liked anecdotes and enjoyed telling them. He was almost always in good spirits and talked with ease and pleasure.

One day, grinning broadly, he entered the Cabinet meeting somewhat late. He said he had just been the victim of a bit of impertinence on the part of a member of his family. This relative had told him: "Sir, you talk so much we never have a chance to say anything." The President laughed as he recounted the episode, then turned to me and said: "Cordell, do you agree with that?"

I replied: "Well, Mr. President, just before I came over for the meeting today, some newspapermen met me at the State Department and said to me:

" 'Mr. Secretary, there's a rumor going about that the White House food is very poor. We'd like to know what you think about it.'

" 'I never eat the White House food,' I answered.

" 'What!' they exclaimed. 'We know you go frequently to the White House for luncheon or dinner.'

" 'That,' I said, 'is true enough. But I always eat luncheon or dinner before I go over there. Then, while the President is eating, I have a chance to do a little talking.' "

The President joined in the general laugh.

Mr. Roosevelt seldom intervened when his Cabinet officers or principal assistants got into quarrels among themselves. He gave the impression almost of being a spectator looking on and enjoying the drama. But occasionally he exerted his personality, generally in a genial way, and brought the dispute to an end. Typical of his method was a difference of opinion he settled between Secretary of the Treasury Henry Morgenthau and me, in the early years of his Administration.

The Treasury had drawn up a set of claims totaling $60,000,000 against Canadian distillers for alleged nonpayment of excise taxes on Canadian whisky imported clandestinely into the United States from Canada during Prohibition. To enforce the claims the Treasury drew up legislation for Congress which would have inflicted penalties on Canadian imports if the claims were not paid.

I consulted with Green Hackworth, Legal Adviser of the State Department, and John Hickerson, Assistant Chief of the European Division, who declared that the claims were legally very dubious. We agreed, however, that any claim against a foreign government, whether dubious or not, generally resulted in a 5 per cent settlement, and we undertook to open negotiations through the Canadian Legation for this amount, $3,000,000.

In due course, we reached an agreement with Canada for $3,000,000. Thereupon a loud outcry came from Mr. Morgenthau that he would not settle for less than $6,000,000. We were then in a quandary, because we could not request Canada to pay $6,000,000, when we had settled for $3,000,000. I accordingly put on my hat and walked across the street to see the President.

I told Mr. Roosevelt the facts in the case.

"What do you think our claims are really worth?" he asked.

"Frankly," I replied, "they're probably worth nothing legally."

Without saying more, the President picked up the telephone and got Morgenthau at the other end.

"Henry," he said, "Cordell is in my office about the whisky claims against Canada. I'd like to have you do a little figuring with me. Can you put a piece of paper and a pencil before you? All set?

"Now put down on the left side of the paper what you say the claims are worth. That's $6,000,000. Now opposite that, on the right side of the paper, put down what Cordell has settled for. That's $3,000,000.

"Now under your own figure I want you to put down a figure I'm going to give you. This is my own estimate of what the claims are worth. Are you ready? All right, put down zero. Now draw a line below your figure and mine, and add them together. What do you get? $6,000,000.

O.K., now that is the sum total of what you and I think the claims are worth. Now take the average. Since there are two of us, divide by 2. What do you get? $3,000,000.

"Well, that balances exactly with what Cordell settled for. How about settling for that?"

There was a moment of silence. Then the President laughed and hung up. He turned to me.

"It's O.K.," he said.

I had no hesitation in standing up to the President on behalf of a few of my associates at the Department concerning whom one or two Cabinet members had lodged bitter complaints with him. On one occasion, Morgenthau and Ickes made various complaints to the President against a chief of one of my divisions, using the facile accusation that he was a Fascist. When the President brought up the subject, I asked him to specify the charges. He seemed unable to bring forward anything specfic, but repeated the general accusation of Fascism on the part of my assistant, which I denied. When the President continued on this general line, I said:

"Why go on talking about my assistant? Why don't you talk about me? Everything that he has done was done by my authority."

I emphasized that a group of extreme New Dealers was intent on attacking me by using the method of hitting me through attacks on my assistants.

The President then calmed down and let the matter drop.

The Secretary of the Treasury, Henry Morgenthau, Jr., who ranked next to me in the Cabinet, often acted as if he were clothed with authority to project himself into the field of foreign affairs and inaugurate efforts to shape the course of foreign policy in given instances. He had an excellent organization in the Treasury Department, ably headed by Harry White, but he did not stop with his work at the Treasury. Despite the fact that he was not at all fully or accurately informed on a number of questions of foreign policy with which he undertook to interfere, we found from his earliest days in the Government that he seldom lost an opportunity to take long steps across the line of State Department jurisdiction. Emotionally upset by Hitler's rise and his persecution of the Jews, he often sought to induce the President to anticipate the State Department or act contrary to our better judgment. We sometimes found him conducting negotiations with foreign Governments which were the function of the State Department. His work in drawing up a catastrophic plan for the postwar treatment of Germany, and inducing the President to accept it without consultation with the State Department, was an outstanding instance of this interference. Another was his negotiation with the British at the second Quebec Conference, in 1944, for credits to Britain totaling $6,500,000,000, without reference to the negotiations the State Department had undertaken with Britain on economic principles. Morgenthau's interference at times misled some portions of the public and seriously impeded the orderly conduct of our foreign policy. I mentioned this habit to the President from time to time; but Mr. Roosevelt had a way of quietly easing by such complaints relating to his intimates, although when the showdown came—as in the instance of the Morgenthau plan for Germany—he almost always delivered an impartial decision.

The later Secretary of War, Henry L. Stimson, and I worked together as would double cousins, even from the time I succeeded him as Secretary of State in 1933. I have never known a higher-class man in every essential respect. A striking example of his broad and nonpartisan attitude, especially in foreign affairs, occurred when, some time before his entry into the Cabinet, he remarked to me, in effect: "You are considered a Democrat and I a Republican; but in all candor I know of no public question of importance on which you and I could not work wholeheartedly together in effecting a common solution." Stimson's name should be most highly regarded in the history of our times. His predecessor, Secretary of War Harry Woodring, was efficient and able, but on some aspects of the international situation he entertained divergent views from those of the Administration as a whole, since he leaned more in the direction of isolation. The Assistant Secretary of War of that time, Louis Johnson, rendered highly useful service in solving numerous questions that threatened to become aggravated, and gave us at the State Department the utmost cooperation.

Colonel Frank Knox made a good record as Secretary of the Navy. He never failed to meet me and other colleagues halfway in handling any matter that required cooperation. He possessed real breadth of view and was intensely devoted to his duties, all of which he performed with high credit. His predecessors, Claude Swanson and Charles Edison, likewise ably filled that office. After Knox's death, James A. Forrestal, Undersecretary of the Navy, succeeded him. My conferences with Forrestal impressed me with his fitness for this high position.

Postmaster General James A. Farley was untiringly active in connection with the high positions he filled, and his work earned the admiration and approval of the country. When Farley, who had qualities of real statesmanship, spoke in Cabinet meetings or elsewhere, he always commanded the full attention of his associates.

His successor, Frank Walker, was an original and highly useful Roosevelt supporter leading up to the 1932 convention. He continued throughout the Administration to bear the reputation of being of unfailing help to the President. No request of Mr. Roosevelt was difficult enough to cause him to hesitate in responding to it. He was one of the very able and useful public servants of this period. No person loved his country more dearly or was more ready to give his services unstintingly.

Secretary of the Interior Harold Ickes was always quite active and had numerous achievements to his credit. He was often quite far to the left and hence frequently out of line with many of us, and he had an unfortunate approach to problems which not infrequently antagonized others. He was one of the three Cabinet members who at times undertook to interfere with other Cabinet functions; but he did not often interfere, and in cases concerning the State Department I credit him with honestly believing that he did so because of overlapping jurisdictions.

My long association with Attorney General Homer Cummings in public affairs and on the Executive Committee of the Democratic National Committee (each of us having been at times chairman of the National Committee) enabled me to appraise him as being exceedingly able, well poised, always vigilant, and possessing the essential equipment of an outstanding lawyer in the nation. He rendered long and capable service.

The later Attorney General, Robert Jackson, had a remarkable rise in the legal world and had moved with ease from one important post to another still higher. He was an agreeable man to work with and possessed an impressive personality.

Henry A. Wallace, Secretary of Agriculture and later Vice President, was extremely energetic and possessed considerable ability, but was in many respects an extreme leftist. He was inclined to explore new theories and to embrace them if they appeared plausible. This habit from time to time led him into difficulties, if not embarrassing positions. He was so active that his tendency at times was to trench on the jurisdiction of his colleagues, including myself, and to interfere with their policies. On the other hand, he and I worked wholeheartedly together in support of my broad economic and trade policy.

Jesse H. Jones, the Secretary of Commerce, had risen by sheer force of intellect, energy, and sound judgment from poverty in the rural sections of Tennessee to one of the highest levels of business and financial achievement, statesmanship, and public accomplishment in political and economic affairs. Few Americans have been more public-spirited.

Miss Frances Perkins, Secretary of Labor, has never received the full credit she deserves for her ability and public services. She was unusually able, very practical, and brought vision and untiring energy to her work.

In general, my relations with almost all the Cabinet members were cordial and cooperative.

15: Congress, Public, and State Department

NO PRESIDENT or Secretary of State who has sought to play a positive role in foreign affairs has emerged unscarred by battles with Congress. The viewpoint of the President or Secretary of State differs at times, by the very nature of their offices, from that of Senators and Congressmen. The Executive Department looks on a question of foreign policy, first from a national and then from an international viewpoint. Many Congressmen look on the same question, first from the viewpoint of their district or State, second from the national point of view, and third from the international point of view. The attitude of a Congressional district or a State is often, and naturally, at variance with the other two attitudes. The national good may not be immediately the good of the particular district or of the State, although ultimately it will; and the international good may not be immediately the good of the nation, although ultimately it will.

I had important victories in Congress, but I also had important defeats. Both the President and I were strongly inclined toward international cooperation, sharply opposed to extreme nationalism and to isolation. But we were ahead of Congress as a whole. In many instances in the years to come, Congress narrowed the range and importance of our efforts to make the United States a more integral part of world affairs. Congress was slower on many occasions than the Executive in seeing the dangers looming to world peace and in taking appropriate steps to meet them.

After twenty-four years in Congress, I had the best of personal and working relations with numerous key Members of the House and Senate. These included the official leaders of the two Houses and the more active and capable members of the committees having jurisdiction over legislation pertaining to foreign affairs. Their personal friendship, however, was no sure guarantee of their vote on crucial foreign issues.

Not all the questions involving Congressional jurisdiction in foreign affairs have been fully determined. The President has the constitutional function of initiating and negotiating treaties with foreign governments. These become effective only with the consent of the Senate, two-thirds of those present voting in the affirmative. Numerous claims have been made, however, by Members of the House of Representatives to a share in Senate treaty jurisdiction. Such claims arise in connection with the approval of treaties involving the exercise of the power of taxation or requiring appropriations which must be initiated in the House of Representatives.

Advocates of greater House of Representatives participation in foreign affairs suggest that this procedure permanently replace the Senate two-thirds vote requirement, and that treaties be approved by a majority vote of the two Houses. Others suggest a majority vote of the Senate.

I believe that a majority vote in the Senate in the case of treaties would be more practical than the two-thirds vote. The constitutional two-thirds requirement gives excessive power to minorities, the possession of which has been much more hurtful than helpful. Such abuses occurred in the rejection of the League of Nations and the entire cause of future peace, and of the World Court and a number of important treaties.

Action by a majority vote is all that is required in other extremely important actions such as declaring war. A majority vote requirement would hamper the practice of filibusters by small minorities. The Senate, however, would still have its constitutional rights and privileges preserved. A change in the two-thirds rule will not occur until sufficient interest is aroused to obtain a constitutional amendment. The House, of course, must come into the legislative picture when it is necessary to implement treaties, as by appropriations or loans.

Recent decades have seen a pronounced trend toward executive agreements with foreign Governments, many of which are more important than the average treaty. These are not submitted to the Senate for its advice and consent. Some agreements have been negotiated by blanket authority granted by Congress, such as the trade agreements under the Act of 1934. Others have been negotiated without such authority, such as the exchanges of letters whereby we recognized Soviet Russia in 1933, the Ogdensburg agreement of 1940 between the President and Prime Minister Mackenzie King of Canada, creating a permanent joint-defense board, and my exchange of notes with the British Ambassador in 1940, trading over-age American destroyers for leases to bases in British possessions in the Western Hemisphere. During the first fifty years under the Constitution, 60 treaties became law and 27 executive agreements were signed; during the next fifty years there were 238 executive agreements compared to 215 treaties, and during the third fifty years, 917 executive agreements compared to 524 treaties.

There is a twilight zone between the policy relating to executive agreements and the constitutional authority relating to treaties. There is no clear-cut standard by which to test the two processes. The question of where to draw the line is not without its difficulties. It is a matter of judgment on the part of lawyers and others capable of passing on the scope and nature of treaties on the one hand and of executive agreements on the other.

Generally executive agreements are not of such importance or of such a nature as would call for formal Senate consent. Sometimes an executive agreement is signed when an important time element prevails which would be sacrificed if several months were to pass until Senate approval could be obtained. It would be impossible to put all the executive agreements in the form of treaties and expect the Senate to approve them.

The policy on which executive agreements is based is good from the practical viewpoint, just as the constitutional authority for treaties is good from the legal viewpoint. It is possible that in some instances executive agreements have been entered into which might properly have gone to the Senate for approval as treaties. These are in the borderline area. At one time I examined this question in detail. I then gave specific instructions to the Legal Adviser's office and to other important officials that each case that might raise a question of whether it was a treaty to be ratified or an executive agreement must be subjected to the fullest possible examination, and if there were any reasonable doubt, the matter should be sent to the Senate for its advice and consent.

The State Department is the only department not required to make annual reports to Congress. There is the best of reasons for this policy, adopted at the outset of our Government. It is impossible to conduct foreign relations in many important respects with wide-open publicity. Were we to do so, foreign nations would promptly refuse to discuss matters of a delicate or serious nature with us. As an inevitable result, it would be impossible to carry on diplomatic conversations any portion of which the other interested countries would desire to be kept secret. We would soon cease to be on speaking terms with other nations if we should make public, at the time, the confidential details of the conversations taking place between us.

President Washington quickly discovered the necessity for secrecy in many respects in negotiating treaties with other Governments. When he was requested by a resolution of the House of Representatives in 1796 to lay before the House copies of the documents and correspondence relating to the treaty with Great Britain, he refused, saying:

"The nature of foreign negotiations requires caution, and their success must often depend on secrecy; and even when brought to a conclusion a full disclosure of all the measures, demands, or eventual concessions which may have been proposed or contemplated would be extremely impolitic; for this might have a pernicious influence on future negotiations, or produce immediate inconveniences, perhaps danger and mischief, in relation to other powers. The necessity of such caution and secrecy was one cogent reason for vesting the power of making treaties in the President, with the advice and consent of the Senate, the principle on which that body was formed confining it to a small number of members. To admit, then, a right in the House of Representatives to demand and to have as a matter of course all the papers respecting a negotiation with a foreign power would be to establish a dangerous precedent."

In accordance with experience and sound judgment, this Government, therefore, early adopted a fixed policy on supplying official information on foreign affairs even to one or both of the two Houses of Congress. Washington's precedent was followed by later Presidents. A formula was early devised for the protection of the State Department whereby any Congressional request to the President for information on foreign affairs contains the words, "if in his judgment not incompatible with the public interest." The policy embodied in this clause enables the State Department to impart to Congress the fullest possible information within its possession, with the exception of such facts and records as it would be "incompatible with the public interest" to disclose.

There were instances during the Roosevelt Administration when Congressmen sought to force the hand of the President and State Department by introducing resolutions requesting that certain actions be taken in foreign affairs. I was in office less than a year when a resolution was introduced in the Senate which would have requested the President to make a formal protest to Germany over the persecution of Jews. Here would have been a case of Congress taking an initiative that constitutionally belonged to the President. At the State Department we prepared a memorandum for the Senate Foreign Relations Committee pointing out this fact. The resolution was buried.

In my efforts to cooperate to the fullest practicable extent with Congress in furnishing information requested, I made it a rule at the State Department that, when requests from Congressmen presented difficult questions, I should be informed. I then got in personal contact with the Members of Congress immediately interested. In that way I could talk over the question with them and, as a rule, reach a mutual understanding.

I also made it a practice to appear personally before Congressional committees or important group conferences, which I did scores of times during my stay at the State Department. In other instances, where the questions involved technical subjects, I sent the Department experts to the Congressional committees concerned, generally accompanied by such key men as an Assistant Secretary or the head of a division.

I made it a rule with my assistants at the State Department that they should not engage in "cussin' matches" with Congressmen who opposed our views. On one occasion, after the minority members of a Congressional committee made a sharp attack on trade agreements, several of my assistants wrote up a statement in which they attacked those Congressmen. They asked if I would read, approve, and issue it. After reading it through, I put it away and said to them: "Don't forget, you may need some of those fellows some day."

In my rather frequent visits to the Senate, especially to the Senate Committee on Foreign Relations, or whenever I met Senators anywhere, I always invited them to visit me at the State Department. My idea was that they could ask me any question they had in mind and I would be near any documents that might throw light on their difficulties. Also, I could give them a picture of our foreign policy and our objectives.

My relations with the Senate were complicated in some instances by the fact that my views differed at times from those of Democratic Senator Key Pittman, chairman of the Senate Foreign Relations Committee, as well as from those of isolationist Senator William E. Borah, ranking Republican member of the committee and its former chairman.

Pittman was one of the able Senators of the period. Prior to 1933 I had had no special legislative relations with him, but he and I had traveled with John W. Davis in the 1924 campaign and were warm personal friends. That friendship was somewhat impaired during the London Economic Conference in the summer of 1933. Thereafter we kept up wholehearted working arrangements, but our hitherto close ties were never fully repaired. Pittman declined to go along with the President and myself on such important issues as the World Court. He strongly opposed my trade-agreements program from start to finish and voted against it, though it is due him to say that his State, Nevada, demanded the highest tariff protection, especially for her sheep and cattle. He was largely responsible for the appointment of Senator Nye as chairman of the Nye investigating committee which had such disastrous effect in the stimulating of further isolation.

Pittman was jealous of his prerogatives as chairman of the Foreign Relations Committee and at times keenly resented any effort by the State Department to draft or suggest legislation concerning foreign affairs. During the neutrality battles between 1935 and 1939, he showed a disposition to want to work with the State Department but disliked any too close relationship with the Department. He felt he could be more effective in handling a pending bill in the Senate if the Executive Branch remained aloof and were not known as its originator or supporter. This overconfidence had a tragic result in our unsuccessful efforts to lift the arms embargo in the spring and summer of 1939.

Senator Borah, when chairman of the Committee on Foreign Relations, and later as ranking Republican member, was in a position to render incalculable injury to the cause of international cooperation—which I think he did. His position of leadership and his integrity, sincerity, patriotism, and great ability, together with his pleasing personality, played their full part in the effect of his implacable opposition to all efforts at international cooperation to preserve the peace and improve economic standards. He held regular news conferences not unlike those of the President or Secretary of State and kept the newspapermen completely fed on his isolationist ideas. He rarely lost an opportunity to strike a blow at any act or utterance in the direction of broader international relations. He was isolationist in his very blood. He followed Senators Lodge, Brandegee, and Reed in their fight against our sharing in the League of Nations and international cooperation. He continued his bitter opposition throughout the two decades that followed until his death.

Personally, Borah and I were friends. We had long believed in the same progressive domestic issues such as income and inheritance taxation and election of Senators by the people. We came to Washington in the same year, 1907, and I met him at the Raleigh Hotel upon our arrival. He was always very democratic and rather broad in his domestic views, taking a wide interest in almost all progressive measures. He was of impressive personal appearance which, along with his marvelous capacity for gesture, contributed fully to the effectiveness of his powerful oratory. He was a great orator. During my years at the State Department I frequently saw Borah and invited him to visit me at my office, intending to lay before him the facts I possessed on the international situation—but he never once appeared.

Other Senators who were outstanding in their opposition to anything resembling international cooperation were Hiram Johnson, Gerald Nye, Burton Wheeler, and Henrik Shipstead. Wheeler and I were always personal friends, although we differed widely as the poles on isolation and also on tariffs, he having the copper, sheep, and other interests among his constituents to look after. I first met him at a Democratic meeting I held in Montana in 1922, when he was preparing to run for the Senate. He was able and, I believe, sincere in his beliefs. Bennett Clark, who differed with me vehemently on isolationist questions, strongly supported my trade agreements and was disposed to defend me from personal attack even though he might disagree with me on the issue involved.

The isolationists struck me on the whole as an honest, though mistaken, group. I thought, however, that Senator Nye kept up his performance as chairman of the Nye investigating committee as long as he thought there were votes in it, but kept it up too long. On the whole the isolationist leaders of the thirties seemed to me different from Senator Lodge and his group of purely selfish isolationists of 1919 and 1920 whose policy was rule or ruin.

Fortunately these isolationists were opposed in Congress by a strong and able group of Senators and Congressmen. The Administration received valuable aid in its relations with Congress by reason of the Senate leadership which for some years comprised Vice President Garner and Floor Leader Joseph T. Robinson. It would not be fair to mention them in this connection, however, without referring to the broad-gauged and able Republican floor leader, Charles McNary, who would not permit the partisans to jockey him around. Senator Robinson was at his death succeeded as floor leader by one of the most intelligent statesmen with whom I have been privileged to serve—Senator Alben W. Barkley of Kentucky, a model patriot. Among notable chairmen of important committees whose cooperation often was indispensable was Senator Pat Harrison of Mississippi, who, among other capacities, was a great popular stump speaker.

In the House I had cooperation from Speaker Sam Rayburn, Democratic Floor Leader McCormack and even, in rare instances, from Joe Martin, the Republican floor leader. I was fortunate in that my Tennessee colleague and friend, Sam D. McReynolds, was chairman of the House Committee on Foreign Affairs during the first six years of my tenure until his untimely death. His personal and official cooperation with me could scarcely have been more wholehearted and efficient. He was broad-minded and patriotic,, and, above all, he had integrity. He was succeeded by Sol Bloom, who was always alert and likewise worked closely with me. Bloom's ability, energy, and familiarity with the matters involved made his services exceedingly valuable. Congressman Luther A. Johnson, Democrat of Texas, and Congressman Charles A. Eaton, Republican of New Jersey, were among the highly capable and cooperative members of the committee on whom I relied. Hamilton Fish, Republican ranking member of the committee and an isolationist to the hilt, always opposed me, although he and his family were thoroughly friendly toward me and mine.

During my entire stay in the State Department I received uniform support of my policies from the Tennessee Senators led by my able former colleague, the veteran Senator Kenneth D. McKellar. The Tennessee Democratic Congressional delegation—and much of the time the Republican members as well—likewise gave me their constant cooperation.

Generally, the fact that I kept foreign affairs away from domestic controversies won me the support of Republicans disposed toward the international view, as well as Democrats of like persuasion. This included some of both Parties who were bitter against President Roosevelt on either personal or official grounds.

Behind Congress stood the American public, comprising another problem in our foreign relations. One of the basic principles I set myself for the conduct of foreign affairs was to stimulate an informed American public opinion on international events. Naturally, if I could not furnish full information to the Senate on certain negotiations, I could not furnish even as much to the general public. But I intended to be as liberal as possible in making the working of our foreign affairs visible to the people. I wanted them to see what was going on so that they could realize the nature of the new forces rising abroad and the vital stake their nation had in the peace of the world.

For the first time in the history of the State Department I began to hold daily press conferences. No matter what the congestion of my engagements, I had a certain hour set six days a week at which to receive the news and radio correspondents and answer their questions to the best of my ability. I have no doubt the correspondents were often disappointed, but in general they understood that to talk of certain negotiations meant to defeat them. Throughout my twelve years at the State Department I felt I had the support of the great majority of newspapers in all our foreign policies. At times, as at the close of the London Economic Conference, this support was estimated at more than 90 per cent.

Occasionally, when a correspondent or a member of the Government sought to get me to tell him something I was not at liberty to tell, I would remind him that Stonewall Jackson, at the time of the Seven Days' Battle with McClellan, rode to Charlottesville, Virginia. A man recognized him, hastened over and engaged him in conversation, wanting to know what the General was doing there, where he was going, and what the prospects of battle were.

Jackson leaned confidentially over to him and asked: "Can you keep a secret?"

The man said eagerly: "Sure, I can keep a secret."

"Well," replied Jackson, "so can I."

On one occasion, at the appointed moment, I walked with Harry McBride from my office to the press-conference room where hung the portraits of my immediate predecessors, Stimson, Kellogg, and Hughes. McBride threw open the door and we walked into an empty room.

"Well," I remarked, "this is not the first time I've talked to an empty house."

We returned to my office to be informed that the conference had been shifted to another room that particular morning.

Among my many newspaper friendships, I took special pride in that of Adolph Ochs, publisher of the New York *Times*. I had known him for many years, from the time he was launching out with the Chattanooga *Times*. I saw him in Washington or New York at reasonable intervals, and found that he, his staff, and I virtually always entertained the same ideas on international questions.

I can state it as a fact that no Foreign Office in the world comes anywhere near the State Department in the volume or importance of the information on foreign policy released to the public. I did everything I could to encourage this trend. Ten years after I came into office, the volume of press releases had doubled. We were to be the first Government to issue a full-sized volume—"Peace and War"—on the diplomatic history leading up to Pearl Harbor. This, compiled largely by my very able assistant Carlton Savage, was translated into many languages, and was also published as an official document by the British Government. Including the volumes in the series "Foreign Relations of the United States," issued under the direction of Cyril Wynne and later E. Wilder Spaulding, I find that, in the tenth year after I entered the State Department, we published 6,641 pages of documents contrasted with the average of 2,634 pages annually in the decade preceding 1933.

Nevertheless, I soon was to discover that there were carping political critics and chronic critics apart from those who were friendly and constructive in their criticisms. A small willful element centered its attacks on the State Department relatively more than on any other department— even during the delicate period of the war. They knew that the general public was less familiar with international affairs, to which the work of the State Department related, than with domestic affairs presided over by other departments, and that, if they should misstate the fact or state a deliberate falsehood, the public would have less chance to discover whether it were true or otherwise, than if it were a domestic matter that could be publicized more freely. A lie will gallop halfway round the world before the truth has time to pull its breeches on.

I learned, in my twelve years in the State Department, that criticism came easily. I used to console my associates who came in for such criticism by telling them a story.

"About twenty-five years ago," I said, "Mr. Bourke Cockran was sitting in front of me in the House of Representatives—a wonderfully fluent speaker. A gentleman, Congressman Alexander of New York, got up on the other side of the House to speak under the five-minute rule. Pretty soon Mr. Cockran rose from his seat and put his eye on the gentleman. A Member sitting by Mr. Cockran asked: 'Which side are you going to take?' Cockran replied: 'I don't know until I see which side Alexander takes—I'll take the other.' "

This brings inescapably to mind the greatly increased responsibilities of the distributors of news to the public. One of our great newspaper owners and writers stated publicly several years ago that 15 to 20 per cent of the editors, columnists, and broadcasters put out false, misleading or prejudicial news or information enough to confuse the public mind, divert it from the true course and even array it against the wisest policies and acts of the Government during the most critical times. The gentleman making this statement—former Governor James M. Cox—has been, like myself, a strong champion of the precious human freedoms of the press and of speech, but it is evident that an increasing number of abuses have grown up during recent years.

A perfect illustration is the case of some second- or third-rate person who looks about until he finds enough backing to enable him to climb up to a microphone, and thereupon in the minds of a surprising portion of the people he instantly and automatically becomes an important international expert. His utterances are too often based on ignorance, confusion, or prejudice; but millions of people hang on his sensational and false statements as if he were a competent, genuine broadcaster instead of a fraud. He manufactures false sentiment and in some instances handicaps the conduct of both domestic and foreign affairs.

I pay the highest tribute to the other 80 to 85 per cent of the editors, columnists, and broadcasters, but in all candor I believe the time is overripe for the vigorous reformation of these terrible abuses that are flourishing more and more. A peaceful and orderly postwar world imperatively requires some improvement in this respect. Otherwise there will be no adequate, unified, informed, and aggressive public opinion to support a great, efficient world peace organization or even sound domestic institutions.

16: We Tackle Disarmament

DISARMAMENT WAS one of the first major questions we had to tackle in the spring of 1933. My associates at the State Department and I, working with the President, took the liveliest interest in the problem and its possible solutions. The President and I had the same views. We knew there could be no peace without suitable reduction and limitation of armament—"disarmament," as this process came to be popularly known. We knew this was not possible except under a world policy strongly supported by universal public opinion. Even then there could easily be failure—and such was to be the event.

To my mind disarmament was both a terrific undertaking and an essential element of peace. To me there were three main points to disarmament. In the first place, it would prevent races in armaments and the exhaustion of nations' material resources. In the second place, unlimited races in armaments as a rule resulted in war. In the third place, it had to be by all nations. You could not have some disarming, others not.

For these reasons I was convinced that any peace to last must be accompanied by disarmament under a world agreement. The concept of peace based on disarmament was comparatively new, having been in vogue only after the First World War.

When the Roosevelt Administration came into office, the Disarmament Conference at Geneva, which had convened February 2, 1932, was still in session. It had spent more than a year in discussions that produced anything but disarmament. There was every evidence that Nazi Germany was feverishly rearming. France and other neighbors of Germany were consequently reluctant to reduce armaments unless they could get a security agreement binding other nations to help them if Germany attacked them. The situation was becoming ever more acute, and in March, 1933, the conference seemed in danger of breaking up.

I had not been too much impressed by previous disarmament conferences. I have already cited my objections to the Washington Conference of 1921–1922. During the 1920's everybody stood for a policy of peace with disarmament, but the Administration in charge of the Government made clear that we would shun the League of Nations and refrain from what was termed political alliances and any foreign involvement objectionable to an isolationist mind. In Europe, Britain and France were dominating the League of Nations, sometimes from the viewpoint of their own individual welfare and purposes. As early as 1927 the Japanese violently reproclaimed their long-standing policy of expansion and imperialism, which had been interrupted by the Nine-Power Treaty of 1922. Agitation steadily grew in Japan. The naval disarmament conference at Geneva in 1927 failed. When the London Naval Conference of 1930 decided on a 10–10–7 ratio of cruisers for the United States, Britain, and Japan—a concession to Japan—I was not too well pleased with its very limited accomplishments. I could not help contrasting these results with Japan's more and more noticeable ambitions and the sight of the Germans, apparently inactive but silently watching and working for a way out from under the heel of their conquerors.

Hoover and Stimson had taken some broad-gauged steps to help the Disarmament Conference of 1932. They had advocated the extension of the Washington and London naval agreements and the further reduction of those upper limits; the total abolition of submarines, gas, and bacteriological warfare; protection of civilian populations against aerial bombing; special restrictions for offensive armaments; and limitations on expenditures for arms.

My preoccupation with disarmament began only a day or two after I took the oath of office. Ambassador Hugh Gibson telegraphed me from Geneva that tempers were exasperated, and that, amid general discouragement, the conference seemed likely to adjourn, an adjournment the equivalent of a complete breakdown. In that case, he thought, Germany would feel herself free from the disarmament obligations of the Versailles Treaty and begin to rearm in earnest. The problem therefore became one not merely of disarmament but an even more basic one of the entire relations of European nations one to another.

Gibson pointed out that no disarmament on our part would affect the situation. We could scrap our Navy and abolish the Army and Air Force, but this would not alter the European view toward disarmament. European nations like France were not worried about our armaments; they were worried about Germany. They were not concerned about our disarmament but about our political position toward Europe. They wanted us to agree to advise with them in case of a breach of the peace and then to decide on our own whether we would refrain from interfering with such collective measures as they would take following the breach.

To put it concretely: if Germany or Italy became an aggressor and the other nations imposed sanctions, would we still uphold our rights as a neutral and our traditional policy of freedom of the seas? Would we insist on maintaining commerce with Germany or Italy and permitting our citizens to export arms to them? Gibson indicated he favored our refraining from action that would defeat sanctions. In return for this concession, we should get a good *quid pro quo* in the way of real disarmament at Geneva, especially from France.

As these telegrams began coming in, Norman Davis and I held a series of conferences. On March 14, President Roosevelt named Davis, whom I heartily recommended, as our new delegate to the Disarmament Conference, with the rank of ambassador. Davis soon afterwards sailed for Geneva, where he rendered outstanding service during the later disarmament discussions.

A Tennessean by birth, Norman Davis had early accumulated substantial properties, and thereafter, beginning with his service in the United States Treasury during the First World War, dedicated his life primarily to the promotion of peace with disarmament and to the reduction of trade barriers and the increase of trade, consumption, and employment. This ability and experience made his services much sought after by both Republican and Democratic Administrations, especially those of Hoover and Roosevelt.

Not a showy person, Davis had real wisdom and had developed an intimate knowledge of the world's complications. He would come in on any conference I was having—unless it was a direct meeting between an ambassador and myself—and shed some light upon it. He came and went in that fashion. He would push the door open, see whether I was engaged, and in ordinary proceedings would always come in. He occupied a unique position, was a great help, never for an instant gave away a secret, and could be sent anywhere. He was a strong supporter of the League of Nations.

No person could have represented our Government more capably at the Disarmament Conference than Norman Davis. But no one living person could have achieved the desired disarmament results during those hectic years.

When Davis reached Paris he telegraphed me information that the high costs of heavy armaments were beginning to react on the French. Tired of such huge expenditures, they would like to reduce armaments and to satisfy Germany somewhat, provided they could at the same time form a collective security system to act if Germany ran amuck.

Davis asked me whether we were prepared to agree to consult with the other nations in case of a threat to peace and to refrain from action that would defeat collective action by the European nations. By that time we were making ready for a series of talks in Washington with the leaders of eleven nations preparatory to the forthcoming London Economic Conference. Davis pointed out that failure of the Disarmament Conference would prejudice the discussions to be held in Washington and also the Economic Conference. There was no doubt that all these questions were intimately linked together. Unless the chilling fears creeping over Europe were dissipated, we would get nowhere with either military or economic disarmament, and Europe would head straight for war. I was to realize again and again in the years following how intimately one question of peace was interlocked with another, how closely one threat to or breach of the peace in any part of the world affected the relations of nations in all other parts of the world.

I immediately sent Davis's recommendations to the President. If we agreed to take the advanced steps he suggested, it was obvious that some decisive method to make them known had to be determined upon. But a few days later I was obliged to cable Davis that, although the President had had the recommendations for three days, he had been so occupied with monetary and other economic problems as to find it impossible to give the policy the careful study so important a decision required.

At that point British Prime Minister Ramsay MacDonald arrived in Washington for conversations on economic topics and debts. He discussed the Disarmament Conference with the President and myself. MacDonald had presented to the Disarmament Conference at Geneva on March 16 a comprehensive plan for disarmament. As one of his points, he advocated that all nations confer in case a dispute broke out, and determine the responsible party. He sought to set up a permanent commission to conduct investigations in the territory of a country suspected of rearming. He cited definite upper limits for the armies of the major countries. MacDonald appealed to us for support of his plan. In general, we listened with sympathy.

MacDonald agreed with the emphasis placed by Davis on the dangerous consequences that would follow an adjournment of the conference. I cabled to Davis that public opinion would regard adjournment as equal to a breakdown and told him we counted on him to exert every effort to keep the Conference in session.

Finally, nine days after the arrival of his recommendations, I was able to cable him the President's decision. We felt that disarmament should rest upon more than a European agreement—that is, a regional one—and should be universal. After all, we also had to consider the Far East, then in chaos because of the Japanese invasion of northern China. But we were willing to make a declaratory statement whereby the United States would refrain from action tending to defeat collective efforts—sanctions—by the European nations, provided disarmament were agreed to generally. Bearing in mind the isolationist sentiment in the United States, this was a far-reaching decision. We next had to decide how to communicate our views with as much effect as possible.

On May 6, 1933, the President talked with Dr. Hjalmar Schacht, president of the German Reichsbank, who came here for economic discussions. Mr. Roosevelt sent me a note saying he had told Dr. Schacht that the United States would insist that Germany remain at her present level in armament, and that "we would support every possible effort to have the offensive armament of every other nation brought down to the German level." Also, that "we regard Germany as the only possible obstacle to a Disarmament Treaty." The President asked him to give this point of view to Hitler as quickly as possible.

It was one of our prime viewpoints that equality of armaments should be sought not by raising those of the defeated nations of the World War to the level of the victors, but by reducing the victors' level to that of the conquered countries. Otherwise, it would have been a rearmament, not a disarmament, agreement. Hoover and Stimson had maintained the same view.

A few days later Berlin announced that Hitler would address the Reichstag on May 17. All major capitals believed that the speech would center on the Disarmament Conference and possibly announce Germany's intention to rearm in earnest. The moment seemed to have arrived for the United States to speak out.

On May 15 Davis cabled me and took up the question whether our statement should be made before or after Hitler's speech. If before, it would take the wind out of Hitler's sails. Or should we wait until after Hitler had spoken and the French and British had expressed their reactions, and then use our statement to clear the atmosphere and to find a basis for reconciling the conflicting viewpoints? Davis favored the former.

When Davis's cable arrived, the President was already preparing his statement. I had been sending him Gibson's and then Davis's cables and discussing the matter with him. He determined to make the statement in the form of an appeal to the heads of the fifty-four nations represented at the Conference. We at the State Department cooperated in its preparation and dispatch. We hastened its delivery so as to place it in Hitler's hands in ample time before he made his much-heralded speech to the Reichstag.

The President's message, dated May 16, suggested that all nations eliminate offensive weapons, agree upon the MacDonald plan, enter into a nonaggression pact, and promise not to send any armed force across their frontiers. In case any strong nation refused to join in such agreement, he said, the world "will know where the responsibility for failure lies."

At Geneva they had been discussing for ten years a definition of an aggressor. Every sort of definition was suggested. One was the simple phrase that an aggressor was a nation whose armed forces crossed the borders of another country. The President and I and my associates in the State Department had repeated discussions of this point. Mr. Roosevelt and each of us agreed that the simple phrase was the best that could be used at this time, and we so employed it in his message.

No doubt the President's appeal had some influence with Hitler because the latter's speech turned out, in general, to be conciliatory. Four days later, Davis cabled that the moment was now ripe for decisive developments, following the President's message. He thought a meeting among Hitler, MacDonald, French Premier Daladier, and Mussolini could be arranged, and asked whether he could take the initiative. The following day, May 22, I cabled Davis that the President and I were glad to give him full discretion toward bringing about such a meeting if and when he felt it would be justified. But the political atmosphere was not propitious, and nothing came of his efforts.

I also cabled Davis our authorization to make an additional statement to the Disarmament Conference to supplement the President's appeal. On May 22 he presented a comprehensive statement of how far we were ready to go to keep the Conference alive and achieve disarmament. The United States, he said, was prepared:

(1) To bring all armies down to the level of domestic police forces.

(2) To accept the MacDonald plan.

(3) To consult with other nations in the event of a threat to the peace.

(4) To refrain from any action tending to defeat a collective effort

of the nations against a nation guilty of a breach of the peace in violation
of its international obligations, provided that the nations, in conference,
determined that such nation was guilty and we concurred in their judgment.

(5) To assist in formulating a system of supervision of the nations'
armaments. "We are heartily in sympathy with the idea that means of
effective, automatic and continuous supervision should be found, whereby
nations will be able to rest assured that, as long as they respect their
obligations with regard to armaments, the corresponding obligations of
their neighbors will be carried out in the same scrupulous manner."

All the above was to be contingent upon the Conference reaching a
substantial reduction of armaments by general international agreement.

Here, two and a half months after the new Administration came into
power, was a radical change in the traditional attitude of this country
toward two old principles—neutrality, and freedom of the seas. It meant
that, if the other nations instituted sanctions against a nation they
deemed an aggressor, we would do nothing to interfere with such sanctions
if we determined on our own that the other nations had made the right
choice of the aggressor. Concretely, we would not insist on upholding
the freedom of the seas or our rights as a neutral so as to continue our
trade with that country. We would put the offending nation in Coventry
just as the other nations were doing. In the 1932 Democratic platform
we had advocated consultation and conference in case of threatened
violations of treaties, but in the May 22 statement we were going well
beyond that point.

Our agreeing on supervision of armaments was also a decided change
in policy. This meant we were willing that an international inspection
committee should enter the United States, as well as any other nation,
to see whether we or someone else were carrying out the provisions of a
disarmament agreement. This obviously meant a certain voluntary abridg-
ment of sovereignty in the interests of international peace.

In an effort to implement our promises we sought Congressional
approval of legislation to give the President the right to embargo shipments of arms to an aggressor nation. This legislation had been proposed
under the Hoover Administration. We at the State Department, who
were never ceasing to try to find the right way toward international
cooperation, took it up and championed it. Since their own Administration had supported it, we hoped it would have the backing of Republicans
as well as Democrats.

Congressman McReynolds, chairman of the House Committee on Foreign Affairs, in agreement with me introduced the resolution in the House. On April 5 I wrote Mr. McReynolds, urging its passage: "In justice to the firm convictions of the American people and to its own dignity, this Government should no longer be left in the position of being unable to join the other governments of the world in preventing the supply of arms and munitions for use in an international conflict when it is exercising its diplomacy and the whole weight of our national influence and prestige to prevent or put an end to that conflict."

The resolution passed the House in the form we wished, and went over to the Senate. I thereupon sent a memorandum to the Senate Committee on Foreign Relations to answer objections that the resolution might result in involving us in war. I pointed out that the action permitted would "certainly not be adopted by this Government without such effective guarantees of international cooperation as would safeguard us against the danger of this country's being involved in the conflict as a result of such action."

I told the Senate committee that if the resolution were passed the Government, in cooperation with other Governments, would embargo the shipment of arms to Paraguay and Bolivia. It would not, however, embargo arms shipments to China and Japan. Such an embargo would not be effective in restoring peace. Japan could supply her own needs by her own industries. China was dependent upon imports. An embargo against both would militate against China and in favor of Japan. An embargo against Japan alone would probably result in a Japanese blockade of China's ports.

"It is not our policy to have this Government posing before the world as a leader in all the efforts to prevent or put an end to wars," I said, "but on the other hand it is not our policy to lag behind the other nations of the world in their efforts to promote peace. The passage of this Resolution is necessary in order that this Government may keep pace with other Governments of the world in this movement."

The Senate committee, however, amended the resolution to require the President to embargo arms shipments to all the nations involved in a conflict. We would therefore be unable to single out the aggressor. On May 27 I wrote the President:

"I gathered the impression from Key Pittman that he had conferred with you about a compromise amendment to the arms-embargo resolution pending before the Committee on Foreign Relations in the Senate, and that Pittman had decided to make the measure apply to both parties to any particular conflict. I did not learn whether you had finally and definitely agreed to this proposal.

"If you have not committed yourself definitely, I would suggest that, since the proposal is directly in conflict with our position at Geneva as expressed by Norman Davis, it would be well for the Government to deal with the matter in the light of this situation.

"If, in other words, certain extremists among the Senators desire to take the responsibility of preventing the adoption of the policy of peace that is being pursued by every other enlightened nation, they might be given the privilege of tying up proposed peace legislation over the next few months."

Pittman's committee, however, was obdurate in insisting that the embargo apply to both parties to a conflict, to the victim as well as to the aggressor. Consequently, we ceased to urge the passage of the measure, and it died. This was a real disappointment to me. It was the first of a series of efforts we made toward international cooperation which failed in Congress.

The Senate's action, together with the continued truculence of Germany and the unwillingness of France and other neighbors of Germany to disarm without adequate security pledges, deprived our proposals at Geneva of the force we intended they should have. The Disarmament Conference struggled on, but in vain. On October 9, when the German Ambassador, Dr. Hans Luther, a very agreeable man personally who I believe was anti-Nazi, called at my office, I told him the primary purpose of our Government was the promotion of general disarmament. "We should wage a steady contest for the disarmament of the heavily armed nations, rather than become parties to a plan for others to proceed to rearm," I said. I believed that Germany could, in the course of a few years, obtain parity of arms with other nations if she would be patient, cease the rearmament measures she was already undertaking in violation of the Versailles Treaty, and await the disarmament of other countries.

But patience to Hitler was an unknown attribute. On October 14 Germany withdrew from the Disarmament Conference. The armaments race was now on in earnest, and the Second World War came less than six years later.

The following day I told the press we were still firmly opposed to German rearmament, and I blamed Germany for taking a step that gravely imperiled the movement for the organization of peace. On October 17 Norman Davis, on our instructions, told the conference we would take part in disarmament discussions as long as there was any prospect of their being continued with success. Our Government, however, was not interested in the political elements of the purely European aspects of disarmament, and Europe, not the United States, must decide whether conditions were favorable for continuing the attempt to reach an agreement.

Some days later the conference adjourned until 1934. Disarmament was dead. Germany's disarmament was to occur under a rain of American and British aerial bombs nine, ten, and eleven years later.

On November 2 I saw Ambassador Luther again and said: "The outlook in Europe at this distance for disarmament or for peace does not appear very encouraging. A general war during the next two to ten years seems more probable than peace." I added that I felt "somewhat discouraged."

With Germany absent, the Disarmament Conference limped along for more than a year. Basic differences rose between the British and the French. The British were willing to grant Germany equality of land armaments. The French argued that such equality meant inequality for France because of Germany's superior power for manufacturing the weapons of war.

Seeing little hope of any substantial agreement on disarmament, my associates and I at the State Department turned our attention to one aspect of the problem—international supervision over the manufacture and trade in arms. When I entered the State Department, the Senate still had before it for approval the Convention for the Supervision of the International Trade in Arms and Ammunition and in Implements of War, which the United States had signed at Geneva in 1925. This set up controls over the export and import of arms and provided for full publicity on the international arms traffic. Previous Administrations had sought, unsuccessfully, to obtain its ratification.

On April 12, 1934, I wrote Senator Pittman, chairman of the Senate Foreign Relations Committee: "The ratification of this convention is an important contribution which the American Government and people can make at this time to the cause of world peace; its remaining unratified cannot fail to produce, with justification, the impression that we are indifferent to the important problems with which the Convention deals."

Several other Governments had made their ratifications conditional upon ratification by the United States. If we ratified, a sufficient number of other nations might ratify to bring the convention into force. This was particularly important because of the uncertainty as to whether the Conference at Geneva would produce a general disarmament convention, which we had hoped would include a section on the control of the international traffic in arms.

On June 15, 1934, the Senate approved the convention, but with a reservation that we did not thereby deny any right of sovereignty which Persia might have in and to the Persian Gulf. Few items were ever to cause us so much trouble as this clause. It had been introduced by Senator King of Utah, at the instance, it later developed, of the Persian Minister Ghaffar Khan Djalal. The Minister had gone direct to him over the head of the State Department.

The reservation was unacceptable to the State Department, as I wrote Senator Pittman and Senator Robinson. It appeared to recognize alleged Persian rights; whereas the Persian Gulf's shores were shared by eight powers. The reservation, I felt, would indefinitely delay the coming into effect of the convention, since we could never conceivably obtain consent to it by the other signatory powers.

I called in the Persian Minister and told him our foreign affairs were conducted primarily through the State Department and it was inexcusable for him to go directly to members of the Senate with his views. "No Government," I said, "can conduct its foreign affairs in this fashion. Any repetition of such a practice will necessarily be treated much more seriously than in the present instance."

We communicated the reservation to our Ambassadors in London and Paris and our Minister to Switzerland, Hugh Wilson, to get the informal reaction of other Governments. The reaction was unfavorable. I then recommended to the President that the convention be returned to the Senate for reconsideration of the reservation. The President first decided to wait, but then agreed. Protests continued to arrive from Persia. It was not until June 6, 1935, that the Senate approved the convention without the King reservation. A valuable year and more had been lost. The psychological moment was gone, an insufficient number of countries ratified, and the convention never went into effect.

Meantime, on May 24, 1934, I cabled Minister Wilson in Geneva that, while I had not lost hope in negotiating a general disarmament agreement that would include provisions for supervising and controlling the trade in and manufacture of arms, our Government was now willing to participate in a new and separate convention covering this one point.

Our previous attitude, as expressed in 1933, was that our willingness to take part in such international control would depend on a general disarmament agreement being reached.

Discussions lasting several months followed with other nations. Finally, on November 20, Minister Wilson presented our draft of a treaty. Difficulties had risen on this side between the State Department and the War and Navy Departments, which objected to the idea of inspection of arms manufacture and traffic by an international body. I therefore on November 22 wrote the President, who was then at Warm Springs. Pointing out the provisions of the treaty presented at Geneva, I said: "I felt that I was acting in accordance with your policy and with the ideas which you have expressed on several occasions. . . . Before proceeding further in the negotiation of this Convention, I should be grateful if I could receive your assurance that I have indeed reflected your views."

The President replied: "I see no reason why you should not tell the War Department that supervision and inspection must be all-inclusive, including all plants in all nations. That is my policy. . . . I entirely approve of the draft and am glad you have authorized Mr. Wilson to present it to the Bureau."

On February 14, 1935, the Disarmament Conference's committee on the regulation of the manufacture of and trade in armaments unanimously adopted our draft convention as the basis for its discussions. But on April 13 the committee adjourned without setting any date for its next meeting. It recognized the impossibility of continuing its work under the adverse conditions then existing.

We could at least exert pressure to prevent the export of arms from this country to Germany. Inquiries kept coming to the State Department from armaments manufacturers as to our attitude toward the export of arms to Germany. On September 18, 1934, I issued a statement saying: "The Department of State has heretofore stated to manufacturers who inquired concerning the attitude of the Department of State toward the exportation of arms or munitions of war from this country to Germany that this Government would view such exportation with grave disapproval." I appended to this statement a letter I sent to an American airplane company on the subject, pointing out that the export of military planes from the United States to Germany would violate the peace treaty between the two countries, which incorporated certain provisions of the Treaty of Versailles dealing with the disarmament of Germany.

The story of disarmament efforts between the First World War and the Second is tragic indeed. While the doctrine of peace based on disarmament was a somewhat new idea, it was generally accepted by the nations, including the United States. This was especially true since all the nations assumed that, under the leadership of the League of Nations, the law-abiding forces of the world would keep the peace, with the result that important nations could reduce their armaments by mutual agreement without endangering their security.

But the movement for general disarmament was found to be far more difficult in practice than in theory. Literally years of discussion produced comparatively minor results. The best efforts of many leading statesmen were absorbed in the disarmament conferences between 1922 and 1935, with slight avail. The very number of such conferences illustrates the work that went into an almost useless effort. The Washington Disarmament Conference of 1921–1922 was followed by the Geneva Small Arms Conference of 1925, the Geneva Naval Conference of 1927, the London Naval Conference of 1930, the General Disarmament Conference at Geneva of 1932, which was prolonged by numerous recesses through the three following years until it gradually faded out of existence, and the London Naval Conference of 1935, following a preliminary conference in 1934. Any clear-sighted statesman could see that increasing armaments meant increasing the chances of war. But an infinite number of rivalries, diversities of view, and subterfuges prevented any real achievement. Disarmament had died, and with it passed the hope of peace through disarmament.

In a speech to the Canadian Society of New York on February 16, 1935, I set forth four pillars of a sound peace structure: "First, the renunciation of war as an instrument of national policy; second, a promise of nonaggression; third, consultation in the event of a threat to peace; and fourth, noninterference on our part with such measures of constraint as may be brought against a deliberate violator of peace."

I added, however: "I should emphasize . . . that these four pillars might readily crumble were they to be built on the shifting foundations of unrestricted and competitive armaments. We have therefore insisted that a real limitation and reduction of the instruments of warfare must be an essential concomitant of any such peace program as I have outlined."

The President and I were willing to help erect all four pillars. But certain nations had other ideas. Europe even then was hell-bent toward war.

17: Germany Equals Trouble

THERE WERE MANY discouraging elements in the European situation, but the most troubling was Hitler's Germany. All the reports from Germany that flowed to my desk pointed to the dangerous change that had taken place with the advent of Hitler. There could be no shadow of doubt that Germany was rearming, with all that such rearming meant in the way of political disturbance and, eventually, war.

What was even more perturbing, however, was the vicious, new spirit engendered in Germany. A militant, Spartan psychology was permeating the German people, already intoxicated by the Prussian teachings that all Germans constituted a superior race. The Nazi leaders were seeing to it that everyone in Germany able to do so was out in the streets or fields drilling, from boys of six to eight on up to men on the edge of old age. Civilians were being trained in air and gas attacks. Hitler and his gang were in a frenzy to get the Germans to believe they had always had the world against them and were in danger from their neighbors.

Germany, like the rest of the world, was in the grip of an economic panic. This afforded Hitler greater opportunity to remake Germany in his own image. The fact must not be overlooked that the most moving and impelling influence supporting dictators' ambitions is unemployment and distress among the masses. While there is an exception now and then, it is a general rule that the largest single cause of riots, revolutions, and wars of aggression is a people in severe economic distress.

The same basic lack of honesty that frequently displayed itself in Hitler's later international dealings was already apparent in his efforts at rearmament. Germany pleaded piously at Geneva that the Nazi organizations were not military units. Nevertheless they were constantly being drilled and given military training through maneuvers, night marches with heavy knapsacks and steel helmets, map-reading, signal exercises, and rifle practice. And some factories were being quietly converted to the manufacture of weapons.

Less than three months after I entered the State Department, our Consul General at Berlin, George Messersmith, one of our ablest officials, reported to us: "I think the Department must be exceedingly careful in its dealings with Germany as long as the present Government is in power as it has no spokesman who can really be depended upon, and those who hold the highest positions are capable of actions which really outlaw them from ordinary intercourse."

He wrote also: "I think we must recognize that while the Germany of today wants peace, it is by no means a peaceful country or one looking forward to a long period of peace. The present German Government and its adherents desire peace ardently for the present because they need peace to carry through the changes in Germany which they want to bring about. What they want to do, however, definitely is to make Germany the most capable instrument of war that there has ever existed."

Messersmith, with keen insight, drew a horrifying picture of Hitler and his governing clique. "Some of them are psychopathic cases and would ordinarily be receiving treatment somewhere," he said. "Others are exalted and in a frame of mind that knows no reason. The majority are woefully ignorant and unprepared for the tasks which they have to carry through every day."

As my conversations with German Ambassador Luther got under way, Messersmith wrote: "Dr. Luther may talk bravely and fairly about Germany in the United States, but he can't tell what he knows, and even if he would, there is a great deal that he does not know. There is a real revolution here and a dangerous situation."

That revolution had repeated repercussions in the United States. Right from the beginning we faced one problem after another in our relations with Germany. I found myself calling in the German Ambassador time after time to protest against violations of the rights of our citizens, against persecution of the Jews, and against maltreatment of Americans by Nazi bullies. Feeling was rising in this country, and Ambassador Luther on his part came in to protest about boycotts by private American organizations against Germany and statements denouncing the Nazi leaders.

In March, 1933, I asked our Embassy for a full statement on the anti-Jewish movement in Germany. On May 3 I called in Dr. Luther and opened our conversation by pointing to a heap of memorials and letters by Americans of all religions and races received at the White House and State Department protesting against the mistreatment of Jews in Germany. Here was the beginning of what was soon revealed to be Hitler's amazing movement of both persecution and destruction of the Jews.

"These communications," I said, "ask my Government to take all possible steps to terminate this mistreatment. Some of them ask us to make very definite and more or less peremptory demands of your Government itself. Now this is an internal problem within Germany. Hence I have not undertaken bluntly or definitely to make complaint directly to your Government. Nevertheless, I've tried, through various representations and dispatches, to draw your Government out in a favorable direction and to encourage a return to normal conditions."

Dr. Luther then made a surprising statement. "The worst of the Jewish troubles has been over for some time," he said. "The situation is constantly improving. Germany has no purpose to expel the Jews as a race. Many laws and court agencies are becoming more and more available from week to week to protect Jews and Jewish rights and properties. And it will only be a question of a reasonable time when normal conditions and relationships will, to a measurable extent, be brought about."

How wrong he was!

I ended the conversation by emphasizing the deep-seated feeling in this country and expressing an earnest hope that every possible step be taken to relieve the anti-Jewish situation in Germany. Naturally the Ambassador would be expected to communicate these sentiments to his Government.

On May 8 Dr. Schacht, head of the German Reichsbank, who was in Washington on an official visit to prepare for the London Economic Conference, announced that his Government would cease payments abroad on Germany's external debts, totaling $5,000,000,000, of which nearly $2,000,000,000 were held by Americans. The following day I called Dr. Schacht into my office, determined to speak some bare-fisted words.

I found Schacht simple and unaffected, thoroughly approachable. He readily impressed me as one of the shrewdest persons with whom I came in contact among the delegations visiting this country prior to the London Economic Conference. Some leading Americans were convinced that Schacht was not at heart with Hitler and the Nazi programs, and remain so convinced to this day. It seemed to me that Schacht could have been like many statesmen in the South who were violently opposed to Secession but, when Secession actually came, went along with the Secession forces and played their full part. Later, during the war, I was to get indirect communications from Schacht indicating that he was not in sympathy with Hitler; but I assumed these were a maneuver to confuse us.

The moment Schacht sat down alongside my desk, I went right to the point and said, with some anger:

"I was never so deeply surprised as I was yesterday afternoon by your announcement. My Government is exercising every ounce of its power to bring the nation out of the depths of awful panic conditions, back in the direction of normal prosperity. Just as real progress is being made, you come over here and, after sitting in confidential conferences with our officials relating solely to preparations for a successful world economic conference, suddenly let it be given out from our doorstep that Germany has suspended these payments. This is to be the strangest possible course. It is greatly calculated to check and undermine American efforts to restore domestic business conditions."

I felt outraged at such a bald attempt to involve this Government in so odious an act by Germany. I said that trouble-making persons could prejudice Americans against the efforts of the Roosevelt Administration to promote better business conditions by falsely hinting that there might be some relationship between our conversations with him and his announcement that Germany had abandoned transfers to her creditors. "Any person ought to realize the serious possibilities of such steps," I added.

Dr. Schacht kept protesting that he had not foreseen or grasped these reactions. "I am extremely sorry," he said.

I gave Dr. Schacht a written memorandum which stated: "The President has directed me to say to you in regard to your communication as to the decision of the German Government to stop transfers on obligations externally sold or externally payable that he is profoundly shocked."

My vigorous conversation with Dr. Schacht had some effect in moderating this decision. At London, during the Economic Conference, we told Schacht that, if Germany's foreign exchange holdings were low, the obligations held by private citizens should be paid first, banks later. Schacht seemed in agreement, but afterwards his policy was exactly the opposite.

Hitlerite Germany's attitude toward her financial obligations to American citizens was typical of her attitude toward her obligations generally. Hitler and his financial crowd had worked out what they considered an ingenious system to enrich and rearm Germany at the expense of others. Following the Dawes loan in 1924, American private investors subscribed in the next six years—that is, until the panic—to over $1,000,-000,000 in bonds of the German Government, states, and corporations. American banks advanced German borrowers another $1,000,000,000 in short-term credits. Even after the panic, Germany continued payments on this indebtedness, but when Hitler came into power he soon manifested an intention to suspend payment on all foreign debt.

Toward the end of 1933, the German Government perpetrated one of its numerous colossal frauds. It announced it would pay 50 per cent of the interest on its foreign bonds in cash and 50 per cent in scrip. The scrip could be sold to a German Government-controlled bank for reichsmarks at half its face value. Germany was therefore paying only 75 per cent of the interest payments. The remaining 25 per cent was turned over to German exporters to subsidize exports. Later on, interest was discontinued altogether.

What then happened was that German bonds over here fell to very little. The Germans said they did not have enough dollar exchange to make the interest payments but, when the bonds fell, they released enough dollar exchange to buy their depreciated bonds in the open market. They permitted their exporters to keep part of the dollars they received from their exports to America and to buy the bonds at low prices with this exchange. The exporters could then sell the bonds to the German Government at par in reichsmarks, and utilize their profits to subsidize further exports. In this way 85 to 90 per cent of these bonds were repurchased in America by Germany at great loss to American investors. In devilish fashion the Germans tied in nonpayment of bond interest, depreciation of bond prices, redemption of bonds at these low prices, and subsidization of German exports. And at the same time they were able to continue their enormous purchases of material that went into armaments.

In the same way the value of American-owned factories in Germany, estimated at about $250,000,000, greatly declined because the German Government would not permit the profits of the companies to be converted into dollars and brought over here. These factories were later to prove of high value to Hitler's war machine. Germany also discontinued payments on her $400,000,000 debt to our Government for the Mixed Claims Commission. In general, what payments she did make on her indebtedness she made more liberally to other countries, thereby discriminating against us. Of the creditor countries we were in the most disadvantageous position because the others bought more from Germany than they sold to her, and could, if they desired, impound the difference for the payment of German interest.

This was a wholesale dishonest and fraudulent policy of the German Government to rearm on a gigantic scale by robbing and defrauding all other governments and their citizens of every possible penny. It was a gross fraud to acquire money and materials for virtually nothing in order to promote Germany's scheme of rearmament without precedent in magnitude. A government, in my opinion, has no more privilege than a private citizen to be dishonest. In fact a government has even less privilege, because the private citizen can have recourse to the courts, while there is much less recourse against a foreign government.

Germany was using every cunning currency device known to perverted economic minds to obtain unfair advantage over other nations. She invented nearly a score of different types of reichsmarks with varying exchange rates and methods of conversion into other currencies. A nation that made an economic agreement with Germany seldom knew what it was getting in return. Confusion was the prime commodity. Suppose the United States had nearly twenty different kinds of dollars, one for use within the country, one for the use of tourists coming here, others for certain types of imports, still others for certain countries!

At the London Economic Conference I was too occupied with the work of the Conference to conduct particular discussions with the Germans on our relations with their Government. When I returned to America, however, the criminations and recriminations went on.

On August 11, 1933, the German Chargé d'Affaires, Rudolf Leitner, called on me to protest against a boycott of German commerce because of the Jewish situation in Germany. "The best remedy," I told him, "will be for the German people or German Government or both to stop whatever may be their activities against the Jews. This will enable us to make suitable appeals to discontinue the boycott."

On September 5 I called in the German Chargé to protest against an unprovoked Nazi attack on two Americans in Germany. There had already been many similar attacks on Americans, generally because they did not give the Nazi salute. I told him these attacks occurred when police were present who took no action against the Nazi assailants. The Nazis remained unpunished. "I think you will agree," I said, "that continuance of these assaults on American citizens will very soon compel this Government to make formal, vigorous, and open protest to your Government."

"It is the custom of many countries," Dr. Leitner replied, "for foreign visitors to salute the flag of the country on all proper occasions."

"Having served in the Army," I rejoined, "I early learned this propriety. But, while a vast number of Americans observe this practice both at home and when traveling abroad, there are also a large number, including supposedly intelligent persons, who, to my knowledge, violate it here at home. They would naturally fail in the same manner when traveling abroad."

Dr. Leitner said that, so far as he knew, his Government was disposed to be diligent in guarding against such assaults as I complained of and in punishing the offenders.

I wound up the conversation by saying: "I am seeking to keep a hundred miles away from an emergency that would cause my Government to feel obliged to warn all Americans to stay out of Germany."

When Ambassador Luther came in on September 21 to make further protest against the boycotts against German goods, I said to him: "We have undergone the most bitter criticism in our efforts to refrain from criticizing the German Government on account of its internal Jewish policies. More than once I have sent for Congressmen and Senators and urged them not to go beyond the proper bounds. My hope was that we might all the sooner secure readjustments of this delicate situation in Germany. Also that we might avoid the possible risk of causing increased mistreatment of the Jews instead of lessening it.

"When Congress meets next January," I warned, "there will likely be a flood of denunciation of the German Government and nationals on account of their attitude toward the Jews in Germany, unless the facts entirely change. If the German Government will bring about a cessation of this treatment of the Jews, it will then be possible to check boycotting and similar incidents in the United States."

The subject of additional assaults on Americans in Germany came up, and to test him out I asked the Ambassador: "What do you think about the idea of my Government making an announcement that unless Americans intending to visit Germany do give the Nazi salute on appropriate occasions, they must not expect the protection of the American Government if they are assaulted?"

"I think that is too drastic," he replied hastily.

On October 14 Germany withdrew from the League of Nations. On November 23 Consul General Messersmith wrote the Department from Berlin: "Everything that is being done in the country today has for its object to make the people believe that Germany is threatened vitally in every aspect of its life by outside influences and by other countries. Everything is being done to use this feeling to stimulate military training and exercises, and innumerable measures are being taken to develop the German people into a hardy, sturdy race which will be able to meet all comers. The military spirit is constantly growing. It cannot be otherwise. The leaders of Germany today have no desire for peace unless it is a peace which the world makes at the expense of complete compliance with German desires and ambitions."

Messersmith pointed out that Germany would attempt particularly to embarrass France by making protestations of her willingness to do all sorts of things with the hope of making trouble between France and England and the United States. This became, in fact, one of the motives of Hitler's later mancuvers to split France and Britain, to split Britain and the United States, and to split all three from Russia.

In my first year in the State Department I had no doubts as to Hitlerite Germany's intentions and capacities. But, had I had any, the events of 1934 and the first half of 1935 would have completely removed them.

Hitler's ruthlessness was written in blood in the purge of June 30, 1934, when he had nearly one hundred persons of influence executed, including former Chancellor Kurt von Schleicher and Captain Ernst Röhm, commander of his Storm Troops. Whatever may have been his justification in the alleged plotting of these men against him, the methods he employed shocked the world. They were a portent of the disregard for human life he was later to evince.

Since this was an internal German event, not affecting the United States or our citizens, there was no step we could take. I was drawn into it indirectly, however, by an impulsive speech of condemnation made by General Hugh Johnson, head of the NRA, in consequence of which the German Chargé d'Affaires, Dr. Leitner, protested. I told Dr. Leitner that it was to be regretted that the position in the Government occupied by General Johnson made it possible for remarks uttered by him as an individual to be misconstrued as official. I then issued a statement to this effect and wirelessed it to the President, aboard the cruiser *Houston,* with this ending: "I hope you approve." The President replied the following day: "Your July 13 [message] cordially approved."

Many of our ambassadors abroad cabled me the conviction of the Governments to which they were accredited that the June 30 purge meant the beginning of the end of Hitler. Ambassador Bullitt in Moscow quoted a very high Soviet official as saying he did not expect Hitler's regime to last long, that Hitler would henceforth be compelled to rely solely on the German Army and big industrialists, and that the economic future of Germany was hopeless. I did not share this optimism.

In July, 1934, occurred the assassination of Austrian Chancellor Engelbert Dollfuss, engineered by Germany and Austrian Nazis. The

President and I telegraphed our regrets and sympathy, but there was no other move to take. Here again the new Nazi mentality was revealing that any means were licit, however despicable, toward achieving its aims, however illegal.

President Hindenburg of Germany died August 2, 1934, whereupon Hitler assumed Hindenburg's authority and merged the office of President with that of Chancellor. There was now no authority in Germany to challenge his ambitions.

On March 16, 1935, Hitler announced the reinstitution of military conscription. Germany thereby tossed overboard the military clauses of the Treaty of Versailles. She announced that her army would embrace thirty-six divisions, or more than a half-million men. She was clearly preparing for conquest.

The United States was not a signatory to the Treaty of Versailles, but on March 22 I told a press conference: "Everybody knows that the United States has always believed that treaties must constitute the foundation on which any stable peace structure must rest. All who believe in peaceful settlement of international problems of all kinds have felt increasing concern over the tendency to fail to live up to the letter and spirit of treaties. I believe that the moral influence of the United States and its people must always encourage living up to treaties."

Britain, France, and, to some degree, Italy were conferring among themselves and making representations to Germany. I told the press conference that we were closely following their efforts and hoped they might succeed in their purpose to effect some settlement. Their efforts, however, were fruitless.

German Ambassador Luther came to see me on March 28 and began his conversation by saying: "I hope there will be no misunderstanding about the true attitude of my Government on political and peace questions." He left this general statement hanging in the air, without any attempt to put supports under it.

I thereupon remarked: "Your Government right now has a greater opportunity than any within two generations to make a remarkable showing of leadership. The leadership I mean is with a program that will gradually bring Western Europe to normal political, social, and peaceful relations. Now the nations can either take this course or they can continue aloof from each other and misunderstand each other's motives and objectives. The result will be that each country will go on and arm to the teeth on an ever increasing scale. And then perhaps some local incident will ignite a spark that will start a conflagration which ultimately will not leave a vestige of Western civilization."

Hastily the Ambassador interposed: "My Government follows no other course than that of peace."

"We are simply speaking here as individuals interested in the peace and progress of the world," I went on. "But it would be wonderfully interesting to see whether the statesmanship of Europe goes forward with high purposes and objectives and the spirit necessary to reach them or whether it becomes bankrupt and collapses and swims with the tide toward more friction, fear, suspicion, and opportunities for war."

I then ran down the list of reported German objectives—Polish Corridor, Austria, Memel, part of Czechoslovakia, and the like. As I mentioned each one, Dr. Luther promptly disclaimed it as an objective and said, "Germany favors peace."

"What about disarmament?" I asked.

"My Government is willing to disarm on relative equality with other governments."

I repeated that his Government had an almost unprecedented opportunity for leadership with a program back to normal peace conditions. At the same time I emphasized: "It is easy to lose this opportunity or to throw it away amidst the many difficult and chaotic things that are being said, done, or threatened. It will take a resolute person, strongly bent on the goal of stability in international affairs, if such leadership is to succeed."

No doubt Ambassador Luther reported this full conversation to the German Foreign Office. But my exhortations had no effect. Hitler had leadership in mind, all right, but a leadership directed toward conquest and domination.

Ominous indications began coming to me in those early years of closer and closer relations between Germany and Japan. A note from the Military Attaché in our Berlin Embassy, dated May 17, 1934, stated: "For some time past evidence has been accumulating which tends to show the existence of unusually close and friendly relations between Germany and Japan even to the extent of a possible secret alliance. Japan has apparently taken the more active part in establishing these relations, but she has met with a ready response from Germany, especially from the Nazi Government."

On March 22, 1935, Ambassador Dodd cabled me from Berlin concerning a conversation he had with the Japanese Ambassador to Germany.

The Japanese revealed he had been in three conversations in one week with officials of the more belligerent wing of the German Cabinet and said that Japan was pressing the Germans to ask for the restoration of German naval strength.

It was therefore obvious that we had to watch not only a rapidly rearming Germany or a militant, conquering Japan, but a combination or alliance of both, working hand in hand to bring pressure to bear on other nations at strategic moments and places, and being joined in due course by Fascist Italy. The events to come were assuming shape.

In an address on May 5, 1934, to the alumni of my alma mater, Cumberland University, I said: "Today numerous nations are feverishly arming. They are taxing all of their citizens beyond the limit of ability to pay, and in many ways developing a military spirit which, regardless of present motives of self-defense, may probably lead to war, unless past human experience is to be reversed. . . . It would be both a blunder and a crime for civilized peoples to fail much longer to take notice of present dangerous tendencies which negative every idea of friendliness and of the spirit of the good neighbor."

My first few months in the State Department forecast our relations with Germany in the years to come. It was evident that a German Government without any regard for the rights of their own citizens or the citizens of other countries was in power. It was clear that the usual methods of approach to such a Government were of little avail. It was already manifest that Hitler was arming for a later trial of strength. And it was more than clear that our difficulties with Germany would multiply as time went on.

The last thing I had in mind was to be easy toward Germany. Having closely followed the course and methods of Germany from the inception of the World War and especially from the time of Hitler's assumption of power, nothing was more convincing to me than that the German Government was pursuing policies of gross unfairness, discrimination, fraudulent manipulation, and swindling of other nations out of billions of dollars by subterfuge and false representations while Hitler went forward feverishly with the work of building up vast military strength. It was therefore clear to me that we should on every possible occasion emphasize to our own people and to the democracies of Europe the dangers inherent in this new and terrible Germany, and to take all steps possible to show to the German Government our unalterable opposition to all plans of aggrandizement based on force or threat.

18: Economics and the Conference

EVERY BLOSSOM that unfolded in Washington in the spring of 1933 seemed to contain an economic problem. The President was struggling with terrific domestic conditions and seeking the best possible remedies. A feeling existed that extremely drastic remedies had to be adopted, including some that might help only temporarily.

The string of tremendous questions forcing themselves on the attention of our Government related both to the domestic and to the international situation. There was opportunity in this connection for differences to rise between those in the Government dealing with domestic economic problems and those dealing with international economic problems. This, in some vital respects, is what later occurred.

In the very center of the international highway lay the granite rock of political and economic isolation, in this as well as in other countries. As we sought to budge this boulder, such problems as exchange stabilization, debts, reparations, monetary difficulties, disarmament, trade barriers, and the increasing activities of dictators, rapidly becoming of serious concern to peaceful nations, pressed upon us.

As I entered the State Department our Government was already preparing for the Economic Conference to be held in London. The preparatory meetings under the auspices of the League of Nations had been held at Geneva, and an elaborate agenda drawn up. By way of further preparation, the President invited eleven nations with whom we had large commercial relations to send representatives to Washington to discuss economic questions with us. With Prime Minister MacDonald leading off in point of time, Edouard Herriot of France, Richard Bennett of Canada, Guido Jung of Italy, Hjalmar Schacht of Germany, T. V. Soong of China, and Viscount Ishii of Japan, among others, came to us. With those concerned we entered into detailed discussions of the Disarmament Conference, war debts, stabilization of currencies, and lowering of tariff barriers.

The President, in a radio address on May 7, 1933, listed four objectives in the talks. They were: reduction of armaments; cutting down of trade barriers; stabilization of currencies, in order that commercial firms could make contracts ahead; and reestablishment of friendly relations and greater confidence between all nations. In addition, the President and MacDonald had a special conference on war debts, with no results accomplished.

My participation in war debts was small. The President had confided this subject to Assistant Secretary Moley. It was more a Treasury than a State Department question, I felt, and besides, I believed war debts were becoming a dead horse. I was content not to be too involved.

At about this time Moley came one morning to my apartment. His face was serious, and he proceeded to say to me that he did not seek my position as Secretary of State, contrary to any rumors to that effect. After he left I remarked to another visitor, "Moley at least has the subject on his mind." This was later confirmed in numerous ways, culminating at the London Conference.

The talks with the visiting foreign leaders were most interesting— and most unfruitful. They were not intended to reach agreements but only to prepare for the London Conference. Each of the conferences was without particular controversy, whatever may have been in the back of the minds of the leading participants. The communiqués issued on each occasion were in line with this view—and contained little substance. The sum total of them all was almost precisely nothing. Moreover, the time taken up in talking to and entertaining these foreign delegations cut down the time available for the careful preparation of our Government's policies for the coming world conference and the instructions for carrying out these policies. Still more time was absorbed in discussions with the ambassadors or ministers of forty-two other countries who had been invited to discuss their views with us though not to send special representatives.

Each Government not only had differing attitudes on a number of the main topics, but each was changing or modifying its previous attitude. This Government, after discussing war debts with MacDonald and others, decided that the American delegation should not deal with debts at the London Conference. After debating both temporary and permanent stabilization and favoring action especially on the former, the Administration later instructed the American delegation to London to have nothing to do with temporary stabilization, which seemed uppermost in the minds of certain other important Governments. After elaborately discussing trade barriers, with tariff reductions the central point, and expressing a favorable attitude toward them, the Administration later modified its position.

The truth of the whole pre-conference situation was that nations were extremely active in discussing the important topics on the agenda, but with an astonishing amount of confusion and lack of system or orderly procedure designed for deliberation and clean-cut decisions. The proceedings prior to the conference grew increasingly unstable and almost chaotic. It was in this state of turmoil, cross-purposes, and frequent changes of positions by Governments that the Conference was to meet.

For a time before I left for London, it looked as if no serious obstacles would arise to my putting into effect the ideas I had entertained for nearly thirty years on the necessity for lowering tariffs and other trade barriers. At the State Department we began to draft a bill for submission to Congress authorizing the Executive to negotiate reciprocal trade agreements based on the unconditional most-favored-nation principle. This principle meant that when mutual tariff reductions were made by this and another country, we automatically extended them to other nations provided those nations gave us the same nondiscriminatory treatment. The effect would be to spread trade relations wider and wider over the world as such agreements based on the most-favored-nation doctrine went into effect.

It was my understanding with the President that he would present the bill to Congress shortly. This bill was similar to our later Trade Agreements Act of 1934, but contained the additional proviso that any tariff-reduction agreements entered into would be subject to veto by Congress within sixty days and would become fully operative if Congress did not act within that time.

There were some signs of approaching trouble in the fact that the new agencies, National Recovery Administration and Agricultural Adjustment Administration, were coming into being with their own remedies for recovery. Basically, they believed in cutting the United States off from the rest of the economic world, which they regarded as of little importance. They wanted to concentrate on lifting prices and restoring business in this country by purely domestic measures. As prices rose they felt the need for import embargoes and higher tariffs to keep out imports from abroad which would interfere with the increasing price scale.

The United States went partly off the gold standard on March 6, 1933, with a prohibition against the export of gold, and entirely off the gold standard in April. The President's financial advisers believed they could lift and control prices by changing the gold content of the dollar. With the dollar fluctuating wildly in terms of other currencies, our chances of negotiating trade questions with other nations were rendered all the more difficult. But on April 3 the President, in a message to Congress on farm-mortgage refinancing, said he would ask for authority to initiate "practical reciprocal tariff agreements . . . to break through trade barriers and establish foreign markets for farm and industrial products."

At the beginning of May, 1933, with the President's concurrence, I instructed Mr. Norman Davis, then in London, to propose a temporary tariff truce to the organizing committee of the London Economic Conference. Other nations backed and filled but finally accepted, with various reservations and interpretations.

On May 20 Moley suddenly made a radio speech without consulting me in any way, before or after, in which he definitely discounted the beneficial results to be obtained at London, even if the conference should be successful. He said foreign trade was of little importance. This speech was broadcast throughout America as the actual position of the Administration—to the prejudice of the position later embodied in the instructions to the American delegation to London. And it was broadcast repeatedly through Europe, thereby impairing the standing of the American delegation, especially myself. In the circumstances Moley deserved a severe call-down from the President, but unfortunately Mr. Roosevelt sometimes gave his intimates undue liberties over his other friends.

Only when the American delegation, which I headed, was ready to sail for London at the end of May was the question of a conflict between the reduction of tariff and trade barriers at London and the high-tariff demands of the NRA. and AAA., especially the former, raised and briefly discussed. I stood firmly for the purposes I had in mind for the London Conference, principally tariff reductions, and no action was taken to the contrary until after we were on the high seas.

On May 30 the President received the delegation consisting of five other members in addition to myself: former Governor James M. Cox as vice chairman; Senator Key Pittman, Democrat of Nevada; Senator James Couzens, Republican of Michigan; Representative Samuel D. McReynolds, Democrat of Tennessee; and Ralph W. Morrison, retired banker and cotton dealer of San Antonio, Texas. The President had appointed these members without consulting me.

Mr. Roosevelt gave us a memorandum on policy to be followed in London. The major problems he requested us to take up at once with the conference were: a tariff truce for the duration of the conference; establishment of general principles of a coordinated monetary and fiscal policy; removal of foreign-exchange restrictions; an international monetary standard; basic agreement for gradual abolition of artificial barriers to trade and for reduction of tariffs; agreement for control of production and distribution of certain basic commodities. I took with me six resolutions covering these topics to introduce at London.

As I sailed aboard the steamship *President Roosevelt* from New York on May 31, I had in my pocket a copy of the reciprocal Trade Agreements Bill which was now on the President's desk. I expected to be able to show this to other delegations at London and to use it to prove to them we were sincere in our efforts to reduce tariffs and also had the power to do so. I hoped that by the time the conference was well under way the President would have submitted the bill to Congress and that it would have been passed. As events developed, I was not in a position to bring it up except for information.

During the trip I began a custom I followed on many similar boat trips to and from conferences in the following years—hard work aboard ship. I have been lucky enough never to be seasick. In the roughest weather I have been able to read and write with facility. I took exercise in long walks around the deck and an occasional game of deck golf. I conducted several conferences each day with the delegates and experts on board and kept in touch with Washington by wireless.

I reflected that, of the three chief economic questions interesting the larger nations at that moment, I was really able to discuss only one at London. The three were war debts, immediate stabilization of currencies, and reduction of trade and tariff barriers. War debts were ruled out completely. Stabilization of currencies was to be discussed at London, but only by Treasury and Federal Reserve experts apart from the conference, not by the American delegation. There still remained the reduction of trade barriers.

Thereupon I began receiving aboard the steamer wireless messages from Washington concerning new legislation to raise—not lower—tariffs and impose import quotas, and indicating that the President would not submit the Trade Agreements Bill to Congress. A week after sailing I wirelessed the President, on June 7:

"I earnestly trust reports are unfounded that Congress will not be asked for executive authority to negotiate reciprocal commercial treaties based on mutual tariff concessions with right of Congressional veto included as per State Department draft of bill. My deliberate judgment is that, in addition to most seriously handicapping the mission of our delegation to the London Economic Conference, it would be a major error to defer until 1934 any authority thus to negotiate this type of commercial treaty.

"My profound belief is that by the end of the first year of your Administration the American accomplishments possible at the London Conference, even if only moderately successful at this first session, will constitute the most outstanding single achievement of your Administration. The attitude of your Government on this vital matter will naturally greatly affect the nature of my address at the opening of the conference. Furthermore, it seems to me that such an eventuality would necessitate serious alterations in your instructions to the delegation and that the delegation would be reduced to a passive role at the conference rather than the active role contemplated."

The President replied:

"I wholly understand and approve your anxiety for tariff action at this session. The situation in these closing days of the session is so full of dynamite that immediate adjournment is necessary. Otherwise bonus legislation, paper money inflation, etc., may be forced. . . . Therefore, tariff legislation seems not only highly inadvisable, but impossible of achievement.

"You have full authority to negotiate in London general reciprocal commercial treaties based on mutual tariff concessions. Negotiation requires no prior Congressional authorization. In addition, there is no reason why you cannot arrange for conferences to be held in Washington looking to definite reciprocal agreements with individual nations. All such agreements, both general and bilateral, would be submitted for approval as soon as Congress reassembles."

This message was a terrific blow. It swept from under me one of the prime reasons for going to London, one of the chief bases I had for hoping that real results could be achieved at the conference to lift the nations, albeit gradually, out of the world depression. The fundamental difference between my position and what the President advocated in his telegram was as follows.

To me it was essential that Congress grant the Executive authority to negotiate reciprocal trade agreements embracing tariff reductions within certain limits, such agreements to enter into effect without Senatorial approval. This was what was done later, in June, 1934. But what the President suggested was the negotiation of tariff treaties on the old basis, which meant they had to be submitted for Senate approval by a two-thirds majority. This method offered me no aid or encouragement because no American Senate had ever approved a trade treaty negotiated by the Executive which materially reduced tariffs, especially when negotiated without prior Congressional authority. Such a tariff reduction proposal was always beaten outright or filibustered to death after the protected interests brought pressure on their Congressmen.

This, therefore, was the only leeway open to the delegation, to propose to another country or countries to negotiate for tariff reductions, but subject, in the case of the United States, to Senate consent. It was a dismal and hopeless prospect. To add to this discouraging outlook, the advisers of the President reached the conclusion that some of the domestic measures for business and industrial recovery would require either an actual tariff embargo or full discretionary authority vested in the President to increase tariff rates when domestic policy might call for it.

When I arrived in London, I found that delegations of other countries were well aware of the severely handicapped situation in which the American delegation was thus left. The President announced on June 9 he was not going to send tariff legislation to Congress. The other delegations promptly shied away from any treaties that would be left indefinitely in the lap of Congress. I could talk to the conference about a reduction of trade barriers and urge steps that seemed feasible in addition to the tariff truce that was agreed to for the duration of the session —but the other delegations considered this but little more than mere talk. Our inability to offer a practical program of tariff reduction was one of the major reasons for the constant criticism heaped on the American delegation, especially by the London and Paris press. I had represented to Washington that the hands of the delegation would be virtually tied in the circumstances and under the plans of our Government—and they were tied indeed.

On June 11, the day before the conference opened, the President cabled me:

"Please do not worry about situation here in regard to tariff reductions and removal of trade obstacles. The eleventh-hour rows in Congress over domestic problems made general tariff debate dangerous to our whole program.

"I am squarely behind you and nothing said or done here will hamper your efforts. There is no alteration of your policy or mine. Remember, too, that if we can get treaties signed we can call special session of Senate alone in the autumn to consider ratification."

But there was no hope here for me. The President was behind me in words, but I needed actions, too, if I was to have any success in London.

The highly important fact, however, should not be overlooked that wide divergencies existed between almost all nations about an acceptable method of reducing trade barriers. Great Britain was moving toward a quota system. Some of the gold-standard countries like France, Belgium, Holland, and Switzerland were demanding temporary stabilization of currencies before they would consider tariff reduction. Others demanded other prerequisites such as war-debt relief.

It is possible, although no one can make a certified prediction on this point, that, had the American delegation been clothed with full authority to function and to furnish leadership with a definite program of tariff revision, something real might have been accomplished. Certainly most of the nations assembled at London faced domestic and international difficulties similar to ours, which urgently called for remedy. If the United States delegation, right from the beginning, could have offered definite workable proposals for trade-barrier revisions downward, with aggressive leadership in support of them, it would have greatly encouraged the whole spirit and doctrine of international cooperation. This might have meant a splendid beginning, with greater possibilities ahead.

But powerful special-privilege groups, clinging desperately to high tariffs to protect their interests, were never more active in each country, including our own, than before and as I arrived in London. The isolationist and ultranationalist groups kept pace with their movements. Numerous individuals and minorities were peddling their economic remedies which, in the main, were absurd or hopelessly unsound. There was never such a mix-up of discordant elements, of isolationism, or such utter working at cross-purposes and such lack of stable plans and ideas.

In my own country the people, already extremely nationalistic before the panic, had, if possible, in their desperation and distress, become more so. The Government, which had looked favorably on temporary stabilization, removal of excessive trade barriers, and some discussion of debts, found domestic conditions so chaotic by the time the conference convened that its mind was first centered entirely on finding some way to increase prices of commodities. The gold-standard countries, such as France, became consumed with the idea that temporary stabilization was an indispensable prerequisite to consideration of the conference's agenda.

Little wonder is it that, when the delegates reached London with all this background of indescribable confusion, the conference was not able to function with much definiteness or satisfaction. Never in my life have I witnessed such bewildering movements and utterances containing the most surprising changes of opinion without a moment's notice to anyone. There was never so much milling around and tugging and pulling as characterized this conference. It seemed to be moving and operating most of the time in a dense fog. Here the demagogue, the agitator, the perverse person, and the chronic critic could keep thoroughly busy.

These contradictory views and attitudes characterizing the London Conference extended into the American delegation. There were high-tariff members such as Senator Key Pittman; there were conflicting approaches to the currency stabilization question and virtually all other questions. Few mistakes can be more unfortunate than for the official head of a delegation to a world conference not to have a chance to consult with the President on the selection of the entire personnel—or at least let the personnel have that distinct impression. Otherwise there is little sense of loyalty or teamwork on the part of some, and open defiance from others. This has been my experience.

My own belief was that we really could carry out international measures to lift the economic level of the world without interfering with domestic measures. I saw no real reason why our domestic program should interfere with orderly reduction of trade barriers in London. The fact was that, in the preceding three and a half years, world commerce had fallen from fifty billion dollars per year to less than fifteen billions, and our share of that huge loss was about one-sixth. If we could regain the previous figure of fifty billions, we would take long strides out of the gully of depression.

Some of the President's economic advisers at home evidently did not grasp fully the methods I had in mind for lowering or removing in the most cautious manner and over a period of time the objectionable trade barriers existing everywhere. Therefore they recommended that the London Conference, in effect, abandon any serious interference with trade barriers and restrictions which were dragging the world to its knees. They did not realize that these reductions or removals, if permitted to be undertaken, could be effective. They were unable to look ahead and see how our own American trade-agreements program, begun in 1934, avoided shocks to industry or agriculture and took account of lack of time for readjustment by pursuing a practice of the most careful administration over a period of some years. It was such a practical course as we later pursued with our trade agreements policy that I was most anxious to see adopted and projected into the future by the London Conference.

I left for London with the highest of hopes, but arrived with empty hands.

19: The Conference Fails

KING GEORGE V opened the Monetary and Economic Conference in London on June 12, 1933, and Prime Minister MacDonald followed him on the rostrum. It had been definitely agreed before the conference that war debts would not be discussed or mentioned in the course of the proceedings. MacDonald, however, baldly referred to these debts and supported the British view advocating their reduction. This created among the delegates a commotion bordering on dismay.

I suggested, and my delegation was of the same mind, that we ignore MacDonald's transgression, and I would deliver my speech accordingly. The text of my address was then in Washington to receive the President's approval. Mr. Roosevelt's changes did not arrive in time for me to speak at the scheduled hour, and my speech had to be postponed. This was wrongly interpreted as indicating resentment at MacDonald's mention of war debts.

I was not able to speak until June 14. I no longer had much to offer concretely, but at least I could make an effort to inspire the delegates of the sixty-six nations with the ideas of economics and peace for which I had fought, especially since 1916. "The cherished idea of the extreme type of isolationist," I said, "that each nation singly can, by bootstrap methods, lift itself out of the troubles that surround it has proven fruitless. Each nation by itself can to a moderate extent restore conditions by suitable fiscal, financial, and economic steps. Thus the Administration of President Roosevelt has within three months adopted an effective domestic program to promote business improvement in the fullest possible measure. The equal necessity for an equally important international economic program of remedies is clear."

Although I was arguing against some economic isolation prophets in my own country as well as abroad, I went on: "The more extreme proponents of these disastrous policies in operation during the postwar period, in a spirit of mistaken selfishness or unreasoning fear, have insisted strenuously upon the very minimum of economic contacts with other nations. Their slogan has been the talismanic word 'prosperity,' and each nation living by itself was to grow rich and the people everywhere were to wax fat and be clothed in purple and fine linen. In their eyes it was unpatriotic not to buy homemade goods regardless of costs."

256

I urged that the conference "should proclaim that economic nationalism as imposed upon the various nations is a discredited policy; and from those who insist that the world should continue in this discredited policy the conference must turn aside. Many measures indispensable to full and satisfactory business recovery are beyond the powers of individual states. The extreme difficulty is manifest of one nation by itself undertaking largely to reduce its tariffs or to remove exchange restrictions or to stabilize its exchange and currency or to restore the international financial credit and trade structure."

Hundreds of thousands of words were to flow from that same rostrum in the following weeks. But there were few constructive actions. We moved in vicious circles. I wanted tariff reductions but could offer nothing satisfactory myself. France and the gold-bloc countries wanted currency stabilization before they would consider tariff reductions, but I could not talk about it. Britain and others wanted debt settlement, but I could not discuss it.

A Secretary of State at the head of a delegation to a great world conference is under a heavy handicap if his hands are thus bound. It is often most important to him to know the state of mind of other delegations regarding some portion of the program. But he cannot get to know this state of mind accurately if the ideas of those delegations are influenced by the status of other negotiations pending between their governments and ours, into which he may not enter.

I was in no sense impressed by my surroundings. I felt that the fundamentals of the problems and remedies were not being dealt with properly. I knew that our country and others, from the overthrow of Wilson's program, had been consistently pursuing a policy of nationalism, economic and political, which was becoming ever more narrow. This policy of each nation living in a separate compartment by itself was a chief, if not the chief, factor in bringing on the panic at the end of the 1920's.

To pursue this course still further, instead of carrying out the economic hopes of the London Conference, seemed to me to be treading farther on a disastrous course. All nations were thinking only of themselves, forgetting that in a betterment of world conditions lay the possibility for their own advancement. Since surplus-producing countries had their surpluses dammed up by hopeless obstructions on every international boundary, with resultant widespread unemployment and vast distress because universal embargoes prevented their securing adequate necessities, I believed there was no domestic program that should prevent careful, gradual, and reasonable steps at London to restore international commerce.

As the conference began to organize, other leading Governments proposed that I be made chairman of the economic committee which embraced tariffs and trade barriers. Anxious as I would have been for this position in other circumstances, I promptly declined because the American delegation had been stripped of any real authority to function in this field.

Governor Cox was then suggested as chairman of the monetary committee, to which I agreed. Cox and I had been colleagues in Congress and warm personal friends throughout the years. I entertained the highest regard for his great ability and equipment for the duties of chairman of this committee. He exercised splendid tact and skill in dealing with the numerous ticklish monetary questions that came up. He was hopelessly handicapped, however, in the light of the kaleidoscopic moves taken by different Governments to improvise some sort of monetary arrangement to pull them out of the panic.

Discouraging as it was, the conference had a few lighter shades. Mrs. Hull and I attended King George's reception. We had also planned a much-needed little outing that required us to go from the reception to a country place some miles distant. The strain of trying to build something at the conference with inadequate materials was wearing me down, and I felt obliged, in justice to my condition, to get this rest at all hazards. The crowd at the King's reception, including delegates from the sixty-six countries, was so tremendous that, after waiting for a considerable time until further delay would render my trip impossible, I suggested that my associates and I depart quietly. I had failed in an effort to reach the King by a near cut. I learned later that I had scarcely left when the King sent for me but was told I was not on the grounds.

I thereupon made known to the proper British officials my desire to call on the King at his pleasure. An immediate, favorable reply came back. I found the King very democratic. He received me cordially and spoke highly of the American people. We then had an easy, friendly conversation of some thirty minutes on the conference and its objectives. We agreed on the importance of the topics listed on the agenda and the necessity for a suitable solution of each. King George remarked that he expected to see me further at a later stage of the conference. That moment, unfortunately, did not arrive.

A delegation from the Pilgrims of Great Britain invited me to attend their luncheon. I promptly declined, saying I was too busy and that to make a speech would require more preparation than I could afford to give to it at that time. They insisted, however, that the luncheon was informal, I would not have to make a speech, and need only shake hands with the personages present. On those conditions I consented.

When the day arrived, I found that luncheon a very elaborate affair, with an immense crowd of top notables. I sat on one side of Lord Derby, president of the Pilgrims, with MacDonald on the other. Toward the close of the luncheon, I saw Lord Derby reach in his pocket and draw out a manuscript.

"What's that?" I asked.

"That's my speech of introduction," he replied. "First I shall introduce MacDonald, who will make a speech. Then I shall introduce Lord Reading, who will make a speech. And then I shall introduce you, and you can say what you like."

I felt as if ten cannon had been fired at me. I said nothing more but drew myself together as if I were dodging a bullet. I began to jot down notes on the back of my menu. And then, before I knew it, Lord Derby was introducing me.

I rose. Instead of talking just a few seconds to say how glad I was to be present, I proceeded to talk for twenty minutes. I went directly into my views, first on democracy, then on economics, on isolation, and on what I thought the conference should accomplish. A moment after I sat down two notes were passed up to me, one from Governor Cox, the other from Senator Pittman. Each said, "Best speech I ever heard you make."

The conference began to show unmistakable signs of bogging down. At that moment we got word that the President was sending Raymond Moley to London as a liaison man to inform us about the latest developments in Washington. Vivid press dispatches began to flow in about Moley's dramatic airplane flight to see the President on Mr. Roosevelt's yacht and the bustle and speculation attending Moley's departure from Washington and New York. It was made to appear to the public everywhere that he was coming with new instructions or a message from the President or possibly even to take over the American delegation. From that moment on, for the seven days he was on the high seas, the conference marked time. The press in London carried big headlines that Moley, "the man who controlled Presidents," was on his way to London to look after American interests there. The Paris press became highly wrought up and rawhided me in rough fashion, indicating that I had proved incapable of handling the situation for my Government.

Moley's reception in London was surpassed only by those given to kings. Delegations of high officials, newspapermen, and others, their emotions roused, hurried down to Plymouth to meet him and vie with one another in paying him tribute. Upon reaching London he called at my office, shook hands, paid his respects, and met the delegation. The press desiring to interview him, I accompanied him to the meeting but kept in the background while he appeared as the only person among the Americans whom they had the slightest interest in seeing. Therefore I saw little of Moley until the explosion occurred. I decided to give him all the rope he might want and see how long he would last in that London situation.

Soon after his arrival, Moley sent word to me requesting that I convey to the delegation a message to the effect that he intended giving his attention to the currency stabilization question. He immediately launched into conversations with the Chancellor of the Exchequer, Neville Chamberlain, and Sir Frederick Leith-Ross, Chief Economic Adviser of the British Government. The first meeting was reported to have taken place at the American Embassy, where Moley was stopping.

During the few days that followed, prime ministers and other top officials of governments flocked after Moley as if he were the Pied Piper. I continued to keep in the background as if I were the most insignificant individual hanging about the conference.

MacDonald asked me, at one time: "Can you send Moley over to me? I'd like to talk to him." Then he added, as an afterthought, "And you can come too, if you like."

Some days later, MacDonald called me aside and spoke to me like a schoolmaster lecturing a pupil. "Do you know," he said, "that it is not customary to issue press statements at a conference like this?" (I had issued one or two.) "It just isn't done."

I retorted: "It's no more unusual than for the chief of another delegation to go over my head and follow after and confer directly with a subordinate of mine."

All in all, however, MacDonald was an admirable man, with fine ability, and fluency in speaking. In any group he would soon attract attention. He was an omnivorous reader and possessed a marvelous fund of general information, especially in relation to government.

Some years later Canadian Prime Minister Bennett told me Mac-Donald and others had asked his opinion as to whether they should deal with Moley or myself, and whether Moley bore a message from the

President authorizing him to stabilize the dollar. Bennett said he told them I was the Secretary of State and chief of the delegation and they had better deal with me. MacDonald and the others were trying to find out whether Moley would give his supposed message to me to give to them or give it direct to them himself. Bennett said Moley had given them to understand he would give any Presidential message direct to them. In any event, Moley was with MacDonald and others for lengthy conferences.

Moley early discovered that some of the leading foreign delegates and some of the foreign press were saying freely that he had come to London not merely as a liaison person but as the representative of the President, clothed with full powers which would supersede those of the delegation. While this sort of publicity, which spread rapidly over Britain and the Continent, was injurious to the delegation and especially myself, Moley, courted by prime ministers and other high dignitaries, appeared to act as if he were in entire charge for the United States Government, notwithstanding his transparent protests and denials as to his occupying such a status.

Moley negotiated an agreement to stabilize currencies, and cabled it to the President for his approval. So sanguine was he that the President would accept his ideas that he informed high officials of Britain and other Governments that he would meet them at Number 10 Downing Street at a certain hour in the late afternoon of June 30. Soon he telephoned me at my hotel and very earnestly requested me to go to Downing Street to sign what he said was the forthcoming agreement. I quickly and bluntly declined to go and stated decisively that, as a delegate to the London Conference, I had nothing to do with the stabilization question. He pleaded with me, but I choked off his further attempts at conversation.

There was obliged to be a showdown and end of this grotesque performance. It came with a telegram from the President rejecting Moley's proposed agreement. At that moment I was starting for Cliveden. As I walked out to the head of the steps leading from the hotel, Moley rushed down to meet me and said: "There's a cable coming in from Washington, and it is unfavorable on stabilization. We've just got to do something about it."

I then turned on him. I saw he had reached the end of his rope and was through. I proceeded to talk to him. I started in by saying: "You had better get back home. You had no business over here in the first place." I elaborated along those lines. I then walked to my car to spend the week end in the country, which I had promised to do after many urgent invitations.

Upon my return to London, the President's famous "bombshell message" arrived, which vigorously rejected Moley's stabilization proposal and spoke out to the conference in strong fashion. The President said he would regard it as "a catastrophe amounting to world tragedy" if the conference allowed itself to be diverted from its broader problems by the proposal of a purely artificial, temporary experiment affecting the monetary exchange of a few nations only. This was the message that threw the conference into an uproar.

A few hours after it arrived, Governor Cox, who I had arranged should see MacDonald every day, came rushing to my office. Very much wrought up, he said: "The British and other important countries are so aroused by the President's message that they have decided to call a meeting of the steering committee this afternoon, let it convene the conference in full session tomorrow, and then and there declare the conference adjourned indefinitely. In their resolution they will hang around the President's neck the sole responsibility for wrecking the conference." He hastily added that he was going to call President Roosevelt over the transatlantic telephone at once.

I suggested that he hold off doing so, and meantime I would see what could be done to avert the action he predicted.

During the afternoon I was informed that the steering committee, comprising the chief delegates of the sixteen leading countries, would meet at six o'clock that evening. Also that the gold-standard countries—France, Italy, Belgium, Holland, and Switzerland—in addition to the British delegation, including MacDonald, along with other Continental countries, were openly and severely criticizing the President's message, especially its tone. They were proclaiming on all sides that the conference could not go on in view of the injurious effect of the President's message.

I concentrated on an effort to checkmate this movement and to quiet the situation before it got out of hand. I first requested MacDonald to defer the meeting of the steering committee until the following day, but he was blunt and obdurate in refusing. I authorized Cox, William C. Bullitt, an adviser of the delegation, and others, to use any possible efforts to calm the angry waters.

I then hastened to the conference building where the steering committee meeting was to be held. As soon as I arrived, one of the high officials of the conference handed me a memorandum of what had occurred at the morning meeting, which revealed that the situation was really acute. The representatives of the leading nations, excepting the Americans, had agreed that "the American statement on stabilization rendered it entirely useless to continue the conference." A small committee, consisting of Chamberlain of Britain, Jung of Italy, Bonnet of France, and Colijn of Holland, was appointed to draft a document showing "the exact present status and the reason therefor."

This subcommittee was expressly instructed that the document should contain, first, the extract regarding stabilization contained in President Roosevelt's message of May 16 to the heads of governments, and, secondly, the passage opposed to stabilization contained in his present message to the conference.

I hurried to the room where the steering committee was to meet, hoping I might individually persuade its members to postpone their session until the next day so that the feeling that was manifest on all sides might have time to subside. I found, however, that the atmosphere was frigid. The members had been deeply aroused and had not the slightest disposition even to discuss a postponement of the meeting. It was evident that in their wrought-up state they were bent on presenting the resolution which had been drafted by the subcommittee and having it printed the next morning in every important newspaper in the world. The only member I could find at all sympathetic was Prime Minister Bennett of Canada.

When the committee convened at six o'clock—this was July 4—the president of the conference, MacDonald, launched into a terrific speech. He said the conference had been brought to a practical end by the conduct of one country relative to certain currency matters, thereby making it impossible to proceed. There was nothing to be done, he concluded, except to adjourn subject to the call of the President, which might be made if and when the causes necessitating the adjournment had been removed.

I was utterly astonished at MacDonald's bitter tone and sweeping condemnation. He boldly placed sole responsibility upon the American Government.

At the conclusion of MacDonald's excoriating speech I obtained the floor. It now seemed inadvisable at the outset to offer a motion to recess until the next day. The state of feeling was such that it evidently would have been promptly and overwhelmingly voted down.

I proceeded instead to confront MacDonald with rather technical questions. I avoided arguing with him, but I asked for a more definite statement as to just what "currency" matters or causes would have to be dealt with and removed before the conference could be reconvened.

The Prime Minister was not at all definite in his reply.

I suggested to the meeting then that, since the able Prime Minister found great difficulty in defining the circumstances in which the conference could be reconvened, the occasion was so momentous that I felt we should pause long enough to realize fully the high mission we were here to perform.

I continued to propound further technical questions to MacDonald, each in the most courteous and friendly manner possible. It so happened that his reply to each was not clear and definite.

Among other points, the Prime Minister had announced that the message from Washington prevented consideration by the conference of any monetary questions contained in the agenda, and that tariffs and other trade barriers could not be dealt with without first dealing with the monetary question. But he added that the conference would be obliged to adjourn with the possible appointment of some sort of committee of experts to conduct work pertaining to the agenda during the adjournment period.

I inquired of MacDonald how the committee could perform any work pertaining to trade barriers if the conference could not consider them.

His reply fell hopelessly short of what the members expected.

As a result, by this time I felt justified in making my motion for recess of the steering committee, which I did.

From a seat two or three chairs to my rear rose Neville Chamberlain, Chancellor of the Exchequer. It was understood he had in his pocket the resolution denouncing Roosevelt and declaring the conference adjourned indefinitely. To my great surprise and relief, he stated he had been considering the matter in the light of all that had been said and he had reached the conclusion that "Mr. Hull is right." Therefore, he would ask for a recess of the meeting until the second day following.   ,

Prime Minister Bennett followed in my support. It was now apparent that the opposition was rapidly collapsing in so far as it contemplated summary action and publicity for the resolution. The members agreed to recess the meeting until ten o'clock in the morning two days later.

Meantime I saw MacDonald. I most earnestly urged him to modify his attitude and say a few words in favor of continuing the conference in regular session. He very sharply stated he had no notion of doing so.

He complained bitterly that the President's message, by shattering the conference, had destroyed his, MacDonald's, entire political position, which he had expected to be bolstered by a successful conference. I had received reports that, in private conversation, MacDonald had said he probably would now be obliged to resign as Prime Minister.

When the steering committee reconvened, the outlook was little more encouraging. It had not been possible to secure any definite expression from either MacDonald or Chamberlain, while the Little Entente of Rumania, Yugoslavia, and Czechoslovakia, feeling under special financial obligations to France, had become aligned, like Spain, with the five gold countries in favor of abrupt adjournment and placing all blame on the United States Government. The gold countries claimed to have the votes of forty delegations. The French had called on the various delegations at their hotels and sought to line them up, thereby reminding me of the activities of a national political convention where the rivalry was keen.

The chances for a favorable outcome did not look to be more than one in a hundred.

I sought and obtained the floor for some twenty minutes for an opening address. I rested my main position on the ground that sixty-six nations of the world had unanimously agreed on the absolute necessity for holding the conference and on its taking action to solve the numerous financial and economic problems imperatively calling for remedies unless the whole international structure was to collapse even more completely. When we came here we represented to everyone that we were competent to solve these terrific problems and implement our solutions.

"Thus far," I said, "we have not scratched the surface with respect to the many pressing questions we have been sent here to deal with. The question is whether we shall now, at this early stage of the conference, confess before the world that, after all, we are incompetent to meet our responsibilities as delegates. Are we to confess that we are taking advantage of an incident limited in its scope and possible effects in order to break up the conference? Are the delegates then to scatter off in every direction carrying with them the puerile plea that they were not competent to proceed further? It will be an amazing spectacle if this incident causes the members, in a spirit of pique, suddenly to pick up their hats and disperse."

The delegates who followed alternated in their support of MacDonald or me. Prime Minister Bennett of Canada, Viscount Ishii of Japan, and the Swedish delegate strongly supported my position. Neville Chamberlain, too, came out in my favor.

The arguments we marshaled in opposition to adjournment were sufficiently appealing to break down the plans of the British and French. The outcome was as sudden as it was surprising to me. Even Prime Minister MacDonald backed away from his original position and joined the movement in the opposite direction. After two hours of argument, the meeting agreed that the conference should remain in session. By a desperate defense I had succeeded in thwarting the virtual certainty that the conference would formally fasten upon the President the blame for its failure.

The three weeks that followed were a kind of paper chase during which we sought to find odds and ends of topics that could be discussed. Perhaps agreements could be reached, however general, which would later serve as a basis for more concrete action. Perhaps a few charred planks could be drawn from the wreckage of the conference.

I personally discussed with many delegates the basic ideas I had in mind for the reciprocal trade agreements program. I thought I might begin to enlist the later support of important commercial countries for this method which I considered the most practical plan for attacking trade barriers.

One night I went to the hotel room of the Dutch Prime Minister Colijn, who was chairman of the economics subsection of the conference. I sat down with him for hours and went over my ideas in great detail. Generally I received a favorable response from the commercial nations; but I could get little further because the situation at home did not make it possible for me to introduce this economic program for consideration and action by the conference. Also, as the days passed, the delegations became more and more discouraged over the possibility of taking any important action.

Moley departed for home after sending the President a telegram that was in the nature of a rigid inspection report on the delegation. He pronounced the entire delegation incapable of representing the President at the conference except Key Pittman, who, in fact, rendered about the least service apart from his resolution on silver in which few were interested. Moley naïvely sent the telegram in State Department code, and its contents became known to the American delegates, each of whom, except Pittman, resented it strongly.

Toward the close of the conference, Sir Maurice Hankey, Secretary of the British Cabinet, visited me and apologized for the conduct of the

British delegation in ignoring me and the American delegation for some days and running off after Moley. He then recounted Moley's numerous contacts with the British delegates, especially MacDonald, which corresponded to what I already knew, in addition to other acts and utterances which occurred under my own observation.

After three weeks of desultory conversations the conference recessed indefinitely. Delivering my closing address on July 27, I said that the progress of the conference "has corresponded with the difficulties of its task. Human ingenuity could scarcely have devised a more complete jumble and chaos of business and general economic conditions than those facing the nations and the conference when it convened and still challenging solution. A multiplicity of other circumstances has further impeded the progress of the conference, such as the lack of an international public opinion, the malignant opposition of those who blindly or selfishly oppose all international economic cooperation, and the engrossment of many nations with the more or less temporary phases of their domestic programs for the emergency treatment of panic conditions."

The conference had not succeeded, but I refused to be utterly pessimistic. "There are after all only two ways of reaching international agreement," I continued. "One is by imposing one's will by force—by war. The other is by persuasion—by conference. Even by the violent means of war—which we have all renounced—no one would expect agreement in six weeks. How can it then be said that the conference—this method which has killed no man—has already failed? Many actual wars of the past growing out of bitter trade controversies would have been averted had there been more peacetime conferences." And I ended by saying: "We cannot falter. We will not quit. We have begun and we will go on."

That night I sailed on the steamship *President Harding* for home. Prior to leaving London I received a cable from the President: "Before you sail I want you to know once more of my affectionate regard for and confidence in you. You have admirably faced great difficulties and through your own courage and sincerity saved the principle of continued international discussion of perplexing world problems from a collapse which would have made further deliberations impossible. When you get to New York next week I shall be at Hyde Park and I much hope that you and Mrs. Hull will come there for the night when you arrive."

The State Department cabled me that the American press had strongly and overwhelmingly supported my position at the conference, especially during its closing phases.

At Hyde Park I gave the President a running narrative of the conference's proceedings, concentrating mainly on the high spots. The President did not go into his reasons, which were mainly technical, for sending his "bombshell" cable to the conference. We did not then discuss the questions of trade barriers. In fact, the disappointments encountered at the conference did not conduce to lively conversation, beyond some emphasis I put on what the American delegation had sought to do and on the disagreeable experiences we had met.

I found that the President was well aware of Moley's activities in London. He knew about his telegram concerning the members of the delegation and about the resentment of these members. He was cognizant of Moley's activities in officially taking charge of the temporary stabilization matter and undertaking to secure an agreement and to prevail on the President to approve it. He was aware that Moley had handled himself so as not in the least to dispel the impression, widely circulated by the European press and many foreign delegates, that he was supreme in London over the delegation as the direct, authorized representative of President Roosevelt.

It is due the President that I should say that he then and always thereafter insisted strongly that he had had no thought of giving Moley any special powers, much less any authority over the United States delegation. He said he merely meant for Moley to drop over to London as a liaison man to take any information the delegation might be interested in securing, and to return to America within a few days with such information from the delegation as the President might be interested in. He told me that the great blare of trumpets and the dramatization that Moley either promoted or acquiesced in, or both, with an enthusiasm apparent to the public, surprised him greatly. The President gave Moley some outside work and within a few weeks transferred him from the State Department.

I believed then, and do still, that the collapse of the London Economic Conference had two tragic results. First, it greatly retarded the logical economic recovery of all nations. Secondly, it played into the hands of such dictator nations as Germany, Japan, and Italy. At that very time this trio was intently watching the course of action of the peace-seeking nations. At London the bitterest recrimination occurred among the United States, Britain, and France. The dictator nations occupied first-row seats at a spectacular battle. From then on they could proceed hopefully: on the military side, to rearm in comparative safety; on the economic side, to build their self-sufficiency walls in preparation for war. The conference was the first, and really the last, opportunity to check these movements toward conflict.

History, which is filled with might-have-beens, picked up another at London.

20: The Far East Confronts Us

ON FEBRUARY 24, 1933, the very day I issued my first public statement after the President-elect named me Secretary of State, Yosuke Matsuoka, chief of the Japanese delegation at the League of Nations, walked out of the Assembly at Geneva as a result of the League's condemnation of Japan's invasion of Manchuria. A month later, March 27, Japan formally resigned from the League.

One of the basic points of my statement was that there should be no laxity on the part of any nation in observing both the letter and spirit of treaties and of international good faith. The President-elect had also spoken to the same effect. Secretary Stimson, in my long conferences with him, had emphasized the policy he was pursuing, of opposing Japan's advance into China by all the diplomatic means at his command, including a refusal to recognize Japan's acquisition of Manchuria.

Stimson gave full credit to William Jennings Bryan for providing him a precedent on nonrecognition in the Far East. Secretary of State Bryan in 1915, at the time Japan made her infamous Twenty-one Demands on China, notified China and Japan that the United States would not recognize agreements that violated our rights under the Open Door policy. Stimson himself deserves full credit for taking this principle, broadening it and seeking to gain it world adherence. Since Japan's undeclared war in China was in flagrant violation of the Nine-Power Treaty signed at Washington in 1922, Mr. Roosevelt and I wanted our statements to reflect our intention to continue unchanged the opposition of this Government to Japan's expanding ambitions.

As I entered the State Department I had two points on the Far East firmly in mind. One was the definite interest the United States had in maintaining the independence of China and in preventing Japan from gaining overlordship of the entire Far East. The other was an equally definite conviction that Japan had no intention whatever of abiding by treaties but would regulate her conduct by the opportunities of the moment.

Japan's diplomatic record was that of a highway robber. She warred against China in 1894 in order to get hold of Korea. She fought Russia in 1904 and obtained Russia's lease of the Liaotung Peninsula in Manchuria and a transfer to herself of the South Manchuria and other railways. She took advantage of the Western Powers' absorption in the First World War to present her notorious Twenty-one Demands against China which would have given her control of China. She declared war against Germany solely to get possession of German concessions in China and islands in the Pacific. She tried to annex Siberia east of Lake Baikal while Russia was engrossed in the Soviet Revolution.

When the war ended, the United States took the lead in demanding that Japan abandon her demands and gains. Japan complied like a thief who had been caught up with and made to give up his loot. With as much face-saving as she could muster, she abandoned her chief advantages but clung to some that gave her substantial advantages in the Orient during the years that followed. It was under these circumstances that the United States and Britain decided upon a disarmament conference in 1921 which had the Atlantic area of the world largely in mind. As the proposal developed, however, the Western nations decided it would be wise also to safeguard the Pacific which Japan had shown every disposition to disturb.

At the 1921–1922 Washington Conference Japan, for the first and only time, submerged her steady policy and plans of expansion. She acquiesced in the decisions of the Disarmament Conference, although without enthusiasm. The Nine-Power Treaty she signed at Washington embraced the Open Door policy for China proclaimed by Secretary of State John Hay in 1899. This policy was twofold: equality of commercial opportunity for all nations in dealing with China, and, as a necessary corollary, the preservation of China's territorial and administrative integrity. It had been reenforced by the Root-Takahira exchange of notes between the United States and Japan in 1908.

Japan's attitude of inactive acquiescence ended five years after the Washington Conference when the cabinet of General Tanaka began to adopt a "positive" policy toward China, meaning interference in China's internal affairs. Japanese spokesmen commenced to speak of Japan's chosen mission to rule the Orient. Words changed to actions when Japan invaded Manchuria in 1931 and set up a puppet regime called "Manchukuo."

Japan thereby created a world danger extending beyond the confines of a conflict between Japan and China. Here was the first open violation of treaties since the Treaty of Versailles ended the First World War. To permit this bad example to pass unnoticed at a moment when dictatorial movements were rising in Europe would have been foolhardy.

I had no hesitation in agreeing with Stimson on the wording of the message he sent to the League of Nations on February 25, 1933, joining in the League's condemnation of Japan's actions. But, as I entered my new office, I found confronting me a decision that meant going still further. The League, on February 24, had invited the United States, although not a member of the League, to cooperate with the Advisory Committee set up to handle the Far Eastern Situation. The President and I decided to go this extra distance.

On March 11 I notified Sir Eric Drummond, Secretary-General of the League, by cable: "Believing that participation by a representative of this Government in the deliberations of the committee would be helpful, I am instructing the American Minister to Switzerland, Mr. Hugh R. Wilson, to be prepared so to participate, but without right to vote, if such participation is desired."

In making public announcement of this decision, I said: "We believe that the importance of the problem which is of common concern in this connection to the League, to the League Powers, and to the United States, calls for promptness and accuracy in exchange of information and views; that the dictates of common sense call for consultation with friendly and frank discussion among the nations; and that the procedure thus suggested will contribute toward the serving of those ends—in the interest both of the United States and of all other countries concerned." This statement indicates the caution with which, owing to the isolationist sentiment at home, we had to proceed in any move in the direction of the League.

On March 31 I received Matsuoka as he passed across the United States en route to Japan from Geneva. After leaving the League, Matsuoka had made unfriendly statements to the press concerning our country. I had little inclination to engage in a political discussion with him, and I so told Japanese Ambassador Debuchi, who passed on the word to Matsuoka. Matsuoka came to my office alone, unaccompanied by Debuchi. Bespectacled, with a black mustache, he looked like a businessman of his race, which he was. He spoke English by virtue of a few years spent in the United States, to which he had migrated at the age of thirteen.

He was affable enough, did not try to discuss political matters, uttered a few casual words of greeting, and then rose to go. Once on his feet, however, he could not resist the temptation to make some political statement. He said he and his country regretted having felt obliged to quit the League. He handed me a printed pamphlet of his speeches and asked me to read it, which I promised to do. As he moved toward the door he said he did not want war to come between the two countries. He urged that Japan be given time in which to make herself better understood, and said he would undertake personally to do his full share toward this end when he reached home. I refused to be drawn into a discussion and merely wished him a pleasant journey.

When Matsuoka arrived home he received a public patriotic demonstration seldom seen in Japan. It was whipped up to show Japanese antagonism to the League. Later in the year Matsuoka resigned from the Seiyukai Party and from the Diet and proclaimed his opposition to party government, meaning his advocacy of a dictatorship. He was to prove one of our major enemies when he became Foreign Minister in 1940. It was while he was Foreign Minister that Japanese troops invaded French Indo-China and that Japan entered into the Tripartite Alliance with Germany and Italy aimed directly at the United States. My distrust of Matsuoka in 1933 was to prove correct.

The sentiment in Japan as I came into office was predominantly anti-American. On April 21 Ambassador Joseph C. Grew, one of our ablest diplomats, who was to render highly valuable service at Tokyo through the years until Pearl Harbor, sent me from Tokyo a long list of cases of anti-American demonstrations in Japan. "There is no doubt in my mind," he said, "that these incidents are due in some cases directly and in practically all cases at least indirectly to military propaganda. In order to justify the immense appropriations asked by the War Office for carrying out the campaign in Manchuria it was in the interests of the army to create a war psychology in the country. Sometimes openly and at other times in scarcely veiled language the people have been given to believe that the United States is preparing for an eventual attack on Japan."

When President Roosevelt addressed his appeal to the heads of nations on May 16, 1933, and when Norman Davis presented our proposals to the Disarmament Conference at Geneva on May 22, we made every effort to extend their application to the world rather than limit it to Europe. We wanted to leave no doubt that we had Japan in mind as well.

On May 24 Japanese Ambassador Debuchi called on Under Secretary Phillips and began fishing by saying it was his opinion that the President's message was intended primarily for European consumption, and in particular for German consumption. Phillips hastened to emphasize that it was applicable to the Far Eastern situation as well. Debuchi then made the surprising statement that the Emperor would be obliged to delay sending his response to the President's message because his position did not correspond to that of the President and the reply would therefore have to be carefully considered by the Government. He thought, in view of the situation in China, that there would be some embarrassment in answering the President's communication. The Emperor's answer came in due course, however, and whatever may have been his embarrassment, he agreed in general terms to the President's proposals.

Debuchi told us in May that Japanese sentiment toward the United States had been improving during the last two months. He gave two reasons for it, one being a feeling of confidence in the President, the other that there had been a "quiet period" in exchanges of communications between Japan and the United States.

There was, in fact, a slight betterment of relations during the remainder of 1933 and into 1934. Toward the end of May, Viscount Ishii held friendly conversations with the President and myself, almost entirely on economic subjects, before going to the London Economic Conference, at which he generally supported me. On May 31 Japan and China concluded the Tangku Truce whereby the Japanese were to keep north of a line generally marked by the Great Wall of China, and the Chinese to the south. I was convinced, however, that Japan was merely marking time until she could consolidate her gains in Manchuria and then advance farther.

In June I received a circular letter from the League of Nations asking our adherence to specific steps to show our nonrecognition of Manchukuo. We could not agree with some of the steps, but in September I cabled the new Secretary General of the League, Mr. Avenol: "I am happy to inform you that the views of the American Government with regard to the principle of non-recognition remain unchanged and that the American Government concurs in general in the conclusions arrived at."

League members were joining together to aid China, and the United States kept pace by agreeing to extend $50,000,000 in credits to China with which to purchase cotton and wheat. On August 10, 1933, Debuchi came to see me and said China intended to sell the cotton and wheat at a discount and use the proceeds against Japan. He requested that we consult with Japan before taking any steps that might affect her interests. I simply told him we had made the credit to aid our price situation at home and had no purposes in mind to affect adversely Japan's affairs. I gave him no promise to consult with Japan before making such arrangements with China.

In October Ambassador Grew cabled me a suggestion from Foreign Minister Hirota that Japan send a good-will mission to the United States. Grew said he advised Hirota against it. He told the Foreign Minister that the American public viewed organized foreign propaganda with distaste, was then far more occupied with domestic problems than with any foreign questions, and in certain quarters a latent distrust of Japan existed which organized Japanese propaganda would enhance.

I cabled Grew my approval of his position and suggested he might find opportunity to turn Hirota's "attention to the situation whereby the Department is confronted with increasing evidence of discrimination, actual or likely to develop, by the authorities of Manchukuo against American and other foreign commercial interests in Manchuria, and of acts by these authorities prejudicial to the treaty rights of the United States." I added: "If the Japanese authorities could discourage successfully the discriminatory and other objectionable practices in Manchukuo, it would contribute substantially to maintaining and promoting good will between the United States and Japan, and at the same time efforts along that line would contribute more than any gesture of a good-will mission."

Our objections to Japan's discrimination against American business in Manchuria and the establishment of monopolies there were the subject of repeated diplomatic notes I sent to Tokyo throughout 1934. Japan pursued her usual devious course by denying discrimination or by evading responsibility and requesting that representations be made direct to the so-called Manchukuo Government, which in reality was a Japanese puppet unrecognized by us.

Japan was flagrantly dishonest in her statements regarding Manchuria. She had conquered Manchuria, set up a puppet Government there with the strings manipulated by her army, and occupied it with her troops. Yet Hirota had the audacity to say, in a memorandum to us on November 5, 1934: "The plan of the Government of Manchukuo for the control of the oil industry is a project of that Government itself and is not within the knowledge or concern of the Imperial [Japanese] Government, and the Imperial Government is not in a position to give any explanation with respect to it."

It is difficult to see how Japan could expect other countries to believe such a statement or not to resent it. We replied on November 30: "The American Government finds unconvincing the statement . . . that the proposed control of the oil industry in Manchuria is not within the knowledge or concern of the Japanese Government. The American Government must of necessity assume that a project of such major importance to all concerned and one with regard to which Japanese interests, including a quasi-official organization, apparently are taking so active and so prominent a part, cannot escape either the knowledge or the concern of the Japanese Government. Likewise, for obvious reasons the American Government cannot accept the implied disclaimer of responsibility on the part of Japan in relation to the industrial policy in Manchuria."

The Japanese were carefully watching developments pointing toward American recognition of Soviet Russia, which was to take place in November, 1933. Relations between Japan and Russia were strained, partly over which one should own the Chinese Eastern Railroad running through Manchuria. Japan had no desire to see the formation of diplomatic ties between the United States and Russia.

On October 24, 1933, Ambassador Grew cabled me a statement made to our Counselor Edwin L. Neville by Saburo Kurusu, chief of the Commercial Bureau of the Foreign Office, who was to be one of the ill-famed negotiators in Washington at the time of Pearl Harbor: "If American recognition of the Soviets were to lead to a belief on the part of the Russians that the United States would support them in their discussions with the Japanese, or if the Chinese were to believe that the United States would support Russia in the Far East, the Foreign Office felt that it might have its work with the Military to do all over again."

Here in this last phrase lay one of my difficulties in dealing with the Japanese in the eight years to follow. Japanese diplomats always took care to represent to us that there were two elements in Japan: one, liberal, peaceful, and civilian; the other, military and expansionist. There was always a neat balance between them, they argued, which our actions could affect. If we did not irritate the military element by denying them the right to expand in the Far East, the peaceful element could eventually gain control of the Government and ensure peace. It was therefore up to us to prevent the worst from happening in Japan.

But there were two fallacies to this position. One was that the military could whip up the population at any time by propaganda and desperado actions. When I came into office, trials were pending in Japan against a group of military terrorists who had assassinated the previous Prime Minister Inukai in protest against Japan's signing the London naval limitation agreement of 1930. In November, 1933, they were given amazingly light prison sentences in deference to Japanese public opinion. And the other was the fact that the appetite of the Japanese militarists grew with eating, and their prestige rose in the country as they gobbled up section after section of China. The all-powerful military element, always in control when it desired to control, maintained its supremacy by fair means or foul such as brutal assassination of influential persons or officials who were getting in the way of the rule-or-ruin group.

A new Japanese Ambassador, Hirosi Saito, a rather young man belonging to the aggressive group in Tokyo, arrived at his post here in February, 1934, and handed me a personal message from Foreign Minister Hirota. This said that Hirota believed that "no question exists between our two countries that is fundamentally incapable of amicable solution. I do not doubt that all issues pending between the two nations will be settled in a satisfactory manner, when examined with a good understanding on the part of each of the other's position, discussed with an open mind and in all frankness, and approached with a spirit of cooperation and conciliation."

I cordially replied in a personal message to Hirota, fully concurring in his views. But I also expressed my earnest hope "that it may be possible for all of the countries which have interests in the Far East to approach every question existing or which may arise between or among them in such spirit and manner that these questions may be regulated or resolved with injury to none and with definite and lasting advantage to all."

Within the lines of this paragraph lay another of the major differences of attitude between ourselves and the Japanese. During my years at the State Department, Japan repeatedly suggested direct agreements in general terms between Tokyo and Washington. We, instead, stood for broader agreements embracing all the powers interested in the Far East. Japan was already worming out of the Nine-Power Treaty and the Four-Power Treaty signed at Washington in 1921–1922, and disliked any accord that brought the Western Powers together with regard to China or the Far East generally. Japan wanted to deal with the Western Powers and with China separately.

But of what use was a direct agreement between Japan and ourselves if Japan intended, as she did, to continue to absorb China? Japan and the United States could agree not to attack each other, but this would not prevent Japan's going right ahead in China. On the contrary, it would encourage her.

The Japanese Foreign Office was trying to continue with me the same policy it had pursued for twoscore years. Soon after a military conquest,

Japan had always sought to calm the other powers by diplomatic agreements which had the implicit effect of recognizing Japan's gains. She thus tried by means of diplomacy to consolidate acquisitions made by means of arms.

Nothing could have been more discouraging to China, or more disastrous later to us and other countries interested in the Pacific area, than for us to sign a pact with Japan. It would have been a sort of underwriting of Japan's ambitions in China. It would have made us a kind of silent partner in Japan's aggressions. And nothing could have been more disruptive of the united front we hoped to secure in the Far East—including Japan if she were willing to mend her ways.

In March, 1934, we took an initiative in the Far East sharply in contrast to Japan's attitude toward the other peoples of the Orient. The President signed the Tydings-McDuffie Act agreeing to grant Philippine independence. I was fully in support of it. Back in my Congressional years I had stood against imperialism and colonial expansion. When I was on the Ways and Means Committee of the House, I assisted in the appointment of a committee to consider the question of Philippine independence. The chairman was Congressman W. A. Jones of Virginia. The result was the enactment of the Jones Bill in 1914, by a large majority. This contained a pledge by this Government that the Philippines would be granted independence as soon as they were deemed ready to govern themselves. It was in accordance with this Act that the Philippines were decided capable of self-government by the Tydings-McDuffie Act, and 1946 was set as the year for their independence.

In the same month of March, 1934, I seized upon the occasion of the eightieth anniversary of the negotiation by Commodore Matthew Perry of a treaty of peace and amity with Japan to make a gesture of friendship toward Japan. I addressed a letter to the Chamber of Commerce of the United States in which I said that Perry's treaty "firmly laid a foundation upon which there has been erected a structure of enduring friendship and reciprocal benefits . . . the trade between the two countries has reached conspicuous proportions and continues to increase. In the field of industry, each nation has its own distinctive genius: both countries are able to contribute, each in its own way and without injury to the other, toward the welfare of mankind. . . . Today, as eighty years ago and always, it is our desire to cooperate cordially and helpfully with Japan in all peaceful constructive lines of endeavor, to the benefit of this country, of Japan, and of the rest of the world."

But in April, 1934, came the notorious Amau statement—a rude surprise to me though not a shock. Eiji Amau, spokesman of the Foreign Office, made a long statement to the press the gist of which was that Japan had special responsibilities in East Asia and might have to act alone on her own responsibility. Japan, he said, was opposed to any joint operations by foreign powers with respect to China, even technical or financial assistance, because these would have political significance and might have most serious repercussions upon Japan and East Asia.

The Amau statement received world publicity. It simply meant that, after pretending for a brief period to harbor peaceful intentions, Japan was in fact—and for the period up to Pearl Harbor—merely settling back into her fixed notorious course of armaments, treaty breaking, and aggression. Although Hirota watered down Amau's statement by official explanations, the basic note of Japan's special claims in the Far East remained, and we could not let it pass.

On April 28, 1934, I sent Hirota a note calling attention to the fact that the United States, by virtue of existing treaties, had certain rights and obligations in China and was associated with China, Japan, and other nations in multilateral treaties relating to the Far East. "In the opinion of the American people and the American Government," I said, "no nation can, without the assent of the other nations concerned, rightfully endeavor to make conclusive its will in situations where there are involved the rights, the obligations, and the legitimate interests of other sovereign states."

The British Government, with which we were in contact, had delivered a similar note to Tokyo. Here was an example of the parallel action we were to pursue in the years following. The President and I stayed clear of joint action with Britain because few courses so stirred up the isolationists here as any mere hint of an agreement between Washington and London. But there was no reason why, if our policies coincided, we could not take the same kind of action, provided we acted independently. Since we were signatories to the same treaties that were being violated, it was but natural and logical that we should ascertain one another's views. And, since our views generally concurred, it was equally natural and logical that our actions based on such views should be similar.

Paris frequently followed the same procedure too. In the years to follow, the American, British, and French Ambassadors in Tokyo were frequently to call at the Japanese Foreign Office at different hours on the same day or the day after and present notes which, in substance, were the same. Such action was stronger than if the major Western Powers pursued different courses, and it prevented the Japanese from playing off one against another.

In the present instance, however, Sir John Simon, British Foreign Secretary, although sending Tokyo a strong note, made a statement in the House of Commons in which he indicated Japan had some special rights in Manchuria and in portions of China. I thereupon called in British Ambassador Lindsay and told him: "Frankly, I am somewhat disappointed to find this clause in Sir John Simon's statement. Britain is more interested materially in the Orient than the United States is, and it is Britain's full privilege to treat this Japanese publicity as she thinks best. But all the Governments signatory to the treaties operative in the Orient are in the same boat with respect to the observance of the treaties. I myself feel that, since none of the countries were planning pronouncements that would call for the use of force, clear-cut and unequivocal statements from each Government relative to their rights, interests, and obligations in the Orient—such statements being made separately and independently—would offer the best possible method of dealing with such Japanese utterances by arousing the moral sentiment of the world."

The Ambassador answered that he thought Sir John Simon was thoroughly justified in making the statement he did. I replied: "In stating a broad, fundamental position relating to rights, interests, and obligations of all nations signatory to the treaties involved, there is no occasion whatever for singling out some one of numerous, purely minor or local conditions for the purpose of making an exception in favor of Japan and of Japan's alleged rights." I utterly detested this sort of strategy.

Our policy of parallel action with Britain worked out generally, however, with a great degree of smoothness and efficiency. Each Government kept the other well informed of its views and projects with regard to the Far East. We did not always see eye to eye, but the similarity of our basic principles tended to overcome our minor divergencies.

21: Japan Tears Up Naval Treaty

JAPANESE AMBASSADOR SAITO handed me in May, 1934, a proposal for a Japanese-American agreement which unfortunately demonstrated the narrow thinking of his Government. For some days he had indicated his wish for what he called a highly secret and highly important conference with me. He did not want to come to the State Department—that was too prominent. He wanted to come to my apartment. The conference was to be so secret that neither of us was to take any notes on it or communicate anything about it to his Government. I agreed to the conference without committing myself to his stipulations.

Saito came to my apartment, therefore, on May 16. He had the air of being about to communicate a secret of tremendous import. Despite his wish that nothing be put on paper concerning the conference, he had evidently been doing some intensive thinking about relations between the United States and Japan and, to marshal his thoughts, had put them on paper in the form of an eight-point memorandum, which he handed me. It began: "These are entirely my private thoughts."

Saito's eight points outlined what he considered American suspicions of Japan and Japanese suspicions of America, and pleaded that each country should repose full confidence in the sincerity of the peaceful motives of the other. They contained a proposal for a joint Japanese-American declaration on the Far East whereby the two Governments would promise to cooperate with each other to promote trade to their mutual advantage, to respect the territorial possessions and rights and interests of each other. Also:

"Both Governments mutually recognize that the United States in the eastern Pacific regions and Japan in the western Pacific regions are principal stabilizing factors and both Governments will exercise their best and constant efforts so far as lies within their proper and legitimate power to establish a reign of law and order in the regions geographically adjacent to their respective countries."

It did not require much thinking to determine where this paragraph would lead us. To agree to Japan's establishing "a reign of law and order" in regions "geographically adjacent" to her meant giving our blessing to her sending troops into China and elsewhere. Here was a start along the line of later Japanese propaganda that what she wanted was a "Monroe

Doctrine" in the Far East pretendedly such as our Monroe Doctrine for the Western Hemisphere.

Japan violently and fraudulently misrepresented the idea of the Monroe Doctrine, deliberately forgetting that that doctrine did not give us the right to conquer and occupy or dominate sections of the Western Hemisphere or close them off to the trade of other nations. And she ignored the basic concept of the Monroe Doctrine, which was to preserve the security and independence of the nations of the Western Hemisphere. Also, the Monroe Doctrine was designed to prevent foreign nations from making conquests in this Hemisphere, whereas the Far East was being threatened by no foreign nation whatever.

There was no resemblance at all between the Japanese "Monroe Doctrine" and our own. Japan's "Monroe Doctrine" would have given her domination, for political as well as economic purposes, of nearly one-half the world's population, all under the guise of a doctrine that Monroe had proclaimed for self-defense. This was an impossible situation to the other nations. It meant they would be frozen out of the Pacific area and could not enter it except under such arbitrary terms and exactions as Japan might impose.

Saito talked to me at length about his proposal. I told him I would study it carefully and asked him to call upon me in a few days. I then commented: "We are living in a highly civilized age, and my country is exerting every effort to condemn and discard every practice, policy, or utterance that might give reasonable grounds of complaint to any other people or country. We are abandoning practices toward Latin-American countries which gave rise to friction, misunderstanding, and ill will between us. Human progress and civilization call for just such reforms, and this is the way my government and people feel. We have no notion of turning back to those trouble-breeding methods which at times my government applied to some Latin-American countries."

Remarking that an American citizen (Wiley Post) had stepped into an airplane and sailed away, flown over Japan and around the world, and within eight days alighted at the airport from which he had started, I said: "Until very recently, England, with the Channel between her and Western Europe, felt herself isolated and secure from any ordinary interference. Now it's patent that a fleet of two thousand bombing planes, probably carrying explosives infinitely more powerful than any heretofore used, could fly to London from many capitals of Western Europe with perfect ease, blow London off the map, and return within a few hours to their base. Twenty years ago no human being, with the wildest stretch of the imagination, could have visualized the smallest part of the amazing changes that have taken place in every part of the world. Only the Lord can begin to visualize the even more startling changes that may take place during the next twenty years."

I drew the conclusion for Saito that the more highly civilized nations, therefore, had correspondingly greater responsibilities and duties, both from the viewpoint of their own progress and well-being and from that of the world—and these could not be dodged. No notion need be entertained for a moment that his country or mine, or any one country, no matter how highly civilized, could keep itself above the much lower level of the world, leaving them and the people of other countries to undergo a steady decline and even collapse without being drawn itself down into the vortex.

"Since there are no two more highly civilized countries than Japan and the United States," I continued, "their own self-preservation, as well as their world responsibility, calls for the utmost breadth of view and the profoundest statesmanship that their biggest and ablest statesmen can offer. It's all-important that your statesmen and mine should be broad-gauged enough to understand each other's problems and conditions, as well as those of the world. It's all-important that they should have the will to deal with them so capably as to avoid misunderstanding or material differences and promote both national and world progress. In no other way can countries like Japan and the United States, which are at present the trustees of the greatest civilization in history, make such a showing as would give them a creditable place in the future history of the world."

Great Britain, and other countries too, I remarked, had a wonderful civilization, but Britain was deeply engrossed with the dangerous political, economic, and peace problems of Western Europe.

When Saito came back to me on May 19 for an answer, I made it quite clear to him that the proposal for a joint declaration was unacceptable. Saito repeated to me the same formula his Government had been putting out for some weeks about the superior duty or function of his Government to preserve peace in what he called "Eastern Asia."

After telling him I saw no reason why our two countries should not, in the most friendly and satisfactory way, solve every present or future question, I said to him: "In my opinion, your country can conduct its affairs in such a way that it will live by itself during the coming generations—or it can conduct its affairs even more profitably by retaining the perfect understanding and friendship of all civilized nations." I added that everywhere there was considerable inquiry as to just why Japan singled out the formula about Japan's superior and special interests in peace in "Eastern Asia," and whether this implied an overlordship of the Orient or Japanese preferential trade rights.

The Ambassador replied that Japan did not contemplate interference or overlordship.

"Today," I said, "there is universal talk and plans about armaments on a steadily increasing scale. Japan and Germany are the two countries considered chiefly responsible for that talk. If the world understood the absence of any overlordship intentions or other unwarranted interference by your Government, your country would not be the occasion of armament discussion in so many parts of the world."

I emphasized that, in this awful crisis through which the world was passing, debtors everywhere were not keeping faith with creditors, and the sanctity of treaties, especially in Western Europe, was being ignored and violated. Hence, this was peculiarly a time when our civilized countries should be especially vigilant to observe and preserve both legal and moral obligations.

I saw Saito again on May 29 and, when he brought up the subject of his proposed joint declaration, I replied: "The conclusion between any two countries of a special agreement on political lines tends to imply that the relations between the two are closer than those between each of them and other countries. A joint declaration would not have the effects you propose. The American people have always been adversely disposed toward the theory and practice of political alliances. A number of agreements are already in effect to regulate relations between Japan and the United States."

Saito having said that the United States and Japan should repose full confidence in the sincerity of each other's peaceful motives, I remarked: "Japan and the United States can best convince each other that their motives are peaceful by making both their words and their courses of action those of peace."

This divergence between the words and the actions of the Japanese Government plagued our relations in the years to follow. Tokyo was liberal with protestations of peace while, often at the very same moment, engaging in new military actions and planning further ones, or in flagrantly violating the persons and rights of Americans in the Far East.

I sent the President a memorandum of my conversations with Saito and wrote him: "At this moment we have indications that the Ambassador is not inclined to accept as final my expression of the view that we cannot act upon his suggestion that there be made a joint declaration, and that he may be contemplating appealing to you in the hope that you will be more responsive to his effort." I recalled to the President that Viscount Ishii had done this very thing in 1917 when he appealed to President Wilson after Secretary of State Lansing had refused Ishii's proposal of a joint statement recognizing Japan's "special interests" in China. The consequence, I said, "was the Lansing-Ishii Agreement—which Agreement resulted in no end of confusion and embarrassment. I feel that it is highly desirable that you give the Ambassador no encouragement to think or to report to his Government that you are favorably disposed toward his project."

This was the Viscount Ishii who visited us in 1933 prior to the London Economic Conference. I recalled to the President that on that occasion certain Japanese newspapers stated that Mr. Roosevelt had made a promise to Ishii, relating to a special position of Japan in the Far East, which the American Government did not keep. "You of course made no such promise," I wrote, "but the likelihood is that the slightest indication of willingness to take the matter under consideration will be construed or be represented by Japanese officials concerned as a favorable assurance."

The President was out of Washington at the time. On his return he wrote me a note in longhand: "I find your memorandum in regard to Japan and Saito's proposal on my return from the *Sequoia* this evening. Your replies to his eight points and your general position are magnificent and I most heartily approve and congratulate you. If Saito comes to see me I want you to be there."

This episode illustrates the policy I had of carrying on foreign affairs and making decisions when the President was away, sure that he would approve what I did. I knew his general views toward the problem of Japan and the Pacific.

Ambassador Saito did see the President before returning temporarily to Japan in June, and I was present at the meeting. He did not, however, raise any political question. He came in merely for the usual formula of saying goodbye.

Saito was annoying to us generally in that he continually put out statements and made speeches in this country emphasizing his Government's alleged special rights in the Far East and virtually criticizing the attitude of our Government. I could have requested him to cease this practice, but decided not to. I did not want to give Tokyo an opportunity to believe or say that we were muzzling their Ambassador.

In June I gave a luncheon for Prince Fumimaro Konoye, president of the Japanese House of Peers, and we had a most cordial conversation. Konoye was supposed to be of the liberal as opposed to the military element in Japan. Yet it was while he was Premier of Japan that Japan invaded China in 1937, signed an alliance with the German-Italian Axis in 1940 and invaded French Indo-China in 1941. He committed suicide after American forces occupied Japan in 1945. He was an outstanding illustration of how fallacious it would have been to put all our diplomatic eggs in the Japanese liberal basket.

Japan's exuberant trade expansion with cheap goods created difficulties between our two countries then and in the years to follow. We were less affected than the British Commonwealth, but were forced to put increased duties on some Japanese products. Saito came to see me in June, gave me a memorandum on the subject, and argued in favor of an even balance of trade between the two countries. I told him I would see what I could do on the specific items he mentioned, but I emphatically spoke against bilateral bargaining between any two countries for the purpose of balancing imports and exports between them.

"This," I said, "eliminates all triangular and a number of other trade methods and policies which are vital to the development of full and normal trade between nations. The trade of most important countries of Europe, such as France, Germany, and Italy, under narrow bilateral bargaining plans, attempting to equalize trade between every two countries, shows an actual loss in their respective exports, while the sum total of trade barriers shows a net increase in height." The alternative, I suggested, was the reciprocal trade agreement which lowered tariffs mutually and extended such reductions to other nations under the most-favored-nation principle.

Underlying all our relations in the early years of my contact with the Japanese was the question of naval armaments. When the Roosevelt Administration came into office it found our Navy well below the British in strength and about on a level with Japan. The ratio of 5–5–3 established at Washington in 1922 for the battleships and aircraft carriers of Britain, the United States, and Japan, respectively, supplemented by the ratio of 10–10–7 established at London in 1930 for light cruisers and destroyers, with heavy cruisers at 5–5–3, had not been built up to by our country, whereas Japan had engaged in steady replacements as warships became overage. On March 4, 1933, our Navy was approximately at 65 per cent of treaty strength, whereas the Japanese Navy was at approximately 95 per cent.

Several days after the President's inauguration, Secretary of the Navy Claude Swanson announced this Government's intention to build the Navy up to treaty strength. He also said the fleet would be retained for the time being in the Pacific, where it had been concentrated since January, 1932. I went along gladly with these decisions. In June, 1933, the President allocated $238,000,000 from the National Industrial Recovery Act appropriations for the construction of new warships conforming to the types established by the London Treaty. The following March the Vinson-Trammell Act authorized additional naval building.

The reaction that came to me from Japan was twofold. On the one hand the army and navy chieftains made use of it to inflame the Japanese public so as to obtain funds to complete their armaments program. They succeeded in getting backbreaking military appropriations. Japan's "national defense" budget doubled between 1931 and 1934. In November, 1934, the Tokyo Cabinet approved the largest army appropriations in Japanese history. Military expenditures were rising to nearly half the total national budget.

On the other hand, the naval leaders felt disappointed in their expectation of going to the London Naval Conference to be held in 1935 and there obtaining parity with the United States and Britain. They had figured that, with their own navy built up to the treaty limits and with the United States fleet probably at 75 per cent of treaty strength at that time, parity could easily be obtained. Now they had to decide whether to denounce the naval limitation treaties and engage in a naval building race with the far wealthier United States and Britain, or to agree to continuance of the treaty ratios and risk the anger of a public opinion against naval limitation which they had already created through assassinations of Premier Hamaguchi and Premier Inukai, and ceaseless propaganda.

Reaction was not confined to Japan. On September 14, 1933, the British Chargé d'Affaires, F. D. G. Osborne, handed me an aide-mémoire from his Government which asked us to abandon our plans.

I made my reply immediately. "I can say to you now," I said, "that my Government does not have it in mind to enter upon an armaments race with any other nation or nations. We have 12,000,000 unemployed, and it is perfectly natural for our Government to absorb some of this unemployment in filling up some of its quota under the London treaty.

We have no substantial interest or motive whatever to enter upon a naval race with Japan. There is nothing that need take us to the Orient, much less to induce us to prepare for naval conflict on account of any Oriental considerations. The United States Government wants nothing in any part of the world that would call for an increase of the Navy or the Army for purposes of conquest."

The American Government, I said further, had sent delegations to Geneva and London to make earnest pleas with other Governments for both military and economic disarmament but both efforts were very disappointing and trying. "President Wilson once said to me," I remarked, "that 'the only alternative to disarmament is armament.' Hence the policy on the part of nations of refusing to enter into suitable disarmament agreements is suicidal."

Here I faced a difficult point of policy. At home the isolationist sentiment was so overwhelming that there was utmost opposition to any armaments building, however necessary in the light of world conditions. Abroad we were still endeavoring to carry forward the movement for disarmament in the interests of peace. It was therefore doubly important to dispel the slightest impression that this Government was sufficiently affected by conditions anywhere to impel it virtually to abandon and undermine the movement for disarmament and to engage in a naval race with Japan when the Roosevelt Administration had been in power but a few months.

We were, in fact, starting to build a larger navy, simply because we were dangerously below treaty limits—a danger accentuated by Japan's open military movements in the Orient and Germany's military preparations in Europe. But we had to be careful neither to antagonize the isolationists at home nor to discourage those nations abroad which still strove for disarmament.

In April, 1934, the President transferred the United States Fleet from the Pacific for maneuvers in the North Atlantic. The Japanese, who regarded the presence of the fleet in the Pacific as directed at them, appeared relieved on the surface. But not in the slightest did they slacken their efforts at naval building. On September 18, 1934, Foreign Minister Hirota informed Ambassador Grew that Japan had definitely decided to give us notice before December 31, 1934, to terminate the Washington Naval Treaty. In November our fleet was back in the Pacific.

Preliminary conversations began in London in October, 1934, for a renewal of the 1930 naval treaty due to expire December 31, 1936. Norman Davis was our chief delegate, with Admiral Standley the ranking

American naval representative. The Japanese quickly put forward their claims to parity. They wanted a common upper limit in tonnage for the navies of Britain, the United States, and Japan, and the right to build ships of any category within that tonnage. They had advanced a similar claim in 1930, but eventually acceded to the 10–10–7 ratio which soon brought actual or political death to the Japanese leaders who agreed to it. Now they were adamant. They argued that parity was necessary to their prestige. They failed to see that the United States did not consider its prestige impaired by the fact that our Army was many times smaller than that of Japan.

Our position was that the Washington and London treaties were based on the principle of equality of security. This meant that each navy was supreme in the defense of its own area. With the ratio Japan had secured, she could successfully defend herself. The United States and Britain had longer coast lines and more possessions to defend and hence needed larger fleets. We also argued that the United States had made great sacrifices to obtain the Washington Treaty by scrapping warships that would have given us twice and more the fleet of Japan. Moreover, we had made other sacrifices in the accompanying Four-Power Treaty whereby we agreed not to fortify Guam or the Philippines.

It was soon evident that no agreement would be reached. I cabled Norman Davis on November 13, 1934: "We are convinced by the conversations which have taken place over the past three weeks that practically no chance exists of bridging the definite disagreement between the Japanese delegation on the one hand and the British and ourselves on the other with regard to the fundamentals of future naval limitation. Every opportunity has been afforded the Japanese to explain and to justify Japan's demands; we have not forced the pace and we have not refused them a chance to 'save face.' We should continue to emphasize our thesis that maintaining the treaties as a basis for future naval limitation rests on the equality of self-defense, equality of security, and on a united purpose to avoid competition in armaments. The only construction we can place on the Japanese thesis is that it represents a desire to obtain overwhelming supremacy in the Orient, opening the way to preferential rights and privileges and destroying the delicate balance in Asia, both economic and political, which is represented by the other basic principles and policies that are embodied in the Washington and other treaties."

There was little point in trying to placate the Japanese. On November 26, 1934, I cabled Davis: "For the last three years, with conspicuous lack of success, the idea has been tried that the moderate Japanese element, now silent and in eclipse, would, through concessions made to Japan, be encouraged to oppose the Japanese military elements. According to our belief and information, furthermore, military psychology and military elements are stronger today in Japan than has been the case for a long time."

The preliminary conference adjourned on December 19, and ten days later Ambassador Saito handed me his Government's notification ending the Washington Treaty. Two years were still to run until December 31, 1936, before Japan would be free of her obligations under the treaty, but the barrier was down on the race for naval armament.

In a public statement on December 29 I said: "We, of course, realize that any nation has the right not to renew a treaty; also that any movement toward disarmament, to be successful, must rest on agreements voluntarily entered into. This notification is none the less a source of genuine regret to us, believing as we do that the existing treaties have safeguarded the rights and promoted the collective interests of all of the signatories."

I also expressed our willingness to enter into new negotiations whenever there was prospect of arriving at a mutually satisfactory conclusion. But that prospect was never to arrive. No new ratio was to be set for the Japanese Navy until American bombs and shells fixed it at zero.

We were now at the Oriental crossroads of decision. There were two courses open to us. One was to withdraw gradually, perhaps with dignity, from the Far East. This meant acquiescence in the nullification of our treaty rights, the closing of the Open Door, further Japanese appropriation of pieces of China and other territory, relinquishing the protection of our citizens and abandoning them to unequal competition with Japanese-operated monopolies. This course clearly would mean our turning over to the domination of Japan the entire Pacific Ocean west of Hawaii where lived nearly one-half the population of the world. It further would mean that the same aggressive, lawless military element in Japan would continue in supreme control and extend their power throughout the Pacific so that this country could not land a boatload of goods on the other side without falling under the arbitrary authority and harsh rules of Japanese domination. There were many who would support us in such a policy, believing that war might thereby be avoided, while the United States could continue to exist without the trade of the Orient.

The other course was to continue to insist on the maintenance of law, on our legitimate rights and interests in the Far East, and on observance of the treaties and declarations that guaranteed an independent China and pledged equality to all nations, nonintervention, nonaggression, and peaceful settlement of disputes in the Orient. This meant a firm, though not an aggressive, policy toward Japan, especially in the light of her evident plans of territorial expansion by force. It meant adequate military preparedness. Recognizing the inferiority complex of the Japanese, generally manifested by blustering superiority assertions and actions, this policy meant a delicate day-to-day operation of diplomacy. It meant close contact and parallel action with the other powers interested in the Orient, particularly Great Britain. It meant friendship and cooperation with China.

By the first course, one of patent appeasement in its worst sense, we could, by concessions and by surrendering both rights and solemn treaty obligations, postpone the virtual certainty that Japan would gradually secure domination of what she later called Greater East Asia. This meant the entire Pacific, beginning with the East Indies and coming clear across, both south and west, to and embracing the mandated islands.

By the second course we would frankly face and resolutely deal with the not distant dangers of territorial and other aggression, cling steadfastly to all our basic policies and obligations in the Pacific area, and govern our attitude toward Japan accordingly.

The President and I chose the second course. As a great and enlightened nation, seeking to uphold and spread the doctrine of world order under law, liberal commercial policy, and other basic principles on which alone the world could live in peace and economic well-being, the United States could choose no other.

22: Speaking Terms with Russia

IN A RIGHT-HAND DRAWER of my desk, letters began gathering from my first day in office, requesting us to—or not to—recognize Soviet Russia and establish diplomatic relations with her. For sixteen years we had had no formal ties with Moscow. The new Administration was confronted with a question that had many ramifications both at home and abroad.

I kept these letters close at hand because I felt that the subject itself was close at hand. I was receiving delegations from various organizations presenting compelling reasons why Russia should—or should not—be recognized. Many ambassadors and ministers, whose countries' policy might be determined by our action, questioned me on our intentions. The matter was under discussion in Congress. Previous Administrations had had it under consideration—but decided against it.

It was an ironic moment in history. In 1781 the Continental Congress sent Francis Dana, Chief Justice of Massachusetts, as our envoy to Russia, with John Quincy Adams as his private secretary. The autocratic Catherine the Great refused to receive these representatives of what she regarded as a dangerous revolutionary government. They languished in Moscow two years, then returned home without recognition. It was not until twenty-eight years later that Czar Alexander I agreed to recognize the United States, and John Quincy Adams was sent to Moscow as the first American Minister to Russia. Now we ourselves were debating whether Soviet Russia was too dangerously revolutionary to be recognized.

We had rich food for debate. The Communist International, under direction from Moscow, was spreading communistic propaganda in the United States, seeking to overthrow the Government. Şoviet Russia had refused to honor debts incurred by the Czarist Government to the United States Government and American citizens. Foreign citizens in Russia had been thrown into jail on slight pretext. Religious freedom was denied. Other large nations, among them Britain, France, Germany, and Italy, had recognized Russia, but their relations with Moscow had not been wholly happy.

Certain conditions were arising, however, which were not fully present under previous Administrations. Russia, emerging from her seclusion, showed signs of willingness to cooperate with the Western Powers. She attended the Disarmament Conference at Geneva, beginning in February, 1932. Her relations with Japan were strained, and it was simultaneously apparent to us both that Japan was on the highroad to conquest and aggrandizement. Russia indirectly indicated to us on numerous occasions that she desired a restoration of diplomatic relations between us. She badly needed American credits to assist in her industrial revolution. She had established a trading organization in New York and had an informal representative in Washington.

If I may jump forward a few years, I clearly expressed the ideas I held in 1933 during a conversation with Soviet Foreign Commissar Molotov on June 3, 1942, in Washington when we were both at war with Germany. "When I came to the State Department in 1933," I told him, "I recommended recognition of the Soviet Government on several important grounds. Probably the most important was the great need and opportunity for cooperation between our two Governments during the years ahead for the purpose of promoting and preserving conditions of peace in the world. My further grounds were the traditional friendship between the peoples of the two countries and the fact that it was contrary to the best interests of two great nations such as the Soviets and ourselves not to be on speaking terms diplomatically in view of the existing circumstances in the international field."

When President Roosevelt addressed his May 16, 1933, cable appeal for military and economic disarmament to the heads of fifty-four nations, one of his messages went to President Mikhail Kalinin of the Union of Soviet Socialist Republics. To some it seemed anomalous to address the head of a Government we refused to recognize, and to others it seemed a species of recognition. Actually, it did not change the situation.

From time to time I talked with the ambassadors or ministers of countries that had recognized Russia, and sought to learn from them all possible details of their negotiations with Moscow and their impressions of the results achieved through relations with the Soviet Union.

While I was at the London Economic Conference in June and July, I discussed the same question elaborately with a number of foreign ministers attending the meeting. I tried to have a long talk with British Foreign Secretary Sir John Simon on the subject, because Britain had recognized Soviet Russia some years before and I wanted to get from him different angles on how it had worked out. But, for some reason or other, Simon would talk but very little.

In London I also conferred with Soviet Foreign Commissar Maxim

Litvinov, and found him a thoroughly capable diplomat and international statesman. He had been one of Russia's principal peace advocates, and he was later to become a world figure by reason of his constructive support of peace at Geneva. Round-faced and rugged, and of more than normal weight, he possessed an agreeable personality. He was more interesting in conversation and in his ideas than the average diplomat, though he was guarded in what he said. I was too busy to do more than emphasize economic principles in our conversations, but the groundwork was laid for our later personal discussions at the time of recognition.

On my return from London in the first week in August, I told President Roosevelt at Hyde Park about my talks with Simon and Litvinov. We discussed Russian recognition in a general way, but did not reach any conclusions.

In Washington I found that a number of persons were active in favor of immediate recognition of the U.S.S.R. I kept an open mind on the subject myself, and while leaning strongly toward recognition, declined to agree to any final action until this Government had first satisfied itself on certain vital points.

In the following month, on September 21, I sent the President a long memorandum outlining the whole question and explaining the moot points at issue which, if settled, would open the door to recognition. The stumbling blocks to recognition, as I saw it, were the operations carried on in this country under the direction of the Communist International at Moscow, freedom of religion for American citizens in Russia, fair treatment of Americans in Russia, and satisfactory settlement of governmental and private indebtedness due from Russia. My memorandum prescribed the nature and extent of these obstructions and indicated that, with them out of the way, recognition would follow. The Soviets were then pressing hard for loans or credits, governmental or private, in the United States, to enable them to buy machinery for their industrialization.

"As you know," I wrote the President, "recognition of the present regime in Russia has been withheld by the Government of the United States on account of the failure of the Soviet Government to carry out certain international obligations which are considered essential to the maintenance of friendly and mutually advantageous relations between the United States and Russia. The Soviet Government, for instance, has repudiated Russian obligations held by the United States Government and by American citizens, and has confiscated the property of American citizens invested in Russia. More important still, the present regime in

Russia has been unwilling up to this time to discontinue its interference in the internal affairs of the United States. Furthermore, there are a whole series of questions arising out of differences between the economic and social structure of the United States and Russia, especially the existence of a state monopoly of foreign trade in Russia, which require settlement by agreement.

"I think that there is no question that until these fundamental problems have been settled through agreement in a manner satisfactory to the United States, there will be lacking any sound basis for friendly cooperation between the Governments of Russia and the United States and for the development of mutually beneficial trade and intercourse between the two countries."

I pointed out to Mr. Roosevelt that Russia was "very eager" to get two things from our Government—credits or loans, and recognition. I stated bluntly that the Soviet position toward payment of debts was very bad. With regard to the second desire, recognition, I said:

"It is to be noted that recognition by the United States is greatly desired by the Soviet authorities, since they are apparently convinced that recognition by the United States would be a factor in preventing a Japanese attack on the Maritime Provinces. The Soviet Government also appears to believe that recognition by the United States would open the private banking resources of the United States to the Soviet Government and facilitate the obtaining of credits in other countries. Finally, there is no question but that the Soviet authorities realize that recognition would strengthen the prestige of the Soviet Government not only abroad, but also at home, where it is faced with tremendous difficulties in carrying out its industrial and agricultural programs."

Consequently, I told the President, we had "two powerful weapons which can be used to bring about a favorable settlement of some, if not all, of our outstanding problems with the Soviet Government. I am convinced, from the experience of other countries, that, unless we utilize every available means of exerting pressure on the Soviet Government in order to obtain a settlement of outstanding problems, there is little likelihood that such problems can be satisfactorily solved. It is evident that if loans of any considerable amount should be extended to the Soviet Government, except as a part of an agreement involving a satisfactory settlement of such problems, one of our most effective weapons would be taken from our hands—possibly the most effective—since the Soviets, it is believed, prefer at the moment credits to recognition." I concluded by recommending that no loans be extended "except as part and parcel of a final settlement of our relations with Russia."

Thus our approach to the question was different from that of other nations then maintaining diplomatic relations with Russia. Those nations recognized Russia first and then began to discuss the questions in dispute between them. The results were generally disappointing. Having obtained part of what she wanted, Russia became less disposed to make concessions to obtain the remainder.

In some respects we stood to gain more than Russia by a restoration of diplomatic relations. Without relations, the Russians were probably much better informed about conditions in America than we were about the situation in Russia. The Soviets were in close touch with what was going on here through their Amtorg, or trading office, in New York, an Information Bureau in Washington, and the American Communist Party.

The chief of the Information Bureau, Boris Skvirsky, had numerous contacts with American citizens. His relations with members of the State Department were limited, but his large house on Massachusetts Avenue became a rendezvous for some American newspapermen and other persons, a number of United States Senators and Representatives, and a few officials of executive departments other than the State Department. After we resumed relations with Russia, this house became the temporary Soviet Embassy and Skvirsky became the Soviet Chargé d'Affaires.

Moreover, it was easier for Russians to do business in the United States without diplomatic protection than it was for Americans to do business in Russia. With few American citizens and no diplomatic officials to consult in Russia, the American businessman yielded too readily to Soviet demands.

For some time we had informally exchanged views with Russia through two media—American citizens in contact with the Soviet Government, and the informal Soviet representatives in the United States. I frequently received some of these Americans, including engineers working on industrial projects in Russia, who strongly favored recognition.

William C. Bullitt, an intimate friend of the President and my special assistant, was in close touch with the Soviet representatives here. A brilliant person, well versed in international affairs, he was particularly friendly toward Russia and was an ardent proponent of recognition. He so expressed himself to the President and to me.

Our informal exchanges with the Russians were directed toward getting some indication from them that they were willing to make the concessions we required prior to recognition. They gave the impression of moving more and more in our direction.

During a visit I made to the President a few days after my memorandum to him, he casually picked up a sheaf of papers from his desk and handed them to me. "These are letters and petitions, pro and con, on recognition of Russia," he said. "Will you look them over and any others you have and give me your opinion on what we should do?"

I did not tell him that my opinion was already virtually formed. I took the papers and returned to the State Department. There I completed examination of the great mass of material I had on the same subject. A couple of days later I went back to the President.

"I favor recognizing Russia," I said, "although our correspondence reveals that great numbers of people are opposed to it. Russia and we had been traditional friends up to the end of the World War. In general, Russia has been peacefully inclined. The world is moving into a dangerous period both in Europe and in Asia. Russia could be a great help in stabilizing this situation as time goes on and peace becomes more and more threatened."

The President, without a moment's hesitation, replied, "I agree entirely." He then added: "Two great nations like America and Russia should be on speaking terms. It will be beneficial to both countries to resume diplomatic relations."

We then ran over again the various points at issue between the United States and Russia, and talked about the steps to be taken toward recognition. I earnestly argued that three questions—no Soviet interference in our internal affairs; freedom of religion for Americans in Russia; and debt settlement—should be thoroughly taken up and satisfactory understandings reached and put in writing, by informal conferences between the two Governments, before we should invite the Russian Government to send a representative here with a view to recognition. Meantime not a single word should be uttered publicly about recognition.

The President, however, decided otherwise. His view was that we would invite Russia to send a representative here and could then discuss the questions at issue and thereafter agree upon recognition.

The President decided he would send a letter direct to President Kalinin. I would have preferred having the message sent through State Department channels, but the President on many occasions was a believer in the beneficial effects of communications directly between the heads of Governments rather than through the foreign offices, as he had already shown by his messages on May 16.

Numerous occasions were later to arise when the President preferred thus to communicate directly with the heads of other governments instead of having the governments communicate through their respective foreign offices. In many instances I doubted the wisdom of this course.

On October 10 the President addressed a letter to President Kalinin. He said he had contemplated "the desirability of an effort to end the present abnormal relations between the hundred and twenty-five million people of the United States and the hundred and sixty million people of Russia." He added: "The difficulties that have created this anomalous situation are serious but not, in my opinion, insoluble; and difficulties between great nations can be removed, only by frank, friendly conversations. If you are of similar mind, I should be glad to receive any representatives you may designate to explore with me personally all questions outstanding between our countries."

We were careful not to put any promise or commitment on recognition in the message. The word itself was not used. President Kalinin replied cordially and said he would send Litvinov. "There is no doubt," he said, "that difficulties, present or arising, between two countries, can be solved only when direct relations exist between them; and that, on the other hand, they have no chance for solution in the absence of such relations." There was an implication here that the questions in dispute between us could be solved only after direct relations were established. Our position was that the questions had to be solved or direct relations would not be established.

Kalinin said also: "I shall take the liberty further to express the opinion that the abnormal situation, to which you correctly refer in your message, has an unfavorable effect not only on the interest of the two states concerned, but also on the general international situation, increasing the element of disquiet, complicating the process of consolidating world peace and encouraging forces tending to disturb that peace." This sentence worried the Japanese, as Ambassador Grew cabled me, because they believed it referred to the turmoil in the Far East and Russia's intention to bring Moscow and Washington in line to face it.

The next few weeks were busy ones in the State Department. I was preparing for my departure for the Pan American Conference at Montevideo, Uruguay, in December. And I was also going over draft after draft of the agreements we hoped and expected the Russians to sign before we would grant recognition. The Division of Eastern European Affairs—under Robert F. Kelley, a thoroughly capable and useful official —made as many as twenty drafts of some of the conventions. We had to be sure both that they were ironclad guarantees of the rights of our citizens in Russia and also that they would be agreed to by Litvinov.

Kelley and his assistants made a close study of every treaty Soviet Russia had signed with other governments. They particularly concentrated on the treaty of 1925 between Russia and Germany, which was the most favorable of all the treaties Russia signed. We paid special attention to the agreement whereby Russia would promise to refrain from internal interference in the United States. The Eastern European Division prepared this draft by taking a phrase here and a sentence there from twenty-six similar treaties Russia had signed with other countries, ranging from Germany to Afghanistan. When it was finished, there was not a single word in the draft that had not already appeared in some treaty to which Russia had affixed her signature and seal. I insisted, however, that the agreement be much broader than the usual agreements the Soviet Government signed, which bound only the Government itself not to conduct propaganda and left all individuals in Russia free to do so, including the Communist International.

The principal agreements prepared were in the form of exchanges of letters between the President and Litvinov or statements by them. In addition to that dealing with interference in the internal affairs of each other's country, the remainder embraced, in general:

Establishment of diplomatic relations and exchange of ambassadors. Freedom of conscience and free exercise of religion. Legal protection for the citizens of each country equal to that granted the citizens of another nation having the most favorable rights in this respect. (In this case the treaty between Russia and Germany was specifically cited.) A definition by Litvinov of economic espionage, to protect American citizens against prosecution if they sent out ordinary information on Russian economic developments. A statement by Litvinov waiving any claims arising out of activities of United States military forces in Siberia subsequent to January 1, 1918, following his examination of certain documents of the years 1918 to 1921. These latter documents made clear to Litvinov that American forces had not been in Siberia to wrest territory from Russia, but to ensure the withdrawal of the Japanese, who had a far larger force in Siberia with the intent to occupy it permanently. The

Treasury Department took part in the drafting of a statement on Russian debts, and on the extension of a loan to Russia.

The Rumanian Government tried to induce us to inject an outside element into the forthcoming discussions. It requested that we induce Russia to guarantee Rumania possession of Bessarabia, the province Rumania had obtained from Russia at the end of the World War. I had no intention to muddy the waters which were already agitated enough, and refused.

I sent a memorandum to the President suggesting that I defer my departure for Montevideo—originally scheduled for November 5—for one week in order to participate in the Litvinov conferences. I told him I especially wanted to be sure that the agreements on no Soviet propaganda and interference in the United States and on religious freedom for Americans in Russia were agreed to before I left. The President consented.

Litvinov was due to arrive November 7. The day before his arrival, I met with the President, Secretary of the Treasury Henry Morgenthau, Under Secretary of State Phillips, and William Bullitt in the White House. We went over the subjects to be discussed with Litvinov, and agreed that the two most important were precautions against Soviet propaganda and illegal activities in the United States and freedom of worship for Americans in Russia.

Litvinov arrived in Washington as scheduled, and I had two long conferences with him on November 8 and also attended a luncheon given him by the President. On November 9 we had another conference and I gave a luncheon for him.

Right off, Litvinov gave us to understand he expected us to agree on recognition, and then we would begin to discuss the moot questions. He and his Government had drawn this conclusion from the President's letter, although the letter had made no such commitment. He had drawn it also from the fact that the twenty-six other nations that recognized Russia had done so unconditionally and had then proceeded to discuss their mutual difficulties. I had to disabuse him of this idea before we could get down to real business.

When I showed him the agreement on abstention from interference in our respective internal affairs, he read it and said: "We can't agree to this."

"But you have agreed to it," I replied.

"How?" he exclaimed.

I then pointed out how we had prepared it, using entirely the wording of treaties that Russia had already signed. He was greatly impressed and agreed to study it further.

When I handed him the agreement on freedom of religion for Americans in Russia, he first objected that this was impossible. It shortly developed that, although he spoke English quite well, he had misunderstood our objective to be freedom of religion for Russians as well as Americans. After that had been cleared up, I told him that reports were still coming in from Russia that our citizens were being denied proper protection in the exercise of their religious rights. "What guarantee can you furnish for removing this serious difficulty?" I asked. "Would you look at this draft and say whether it meets with your approval?"

He read it. "Russian laws are sufficient for the purpose indicated," he commented. "I have no authority to say they will be changed."

I then asked him to consider the draft and give us his comments in writing, but he said: "I prefer to do it right away. I'll write my comments on it here." This he proceeded to do.

At the end of an opening sentence stating that Americans should be permitted to exercise full liberty of conscience and be protected in the free exercise of religious worship, he wrote "Yes." He wrote in several exceptions to later sentences which had to be ironed out in further conferences, and he left his copy of the draft with me.

Our conversations gave promise of leading to results. Litvinov and I reached specific agreements to the entire satisfaction of this Government on religious protection in Russia and discontinuance of propaganda here by all Soviet agencies. I had made it perfectly plain to Litvinov that, unless he agreed to straighten out the differences existing between us, there would be no recognition and no diplomatic relations, and of course no loan or credits. I was then obliged to withdraw from the conferences in order to leave for Montevideo on November 11.

On November 10 I went to the White House for a final conference with the President, Phillips, Bullitt, and Assistant Secretary of State R. Walton Moore. I outlined the progress made thus far in the negotiations with Litvinov and the difficulties that still remained, among which was an agreement on the Soviet debt. I then turned the negotiations, so far as the State Department was concerned, over to Assistant Secretary Moore. I had served for some years in Congress with Judge Moore and we had become warm personal friends. Head of the Virginia bar for years, he was a person of unusual ability and high purpose, a profound student of both domestic and international affairs, and possessed character and patriotism of the highest order. The conferences shifted to the White House, with Judge Moore, Bullitt, and Kelley working under the President. Before I left, the President and I agreed that, if the negotiations succeeded, Bullitt should be our first Ambassador to Soviet Russia.

The agreements were announced November 17 while I was on the high seas aboard the steamship *American Legion*. A telegram to this effect arrived from the State Department during the middle of the night while I was asleep. Awakened at once by my assistant, Hugh R. Cumming, I read the message joyfully, remarked, "I hope it lasts," and, sitting up in bed, composed this statement which was issued on November 18:

"I am gratified to learn that the peoples of the United States and Russia, after a frank exchange of views at Washington, have resumed normal relations and that the primary basis agreed upon is substantially that indicated before I left Washington. The badly confused world situation will be improved by this natural and timely step which is proof of the marked progress possible in all international dealings when there exists such splendid initiative as that displayed by the President and the mutual disposition and will to approach serious world problems in a friendly and fearless spirit."

At Montevideo I was approached by various Latin American Governments which had not yet recognized Soviet Russia. They wanted to learn the details of our handling of the problem, and what success we had met with, so as to determine their own attitude. I gave them all the information available.

When I returned to Washington in January, 1934, I found a dispatch from Bullitt, who meantime had proceeded to Moscow, recounting a meeting he had with Stalin and a conversation with Litvinov. Stalin introduced his Chief of Staff General Egorov to him as "the man who will lead our army victoriously against the Japanese when they attack us." He asked Bullitt for 250,000 tons of old American railroad rails for eastern Russia. "Without the rails we shall win that war," he said, "but it will be easier with them."

Bullitt reported that a Japanese attack on the Soviets was regarded as certain by all members of the Government and the Communist Party. Litvinov told him Russia did not fear an immediate invasion by Germany but that, if the probable war with Japan should drag on for two years, Germany, acting in concert with Japan, would attack. Litvinov said he knew preliminary conversations toward this end had already taken place.

The first Soviet Ambassador to the United States, Alexander Troyanovsky, was already in Washington when I returned from Montevideo. The discussions between the President and Litvinov on debt settlement had failed to reach an agreement, hence this was the first important subject I took up with the Ambassador. On our part we were ready to extend credits to the Soviet Union. An Export-Import Bank of Washington was incorporated on February 12 for this purpose, with a capital of $11,000,-000. But it was soon evident that Russia was not equally ready to settle her debts. The conversations between the President and Litvinov had narrowed the debts down to between $75,000,000 and $150,000,000, and Litvinov said his Government might be willing to pay as much as $100,-000,000. It now developed, however, that there was a complete disagreement on the subject of interest on the debts, which had already run for twenty years. We wanted the interest paid; the Soviets wanted to ignore it.

On March 26, when Ambassador Troyanovsky called on me to ask why the Export-Import Bank had not begun to extend credits to Russia, I told him: "I must be entirely frank with you. The President, Mr. Bullitt, Assistant Secretary Moore, and others who took part in the Russian debt conversations with Mr. Litvinov, were greatly surprised and keenly disappointed to learn that Mr. Litvinov has offered a contention and version of the debt understanding entirely different from anything our officials thought they were discussing. It is entirely different from anything they were thinking about. The misunderstanding is so wide that perhaps it would be best to bring all commercial and financial relations to a standstill until it can be clarified."

The following month the situation became further complicated by the enactment of the Johnson Act, which prohibited loans to foreign governments in default on indebtedness to the United States. I asked Attorney General Homer S. Cummings for an opinion on whether the Soviet Government could be considered in default as the successor of the previous Russian Government when it was negotiating a settlement of its debt. He replied in the affirmative. The Johnson Act contained an exception whereby Federal Government agencies, such as the Export-Import Bank, could still extend credits to countries in default, but the bank issued a statement that it would extend no credits to the Soviet Government until its indebtedness to the United States Government and American citizens had been satisfactorily adjusted.

An unbreakable deadlock ensued, despite months of patient negotiation. The Soviet Government knew that payment of its indebtedness was unpopular in Russia but had hoped to offset this unpopularity by the credits it would obtain here. No credits were forthcoming, and no agreement could be reached on the payment of interest on the Soviet debt. Hence the Soviets were never to make a debt payment, and the Export-Import Bank was never to function with regard to Russia. The Soviet Union was actually in a worse position than other countries. Private corporations and banks of other nations in default could obtain credits in the United States, but all corporations and banks in Russia were government-owned.

The effect on our relations with Russia was unfortunate. Instead of the friendship I expected, a large number of points of friction and suspicion developed in the years to follow. The beneficial influence I had expected Russo-American cooperation to have on the political situation both in Europe and in Asia did not materialize. I argued again and again with Soviet ambassadors that it was disastrous to let the comparatively small sum of Soviet indebtedness and other modest differences stand in the way of our thoroughgoing political relations. I pleaded with them again and again that if only the United States, Russia, Britain, and France could present a common moral front to the aggressor nations, Germany, Japan, and Italy, war might be prevented. I warned them again and again of the dangers threatening us all. But a common front did not come until long after war had begun.

In September, 1934, Russia joined the League of Nations, and in December Litvinov proposed to the President and me, through the Soviet Embassy, that the United States join with him in a project for a permanent disarmament organization to sit at Geneva. His point was that the Kellogg Antiwar Pact of 1928 provided no machinery for consultation in the event it were violated, and that such an agency as he proposed could provide such machinery, and could offer the United States, not a member of the League of Nations, a place in which to present her views. But the political implications were such that the isolationist sentiment in America would have been aroused. I regretfully had to tell him, No.

I still hoped that something might be salvaged in the way of increased trade between the two countries. After the Trade Agreements Act was enacted June 12, 1934, and trade agreements began to be concluded with a series of nations, I had to decide whether to extend the tariff reductions, under most-favored-nation treatment, to the Soviet Union, which exercised a government monopoly of foreign trade. There was no such thing as freedom of trade in Russia.

Desirous of doing everything possible to better our relations, I agreed in July, 1935, that Russia should enjoy the benefits of our tariff reductions granted to other nations. In exchange Russia agreed to purchase $30,000,000 worth of American products during the next twelve months, compared to the three-year average of $12,000,000 annually.

But our efforts toward closer relations were again to be negated. The Communist International, with headquarters in Moscow, continued to support Communist propaganda and activities in the United States. We made verbal complaints to Moscow, without result. Finally Russia permitted the holding of an All-World Congress of the Communist International in Moscow from July 25 to August 20, 1935. American Communists attended and took part in discussions and plans for the development of the Communist Party in the United States. Here was a flagrant violation of the pledge of noninterference given us on November 16, 1933, and we could not let it pass without protest. By agreement with the President, I sent through Ambassador Bullitt a strong note to the Soviet Government:

"The Government of the United States would be lacking in candor if it failed to state frankly that it anticipates the most serious consequences if the Government of the Union of Soviet Socialist Republics is unwilling, or unable, to take appropriate measures to prevent further acts in disregard of the solemn pledge given by it to the Government of the United States."

But the Soviets replied with the astounding assertion that "it is certainly not new to the Government of the United States that the Government of the Union of Soviet Socialist Republics cannot take upon itself and has not taken upon itself obligations of any kind with regard to the Communist International." They refused to accept the protest. In other words, the Communist International, although intimately connected with the Soviet Government, could do what it wanted in American internal affairs without interference from that Government.

In publishing both notes, I issued a statement in which I said: "In view of the plain language of the pledge, it is not possible for the Soviet Government to disclaim its obligation to prevent activities on its territory directed toward overthrowing the political or social order in the United States. And that Government does not and cannot disclaim responsibility on the ground of inability to carry out the pledge, for its authority within its territorial limits is supreme and its power to control the acts and utterances of organizations and individuals within those limits is absolute. . . . If the Soviet Government pursues a policy of permitting activities on its territory involving interference in the internal affairs of the United States, instead of 'preventing' such activities, as its written pledge provides, the friendly and official relations between the two countries cannot but be seriously impaired."

.We were now back almost to where we had started. We had official relations with Moscow, but they rested on no bedrock of friendship and cooperation. Try as I might, I could not establish the sound relationship I deemed so necessary not only for the two countries but also as a counter-weight for peace in the scales tipping more sharply toward war.

As long as I was in the State Department, however, I was never to relinquish efforts to promote two-way friendly relations with Russia. I did not abandon my original idea that Russia and the United States, especially after the agreements reached at the time of recognition, had no conflicting national aims, and that the two countries, working together and in harmony with other countries opposed to war, could have a beneficial influence on the world. I recalled the fact that, especially since our Civil War, Russia and the United States had enjoyed thoroughly friendly relations, without interruption, and also that Soviet Russia, at the time of our recognition, was pursuing a strong disarmament and peace policy as a member of the Disarmament Conference at Geneva.

But I knew that much time and more patience would be required. Russia had not yet forgotten that the nations of the West had strenuously opposed the Bolshevik Revolution. She remembered that, when the war ended, the troops of the Allies remained on her territory for many months thereafter. Long isolated in her northern snows, she did not have the knack of dealing with other nations on a basis of understanding, friendliness, and freedom from suspicion. The efforts of the Comintern to overthrow other governments and the fact that Stalin in effect controlled both the Comintern and the Soviet Government—however much his Government sought to make it appear that there was no connection between the two—doubled our difficulties in dealing with Moscow.

No nation has the right to send money and organizations into a country to undermine and overthrow its government. Every nation has the right to preach its ideas anywhere in the world and to convey information regarding its government and the basic ideas underlying it to other peoples or countries; but those peoples or countries must have the chance to decide independently on their own form of government. This doctrine applies to all nations as well as to Russia.

During the years following our recognition, Russia did not pursue a stable course based on fundamental policies. The comparatively new Soviet regime seemed at this stage not to have settled on a solid, permanent, straightforward course in the conduct of its foreign policies. We noticed a careless or indifferent observance by the Soviet Government of some of the agreements and understandings our two Governments had entered into. There was a disposition to haggle over little things and to debate seriously and interminably over wholly minor matters which developed numerous pinpricks. Some questions of major importance were also to arise on which Russia's attitude was difficult to understand.

Negotiating with Russia, therefore, was not like negotiating with other great powers. In every approach to Moscow I had to bear these facts in mind.

23: A Good Neighbor Moves In

ARMED WITH the President's declaration of our Good Neighbor Policy, I moved into the Latin American field in 1933 only to find manifold impediments in the way of the development of cooperative relations among all the twenty-one American Republics. Over a long period until almost 1933 the United States had pursued policies toward some of the Latin American nations of so arbitrary—and what some of those countries considered so overbearing—a nature that prejudice and feeling throughout Central and South America against our country were sharp indeed.

Our inheritance of ill will was grim. It was probated under the name of Intervention: intervention in Panama to separate Panama from Colombia and build the Panama Canal; intervention in Mexico; intervention in Cuba; intervention in Haiti; intervention in Nicaragua.

Piled high on political antagonism was economic resentment. The high tariffs of preceding Administrations, coupled with the panic of 1929, had brought grave economic distress to the Latin American countries. In 1929 the value of our imports from Latin America was a little more than $1,000,000,000, and our exports to Latin America slightly less. In the year ending June 30, 1933, the value of imports from Latin America had fallen to $212,000,000 and our exports to $291,000,000. In other words, our total trade with Latin America in four years had dropped to just one-fourth of what it had been. In 1932 certain Latin American countries, stung by our high tariffs, actually conferred with one another to form a customs union for defensive action against us.

I retained a vivid, uncomfortable memory from reading of the pyrotechnic clash between our Government and Argentina at the Pan American Conference at Havana in 1928. The United States delegation, headed by former Secretary of State Hughes, sustained repeated attacks from the Argentine delegation, largely over the issue of intervention. Hughes had delivered an extensive argument supporting our right to intervene. The statesmen and politicians of Argentina had for some years undertaken to assert leadership of the hemisphere by rallying all possible elements against the United States. A powder magazine was built at Havana which could easily explode into numerous discordant factions among the twenty-one American nations.

Secretary of State Stimson had taken two or three steps under the authority of President Hoover in the direction of fair treatment of other American nations. One of the most outstanding was the withdrawal of our Marines from Nicaragua two months before I came to the State Department. Unfortunately, these wise political acts were not sufficient to impress Latin America in our favor. Nor was Stimson, in the bosom of a high-tariff Administration, able to do anything for Latin American trade.

Intensifying the bitterness in the Western Hemisphere as I crossed the threshold of the State Department was the fact that the Latin American republics were falling out among themselves. The Chaco War, one of the most violent ever fought in the New World, was raging in the jungles between Paraguay and Bolivia. A border conflict had broken out between Colombia and Peru and threatened to develop into real war. In Cuba the government of dictatorial General Gerardo Machado was slipping its cinch after twelve years in the saddle, and revolution was plotting.

The very day before I became Secretary of State, Stimson had rejected Argentina's invitation to sign the Antiwar Pact composed by Foreign Minister Saavedra Lamas. His thought was that it impaired the vigor of the Kellogg Pact, engineered by his predecessor, Secretary Kellogg. Argentina, on her part, had refused to sign the Kellogg Pact.

Facing me was the prospect of a Pan American Conference scheduled to meet at Montevideo at the end of the year. The conference should have met in December, 1932, but so poor was the prospect of effective cooperation in the Western Hemisphere that it had been postponed for a year. And now there was insistent talk of further postponement.

The entire outlook, charged with pent-up bitterness, seemed thoroughly discouraging. I therefore knew that implementing the Good Neighbor policy proclaimed by President Roosevelt would involve a tremendous undertaking in the Western Hemisphere. But this fact was also a challenge. I felt that our principles could have little effect in the world unless they produced a bounteous harvest in our own neighborhood. We could not look for closer cooperation throughout the world, we could not hope to point the better road to nations like Germany and Japan, unless we first showed that cooperation could work in the areas of the Monroe Doctrine. In the years following 1933, the Good Neighbor Policy, in the eyes of the public, took on a special significance for the Western Hemisphere, but when President Roosevelt first stated it in his inaugural address he meant it to apply to the other continents as well.

Long before March 4 I had resolved that one of our principles in dealing with Latin America would be religious adherence to the principle of nonintervention. I felt we could never be real friends with the Latin Americans so long as we maintained the right to intervene in their internal affairs. I had helped write the planks in the Democratic platform of 1932 which stated, "No interference in the internal affairs of other nations" and also "Cooperation with nations of the Western Hemisphere to maintain the spirit of the Monroe Doctrine." President Roosevelt was in thorough agreement with me on these points, and for some years we had already been thinking on the same line.

Our program toward Latin America, I knew, had to embrace a broad and basic set of mutually beneficial policies and principles, political, economic, and moral. But policies and principles were not enough. The Latin American nations had heard them enunciated by previous Administrations, and alleged breaches of such principles had brought doubt and misgivings in every corner south of the Rio Grande. We should have to give them acts as well as words. They were judging us now by their interpretation of our previous acts. They would continue to judge identically.

But action, even though right, was not enough. It also had to be highly delicate and tactful. We had to take the initiative and leadership to effect contacts and conference calculated to remove the grievances held against us. By deeds done carefully in the right way we had to pave the way for the gradual restoration of confidence and friendliness and steadily increasing cooperation on the part of all the Latin American nations—not only with us, but also among themselves. Actually, our task was to create a whole new spirit.

My first action was called forth in March, 1933, by the Leticia border conflict between Colombia and Peru. Peruvians had invaded and occupied the Colombian border town of Leticia on September 1, 1932. At first the Peruvian Government disavowed the movement and promised to evacuate its citizens from Leticia. But internal difficulties in Peru prompted that Government to reverse its position. Both countries began to marshal their armies for a real trial of strength. Leticia, a town of several hundred souls, unknown to the world before the dispute began, sadly exemplified the basic lack of friendship throughout the Western Hemisphere which could so quickly nurture an insignificant pinprick into a probable war.

I had not been in office a fortnight when an invitation arrived from the League of Nations to join with its Advisory Committee handling this incipient war. The decision we had to make was delicate. Were we to acquiesce in the League's assumption of jurisdiction over a controversy in the heart of the Western Hemisphere? Would any precedent thereby be set infringing in any way on the Monroe Doctrine, assuming that the League members' action might eventually result in military sanctions against one of the disputants?

The President and I, after consultation, decided to cooperate with the League. On March 18 I telegraphed the Secretary General that the United States would take part in its committee to the extent of having a representative participate in its deliberations, although without the right to vote. Thus within one month I assisted in placing the United States side by side with two League committees, one for the Far East and one for the Leticia dispute.

Our acceptance signified our willingness to cooperate with other nations in the settlement of Latin American questions. Unilateral action on our part was now in the discard. We began to apply a principle to which we adhered in the years to follow. This was to refrain from acting until after having consulted with all the other interested nations. Only in this way could we work from under the deep-seated resentment engendered in Latin America by previous one-sided actions of our country.

The Leticia dispute dragged on until the following year, but it was eventually settled happily without recourse to war. Spain, the United States, and Brazil formed a League Commission to go to the Leticia area and oversee the evacuation of Peruvian and Colombian troops from contested areas. For the first time in history, a banner of the League of Nations, a white rectangle, emblazoned in dark blue letters, "League of Nations Commission, Leticia," waved over a portion of New World territory.

On the afternoon of April 11, 1933, the White House telephoned the State Department requesting that a speech be prepared for the President to make the following morning at the Pan American Union in celebration of Pan American Day. I accompanied Mr. Roosevelt to the Union the next morning. "The essential qualities of a true Pan Americanism," said the President, "must be the same as those which constitute a Good Neighbor, namely, mutual understanding and, through such understanding, a sympathetic appreciation of the other's point of view. It is only in this manner that we can hope to build up a system of which confidence, friendship and good will are the cornerstones. Each one of us must grow by the advancement of civilization and social well-being, and not by the acquisition of territory at the expense of any neighbor."

I had been elected chairman of the Governing Board of the Pan

American Union on April 5, a post customarily held by United States Secretaries of State. In accepting the chairmanship I stated: "I have for many years past felt the deepest interest in the establishment of closer cultural and economic ties between the republics of America and in cementing the bonds of friendship between them. I have always believed that you can measure the political, social, and other standards of a people by the amount of commerce they produce and create, among themselves and with other countries. I think you can determine the standards of civilization itself more accurately by a careful analysis of the economic ideals and aims and purposes of a people and the extent to which they develop those objects and purposes. I think that commerce will develop and progress more during the next generation through the leadership of the people of North and South America than that of any other people on the planet."

That same month a new decision was called for in line with our changed attitude toward Latin America. The American collector of customs at Port-au-Prince, Haiti, who was maintained there by virtue of a treaty between the two countries to collect customs duties applicable to Haiti's debt to the United States, was found guilty of fraud, and confessed. He was an American citizen, also a treaty official, and we could have brought him to the United States for trial. Instead, in token of our recognition of Haiti's sovereignty over her own soil, we surrendered him to the jurisdiction of the Haitian courts.

Four months later, following my return from the London Economic Conference, we signed an executive agreement with Haiti providing for the withdrawal of United States Marines before the end of October, 1934. They had been stationed there since 1915.

Cuba, Haiti's neighbor in the Caribbean, was giving us good cause for anxiety. Popular resentment against the brutal dictatorship of General Machado, who had been in power since 1925, was growing acute. It was becoming evident that either Machado would resign or a revolution would force him out. Bomb explosions and shootings were occurring in Havana, sugar mills and cane fields were being burned, schools were closing, and guerrilla bands, left over from the unsuccessful revolution of 1931, were operating in the hills. Political exiles streamed to the United States. Added to the political unrest was economic distress, partly caused by high United States tariffs. It was a hair-trigger situation.

By the so-called Platt Amendment to the Treaty of 1903 the United States had the legal right to intervene in Cuba to preserve Cuban independence or to maintain a Government adequate to protect life, property, and individual liberty. But the President and I were determined that we would not intervene in Cuba. Despite the legal right we possessed, such an act would further embitter our relations with all Latin America. It would undo all our protestations of nonintervention and noninterference. It would feed our traditional enemies whom I hoped to starve.

On April 15 I made to a press conference my first public statement on Cuba. "No consideration," I said, "has been given to any movement in the nature of intervention. Nothing whatever is going on that would call for the slightest departure from the ordinary relationships and contacts between two separate and sovereign nations."

President Roosevelt and I agreed to send Sumner Welles to Cuba as Ambassador and also as the President's mediator among the various factions in Cuba, if they appeared willing. At the President's suggestion, to which I agreed, Welles had been made an Assistant Secretary of State April 6, 1933. He had good ability and experience, along with much ambition. In later years we were to differ sharply on questions of judgment. In the earlier years I found myself in agreement with my other associates more often than with Welles on important questions of policy. I, of course, had the responsibility for all decisions, and I endeavored in every instance to meet it.

Welles left for Cuba in May, bearing with him instructions from me, dated May 1, which said: "You will always bear in mind that the relations between the Government of the United States and the Cuban Government are those existing between sovereign, independent, and equal powers; and that no steps should be taken which would tend to render more likely the need of the Government of the United States to resort to that right of formal intervention granted to the United States by the existing treaty between the two nations." I instructed him to extend what assistance we could to better Cuba's economic conditions, to negotiate a trade agreement with Cuba, to offer his friendly mediation, and to express to President Machado our earnest hope that he would take steps to end the state of terrorism.

At the close of that month I departed for the London Economic Conference. When I returned to Washington in August, the situation in Cuba had worsened. Writing to Ambassador Bingham in London on August 11, I said: "The Cuban trouble was inherited from the preceding Administration. I find it in an ugly situation on my return. I am striving desperately to avoid the almost unthinkable step of intervention. I have some hope that I may succeed, although conditions are very critical."

On the following day General Machado took leave of absence, and on the day thereafter Dr. Carlos de Cespedes, former Secretary of State, formed a coalition Government. Widespread disorders and attacks on persons and property followed Machado's exit. President Roosevelt ordered two destroyers to Cuban waters, but said this involved no possible question of intervention or of the slightest interference with the internal affairs of Cuba.

We decided it was not necessary to grant President de Cespedes formal recognition, since the change of Government had been achieved by constitutional process. Ambassador Welles was working hard, keeping in touch with all factions, and on August 12 the Department cabled him warm congratulations and "appreciation of what you have done" from the President and myself.

I held frequent conversations on Cuba with the ambassadors of important Latin American countries. This was in line with the decision I had reached that whatever diplomatic actions were called for on our part in Latin America would be taken only after consultation with the interested countries to the south of us. We would no longer make single-handed moves.

Acting in conjunction or consultation with other Latin American countries gave us two advantages. It strengthened the move we had in mind. And it prevented or lessened the resentment that so often rose in Latin America when the United States acted by herself in the Western Hemisphere. The President was fully in accord with this method of approach. After conferring with representatives of Argentina, Brazil, Chile, and Mexico, Mr. Roosevelt issued a statement on September 6, saying:

"The United States desires that complete and constant information about Cuba shall be available for the Latin American countries.

"The United States has absolutely no desire to intervene, and is seeking every means to avoid intervention.

"The key of American policy in regard to Cuba is that Cuba shall obtain quickly a Government of its own choosing, and one capable of maintaining order."

The situation hurried to a climax, with widespread rioting and growing mutiny in the Cuban Army. The Cespedes Government collapsed following a revolt within the army led by the rank and file under Sergeant

Fulgencio Batista. At that moment, September 7, I received a long telegram from Ambassador Welles suggesting that a considerable American
armed force be landed at Havana and smaller forces in other Cuban
cities.

"What I propose," he telegraphed, "would be a strictly limited intervention of the following nature. The Cespedes Government should be
permitted to function freely in exactly the same manner as it did until the
time of its overthrow, having full control of every branch of the Government. It is obvious, of course, that with a great portion of the army in
mutiny, it could not maintain itself in power in any satisfactory manner
unless the United States Government were willing, should it [the Cespedes
Government] so request, to lend its assistance in the maintenance of
public order until the Cuban Government had been afforded the time
sufficient . . . to form a new army. . . . Such a policy on our part would
presumably entail the landing of a considerable force at Havana and
lesser forces in certain of the more important ports of the Republic."

Ambassador Welles said further: "The disadvantages of this policy
as I see them lie solely in the fact that we will incur the violent animosity
of the extreme radical and communist groups in Cuba . . . it would
further seem to me that since the full facts of the situation here have been
fully explained to the representatives of the Latin American countries,
the landing of such assistance would most decidedly be construed as well
within the limits of the policy of the 'good neighbor' which we have
done our utmost to demonstrate in our relations with the Cuban people
during the past five months."

The moment I finished digesting the telegram I took it myself to the
President at the White House and had him read it. I then strongly expressed to him my opinion that we could not and should not think of intervening in Cuba even to a limited extent. It seemed to me that Welles was
overinfluenced by local conditions in Cuba and misjudged the disastrous
reaction that would follow throughout Latin America if we agreed to his
request. From my previous conversations with the President I knew that
he was as resolved as myself to stay out of Cuba. Mr. Roosevelt readily
agreed with my viewpoint. He said he would merely send a cruiser to
Cuban waters, where we already had some light units. The naval vessels
were strictly forbidden to send forces ashore unless it were necessary to
evacuate American citizens caught between the contending Cuban factions.

After my conference with the President I went to my hotel—it was
already late in the day—to compose the reply to Welles. When it was

completed I returned to the White House, where the President and I quickly agreed on the draft. I then went to the State Department and at eight o'clock in the evening sent the answer we had agreed upon, as follows:

"We fully appreciate the various viewpoints set forth in your telegram. However, after mature consideration, the President has decided to send you the following message: 'We feel very strongly that any promise, implied or otherwise, relating to what the United States will do under any circumstances is impossible; that it would be regarded as a breach of neutrality, as favoring one faction out of many, as attempting to set up a government which would be regarded by the whole world, and especially throughout Latin America, as a creation and creature of the American Government.' The President's conversations with the Argentine, Brazilian, Chilean, and Mexican representatives have received widespread approval in the United States and throughout Latin America and any action contrary to the policy outlined therein would have disastrous results.

"The above does not mean, of course, that you should do anything to block or in the least affect any movement by any section; in other words, strict neutrality is of the essence."

Indicative of the storm we should have aroused to the south if we had intervened in Cuba was a note handed me from the Argentine Government just two days later expressing its hope that we would not intervene, "no matter what may be the course of events," because "no state arrives at the maturity of democracy and the fullness of destiny without experiencing, as a necessary accompaniment, the travail of difficult conflicts."

Josephus Daniels, our Ambassador to Mexico, telephoned me to give me Mexico's attitude and to urge us not to budge from nonintervention. A day or two later I received a letter from him dated September 9, saying: "It was good to hear your voice over the telephone today. Sometimes I get lonesome for the voice of a friend in our country. It cheered me greatly when you said, 'I would rather walk from here to the South Pole than to have to intervene.' "

On September 11 I cabled to our representatives in the major European capitals, in Tokyo, and in all Latin American capitals except Cuba: "This Government, in view of disturbed conditions in Cuba, has sent ships to that country solely as a precautionary measure, and there is not the slightest intention of intervening or interfering in Cuba's domestic affairs. It is our earnest hope that the Cubans themselves will work out a solution of their own difficulties. . . . We shall not attempt to influence the Cubans in any way as to choice of individuals in the Government."

The De Cespedes Government having fallen, Dr. Grau San Martin became President. We delayed recognition of his Government to see whether it could establish order. Fighting among the factions continued. Such was the situation when I sailed for the Montevideo Conference. Two weeks after my departure the President issued a statement expressing the willingness of our Government to reopen the treaty of 1903 which gave us the legal right to intervene militarily in Cuba. Our record on nonintervention was therefore to be clear to the world as the Montevideo Conference opened.

Lack of confidence in the ability of the Montevideo Conference to achieve results was abysmal, especially in South America. Two vitally important world conferences had already failed in the space of six months —the London meeting to achieve economic disarmament, and the Geneva meeting to achieve military disarmament. One war and a near-war were raging in South America, Cuba was in revolt, and all the twenty-one American Republics labored in acute economic distress.

Several months before December 3, 1933, when the conference was to convene, the Governments of Argentina, Brazil, Chile, and Colombia cabled us that the time was not ripe for a successful conference and it should again be postponed. Argentine Foreign Minister Saavedra Lamas was particularly emphatic. Recounting the conflicts then raging, he pointed out that Uruguay, where the conference would be held, was also unsettled politically, and that to go to Montevideo was "like walking into a burning house." On the other hand, the Uruguayan Government strongly urged that the conference be held and emphatically suggested that I head the American delegation, thereby inducing other countries to send their foreign ministers to the conference and thus increase its importance.

At that point several old friends came to me and said: "You must not go to the Montevideo Conference. The Latin Americans are ganging up on us again. You can't afford two failures." The first failure had been the London Conference.

"No," I replied, "I feel I must go. We are going to start international cooperation right down here with our neighbors."

We had failed to make headway with any economic proposals at the London Conference. I had no assurance whatever that I would be able even to offer at Montevideo the economic proposals I had had inserted in the record at London solely for the information of the various delegations.

All nations were still moving, some slowly, some rapidly, in the direction of the most extreme economic nationalism. And the United States was engrossed with the NRA, AAA and numerous other domestic undertakings the logic of which, if permanently pursued, meant economic nationalism in this country as a long-term policy, with its manifold evils both at home and abroad.

I thereupon went to see the President at the White House. I told him of the views of the Latin American countries about the conference and mentioned the difficulties inherent in the present economic situation. "No country," I said, "seems to have any real program or plans looking toward peace or economic betterment. Many Latin American countries still cherish their old bitterness toward the United States on the score of intervention and overlordship. They have largely lost faith in our pretensions in favor of an entirely different course in the future."

The President agreed, but insisted that our Government should not take the responsibility for postponement of the conference. I concurred and said that the responsibility should be a joint one embracing the other Governments favoring postponement as well as the United States.

I then returned to the State Department, and during the following days I debated the prospects of the conference. Finally I came to the conclusion that it were best that the conference, already once postponed, should be held as scheduled, and that I should head the American delegation. This would be the first time that an American Secretary of State had ever headed a delegation to a Pan American Conference. Mr. Hughes had been chief of the delegation to the Havana Conference, but he was a former Secretary of State at the time.

President Roosevelt agreed. I accordingly informed the other American nations of our intentions. This changed their attitude toward the conference. They agreed to attend, and many said they would send their foreign ministers. Argentina remained dubious until the last moment.

During and after the London Economic Conference I had not hesitated to emphasize to the President how disastrous it had been to appoint the American delegation without prior consultation with me. He was thoroughly aware of the lack of discipline displayed by the delegation at London. He knew that some of the delegates had spoken out of turn, had fought among themselves, and had prejudiced the work of the delegation as a whole. Now he permitted me to select the delegation to Montevideo and also the accompanying experts.

My idea was to take a small number of delegates and personnel

generally from Washington, and to recruit from the most expert persons
in our service in Latin America. The delegation was composed of myself
as chairman; Alexander W. Weddell, our Ambassador to Argentina; J.
Reuben Clark, Jr., who had been Under Secretary of State and later
Ambassador to Mexico under President Hoover; J. Butler Wright, our
Minister to Uruguay; Spruille Braden of New York, a businessman in
Chile; and Sophonisba P. Breckinridge, University of Chicago, who would
represent women's interests. This delegation was to function with high
efficiency; I could not have asked for better cooperation.

A few days before I sailed, Louis Howe, the President's assistant,
came to me on behalf of the President and said: "We don't think you
need to undertake much down at Montevideo. Just talk to them about
the Pan American highway from the United States down through Central
and South America."

The outlook for a successful conference was so completely sterile
that I asked the President to issue a statement that would serve to squelch
too much optimism as to its possibilities. He thereupon gave out a sweeping release which went well beyond what I had in mind and seemed to
close the door to any real achievement at Montevideo. Nine-tenths of
it was taken up with the subject of improving transportation. It then
stated: "Internal economics in nearly every country concerned have made
necessary certain temporary policies regarding a number of important
phases of economic and trade conditions which will obviously render impracticable at this time useful conclusions as to some items on the old
agenda. . . . Unsettled conditions, such as European commercial-quota
restrictions, have made it seem desirable for the United States to forgo
immediate discussions of such matters as currency stabilization, uniform
import prohibitions, permanent customs duties, and the like."

As I left Washington, therefore, it seemed that most avenues to success at the Conference were barred. Was Montevideo thus to be another
London? The London Conference had convened with high hopes, and
failed. The Montevideo Conference was convening with low hopes—and
just had to succeed. It was a case of "It can't be done, therefore we will
proceed to do it."

As I went aboard the ship in New York I gave out a statement that
was definitely more optimistic than the White House release. "A more
substantial step forward in Pan American unity can and, I believe, will
be taken at the Montevideo Conference than at all others within two
decades," I said. "I am speaking of the possibilities of mutual economic

national and international planning. While serious impediments do exist, the need and the opportunity are far greater than ever before. . . . I have confidence that our twenty-one American nations, with their 240,-000,000 population and their younger civilization, will be able to furnish an example of high accomplishment at Montevideo by which the European nations, with their 450,000,000 population and their far older civilization, may greatly profit." It was with the European nations that we could not agree at London. Now we were to see whether we could agree with the Latin American nations.

Once our ship, the *American Legion,* pulled out, I began to ponder, and by degrees to develop, a plan and program to implement the President's Good Neighbor Policy in a broad, practical way. I had carried along with me several trunks and boxes of books, pamphlets, and documents relating to Latin America and our relations with it to date. I called the delegation together and organized it into groups for systematic study and preparation along specific lines. We usually had daily meetings throughout the voyage.

On the same ship were the delegations of several Latin American countries. I made it a point to confer with them cordially and to see as much of them as possible. Of particular importance was my conference with the Haitian delegation with regard to the progress of our program to withdraw completely from Haiti.

I early determined to introduce a comprehensive economic resolution calling for lower tariffs and the abolition of trade restrictions. I decided to use as its basis the proposal I had introduced into the record at London as an "American suggestion for the further development during the recess and later stages of the conference of a program on commercial policy."

This provided first for a tariff truce. Next, the signatories agreed to initiate bilateral or plurilateral negotiations for the removal of restrictions on commerce and for the reduction of tariff rates. The Governments were to direct their greatest efforts toward eliminating restrictions and reducing duties which most clearly lacked economic justification. Lastly, the Governments agreed to incorporate in their trade agreements the most-favored-nation principle in its unconditional and unrestricted form, this to be applied to all forms and methods of control of imports and not only to import duties.

I spent many days writing this resolution myself for introduction at Montevideo. Like other projects for the conference on which I was working I endeavored to make the resolution world-wide in its possible application. In carrying out our policies toward Latin America, it was never my wish to make them exclusively Pan American. I always had the hope that what was accomplished in the New World could be achieved in the Old as well. Measures like my economics resolution could have been applied as logically to the Eastern Hemisphere as to our own.

I wirelessed my text to Acting Secretary of State Phillips for submission to the President. There followed several exchanges of telegrams which continued after we landed at Montevideo. The resolution was meeting with opposition in Washington, and it was evident I should have to fight for it.

On December 6 Phillips saw the President and then cabled me: "You would naturally be forced to include exceptions to cover possible actions by the NRA and AAA. Other Governments would thereby put forward other exceptions and your proposals could only be valuable from the point of view of expressing ultimate objectives rather than from the point of view of practical and immediate progress. It seems to us that all possible emphasis on the immediate undertaking of bilateral negotiations would be more useful during this period of unsettled government finance and of sharply fluctuating exchanges, and we wish to submit this for your consideration."

It was thus manifest that the old struggle between the nationalistic philosophy of the New Deal group about the President and my international philosophy of economics was still acute. The bilateral negotiations Phillips referred to, of course, were the same the President had suggested in his telegram to me when I was en route to London. These would involve treaties which would have to be submitted to the Senate and, if they involved substantial tariff reductions, had no chance on earth of being approved.

The following day I telegraphed Phillips for the President: "I would consider it unfortunate if our Government should not thus keep alive the foregoing broad proposal, with the exceptions and reservations mentioned. The alternative would offer a very narrow and limited domestic policy alone with no indication of any other for the future. I feel constrained to offer this frank opinion which is based upon the assumption that we ultimately expect to reenter foreign trade. If this is not in mind it of course would not be necessary to keep alive any policy for the future."

Then, on December 8, Phillips replied: "In talking with the President he asks me to tell you that he is wholly sympathetic to any long-term plan with adequate exceptions and reservations covering possible actions found necessary during this period of readjustment, especially actions under the NRA and AAA. With this safeguard he gladly approves your effort to keep alive, as a permanent objective, the idea of liberalizing tariff barriers by simultaneous action of many nations."

I was delighted. Already I was well ahead of myself at London.

Going down on the boat I observed that there were five peace agreements floating around in this hemisphere without full ratification. These were the Treaty to Avoid or Prevent Conflicts Between the American States, signed at the Fifth Pan American Conference at Santiago, Chile, in 1923; the Kellogg-Briand Pact of 1928; the Convention of Inter-American Conciliation and the Convention of Inter-American Arbitration, signed at Washington in 1929; and the Antiwar Pact of Saavedra Lamas, signed by six Latin American countries at Rio de Janeiro on October 10, 1933.

It seemed to me that the time was both ripe and urgent for vigorous, concerted action by the negligent governments to ratify these five instruments of peace. The Chaco War and other threatening conditions pointed up the need for action. Bolivia and Paraguay, the Chaco belligerents, were signatories to none of the five treaties; hence these treaties could not be called upon to aid in effecting a settlement of the war. I accordingly prepared a resolution that I intended to introduce at Montevideo, pledging each of the twenty-one nations to proceed at once to ratify all these peace treaties.

We ourselves had declined to sign Saavedra Lamas's treaty, just as Argentina had refused to sign the treaty in which the United States had taken principal part—the Kellogg-Briand Pact. Argentina, in fact, was one of the most negligent in ratifying the existing peace machinery agreements. A fortnight before I sailed for Montevideo the Argentine Ambassador, Dr. Felipe Espil, came to see me and said that if we desired to win Saavedra Lamas over to our side at Montevideo we could do so by adhering to his Antiwar Pact. "You can do so with reservations, if you like," he told me. "Saavedra Lamas won't object to reservations—what he is interested in is having the United States adhere to his pact." Saavedra Lamas had long been one of the most outstanding and irrepressible opponents of the United States.

I believed that, if we could make a friend of Saavedra Lamas at Montevideo and at the same time get him to sign the Kellogg Pact, we could well sign his Antiwar Pact. His pact condemned acts of aggression and settlement of territorial questions by violent means, and provided for: differences to be submitted to peaceful settlement; conciliation commissions to deal with disputes; nonrecognition of territorial arrangements unless effected peacefully; the exercise against aggressors of all political, juridical, and economic measures authorized by international law.

The question of interference in the internal affairs of other countries was certain to be raised at Montevideo, I knew; but I did not believe it should throw difficulties in our way, because we ourselves were fully prepared to go along with any agreement on noninterference.

It was also clear that the question of the Chaco War would be broached at Montevideo and an effort made to solve it; and there, too, I was prepared to play as helpful a part as possible.

Aboard the ship I said to our delegates that I intended to call personally upon the delegations of other countries after we reached Montevideo. It seemed to me that a large part of our mission to Montevideo was to make friends and to overcome the deep suspicion Latin American statesmen entertained toward the United States. My suggestion was not too enthusiastically received. It may have seemed to my associates that the United States, being by far the largest nation attending the conference, should be in the position of receiving visits, not making them, and that I should be lowering my dignity by taking the first step. I did not pursue the subject further—but I did not change my mind.

Our ship called at Rio de Janeiro before proceeding to Montevideo. There I made a statement on landing to carry out the thought I cherished that the New World had a Heaven-sent opportunity to provide a good example to the Old. "We must take stock," I said, "of all our blessings in this favored part of the world—all our cultural, political, social, and material assets—and bring them to bear, by united efforts, to help right a topsy-turvy civilization. Let the Americas show the way. By being the best of good neighbors let us offer the finest possible example for a jaded and disillusioned world."

I talked with many members of the Brazilian Government, emphasizing our traditional friendship and paving the way for effective cooperation at Montevideo. In order to see at close hand as many aspects of Brazilian life as possible and also to show the interest we felt in Brazil, I went by the night train to São Paulo and also drove some forty miles farther to Santos, the great coffee shipping port. As we approached Santos we saw huge columns of smoke rising into the sky. The Brazilians were burning the surplus coffee they could no longer export. Tens of millions of dollars' worth of coffee was changing into useless heat and smoke. It was a graphic commentary on the world's economic dislocation, and I dug my toes in deeper, determined to try to do something about it at Montevideo.

But when we landed at Montevideo, four days before the opening of the conference, it was at once apparent that a stupendous work lay ahead of us if we were to win the cooperation of the other American nations. One of my first sights from the ship was billboards with the huge words: "Down with Hull." And some of the first newspapers shown me spoke of the "big bully" who had come down from the North, and wondered what he was up to now. Most of the press of Montevideo and Buenos Aires across the Plata River rawhided our country and our delegation, called us names, and threw out the idea that we were down there, as usual, for purely selfish, narrow purposes. They said, in effect: "We have heard of the Good Neighbor Policy, and it sounds all right; but we have heard similar talk before."

The whole atmosphere and surroundings were like a blue snow in January.

24: The Good Neighbor Functions

MY FIRST CALL in Montevideo was on President Gabriel Terra of Uruguay. As I approached his palace I could see guns glinting amid the bushes, and guards were everywhere. Uruguay was tense with latent civil war, as a bitter minority sought opportunities to overthrow the Government, notwithstanding Señor Terra had taken many highly useful steps for Uruguay. This reasonably short, stout man did not appear too much disturbed, however, and, with suitable military protection for himself and his Government, was going steadily forward with additional plans for improving conditions in Uruguay. When I saw him he was unperturbed, calm, and courteous. A few weeks later he was wounded by an assassin.

We spent an hour discussing all aspects of United States and Uruguayan affairs and relationships, present and prospective. We were agreed that closer cooperation was imperative. President Terra then remarked: "I am greatly apprehensive about the probable failure of this conference. I am doubly concerned about it because my Government and I are the hosts." He added: "How long do you expect to attend the conference?"

"I expect to remain as long as there are any real prospects of material accomplishments," I replied. "But I plan to leave early if no such prospects are presented."

He earnestly besought me to stay on. "Quite a number of delegations headed by foreign ministers are coming," he said, "because the United States has sent a delegation, headed by yourself. There will be ten foreign ministers here. Many or most of these will leave if you leave."

"In the past," I responded, "these conferences have been accustomed to continue for five weeks. If this conference can be cut down to three weeks and the work thoroughly organized on an effective basis, and if, during these panic conditions, we can omit all formal dinners so as to save time as well as expense to the delegations, I'll be disposed to stay on and work earnestly for the success of the conference."

President Terra wholeheartedly agreed. Later I often conferred with him privately. I invariably found him ready to do teamwork with me, giving full support to all propositions I suggested for the consideration of the conference.

As other delegations filtered in, I went to call upon them at their

hotels. I made no appointment with any of them,
secretary telephone them after I left my hotel, statin
way to call. I moved in somewhat unceremoniously.
from little Panama to big Brazil. Some of the dele
most reserved.

Invariably one of the first sentences the other
uttered was: "I was just intending to call upon you

To which I invariably replied, "It is as much m
you as your duty to call upon me, and my people feel
and your people."

Generally a thirty- to forty-minute conference
the way to better understanding, more uniform ob
measure of cooperation to attain them. I assured each
is nothing my Government wants or is seeking down
forward the doctrine of the Good Neighbor. We simpl
fully with all Latin American countries in promotin
economic ideals in which we are all alike equally and n

I sought to discuss with the delegates pleasant r
able subjects and to convince them of my absolute go
to the meeting. Having ascertained in advance what
most interested in, I made that an important part o

Most delegations had difficulty concealing their
and manner of my call; but they appeared please
receiving return calls from the other delegations in an
atmosphere.

I then had my first experience with the Argentin
long been familiar with the history of Argentina an
genuine admiration for that country and its people,
knew that the Argentine Government had been a t
of the United States and for nearly a generation had
of organizing as many of the Latin American countries
the United States whenever a Pan American Conferen
were now indications that at Montevideo the Argenti
their efforts to lead other American nations against the
would utilize toward this end any one of a number of
as intervention, methods of promoting peace, and the

I fully realized the disastrous effects that would f
and throughout the hemisphere if the meeting at Mo
sult merely in another bitter Havana fight, with Ar

24: The Good Neighbor Functions

MY FIRST CALL in Montevideo was on President Gabriel Terra of Uruguay. As I approached his palace I could see guns glinting amid the bushes, and guards were everywhere. Uruguay was tense with latent civil war, as a bitter minority sought opportunities to overthrow the Government, notwithstanding Señor Terra had taken many highly useful steps for Uruguay. This reasonably short, stout man did not appear too much disturbed, however, and, with suitable military protection for himself and his Government, was going steadily forward with additional plans for improving conditions in Uruguay. When I saw him he was unperturbed, calm, and courteous. A few weeks later he was wounded by an assassin.

We spent an hour discussing all aspects of United States and Uruguayan affairs and relationships, present and prospective. We were agreed that closer cooperation was imperative. President Terra then remarked: "I am greatly apprehensive about the probable failure of this conference. I am doubly concerned about it because my Government and I are the hosts." He added: "How long do you expect to attend the conference?"

"I expect to remain as long as there are any real prospects of material accomplishments," I replied. "But I plan to leave early if no such prospects are presented."

He earnestly besought me to stay on. "Quite a number of delegations headed by foreign ministers are coming," he said, "because the United States has sent a delegation, headed by yourself. There will be ten foreign ministers here. Many or most of these will leave if you leave."

"In the past," I responded, "these conferences have been accustomed to continue for five weeks. If this conference can be cut down to three weeks and the work thoroughly organized on an effective basis, and if, during these panic conditions, we can omit all formal dinners so as to save time as well as expense to the delegations, I'll be disposed to stay on and work earnestly for the success of the conference."

President Terra wholeheartedly agreed. Later I often conferred with him privately. I invariably found him ready to do teamwork with me, giving full support to all propositions I suggested for the consideration of the conference.

As other delegations filtered in, I went to call upon them at their hotels. I made no appointment with any of them, but simply had my secretary telephone them after I left my hotel, stating that I was on my way to call. I moved in somewhat unceremoniously. I called on them all, from little Panama to big Brazil. Some of the delegations were at first most reserved.

Invariably one of the first sentences the other chiefs of delegation uttered was: "I was just intending to call upon you at your hotel."

To which I invariably replied, "It is as much my duty to call upon you as your duty to call upon me, and my people feel that way toward you and your people."

Generally a thirty- to forty-minute conference followed, preparing the way to better understanding, more uniform objectives, and a full measure of cooperation to attain them. I assured each delegation: "There is nothing my Government wants or is seeking down here except to carry forward the doctrine of the Good Neighbor. We simply want to cooperate fully with all Latin American countries in promoting the political and economic ideals in which we are all alike equally and mutually interested."

I sought to discuss with the delegates pleasant rather than disagreeable subjects and to convince them of my absolute good faith in relation to the meeting. Having ascertained in advance what each delegation was most interested in, I made that an important part of our conversations.

Most delegations had difficulty concealing their surprise at the fact and manner of my call; but they appeared pleased, and soon I was receiving return calls from the other delegations in an increasingly cordial atmosphere.

I then had my first experience with the Argentine delegation. I had long been familiar with the history of Argentina and had developed a genuine admiration for that country and its people, even though I also knew that the Argentine Government had been a traditional opponent of the United States and for nearly a generation had been in the habit of organizing as many of the Latin American countries as possible against the United States whenever a Pan American Conference was held. There were now indications that at Montevideo the Argentines would continue their efforts to lead other American nations against the United States and would utilize toward this end any one of a number of alleged issues such as intervention, methods of promoting peace, and the Monroe Doctrine.

I fully realized the disastrous effects that would follow both at home and throughout the hemisphere if the meeting at Montevideo should result merely in another bitter Havana fight, with Argentina aligned on one side and the United States on the other. If we were to have a conference, it was supremely important, especially from the long viewpoint of the future, that it should be a unified, harmonious conference of all the twenty-one American Republics.

It seemed to me that, with Europe plainly showing signs of preparing for another war, and with the Far East already at war, there was no excuse for an issue on the Monroe Doctrine—just the contrary. There could be no issue between us on intervention, for our thoughts were the same. Finally, I knew that the Argentine leaders and ourselves were equally strong in support of peace and what we deemed the most effective methods of promoting and preserving peace, and no conflict could arise on this point.

It was therefore a shock to learn from our Ambassador to Buenos Aires, Alexander Weddell, one of our most valuable delegates, that, although Argentina on October 31 had accepted the invitation to attend the conference, she had not decided until almost the last hour to send a delegation. She had planned to conduct a fight from across the river against every important move the United States delegation might undertake.

It was only on the Thursday I arrived in Montevideo that the Argentine Government appointed a delegation, headed by Foreign Minister Saavedra Lamas. Without any time for preparation, the delegation reached Montevideo by boat Saturday morning, the day before the opening of the conference, and went to a resort hotel fourteen miles down the coast.

They had scarcely reached their hotel when I left my hotel to call on Saavedra Lamas after instructing my secretary to telephone him that I was on my way. On my arrival at his hotel I found his delegation in considerable excitement over my visit. I saw Saavedra Lamas at once, however. He was short and dapper, excellently dressed. His black-mustached, thin, dark face surmounted a very high stiff collar. He received me most courteously, but exhibited a noticeable degree of reserve and aloofness, with outcroppings of skepticism as to my purposes.

I approached him somewhat in circles. I first assured him that my Government wanted nothing for itself except to put into practice the doctrine of the Good Neighbor. This included the fundamentals of all those relationships between the nations of this hemisphere which should be asserted and scrupulously maintained. It embraced the doctrine of territorial and political integrity of each nation, the freedom of their citizens and their absolute sovereignty. It also included the promotion of peace and economic welfare.

In that and the next conversation we had, Saavedra Lamas was highly nervous, which was customary with him. He smoked cigarettes incessantly, lighting one from another. I found him very brilliant, with many attractive personal qualities, showing himself in conversation to be a talented and experienced diplomat. I told him that in the United States he was considered the outstanding Latin American statesman and advocate of peace. "I am here," I said, "to seek your counsel. I know from your past record that you will help us take the right direction and do so in a thoroughly practical and efficient manner."

I then said to him: "The world peace situation can scarcely be more discouraging or at a lower ebb. The world organization has failed to function on disarmament at Geneva. The entire method of settling questions or conducting movements by international conferences is literally hanging in the balance since the failures at London and Geneva. The nations of the Old World are now looking to us to redeem the situation by holding a successful conference and accomplishing something real. With the Chaco War almost within hearing distance, this conference will be utterly discredited unless we not only speak but also act in so aggressive and determined a manner that our avowals of peace and demands for peace there and everywhere carry conviction."

I told Saavedra Lamas that two broad, comprehensive resolutions should be introduced at the conference and passed. One should propose a constructive economic program for business recovery. The other should call upon each of the delegations present to pledge its Government to sign all the five largely unsigned treaties which comprised a wonderful basis for the promotion and maintenance of peace in the Western Hemisphere. "World opinion," I said, "feels that the Chaco War would not have broken out if these treaties had been promptly signed some years ago when they were proposed. We cannot excuse ourselves unless we do everything humanly possible to stop the war in the Chaco and to secure governmental pledges for signature by all the countries that have not signed these treaties."

Saavedra Lamas listened intently, smoking furiously and constantly shifting position in his easy-chair. He sat up straighter when I said, "The United States is ready to sign your Antiwar Pact." I told him I had tentatively prepared the two necessary resolutions, one on economics, the other on the peace treaties. I then said: "You yourself are the one person who should introduce the peace resolution. You are known throughout the world as the author of the Antiwar Pact and as an advocate of peace. You are the one outstanding person who can furnish leadership for this resolution. Deliver a ringing speech in presenting it, and let us have a real peace revival in the conference, with all the fervor of a religious revival. I will give you my utmost support."

These two drafts were mine to introduce to the conference myself, or, if the unity of the conference could be advanced, I could request some one like Saavedra Lamas to offer one or both.

I waited a moment. He was thinking, silently, and smoking hard. I went on, "Of course, if you should not see fit to do so, it will be necessary to select the next most suitable person for this outstanding task." I had in mind Mello Franco, head of the Brazilian delegation, a great international lawyer and a strong peace advocate.

Saavedra Lamas was becoming more cordial, more interested. "Give me twenty-four hours to consider," he said. "I'll come to see you and let you know then."

I readily agreed.

In less than twenty-four hours Saavedra Lamas came to my hotel apartment. He seemed very happy. "I'll be glad to offer the resolution," he said, "and to deliver a speech in support of it and of the cause of peace generally." He had in his hands a copy of the speech he intended to make and of the resolution he would introduce, which was a slightly modified form of my resolution. "And I'll support your economic resolution," he said, "although my government is not very favorable to certain portions of it." This last was doubly important because Saavedra Lamas was chairman of the committee in which the resolution would be presented.

Then he smiled and said, "We shall be the two wings of the dove of peace, you the economic and I the political."

Throughout the conference I could not have asked for more cordial and understanding cooperation on all important questions than I received from Saavedra Lamas. I later urged him for the Nobel Peace Prize, although my own candidacy had also been proposed, and he received the award.

By this strategy at Montevideo, a big and necessary step toward uniting the Argentines with ourselves and other delegations for the work of the conference was accomplished. In the years to follow I continued a constant effort to keep Argentina included in cooperative relations on a basis of unity among all the twenty-one American Republics.

The result of all my calls on the other delegations was that, by the time the conference opened, there was a considerable lessening of the tension and animosity against the United States.

The conference was divided into twelve committees, but our delegation neither sought nor obtained the chairmanship of any of them. For my part I wanted to remain footloose and not be tied down to one committee. I was carrying on the same thought I expressed to Franklin D. Roosevelt at Hyde Park in 1932 when I refused the chairmanship of the Platform Committee for the Chicago convention. I believed I could render better service by being available to take part in the work of any committee.

Furthermore, it was part of my policy to steer wholly clear of even the appearance of pushing my country or myself forward. The antagonism to the United States would have bristled at any attempt to claim position or honors. Besides, I went to Montevideo with the hope of introducing policies and principles of international relations on the broadest practical basis. If such a program of policies based on morals and friendship could be adopted, it would constitute the most solid foundation for international cooperation and a hemispheric structure equally desirable, mutually profitable and advantageous to each of the twenty-one nations.

The last thing I was interested in at Montevideo was to engage in rivalries or controversies with one or more other countries on some minor issue and to center attention on a victory by some country or individual. I felt that basically all the twenty-one Republics were in agreement with respect to the fundamentals of international cooperation, and no delegate had any excuse to oppose the broad movement for which I and others stood at the conference unless he were willing to assume a very narrow, selfish, and trouble-making attitude. There was therefore no occasion for any personal or diplomatic victories on a minor, single scale, but only the victory of the harmonious, united twenty-one nations working wholeheartedly together.

Moreover, was not the whole concept of conferences at stake, following the failure of the League of Nations in the Far East and the breakdown of the London Economic and Geneva Disarmament conferences? If the Montevideo Conference failed, the world's faith in the idea of conferences to establish peaceful working relations among nations would be shattered. My study of conferences disclosed that some had been wrecked because nations or individuals tried to use them as battlegrounds for the winning of narrow and selfish spectacular victories. The United

States had gone to some previous Pan American conferences with the same thought in mind. The differences heretofore existing between us still afforded glorious opportunity for real fights, sham fights, and shadow boxing, and otherwise a Paradise for self-seekers or notoriety-prospectors.

But I firmly believed in the principle that "there are no real triumphs in diplomacy." I felt that true success could come only by inducing our opponents to become our allies through convincing them that basically our ideas were their ideas. Occasionally this meant giving statesmen of other countries credit for the ideas I myself entertained. I have already pointed out how, in Congress, I often permitted fellow Members to make use of my ideas and information and christen them with their own names. I transplanted this practice into diplomacy as well. I could have introduced into the conference the peace resolution I had prepared, rather than give it to Saavedra Lamas, and perhaps I could have secured a majority in its favor. But, had I done so, Argentina doubtless would have fought it on some technical ground, and the unanimity it needed would have vanished. I believed it wiser in the circumstances for the head of the Argentine delegation to offer it.

A conference is always a delicate device because, owing to the publicity it obtains, it furnishes a temptation to the statesmen represented there to reap renown back home for themselves and their countries, and nothing attracts publicity so much as conflict. The most successful conferences are those in which the representatives are willing to submerge themselves in the general interest of obtaining real agreements. And real agreements are seldom "triumphs." They are real only if, when the conference ends and the delegates scatter, the nations concerned continue to believe that they entered into them wholeheartedly, without duress or loss of prestige, and enthusiastically intend to implement them.

When I introduced my economics resolution on December 12, Saavedra Lamas, along with others, supported it magnificently. His speech was longer than mine. Other delegations were somewhat surprised at the sweeping nature of my proposals, since many believed that the delegation would be hamstrung by the White House statement prior to our sailing, which virtually eliminated economic topics from our consideration.

The day after I introduced the economics resolution, President Roosevelt was asked at a press conference whether he thought the time was approaching when tariff reductions would be advisable or practicable. He said, for background, that one could have this objective and yet not feel particularly optimistic about getting very far with it. Under present world conditions, he continued, we were not much in sight of that except through bilateral treaties which might be extended to include other countries. Any general tariff agreement among nations, he said, would have a pretty slim prospect for the next few months.

This caused some delegations at Montevideo to hesitate, but the resolution was approved in due course unanimously. When, exactly six months later, our Trade Agreements Act was enacted, this resolution, having committed the Latin American nations to the principles that formed the basis of the Act, was of material help in our first negotiations with the Latin American countries.

On December 14 Acting Secretary Phillips cabled me on behalf of the President that "it seems good psychology to reinforce the excellent groundwork you are building up for future better commercial relations with South America, and which the press of this country are commenting upon most favorably, with some definite, concrete, and immediate action in establishing better and more rapid communications which lie at the foundation of increased trade." The President suggested that I offer, on behalf of the United States, to create a $5,000,000 non-profit-making, semipublic engineering corporation financed by the United States to erect the necessary radio stations, beacons, and landing fields to make night flying possible.

But five days later I was forced to cable in reply that the reaction to any offer of money was unfavorable. "One reaction," I said, "is that of inquiring at once what the United States is after now. This warped state of mind, which seems to be widespread just now, does not look with favor even on benefactions or accommodation loans or advances to these people, especially by our Government." In other words, no dollar diplomacy whatever.

I was able to induce the conference to refer questions of transportation, such as the Pan American Highway, and communications, to committees of experts for study.

When Saavedra Lamas introduced his peace resolution on December 15 I rose to second it, in accordance with our previous understanding, and made a much longer speech in favor of it than I had when introducing my economics resolution. "The adoption of this resolution and the agreement to sign these five splendid peace instruments," I said, "will thoroughly strengthen the peace agencies of the twenty-one American states and make peace permanently secure in this hemisphere. This wholesale affixing of signatures to five treaties through conference action within itself thoroughly vindicates the policy of international conference. . . . Universal peace has been the chief aim of civilization. Nations fail or succeed according to their failure or success in this supreme undertaking. I profoundly believe that the American nations during the coming years will write a chapter of achievement in the advancement of peace that will stand out in world history."

I also called attention to the efforts of the Roosevelt Administration to end the policies which the Latin American nations regarded as interference in their internal affairs. "My Government," I said, "is doing its utmost, with due regard to commitments made in the past, to end with all possible speed engagements which have been set up by previous circumstances. There are some engagements which can be removed more speedily than others. In some instances disentanglement from obligations of another era can only be brought about through the exercise of some patience."

At about that time I received a letter from former Secretary of State Frank B. Kellogg asking me to induce Argentina and Brazil, along with several Central American states, to sign his pact. He wrote from the Hague, where he was a member of the Permanent Court of International Justice. I was able to reply that all the Latin American countries which had not already done so intended to sign.

Nonintervention was naturally a point of keen debate at Montevideo. It had formed one of the battlecries of the tumultuous 1928 Havana Conference. Although the Latin American nations were beginning to place more faith in the new intentions of the United States Government, they still wanted to wrap up nonintervention in a copper-riveted guarantee. One of the conference's committees prepared a convention on the rights and duties of states, Article 8 of which declared: "No state has the right to intervene in the internal or external affairs of another."

I sought to make our own position clear from the start. I was as much in favor of nonintervention as any of them. I tried to put this point over as emphatically as I could in my preliminary conversations with delegations so that no representatives need feel a desire to line up for a fight against the United States. Several attacks on us did come from Cuban and Haitian delegates, but they were actually not so strong as many had expected. The Cuban chairman, Dr. Angel Giraudy, was good enough to recall the small part I had taken in Cuban independence in 1899.

On December 19 I made a formal statement on the subject of nonintervention to the committee considering the convention. "The policy and attitude of the United States Government toward every important phase of international relationships in this hemisphere could scarcely be made more clear and definite than they have been made by both word and action especially since March 4," I said. "Every observing person must by this time thoroughly understand that under the Roosevelt Administration the United States Government is as much opposed as any other government to interference with the freedom, the sovereignty, or other internal affairs or processes of the governments of other nations.

"In addition to numerous acts and utterances in connection with the carrying out of these doctrines and policies, President Roosevelt, during recent weeks, gave out a public statement expressing his disposition to open negotiations with the Cuban Government for the purpose of dealing with the treaty which has existed since 1903. I feel safe in undertaking to say that under our support of the general principle of nonintervention, as has been suggested, no government need fear any intervention on the part of the United States under the Roosevelt Administration."

One week later the conference met in plenary session to receive and adopt reports of committees. The report embracing nonintervention provided an opportunity for some fiery orators who were accustomed to ringing the changes on this question at every Pan American meeting. When the criticism of the United States became violent, a United States delegate on my left almost exploded and insisted in whispers that I rise up and thoroughly denounce our opponents. Another delegate on my right, who, like myself, was a strong believer in nonintervention and knew my position, handed me notes from time to time stating that I had better just sit still and say nothing. It was one of the most uncomfortable and disagreeable experiences I have ever had in a public meeting.

Saavedra Lamas found himself, too, in a peculiar situation. At prior Pan American Conferences the Argentine delegates had taken the lead in denouncing the United States on the subject of intervention. At Montevideo, Saavedra Lamas was faithfully carrying out our understanding that we would work together in every way throughout the conference. He now knew beyond question that, at roll call at the end of the discussion, I would vote for nonintervention and express myself accordingly. But he could not rise in his place and reveal this fact beforehand. Nor could he speak at all without making some reference, as all the other speakers were doing, to the transgressions of the United States Government in the past. As a result, he got up and said just enough in an adverse way to escape censure by his colleagues who had followed Argentina's leadership in such denunciations in the past.

When my turn came I simply said that the United States was glad to sign the convention. Then, having had no time, in the rush of discussion, which had been carried on in Spanish, to understand some of the hairsplitting language indulged in by other speakers, I said that, in signing, I wished to append in clarification of my action the remarks I had made on December 19. Thereafter, the meeting calmed down.

The moment the meeting adjourned, I went out of my course to step across the aisle and shake hands with Saavedra Lamas. "I know," I said, "there was nothing else you could have done in the circumstances." He smiled broadly and thanked me, undoubtedly relieved that I was not taking serious exception to his words. After that slight exception, he worked with me as closely as I could have wished.

Another crisis rose when Dr. Puig Casauranc, Foreign Minister of Mexico, introduced a resolution on debts. Under his plan, debtors were to receive seven to ten years' moratorium for the asking, interest rates were to be slashed to about 3 per cent, and the principal scaled on almost any pretext. Debts were not on the agenda, but Dr. Puig sought to get a full discussion and acceptance of his proposal. He had already discussed his views with the foreign ministers of other countries and had visited me in Washington before my departure for Montevideo. I told him at that time that I could make no commitment, since the debts he was dealing with were from Latin American countries to private American investors, not to the American Government. The President had sponsored the creation of an unofficial Protective Bondholders Committee, composed of noted citizens like Newton D. Baker, Governor Philip F. La Follette, and former Governor Frank Lowden, to represent the American creditors. Thus the question was being taken from the hands of the United States bankers who had originally floated the loans and then sold the bonds to private investors.

Dr. Puig delivered a long, fiery speech. He was applauded wildly as he dramatized the distressed debtors oppressed by conscienceless corporations in Wall Street. He demanded and secured the appointment of a special committee, of which he was named chairman and to which his proposal was referred. It looked as if he would carry everything before him. No delegate dared throw himself in front of Dr. Puig's avalanche. Many speakers who followed him referred kindly to the Roosevelt Administration, but much doubt was strewn about as to whether we could deal with the soulless corporations and see that the oppressed everywhere were given deserved relief. Frequently the audience cast its eyes on me as if I were the villain in the show.

Finally I rose and outlined the situation as I saw it, calling attention to the formation of the Protective Bondholders Committee. I expressed my willingness that there should be the broadest, frankest discussion of Dr. Puig's proposals. But I said that, since my Government had no authority to treat with private contracts, I could not vote yes or no on the proposals.

At that point Saavedra Lamas came to the rescue. He said that a general moratorium on debts was impossible, that the conference did not have the time or ability to enter into its details, and that the whole question should be referred to a commission to meet later at Santiago, Chile. The conference so decided.

Over the whole conference hung the cloud of the Chaco War. This horrible jungle conflict had been raging intermittently since 1928, and was now reaching a climax. In proportion to the size of the nations involved, it was one of the most deadly in all history. Various methods to solve the dispute had been tried without success by a Commission of Neutrals of which the United States was a member; by a group of neighbors—Argentina, Brazil, Chile, and Peru; and by the Council of the League. The very multiplicity of agencies that sought to settle the conflict was one reason why it persisted.

When I arrived at Montevideo I found that a Commission of the League of Nations had just reached the city. I also found that President Terra of Uruguay was beginning discussions with the Paraguayans and Bolivians in an effort to bring the two countries together in peace. Subsequently the conference appointed a subcommittee composed of seven foreign ministers to work with President Terra. Although not a member of the subcommittee, I was invited to attend its meetings.

My own thought was that every effort should be made at the conference to compose the Chaco War. The nearness of Montevideo physically to the war and the war's immediate impact on the peace machinery we were seeking to set up rendered it imperative that the combined pressure of all the other American nations be applied to dispose of it. However, I did not feel that the question had any proper place on the conference agenda. I told the Conference that the League of Nations Commission was the only body that had an authoritative mandate to act in the dispute. The League Covenant was the only peace instrument that both Paraguay and Bolivia had signed. Therefore any move taken by the conference or by the delegations individually should be directed toward helping the League Commission arrive at a peaceful solution and toward urging the belligerents to accept it. Here was the third instance in 1933 when I, in concurrence with the President, was anxious to bolster the authority of the League.

The conference subcommittee followed this line of approach. On December 15, as a result of suggestions on our part, the Presidents of Argentina, Brazil, Chile, Colombia, Mexico, Peru, and the United States telegraphed the conference urging that every step possible be taken to effect a friendly solution of the Chaco War. President Roosevelt took care to mention the League of Nations in this message.

Four days later Bolivia and Paraguay signed an armistice; but the conference continued its efforts to obtain a definitive settlement of the war. How precarious was the truce was indicated by the explosion that occurred when Paraguayan troops occupied a key fort apparently a couple of hours after the armistice began. President Terra called a meeting of the committee of foreign ministers, at the Uruguayan Foreign Office, behind closed doors. There the Bolivians announced that if the conference failed to take action they would denounce it as not being seriously for peace, and they would walk out. This was some forty-eight hours before the conference was to adjourn.

President Terra suggested that the representatives of Paraguay and Bolivia be called in and told the view of the committee that Paraguay's action undoubtedly was a misunderstanding and should and would be worked out amicably. He believed this would require some days and that the conference should be held in session until it was concluded.

I proposed instead that telegrams be sent immediately to the Presidents of Paraguay and Bolivia asking them to settle the incident by agreeing to the appointment of a special committee to handle it. I pointed out that delegates even now were beginning to drift away from the conference, that it would not be possible to hold the conference in session, and that only a ragtail assembly would remain in Montevideo after a few more days. I emphasized that the controversy had been projected into the conference, and that actually the League of Nations Commission was handling the matter officially and could continue to do so.

The discussion went on for nearly three hours. The Paraguayan and Bolivian delegates were called in separately from time to time. The Bolivians boldly insisted that the conference could not go on until the controversy was taken in hand and settled. Finally, the meeting was coming to an end—some of the members had already risen—when I got up and literally shouted, "If we permit these two countries to break up the conference, after so many far-reaching accords have already been reached, we will become the laughingstock of the world. Let us convene in plenary session tomorrow and notify these two delegations that if they give trouble they will be virtually thrown out of the window. The conference must not be intimidated or bluffed in any such manner."

When I concluded, President Terra dictated to his stenographer a telegram to the Presidents of Bolivia and Paraguay, as I had suggested. Thereupon the meeting adjourned. Later that night some other delegates told me I had broken up the conference. I replied that I was entirely willing to take the responsibility in the circumstances. Early the next morning I heard that the Bolivian delegates were going from delegation to delegation, strongly insisting that they would carry out their threat to break out of the conference. But at about eleven o'clock that morning replies came in from the Presidents of Paraguay and Bolivia agreeing to the appointment of a commission to consider this specific controversy. Thus terminated what looked like a very serious situation.

At the last session of the conference I introduced a resolution, which was adopted unanimously and enthusiastically, reminding Bolivia and Paraguay of their obligations under the Covenant of the League and requesting them to accept juridical methods for the solution of their dispute. In presenting the resolution, I said: "The useless shedding of blood has no place in the age in which we live. With the innumerable agencies for the peaceful settlement of disputes between nations, war is useless as well as odious, repulsive, and a challenge to organized society. The present war is as deplorable as it is dangerous in its consequences to all neighboring countries."

The conference thus ended with fighting between Bolivia and Paraguay suspended. Unfortunately the truce was not to last. While I was on my way back to Washington fighting broke out again on January 6, 1934. Our efforts to end the Chaco War were to drag on through 1934 and well into 1935.

On Christmas Eve I cabled the President and Phillips: "A better state of feeling exists than at any time within a generation in the judgment of old attendants . . . The American delegation has succeeded in all its plans and has worked as a unit at every stage."

The outstanding social event of the conference was a full-dress dinner given by President Terra in the legislative palace, at which occurred probably the oddest episode of all the state dinners I have attended. Since all Latin American dinners begin late, we were invited for nine o'clock that evening. Shortly after nine all the guests, including all the major delegates and the members of the Uruguayan Government, and their wives, were assembled. We stood about in groups talking and waiting for the dinner to be announced. We stood, and stood, and stood. A half-hour passed, an hour passed, and the guests, many of them no doubt hungry, hoped the announcement would come any moment. But another half-hour passed and then an hour, and still no announcement. Many of the guests, tired of standing, were sitting down. Something seemed to have gone wrong, but no one was impolite enough to ask why the dinner was not forthcoming. Another half-hour and yet an hour passed, and then, at midnight, dinner was announced and we filed into the dining hall. To our surprise, we found no placecards at the tables. The hundreds of guests milled about for many minutes seeking to learn where they were to sit. Finally, word was passed around to sit anywhere, and the guests took whatever places were nearest them. We did not rise from table until two o'clock in the morning.

Later I was informed that the Uruguayan Chief of Protocol had arrived at the palace late in the afternoon to arrange the place cards. He found the task so hopeless that he became ill and went home. When the dinner hour arrived there were no place cards and no Chief of Protocol to be found. After much telephoning, it was learned he was in bed thoroughly exhausted. No doubt the chef was as unhappy as the Chief of Protocol and the guests.

Having gone to Montevideo via the east coast of South America, I returned to Washington via the west coast so as to visit as many Latin American countries as possible and place a few more solid stones on the foundation of friendship and cooperation built at Montevideo. With Mrs. Hull and many members of the delegation, I sailed from Montevideo for Buenos Aires on December 26. We had two cordial days in the Argentine capital, conversing with many Argentine officials.

While I was in Buenos Aires President Roosevelt made an important speech December 28 to the Woodrow Wilson Foundation in which he said: "The definite policy of the United States from now on is one opposed to armed intervention. The maintenance of constitutional government in other nations is not a sacred obligation devolving upon the United States alone. The maintenance of law and the orderly processes of government in this hemisphere is the concern of each individual nation within its own borders first of all. It is only if and when the failure of orderly processes affects the other nations of the continent that it becomes their concern; and the point to stress is that in such an event it becomes the joint concern of a whole continent in which we are all neighbors." This last was in line with the course we had been pursuing; namely, that any action on our part in Latin America had to be coordinated and conducted jointly with the other nations of the hemisphere.

The President also said: "A better state of feeling among the neighbor nations of North and Central and South America exists today than at any time within a generation. For participation in the bringing about of that result we can feel proud that so much credit belongs to the Secretary of State of the United States, Cordell Hull."

We next took the train for a magnificent trip across the Andes to Chile. Our reception in Chile could not have been friendlier. I spoke to the Chilean Congress. We then visited Peru. Wherever we stopped I issued statements or made speeches emphasizing our Good Neighbor policy and promoting friendship.

During a dinner given by President Benavides, at Lima, which was to be the seat of the next Pan American Conference in 1938, I pointed to one of the factors of our success at Montevideo. "We have just had a great demonstration at Montevideo," I said, "a demonstration that common sense and sincerity can surmount all obstacles when men of good will approach problems in a spirit of mutual helpfulness. That conference was a convocation of good neighbors. It was no place for demagogues and troublemakers, for backbiters and detractors, for petty suspicions, for the harangues of mere place-hunting politicians. The republics of this continent sent to the conference men, in a majority of instances, of high attainment—men who had won eminence as lawyers, scholars, statesmen, or as other distinguished workers in the fields of science, letters, and politics in the true sense of that word. Largely because of this, it was possible in the beginning for the conference to assert on behalf of the republics represented there a spiritual partnership that became the underlying force of all our efforts."

We went on to Ecuador, Colombia, and Panama, where we were cordially received, and then sailed aboard the cruiser *Richmond* for Key West, Florida. I transferred from the steamer because it was going on to Havana and, at that critical moment in Cuba, with the Cuban Government still unrecognized by us, I did not feel justified in visiting the Cuban capital. The *Richmond* took me to Key West, where I conferred on the Cuban situation with Jefferson Caffery, who had become Ambassador to Cuba, replacing Welles whom the President had named Assistant Secretary of State. Caffery proved himself one of our outstandingly capable representatives. His record at Havana was to attract considerable attention, while his subsequent services as Ambassador to Brazil were to be especially valuable to us. On the basis of his performance I later suggested to the President that Caffery be named our first Ambassador to liberated France, in which post he sustained the fine reputation he had already acquired.

At Key West I took the train for Washington, where I arrived January 21. I had been gone nearly two and a half months. But in that time a hemispheric seal was set on a new policy, and the Latin Americans came to believe that the United States was a nation among them, not over them. My next task was to implement this policy by appropriate actions, to mold the flesh and blood of deeds on the skeleton of words.

25: A Good Neighbor Keeps Promises

WITH THE END OF the Montevideo Conference and my return to Washington, the eyes of Latin America turned toward our capital to see whether we meant to carry forward concretely the agreements we had signed and the basic policy of the Good Neighbor. The next few months, in fact, were a delicate period. We had reached a climax of cooperation at Montevideo. Any faltering on our part now would revive old suspicions and antagonisms as acutely as before, if not more so. On the other hand, definite actions in the right direction would solidify the friendship attained for years to come.

After my return to Washington I conferred with the President, and then made a public statement, saying: "When our delegates, acting under the instructions of President Roosevelt, figuratively took off their coats, invited the other delegates into their confidence, and dispensed with all possible formality in approaching the work of the conference, an immediate response was evoked. When the President, supporting the actions of the delegation, emphasized the assurance that the United States disavows and despises all the old themes of conquest or armed intervention, it became evident that solidarity of purpose of all the Americans could be attained. For the first time in the history of such conferences, there was no imposing bloc arrayed against us. Individual carpers and quibblers were thwarted. Suspicions were disarmed. Understandings of a genuine sort became the pervading element of the proceedings and cooperation a significant reality."

Cuba was to be the kernel of our new and positive policy toward Latin America throughout the year. Our actions toward Cuba would prove to the rest of Latin America whether we were sincere in our protestations of nonintervention. While I was en route to Washington, the Grau San Martín Government in Cuba had faded out and Colonel Carlos Mendieta, leader of the Nationalist Party, became President. My conversation at Key West with Ambassador Caffery dealt with the question of recognizing Mendieta.

Following this conversation I telephoned the President in Washington and expressed my support of Caffery's view that the Mendieta Government should be recognized. The same day I received a message from Phillips stating that the President would invite the Latin American representatives in Washington to meet with him in the White House Tuesday or Wednesday of the following week. The President would tell them that the requisites we had laid down for recognition of a Cuban Government had been met by the popular and political support obtained by Mendieta and the apparent ability of the Government, with the help of the Cuban armed forces, to maintain public order.

Two days after my return to the State Department, with the concurrence of the President I telegraphed our Embassy at Havana: "Under authorization of the President you will please extend immediately to the Government of Cuba, on behalf of the United States, a formal and cordial recognition."

The State Department now hastened the preparation of a new treaty to take the place of the treaty of May 22, 1903, between the United States and Cuba, which incorporated the Platt Amendment giving us the right to intervene militarily in Cuba. Negotiations were opened and on May 29, 1934, I, along with Assistant Secretary Welles, and the Cuban Ambassador Manuel Marquez Sterling, signed the new treaty. Welles had made an earnest plea to me to be allowed the privilege of signing it with me, although this was not customary. He had taken a considerable part in the negotiations, hence I agreed.

By this treaty we gave up the right to intervene and also rights relating to Cuban financing and sanitation. We retained only the right to continue our naval base at Guantánamo, Cuba. Foreign Minister Torriente and I, on behalf of our respective Presidents, exchanged messages of congratulation and friendship. Significantly, messages of congratulation came to me from other Latin American nations as well.

President Roosevelt sent the treaty to the Senate on the same day with a message saying: "Our relations with Cuba have been and must always be especially close. They are based not only upon geographical proximity, but likewise upon the fact that American blood was shed as well as Cuban blood to gain the liberty of the Cuban people and to establish the Republic of Cuba as an independent power in the family of nations. I believe that this treaty will further maintain those good relations upon the enduring foundation of sovereign equality and friendship between our two peoples."

In the remarkable time of two days the Senate voted its consent. Ratifications were exchanged on June 9, and the Cubans declared a three-day festival in celebration.

That same month I addressed a letter to the President suggesting his approval for an embargo on the shipment of arms to Cuba except those licensed by the State Department on the basis of a request from the Cuban Ambassador. This was designed to prevent a resurrection of armed strife in Cuba. The President accordingly signed and issued a proclamation prepared by the Department.

But a new political relationship was not enough to bring Cuba up to the surface of normality. Economic assistance was needed as well. As one means to help, the President created the Second Export-Import Bank in March to finance exports to Cuba. In May he reduced the tariff rate on Cuban sugar 25 per cent. Following the passage of the Trade Agreements Act in June, I started negotiations with Cuba which ended with the signing in August of our first trade agreement. This lowered the tariff on Cuban sugar 40 per cent more. In the remaining four months of 1934 our trade with Cuba developed phenomenally. Exports to Cuba increased 129 per cent compared with the last four months of 1933, and our imports from Cuba increased 155 per cent.

In summation, if the case of Cuba was to be the focus of Latin American scrutiny of our acts and intentions, a happier one could scarcely have been chosen.

Our next step in furtherance of the Montevideo agreements was to adhere to Saavedra Lamas's Antiwar Pact. Ambassador Weddell presented our adherence to the Argentine Government on April 27 with the reservation that we did not thereby waive any rights we might have under other treaties or conventions or under international law. Our adherence was conditioned upon the approval of the Senate, which was duly given in July.

Saavedra Lamas then requested my help in inducing nations outside the Western Hemisphere to adhere to his pact. Since it was my ideal that the efforts of the nations of this Hemisphere toward peace should not be restricted to the New World but serve as an example in which the rest of the world could join, I readily agreed. I sent instructions to our representatives in many European capitals to inform those governments that we had ratified the Saavedra Lamas Antiwar Pact, sincerely believed in its efficacy, and hoped they would become signatories to it. A few other governments duly signed.

Panama received considerable attention from my associates and me following the Montevideo Conference. Panama nourished certain grievances against us by virtue of the 1903 treaty with us. This treaty, signed when Panama was still in the cradle, gave us privileges that she regarded as incompatible with her sovereignty, such as the right to intervene to maintain order in Panama City and Colón. She was also grieved because we were paying her the annual $250,000 rental for the Panama Canal Zone in devalued dollars instead of the gold coin called for by the treaty.

When I passed through Panama while returning from Montevideo, I went thoroughly into these questions with officials of the Panamanian Government so as to lay the groundwork for a revision of the treaty. I carried on similar conversations with the Panamanian delegates at Montevideo, and with the Panamanian Minister in Washington. I felt it was very important to agree upon a new treaty if we were to establish better relations with the people of Panama and to some extent with the people of Colombia, who still kept contact with the citizens of Panama, which formerly had belonged to Colombia.

Formal negotiations to overcome our difficulties began in the spring of 1934, with Welles directly in charge. I had assigned Welles to the immediate direction of Latin American affairs. I closely followed the negotiations myself, and took part whenever I could be helpful. They continued throughout the year and reached a satisfactory agreement in 1935 which effectively removed any possible infringement on Panama's sovereignty. Welles and the Department officers working with him creditably carried out their task.

When the treaty came up in the Senate for approval, some Senators rose in vigorous opposition to a few of its provisions. I kept in close contact with the Senate until a favorable two-thirds vote was obtained.

Haiti offered another focal point of friction with Latin America which I worked to remove. Our agreement of August 7, 1933, with Haiti had provided for the withdrawal of our troops in October, 1934. President Roosevelt, during a Caribbean trip in July, visited President Vincent of Haiti, and agreed to move it up two months.

On August 15 the American flag was lowered and the Haitian flag hoisted in its stead. "In the nearly twenty years during which our marine and naval forces have been stationed in Haiti," I said in Washington, "they have rendered invaluable, disinterested service to the Haitian Government and people. At this present moment they are withdrawing from the island in an atmosphere of great friendliness and the best of understanding. We wish for the Government and people of Haiti stability, progress, and all success."

President Vincent had already visited President Roosevelt in April, 1934, to discuss the discontinuance of the financial controls maintained in Haiti to ensure the allocation of duties and other revenues to the payment of Haiti's debt to American investors. As a result, an agreement was made that month whereby the National City Bank of New York sold its National Bank of Haiti to the Haitian Government and the bank took over the supervision of finances then carried out by American officials.

In the period following Montevideo no question proved so cantankerous as the Chaco War. The truce we had obtained at Montevideo lasted eighteen days. The fighting that followed in 1934 was bitter. The League Commission returned to Geneva and made its report in May. On May 20 I received a telegram from the League informing us that the League Council recommended an embargo on arms shipments to both Bolivia and Paraguay and asking whether the United States would take part.

Two days prior to the receipt of this telegram I had asked Senator Pittman, chairman of the Senate Foreign Relations Committee, and Congressman McReynolds, chairman of the House Foreign Affairs Committee, to introduce a joint resolution authorizing such an embargo. I wrote them that Bolivia and Paraguay had refused to accept the carefully considered proposals for the restoration of peace, and that further efforts at conciliation, unaccompanied by more direct measures, would be fruitless.

"The United States," I said, "should be willing to join other nations in assuming moral leadership to the end that their citizens may no longer, for the sake of profits, supply the belligerent nations with arms and munitions to carry on their useless and sanguinary conflict. . . . I have reason to believe that the arms-producing nations of the world will find it possible to join in this movement, and that the selfish interests of manufacturers and merchants of arms and munitions will not be permitted to stand in the way of concerted action sponsored by the enlightened opinion of the world."

On May 23 the House passed the resolution; and the Senate approved it the following day. It was significant that Congress had given us authority to join in a League action without precedent, for this was the first time the League had ever imposed an embargo against both belligerent nations.

Our actions in Latin America following the Montevideo Conference were given effective backing by Congress. The almost incredibly rapid passage of the legislation on the Chaco embargo and the Cuban treaty, as well as on Haiti and the Argentine Antiwar Pact, showed that Congress too was convinced of the validity of the Good Neighbor Policy and the need to implement it with acts.

The Chaco War, however, dragged on throughout the year and into

1935. On December 7, 1934, in response to a League invitation, the United States agreed to appoint a member of a Neutral Supervisory Commission set up by the League. This commission, composed of American states only, would have the task of supervising the neutrality of a zone to extend between the forces of Paraguay and Bolivia in the Chaco.

Paraguay, however, refused the League plan of settlement and withdrew from the League. Thereupon the League recommended retaining the arms embargo against Paraguay but lifting it as to Bolivia, and transmitted its recommendations to me. For the United States to pursue the same action meant a new Act of Congress, and experience had already shown us that Congress was not disposed to grant the President authority to impose an embargo against one country, the aggressor. Furthermore, the League's recommendation, being a partial imposition of sanctions in Latin America, quickly aroused resentment among our neighbors to the South, who did not hesitate to point out that the League was dealing more harshly with a small South American country than with Japan in 1933. We accordingly did not agree, but continued the embargo against both countries. In fact our action was still helpful to the League, because, if we had lifted the embargo and permitted the sale of arms to both belligerents, we should have impaired the League's efforts.

Argentina and Chile now took the lead in negotiations with Paraguay and Bolivia, and the United States, along with Brazil, Peru, and Uruguay, joined them. I named Hugh Gibson, our Ambassador in Rio, to represent us. The mediators met at Buenos Aires in May, 1935, were joined by representatives of Paraguay and Bolivia, and, at long last, were able in June to induce the belligerents to accept an agreement ending the conflict and providing for immediate demobilization. The most savage fighting in the Western Hemisphere in more than a half-century had come to an end.

All our political acts in the direction of Latin America, however, would have lost their true effect if we had not been able to back them up with economic acts. It was not for naught that President Terra of Uruguay, in his opening address at Montevideo, had said, in quoting President Roosevelt, that "the Smoot-Hawley tariff closed almost completely, beginning three years ago, the foreign markets for our industry and agriculture, has served to impede the payment to us of our public and private debts, increasing taxation in order to cover the expenses of the government, and, finally, has closed our factories."

The American nations, somewhat surprised that I should have introduced a broad-gauged liberal commerce resolution in the light of the

White House statement prior to my sailing for Montevideo, and somewhat skeptical following the President's press conference the day after I introduced it, now were waiting to see. Could I, following the Montevideo Conference, succeed where, prior to the London Conference, I had failed? The Trade Agreements Act, less than five months after my return from Montevideo, was the answer.

The subject of transportation and communications, which the White House statement of November 9, 1933, had made the center of all discussion at Montevideo, formed a considerable share of our work on Latin America in 1934. On March 5 I transmitted to the President—and he, the following day, to Congress—a report of a survey of the proposed Pan American Highway made by the Bureau of Public Roads, Department of Agriculture. This survey had begun under the Hoover Administration and had been in progress three years. The report contained a description of the selected route and economic analyses of the effects of the projected highway on the economy of the countries through which it would pass.

On June 18, 1934, the President approved an Act of Congress authorizing $75,000 to continue the surveys. Following our negotiations with Central American republics, where construction of the highway through jungles and over rivers was most difficult, an allocation of $1,000,000 was made in the Emergency Appropriation Act of June 19, 1934, for construction, as well as survey, on the highway. The money was to be used largely in building bridges in Central America, we to provide building materials and machinery, our sister republics to transport the materials and supply the labor.

At this writing, the Pan American Highway is still not completed, though great progress has been made. When it is finished it will be a valuable material link among the twenty-one American States of the Pan American Union, and also Canada to the north. Streams of hundreds of thousands of automobile tourists, flowing north and south, should serve to increase the knowledge by each American nation of the others, and to augment the work of political, cultural, and economic cooperation in binding them all together.

Claims of American citizens against the Mexican Government arising out of injury to Americans or damage to their property over years of revolution and counterrevolution in Mexico furnished another item calling for settlement in the post-Montevideo months. They amounted to several hundred million dollars. We agreed to accept the terms already accepted by six European countries; namely, 2.65 per cent of the principal, the exact total to be ascertained by a commission. Mexico promised to make annual payments of $500,000, beginning in January, 1935. The protocol was signed April 24, 1934, in Mexico City, and Mexico's first payment was duly made the following January. Settlement of these claims, which had been hanging over our relations with Mexico for many years, was of help in our dealings with our neighbor to the south in the years to come.

One of my most delicate tasks in 1934 was to remove the disquietude felt by Brazil over our closer relations with Argentina. At Montevideo, Dr. Mello Franco, head of the Brazilian delegation, had evinced some mild disappointment in the belief that I had consulted Saavedra Lamas too much, himself not enough. This related to the peace resolution I requested Saavedra Lamas to offer. In other respects I had consulted Mello Franco more than any other delegate. Even before I learned of Mello Franco's state of mind, I made a special call upon him and, as frankly and tactfully as I could, laid before him everything I had learned or been connected with since my arrival at Montevideo. He and I worked together thereafter in a thoroughly friendly, cooperative way.

After my return to Washington, Brazil continued uneasy over our friendship with Argentina. Brazil and the United States, almost from the beginning, had been the best of friends. I personally cherished and valued this relationship very highly. Nothing was further from my mind than to say or do anything in connection with Argentina that could indicate the slightest neglect of our good friend Brazil. Argentina's political leaders, however, had so long taken the lead in organizing opposition against us during preceding years that her joining the other nations, including the United States and Brazil, in carrying forward the work of the conference with entire unity, could not but cause comment and speculation. This was unavoidable, especially since Brazil and Argentina had been rivals in many ways and each closely observed the significance of any development concerning the other. During 1934 I was able to convince Brazil that no change whatever had occurred or would occur in our traditionally warm relations.

Throughout 1934 and into 1935 I seldom lost an opportunity, in my conversations with the ambassadors of the major countries in Europe and Asia, to point to the example of Pan America. I assured them that the principles we were laying down and the agreements we were reaching were not exclusive. We should be more than delighted to share them with the nations of the rest of the world. I earnestly besought them to urge their

Governments to observe the same tenets of nonintervention, peaceful settlement of disputes, and liberal, nondiscriminatory commerce.

I said to one after another: "The broad, fixed purpose I had at Montevideo was to lay the foundations for a copper-riveted international cooperative structure such as would afford a model of rules and basic principles to govern normal, peaceful relations among nations. This program of international cooperation is now the basis of our appeal to all other nations to embrace it and make it universal."

Had their Governments heeded our words the remainder of the world might have avoided the tragedy of arms that was to come five years later. But, as I said in an address to the National Press Club, Washington, on February 10, 1934, in summing up the results at Montevideo: "While the American nations were thus consecrating all their efforts and emotions by concrete actions and utterances to the cause of peace, some statesmen in other countries were urging policies and preachments which they knew would probably lead to war, while numerous other statesmen were no longer vocal in support of conditions of peace. When, therefore, would it ever become more important and more incumbent upon the republics of this Western Hemisphere to speak out against war as the supreme scourge of the human race, than at this time?"

A decade of steady implementation of the Good Neighbor policy was now to follow. It was not always to be smooth rafting, and we were to encounter towheads in our stream of friendship. Great patience was required, and disappointments were sure to be encountered. But I had long before realized that the achievement of worth-while aims often called for extreme patience and sometimes serious personal and official embarrassment, and I therefore formed a definite resolution that I would undergo any such experiences for the sake of vitally important long-view accomplishments.

It took even more persistence to put the liberal commercial and trade policy I began urging in Congress in 1916 into practice with the Trade Agreements Act of 1934, eighteen years later. The London Economic Conference had been an acute test of patience. But those who then attributed to me the thought of resigning did not do full justice to the belief I cherished that personal embarrassments weighed little against the ultimate fulfillment of the principles for which I fought. Any other course to achieve the vital, urgent policies I deemed necessary would have gone for naught.

In implementing the Good Neighbor movement in Latin America, one of our most enthusiastic and valuable collaborators was Dr. Leo S. Rowe, Director General of the Pan American Union. He had long been a veteran in the Pan American service, and, with his first-class ability, wide experience, and familiarity with all questions and conditions, he was of immense aid. I found him always honest, sincere, and loyal to every aspect of the Good Neighbor policy. I also received great help from a quiet but useful official in the State Department, Warren Kelchner, one of our technical advisers and later chief of the Division of International Conferences.

Moving steadily forward from Montevideo with ever increasing interest and enthusiasm, we were to develop a marvelous structure of friendly and trusting cooperation among the twenty-one nations of the Pan American Union. They thus prepared themselves for the most effective unity, teamwork, and joint resistance against the external attack by the forces of aggression which was soon to threaten them. The entire structure of relations in the Western Hemisphere had as its most solid foundation a broad moral principle, absolute confidence in one another, and a will to work together to promote the greatest measure of progress on the part of all American nations alike. It has been my profound conviction at all times—which grows stronger, if possible, with the years—that any system of international relations must deteriorate and collapse whenever moral considerations are repudiated and abandoned.

26: Tearing Down Tariff Walls

THE LIFE OF A MAN in politics is a series of conflicts. I have had my full share, but none was longer drawn out and at the same time more successful and important than the fight for Trade Agreements. I was thirty-six years old when in my maiden address in Congress I pleaded for lower tariffs and fewer trade restrictions. I was sixty-two years old when in 1934 we finally won the fight to reduce them, after our temporary victory with the Underwood Act of 1913 which the World War badly handicapped and the Republicans promptly tore to pieces when they came to power in 1921. In all that interval I never ceased urging a liberal commercial policy for the United States. There was never any narrowing or compromising of my attitude; rather it broadened from 1916 on as I saw the effect that a freer flow of commerce could have on world peace. I never ceased attempting, by acts and utterances in and out of Congress, to keep alive and advance my economics and peace policy and to implement it at the earliest possible stage.

In the earlier period I faced two types of opposition. One was from the traditionally high-tariff Republican Party. The other was from a portion of my own Party, exemplified by the Smith-Raskob group. After becoming Secretary of State I faced four types of opposition. In addition to the two already mentioned, the others came from some foreign countries and from a small group of experimenters about the President.

During the course of my talks with Franklin D. Roosevelt when he passed through Washington in the years prior to his nomination in 1932, I gathered the impression that he was entirely favorable in principle to my proposal and to the questions related to it. Our conversations were in the nature of exchanges of information and views about developments and conditions generally, with sufficient definiteness for each to understand the slant of mind of the other, and I had no occasion to seek a definite commitment from him on this or other questions.

My associates and I had already won our fight of 1931–1932 to keep the Democratic Party from sliding into the error of high tariffs. Mitchell Palmer and I had written our views into the platform of 1932, which received Mr. Roosevelt's approval, in these words: "We advocate . . . reciprocal tariff agreements with other nations."

On March 4, 1933, therefore, I had reason to believe that the highway was now open toward liberal commercial policy and reduction of trade barriers. Following his inauguration, the President, in the course of his conferences with foreign delegations, seemed much interested in carrying the idea forward at the London Economic Conference. Gradually, however, the forces favoring high tariffs, together with a number of the President's economic advisers connected with the NRA and AAA, increasingly urged him to abandon the idea of tariff reductions in order that our Government might, if necessary, impose restrictions on imports to enable NRA and AAA to function successfully.

During the days prior to my departure for London I thought I sensed decreasing interest by the President in my program. I was also made uncomfortable by Moley's radio speech a few days before my departure condemning the tariff program, without objection by the President. I often wondered later whether the President gave him permission expressly or by mere silence thus to negate my whole plan.

The failure at London is already known. Following my return to Washington I kept earnestly at work on officials and the public in support of this undertaking. I delivered speeches and gave out statements. I maintained contact with appropriate members of the State, Commerce, Treasury, and other departments of the Government, including the Tariff Commission, and with officials of economic associations, leading economists, and others who showed a disposition to help.

On the day I sailed for Montevideo, November 11, 1933, the President sent letters to me and to the Secretaries of the Treasury, Commerce, and Agriculture, the chairman of the Tariff Commission, and the heads of AAA and NRA, directing that an Executive Committee on Commercial Policy be formed to coordinate our country's international commercial policies. The chairman was to be a representative of the State Department. Under Secretary William Phillips functioned as the first chairman pro tem.

The President, still pursuing the theory of retaining full discretionary authority to fix tariff rates at any height deemed necessary for the successful operation of the AAA and NRA, was slow to embrace my liberal trade proposal at Montevideo. But the success it achieved among the Latin American countries and in the press at home made him more friendly toward it. When I returned from Montevideo, I found that two things had happened. First, the President was favoring a trade agreements program. But, diametrically on the other hand, he had during my absence appointed George N. Peek to head a committee to coordinate foreign trade relations. Peek had been administrator of the AAA, disbelieved in tariff reductions, and favored an embargo fence around the country while the policies of NRA and AAA were applied. His theories, if carried out, meant the death of the trade agreements policy. The appointment was made exactly one month after the creation of the Executive Committee on Commercial Policy.

I immediately began working with the Executive Committee on Commercial Policy to draft a Trade Agreements Bill. I found the committee unanimous that Congressional legislation should be sought directing and authorizing the President to enter into reciprocal trade agreements. It was generally agreed that only this type of executive agreement could succeed. Treaties, which had to be submitted for Senate approval, were hopeless if they contained substantial tariff reductions. While I was at London the President had instructed the State Department to begin the negotiation of treaties calling for Senate ratification, and we duly entered into negotiations with Argentina, Brazil, Colombia, Portugal, and Sweden. Only with Colombia was a treaty signed, and this was not even submitted to the Senate for approval, hence did not become effective.

The tariff truce that we had established at the London Economic Conference was evaded by almost all nations after the conference ended. They increased their tariffs and restrictions, and at the same time negotiated trade agreements one with another whereby the two negotiators sought to balance their exports and imports between them, so that each one bought exactly the same value of goods from the other. I felt that such agreements, bottomed on barter, could not expand commerce but only choke it. They were, I said, "a direct road to economic suicide."

Trade was being readjusted, and we were losing out at every turn. In 1929 the United States' share of the world's foreign trade had been 13.8 per cent; by 1933 it had fallen to 9.9 per cent. All our exports had declined appreciably, some disastrously. Exports of automobiles and parts were down from $541,400,000 to $90,600,000; of iron- and steel-mill products from $200,100,000 to $45,500,000; of copper from $183,400,000 to $24,900,000; of wheat and flour from $192,300,000 to $18,600,000, and of rubber and rubber manufactures from $77,000,000 to $17,800,000.

Many other nations could raise or lower tariff rates by executive order, and thus could negotiate. We could not. Other nations were skeptical about negotiating with us because any accords we reached had to receive a two-thirds vote of the Senate before entering into effect. They were doubly skeptical because they knew the record of the Senate's adverse action in the case of previous treaties containing substantial tariff reductions.

Over and above the economic side of our foreign policy, but closely tied in with it, I believed, hung the political side. To me it seemed virtually impossible to develop friendly relations with other nations in the political sphere so long as we provoked their animosity in the economic sphere. How could we promote peace with them while waging war on them commercially? When I came into the State Department I found in the files no fewer than thirty-four formal and emphatic diplomatic protests presented by as many nations following the passage of the Smoot-Hawley high-tariff Act. Nor had their protests been confined to words. Goaded by what they regarded as almost an embargo keeping out their exports to the United States, they retaliated in kind.

Take, for instance, the case of little Switzerland. The Smoot-Hawley Act had raised duties on practically every major Swiss export to the United States—particularly on watches and clocks, an industry employing one-tenth of Switzerland's population. The Swiss stated they considered the Smoot-Hawley tariff an unfriendly act against them. They forthwith raised their tariffs against our automobiles, tires, gasoline, electrical and household equipment, office appliances, and meat products to virtually a boycott level. In one year thereafter Switzerland's exports to the United States fell off 30.5 per cent, compared to a general decline in her exports of 11 per cent, and her imports from the United States decreased by 29.6 per cent compared with a decrease of 5.4 per cent in her imports from all countries.

The British Commonwealth had indignantly followed up the Smoot-Hawley Act by the Ottawa agreements of 1932 establishing through empire tariffs a high wall around the entire Commonwealth, thereby greatly injuring our trade with the United Kingdom and the Dominions. One comparatively small item of our trade with Canada shows graphically what retaliation in tariff raising can do. Our imports of eggs from Canada were very small, but the tariff on eggs was increased by the Smoot-Hawley Act from 8 to 10 cents a dozen. Eggs imported from Canada then dropped from 13,299 dozen in 1929 to 7,939 dozen in 1932. But Canada retaliated by raising her duty on eggs from the United States from 3 to 10 cents a dozen. What then happened? Eggs exported from the United States to Canada dropped from 919,543 dozen to 13,662 dozen in the same period. Some of this decline can be attributed, of course, to the economic crisis following 1929, but that crisis itself, in my belief, was largely caused and certainly accentuated by our high tariffs.

Before I left for Montevideo, I had agreed with President Roosevelt on the appointment of Francis B. Sayre, son-in-law of President Wilson, as an Assistant Secretary of State, to take charge of economic and commercial policy in the State Department. I had known Sayre only casually in the years prior to 1933, but I had fine reports about him, especially on his work in Siam and other countries. I put him in charge of the preparation of the trade agreements program, and he became the first permanent chairman of the Executive Committee on Commercial Policy. I found him to be conscientious, painstaking, and efficient. He was loyal, and I found I could rely on him to take given matters for me to the President, particularly in connection with trade agreements. He made an excellent record as Assistant Secretary of State.

In earlier years I had been in favor of any action or agreement that would lower tariff barriers, whether the agreement was multilateral, signed by many or all nations, whether it was regional, embracing only a few, or whether it was bilateral, embracing only two. My original proposal of 1916 had meant multilateral action, whereby all nations would agree to reduce their tariffs at the same time to the same extent. I repeated this formula in its broadest sense to Congress in renewing my economic proposal on various occasions during the 1920's. As the London Economic Conference approached I was still prepared to use this method if other nations were willing. The world-wide tariff truce I proposed and saw adopted was a step in this direction. But during and after the London Conference it was manifest that public opinion in no country, especially our own, would at that time support a worth-while multilateral undertaking. My associates and I therefore agreed that we should try to secure the enactment of the next best method of reducing trade barriers, that is, by bilateral trade agreements which embraced the most-favored-nation policy in its unconditional form—meaning a policy of nondiscrimination and equality of treatment.

When I returned from Montevideo I dived in on Congress preparatory to getting trade agreements legislation offered and passed. By the end of February, 1934, we had completed our draft of the Trade Agreements Bill. Ironically, our opponent Peek proved of material aid to us. The original draft was too long and complicated. "Make the bill only two or three pages long, and it will stand a better chance," Peek suggested. We followed his idea. He was right.

On February 28 I attended a conference at the White House, presided over by the President, to consider the draft. Vice President Garner, Senators Robinson and Harrison, Representatives Rainey, Byrnes, and Doughton, Secretary of Agriculture Wallace, Peek, and Sayre took part. The President approved our draft and agreed to send it to Congress with a message from himself. In the message, which we drafted in the State Department, Mr. Roosevelt pointed out that our exports in 1933 had fallen to 52 per cent of the 1929 volume, and to 32 per cent of the 1929 value. He said that "a full and permanent domestic recovery depends in part upon a revived and strengthened international trade" and "American exports cannot be permanently increased without a corresponding increase in imports."

I appeared before the House Ways and Means Committee on March 8 and promised them with emphasis that each trade agreement would be undertaken with care and caution, and only after the fullest consideration of all pertinent information. "Nothing will be done blindly or hastily," I said. "The economic situation in every country has been so thoroughly dislocated and disorganized that the people affected must exercise patience while their respective governments go forward with such remedial undertakings as the proposed bilateral bargaining agreements."

The bill passed the House of Representatives March 20, by a vote of 274 to 111. The Senate Finance Committee held extensive hearings. I went before it to advocate the bill. I said it was "not an extraordinary plan to deal with ordinary or normal conditions, nor an ordinary plan to deal with extraordinary conditions," but was "an emergency measure to deal with a dangerous and threatening emergency condition." The bill, slightly amended by the committee, passed the Senate on June 4 by a vote of 57 to 33. In both House and Senate we were aided by the severe reaction of public opinion against the Smoot-Hawley Act.

Then and later Chairman Robert L. Doughton of the Ways and Means Committee, and Representative Jere Cooper of Tennessee proved towers of strength in support of our trade agreement legislation. Each rendered conspicuous service, and they were ably seconded in their efforts by their colleagues on the Ways and Means Committee.

At 9:15 on the night of June 12 I watched the President sign our bill in the White House. Each stroke of the pen seemed to write a message of gladness on my heart. My fight of many long years for the reciprocal trade policy and the lowering of trade barriers was won. To say I was delighted is a bald understatement.

That night I issued a statement saying: "If human experience has taught any lesson during the past four and a half years, it has demonstrated with certainty that the difficulties of international finance and the decline of international commerce have been among the most destructive factors in the most destructive depression." I urged that other nations join with us in carrying out the new policy "not in a niggardly spirit or upon apothecary scales, but with a broad view of enlightened self-interest."

What was the Trade Agreements Act? It has been my experience in Congress and in the State Department that the general public grasps with much more ease and interest many of the broad political actions of our government in foreign affairs than it does the economic actions. It is not too difficult to understand the meaning of a diplomatic protest, a political treaty, the withdrawal of an ambassador, or the recognition of a new government. It is indeed difficult to understand the interaction of foreign commerce, tariffs, currency exchange, and debts.

First of all, the Trade Agreements Act was an amendment to the Smoot-Hawley Act. It was immaterial, however, whether the Trade Agreements Act was a separate Act or an amendment to an Act. The point was that it was to be fully effective and independently operated just as if it were a separate enactment. Actually it would have been folly to go to Congress and ask that the Smoot-Hawley Act be repealed or its rates reduced by Congress. This had been the old system; and, with the exception of the Underwood Act in 1913, it always resulted in higher tariffs because the special interests enriched by high tariffs went to their respective Congressmen and insisted on higher rates.

Throughout my experience, I found many able Republicans in the House and Senate who, individually, were moderates rather than extremists in their tariff views. For example, I could have sat down with Speaker Nicholas Longworth, Ebenezer J. Hill, or several other outstanding Republicans, and, without difficulty, reached an agreement with them on tariff rates, with few exceptions. But, in practice, the chief tariff beneficiaries who had helped finance political campaigns would come to Washington and demand that the rates be increased rather than decreased, with the result that Republican leaders of moderate view were obliged to yield to ever rising rates as successive tariff revisions took place.

We therefore started with the Smoot-Hawley tariff rates as the upper limit. The President was now authorized to enter into trade agreements with other countries. These would go into effect without the need for

Senate approval or Congressional action. In negotiating such agreements, he was authorized to increase or decrease any of the Smoot-Hawley rates by as much as 50 per cent in return for adequate trade concessions from another country. He could therefore cut in half all existing rates; but we had made it clear that we did not for a moment contemplate such drastic, horizontal action. Although tariff rates could be raised or lowered, it was obvious we would reduce them, since no other country would sign an agreement to increase our tariffs. The purpose of the Act was stated to be to improve our exports.

The President could not transfer to the "free list" any imports now paying duty. That is, he could not remove the duty entirely. Nor could he take any import now on the free list and make it pay duty. However, he could "bind" such an article on the free list. This meant that the Government promised another Government that it would not take the article from the free list.

Any reduced duties were to apply to all foreign countries alike. If any country, however, discriminated against our commerce, the lowered duties need not apply to that country. Our preferential treaty of 1902 with Cuba was left untouched.

Reasonable advance notice of intention to negotiate a trade agreement had to be given so that interested persons could present their views. Before concluding an agreement, the President had to seek information and advice from the Tariff Commission, the Departments of State, Agriculture, and Commerce, and other appropriate sources. Congress excluded from trade agreement negotiations any authority to cancel or reduce foreign debts to the United States. The Act was to expire in three years.

The Trade Agreements Act in itself thus was simple. Basically it contained three main points: Agreements could be negotiated without their having to be submitted to the Senate. Tariffs could be reduced by as much as one-half, but only if we gained corresponding concessions from other countries. Reductions applied to all countries that did not discriminate against us.

The first two points require little explanation. The third has been the subject of much debate. This is the so-called unconditional most-favored-nation clause. The phrase is not of the happiest. It gives an impression of getting or giving favored or special treatment. It merely means: "I won't treat you any worse than the person I treat the best of all, provided you don't treat me any worse than the person you treat the best of all."

As for tariff reductions, it simply meant that, when we reduced the

tariff rates on certain articles imported from country A, we likewise reduced them on the same articles coming in from countries B to Z—
provided countries B to Z gave our exports to them as low rates of duty
and as much freedom from restrictions as they gave any other country.
If country B put higher rates of duty or more restrictions on our products
than on those coming in to her from any other country, then B's exports
to us would still have to pay the high Smoot-Hawley rates—the highest
in American history.

Nondiscrimination in foreign commerce had been a traditional American policy. President Washington stated it in his Farewell Address when
he said "our commercial policy should hold an equal and impartial hand;
neither seeking nor granting exclusive favors or preferences; consulting
the natural course of things; diffusing and diversifying by gentle means
the streams of commerce, but forcing nothing."

Since then we have had what is called a "single-column tariff." That
is, we had only one tariff rate for each dutiable article. Some nations have
two- or three- or four-column tariffs. They apply the first column of
lowest rates to nations getting the best treatment, the next column of
higher rates to nations getting the next best treatment, and so on.

However, in practice, we had applied the most-favored-nation principle in its conditional form until 1923. This meant that, when we made a
tariff treaty with country A, we did not apply our tariff reductions to
countries B to Z unless countries B to Z agreed to give us concessions
equivalent to those given us by country A. Secretary of State Hughes,
under President Harding, began to apply the principle in its unconditional
form.

The conditional form had proved a failure. Why? Trade between any
two countries is virtually never the same, in products or quantity, as
between one of them and some other country. If we make tariff reductions
to country A in exchange for tariff reductions by country A, it is difficult
to say exactly what country A gave us in exchange for any one reduction.
We cannot, therefore, logically go to country B and say, "We will give
you what reductions we gave A if you give us what reductions A gave
us." Country B may not be interested in the products dealt with in our
agreement with A. This system also means an interminable series of negotiations with many countries. During that time our exporters who got
reductions from A are kept in suspense as to what will happen in B to Z,
and meantime B to Z may go on discriminating against them, or actually
take new retaliatory action against them because of our discrimination

in favor of A. And if a new treaty is later negotiated with any other country concerning the same products, the whole series of negotiations must be done over again with all the other countries.

Hence it was that the Trade Agreements Act specifically stated that the unconditional policy should apply. But people have argued that we were thereby giving away something for nothing. They would say: "You reduced our tariffs on imports of horses, seed potatoes, and whisky from country A, and you got reductions from country A on our exports of automobiles, wheat, and lard. That's fine! And then you go and automatically give countries B to Z the same reductions you gave A—and you don't get anything in exchange! That's terrible!"

But the fact is, we get a great deal in exchange. Countries B to Z get the same reductions we have granted A only if they are not discriminating against us. B may be applying its lowest duties only toward Y and Z. But if B wants to benefit from our reductions she has to give us the same duties she is extending to Y and Z. Furthermore, a few months from now B may negotiate a treaty with X whereby she will give X lower duties than she gives Y and Z. Thereupon, if she still wants the benefit of our duties to A she has to give us the same duties she gives X. The use of the term "unconditional most-favored-nation" is therefore somewhat misleading. Other nations get our tariff reductions not unconditionally but on condition that they grant us equality of treatment.

In actual practice this principle has meant scores of millions of dollars to American exporters. We found repeatedly that lower duties were placed by certain countries on their imports from the United States merely because those countries negotiated tariff treaties with other countries embracing such lower duties—and then had to extend them to the United States if they wanted to continue to receive the reductions granted under the trade agreements.

As one example among hundreds, our trade agreement with Belgium reduced the Belgian duty on typewriters weighing less than 110 pounds from 2,012½ Belgian francs to 1,500 francs. A few months later an agreement between Belgium and Germany reduced the duty to 1,150 francs. By virtue of the most-favored-nation clause in our trade agreement with Belgium, American exporters of typewriters instantly and automatically received the same reduction. Had we been operating under the old conditional system, we should have had to negotiate anew with Belgium and offer her additional tariff reductions in order to get the benefit of the reductions she gave Germany.

During the first two years of the trade agreements, our exports safe-guarded from discrimination because of the equality of treatment we received from other countries were valued at $265,000,000.

Other persons have argued that extending tariff reductions to other countries than the one with which we sign a trade agreement would bring in a flood of imports. They say: "Reducing the duty on shoes imported from country A may be all right. But if B to Z send shoes in to us under the same duty we'll be swamped."

The answer is that countries B to Z do not all manufacture shoes for export. Perhaps only one or two do, and the probability is that they are smaller exporters than country A.

If the reduction in duty we granted to A were such as not to injure our own producers with whom A was the principal competitor, it was highly unlikely that our producers would suffer injury from the competition of imports from countries B or C, who were secondary sources of supply.

It is a fact that virtually all countries exporting to us have one or a few articles of which they are the predominant exporters. They are adapted, through climate, inherited skill, or location of raw materials, to make or grow these products better or more cheaply than other countries.

Therefore, in negotiating the trade agreements, we paid special attention to reducing the tariffs on such products, while ignoring other products of which they were not predominant exporters to us. In this way we could get the maximum tariff concessions for our own exports to country A by concentrating on the imports from country A in which A had her largest stake. The products we ignored with regard to A could be taken up in the negotiations with the other countries which were the predominant exporters of them. This became known as the "principal supplier" approach.

In the first two years of the trade agreements, the value of our imports from third countries which, because of equality of treatment, received reductions we granted in agreements, amounted to $30,000,000. Since our exports which benefited from the protection afforded by the same principle amounted to $265,000,000, the ratio of benefit in our favor was nine to one.

During my Congressional years I had repeatedly called attention to the disastrous reprisal effects produced by high tariffs and discrimination. If country A found herself discriminated against in a treaty between B and C she forthwith proceeded to discriminate against B and C. It was a vicious spiral. No country felt the effect more than the United States following the Fordney-McCumber high-tariff Act and particularly after the Smoot-Hawley Act. On the other hand, the nondiscrimination called for under the unconditional most-favored-nation principle had the opposite effect. Trade agreements tended to loosen up constriction in trade and to bring about universal decreases in tariff rates and restrictions. Instead of nations raising their tariffs in reprisals, they had to lower them if they wished to obtain the lower tariffs of other nations.

The most-favored-nation principle, however, could not go hand in hand with almost prohibitive tariffs such as our Administrations in the ten years prior to 1933 had imposed. Since 1923 the United States could say that she had applied her tariffs to all nations alike. But no nation could get over our tariff wall any product at all competitive with ours. We raised tariffs to impossible levels and then told all nations they were equally affected. We saw from the sharp and concrete reaction of other countries following the Smoot-Hawley Act how much value attached to most-favored-nation treatment under such conditions.

This principle as applied under the Trade Agreements Act did go hand in hand with better political relations among the nations. By inducing better economic feeling it brought better political feeling. Nations that entertained and expressed bitter resentment against us became our friends. Nor was this friendship limited to ourselves and specific other nations. By championing the principle, reenforced by substantial tariff reductions we helped extend its observance among other nations. With economic warfare diminished between any two of them, their own political relations were almost certain to improve.

Since 1916 I had been arguing that economic warfare fertilized the growth of political war, and that nondiscrimination in trade lessened the likelihood of war. The Trade Agreements Act was passed in 1934, however, and war came in Africa the next year, in Asia three years later, and in Europe five years later. Someone might therefore say, "You see, trade agreements could not prevent war."

I, of course, never claimed that trade agreements would be an absolute panacea against war. Moreover, by the time the Trade Agreements Act was passed, Hitler had been in power a year and a half and was furiously arming, Mussolini had been in power nearly twelve years and was planning the Ethiopian War, and Japan had been in Manchuria nearly three years and was getting ready to withdraw from the naval limitations treaty. These nations had no use for the liberal commerce of trade agreements, for they were already transforming their commerce to the needs of war. If, as I urged in my speeches during the First World War, something like the Trade Agreements Act could have been passed instead of the Fordney-McCumber Act of 1922 and other nations had seen fit to follow suit at once, the story might have been different.

I did claim, and continue to claim, that:

Economic warfare results in a lowering of living standards throughout the world. It foments internal strife. It offers constant temptation to use force, or threat of force, to obtain what could have been got through normal processes of trade.

A people driven to desperation by unemployment, want, and misery is a constant threat of disorder and chaos, both internal and external. It falls an easy prey to dictators and desperadoes.

In so far as we make it easier for ourselves and every one else to live, we diminish the pressure on any country to seek economic betterment through war.

The basic approach to the problem of peace is the ordering of the world's economic life so that the masses of the people can work and live in reasonable comfort.

Nations cannot produce on a level to sustain their people in well-being unless they have reasonable opportunities to trade with one another.

And this cannot happen in a world of extreme economic barriers, political hostility, and recurring wars.

The principles underlying the trade agreements program are therefore an indispensable cornerstone for the edifice of peace.

When I was a boy on the farm in Tennessee, we had two neighbors—I'll call them Jenkins and Jones—who were enemies of each other. For many years there had been bad feeling between them—I don't know why—and when they met on the road or in town or at church, they stared at each other coldly and didn't speak.

Then one of Jenkins's mules went lame in the spring just when Jenkins needed him most for plowing. At the same time Jones ran short of corn for his hogs. Now it so happened that Jones was through with his own plowing and had a mule to spare, and Jenkins had a bin filled with corn. A friendly third party brought the two men together, and Jones let Jenkins use his mule in exchange for corn for the hogs.

As a result, it wasn't long before the two old enemies were the best of friends. A common-sense trade and ordinary neighborliness had made them aware of their economic need of each other and brought them peace.

Yes, war did come, despite the trade agreements. But it is a fact that war did not break out between the United States and any country with which we had been able to negotiate a trade agreement. It is also a fact that, with very few exceptions, the countries with which we signed trade agreements joined together in resisting the Axis. The political line-up followed the economic line-up.

27: Trade Agreements Start to Work

ALMOST AS IMPORTANT as the passage of the Trade Agreements Act itself was the setting up of the right machinery to make it work. On June 27, 1934, the President created an interdepartmental Committee for Reciprocity Information to hear the views of interested persons concerning any trade agreement. The following day a Committee on Trade Agreements was formed to administer the Act under my supervision. Its nonpartisan membership was composed of representatives from the Departments of State, the Treasury, Agriculture, and Commerce, and the Tariff Commission, with Assistant Secretary Sayre as chairman. It became the guiding committee for negotiating the new agreements.

These two committees provided an example in cooperation among the Government departments that deserves mention. Hitherto coordination among the departments on economic matters had been loose, and conflicts of jurisdiction frequent. The new committees achieved a wholehearted, friendly working together that materially increased their efficiency.

I later named Henry F. Grady chairman of the Committee on Trade Agreements when I brought him into the State Department to take direct charge of the work of formulating and negotiating trade agreements. Grady efficiently carried a large part of the heavy burden of getting the trade agreements under way and in enlisting the support of business and other interests for it. I later named him Assistant Secretary of State.

Harry Hawkins, who became chief of the Trade Agreements Division of the department, served with great energy and ability. No one in the entire economic service of the Government, in my opinion, rendered more valuable service than he. Hawkins was a tower of strength to the department throughout the development of the trade agreements, and especially in our negotiations with other countries, which at times were exceedingly difficult.

The Trade Agreements Committee now surveyed the foreign-trade field to see which countries offered the best prospects for negotiations. It set up a number of "country committees." Each country committee was assigned a specific foreign nation. It studied our trade with that nation, to see which imports from her could receive lower duties without competing unfairly or injuriously with our domestic industry or agriculture, and which of our exports should receive lower duties from her by way of compensation. It studied the tariff system and the quota or exchange control arrangements, if any, of that country. Finally it made its recommendations to the Trade Agreements Committee.

Assuming that the recommendations were approved as to country A, we then approached country A, either through her Ambassador here or our Ambassador in her capital, explained the trade agreements program, and asked if she were prepared to negotiate. We stressed that the negotiations would have to be on the unconditional most-favored-nation basis —that is, equality of treatment.

If country A said "Yes," I then informed the President and asked his approval to initiate negotiations. He approved as a matter of course. Thereupon I issued a public notice of our intention to negotiate. Later on, this notice carried appended to it a list of those imports from country A on which we might consider granting tariff reductions or concessions.

Our purpose in making known these products at this early stage was to enable interested American manufacturers or growers to state their views. We set the date and place for such presentation of views, at least thirty days in advance, and generally much longer. Our imports from country A might embrace a large number of different products, but we might consider granting reductions on only the small number of products of which country A was a large exporter to us. American manufacturers or growers interested in this small number were asked to present their suggestions and views. There was no need for manufacturers or growers interested in the products not included in the list to state their views, because such products would not be touched, at least not in the agreement with country A.

The interested American producers presented their briefs and made their statements to the Committee on Reciprocity Information, which met in the Tariff Commission offices. The committee passed these views on to the Trade Agreements Committee, which considered them after a detailed study and report had been made to it by the country committee dealing with country A. They received full consideration in the ensuing negotiations.

When the groundwork was sufficiently advanced, we arranged for the negotiators of country A to meet with a group representing our trade agreements organization and begin the discussions. In some cases the negotiations that followed were fairly simple. There were few products to consider on either side and few restrictions to be removed. In other cases the negotiations were extremely difficult, dragged out many months, and at various points seemed on the verge of breaking down. At such moments I did not hesitate to communicate with the other Government and say, with all the emphasis I could use, that much more was at stake than a small tariff reduction on this or that product. The whole system of international trade, and perhaps world peace as well, was at issue.

We negotiated our first trade agreement with Cuba, signing it on August 24, 1934, less than two and a half months after the enactment of the Trade Agreements Act. It reciprocally reduced tariffs on a number of products. It was not, however, a typical trade agreement because it did not embrace most-favored-nation treatment. The Trade Agreements Act had continued in force the 1902 Treaty with Cuba, whereby we granted Cuba a reduction of 20 per cent in our general tariff rates and Cuba granted us reductions from 20 to 40 per cent on our products. The agreement was significant, however, because it quickly provided proof of the substantial increase in trade that mutual tariff reductions could produce.

Within three weeks after the signing of the Cuban agreement we announced our intention to negotiate agreements with eleven countries— Brazil, Haiti, Belgium, Colombia, Spain, Sweden, and five Central American Republics.

By October 18, 1934, I was able to say in a statement: "I regard the readiness of so many nations to cooperate with us in an effort to remove the obstacles put in the way of world commerce by excessive tariffs, by quotas and embargoes and other restrictive measures, as extremely gratifying and indicative of a widespread belief that the negotiation of such agreements is an effective method to reduce the economic ills of the world."

But we had difficulties a plenty. One was the questionable practice some countries indulged in of raising their tariff rates or restrictions just prior to the negotiation of an agreement. They hoped later to make an apparent concession to us by lowering their rates to the previous level in exchange for reductions by us. This practice, I said, "has never in the long run produced other than one result—loss of the fair-minded customer and the most worth-while trade. It should be obvious that no bargaining program, based upon a sincere effort for an all-around reduction of trade barriers, can succeed in the face of such practices. . . . Increased harm will result if the 'padded' restrictions are left standing by the breakdown of negotiations."

More difficulties confronted us in our efforts to remove restrictions other than high tariffs. Though nations might apply their tariffs equally,

they could still defeat the idea of equality of treatment by imposing quotas or exchange control or government monopolies. If we and
country A have each been exporting to country B 10,000 sewing machines,
and country B is applying the same tariff rates to both us and A,
country B could still discriminate against us by applying quotas whereby
she agrees with country A to import 15,000 sewing machines from A in
exchange for a similar arrangement by A to import a certain quantity of
B's farm produce. The same purpose is served if country B has an
exchange control system and gives her importers enough foreign currency
to purchase 15,000 sewing machines from A and only 5,000 from us.

When the Trade Agreements Act was enacted, the majority of foreign
nations were using some such devices, which had the effect of nullifying
the principle of equality of treatment.

We therefore had to pay great attention to removing these restrictions, and to stipulate their removal so clearly that there could be no
misunderstanding. Had we not done so, the concessions on tariffs which
we obtained for American exporters would have been largely erased by
such practices.

It was therefore not without significance that the text of each trade
agreement began, not with tariff reductions, but with guarantees of
equality of treatment in all its forms. Usually the agreement contained a
preamble stating that we and country A intended to maintain "the principle of equality of treatment as the basis of commercial relations"
between us. Then followed a number of articles giving legal effect to this
principle. Where we could not eliminate quotas we were able to stipulate
that our quota should guarantee us a fair share of country A's imports
of a certain article. This share would be calculated on our percentage of
the total imports of this article during a certain previous period of years.
We first followed this system for exchange controls as well, and later
insisted that enough foreign exchange be given to country A's importers
to cover their purchases from us under our guaranteed quantity quota.

Because a serious change in the currency rates between the United
States and country A might prejudice our or A's industry or commerce,
most of our trade agreements contained an escape clause. Thereby we or
the other country could propose negotiations to modify the agreement or
could terminate it on thirty days' written notice. A similar escape clause
was provided if, contrary to expectations, a tariff reduction or concession
on a certain article let in a seriously injurious amount of such articles

from some other country which hitherto had not been the chief source of our imports of the product.

The foreign hurdles we had to overcome abroad were paralleled by others at home. The trade agreements had not even begun to go into effect when an avalanche of protests against possible tariff reductions began to pour in to us from the special interests which thought that higher tariffs helped them. We were "selling them down the river" or "across the seas." Some protests were justified and were given full weight by the Trade Agreements Committee. Others were based on vague fears or on selfishness. Among the loudest complainers were a few very small industries employing two or three hundred persons which could supply only a tiny fraction of the country's needs of certain products. Nevertheless, they wanted even higher tariffs which would have increased the cost of such articles to all American consumers. On the other hand, we received welcome support from many manufacturers who knew the value of exports, including the automobile companies and producers of farm products. They could see the fallacy of trying to sell American goods abroad if we were not willing, by lowering our tariffs, to buy goods from abroad and thereby provide the dollars for the purchase of American exports.

But the greatest threat to the trade agreements program came not from foreign countries, not from the Republicans, not from certain manufacturers or growers, but from within the Roosevelt Administration itself, in the person of George N. Peek, former chief of the AAA. In March, 1934, the President had named him Foreign Trade Adviser. If Mr. Roosevelt had hit me between the eyes with a sledge hammer he could not have stunned me more than by this appointment. Personally Peek was most affable and agreeable in his relations with others. He was honest in his views and supported them with persistency. But I was convinced that his economic ideas were unsound, and that it would be a supreme tragedy if they were to displace the sound economic policies on which our trade agreements rested. His efforts, and those of his associates, aided at times by the President, came perilously near supplanting my whole set of international economic policies and my program to extend their application over the world and thereby to promote conditions of economic well-being and peace.

Peek used to take basketfuls of statistics to the White House, and the President would sponsor his statements to the press. He gave the President a memorandum in which he urged he be given control over all foreign-trade policy and negotiations. He would have stripped the State

Department, as well as the Departments of Commerce, Agriculture, and the Treasury of any real voice in foreign commerce. Fortunately, I was able to block this development.

Then Peek turned to the negotiation of barter agreements with foreign countries—precisely the type of practice then going on in Europe which we hoped eventually to eliminate through the trade agreements based on the equality of treatment principle. He started, no doubt, from the honest viewpoint that there were American surpluses that should be disposed of abroad. But he wholly failed to see that such barter agreements and the trade agreements could not both exist at the same time.

The Trade Agreements Act dealt with broad policies and broad trade methods rather than with individual barter transactions. One basis of our trade agreements policy—equality of commercial treatment and opposition to the numerous sorts of discrimination and preference—would have been openly violated by the Peek barter proposals. Our program undertook in a broad way to provide export facilities especially for the more burdensome surpluses such as cotton, tobacco, lard, wheat, and automobiles, by reducing discriminations and preferences abroad and increasing equality in trade treatment. In my view, the maintenance of this policy everywhere was all-important.

Throughout the summer of 1934 my associates at the State Department and I spent much time contesting Peek's theories. The conflict reached a summit when Peek negotiated a barter agreement with Germany in November and December of 1934. Germany was openly in default on her debts of $2,000,000,000 due in the United States; but, while thus guilty of the worst of bad faith toward American creditors, she pretended to desire a fair trade agreement with us. At the same time she was keeping other countries placated for the moment by paying her debts and trade balance due them.

Hitler's economic magicians sent a mission to the United States, and Peek negotiated an accord with them. It had all the characteristics of a typical German deal such as Hitler and Schacht had forced down the throats of other countries. We were to sell Germany 800,000 bales of cotton through the Export-Import Bank. Germany would pay one-fourth of the price in American dollars to the bank. She would pay three-fourths in German currency plus a premium of 22½ per cent. The bank would sell this currency at a discount to American importers of German goods, who could use it to pay for such goods.

While this deal was being negotiated I argued to the President as emphatically as I could against it. I felt that Mr. Roosevelt had lost, to a considerable extent, the interest in foreign-trade policy he had entertained before his election and inauguration. He had little time left to study international economic relations after he had studied domestic reforms. From my contacts with him I did not believe he was following the foreign economic side closely.

On November 19 I received an informal note from him, saying:

"Like most problems with which you and I have been connected during many years, there are two sides to the argument. In pure theory you and I think alike, but every once in a while we have to modify a principle to meet a hard and disagreeable fact! Witness the Japanese avalanche of cotton goods into the Philippines during the past six months.

"I am inclined to think that if you and George Peek, who represents the very hard-headed practical angle of trade, could spend a couple of hours some evening talking over this problem of the most-favored-nation clause, it would be very helpful in many ways."

This, to all practical intents, meant that I should call in Peek and virtually abandon my program and let him take the economic leadership. I was thoroughly convinced that the President and Peek were wrong in this all-important matter. There was no compromise on equality of treatment. Either you had equality or you had inequality. You could not have both operating at the same time. The Trade Agreements Act had laid down the principle of equality of treatment for the trade agreements. If this principle were modified, the "hard and disagreeable fact" mentioned by the President would become harder and more disagreeable.

I did call in Peek. But, as I fully anticipated, our conversation on his proposals was entirely fruitless. On November 28, 1934, I wrote to the President at Warm Springs, Georgia, sending him three memoranda on our commercial policy. "The several departments of the Government . . . are, according to my understanding, in entire harmony with the ideas expressed herein," I said, "with the sole exception of our good friend Peek. The press, as I stated to you on the train, is generally supporting us."

Some days later I left Washington for Nashville, Tennessee, to make an address on agriculture and the trade agreements. While I was returning to Washington, my assistant, Harry McBride, met me at Charlottesville, Virginia, with an urgent letter from Under Secretary Phillips, dated December 13. "With a suddenness which was unexpected," it began, "developments have occurred during the last two days which I know will be distressing to you." He recounted that on December 12 Peek conferred with the President, and thereafter the White House informed the State Department that the President had approved Peek's barter agreement with Germany. Phillips telephoned the White House and got a promise from the President that the final word would not be given until after my return.

When I got back to the State Department my associates and I arrayed together our arguments against the German barter deal, and I presented them to the President. I told him that our trade agreements program would be seriously endangered. Already we had received a protest from Brazil, with whom we were negotiating an agreement. Brazil, also a cotton exporter, said that if we entered into a special preferential accord of this nature with Germany, she would be obliged to do the same and to defer signing the agreement with us.

I pointed out that the deal was a subsidizing of German imports into the United States. By giving importers of German goods German currency at a discount with which to pay for them, they were thus getting the goods at lower prices than the same goods from other countries.

The deal called for the exchange of reichsmarks into dollars at the old gold dollar rate. This meant undoing, so far as Germany was concerned, the devaluation of the dollar.

Our cotton exporters, I said, might not, in fact, be able to get dollar exchange for their sales to Germany. There was no assurance that they would not be forced to sell cotton at a loss. Other losses might be suffered by the United States Government, through the Export-Import Bank.

The barter arrangement, I added, was based on Peek's belief that we could not otherwise sell the cotton to Germany. On the contrary, I felt that Germany needed the cotton so badly that she would buy at least 500,000 bales and find dollar exchange with which to pay for them.

Over and above all these arguments of detail was the fact that the deal was one of discrimination, not of equality of treatment. Every German export to the United States was thereby given a special advantage, and every other country exporting such products to the United States would inevitably protest and possibly take reprisals. The Chilean Ambassador stated to us that, if German fertilizer were given preferential treatment in our market, as this plan provided, Chile would be compelled to dump nitrates here.

"On top of her gross discrimination against American nationals," I said, "this deal would make a very good trade bargain for Germany, but with little gain and large risks for the United States. . . . The proposed plan is almost certain to engender extreme resentment among that large section of the American public which is violently opposed to the Hitler regime."

Fortunately, the President saw the validity of these arguments. He withdrew his approval of Peek's deal. That meant the end, too, of Peek's intention to negotiate similar deals with other countries. From then on, the new proposals contained in the trade agreements doctrines and programs steadily weakened and broke down the Peek program. I kept illustrating to the President the soundness of our plan, particularly the vital necessity of equality of treatment. In a memorandum to him on February 15, 1935, I said: "This country could get in the rut with other countries and confine its trade activities solely to the extremely narrow methods and practices of barter and bilateral bargaining transactions, but with the knowledge that during last year our exports increased $450,000,000, which is as much as the export increase of all the countries of Europe where several hundred of these narrow barter and bilateral bargaining treaty methods and devices were in operation."

I pointed out to Mr. Roosevelt that the first step was to eliminate or reduce excessive duties which excluded competition entirely or practically, or which had been in effect for a considerable time without resulting in domestic production equal to more than 10 to 15 per cent of total domestic consumption. Also duties which applied to notoriously inefficient businesses or industries or to a vast range of novelties, specialties, patterns, designs, luxuries, semiluxuries, articles of materially different qualities to our home production, or commodities of different use, none of which were seriously competitive with American products.

Two months later Peek's office was abolished. The trade agreements program was saved and subsequent results fully vindicated our opposition to Peek's ideas.

On March 28, 1935, I had a curious conversation with German Ambassador Hans Luther. He brought me extracts from an address by Schacht at Leipzig on March 4 in which Schacht emphasized the loss of trade Germany had suffered in her efforts to carry out the purely bilateral bargaining and bartering method of trade with other countries. Dr. Luther said he recognized "the soundness of the economic program being pursued by the State Department." He said his Government favored a suitable trade arrangement with us and wanted to restore normal trade relations. But he failed to appreciate Hitler's determination to steer all German economy toward the building of his war machine. In October, 1934, the German Government had notified us of its intention to denounce the most-favored-nation clause in its commercial treaty with us. After October 15, 1935, German exports to the United States ceased to receive the tariff reductions granted other countries under the trade agreements.

With Germany championing one method of foreign commerce and ourselves another, it is interesting to compare their respective results over a five-year period. Our exports to the sixteen countries with which trade agreements came into effect by the end of 1938 had increased 39.8 per cent between the periods 1934-1935 and 1936-1938. In the same time German exports to the same sixteen countries increased by only 1.8 per cent. Moreover, our method was developing friendly relations whereas Germany a few months later was to plunge into war.

Following the negotiation of the special agreement with Cuba our negotiations with other countries went steadily ahead. The first to be signed was with Brazil. On that occasion, February 2, 1935, I said: "Having once started on the road away from the medieval mercantilism which was strangling the commerce of a new world, progress should now be more rapid and the movement gain momentum."

It did gain momentum. By the end of 1935 we had signed agreements also with Belgium, Haiti, Sweden, Colombia, Canada, Honduras, and The Netherlands including the Dutch colonies. The agreement with Canada was the first formal arrangement between the two countries since the Confederation of Canada in 1867. By the end of 1936 we had signed agreements with Switzerland, Nicaragua, Guatemala, France and her colonies, Finland, and Costa Rica. Negotiations were under way with a number of others.

The results of these agreements gradually began to make themselves felt. Our exports to the fourteen countries with which agreements were in effect during all or a part of 1936 were 14 per cent greater during that year than during 1935. This compared with an increase of only 4 per cent in our exports to all other countries. In 1937, with sixteen agreements in effect during all or a part of the year, exports to those countries were 60 per cent greater than in 1935, compared to an increase of 39 per cent in exports to all other countries. Furthermore our exports to those countries increased more than the increase of exports to them from other countries.

Our imports from the trade agreement countries increased more rapidly in 1936 than from those countries with which we had no agreements, which was a natural and healthful development. In 1937, however, the reverse was true because the drought of 1935 required additional imports of agricultural products from countries with which we had not yet signed trade agreements.

The flood of imports from trade agreement countries, which opponents of our program vociferously feared, did not occur. We continued, however, to receive bitter protests from industrial or agricultural interests which believed we were threatening them with financial death. Investigation usually disclosed that the imports of the products they feared amounted to a small percentage, sometimes even less than 1 per cent, of our domestic production. I never ceased to point out to such interests that we had to import in order to export; that exports helped our domestic situation and enabled Americans to buy more American products; and I usually asked them: "Would you sooner have 100 per cent of a poor domestic market, or 95, 96, or 97 per cent of a rich domestic market?"

It was hard for such objectors, as naturally it is for the average citizen, to understand what shutting out imports does to our exports. Because trade is not bilateral but multilateral, it was also hard to see that if we shut out imports from one country we might affect our exports to another country.

An example was imported whale oil, on which a tax was imposed here in 1934, in addition to the regular duty. Whale oil came to us largely from Norway and was used for making soap. The tax sharply cut down our imports of such oil from Norway. Consequently, our exports to Norway were reduced. But this was just the beginning. Norway looked elsewhere for a market for her oil, and found one in Germany where it is used in making margarine. As a partial result, our exports of lard to Germany dropped from $7,000,000 in 1933 to less than $200,000 in 1935.

The State Department received protests from the iron and steel industry because of tariff reductions granted on iron and steel products in the agreements with Belgium and Sweden. This despite the fact that our imports of such products were less than 1 per cent of our exports of such articles. We had protests because of tariff reductions on glass products. The value of the domestic glass industry's production in 1935, however, amounted to about $284,000,000, while the imports were slightly over $5,000,000 or only 1.8 per cent of domestic productions, and the exports of such products were actually 50 per cent higher than the imports. We even received protests that certain industries had been seriously injured by tariff reduction when, on examination, it developed that no reductions had been made on the products mentioned.

"The pressure which is being currently brought upon both legislators and officials in Washington by those who fear that they are to be deprived of even a small part of the artificial advantage given them by an overindulgent Government, too often at the expense of efficient producers and consumers in general, would incline one to believe that much of the sturdy self-reliance, hardihood, and vigor of this country is definitely on the decline," I said in an address to the Chamber of Commerce of the United States, on May 2, 1935.

Nevertheless, from the date of the enactment of the Trade Agreements Act our whole liberal trade and peace policy was able to stand on its feet, with growing strength and influence in the world until this day. The press of the country was overwhelmingly behind it. It was to become a campaign issue in 1936 and win with ease. The Trade Agreements Act was to come up for renewal in 1937, 1940, 1943, and 1945 and secure the approval of Congress. Agreements were ultimately to be concluded with thirty-seven nations. When many other nations saw its possibilities they embraced such agreements not only with ourselves but also with one another. War on three continents was to interfere with its application, but it came to be recognized among the clear thinkers of all nations as the only way out of commercial chaos and as one of the main factors for peace.

"It is incumbent upon some great nations, certainly the United States as much as any other," I told the Chamber of Commerce in my May 2 address, "to come forward with a broad, constructive program calculated to displace gradually the policies which have proven so futile and so destructive during these past several years. . . . I see not a few evidences of the state of mind of other peoples which give me reason to believe that the program which this Administration is following is beginning to supply the inspiration necessary to induce them to alter their course and to hope that the world can shortly expect a general movement in the direction of international economic sanity."

28: Britain, France, the League, and the Court

IN THE FIRST YEARS of the Roosevelt Administration, when Germany was arming, Japan warring, and Italy preparing for conflict, it was most unfortunate that many differences plagued relations among the major Western Democracies—the United States, Britain, and France. Immediately upon entering the State Department I saw that only a common attitude among these three powers, preferably joined by Russia, could recall the three jingoist countries to their senses. Actually we presented a spectacle of miserable disagreement and recrimination more often than of accord.

Many of the causes of this condition lay beyond the Administration's capacity to remove. Some were imbedded in the domestic policies of the three countries. Some rose from the manifold difficulties existing between Britain and France. And some we inherited from the previous Administration.

Both Britain and France were skeptical of our domestic economic policies embraced in the AAA and the NRA. They resented our going off the gold standard and the battle of the currencies that followed. They were irritated over our insistence on the payment of the war debts. They were antagonized by the Smoot-Hawley high-tariff Act. The British disliked our naval rebuilding program. The French disliked our support of the British plans for a disarmament agreement.

I came into first contact with British and French unfriendliness at the London Economic Conference. There I was rawhided unmercifully. I told Prime Minister MacDonald that the British press was evidently acting under the direction of the British Government in the matter of currency stabilization and suggested that the Government induce the press to cease its vitriolic attacks. I got neither a satisfactory reply nor a denial of my charge. Nevertheless, I refused to consider this misbehavior on the part of the British and the French press, with the express or tacit approval of their respective governments, as an attitude of basic or permanent unfriendliness toward either my Government or myself.

The Economic Conference left a wound that took long to heal. Prime Minister MacDonald felt himself personally offended by the President's telegram chiding the conference for straying away from its basic purposes in the quest for a temporary stabilization agreement, and he did not soon forgive us. Britain remained cool to our trade agreements proposals for some length of time, and was among the last countries to negotiate with us. We had terrific difficulties with the high-tariff element in Britain, which was responsible for bringing on high-tariff protection there and for joining with the Dominions in establishing Empire preference. As a result, we were obliged to commence with some of the Dominions like Canada, and, by a trade agreement with her, to begin chipping off the structure of Empire preference. Only then did our trade agreement problems with Britain lessen.

With the current Prime Minister holding himself aloof, a former Prime Minister, Stanley Baldwin, still felt aggrieved because he believed himself discriminated against in the war-debt settlement he had reached with President Coolidge. Other debtors had received better terms. Both MacDonald and Baldwin thus felt that their own political careers had been affected adversely by American actions.

In our relations with Britain, Foreign Secretary Sir John Simon proved a frequent source of annoyance. Beginning with the invasion of Manchuria, Simon seemed to me to lack a stable, basic course. I believed, from all the information available, that he showed too much consideration for the Japanese, and I still think so. He surprised us by conceding that Japan had some special rights in Manchuria. When the President decided immediately after his inauguration to rebuild our Navy up to treaty strength, Simon requested that we abandon the program lest it lead to a race in naval armaments; but he did not offer to abandon construction of British warships then under way. At the London Economic Conference Simon had been uncooperative. His personality was cold.

Simon's objection in March, 1935, to the principle of international inspection on the spot of armaments production sharply irritated the President. Mr. Roosevelt and I were in accord that we should agree to this principle. I had sent him a telegram of March 8 from Minister Hugh Wilson in Geneva, giving three reasons for Simon's opposition: inspection would reveal to Continental nations the precarious state of Britain's armaments; if they agreed to it they would be giving away their "trump card" with reference to the French, for whom there would then be no incentive to go further and make a general treaty limiting armaments; and detailed publicity on armaments orders would furnish a basis for unfair competition that would prejudice Britain's armaments trade.

In a note to me the following day, March 9, the President commented that this was "a very significant dispatch which I think you should lay aside for possible future need." He went on: "It shows two things: first, the unwillingness of the British, because of alleged armament weakness, to accept the principle of open international armament inspection—thus making it impossible to go along with what we have considered essential in its application to Germany; in other words, the only practical way of keeping German armaments down to an agreed-on level being to inspect German armament supplies, Britain dashes this hope by declining to be inspected herself. The last paragraph is a frank admission that the British decline to accept detailed publicity as to armament orders on the ground that it would prejudice their armament trade."

He then concluded: "At some future time it may be advisable to pull this rabbit out of our hat as proof that the present British Government is not sincere in seeking limitation or reduction of present world armaments or present world trade in warlike weapons.

"I am much discouraged."

In Washington, the British Ambassador of this period, Sir Ronald Lindsay, was difficult to deal with. He confined his contacts with Americans to a restricted set of the highest society, most of whom opposed the Roosevelt Administration. It was hard to make him see our point of view. I got along much better with his abler and more agreeable successors, Lord Lothian and Lord Halifax.

Items of friction came from our side, too. The Nye Committee of the Senate, investigating international traffic in munitions, issued reports in 1934 and 1935 that acutely wounded British feelings. One such report, quoting an unknown source in Warsaw as alleging that King George V had brought pressure to bear on the Polish Ambassador in London to conclude a contract for munitions to be supplied by a British firm, brought from the British Foreign Office one of the strongest protests I had yet received. Sir Robert Vansittart, the Acting Foreign Secretary, expressed his Government's deepest indignation and resentment.

It was ill chance that the question of war debts hung so heavily over our relations in the first two years of the Roosevelt Administration. During the first years of the World War, Britain had been supplying the other Allies with credits and matériel. When we came in, Britain began to call upon us. We proceeded at once to lend to Britain and she, in turn, continued to extend credits to some of the other Allies. Finally Britain asked us to provide credits to the other Allies direct. It was then that the debt mounted quickly to about $11,000,000,000.

After the war, as always happens, the debtor countries began to show a lack of interest in their debts. As the United States called on them for payment, they came in and sought refunding settlements. Then, as the Administration scaled debts way down, great fights broke out in Congress over each settlement. Some Members claimed that the debts were reduced too much under any standard of fair dealing. Others defended the reduction, and still others argued for total debt cancellation on the ground that the conflict had been everybody's war. Books, pamphlets, and magazine and newspaper articles were written supporting one theory or another, and the argument got warm. I voted for some of the settlements and against others. I voted against the Italian settlement because it scaled down the debt too much.

I had long argued in Congress that the war debts could be paid if our tariff barriers were lowered so that the debtor countries could export more products to the United States. Otherwise, I argued, we should have to forget about them. At the London Economic Conference I should have liked to have authority to discuss war-debt adjustment as a lever to induce the debtor countries to agree to more liberal trade throughout the world.

The Executive Branch, however, had been specifically forbidden by Congress to reduce or cancel the existing debts or to alter the schedule of debt payments. The Trade Agreements Act likewise made it impossible to link any debt discussion with the negotiation of trade agreements.

In one of my first conversations with British Ambassador Lindsay on the subject, May 18, 1933, he was rather impatient in referring to what he called the failure of our Government to do any educational work in or out of Congress toward liberalizing the debt situation. I told him bluntly: "I am even more discouraged at the seeming indifference of the British and French toward the big fundamental factors to be dealt with by the world conference for the purpose of world business recovery."

Britain made a token payment of $10,000,000 on June 15, 1933, and of $7,500,000 on December 15, 1933. France paid nothing. People in both countries considered the debts a part of the war; the war was over, and so were the debts. They also argued that payment of debts depended on payment of reparations by Germany. Reparations were at an end, hence debts were too. Reparations had been paid the former Allies by Germany over a period of years by virtue of the loans made her, largely by the United States.

On April 13, 1934, the President signed the Johnson Act forbidding the floating of loans in this country by nations that were in default on their war debts. On February 5, 1934, Sir Ronald Lindsay had come in to complain to me about the Johnson Bill, then under discussion in Congress. "Congress," I told him, "is a coordinate and independent branch of the Government and has an equal right to express its attitude on debts." I said I should be glad to make known his views to the President and to some of my legislative friends, but I added: "The fact that the Johnson Bill has been pending for many weeks and once passed the Senate and then was reconsidered and held on the calendar for two weeks without any complaint whatever from any representative of the debtor governments naturally would lead Congress to conclude that such governments were not seriously concerned about the passage of the measure."

In March, 1934, I suggested to the President that we propose to the debtor governments that for a period not to exceed three years they could meet their interest installments by issuing to our Government short-term negotiable bonds of small and marketable denominations. "Such an arrangement," I said in a memorandum, "would not only afford reasonable time for business recovery, but would offer what debtor governments claim is a major factor in such business recovery. It would also carry with it a reacknowledgment by the debtor governments of their entire debt liabilities. In place of surrendering a single dollar of our debts, it would safeguard the integrity of the debts through the collection of negotiable paper instead of almost nothing as at present."

The Johnson Act, however, furnished the last excuse the debtors needed for not paying anything more. Finland became the only country to meet its obligations. In the years to follow I continued, each June and December, to sign notes to the debtor countries telling of the amounts due and requesting payment. And we continued to receive, on or about each June 15 and December 15, replies that the debtors could not pay but were always willing to discuss the question.

One of our prime difficulties in dealing with Britain and France was the inability of each to deal with the other. Here was a problem over which we had little control. We could endeavor, as we never ceased doing, to reconcile their different viewpoints, principally through Norman Davis at Geneva, but the decision rested with the two countries themselves. The divergencies between Britain and France seemed insoluble until the mounting threat from Germany forced their solution.

Troubles between Britain and France had started at the Paris Peace Conference. France wanted to move her strategic frontier to the Rhine.

She gave this up in exchange for Anglo-American pacts of guarantee that never materialized. From then on, France felt that Britain and the United States were relying on her to defend them against Germany and at the same time demanding that she whittle down the Army with which to make such defense. Britain wanted a stronger, prosperous Germany. France wanted Germany held below French strength. Mindful of Germany's superior industrial strength and distrustful of any German Government, no matter what its composition, France could not agree to anything approaching equality of armaments between herself and Germany. Britain, on the other hand, disliked France's predominant position on the Continent and would have liked more of a European balance of power in which her own strength would be the decisive factor. France, although stoutly opposing British ideas on the Continent, still sought unceasingly to swing Britain into a copper-riveted security pact against Germany.

One of the questions people will never cease asking is: When Britain and France in this period were so superior in strength and Germany so inferior, how did they permit Germany to gain superiority and threaten their very existence? The truth was that neither Britain nor France wanted a preventive war. In Britain the isolationist sentiment was about as strong as it was in the United States. France had tried preventive measures when she invaded the Ruhr in 1923. The result was bitter opposition from Britain and the fall of the Poincaré Government. No French Government thereafter was willing to embark on a preventive war.

Here we were face to face with a basic weakness of democracies, or of governments in which the people have an important voice. With all their riches of God's blessings in so many ways, they most unfortunately have a record of moving slowly—too slowly—in the face of external dangers either imminent or seriously threatening. A pure democracy was the contribution of Athenians to civilization; and yet that little nation sought, in the face of certain danger from abroad, to conduct a popular vote on whether Athens should fight. This lack of leadership and of proper consideration for the guidance of the appropriate Government officials played directly into the hands of the lawless aggressor whose purpose was the capture and enslavement of the Athenians. This weakness proved the undoing and ultimate death of the Athenian democracy.

With due respect for the varying and conflicting opinions of individuals and groups here and in other peace-loving countries during the 1930's, I think that if the nations standing for peace had taken concerted action to arm adequately, they might have demanded a showdown with the bandit nations, Germany, Italy, and Japan, and averted the recent World War.

The state of bad feeling between Britain and ourselves obviously could not last. Responsible persons on both sides of the Atlantic were becoming more and more alarmed. As proofs of German, Japanese, and Italian intentions accumulated, it was clear to all of us that it was suicidal for Britain and the United States to drift along in ever more diverging currents. In October, 1934, Lord Lothian, who as Philip Kerr had been secretary to Lloyd George, came to the United States informally to see what could be done to improve relations. He told us frankly that MacDonald, Baldwin, and Simon were not particularly well disposed toward us, but that the great mass of the British people desired the friendliest relations between our two countries.

In October and November, the preliminary naval discussions in London showed Japan's determination to achieve parity with Britain and the United States and served to bring more into line the ideas of the two Western Powers on the relative strength of various categories of our navies. In the spring of 1935 Germany's official acknowledgment of the existence of a German Air Force shocked Britain into a realization that neither the English Channel nor the British Navy was a sufficient bulwark against Hitler's growing strength.

The MacDonald Government was nearing its end. In May, Stanley Baldwin, soon to succeed MacDonald, and Anthony Eden, then Lord Privy Seal, made speeches in which they stressed the absolute necessity for Britain and the United States to work closely together. I determined to meet them halfway. On May 29 I made a public statement referring to these speeches. "It is heartening," I said, "to note such expressions, which I am happy to reciprocate in full. While we have not in every instance viewed problems eye to eye, yet our common outlook and the many traditions we share have enabled us to work together in appreciation of the importance of a constructive policy favoring the promotion and preservation of peace. Looking back over recent years, I feel that both the British and American Governments have consistently followed such a policy in their relations with each other and with other countries, and I foresee that there will be in time to come many opportunities for similar helpful and constructive collaboration."

On June 7 the British Cabinet was reorganized, Mr. Baldwin becoming Prime Minister. Sir Samuel Hoare was the new Foreign Secretary, and Anthony Eden became Secretary for League of Nations Affairs. Prospects for better working arrangements with Britain grew brighter.

Throughout my career at the State Department, I felt that good relations with Great Britain were more important to us than good relations with any other country. I never varied from this view, and made every possible effort to achieve this end. Though we often differed we never really quarreled. We talked out our differences in calm and friendly fashion, and, if we did not always reach agreement, at least we did not descend to recrimination.

Canada, under the brilliant leadership of Prime Minister Mackenzie King, of whom I write later on, was of immense assistance to both Britain and the United States in our efforts toward mutually friendly relations. When I went to Canada I had the feeling that I was visiting home folks.

With France, our relations were complicated by the war-debt question even earlier than with Britain, for the simple reason that France had ceased making payments before the Roosevelt Administration came into office. On May 12, 1933, I received the new French Ambassador, André de Laboulaye, and indicated to him that we had been considering requesting authority from Congress to renegotiate the debts. However, I told him point-blank: "France's failure to pay her debt has hampered the Administration very much in such efforts."

Our movement toward freer trade with France, however, was more successful than with Britain. The French Ambassador, not long after the passage of the Trade Agreements Act, evinced his Government's interest in negotiating an agreement. This was finally concluded in 1936.

When Ambassador de Laboulaye came in for a conversation on trade agreements on October 9, 1934, I tried to win the support of his Government for a policy of general education among other nations for more liberal trade. "If the French Government," I said, "will assist us in conducting educational work among other countries, as well as in our respective countries, it will be very helpful in reaching our common objective. I think the broad world-wide economic program which was adopted at the Montevideo Conference, and which, in substance, I offered at the London Economic Conference, ought to have the support of the French Government." I then added: "Naturally, if the French Government, as was the case at London, shows no interest in any real step except that of permanent exchange stabilization, it will not be possible to get anywhere Unless France is prepared to support a broad program of liberal commercial policy, It will be frittering away time to expect other countries to enter on this permanent stabilization policy. The chief purpose of exchange stabilization is to facilitate trade, and, since there would be no trade to facilitate, it would be worse than whiling away time to consider stabilization by itself as a single step."

Coincidental with our efforts to improve direct relations with Britain and France as a means of increasing the chances of peace in Europe was our constant attempt to strengthen the prestige of the League of Nations. The President and I, as fervent followers of Woodrow Wilson, had the League close at heart. Many times since 1920 we had both made strenuous but vain attempts to uphold the League in its full vigor by preachments and concrete acts. I had very little hope, however, that we could enter the League because of the strength of the isolationist sentiment here.

When the Roosevelt Administration came into office, the League was suffering from two major blows. One was inflicted by the inability of Britain and France to coordinate their views. The League was hamstrung by their discordant policies, which often were aired on the League floor. The other was inflicted by Japan's invasion of Manchuria, the failure of the League to check her, and her withdrawal from the League in the very month I entered the State Department.

In my first year as Secretary of State the League was repeatedly stopped in its tracks. It sponsored the London Economic Conference, the failure of which was the fault of several of the more powerful commercial nations which no longer treated too seriously the League's authority and directives but based their own courses primarily on domestic considerations. It sponsored the Disarmament Conference, the failure of which was due chiefly to the rebellious attitude of Germany, who left the League before the end of 1933. It also failed to settle the Chaco War. And it was unable to arouse peaceful nations, asleep under the morphine influence of isolation and pacifism, to the seriousness of the dangers that were noticeably developing in Germany, Italy, and Japan.

I chose every legitimate opportunity to put as much American influence behind the League as I could. Three times in my first year in the State Department I, with the concurrence of the President, joined the United States to League commissions handling the specific problems of the Far East, the Leticia dispute, and the Chaco War. I supported the League at Montevideo. We began to take an ever larger share in its economic and other nonpolitical activities.

In an address to the Woodrow Wilson Foundation on December 28, 1933, prepared in the State Department at his request, the President said: "The League has provided a common meeting place; it has provided machinery which serves for international discussion; and in very many practical instances it has helped labor and health and commerce and education, and, last but not least, the actual settlement of many disputes great and small among nations great and small.

"Today the United States is cooperating openly in the fuller utilization of the League of Nations machinery than ever before. . . . We are not members and do not contemplate membership. We are giving cooperation to the League in every matter which is not primarily political and in every matter which obviously represents the views and the good of the peoples of the world as distinguished from the views and the good of political leaders, of privileged classes, or of imperialistic aims."

On one occasion the President remarked to me that he was turning over in his mind the possibility of appointing an American Ambassador to the League. But there were too many obstacles in the way. No other nonmember nation had such a representative; the functions of representation were already capably fulfilled by our Minister to Switzerland, and the isolationists on this side would seize upon the appointment for a dead-center rush against the Administration.

While attempting to buttress the authority of the League, the President and my associates and I made a related effort toward international cooperation by trying to secure the adherence of the United States to the World Court at The Hague. A. Mitchell Palmer and I had inserted into the Democratic platform of 1932 a plank calling for United States "adherence to the World Court with appending reservations." We now sought to fulfill this plank. I felt strongly that the World Court was a valid medium for reviving and sustaining faith in international treaties, which Japan had shattered and Hitler and Mussolini were preparing to violate. Infractions of treaties could be brought before the court for settlement. If the court could be strengthened in the eyes of the world as a recognized agency of law and justice, it would help buttress the whole structure of whatever remained in the way of order under law. The participation of the United States in the World Court would add to its substance and authority.

When I entered the State Department, the question of our becoming a member of the World Court was already ten years old, dating from President Harding's request of February 24, 1923, for Senate approval. Presidents Coolidge and Hoover had made similar requests. Finally, on June 1, 1932, the Senate Foreign Relations Committee had reported out a resolution consenting to adherence; but the Senate took no further action at that time.

In the autumn of 1934 I discussed the World Court at length with Assistant Secretaries Sayre and Moore. We agreed to push it to the utmost. As a first step Sayre and Moore drove to Hyde Park in September to propose to the President that we present a resolution to the Senate at the next session of Congress. Mr. Roosevelt readily agreed.

When Moore and Sayre reported back to me that the President was in agreement, I requested them to draw up the necessary legislation. We agreed that our resolution should be more direct and less restrictive than the resolution that the Foreign Relations Committee had reported out in 1932. Sayre and Moore again saw the President on December 28, this time at the White House, and he gave us the signal to go ahead with our resolution and to contact Key Pittman, chairman of the Senate Foreign Relations Committee.

Pittman, however, had his doubts. He thought the previous reservations should be retained. He predicted a bitter fight on the floor of the Senate. And finally he admitted he was not too much in sympathy with the Administration's views toward the World Court and suggested that we should get another Senator more in sympathy to take the lead in handling the legislation. He mentioned Joseph T. Robinson, Democratic floor leader. We agreed to this suggestion. We then had full conferences with the Senate leaders of both political parties as to the prospects of the legislation. Senator Robinson, after a poll, gave as his best estimate that all the Democrats except seven or eight would support the resolution. Senator McNary, the Republican floor leader, after a similar poll, stated as his best estimate that all the Republicans except eight or ten would support it. That would easily give us the necessary two-thirds majority.

I then proposed a conference at the White House, to which the President agreed. It was held January 5, with the President presiding, Pittman, Robinson, Sayre, and myself attending. The President said he would send to the Senate our resolution, which he did.

The Senate Foreign Relations Committee quickly reported out the new resolution favorably on January 9, 1935. Discussions began in the Senate five days later. On January 16 the President sent to the Senate a message we had largely prepared in the State Department, urging passage of the resolution. "The sovereignty of the United States will be in no way diminished or jeopardized by such action," it said. "At this period in international relationships, when every act is of moment to the future of world peace, the United States has an opportunity once more to throw its weight into the scale in favor of peace." I myself saw many Senators personally to urge emphatically their support.

As the discussion developed, however, we began to note that William Randolph Hearst, the newspaper publisher, and other extreme isolationists were waging a tremendous propaganda throughout the country to defeat the resolution. They stationed a large staff of telephonists and other persons in the Mayflower Hotel in Washington. They spent a huge sum on long-distance telephone calls to all parts of the country to induce leaders of all elements to telephone, telegraph, or write to their Senators, opposing the resolution. Soon sluices of telegrams began to pour into the Senate strongly persuading and violently threatening the Senators. Almost immediately we began to hear of certain Senators wavering in their attitude.

The Senate recessed on Friday, January 25, before which time the vote should have been taken. Over the week end the adverse propaganda increased furiously. Father Coughlin, who was closely listened to and blindly followed by a large mass of uninformed, prejudiced persons, bitterly opposed the resolution. So did the cowboy radio orator, Will Rogers. Neither Coughlin nor Rogers knew the real issues involved, but their opposition hurt painfully.

When the resolution was put to a vote on Tuesday January 29, it failed to receive the necessary two-thirds majority, the vote being 52 to 36 in its favor. Had it gone to a vote on the previous Saturday it probably would have passed. The defeat was another heavy blow to our efforts at international cooperation. The press interpreted it as a major defeat for the Administration, and abroad it was deemed a new indication of continued American isolation. Another gag was thus put in our mouths at the very moment when it was so essential to speak out to the world with authority, to warn it of the dangers ahead, and to recall it to some semblance of sanity.

For several years after the defeat of our resolution we kept tab on the prospects in the Senate for ratification. Had there been any new chance for its passage I intended to get the resolution introduced again. But the forces of isolation grew stronger rather than weaker. The opportunity that seemed so bright in January, 1935, was not to recur.

The mounting threats to peace in Europe and Asia had in America exactly the opposite effect they should have had. They ought to have made a large section of the American public more willing to unite with right-minded nations abroad in bringing pressure to bear on the nations obviously preparing for war. Instead, they caused those Americans, most of whom were honest in their beliefs, to pull back in alarm and to vow they would have nothing to do with the rest of the world. They blindly failed to see that a major war anywhere could not but touch us in many vital points. They wishfully thought we could be immune from any hurricane merely by closing our doors and pulling down our windows. Many of them shut their eyes and refused to see that war was coming.

I myself, with the cooperation of numerous other officials, never ceased trying to point out to my own countrymen, and to foreign governments as well, that the danger to peace was great and was becoming greater. A number of persons even to this day, with apparent surprise and astounding ignorance or forgetfulness, say loudly to those of us in immediate charge of our foreign relations in those days: "What were you doing during the years following 1933? Why did you not discern the foreign dangers steadily developing? Why did you not give the American public notice of such perils and the need for adequate preparations against them? If the isolationist viewpoint seriously interfered with the problem of discovering and making known to America these perils and threats, why did you not bring this tremendously important matter to the attention of the general public?"

The answer to these apparently innocent questions and exclamations is fully set forth in the record. As the dangers of aggression increasingly revealed themselves, I made more than twenty addresses and statements in my first two years in office alone, containing as emphatic warnings of coming danger as the English language could convey.

Some of my warnings I have already quoted. On May 2, 1933, I stated to the American Section of the International Chamber of Commerce: "I fear the policy of extreme isolation as the greatest danger to world peace, and as more seriously threatening the world with bankruptcy than war itself."

To the graduating class of the College of William and Mary, I said, on June 11, 1934: "We are obliged to feel deep concern that across the water, notwithstanding the terrible havoc and wreckage wrought by the war that began twenty years ago, and notwithstanding that the inventions of science will make future wars more terrible, there is so much reason for the gravest apprehension. Regardless of the fact that preparation for war but too often makes war inevitable, and the fact that preparation places a grievous burden on the people, armaments are being momentarily increased, and in practice the theory seems to be abandoned that nations, like individuals, should live not as potential enemies, but as neighbors and friends."

On November 1, 1934, I said to the National Foreign Trade Council, in New York: "Extreme nationalism, if persisted in, is destined soon to wreck our entire structure of western civilization."

To the Pan American Union I said on April 15, 1935: "Many a nation is today continuing to plunge headlong in the direction of extreme nationalism. . . . Under this spell of wild and mad extremism, nations in many parts of the globe are arming to the teeth and are thus more securely blocking business recovery in the world at large." I referred to these as "suicidal movements."

I told the Chamber of Commerce of the United States on May 2, 1935: "The dangerous political situations that exist throughout the world today, the international tension, the recrudescence of the military spirit, the expansion of standing armies, the enormously increased military budgets, the feverish efforts made to invent new instruments of warfare, new weapons for offense and defense—all these have emerged and developed in a world in which the international economic structure has been shattered. . . . It is the collapse of the world structure, the development of isolated economies, that has let loose the fear which now grips every nation, and which threatens the peace of the world."

On June 10, 1935, I stated at the Pennsylvania Military College: "We have seen in certain countries, just as we did prior to the dreadful conflagration in 1914, a military caste working on the popular mind until it glorified, not as a means but as an end, military power and achievement; we have seen that same military caste carrying armaments and the preparations of war to a point that well-nigh paralyzes productive effort within the national borders. . . . there has been set up a vicious circle of greater and ever greater armaments, which in the long run can only lead to impoverishment and economic suicide."

Two days later I said in an address to the Conference of Seaport Cities on International Trade, in New York City: "There are some ominous tendencies present in the world which, if persisted in, cannot fail to bring disaster and to undo whatever progress has thus far been made toward greater world stability. We witness all about us a reckless, competitive building-up of armaments, a recurrence of the mad race which prior to 1914 led the nations of the world headlong to destruction. If persisted in, this course will again plunge the world into disaster."

I continued these warnings in the years to follow. I always paid great attention to the preparation of such public addresses. I knew they would be widely quoted at home and also that foreign governments were likely to read them in full. They were to be an expression of the policies and views of the American Government, not merely of myself.

Sometimes weeks were spent in the writing of one speech. I would call to my office a group of my principal advisers. "I am scheduled to make a speech in such and such a city on such and such a day," I would say. "Here is what I have in mind." I then outlined to them the ideas I had been evolving. I might have some notes before me, sometimes written the night before at my apartment. Then I asked for their opinions and suggestions. Finally I picked one of my associates to draft these ideas into a text of the speech. The head of an important department required to make important statements of all kinds virtually from day to day has literally no time personally to prepare his own texts.

When the first draft of a speech came to me, I revised and rewrote. I then circulated this text to my advisers, with the request that they write in their suggestions or additions. When these came back to me I passed them on, if I accepted them, to the official writing the draft. He rewrote it on the basis of the suggestions. From the time of the first draft I dictated any additional ideas or modifications that occurred to me, and added sentences or paragraphs or took them out of the draft. Since the responsibility for the ideas in the speech was mine, I carefully made decisions, paragraph by paragraph. This procedure went on for days until the address began to assume the shape I intended. I frequently called meetings of a group of advisers to go over it together. Among them were the heads of the geographic divisions that might be concerned by what I was to say. In some cases many successive drafts had to be prepared until the speech satisfied me. Fifteen drafts of one important address were written before I gave my final O.K.

Before delivering a major speech committing the Administration to a certain policy, I made it a point to submit the text to the President in advance of delivery. I usually took it to him myself because I did not want it to get into other hands before he had read it, and because I wanted to be present when he went over it in order to explain anything to him that might arise and also to observe personally his reaction. The President silently read my speech but always commented from time to time as he found something that excited unusual interest. Only in rare instances, however, did he offer suggestions or criticism, and they were not of a fundamental nature.

In addition to these addresses I continued to speak privately in the same tone to the Ambassadors of the major nations. I earnestly adjured them to transmit my thoughts to their Governments. When statesmen or important personages of other countries called upon me in Washington, I never lost an opportunity to tell them that war in Europe and throughout the world was inevitable in the not distant future unless the nations began immediately to adopt an entirely different program.

I was listened to but not heeded. My Congressional experience as a Cassandra in the twenties was being transplanted to the foreign field in the thirties. From the floor of Congress during the twenties I had warned again and again that with economic nationalism trade would fail, debts could not be paid, unemployment would ensue, and collapse would surely come. It came. My voice could not stop it. From the State Department during the thirties I warned even oftener that, with political and economic nationalism, war would surely come. Nor did I stop with words. Along with the President, I proposed or took every action that had a reasonable chance for making the United States a part of the struggle for peace— the arms embargo against the aggressor, adherence to the World Court, participation in League Commissions, our offer not to impede the operation of sanctions, a world nonaggression agreement, support of disarmament plans, the Montevideo accords, implementation of the Good Neighbor Policy as an example to Europe and Asia, and the trade agreements. But the political collapse of 1939 came as relentlessly as the economic collapse of 1929.

Many American citizens of breadth and vision, many groups, organizations, and public officials did their utmost to warn and arouse the country. The press and radio in large numbers echoed these solemn warnings. But all who were thus struggling to alert the nation and the other democracies found themselves hopelessly in the minority.

My first two years in office and until the middle of 1935 form a natural period. Within that time we saw the growth and rearming of Nazism, Japan's movement of conquest, the futility of the major European democracies, the death of disarmament, the illness of the League, the recognition of Russia, the foundation of the Good Neighbor Policy, and the beginning of a movement toward more liberal trade.

On the whole, it was not a happy period. Its frustration was like that of a dreamer who sees a monster approaching but is unable to move his legs to escape or his lips to scream. In these two years and several months there was feverish rearmament in some nations, blindness in others, and assassination was used as a political weapon. Nationalism continued to mount. The League, hope of the world after the First World War, grew faint—but its greatest trial was not to come until the next period. In Europe and Asia there was no real agreement signed among the nations which did not embrace increased armaments or a military alliance.

But still there was peace. It was not until the autumn of 1935 that the peace was broken and a series of wars, invasions, and occupations began which dragged Europe and Asia down the dungeon steps to the torture chamber of the Second World War.

Part Three

TOWARD THE ABYSS

(1935–1939)

29: Neutrality by Legislation

AS THE MIDDLE OF 1935 arrived, the following facts of the world situation had become limpidly clear:

(1) War involving one European power, Italy, and possibly others, was coming soon.

(2) Germany, though rearming feverishly, was not ready for any major aggression and would not be for several years. Meantime she would keep Europe in turmoil.

(3) Britain and France, although alarmed at Mussolini's plans and Hitler's rearmament, still had too many differences between themselves to see and act alike in the face of the common danger.

(4) Japan was consolidating her position in Manchuria and exerting every effort to keep China disunited until Japan was ready for another broad-scale military move.

(5) In the United States an avalanche of isolationism was overwhelming any prospect of inducing the American people to agree to a more vital share in world affairs. Congress, having disavowed the World Court, was seeking ways to legislate us out of possible involvement in the next war which was becoming more and more inevitable.

This last development I shall deal with first, because it was to color our foreign relations up to and after the day that Hitler's armies plunged into Poland and the Second World War began.

My first two years and several months in office, until the middle of 1935, differ from my next four years, until September 1, 1939, in that, in the latter period, international relations in all parts of the world became more closely knit and intertwined. In narrating the events of the first period, as they affected the conduct of our foreign relations, I could discuss countries or groups of countries somewhat individually, one after the other. In this next period I could no longer separate them, because they refused to be separated. What Italy did involved two continents. What Germany did and planned embraced the Western world. What Japan did and planned comprised the Eastern world. What the three planned together included the whole world. Our Western Hemisphere could no longer be considered by itself; it had also to be considered in relation to the Axis Powers' intentions here. Our domestic legislation relating to foreign affairs was influenced by the growth of the war threat in Europe.

The way toward neutrality legislation in the United States was paved by the hearings of the Nye Committee established by the Senate to investigate the manufacture and sale of arms and munitions. It is doubtful that any Congressional committee has ever had a more unfortunate effect on our foreign relations, unless it be the Senate Foreign Relations Committee considering the Treaty of Versailles submitted by President Wilson. Following the publication of articles purporting to reveal details of the sale of munitions by American manufacturers to foreign governments, Senator Gerald P. Nye, Republican of North Dakota, introduced a resolution in February, 1934, to create a committee to investigate. Shortly thereafter reports "from the Hill" were published to the effect that I opposed such an investigation. I told a press conference on February 20 that I was trying to show a genuine interest in the investigation, while leaving the initiative and the policy decision to Congress.

After the Senate allowed the resolution to pass, virtually by default and without more than casual consideration, Nye, a minority Republican member and an isolationist of the deepest dye, was appointed by Vice President Garner to be chairman of the investigating committee. This was a blunder of major proportions, the responsibility for which was Senator Pittman's, himself an isolationist in numerous respects. Ordinarily, when a special committee was created for any purpose, especially an investigating committee, a member of the majority party—in this epoch the Democratic Party—rather than a member of the minority party would be made chairman. Pittman, though chairman of the Foreign Relations Committee, was preoccupied in other ways, and decided to let the appointment go to Nye. The Vice President would have accepted Pittman's recommendation of another chairman, had he chosen to make one.

Had I dreamed that an isolationist Republican would be appointed I promptly would have opposed it, but I expected that a member of the majority party would be named under the usual practice and that he would keep the investigation within legitimate and reasonable bounds and not make it a great propaganda movement.

The appointment of Nye was a fatal mistake because the committee, under his chairmanship, proceeded to enlarge the scope of its inquiry into an attempt to prove that the United States had been drawn into the First World War by American bankers and munitions makers. It ignored or contested the broad reasons for our entry into that war; namely, the

unlawful sinking of American ships and the destruction of American lives
by German submarines, and the danger to the United States of a nation
with principles such as Germany's winning the war. We had had to invoke
the principle of self-defense.

Therefore the majority of the committee, in effect, dug the ground
out from under those of us who had the international viewpoint and who
argued that, if the peace of the world were to be maintained, the United
States had to take its share in the effort. Their view was that, if the sale
of munitions and the granting of loans to belligerents could be prevented,
the United States automatically could avoid war and need not cooperate
with other nations toward that end. The rising dangers in Europe and
Asia were to them merely an impelling reason to withdraw within our
own shores as opposed to doing anything to help other nations resolve
these dangers.

By impugning the motives and honesty of President Wilson in the
First World War, by etching a sordid caricature of our former associates,
Britain and France, and by whitewashing the Kaiser's Germany, the
committee gave the American people a wholly erroneous view as to the
reasons why we had gone to war in 1917. The committee made undoubtedly useful disclosures concerning the traffic in arms, but its effect was to
throw the country into deepest isolationism at the very moment when our
influence was so vitally needed to help ward off the approaching threats
of war abroad.

The committee found the country eager for publicity against the big
bankers and munitions makers. With its appetite whetted by the very
publicity it received, the committee sought for more. Its chief investigator, Stephen Raushenbush, in a large sense constituted the committee and
generally directed its activities. He was eager to get the committee into
the headlines and was very careless about the effect his publicity, which
often consisted of mere rumors and half-truths, would have on other
governments, to say nothing of our own people.

Moreover, the Senators on the committee, as so often occurs in such
situations, were entirely too disposed to permit their chief investigator to
have his own way. The committee was well staffed, including capable men,
some of whom had made a kind of hobby of attacking the big bankers and
munitions manufacturers. This staff was largely responsible for the actual
work of the committee and for the violence of its attacks on bankers and
arms makers. Their publicity director kept a stream of so-called "news"
flowing out to the press of this and other countries.

The committee's activities throughout were extremely isolationist. Its investigation and report revolved around the idea that future peace for this nation could be assured by staying at home and remaining neutral, with no serious thought of resistance beyond our own boundaries, regardless of the danger of aggression.

In the Executive Branch it was evident that no one could withstand the isolationist cyclone. The mere hint of an investigation had met with wide acclaim. The President and I, of course, agreed to cooperate with the committee, especially since its original purpose, to investigate the traffic in arms, was laudable.

I wrote Senator Nye on April 27, 1934: "You may rely upon the fullest and most cordial cooperation of the Department in supplying you with any information in our possession, which may aid you. . . . Should you feel that I personally can be of any assistance to you, please do not fail to call upon me."

I instructed Joseph C. Green, the State Department's expert on traffic in arms, to hold himself at the disposition of the committee. On May 18 the President, in a message to the Senate drafted in the State Department, recommended that the committee receive the generous support of the Senate and promised the cooperation of the Executive departments.

A due regard for the Senate action in creating the Nye Committee made it proper for the Department cheerfully to supply it with all papers, documents, and records that it would ordinarily furnish a committee of Congress. Actually, we went beyond the usual limits in our efforts to cooperate with Nye's group. With the Democratic Senate majority going along with the Nye Committee, the President and I felt that our only feasible step was a sort of marking time. There was no hope of success and nothing to be gained in combating the isolationist wave at that moment. To have done so would only have brought a calamitous defeat and precipitated a still more disastrous conflict on the whole basic question of isolation itself.

The committee, after spending the summer of 1934 in examining documents and amassing evidence, began its hearings on September 4. Almost immediately our difficulties with other countries started too. The Buenos Aires Government protested certain allegations from the committee concerning an Argentine admiral. The British Acting Foreign Secretary Vansittart sent a very sharp protest, already mentioned, over rumored charges concerning King George V. The Mexican Government protested references to President Rodriguez. Other Latin American Governments objected to charges of bribery involving some of their high officials. The Chinese Government presented an *aide-mémoire* denying the testimony that a $10,000,000 wheat loan from us had been used to buy arms.

Consequently I went to see the Nye Committee in person on September 11 and spent over two hours with it. I pointed to the damage being done to our foreign relations as publicity was given to mere rumors involving the heads or high officials of other Governments. Thereupon Senator Nye composed a letter to me in which he deeply regretted that a false impression might have been created by some of the statements introduced into the committee's records. I myself issued a statement that it was not in the mind of the committee or of any official of our Government to give the slightest offense to any other Government or its officials. I transmitted Nye's letter and my own statement to the ambassadors who had protested.

The situation worsened, however, when the Nye Committee began referring publicly to State Department documents the publication of which had not been authorized. According to the universally accepted rules of diplomatic courtesy, a Government receiving a communication from another Government does not usually publish it until the other Government formally approves its release. Through the Nye Committee, therefore, we began getting into hot water with a number of other Governments. I found it very difficult to curb the committee in this careless, exceedingly harmful publicity. I was kept busy explaining or apologizing much of the time to other Governments with hurt feelings.

On February 7, 1935, I wrote Senator Nye: "In granting permission to make public the contents of documents from our files, I have been as liberal as the public interest and the maintenance of cordial relations with other Governments would permit. . . . In view of the embarrassment which the unauthorized publication of such documents may cause the Department, and in view of the very real disadvantage at which it may place this Government in the conduct of its foreign relations, I hope that you will be able to make arrangements which will prevent such inadvertent publication in the future." In reply Nye expressed the regret of everyone concerned over "what may appear to have been gross betrayal of the splendid confidence which we have enjoyed with and through you and your office."

Our difficulties became still more acute, however, when the Nye Committee, plunging into the background of the First World War, began to subpoena records of New York banks which had dealt with the Allies. The

British and French Ambassadors protested repeatedly. The British Ambassador, Sir Ronald Lindsay, sent me a note on March 20, 1935, in which he said that to proceed with the examination of the correspondence of the British Government without warning or without attempting to obtain British consent was an act of "grave discourtesy."

Joseph C. Green, at my instructions, called on Senator Nye to attempt to persuade him to abandon the investigation into documents of nearly twenty years before. Nye refused, but did agree that no document relating to dealings between the former Allied Governments and American banks would be made public until I had had an opportunity to consult the interested Governments.

The next day I saw Lindsay and told him of this agreement. But I added: "Frankly, I cannot agree with you that my Government is required, as a matter of courtesy, to ascertain in advance the nature of an investigation like this and of the matter proposed to be made public, and to hunt up the British Ambassador to lay the entire matter before him for such comment as he and his Government might see fit to offer." To put my position on record, I addressed a letter to the British Ambassador the same day, and expressed my surprise at the position he had taken in his letter of March 20.

I had already tried to enlist the support of the President in my effort to bring the Nye Committee within reasonable limits. I handed him a memorandum on March 15 urging that he summon the Nye Committee to a White House conference to advise the committee "to refrain from any unnecessary agitation in public hearings of questions which would handicap this Government in its relations with other Governments." The President did see the Nye Committee four days later, but for some reason did not mention my request.

What I wanted the Nye Committee members to understand was that Hitler had just thrown out the military clauses of the Versailles Treaty and Mussolini was completing his plans for the invasion of Ethiopia, and the spectacle of the bitter quarreling between Britain and France on the one side and the United States on the other over documents two decades old was certainly not one to deter Hitler and Mussolini from their designs. At that particular time Britain and France were trying to bring Germany into an armaments limitation agreement and dissuade Mussolini from his African aggression, and their efforts were certainly not being furthered by the wave of anti-British and anti-French feeling engendered by the Nye Committee.

I sent another memorandum to the President on April 11 in which I recommended he hold a further conference with the Nye Committee and urge it not to proceed with the examination of the correspondence between the former Allied Governments and American banks. "The proposed action of the committee," I said, "would result in irritating the British and French Governments, and it is difficult to conceive that any useful purpose could be served by a study of these documents. It can scarcely be maintained with reason that such a study is a necessary preliminary to the study of legislation for taking profits out of war, particularly as the committee has already prepared its Bill on that subject."

The President and I met with Senators Nye, Pope, and Clark at the White House on April 18. I asked the Senators at least to defer their examination of the correspondence "until the lessening of the tension in Europe might decrease the likelihood of unintended and unfortunate repercussions." But the Senators continued to insist on examining the correspondence.

Finally the Nye Committee demanded the British and French Governments' accounts with American banks during the last war. The British and French Governments stated that, since there was nothing in their accounts with American banks which they wished to keep secret from the United States Government, they would agree to having the accounts turned over in their entirety to me, to be dealt with as I believed right. I communicated this offer to the Nye Committee and stated I would make the accounts available to the committee on the same basis as I had made documents available from the Department's files. Nye agreed and expressed his appreciation of the Department's efforts and courtesy.

But the worst example of carelessness by the Nye Committee was still to occur. On January 15, 1936, reference was made during the committee's public hearings to the contents of a confidential memorandum given by Arthur J. Balfour, British Foreign Secretary, to Secretary of State Lansing on May 18, 1917, which referred to Britain's secret agreements with other Allied Governments. Nye asserted that both President Wilson and Secretary Lansing had falsified when they said they had no knowledge of British secret commitments prior to the Paris Peace Conference. This was a particularly aggravated breach because we had asked the British Government if they would permit publication of the memorandum; they had refused, and we had so informed Nye on December 23, 1935. I vigorously protested to the Nye Committee, which agreed to return all copies of the Balfour Memorandum to the State Department.

On January 20 I issued a press statement setting forth the State Department's attitude toward the publication of confidential documents from its files. I said it was manifestly impossible for our Government to "undertake to make public confidential communications without the permission of the Government which reposed confidence in this Government." I added that it was "important that this long-established rule of universal application among civilized nations should be observed if we are to have the respect and confidence of other governments, so essential to the conduct of international relations." I concluded by stating that the extent to which the State Department would cooperate with Congressional committees was therefore conditional upon the extent to which such committees cooperated with it.

At a press conference I said: "I served here in an official capacity during Wilson's Administration and, needless to say, in common with the American public, I have the highest—I had and have always maintained —the highest regard for his patriotism and scrupulous honesty."

The Nye Committee hearings furnished the isolationist springboard for the first Neutrality Act of our present epoch, and for this reason I have gone into them at length. I do not decry the benefit they undoubtedly produced in revealing hitherto undisclosed methods employed in the traffic in arms. But I cannot too strongly emphasize their disastrous effects.

The Nye Committee aroused an isolationist sentiment that was to tie the hands of the Administration just at the very time when our hands should have been free to place the weight of our influence in the scales where it would count. It tangled our relations with the very nations whom we should have been morally supporting. It stirred the resentment of other nations with whom we had no quarrels. It confused the minds of our own people as to the real reasons that led us into the First World War. It showed the prospective aggressors in Europe and Asia that our public opinion was pulling a cloak over its head and becoming nationally unconcerned with their designs and that therefore they could proceed with fuller confidence.

Actually, the State Department had begun a study of neutrality legislation before the Nye Committee started its hearings. In June, 1934, Under Secretary Phillips induced Charles Warren, former United States Assistant Attorney General, to make a special study of neutrality for the Department. In August, 1934, Assistant Secretary Moore, with my concurrence, sent the President at Hyde Park, for his information, a memorandum on neutrality written by Mr. Warren. About that time I appointed a committee within the Department to study the question.

The President sent me a memorandum from Hyde Park on September 25, 1934, stating that "this matter of neutral rights" was of "such importance" that he wished I would discuss with Under Secretary Phillips and Moore "the whole subject" with a view to advising him whether to recommend legislation to the coming session of Congress. By December the committee I had appointed formulated a tentative draft of legislation which we submitted informally to Attorney General Cummings and Secretary of the Navy Swanson for their comments.

The President, on February 23, 1935, sent me a memorandum asking me to speak with him "about the advisability of a message (to Congress) on war profits and kindred subjects." On March 15 I gave the President two memoranda concerning war profits, the international traffic in arms and the Nye investigations. Advising against a presidential message at that time, I recommended that he call the Nye Committee to the White House for consultation within the next week or ten days. I suggested he might promise to support the committee on legislation setting up a National Munitions Control Board, with a registration and licensing system to regulate the arms traffic. A draft of a bill to this effect had been prepared by the State Department, at Senator Nye's request, and submitted to the committee on March 13.

The President did call the Nye Committee to the White House; but the conference, at which I was not present, seems to have been devoted in large part to the question of neutrality, and the committee members unfortunately got the impression that the President wanted them to devise neutrality legislation. On March 27 the chief investigator for the Nye Committee, Stephen Raushenbush, informed us that the members had not thought to consider neutrality until the President had "pushed" them into it, and now they were "hot on the trail." I thereupon sent Green to tell Nye that the Department, at the request of the President, had been studying the question of neutrality legislation, had found it to be extremely delicate, had not yet agreed upon a legislative program, and had not yet made a report to the President.

At this point the Foreign Relations Committee, under Senator Pittman, became alarmed that Nye was assuming jurisdiction over a subject which properly fell to that committee. I instructed Green to telephone Raushenbush to this effect, and subsequently the Nye Committee decided not to press for neutrality legislation.

On April 11 I sent the President a memorandum informing him of our draft legislation on neutrality, but I told him I was "not prepared to advocate this or any other specific program of legislation on this subject at this time." I said there was "great diversity of opinion" among the President's closest advisers "as to the proper method of dealing with this subject, and certainly great diversity of public opinion." I was informed "that the leaders in the Senate are opposed to the raising of any question of foreign policy which would result in acrimonious discussions and in delaying action on necessary domestic legislation." Furthermore, I said, "it is contended that in view of the present situation in Europe, discussions of this question at this time would tend to arouse unjustifiable fears of imminent war."

And, summing it all up, I told the President that the subject of neutrality was "so complicated in respect to domestic law, international law, and questions of policy" that he might "deem it unwise for the Administration to commit itself to the support of any specific program of legislation until the subject has been further studied" and until a program could be drawn up on which his advisers were in "substantial agreement."

The fact was, I did not want neutrality legislation. And certainly I did not want the kind, advocated by isolationists like Nye, which would bind the Executive hand and foot and inform any prospective aggressors like Germany, Italy, or Japan that they could declare war on their intended victim and we would then see to it that our citizens did not furnish arms to that victim. The dictator states did not need to worry whether we would furnish arms to themselves, because they knew that, in military preparedness, they would have a long edge on the victims.

I did not want to see legislation which, by telling the world in advance what we would not do in case of war, would prevent our exercising our influence to prevent war; nor legislation which, if war came, would preclude our rendering the least assistance to the world organization, the League of Nations, in its efforts to bring the war to an end.

There was so much confusion in 1935 and succeeding years on the subject of neutrality that I should like to pause at this point and outline the situation as I saw it.

We had to look at neutrality from two points of view. The first was neutrality under international law. Over a period of several centuries, certain rules had become more or less accepted in international law governing the rights and duties of neutral countries during wartime. They enumerated, for instance, the goods that could be considered contraband of war and therefore subject to capture by a warring nation if destined to its enemy.

Then there was the neutrality that was made at home. A nation could impose laws on its citizens preventing them from having certain dealings with the warring nations, believing that therefore it would not be drawn into the war. It was this kind of neutrality that the isolationists in the United States had in mind.

The seventeenth century Dutch jurist, Hugo Grotius, often called the Father of International Law, was the first to lay down a comprehensive set of rules under the first kind of neutrality. But it must be remembered that Grotius, although elaborating a code of neutrality, did not recommend that nations remain neutral. He expected them to examine the right and wrong of a war and to support the nation in the right. He said it was the duty of those not engaged in a war "to do nothing whereby he who supports a wicked cause may be rendered more powerful, or whereby the movements of him who wages a just war may be hampered."

My reasoning partly followed the doctrine of Grotius. I believed that, under modern conditions, a nation need not and should not remain neutral in the full sense of the term. Also, because a war by an aggressor in any part of the world was calculated to affect the security of a peaceful country wherever located, it was our duty to make the fullest practical contribution toward cooperation with other law-abiding nations to preserve peace. This I had in mind in 1933 when I urged the passage of legislation giving the President the right to impose an arms embargo against an aggressor nation in time of war and when I helped formulate Norman Davis's statement at Geneva that we would not impede the operation of League sanctions against an aggressor.

I did not, however, fully accept Grotius's doctrine in regard to determining and acting on the right and wrong of a war and to supporting the nation in the right. This became more or less academic and subordinate except as it might figure in the major question of determining the aggressor. A nation could be in the right in an argument with another nation and still be the aggressor if it went to war. Being in the right in a dispute did not give a nation the privilege of going to war to settle it. Moreover, it was often difficult, in the course of a complicated dispute, to determine which of the disputants was in the right. We could not become involved in such disputes all over the world. But, if the rule of world order under law were broken in any part of the world by resort to arms by an aggressor, such fact affected our security and therefore we would impede the aggressor in order to safeguard our peace.

I did accept the moral viewpoint that a powerful nation like ours, advocating the high principles of peaceful living among nations, could not sit idly by if one country attacked another and do nothing whatever to impede the aggressor or aid the victim. A private citizen, seeing one man make a brutal assault on another, would certainly consider it unchristian to hand each of them the same length of stick or to refuse to give either one anything or say or do anything that might help the victim.

What most advocates of stringent neutrality by legislation forgot, moreover, was that an entirely new situation had entered into world affairs right in their own lifetime. The private citizen, even if he did not wish to run the risk of injury by getting into the fight to help the victim, could at least call the police, and when the police came he could help the officers of the law and certainly would do nothing to impede them. Prior to the First World War there had been no such police for the world. But after that war there came into being the League of Nations, whose members could act together to thwart an aggressor and help the victim.

How then could strict neutrality be reconciled with the existence of the League? President Wilson argued that there could be no reconciliation. He maintained that the only solution was to set up a world system that would prevent war and therefore render neutrality academic. As early as September 2, 1916, in an address accepting the renomination for the Presidency, he said: "No nation can any longer remain neutral as against any willful disturbance of the peace of the world." Then, on October 26, 1916, he said in an address at Cincinnati: "The business of neutrality is over." The United States did not enter the League Wilson created, but the League was there. My predecessor, Henry L. Stimson, also stated his belief that the old idea of neutrality was dead.

If, on the outbreak of war, the members of the League had decided that one of the nations was the aggressor and imposed military or economic sanctions against it, could strict neutrality on our part be logical, moral, or to our best interests? Would we, under international law, continue to insist on giving the same-size stick to both contestants, and thereby tend to defeat the action taken under the League system? Or would we, under our own neutrality law, refuse to give anything to either contestant, and thereby also militate against the victim whom the League was trying to help? And would we regard the League members who took part in military sanctions as warring nations, too, and refuse to have dealings with them as well?

It is undoubtedly true that the League, formed by most nations of the world to preserve peace, did conflict with what previously and literally was considered strict neutrality. Nations not members of the League, such as the United States, were, of course, left free to cling to the theory and observance of neutrality for whatever benefit or protection it might afford, if any, to their security. Five years later the world was to see that international desperadoes, waging wars of aggression, ignored with impunity any consideration of neutrality, as the sad experience of countries like Belgium, Holland, Denmark, and Norway showed.

Any law-abiding nation recognizing the doctrine that war by an aggressor against another country is more or less a threat to the security of all countries, relies no longer on the old doctrine of neutrality, but proceeds with due diligence to cooperate with all other peaceful countries against such an aggressor, and accordingly modifies its former conceptions of neutrality.

Another new fact that required cognizance was that, when the First World War ended, neutral rights under international law were left in what I called a "slumbering, disrupted and dislocated condition." During that war the Allies and the Central Powers proclaimed contraband lists embracing not only arms, ammunition, and implements of war, which was natural, but also all the materials out of which such items were manufactured. Virtually every product entering into international trade could be included in this definition, and be subject to seizure. After the United States entered the war in 1917, we adopted generally the same extensive lists of contraband. When the war ended, most of the Allied nations had no further interest in the discussion of neutral rights because they had joined the League of Nations. A new definition and reestablishment of neutral rights was left to the nations outside the League, and they did little or nothing in that direction.

These were only a few of the many points the isolationists failed to consider. To them the word "neutrality" had something magic in its warp and woof. It was at the same time open-sesame and hocus-pocus. Its mere invocation, coupled with the phrase, "Let's stay at home and mind our own business," was sufficient, in their minds, to keep war a thousand miles away. Some of them did not reflect that neutrality had not prevented us from nearly going to war with France at the end of the eighteenth century, or from warring with Britain in 1812 and Germany in 1917. And others who did realize this fact became all the more insistent on moving farther than neutrality under international law and taking refuge behind adamant legislation of our own.

It was a fatal conjunction that two ill-omened events should have occurred at the same time—one, the Nye Committee and its emphasis on munitions manufacturers and bankers as being responsible for our entrance into the First World War, and the other, the obvious approach of the Italo-Ethiopian War and its possible extension into a European war. Public opinion was swayed, on the one hand, by the spectacular conclusions of the Nye Committee which stirred resentment against makers of war equipment, and, on the other, by an almost frantic desire to make it absolutely impossible for us to be drawn into the approaching war, no matter what happened.

In the spring of 1935 a number of bills relating to neutrality were introduced in both Houses of Congress. Among them were resolutions presented by Senators Nye and Clark which were referred to the Senate Foreign Relations Committee. The President and I asked Pittman to kill these resolutions, and it was our understanding that he was in agreement with our wish. We were surprised, therefore, when Pittman's committee reported out two of the Nye and Clark bills on June 26. We thereupon sent Norman Davis to see Pittman, and the latter agreed to "stifle" the Nye-Clark legislation.

The President and I also saw Pittman, and on July 10 I went before the Foreign Relations Committee. I told them of the work being done in the State Department on neutrality and of the complicated nature of the questions involved. The committee then decided to recall for further consideration the two Nye and Clark bills and to appoint a subcommittee to confer with the Department on the whole subject of neutrality legislation. I still would have preferred postponing neutrality legislation, but it was now evident that the movement in Congress, spurred by isolationist agitation, was too strong.

By July 20 the Department had completed a revised draft of a neutrality bill. This left to the President's discretion the application of an arms embargo in time of war. Other provisions gave the President discretion to prohibit American vessels from carrying arms and munitions; to forbid the use of American ports as supply bases, the American flag by belligerent vessels, and American waters by belligerent submarines; to place an embargo on loans and to withdraw the protection of this Government from Americans traveling on belligerent vessels. The President approved this on the following day.

On July 30 the Senate subcommittee held its first meeting with State Department representatives. In my absence, Under Secretary Phillips read a statement suggesting the desirability of a single comprehensive neutrality law to be applied at the discretion of the President. He urged passage of the National Munitions Control Bill as the necessary basis for this legislation. This bill, applying equally in peace and war, was not strictly neutrality legislation but it was essential for the efficient enforcement of any restrictions on the export of arms. It was also needed so that this Government could carry out its obligations if the Geneva arms-traffic convention were ratified by a sufficient number of powers to give it effect. Phillips pointed out that it was desirable to avoid the impression that our Government had ceased to desire the promotion of peace through disarmament, one element of which was the control of the arms traffic.

Finally, on July 31, Phillips sent to Senator Pittman and to Congressman McReynolds, chairman of the House Committee on Foreign Affairs, the Department's draft of neutrality legislation. It soon became apparent, however, that the strong isolationist element in Congress would not go along with our idea that the neutrality provisions should be applied at the discretion of the President. On August 7 the Senate subcommittee refused to approve our draft.

By the middle of August the neutrality struggle in Congress, particularly in the Senate, was highly confused. Although it was obvious that the Italo-Ethiopian War was only a stone's throw away, it seemed possible that Congress would fail to enact any neutrality legislation prior to adjournment. During the second week in August I went to see the President and urged that he request Congress to pass a discretionary arms-embargo resolution to apply in the event of the outbreak of this war.

On August 19 I backed up my oral statements by handing the President a letter in which I said I felt that the time had come "when we should make a vigorous effort to secure the enactment by Congress of the Arms Embargo Resolution in respect to Ethiopia and Italy." At the same time I gave the President a draft of the resolution and another draft of a letter, for his signature, addressed to Senator Pittman and enclosing a copy of the resolution. I suggested to the President that, if he sent the letter, he might wish to release it to the press because, in my opinion, "public knowledge of the position of the Administration in regard to this matter would . . . serve a useful purpose at this time."

The draft letter to Pittman stated that the President had come to the conclusion that the enactment at that time of a joint resolution "which would authorize the President, in his discretion, to prohibit the exportation of arms to Ethiopia or to Italy or to both of these countries" would "assist in the present efforts toward the maintenance of peace and, in the event of the outbreak of hostilities, would serve the best interests of this country."

The resolution would have given the President the right to apply the arms embargo against the aggressor, and therefore pursued the stand I had taken for more than two years that the President should be in a position to support the collective action of other peace-seeking nations in case of aggression, provided he agreed with their conclusions. But Pittman, bedeviled by the isolationist Senators and himself leaning more toward isolation than toward international cooperation, could not see it.

The President signed the letter to Pittman, but never sent it. After he signed it, the White House talked with Pittman who said he would introduce the resolution if the President formally requested him to do so, but he would refuse to sponsor it. In view of that attitude, it was hopeless to expect the Senate to pass it.

Pittman introduced his own bill on August 20. This took from the President any discretion in applying the arms embargo and made it mandatory. It passed the Senate the following day. On that day the President and I met with Congressman McReynolds and other Representatives. We agreed that the House should approve the Pittman Resolution, but with an amendment whereby the mandatory arms-embargo section would expire on February 29, 1936, six months later.

I undertook on August 22 to give informally to the public, through a press conference, my views on neutrality legislation. I pointed out that the real objective was "to safeguard this country against being drawn into war," but at the same time I said that a vast portion of the American people also desired "to make some kind of feasible contribution to prevent war from coming on."

In other words, we could not just sit back and think thereby to keep war from touching us. We were morally bound to step out as well and try to keep the war itself from breaking out. "If," I said, "we strip ourselves of the slightest discretion and go off and erect in front of us an inflexible structure of statutes—the only country of all the sixty-six countries of the world doing so—and announce beforehand that we have stripped ourselves, that we have tied our hands in every possible way, with no chance to exercise the least discretion and to cooperate in different ways to avoid war, ways that nobody could object to . . . we have stripped ourselves bare of all moral influence we might exercise."

Referring to the questions of commerce involved in neutrality legislation, I said: "When we tie our hands completely . . . we strip ourselves of all voice about the conduct of trade . . . we get clear off of the seven seas." I pointed out that the belligerent controlling the seas could then write his own laws of commerce, of contraband of war, of search and seizure, and the like, while we would "have eliminated ourselves entirely beforehand from saying anything."

I added that we were looking to this "bigger, broader situation" and particularly to the questions "of whether we are going to denude ourselves of any moral influence" and of "whether we are going practically to make Japan, or some other first class country, in case of a general war . . . our broker to buy our great congested supplies for nothing, take them out and sell them in neutral territory contiguous to the belligerents."

The Pittman Resolution was passed by the House on August 23 and sent to the President the next day for signature. Mr. Roosevelt thereupon sent me a note asking whether I had any objection to his approving it. In a letter to the President on August 29, I pointed out that the mandatory arms-embargo section would require him, on the outbreak or during the progress of war, to apply the section, and thereupon it would be unlawful to export such arms as he might designate to any belligerent.

"This provision is, in my opinion," I said, "an invasion of the constitutional and traditional power of the Executive to conduct the foreign relations of the United States. It is an attempt to impose upon the Executive by legislative act a fixed and inflexible line of conduct which it must follow, thereby depriving it of a large measure of its discretion in negotiating with foreign powers in circumstances when Executive discretion and flexibility of policy might be essential to the interests of the United States.

"Furthermore, this provision would tend to deprive this Government of a great measure of its influence in promoting and preserving peace. The question of our attitude toward collective action against an aggressor is only one of the many aspects of a much larger question."

I pointed out deficiencies in other provisions of the resolution, but finally I concluded:

"In spite of my very strong and, I believe, well founded objections to this joint resolution, I do not feel that I can properly, in all the circumstances, recommend that you withhold your approval. Section 1 terminates on February 29, 1936. Section 2 is so manifestly inadequate that it will have to be later amended. I hope that satisfactory legislation to replace these two sections can be enacted at the next session of Congress. I shall at the appropriate time venture to submit, for your consideration, the text of a message on this subject which you may wish to address to the Congress."

I had several reasons in mind in suggesting that the President sign the joint resolution. One was that a veto would have provoked an open conflict with Congress, which might have ended unhappily for the Administration, in view of the strong, rising isolationist sentiment throughout the country. It was readily manifest that Congress did not intend to grant our wish that we be permitted to apply an embargo against an aggressor and not against the victim, or even that the President be permitted to decide whether to apply the embargo or not against both of them.

Another reason was that the joint resolution did contain one feature we had been urging—the setting up of a national system for the regulation of the arms traffic.

A third reason was that the nature of the war to which the joint resolution would undoubtedly apply was already apparent. This was the impending Italo-Ethiopian conflict, which was to break out five weeks later. It was already certain that there was to be a war between Italy and Ethiopia, and it was equally certain which one of the two powers would be the aggressor. It was also becoming evident that the League of Nations powers intended to take some action in the way of sanctions against the aggressor when the war came.

It was easy to see, in advance, that the application of the neutrality resolution, in this case, even though it imposed an embargo on both belligerents, could not but affect the aggressor, Italy, far more adversely than the victim, Ethiopia. Italy had the shipping and money to import arms from us; Ethiopia had not. Italian ships carried on traffic with the United States, and American citizens could be warned against traveling on them; there were no Ethiopian ships.

The question of trade with belligerents, of course, was far larger than the question of shipments of arms—and this the isolationists failed to see. When a nation, like Italy, is in position to manufacture its own arms, is it not more important for that nation to import cotton for explosives, steel for military equipment, and oil for its navy rather than machine guns and shells? The early Embargo Acts under Jefferson did not limit themselves to arms and munitions but embraced all trade. The President and I were to deal in our own way with this aspect of the problem after the Italo-Ethiopian War began.

I wrote a letter to the President on August 29, suggesting the wording of a press statement, if he wished to issue one, in connection with his approval of the joint resolution. My suggestion was:

"I have approved this joint resolution because it was intended as an expression of the fixed desire of the Government and the people of the United States to avoid any action which might involve us in war. This joint resolution may in some degree serve to that end. . . . I hope that Section 1 may be replaced by permanent legislation which will provide for greater flexibility of action in the many unforseeable situations with which we may be confronted.

"It is the policy of this Government to avoid being drawn into wars between other nations, but it is equally our policy to exert the influence of this country in cooperation with other governments to maintain and promote peace. It is conceivable that situations may arise in which inflexible provisions of law might have exactly the opposite effect from that which was intended. . . . Moreover, when this subject is again considered by Congress, it may well be found that the joint resolution may be expanded so as to include provisions dealing with important aspects of our neutrality policy which have not been dealt with in this temporary measure."

Two days later the President, on signing the neutrality resolution, issued the statement I suggested, with some changes of wording. After the point I made that the inflexible provision might have exactly the opposite effect from that intended, he inserted: "In other words, the inflexible provisions might drag us into war instead of keeping us out."

Concretely, what it meant was this: If nation A, with whom we had many economic ties and who, pursuing a policy of peace, had not been arming, were attacked by nation B which had amassed vast armaments, an arms embargo by us against both would react very unneutrally against A, and might lead to strained relations between us and A, if nothing worse.

Moreover, depriving the Administration of a portion of its freedom of action in foreign affairs might in itself promote a war into which we would later be drawn. Nation B, militarily prepared, might be less disposed to attack nation A, militarily unprepared, if it knew that A could get the arms it needed from the United States. Furthermore, our mandatory neutrality legislation actually gave B a control over our foreign policy it did not have before. B would know—just as Hitler knew when he was ready to act—that all it had to do to bring the action it desired on our part was to go to war. That very fact would require the President, under the neutrality resolution, to take an action he might feel fundamentally wrong, ill advised, and contrary to our national interests.

The one feature of the joint resolution that I really approved began to operate within a month after the Neutrality Act came into effect. On September 24, 1935, the National Munitions Control Board established by the Act held its first meeting in my office. The board was composed of myself as chairman, Secretary of the Treasury Morgenthau, Secretary of War Woodring, Secretary of Navy Swanson, and Secretary of Commerce Roper. Since the Neutrality Act placed the administration of the registration and licensing system for arms and munitions in the State Department, I set up a new Office of Arms and Munitions Control in the department under Assistant Secretary Moore and placed Joseph C. Green at its head. Thenceforth manufacturers, exporters, and importers of arms, ammunition, and implements of war were required to register with the Department and to obtain a license for every shipment exported or imported. The department began to publish monthly reports on such shipments.

This was a wholesome development. It put us in position to cooperate in a world movement to control arms traffic if the other nations could agree on an international accord. And it gave us more control over our own foreign policy. Obviously the shipment of arms by American citizens to another nation might well affect the relations of that nation to the United States as well as the relations between the United States and other countries with whom that nation was on friendly or unfriendly terms. In peacetime we could not prohibit such transactions, but at least we knew their extent, their destination, and the identity of the persons promoting them.

On November 6 in a radio address (read for me by Under Secretary Phillips because of my absence from Washington), I summed up my views on neutrality legislation. "The shipment of arms," I said, "is not the only way and, in fact, is not the principal way by which our commerce with foreign nations may lead to serious international difficulties. . . . The imposition of an arms embargo is not a complete panacea and we cannot assume that . . . we may complacently sit back with the feeling that we are secure from all danger. Attempts by a belligerent to exercise jurisdiction on the high seas over trade with its enemy, or with other neutral countries on the theory that the latter are supplying the enemy, may give rise to difficulties no less serious than those resulting from the exportation of arms and implements of war."

Pointing out that every war presents different conditions, I said: "Difficulties inherent in any effort to lay down by legislative enactment inelastic rules or regulations to be applied to every situation that may arise will at once be apparent. The Executive should not be unduly or unreasonably handicapped. There are a number of ways in which discretion could wisely be given the President which are not and could not be seriously controversial. These might well include discretion as to the time of imposing an embargo."

I inveighed against the idea of concentrating entirely on means for remaining neutral. "I conceive it to be our duty and in the interest of our country and of humanity, not only to remain aloof from disputes and conflicts with which we have no direct concern, but also to use our influence in any appropriate way to bring about the peaceful settlement of international differences. Our own interest and our duty as a great power forbid that we shall sit idly by and watch the development of hostilities with a feeling of self-sufficiency and complacency when by the use of our influence, short of becoming involved in the dispute itself, we might prevent or lessen the scourge of war."

But, as I spoke, Mussolini's Fascist legions were already plunging into Ethiopia, and the Neutrality Act was in operation.

30: Mussolini Makes War

FEW WARS EVER CAST their shadows so clearly before them as the Italo-Ethiopian conflict which began October 3, 1935. The aggressor stretched out his long arm toward his victim many months before he struck. Since Ethiopia lay in the heart of another continent, three thousand miles from Italy, and Italian troops en route to East Africa had to pass through the Suez Canal, Mussolini carried out his rehearsals in a theater with all seats filled and the curtain rolled up.

Our Ambassador to Italy, Breckinridge Long, made one of the best records of my time as a diplomat and reporter. He foresaw and reported serious signs of the Italo-Ethiopian War more than a year before the war actually arrived. In August, 1934, the State Department requested comments from our Minister, Addison E. Southard, in Addis Ababa, on a London report that Italo-Ethiopian relations were strained almost to the breaking point. Later that month our Military Attaché in Rome reported that the Italian General Staff had drawn up plans for the conquest and occupation of Ethiopia. In September Ambassador Bullitt informed us from Moscow of his conversation with the Italian Ambassador there concerning agreements reportedly reached between Italy and Britain and France giving Mussolini a free hand in Ethiopia.

On December 5, 1934, skirmishes broke out between Italians and Ethiopians in the frontier area between Italian Somaliland and Ethiopia. When Italy demanded apologies and indemnities from Addis Ababa and refused Emperor Haile Selassie's request to arbitrate, the Ethiopian Government wrote the Secretary General of the League of Nations asking him to call the situation to the attention of the Council and the League members. On receipt of a complete report from our Chargé d'Affaires in Addis Ababa, W. Perry George, I telegraphed him on December 18, 1934, to refrain scrupulously from encouraging any request by the Emperor for mediation by the United States. Since both Ethiopia and Italy were members of the League, and the Emperor had asked the League to take cognizance of the dispute, I felt that it was the League's function to act, if it wished, and that any individual move on our part would only confuse the issue. Believing that the Emperor might base a request for mediation on the Kellogg Pact, outlawing war, I reminded Mr. George that this had last been invoked by members of the League Council in 1931, in connection with Manchuria, and that our Government had acted only after separate communications had been addressed to Japan and China by the members of the Council.

The Emperor stated to Mr. George that he was not requesting mediation but desired some gesture calling attention to the Kellogg Pact. I thereupon instructed the Chargé to explain to the Emperor that, since the League had the issue before it, we did not feel that our Government could properly or usefully take action.

During the following months, as I arrived at my office in the morning I was almost sure to find at least one telegram from any one of half a dozen capitals relating to Italian troop movements and military preparations. In January, 1935, I received rumors—and denials—that, during the conversations between Mussolini and Laval in Rome, Laval had agreed not to interfere with Italian operations in Ethiopia. The Italian Ambassador, Augusto Rosso, came to see Under Secretary Phillips on February 14, 1935, to insist that Italy's troop movements were purely defensive and that Italy had nothing aggressive in mind. He stretched our credulity beyond the point of elasticity.

Two months later, on April 27, Signor Rosso was back in the Department to make the surprising request that we use our influence to prevent the shipment of American motor trucks to Ethiopia. He was told by Wallace Murray, chief of the Near Eastern Division, that the President did not have authority to prevent the export of arms and munitions of war without specific legislation; that, in any event, motor trucks could not legally be considered as arms or implements of war; and, finally, that public opinion here would not sympathize with the Italian request in view of Italy's troop movements to Italian East Africa. A similar request was made to the American Embassy in Rome on June 19, and the same answer given.

During these months Britain and France, and then the League, made many fruitless attempts to compose the differences between Italy and Ethiopia. When Anthony Eden failed, during a personal visit to Mussolini, to obtain agreement to a compromise involving some cession of Ethiopian and British colonial territories, Emperor Haile Selassie called our Chargé, Mr. George, to his palace on July 3. The Emperor told him he felt it his duty to ask the United States Government to examine means by which Italy's observance of her engagements as signatory of the Kellogg Pact might be assured.

There was still no point, however, in taking any step that might impede the action of the League. We had before us the vivid example of what happened in the Chaco War, when a virtual competition rose between the League Commission and conciliation committees formed in the Western Hemisphere, thus enabling the contending nations, particularly Paraguay, to play off one against the other and retard a solution. We drafted a reply, which the President approved, stating that we were gratified that the League had given its attention to the controversy and that the dispute was in process of adjustment. As to the Kellogg Pact, we said we would be loath to believe that either Italy or Ethiopia, as signatories thereof, "would resort to other than pacific means."

Mussolini's propaganda machine distorted this reply into "evidence of the United States' friendliness toward Italy" and American realization that Italy was "justified in its stand." I thereupon called in Italian Ambassador Rosso. I said to him that, while we were not familiar with all the facts or merits of the question at issue between his country and Ethiopia, we were "deeply interested in the preservation of peace in all parts of the world" and particularly in "those international arrangements designed to effect the solution of controversies by peaceable means." I said I felt impelled to impress upon him "my increasing concern" and "my earnest hope that a means may be found to arrive at a peaceful and mutually satisfactory solution of the problem." I added: "A war started anywhere would be awfully dangerous to everybody."

The next day I cabled Ambassadors Bingham in London and Straus in Paris the text of this statement, instructing them to bring it to the attention of the foreign ministers of their respective countries of assignment. The ambassadors were to add that they felt certain that the foreign minister would realize, from the close attention we were giving to the dispute, our deep concern over the rapidly advancing developments.

The same day I requested British and French Ambassadors Lindsay and de Laboulaye to come to the Department. I showed them a newspaper dispatch from London concluding that the Kellogg Pact was dead because we did not invoke it in the Italo-Ethiopian dispute. I said this impression was entirely contrary to the sense of our note to the Emperor of Ethiopia, which emphasized the principles of the pact. Referring to press reports that the British and French Governments might confer on the Italo-Ethiopian situation and be joined by the Italian Government, I said: "It would, of course, be a source of great satisfaction to us if, through the considered action of those nations most directly concerned with the situation, some means could be found of arriving at a peaceful solution." I added that I would be glad to be kept informed of any developments.

Three days earlier, I had asked French Ambassador de Laboulaye about the state of mind of his Government toward the Italo-Ethiopian problem. I said I felt justified in making the inquiry because we were both signatories of the Kellogg Pact and because of Mussolini's recent "extremely warlike utterances" and additional military shipments from Italy to Ethiopia. "A war between Italy and Ethiopia would be bad enough," I said, "but it is entirely within the range of possibility that it would in due time spread back into more than one part of Europe with its unimaginable, devastating effects."

To allay any remaining doubts about our attitude toward the Kellogg Pact, I issued a press statement on July 12 that the pact was "no less binding now than when it was entered into by the sixty-three nations that are parties to it" and that it constituted a "treaty by and among those nations." I said the pact was "a declaration by the governments of the world that they condemn recourse to war for the solution of international controversies, and renounce it as an instrument of national policy in their relations with one another." Furthermore, it was "an agreement and a solemn obligation that the settlement and solution of all disputes or conflicts among nations, of whatever nature or of whatever origin, shall never be sought except by pacific means." The President issued a statement to the same effect on August 1.

On August 16 conversations began in Paris among Britain, France, and Italy under their treaty of 1906 obligating them to cooperate in maintaining the political and territorial status quo in Ethiopia. The previous day I telegraphed our embassies in London and Paris our wish to have all information possible to enable our Government to determine "whether any further action by it within the limits of its established policy and its obligations as a signatory of the Pact of Paris [Kellogg Pact] would be likely to have a beneficial rather than a disadvantageous effect."

The following day I received telegrams from our Chargé in Paris, Theodore Marriner, indicating that both the British and the French thought some such action by this Government, if taken promptly, might reenforce their efforts. I thereupon went to see the President. Whenever we at the State Department felt that the Department had exhausted its efforts in a certain direction, we sought to reenforce them by putting out something in the name of the President. I informed Mr. Roosevelt of the situation. He suggested a message to Mussolini.

Accordingly, on August 18, 1935, I telegraphed Alexander Kirk, our Chargé in Rome, requesting him to see Mussolini and give him this message from me:

"I am asked by the President to communicate to you, in all friend-liness and in confidence, a personal message expressing his earnest hope that the controversy between Italy and Ethiopia will be resolved without resort to armed conflict. In this country it is felt both by the Government and by the people that failure to arrive at a peaceful settlement of the present dispute and a subsequent outbreak of hostilities would be a world calamity the consequences of which would adversely affect the interests of all nations."

Kirk delivered this message on August 19. Mussolini replied that, while he appreciated the character of the message and its expression of friendliness, it was too late to escape an armed conflict since Italy had mobilized one million men and had spent two billion lire. He said there was no reason to fear the consequences of such a conflict if it could be limited to Italy and Ethiopia, but, because of the British attitude, such limitation might prove impossible. Mussolini added that the Anglo-French proposals for settlement made in Paris were entirely unacceptable, be-cause what Italy really wanted was the military occupation of Ethiopia. Regardless of League action, he said, Italy would proceed with her plans. If the opposition of other countries developed into actual interference, Italy would take steps accordingly. In that case, Mussolini commented, the consequences might prove disastrous.

I passed this telegram on to the President. The following day he sent me this note:

"It would be well in any subsequent note or message by us, either to Italy or to other nations, to point out that it is never too late to avoid an armed conflict. The mere fact that Italy has mobilized a million men and spent two billion lire does not mean 'destruction of her prestige in incurring the disdain of other countries who would be ready to accuse her of having attempted to bluff or of having engaged in an undertaking which she found she was unable to carry out.' [This was a phrase from Kirk's telegram.] On the contrary, we could well point out that after all these preparations Italian prestige would be enhanced and not harmed if Italy could take the magnificent position that rather than resort to war, she would cancel the military preparations and submit the whole question to peaceful settlement by arbitration."

It was my view then, just as it is now, that, at that late stage in the dispute, this wording would not have been impressive. Mussolini, in his desperado frame of mind, was not going to be stopped by anything short of decisive force. Seeing the war inexorably approaching, I had, on the previous day, August 19, given the President my letter, outlined in the preceding chapter, suggesting legislation that would give him the right to impose an arms embargo against either Italy or Ethiopia when war came.

At the end of August oil was literally thrown on the troubled waters and, contrary to traditional experience, stirred them still more. Emperor Haile Selassie gave a petroleum concession to the African Exploration and Development Corporation, which was understood to be a subsidiary of an American oil company. The concession was arranged by a British subject, Francis Rickett. The world repercussions of this development were intense because the impression was now created that all the efforts of the British and American Governments to keep Mussolini from plunging into Ethiopia were dictated by the greedy motive to corner the oil prospects in that country. It also gave Italian propaganda a wonderful opportunity.

The State Department began to inquire into the origins of the African Exploration and Development Company and of the concession granted. On September 3 George S. Walden, chairman of the board of the Standard-Vacuum Oil Company, accompanied by H. Dundas, vice president, called at the State Department, stated that the African Exploration and Development Company was a subsidiary of the Standard-Vacuum Oil Company, and offered to adopt any suggestion the Department might make in view of the political complications that had arisen.

Wallace Murray, chief of the Near Eastern Division, with whom they conferred, discussed this visit with me, and then met with them again. He told them, on my instructions, that the oil concession at this time "was a matter of grave embarrassment not only to this Government but to other governments, who are making strenuous and sincere efforts for the preservation of world peace, which is seriously threatened by the Italo-Ethiopian dispute." He added that "this transaction had come as a most painful surprise and had been deeply deplored by the Secretary of State." Murray emphasized the importance of the League Council meeting being held that very day in Geneva and "the painful handicap under which certain governments, particularly the British, were now placed in view of the suspicions and recriminations arising out of the oil transaction." He concluded by saying that "this Government, no less than the British Government, desires to divest itself of any suspicion of selfish interest when world peace is at stake, and the oil transaction has created just such a suspicion."

When Mr. Walden asked what the Department wished him to do, Murray replied that he had been authorized by me to inform him that "only radical action on the part of your company in the form of an immediate and unconditional withdrawal from the concession would meet the needs of the situation."

Mr. Walden left the State Department, consulted with other officials of his company, and then informed Murray by telephone that they would cooperate fully with the Department and withdraw from the concession.

I thereupon called the newspaper correspondents into my own office and said to them that the oil concession had been granted "without this Government having in any way been consulted or informed" and that "the attitude and policy of this Government toward the controversy between Italy and Ethiopia will be maintained hereafter just as it would have been maintained had this reported oil transaction not occurred." I pointed out that our policy was "the preservation of peace—to which policy every country throughout the world is committed by one or more treaties—and we earnestly hope that no nation will, in any circumstances, be diverted from this supreme objective."

We next had to pacify Emperor Haile Selassie, who told the American Minister in Addis Ababa, now Cornelius Van H. Engert, that he would very much regret it if reports were true that the Department had exerted pressure on the Standard-Vacuum Oil Company to withdraw from the concession. The Emperor said he had granted the concession not only because he knew the United States was politically disinterested and technically equipped to contribute to the economic development of Ethiopia, but also as a proof of his friendly feeling toward us and his appreciation of the sympathetic interest we were displaying toward Ethiopia's difficulties.

I therefore instructed Minister Engert to assure the Emperor that his sentiments of cordiality and good will were appreciated and reciprocated and that the advice given the oil company by the Department was no indication of a change in policy. On the contrary, it was intended to be "helpful in the cause of peace" and to "strengthen the hands of those powers, including the United States, which are making strenuous and sincere efforts to that end."

On September 10 the Ethiopian Foreign Office asked Engert whether the United States would be willing to mediate, provided Italy would agree. I replied on September 12 that the suggestion "would not appear to be practicable, coming as it does at a moment when the appropriate agencies of the League of Nations, to which the Ethiopian Government has referred its dispute, are occupied in an endeavor to arrive at a solution." I pointed out that, although mediation had been used to advantage in times past, the creation of the League had changed the situation somewhat by providing a forum "to which disputes between member nations can be submitted for settlement by collective action of the member nations."

I did not want to rest merely with refusing the Emperor's suggestion. The following day I issued a long statement of our attitude in which I recapitulated the steps we had taken up to then in connection with the Italo-Ethiopian dispute. After referring to our desire for peace and the obligations of the Kellogg Pact, I said: "Under the conditions which prevail in the world today, a threat of hostilities anywhere cannot but be a threat to the interests—political, economic, legal, and social—of all nations. Armed conflict in any part of the world cannot but have undesirable and adverse effects in every part of the world. All nations have the right to ask that any and all issues, between whatsoever nations, be resolved by pacific means. Every nation has the right to ask that no nations subject it and other nations to the hazards and uncertainties that must inevitably accrue to all from resort to arms by any two."

This theme—that a threat of hostilities anywhere cannot but be a threat to the interests of all nations—became one of our basic ideas in the years to come. I used it repeatedly, and so did the President. It was an answer to the isolationists who continually exclaimed that we had no business being interested in a conflict thousands of miles away. I continued to insist that our own security and peace, to say nothing of our moral duty, demanded that we do what we could to prevent the outbreak of a conflict, even though thousands of miles away, because if the conflict came it would inevitably affect us. In this instance I was building up a foundation on which later to rest the moral embargo that operated principally against Italy.

Events now moved rapidly toward war. Ambassador Long telegraphed me from Rome on September 17 the substance of a long talk with Mussolini whose mind, he said, was "definitely closed to any compromise of any kind which may be made to him from Geneva or elsewhere," and who was "definitely and irrevocably determined to proceed in Abyssinia" (Ethiopia).

The day before, British Foreign Secretary Hoare informed Ray Atherton, our Chargé d'Affaires in London, that, in the event sanctions were imposed by the League, the United States, as well as other non-League powers, would be approached by the League and asked to co-operate. On that day I held two conferences of State Department officials in my office. We discussed sanctions at length, and I took the position that we should define our position relative to trade with Italy prior to any action by the League, in order to avoid accusations by the isolationist elements that we were following the League. Two days later Ambassador Long telegraphed from Rome that he hoped the United States would not associate itself with sanctions.

On September 20 I telegraphed the embassy in London. Referring to Atherton's telegram of September 16, I said that our Government "would not join in the imposition of sanctions upon any nation involved in the pending controversy between Italy and Ethiopia." As for League action, "it would, of course, be obviously impossible for this Government to arrive at any conclusion with regard thereto before it was placed in full possession of the reasons and bases upon which such collective action by the League was founded and a complete description of the specific measures to be put into effect."

I pointed to our pleasure on learning from Minister Wilson in Geneva that Anthony Eden had given him to understand there would probably not be any discussion with us concerning our attitude in advance of the League's reaching a definite program. I was seeking to prevent a situation arising whereby the League would take action and then ask us to join in. I was anxious that some action should be taken by the United States to hamper the forthcoming aggressor, Italy, but it had to be taken on our own and not in conjunction with the League or treading in the League's footsteps. An identical or similar course pursued by the League and by us would lead to the inference that we, a nonmember, were clandestinely cooperating with it.

British Foreign Secretary Sir Samuel Hoare informed me on September 25 through Ambassador Bingham that Britain, in the event of war between Italy and Ethiopia, would bring economic pressure to bear as far as possible, short of actual sanctions, in hopes of limiting the duration of the war. Hoare trusted that the United States would consider aiding this effort.

I telegraphed Bingham on September 27 to inform Hoare that the Johnson Act prohibited private credits to Italy, that our Government had adopted a policy of not approving credits through the Export-Import Bank for shipments of goods to Italy, that private institutions here likewise were restricting credits to Italian borrowers, and that the recent neutrality legislation would require an arms embargo against both Italy and Ethiopia. I also pointed out that "the clear intention of this Government to assist in the cause of peace" had been amply demonstrated by our intervention in the case of the oil concession; I added that our Government had also "supplemented the foregoing acts and possible acts by moral support which we have consistently given to the efforts made to arrive at a peaceful settlement of the dispute and would continue this support by any act it could take in the light of its limitations as occasions arise."

Hoare had also raised with me the question of possible consultations under the Kellogg Pact. I replied that, while we "would not decline an invitation to consult through diplomatic channels with a view to the invocation of the Pact," we believed that such consultation for any purpose other than "a formal invocation of the Pact of Paris by all the signatories thereto for the purpose of mobilizing world opinion" might "appear to encroach upon the explicit functions of the Council of the League and of the members thereof, and it would therefore appear undesirable to endeavor to utilize the Pact of Paris as a substitute for the Covenant."

Anyone looking at the situation realistically could see there was no hope of halting Mussolini's mad course by words or gestures. Within a week, on October 3, 1935, he pressed the button for the invasion that was to touch off a constant series of wars and invasions until his bullet-ridden body hung head down from a lamppost in a Milanese piazza.

31: Moral Embargo

   MUSSOLINI STARTED HOSTILITIES against Ethiopia without declaring war, thereby following the example of Japan in China in 1931. Because the Neutrality Act required the President to impose the arms embargo "upon the outbreak or during the progress of war between or among two or more foreign states," I telegraphed our diplomatic missions in London, Paris, Rome, Geneva, and Addis Ababa on October 3 asking for information as to the nature of the hostilities. I wirelessed the text of this telegram to the President, who was then aboard the cruiser *Houston* on a fishing trip off the Mexican coast.

Foreseeing the coming of the war, the State Department had prepared a draft neutrality proclamation prior to the President's departure. I had handed this to Mr. Roosevelt on September 25. He signed it without dating and gave it back to me to be kept in the Department for use if hostilities broke out during his absence. On October 4 I received a message from him: "If, when you receive this, you have any official confirmation of Italian invasion and of battles and casualties well within the Ethiopian border, it seems to me that this constitutes war within the intent of the statute and should be proclaimed as such by me." He asked me to send him the draft of a brief public statement to be issued at the same time as the neutrality proclamation. He also asked me to consider whether, if the proclamation were issued, we should make public the names of American citizens sailing from the United States on Italian ships and the cargo manifests of American goods destined for either belligerent.

I wirelessed the President the following day that I expected to have further and official proofs of a state of war by the next morning. I suggested, however, that the proclamation relating to travel on belligerent vessels be "held in reserve, since Ethiopia has no vessels and Italy is not at war with any other country." This was because the Neutrality Act had directed the President to proclaim that Americans who traveled on belligerent ships did so at their own risk, if he found that such travel involved the maintenance of our peace and security, or the protection of American lives or commercial interests. But since Ethiopia had no submarines or other naval vessels, and since no other country was at war with Italy, it was not at all likely that any harm could come to Italian vessels, and our peace and security and the lives and property of our citizens would not therefore be involved.

There seemed little doubt that a full-scale war had begun, but the question then rose: Should we issue our neutrality proclamation, thereby recognizing the existence of a state of war, or should we wait until the League had taken action? My advisers were about evenly divided. Minister Hugh Wilson at Geneva telephoned me on October 5 to tell me that the League Council probably would not reach a decision until Monday the 7th, and to suggest that the first step recognizing the existence of hostilities not be taken by the United States because this "would be a blow to the collective system which Geneva is trying to put through." This suggestion was in line with the views of a portion of my advisers who thought that independent action on our part would either force the hands of the League or would detract from League action.

I maintained the opposite view. I was sure that the League would be forced to recognize that war had broken out, and therefore to consider what steps to take. I was also sure that the United States would have to recognize the same fact and apply at least the arms embargo of the Neutrality Act. I did not want to be in the position, therefore, of waiting until the League took action and then take the same action. This would provide deadly ammunition for the isolationists who would thereupon charge that we had joined the League in some form or other and that our movements were directed from Geneva.

I wirelessed the President on October 5, telling him that I thought we had sufficient evidence of an outbreak of war to justify the issuance of the arms-embargo proclamation, but also informing him of Minister Wilson's comments. "I feel strongly myself," I said, "that our declaration of an embargo in view of the existing state of hostilities cannot be delayed, in the light of present developments, beyond next Monday, but I would like to know your judgment as to whether, in consideration of Wilson's reports and recommendations, we might not well delay the embargo declaration until probably not later than Monday afternoon."

I also wirelessed the President a draft statement to be issued by him at the same time as the embargo proclamation. This declared it to be "the plain duty of our citizens," in order to avoid any possibility of our becoming involved in the war, "to refrain from placing themselves in positions where, were conditions peaceful, they would be entitled to seek the protection of this Government." It stated that the President desired it understood "that any of our people who voluntarily engage in transactions of any character with either of the belligerents do so at their own risk."

I pointed out to the President that the statement did not include measures so drastic as he had suggested (publication of the names of Americans traveling on belligerent vessels and of manifests of cargoes destined to the belligerents), but I said that, in my opinion, it went as far as was advisable at the time. "In the light of further developments," I said, "you might at a later time wish to take successive steps in the line of, first, an appeal; second, a warning that, in the event of acts contrary to your policy of making the utmost effort to prevent our involvement in the war, names and facts might be made public."

Finally, I repeated my suggestion that no proclamation on Americans traveling on belligerent vessels at their own risk be issued. I said that, in the circumstances, the issuance of such a proclamation might subject the President "to criticism on the one hand and might, on the other hand, be regarded by Italy as a gratuitous affront in the nature of sanctions."

Our draft statement went beyond the letter of the Neutrality Act in that it sought to discourage trading of all kinds with Italy and Ethiopia. I knew, of course, that Ethiopia had virtually no credits in the United States and no merchant shipping, and that any increase in shipments of goods to the belligerents would go almost entirely to Italy, the aggressor.

This was also in line with my view that an arms embargo would have slight effect on a belligerent capable of making his own arms and munitions as long as he could import the necessary raw materials. I did not want the aggressor, though forbidden to buy our arms, ammunition, and implements of war, to buy the raw materials out of which he himself could make the sinews of war. Here was the beginning of our moral embargo, so called because it rested on moral rather than on legal foundations. We were to invoke the same principle in subsequent years for other parts of the world.

The President, quickly replying to my telegram, said the embargo proclamation should be issued "immediately in view of the undoubted state of war and without waiting for League action." He entirely approved the suggested statement I had sent him to be given out with the proclamation.

He also said he thought the proclamation concerning travel on belligerent vessels should be issued at the same time. He argued that the intent of the Neutrality Act was "to prevent aid to either belligerent, and American passenger travel on Italian ships gives aid not only financially but also by making access to Italy more easy for Americans seeking commercial advantage." Also, "if Americans continue to patronize Italian ships, there may very easily occur some untoward episode either to or by an individual American or through some commercial transaction which violates the spirit of the arms and munitions proclamation."

The State Department issued the arms-embargo proclamation and the President's accompanying statement late in the evening of October 5. Prior to doing so, the Department gave the Embassy in London by telephone the text of the statement and informed it of the action we were taking. This information could be communicated to the British Foreign Office. We made it clear we were not asking for the British Government's advice or recommendations, but were interested in their general impressions. Sir Samuel Hoare informed us at once that he saw no objection to the issuance of the embargo proclamation and the statement whenever we so desired, the sooner the better. The second proclamation, concerning travel on belligerent vessels, was issued October 6.

On October 10 I made a press statement to combat an impression created by a statement from Secretary of Commerce Roper which appeared to encourage exports to the belligerents. I said that, although there was no legal prohibition against our citizens entering into transactions with the belligerents—except as to arms, ammunition, and implements of war—"the warning given by the President in his proclamation concerning travel on belligerent ships, and his general warning that during the war any of our people who voluntarily engage in transactions of any character with either of the belligerents do so at their own risk, were based upon the policy and purpose of keeping this country out of war. It certainly was not intended to encourage transactions with the belligerents." I added that the speedy restoration of stable trade relations among nations, which could only come with the termination of the war, was "by far the most profitable objective for our people to visualize, in contrast with such risky and temporary trade as they might maintain with belligerent nations."

The League having begun to discuss the application of sanctions, and reports having come to us from Wilson in Geneva that the League intended to invite nonmember nations to join in the discussion, I decided to take the bull by the horns. With the isolationist sentiment so strong, it was impossible to join any League body considering sanctions. I preferred that any action we took should be entirely independent and not even seem to be suggested by the League. I did not want to be in the position of having to refuse a League invitation, which we most certainly would have had to do, thereby throwing water on the League's efforts, whereas, by acting independently, we could take action the effect of which would be to bolster those efforts. Accordingly, I cabled Wilson on October 9:

"In view of our position as shown by our utterances and acts up to the present, fully supported by the public sentiment of this country, we consider that it would be advisable from every standpoint for the League to realize that we have already taken definite steps in line with our own policies and limitations, which include long steps in restricting financial and trade relations with the belligerents, and that we are disposed to pursue our course independently in the light of circumstances as they develop. These steps should be an indication of our course and attitude. From this point of view, it would seem unnecessary and certainly at the present stage inadvisable from our point of view to ask us to participate in such committee as may be set up to deal with sanctions."

The following day Wilson replied that the League Secretary General Avenol, Anthony Eden, and French Foreign Minister Pierre Laval had all agreed to oppose any issuance of an invitation to the United States to take part in the League's discussions.

I wirelessed the President a summary of my telegram to Wilson. He approved it on October 10. He also suggested that we study possible future additions to the list of arms, ammunition, and implements of war contained in the embargo proclamation of October, including such items as processed copper and steel, so as to be ready to make a decision in case the League or Britain or France added articles to their possible sanctions list which were not contained in our proclamation. The President advised that we "try to find out what orders of all kinds are being placed with us by the Italian Government or firms." He said he was opposed to any quota system of exports to Italy and that "we must either allow an export item or disallow it as ammunition."

Referring to exports to neutrals, the President said that, as to those not applying sanctions, "we can require such drastic proof of nontransshipment that in effect such exports by us will be negative." He repeated his earlier suggestion that the names of Americans who, even at their own risk, traveled on belligerent ships or traded with belligerents, be made public. Finally, he said it could and should be made clear at Geneva and in Washington "that the United States cannot and will not join other nation or nations in sanctions but will go as far as laws allow to avoid giving material assistance to belligerents to further their conducting what we have already officially declared to be a war."

I was forced to wireless the President the next day, however, that in our opinion at the State Department, the Neutrality Act did not authorize such additions to the embargo list as he suggested, and additional legislation would be necessary. Such articles did not come under any commonly accepted definition of arms, ammunition, and implements of war, and, in the Senate debate prior to the passage of the Act, such commodities as wheat, corn, cotton, and other food products had been explicitly excluded.

As for publicity on names, I informed the President that both Secretary Roper and I thought it unwise. "I feel it would be wiser," I said, "to proceed slowly and to avoid incurring the criticism and the certain antagonism of traders and travelers when it is not yet evident that they are failing to support our program. It would seem to me that a cooperative method with our public at the moment might probably have more beneficial results."

The question of some form of action under the Kellogg Pact, which had come up before the outbreak of the war, rose again when Sir Samuel Hoare, on October 11, asked our opinion on this point. The President, whom I informed of the development, replied that such action seemed "somewhat farfetched after the horse is out of the stable."

I submitted for the President's approval a telegram to Ambassador Bingham in London, for Hoare, which Mr. Roosevelt termed "excellent" and which was dispatched October 14. I informed Hoare that we had made various statements calling attention to the obligations of signatories to the pact, but that "it would seem to me that the opportune moment for collective invocation of the pact or of any action posited on the pact . . . had gone by. I feel that, many factors being taken into consideration, especially the factor of public opinion in this country, it would be better not to talk of the possibility of holding a conference."

I added that, if other powers wanted to initiate through diplomatic channels a proposal for a concerted or simultaneous utterance by the signatories, our attitude would not be in opposition. I said I doubted the wisdom of any renewed initiative to come from this country, and suggested that four to six important governments in North and South America and Europe could more appropriately originate this step. I repeated my previous view, however, that projecting the Kellogg Pact into the situation might seriously interfere with the League program.

The question of action under the pact did not rise again.

Reports continued to come to us daily that the League still expected to approach our Government with regard to the League's program of sanctions. I cabled the American Consul at Geneva, Prentiss Gilbert, on October 17, to head off such reports by imparting all permissible information relative to our present and prospective course of action. I pointed out that, under my statement of October 10, our influence was being exerted "definitely to discourage any and all economic transactions between our nationals and those of the belligerent countries," and I added that "the American public is making satisfactory response." I said it must be clear to foreign Governments by this time "that this Government is acting upon its own initiative and proceeding separately and independently of all other Governments or peace organizations."

Upon receipt of this telegram in Geneva, Minister Wilson telephoned me to say that the League intended to transmit to nonmember states the recent League documents on the Italo-Ethiopian dispute, and to welcome any views or comments the nonmember Governments might wish to express. I said to Wilson that we could "go along on our course here, which nobody can take exception to at home or abroad, and prosecute it much more effectively if somebody from abroad is not pumping public inquiries into us."

The League's communication and documents did arrive on October 21. Since the question was now officially on our laps, we at the State Department took great pains with the reply we were asked to make. I showed the President a draft of the reply on his return to Washington on the 24th, and he said he was very much pleased with it. After some finishing touches during the course of a number of meetings in my office, it went forward to Geneva on the 26th.

We outlined to the League the various steps we had taken to prevent an outbreak of hostilities between Italy and Ethiopia and our subsequent actions under and parallel with the Neutrality Act. "The course thus pursued," I said, "in advance of action by other Governments, most of which are parties to one or more of the peace pacts to which I have referred, represents the independent and affirmative policy of the Government of the United States and indicates its purpose not to be drawn into the war and its desire not to contribute to a prolongation of the war."

I added that our Government "undertakes at all times not only to exercise its moral influence in favor of peace throughout the world, but to contribute in every practicable way within the limitations of our foreign policy, to that end. It views with sympathetic interest the individual or concerted efforts of other nations to preserve peace or to localize and shorten the duration of war."

On October 30 both the President and I issued statements, which had been prepared in the State Department, relative to trade with the belligerents. At a conference with the President the day before, to which Under Secretary Phillips accompanied me, it was decided that I should make one statement at my noon press conference, and the President would make another that same afternoon. Both statements reviewed the steps we had already taken to discourage trade with the belligerents, and appealed to the American people to forgo this commerce and its profits and to avoid prolonging the war. The President said the Government was keeping informed as to all shipments exported to both belligerents.

Despite our various appeals, there had been some increase in exports to Italy of materials that could be useful in war. Since League sanctions were to go into effect on November 18, we drafted a further appeal which specifically mentioned such commodities. Our thought was that the President could issue it before November 18 so that we could not be accused of having taken these items from the League's list. By agreement with the President, I issued the statement myself, on November 15.

"The American people," I said, "are entitled to know that there are certain commodities such as oil, copper, trucks, tractors, scrap iron, and scrap steel which are essential war materials, although not actually 'arms, ammunition, and implements of war,' and that, according to recent Government trade reports, a considerably increased amount of these is being exported for war purposes. This class of trade is directly contrary to the policy of this Government as announced in official statements of the President and the Secretary of State, as it is also contrary to the general spirit of the recent Neutrality Act."

The League's sanction list, which went into effect November 18, did not include the all-important item of oil. My statement of November 15 did.

For some time I had been evolving the theory of the moral embargo now in effect as to the belligerents and, of course, striking at Italy. I believed that a line should be drawn at normal exports and that exports to a belligerent above that line should be discouraged as strenuously as a Government could do so which had no authority by legislation to forbid them. In working out this theory, I went back to my experiences in the House of Representatives during the First World War, when I was working on various tax methods. There we had drawn a line between normal prewar profits and purely war profits, for purposes of taxation. When I undertook to prescribe a formula that Italy could not reasonably complain against, this tax procedure of separating the volume of war trade from the volume of normal prewar trade came to my mind.

Mussolini's Government had been watching our actions closely. On November 18 Ambassador Long in Rome reported that a noticeable change had come over the Italian Government's attitude toward us and that Mussolini was interpreting our policy of discouraging trade with either belligerent as placing us in the same category as the sanctionist countries. I thereupon cabled Long, for his guidance, an exposition of our policy. The steps we had taken, I said, could in no sense be considered in the nature of sanctions; they were "measures taken independently and on our own initiative in accordance with the spirit and intent of the neutrality resolution" which "clearly embraces essential and primary war materials."

I informed him we had no agreements whatever with other Governments relating to the Italo-Ethiopian War. "It was clearly the part of wisdom," I concluded, "to make the statement I made on Friday last rather than to await similar developments elsewhere and then be subjected to the charge of combining and cooperating with the program of other nations or groups of nations with the resultant reaction in this country."

On November 20 Italian Foreign Under Secretary Fulvio Suvich called in Long to protest against my November 15 statement as "a departure from the strict line of neutrality" and as placing us "in opposition to Italy and in line with the Governments who were applying sanctions."

Then, two days later, the Italian Ambassador in Washington, Augusto Rosso, came in to see me at his own request. I was on friendly terms with Rosso and liked his personality. He had married a girl whom I knew, whose family was from Tennessee, and he was popular in the capital. When I granted his request for the interview I did not know the purpose of his call. He began the interview by reading me a protest from his Government which accused us of violating the 1871 treaty between the United States and Italy guaranteeing to each of the two countries "complete freedom of commerce and navigation." Our embargo, his protest said, was "bound to assume the meaning of a 'sanction' and therefore the positive character of an unfriendly act."

The Ambassador had laid himself wide open to a dead-center attack. After first recalling to him the traditional friendship between our two countries, I said: "The people of this country today do not feel personally unfriendly toward the people of Italy, but they are vigorously and almost wildly against war and are at all hazards in favor of keeping out of the present war. If those participating in this war were double cousins and twin brothers of the American people, the people of this country would be just as violently and eternally against the war and in favor of peace."

I reminded the Ambassador that large groups of people in the United States had wanted primary materials out of which arms and munitions could be made included in the arms embargo.

"Our country," I said, "sent two million men to Europe to fight alongside Italy and other countries at an enormous cost to this Government and this country. We likewise loaned Italy much money at the time and afterwards. We later made almost a nominal settlement with the Italian Government at twenty-five cents on the dollar, all of which, with interest, is due and unpaid. I have been besought during past months to demand aggressively, if necessary, payment by the Italian Government of this indebtedness instead of its spending hundreds of millions in this Ethiopian conquest."

If the American people saw that abnormal quantities of essential war materials were being shipped to belligerents with the silent acquiescence of the proper Government officials, I said, there would probably be a storm of criticism and a loud demand for the immediate reconvening of Congress to take adequate steps. The result undoubtedly would be the swift passage of a drastic act dissolving every possible relationship with the belligerents.

"I'm surprised," I said, "that the Italian Government would make a complaint against this Government, in all the circumstances, in the severe language that it does. Did the Italian Government say anything, and if so what, when Germany prohibited business relations with the belligerents more sweepingly than did this Government?"

The Ambassador said he did not know whether Italy had made any representations to Germany.

"I've seen no published account of any complaint whatever," I commented. "It seems all the stranger to me, therefore, to read this rather harsh complaint against this Government. You and I know that the bitterest critics of the Administration and the most extreme isolationists don't question in the slightest the integrity of the neutrality policies of this Government as they are being carried out in accordance with the letter and spirit of the Neutrality Act. It's really astonishing to find that a Government can't be neutral without being attacked and a demand made to supply war materials to a belligerent under penalty of being charged with an unfriendly act."

Rosso interposed that the manner in which our Government was conducting its policy of neutrality discriminated against Italy.

"Under the law of neutrality in the past," I replied, "any belligerent controlling the high seas was usually at an advantage over its enemy with respect to obtaining goods from neutral countries. A poor belligerent without means of purchasing and paying for supplies from neutrals was at a disadvantage. Likewise, where one country has or can produce its military supplies and another is without such facilities and equipment, the latter suffers under the operation of the neutrality law. Under the policy this Government is now pursuing, neither Italy nor Ethiopia should be securing war materials, with the result that both countries are as nearly on a parity in this respect as it is possible for them to be. The charge of discrimination, therefore, does not apply."

I asked the Ambassador, as I did several times during the interview, why his Government did not sit down with others and work out the dispute in a peaceful manner.

He made a noncommittal reply and then tried to emphasize that the attitude of his Government was not fully understood in this country.

"Your Government might well have thought of all these and other unsatisfactory phases before getting into the war," I replied. "These trading incidents about which your Government complains are trivial compared with the real problems and deep concern which your war causes this Government. You must realize the awful repercussions that make their immediate appearance in remote parts of the world, but which are calculated to give this nation and perhaps others, including Italy, unimaginable troubles for a generation."

"I'm sure," said the Ambassador, "you have the Far East in mind."

I reminded Rosso that the President and I had pleaded and pleaded with Mussolini to keep out of the war. "But he ignored our plea," I said, "and now seems to expect us to furnish him with war supplies while he prosecutes the war ad libitum."

I mentioned to Rosso that during the past three years I had almost worn myself out physically in an effort to aid in world-economic rehabilitation so that Italy and other countries would have an adequate amount of international trade to afford contentment to their respective populations. "You can imagine the deep disappointment I feel," I told him, "at the effort to renew the practice that all nations have recently undertaken to abandon—that of military aggression by any and all countries at any and all times. Of course, if one country is to be allowed to violate this new policy of the pacific settlement of disputes, then every country may do so with consequences that one shudders to contemplate."

I pointed out to Rosso the fact that the League solemnly adjudged an aggressor, while the United States did not; the League sought to aid Ethiopia, which the United States did not; the League sought to embargo all imports from Italy, which the United States did not; and that this Government was pursuing its own separate course. The mere fact that there were some coincidental acts on the part of the League in pursuing sanctions and of the United States in frankly carrying out its policy of neutrality was no basis whatever, in the circumstances, for a charge against the United States of unneutrality and of unfriendliness. When I issued my statement of November 15 I did not know what the League might do to curb exports to Italy of oil and other prime war materials.

I asked Rosso why his Government did not invest $100,000,000 in Ethiopia instead of expending several hundred million dollars in its military conquest and bringing worry and the threat of danger to the balance of the world.

Rosso said Italy had been attempting for forty years to effect colonizations in Ethiopia, but without success.

Taking up his specific complaint that we had violated the 1871 treaty of commerce, I first commented that Italy had violated three or four treaties by invading Ethiopia. I then said I was satisfied that international law and all other law made it possible for either of our countries to remain neutral in case of war on the part of the other.

The interview throughout was on a level plane, despite my point-blank statements. The Ambassador did not attempt any aggressive replies and, on my part, I tried to give him the impression that our nation and most other peace-loving nations were greatly pained and hurt to find their traditional friends, the Italian people, involved in war despite the numerous treaties of peace to which their Government was a party, and despite the awful menace created by their war to the peace of the world.

I sent a memorandum on this conversation to the President, who was at Warm Springs, Georgia, and also telegraphed it to our representatives in Rome, London, Paris, Geneva, Berlin, and Addis Ababa. The President, on November 27, wrote me: "That memorandum of your conversation with the Italian Ambassador on November 22 is a classic. You did a splendid job of making our position clear and, at the same time, pointing out the very untenable position in which Italy has deliberately placed herself. In regard to the 1871 treaty, there is, of course, the undoubted fact that Italy, by a deliberate violation of the Kellogg-Briand Pact, made strict compliance with the old treaty impossible. Furthermore, I much doubt whether the language in the 1871 treaty was even intended to apply to a situation in which one nation was engaged in a war in which that nation was the aggressor."

Ambassador Rosso came back to me four days after the previous interview to know whether we opposed all shipments or just shipments in abnormal quantities. I told him we opposed "abnormal shipments for war purposes of strictly war materials." I then called his attention to press reports of Japanese movements in North China and said: "It's a pity that these tremendous complications had to come on, but they always seem to concur with complicated conditions in the Western World when nations can give little or no attention to other regions."

Rosso returned on December 2 to complain about reports from Geneva that our Government was more or less in agreement with the League. I characterized this as "All bosh!" and stressed the complete independence of our course, saying that our representatives in London, Paris, Rome, and Geneva had had this position of ours hammered in on them many times. I added: "Personally, officially, and selfishly, I have every possible motive to refrain from such agreements or collaboration for the reason that our separate course is satisfying the peace people and the bitterest critics of the Administration in and out of Washington, and is therefore avoiding terrific controversies such as those that grew out of the League of Nations situation in 1920."

Rosso asked me if we had taken up with Japan the situation in North China. I immediately jumped him and said that the Italo-Ethiopian conflict was the most serious single factor in precipitating the Japanese-Chinese crisis. I also pointed out that the Italo-Ethiopian War was responsible for "the complete slowing down and almost the stopping in its tracks of the trade agreements program for the restoration of international finance and trade to their normal volume." Continuation of the war, I said, meant a steadily increasing danger of its spreading and thus involving other nations, including the United States.

I felt it was ungracious for a Government voluntarily participating in a war that was the approximate cause of the Far Eastern crisis to turn around and complacently inquire of this Government what it was going to do regarding that crisis. Our Government had infinitely more ground to request the Italian Government to desist from war than the Italian Government had to call on this Government to deal with some of the natural consequences precipitated by that war.

Though oil remained on our moral embargo list of five primary war supplies, the League, influenced by Laval, one of the most sinister figures of my time, had not put it on the sanctions list. On November 29 the Secretary General of the League raised the question as to what effect the League's postponement of the issue would have on our position on the export of war materials, particularly oil.

I telegraphed Consul General Gilbert at Geneva on December 2 that "to predict as to the nature and duration of the present ban of our Government on the shipment of war materials would at once be heralded abroad as a promise to the League or to other nations," and that "this would violate our pledges to the people as to our independent course." Any talk of cooperation or of the slightest agreement or understanding, I added, was "not only false and misleading," but seriously embarrassed us in prosecuting our own neutrality program.

Two days before, British Ambassador Sir Ronald Lindsay came to my office to express his Government's appreciation of our policy toward the war. On December 2, in speaking to Lindsay, I referred to press reports that this Government felt itself "out on a limb" because of the League's postponement of oil sanctions, and also to expressions of regret from Britain that we had been "thus disappointed." I assured Sir Ronald that, while I greatly appreciated the kind consideration of our British friends in this respect, there was really no occasion for them to feel thus or to imagine that we were in the least disappointed or our plans in the slightest interfered with.

Then, on December 5, Sir Ronald came in to ask, on behalf of his Government, if our Government was in position to take effective action to prevent increased oil shipments to Italy in case the League imposed an oil embargo or the British themselves took steps to prevent increased shipments to Italy. The Ambassador pointed out that such measures meant the loss of the entire Italian oil market to the United States unless we were in position to take appropriate action.

I gave Sir Ronald a written reply to his query, in which I repeated that this Government "definitely opposes to the extent of its influence the shipment in abnormal quantities" of the war materials that I specified on November 15. I said, however, that "those interested must use their own good judgment" in attempting to forecast "the probable attitude and action of Congress toward the abnormal exportation of such essential war materials as those referred to, when it convenes."

I was then turning over in my mind the project of requesting such legislation from Congress. Thus far the embargo on essential war materials —other than arms, ammunition, and implements of war—was solely moral. If manufacturers or exporters chose to challenge it, we had no legal means to enforce it. The policy of preventing abnormal shipments of essential materials to belligerents, I felt, was good, and I would have liked to see it embodied in legislation.

Sir Ronald came back to my office on December 7 to discuss my reply to his inquiry. I had no more to tell him about our future course and attitude, but I did raise a question. The question was whether "fifty-two nations, with their own carefully defined program relating to the war situation and operating under the collective peace system originating after the World War, the very life of which depends on its success in this undertaking (sanctions), are going to hesitate or halt. Also, whether they were going to seek to make the impression that they would not even attempt to go further unless some important country outside the League first gave them some assurance as to what its course and policy might be during coming months with respect to the shipment, especially in abnormal quantities, of oil and certain other essential war materials."

In other words, let the League members cease their backing and filling and take a resolute course. We had gone as far as we could. Exports of oil from the United States to Italy were morally embargoed. The League members, particularly France at the instance of Laval, hesitated to include oil in their sanctions list for fear of additional trouble with Italy. But I did not relish their using the fact that the United States Government did not have legal authority to impose an oil embargo as an excuse for their not taking action.

Sir Ronald said he did not disagree at all with my views, nor was he disposed to make any further inquiry.

At about this time we began to get a series of reports that Britain and France were negotiating a settlement of the war. Early in December, Sir Samuel Hoare left London to confer with Laval in Paris, and on December 7 Ambassador Straus in Paris informed me that Laval told him he had concluded that oil sanctions must not be applied by the League since they would undoubtedly result in a general European war. Laval also said he intended to try to persuade the British to be more generous to Italy.

Then suddenly came the Hoare-Laval plan, presented to the Italian and Ethiopian Governments on December 11. It involved substantial cessions of territory by Ethiopia to Italy. When it was communicated to me I strongly felt it was at direct variance with the rights of Ethiopia and with the obligations of peaceful nations under agreement to refrain from aggression and to preserve the peace. I was definitely opposed to it. I had it analyzed by Wallace Murray, chief of the Near Eastern Division, who commented that it seemed "almost to place a premium on aggression, since the Italians would gain from the proposal more than they were offered by the Committee of Five [of the League] before hostilities broke out."

The storm of public protest aroused by the Hoare-Laval plan in England, France, and the other League countries killed it. Hoare was swept out of office, replaced by Anthony Eden, and Prime Minister Baldwin assured the House of Commons on December 19 that the proposals were "dead" and no attempt would be made to "resurrect them."

The war went on.

32: Japan Demands Parity

IN THE MIDST OF the Italo-Ethiopian War, the London Naval Conference, embracing the United States, Britain, Japan, France, and Italy, convened on December 9, 1935, and went on to the end of March, 1936. Thus a curious but unfortunate parallel pursued the Disarmament Conferences that took place during the 1930's, for the General Disarmament Conference at Geneva had also been conducted in the midst of a war, the Sino-Japanese conflict. With bitter battles raging and requiring increased armaments, it was almost impossible to engender a spirit favoring limitation, to say nothing of reduction, of armaments.

Few international meetings have .convened in unhappier circumstances than the London Conference. In addition to the fact of the Italo-Ethiopian War, the Geneva Disarmament Conference had failed and a race in land and air armaments was under way in Europe. Japan had denounced the Washington naval limitation agreement of 1921-1922, which therefore would come to an end on December 31, 1936. She openly was demanding naval parity with the United States and Great Britain. And the preliminary naval meetings held in London in November, 1934, described in a previous chapter (21), had ended in failure. Moreover, our relations with Japan offered little foundation on which to base an agreement.

Since her invasion of Manchuria in 1931 Japan had never for a moment been idle. She first concentrated on consolidating her hold in Manchuria and freezing out the commercial firms and individuals of other countries. But she never lost sight of a still greater objective—China proper. Her policy was one of piece-meal encroachment. Her project of creating an "independent" Manchuria worked so well that she sought to apply it to other portions of China. Throughout 1935 we received well founded reports that the Japanese were sponsoring an autonomous movement in North China designed to detach it from China and bring it under the control of Tokyo.

China, which once had a great, unified, and central Government, had over many generations deteriorated and degenerated politically into almost numberless regional groups, each purporting to conduct some sort of government of its own. This tremendous area, embracing one-fourth of the world's population, had steadily moved toward economic chaos and political anarchy, with deaths from starvation running into the millions. Many of the detached and discordant elements into which China was split, however, still made an effort to preserve law and order and to carry on commercial relations with other countries, especially with private traders.

After the shock of the 1931-1932 war with Japan, the slow but perceptible movement toward unity in China, which had started in the middle 1920's, commenced anew. The President and I were agreed that we should afford this movement any help we could. It was not our thought to create a unified China to war on Japan, but to help China unite for her own well-being and that of the Far East. China in chaos was a danger to peace in the Orient. China united and contented could be an element in bettering Pacific relations. We felt that any forward-looking countries such as the United States must be deeply concerned about the threatened state of anarchy in China, and anxious to collaborate with other nations and with any important groups in China to check the drift, restore law and order, and unify the scattered, independent elements throughout the country.

The record of Japan, however, made it clear she was pursuing exactly the opposite course. She was doing all she could to increase disunity in China and render the Chinese helpless to resist her fixed policy constantly to prey on the Chinese people, rob them of their substance, and plunder each community with impunity, seizing Chinese territory as she became prepared militarily to do so.

Japan's machinations in North China presented a serious problem. The five northern provinces contained the important cities of Peiping and Tientsin, a population estimated at 90,000,000, and about half the coal resources and cotton area of China in addition to some iron ore. The temptation was too much for Tokyo. Japanese spokesmen, of course, made it appear that the separatist movement in North China was entirely spontaneous and under Chinese auspices. 12/9/35

Three days before the London Naval Conference opened, I issued a statement in which I said: "There is going on in and with regard to North China a political struggle which is unusual in character and which may have far-reaching effects. . . . The fact stands out that an effort is being made—and is being resisted—to bring about a substantial change in the political status and condition of several of China's northern provinces."

I added that unusual developments in any part of China are "rightfully and necessarily of concern not only to the Government and people of China but to all of the many powers which have interests in China. For, in relations with China and in China, the treaty rights and the treaty obligations of the 'treaty powers' are in general identical. The United States is one of those powers."

Throughout the statement I did not mention Japan. It was unnecessary to do so. Tokyo, as well as the other capitals, knew of whom I was speaking when I concluded: "It seems to this Government most important in this period of world-wide political unrest and economic instability that governments and peoples keep faith in principles and pledges. In international relations there must be agreements and respect for agreements in order that there may be the confidence and stability and sense of security which are essential to orderly life and progress. . . . This Government adheres to the provisions of the treaties to which it is a party and continues to bespeak respect by all nations for the provisions of treaties solemnly entered into."

On the same day Great Britain took parallel action through a speech by Foreign Secretary Hoare to the House of Commons, expressing identical thoughts.

Unfortunately our Government was at this very time unsettling internal conditions in China through its silver purchase policy based on the Act of Congress of June 19, 1934. As the Treasury purchased silver in the world market at rising prices, China, which was on the silver standard, found herself in the throes of a disastrous flight of silver from China to the United States. While protesting formally and vigorously to the State Department against this policy, she tried to counter it with an export tax on silver varying with the world market price of silver. This was partly defeated by smuggling, conducted largely by Japanese, who thus turned the silver purchasing policy to Japanese advantage and Chinese disadvantage. In November, 1935, the Chinese Government was forced to go off the silver standard, call in all silver currency, and replace it with paper. It was not until May, 1936, when the Chinese Government reached an agreement with the Treasury for the purchase of gold with silver, that the confusion in China began to be resolved.

Although we could have few hopes of reaching a disarmament agreement with Japan, we sent a strong delegation to the London Naval Conference, composed of Norman Davis as chairman, Under Secretary of State William Phillips, and Admiral William H. Standley, Chief of Naval Operations. We still had to indicate to the world that we believed in the principle of disarmament, however obscure appeared the prospects for attaining it.

The London Conference was called by virtue of a provision in the London naval limitation treaty of 1930, which, like the Washington Treaty, was due to expire December 31, 1936. On November 26, 1935, I sent a memorandum to Norman Davis embracing comments and views of the Administration toward the conference. These were in the form of questions and answers arrived at during discussions between members of the delegation and representatives of the State and Navy Departments and approved by the President.

In the memorandum we stated that our controlling concept should continue to be parity with Britain and no parity with Japan or increase in Japan's treaty ratio (10–10–6 for battleships and 10–10–7 for cruisers). The principles and methods of the Washington and London treaties should be retained as a means of stabilizing the world naval situation. Our objective should be to reduce or at least not to increase naval armaments. We should strive for a five-power agreement (United States, Britain, Japan, France, and Italy). But we would accept a four-power or even a three-power treaty without Japan if it contained an "escape clause" permitting us to build warships beyond the treaty limits in the event of undue construction by any noncontracting power, meaning Japan.

We did not want to make any bilateral treaty with Britain, we pointed out, particularly in relation to the Far East, in order to influence her attitude toward naval limitation. Such a treaty would have impinged violently on the isolationist sentiment in the United States. Even without a treaty, we felt that the United States and the British Empire were likely, in their own interests and in those of the community of nations, to follow a parallel though independent policy, particularly in the Far East, for the maintenance of treaties and treaty rights, the observance of the Open Door policy in China, and opposition to expansion by means of military aggression.

I believed it should be the policy of our Government not to depart from the broad policies such as the Nine-Power Pact, to which all Governments having interests in the Pacific were parties. Bilateral treaties of alliance had become very unpopular in this country, partly by reason of the alliance between Britain and Japan which lasted for a number of years prior to its annulment under the Washington treaties, and partly because of the secret treaties entered into by a few of the Allies during

the First World War. The President and I agreed with the American
public that political alliances were seriously objectionable.

We were willing to accept the continuance of the provisions in the
Washington treaty forbidding the fortification of bases in the Far East,
provided these were incorporated in a naval limitation treaty preserving
the ratio with Japan. We wanted France and Italy included in a new
treaty and would assist in a mediatory capacity between them and Britain.
As for Germany and Russia, we thought they could be included in the
later stages of the conference and be of value in obtaining the adherence
of Japan to an agreement, but we felt that the question was one primarily
for the British; also, that before invitations should be extended to them,
a fairly close agreement was desirable among the United States, Britain,
France, and Italy.

Our memorandum pointed out to the delegation that basic differences
lay between the United States and Great Britain on the one hand and
Japan on the other, although the British, preoccupied with the European
situation, had, at times, taken a less strong stand than ourselves against
excessive Japanese claims. We felt that a common point of view with the
British should be sought, but at the same time giving no impression of a
common front against Japan. We believed that every effort should be
made to demonstrate to the Japanese the reasonableness and equity of
our position and to find such elements of agreement or approaches to an
agreement with them as might be possible.

We attended the 1935 London Conference and presented an elaborate
set of policies with virtually no hope of Japanese cooperation, but in order
to explore and ascertain just where Japan stood with respect to our proposals. At the very outset of the conference, our delegation held a satisfactory meeting with the British in which the British stated their opinion
that patience and tact with firmness were essential in dealing with the
Japanese but that no concessions should be made to the Japanese as to
the naval ratio. They said the French and Italians had already agreed not
to support the Japanese for a common upper naval limit.

On the following day, however, the Japanese formally presented their
demand for parity with Britain and the United States. They also stated
that this common upper limit should be fixed as low as possible and that
offensive arms should be reduced to the minimum. They carried this
thought into more detail in December 17 when they called, at their own
request, on Davis and our delegation. They said that, under the existing
ratios, the United States could take aggressive action against Japan and

there was no way to remove the sense of apprehension of the Japanese except by establishing parity between the two countries. Davis stated our counterview that parity would be tantamount to our surrender of the power to defend Alaska and the Philippines. He said that, in view of the war in Ethiopia, Japanese armies marching in China, and general world misgivings as to the immediate future, the time was not opportune to abandon the security given by the existing naval treaties. He suggested that Japan preserve the balance produced by the treaties and agree upon building programs for the next five years.

When the conference adjourned on December 20 for the Christmas holidays, little, if any progress, had been made. Two proposals had been discussed: the Japanese for a common upper limit and the British for a limitation of naval armaments by means of voluntary declarations by each power concerning future naval construction for a certain period of years. The British and ourselves could not agree to the Japanese proposal, and the Japanese would not agree to the British proposal. On that day Davis told us he saw no hopes for agreement.

On January 7, 1936, the day after the conference reconvened, I sent the President a note saying: "It is obvious that the Japanese have no intention of accepting any agreement in London which will not recognize their demand for parity with the American and British Navies and it seems perfectly clear to me that there is very little use in continuing the discussions too long in London in the face of this apparently fixed attitude of the Japanese Government."

With the note I submitted to the President a draft telegram to our delegation in London, which he approved. We informed the delegation of our conviction that Japan would not agree to a treaty that did not recognize her demand for a common upper limit. Therefore it seemed advisable to have as early as possible a clear-cut decision on whether the Japanese would be willing to reach an agreement on any phase of the naval situation. I expressed my belief that the conversations should not be permitted to drag on and on because this would confuse the public mind and also give the Japanese an opportunity to use the news from London in Japan to justify the aims of the militarist element there and intensify antagonism toward the United States. I requested Davis to confer toward this end with Anthony Eden, who had replaced Hoare as chairman of the conference, as British Foreign Secretary, and chairman of the British delegation.

As the conference reopened, the Japanese delegation refused to discuss any naval matter whatsoever until 'their demand for parity had been met. The British delegation thereupon suggested to us a nonaggression pact for the Far East which might make it possible for the Japanese to continue the status quo of the Washington and London treaties. But there was no prospect whatever that the Japanese Admiralty would agree to anything but parity. We told the British we could not consider such a pact. The British then suggested a consultative pact. They admitted it would really be meaningless but would help save the pride of the Japanese. We replied that it would be difficult to explain to our Senate why we had signed a treaty that had so little meaning and that it would also raise questions involving China, the Dutch East Indies, and Russia, besides all other powers interested in the Far East.

Actually, the existing accords relating to the Far East, such as the Nine-Power and Four-Power treaties signed in 1922, covered that area sufficiently, if Japan observed them, which she did not. What prospect was there that Japan would honor a new political treaty any more than the present ones?

I telegraphed Davis, however, and, after calling attention to the consultation and cooperation clauses of the Nine-Power Treaty, I suggested that he should not definitely object to the British proposals lest the British delegation feel we were blocking efforts that might offer promise.

Meantime Davis had received my long telegram of January 7 and presented its ideas to Eden, who said they were sound. Eden agreed to bring the conference to a head, one way or the other. On January 15 the question of parity for Japan was formally raised, the powers other than Japan voted against it, and she withdrew from the conference. By agreement with the other powers, including the United States, she left an observer at the conference for the remainder of the session.

With Japan out of the conference, discussions limped along for two more months. On January 18 I cabled Davis my impression that "the withdrawal of the Japanese has caused our interest in the conference to become considerably less." I said I believed that "the primary interests concerned from now on will be European and the questions discussed will be of primary importance to Great Britain and the continental nations, particularly the former. . . . We should not take a leading part in the activities of the conference, but should rather leave the initiative to other powers and continue as a friendly and responsive participant without taking the lead.

"You are fully aware, I am sure, of the sentiment now prevailing in this country against becoming involved in any European affairs. Therefore, I think it would be well not to take any steps which might be construed as indicating an unwarranted initiative in European questions or a desire or willingness on the part of our Government to do so."

The discussions now centered on whether limits were to be placed on the size of ships, whether battleships should have 16- or 14-inch guns (we favored the former, the British the latter), and whether the British should have more cruisers. The President suggested that any increase in British criusers should be compensated for by reduction of tonnage in other categories of ships so that the over-all tonnage in existing treaties could be retained.

Mr. Roosevelt took a lively interest in the progress of the conference. Virtually from infancy he had had wide experience with ships of all kinds. Even as a boy he had been particularly attracted to naval vessels passing in the vicinity of the New England shore. When he came to Washington as Assistant Secretary of the Navy in Wilson's Administration, he reveled in naval problems, tactics, facts, and administration. He left that office a deep student of all important naval affairs and with an affection for the Navy.

When he became President, he probably knew more about the Navy than any of his predecessors. Throughout his Administration I found him giving preferential attention to every question arising in regard to the Navy. He himself made most of the more important decisions with respect to naval affairs. During the London Naval Conference the President exhibited a rare knowledge of all the technical phases. He was well equipped to discuss the merits of the most complex developments and to offer suggestions. The oldest, most experienced admirals had great respect for his far-reaching knowledge of their profession.

The President was devoted to his collection of ship models. Frequently, when I went to his office, I would see a new one riding anchor on a corner of his desk. On one of our conference trips to South America, Mrs. Hull bought, on the shores of Lake Titicaca high up in the Andes, a balsa-wood model of the type of sailing craft used on the lake, and gave it to the President on our return to Washington. It cost only fifty cents but was an unusual type of ship. A short time later, during a reception at the White House, the President said to Mrs. Hull: "If you want to see something interesting, go upstairs and look at the glass case just outside the door of my room." She did so and there saw her gift beautifully mounted.

In the telegrams I sent the President and in the verbal discussions we had on the London Naval Conference, the words "quantitative" and "qualitative" in connection with limitation of naval armaments were used scores of times, the former meaning limitation by total tonnage and the latter meaning limitation by the size of specific types of ships and guns. One day the President exploded. "Quantitative, qualitative, quantitative, qualitative!" he exclaimed. "I get sick and tired of hearing these words. Can't we find something to take their place?" But we never did.

The lesser naval powers, France and Italy, complicated the conference with their own issues. France wanted to tie a naval limitations agreement in with a European political accord. We could not agree. Italy stated she would not sign because of the sanctions imposed upon her during the war with Ethiopia, which was then approaching its climax.

The question as to whether Germany should become a signatory to the treaty was also a delicate one. On June 18, 1935, Great Britain and Germany had concluded an agreement fixing the German Navy at 35 per cent of the Navy of the British Empire. Since this was three times the naval strength permitted Germany under the Treaty of Versailles, France and Italy protested strongly. We, on our side, remained noncommittal because the Anglo-German agreement was essentially a European one and because we were not signatories to the Treaty of Versailles. When Britain proposed that Germany be brought into the London Naval Conference, France objected unless such entrance were coupled to an accord with Germany on the Rhineland and with Britain on mutual assistance.

The President felt that a better solution could be arrived at if Britain negotiated a separate accord with Germany whereby the latter could accept the conclusions of the London Conference. On February 29, 1936, I sent Norman Davis a telegram into which the President wrote this paragraph in longhand: "As far as Germany is concerned, an American-Anglo-German Treaty seems inadvisable. I suggest the British be informed that in view of the essentially European aspects of the German Navy and the fact that the German Navy even under the proposed Treaty would not exceed more than approximately a third of the total British naval force, the United States would greatly prefer a bilateral British-German arrangement, if based essentially on their ratios as at present agreed on."

Hitler summarily settled the discussion concerning the Rhineland by occupying that region with German troops on March 7, 1936, in violation of the Treaty of Versailles and the Locarno Pact. At that moment the London Conference was drafting the text of the final agreement. The invasion of the Rhineland was a European development in which we were not involved, and no action was called for in Washington. But it was obvious that it was another seven-league step toward war. I cabled Davis on March 9, asking for his comment in view of the new European situation created and in view of the possibility of rumors or news stories that might connect the United States with developments there. I added: "In any event, we are unquestionably entering into a period of increasing tenseness in European affairs."

The President had made another suggestion on February 28 which he sent to the Department in a memorandum and which we cabled to Davis. This suggestion crystallized in a section of the London Treaty that became one of the most important developments of the conference. "What would you think," said the President, "of sending a telegram to Davis asking him to try to get even a gentlemen's agreement from Great Britain, France, Italy (and through England from Germany) whereby each nation would agree to notify the other of every decision to lay down naval vessels of any size over one hundred tons? If such a gentlemen's agreement could be obtained, these four or five powers could then jointly or severally invite Japan to do the same thing?"

By March 20 we had submitted the final draft of the treaty to the President. Because of Japan's withdrawal there was no agreement on over-all naval tonnage. Battleships were left at an upper limit of 35,000 tons each, but guns on future battleships were to be 14 inches instead of 16. The age limit for battleships was increased by six years, thus prolonging their life and effecting substantial savings in their replacement. Warships in between the categories of heavy cruisers and battleships were not to be built. This was designed to prevent the development of new types of "pocket battleships." The size of aircraft carriers was reduced from 27,000 to 23,000 tons, and the maximum size of submarines fixed at 2,000 tons. A six-year naval holiday for heavy cruisers was agreed upon.

Part III of the treaty provided for an exchange of information among the signatories to the treaty concerning their annual programs of construction of capital ships, aircraft carriers, light surface vessels, and submarines. No ship in these categories could be laid down until four months after the date of the announcement. This was a new provision since nothing of this nature was contained in either the Washington Treaty of 1922 or the London Treaty of 1930. It was important in that it brought the navies of the United States, Britain, and France more closely together in knowledge of one another's plans, in cooperation and confidence. The former treaties merely required their signatories to exchange information after a ship had been laid down and also after it was completed. Now sufficient advance notice was to be given to enable the other signatories to take similar action, if they wished.

The treaty contained safeguarding clauses, one of which permitted the signatories to exceed the limits imposed by the treaty if any non-signatory nation were found or believed to be exceeding them. This had Japan in mind, and had to be invoked two years later.

The President approved the treaty but made a suggestion, which we passed on to Davis on March 20, that Davis should state "that the American Government and delegates are deeply disappointed that the new treaty does not provide for quantitative [over-all tonnage] limitation. While qualitative [as to specific types of individual ships] limitations have their value, nevertheless this Government has been working for many years towards both phases of reduction and limitation of naval armament. The President also suggests that you say we have no intention of abandoning our efforts in both directions."

On March 23 I cabled Davis the President's thought that Davis and Admiral Standley (Phillips had returned to Washington in January) should sign a letter of thanks to Eden, head of the British delegation, "expressing pleasure and satisfaction over their association during the conference and incidentally to mention the fact that, while no quantitative limitations are provided in the new treaty similar to the provisions in former naval treaties, this Government desires to avoid competition with the British in naval construction; that the British Empire and the United States accept as a well recognized and established principle fleet parity; that conditions and circumstances are such that the two Governments should continue on the principle of parity; and that adherence thereto would contribute to friendly relations of the two Governments and to world peace." The British could reply in the same strain.

This had no sooner been done than the news leaked out, and various articles were published about a "secret understanding" on cooperation between the British and American Navies. Minister Wilson in Geneva informed me that the "leak" originated from the Japanese observer at the conference who was kept informed, in confidence, by the British. We accordingly arranged for the release of both letters.

The London Naval Treaty of 1936, even though it did not set upper limits of total naval construction, could still have been of great value if

Japan had seen fit to adhere to it. But the position of Japan, as we early foresaw, was quickly made clear. In May, 1936, Japan notified the British Government that she would not sign the treaty. After December 31, 1936, when the London 1930 and the Washington treaties expired, Japan would be free to build whatever number and size of warships she wanted. By walking out of the London Conference she walked out of the status quo in the Pacific which had kept the major powers, at least in a naval sense, in comparative tranquillity since 1922. Beginning on January 1, 1937, the powers would also be free to fortify their Far Eastern possessions such as the Philippines and Hong Kong, if they wished. The end of the special regime in the Pacific, set up as an aftermath of the First World War, was now at hand, and was to hasten the coming of the Second World War.

When Norman Davis came back from London in April, 1936, he and I had a long talk on the world situation. We went over the major developments since I entered the State Department. Before us lay a tremendous problem and responsibility which our Government was obliged to meet. It involved the accurate determination of when, in the light of chaotic conditions in many areas of the globe, this nation should abandon the undertaking to preserve peace through disarmament and proceed rapidly to arm sufficiently to resist the plainly visible movements toward military conquest by Germany, Japan, and Italy.

For over a decade the tendency of the world in general had been toward disarmament. But in the last several years we had seen acts and utterances by Japan, Germany, and Italy definitely revealing intentions of aggression. We saw these countries repudiate all disarmament undertakings and every written obligation to keep the peace. At the same time we saw wild, runaway races in armaments with these aggressor nations as the chief offenders, accompanied by loud, brazen threats of conquest.

As Norman Davis and I talked over these developments, it became clearly manifest that peace on the basis of disarmament was next to impossible. The question that then presented itself was whether and to what extent there could be suitable cooperation by the law-abiding nations to curb the rapidly developing plans of military aggression. But our Government, we knew, was obliged virtually to ignore this possible method of preserving the peace for the patent reason that public opinion here was, in majority, militantly and almost violently against our entering any such joint undertakings.

The only alternative remaining was for the United States, while continuing to preach and practice peace, and urging like policies on all nations, especially the avowed aggressors, to take immediate notice of the aggressors' movements and arm our nation without delay to the extent adequate for our security.

At the beginning of 1935 I had already communicated to the President my fervent belief that we should hasten construction of a larger Navy, particularly because of the situation in the Far East. On January 22, 1935, I sent him a memorandum enclosing a copy of an excellent dispatch from Ambassador Grew in Tokyo giving a comprehensive view of the outlook in the Orient, and a copy of a memorandum prepared in the State Department on the Far East. "The views expressed by Mr. Grew," I said, "with regard to the present situation and the importance of American naval preparedness are absolutely in accord with views which have been expressed to me from time to time by my assistants who are concerned with those questions here in the Department. With their deductions and conclusions and those of Mr. Grew, I am absolutely in accord."

One paragraph of the Department memorandum read: "We should speed our efforts toward possessing a navy so strong that no other country will think seriously of attacking us; and we should let it be clearly seen that, while not wanting to fight and having no reason for attacking any other country, the people of this country not only are *not* 'too proud to fight' but, *given certain situations, would be too proud not to fight.*"

I wrote the President that "at some time in the near future I should like to discuss with you ways and means for bringing these matters discreetly and in confidence to the attention of certain Members of the Congress." I wrote Grew that I expected to make careful use of his dispatch, on which I congratulated him, "in seeing that leaders of the Administration have a sound understanding of the situation in Japan and of the need of American naval preparedness."

After my talk with Norman Davis, I seldom lost an opportunity to urge substantial rearmament upon the President and appropriate members of the Cabinet. I said to them that, with the other nations of the world furiously rearming, with large areas of the earth already in the throes of war, the United States should keep pace in promoting her national defense. I also knew that, during serious periods of international relations, the diplomatic establishment of our Government was no stronger than the military forces behind it. Decisions by aggressor or potentially aggressor governments on diplomatic matters were determined by the size and strength of the armed forces of the peaceful nations on whom they had designs or who might attempt to thwart them.

When I came to the State Department I thought for a time, when talking to Axis diplomats, that they were looking me in the eye; but I soon discovered that they were looking over my shoulder at our armed forces and appraising their strength. Here, I came to feel, was the controlling factor in their acts and utterances toward us.

In 1936 I began to urge on numerous members of the Government and leading individuals the immediate need to construct three new battleships and two aircraft carriers, giving as reasons the serious dangers steadily increasing abroad. Some Cabinet members thought it strange that the Secretary of State should be recommending the building up of the Navy. A mutual friend of the President and me, Bernard Baruch, told me one day that the President expressed surprise that I should be "plugging" for a bigger Navy.

In 1935 I had begun to plan how to build up a stock-pile of tin, a strategic material not produced in large quantities in the United States, which would be essential to the War and Navy Departments in the event of war. Through Dr. Herbert Feis, Economic Adviser of the Department, who elaborated the plan, I communicated with British Ambassador Sir Ronald Lindsay and laid the project before him. Basically it was that the British Government should procure and deliver to our Government a given quantity of tin, the value of which would be credited to Britain's indebtedness to this Government.

After Sir Ronald had digested the plan, he came in to see me on June 6, 1935, and said he was forwarding the suggestion to London. I informed him that certain persons in this country interested in high tariffs on commodities such as manganese, quicksilver, nickel, and tin not produced to any large extent here had the habit of predicating their demands for high tariffs on the necessity for building up supplies of these commodities for emergency or war purposes. I reminded the Ambassador that a House of Representatives Committee had recently conducted an investigation with respect to tin. I said that the idea of bringing the subject of tin to the attention of the British Government had come into the minds of Dr. Feis and myself, and the President had approved my recommendation that it be taken up with Britain.

Sir Ronald was most gloomy. He said the British people considered the debts done with, and that the British Government would have difficulty getting appropriations with which to pay for the tin to be delivered to us.

I reminded the Ambassador that the chief supply of tin in the world was under the control of British capital. Some little payment in kind, such as we proposed, would be a revival of and in harmony with the spirit behind the token payments that his Government had been cheerfully making until the unfortunate results of the Hiram Johnson Act were created. This move would have a pleasing effect on the state of mind of our people toward the British Government.

But Sir Ronald did not think the proposal would be received favorably even by the British Foreign Office. He was right. The answer from London was a complete refusal. It was not until four years later, three months before the outbreak of the European War, that we were able to negotiate an agreement with Britain whereby, through exchanging cotton for rubber and tin, we began to create reserves of strategic materials.

In addition to these recommendations within the Administration, I made numerous references in public addresses to the need for adequate self-defense. On June 15, 1936, speaking at Brown University, I said: "It is true that war is still a part of our life and that circumstances may arise under which we may have to fight. So long as that remains true, common sense and prudence require each nation to be ready to meet its responsibilities." On September 15, 1936, I said in an address before the Good Neighbor League, in New York City: "Of late we have increased our defense forces substantially. This has appeared essential in the face of the universal increase of armaments elsewhere and the disturbed conditions to which I have alluded. We would not serve the cause of peace by living in the world today without adequate powers of self-defense. We must be sure that, in our desire for peace, we will not appear to any other country weak and unable to resist the imposition of force or to protect our just rights."

But each statement I made advocating rearmament, and each move the Administration took in that direction, brought forth the never failing opposition of the isolationists, who had powerful segments of public opinion behind them. Honest, well-meaning pacifists were still clinging to the idea of peace by disarmament, by the Kellogg Pact, and by peace organizations. One group among them always opposed heavy expenditures for armaments during peacetime on the theory that such a policy was dangerous to our peace. They all promptly set up a loud cry of warmongering and accused us of deep-laid plans to drag this nation into foreign wars.

In 1937 I followed up the recommendations for rearmament which I had been making orally to the President and several members of the

Cabinet, by sending to the President, on December 8, a suggested draft for a portion of a message to Congress, possibly his forthcoming message in January, 1938. I suggested that he say:

"In a world of tension and disorder, in a world where stable civilization is threatened, it becomes the responsibility of each nation which strives for peace to be strong enough to assure the observance, in so far as its legitimate interests are concerned, of those fundamental principles of peaceful solution of conflicts which constitute the only possible basis for an orderly existence. Fearless in spirit, unafraid, resolute in our determination to respect the rights of others, and to command respect for our own, we must keep ourselves adequately strong in the matter of self-defense."

I concluded by suggesting that he make this specific recommendation: "Accordingly, in order that our national defense may be adequate and be able to prevent encroachment or attack by any forces which might seek to jeopardize our security and right to live in peace, I recommend that Congress enact the necessary legislation to provide for the laying down of three capital ships and two aircraft carriers of modern type."

The President adopted the spirit of my suggestions for his message to Congress of January 28, 1938, using his own language. However, he cut my proposal of three battleships to two and omitted the aircraft carriers.

33: "Neutrality" Intensifies

AS THE LONDON NAVAL CONFERENCE approached its end and the Italo-Ethiopian War neared its climax, the Neutrality Act of 1935 was running out its six months' course. Its expiration on February 29, 1936, required new legislation in the light of the lessons its application had taught us. The President and I had reluctantly agreed to what we considered undesirable features of this Neutrality Act such as the mandatory provision requiring him to impose the arms embargo against all belligerents, aggressor and victim alike. The Act was a temporary measure and we hoped we could have it modified at the next session of Congress.

The Act had been in effect just one month when we at the State Department began to study means of improving it. It was soon obvious that it could not simply expire and not be replaced by new legislation. For one thing, the Italo-Ethiopian War would probably still be raging on February 29, 1936. Another reason was that public opinion, more and more alarmed by warlike developments in Europe and Asia, would insist on neutrality legislation as a means, however fallacious, of keeping us out of war. Furthermore, legislation necessary to control the arms traffic had been incorporated in the Neutrality Act and had to be preserved. In 1934 and early in 1935, I hoped that neutrality legislation would not be passed and that the hands of the Executive would not be tied. Toward the end of 1935, with a war being fought in East Africa and threatening to extend to Europe, with Japan stirring up trouble in China, and with large seg-ments of public opinion over here indulging in isolationist hysteria, such a hope was no longer possible.

On October 1, 1935, I held a meeting in my office with Department officials and Charles Warren, former Assistant Attorney General, who had prepared a memorandum on neutrality for us in 1934. Shortly thereafter we began working on the draft of a neutrality bill for consideration by Congress at its next session, beginning January 3, 1936.

My associates and I decided to make an effort to induce Congress to incorporate our moral embargo in the new Neutrality Act and thereby give it legal standing. The moral embargo had been reasonably successful. While exports to Italy of materials that could be used in making weapons and munitions had sharply augmented, the increase undoubtedly would have been many times greater had it not been for the moral pressure exerted by the Administration and by public opinion. A moral embargo is effective only as to persons who are moral. It could not be expected to touch those who placed personal profit above considerations of prolonging a war, aiding an aggressor or adding to the toll of killed and wounded; although over a long period even such persons might be affected by mounting public scorn and resentment.

To make such an embargo completely effective, legislation was necessary. I wanted to express in legal terms the idea of abnormal exports we had applied in my public statements in October and November. Using a certain period of prewar years as a normal level, let exports up to those levels continue to the belligerents, but let exports above such levels be embargoed. Normal exports could continue because they had been needed and used by the belligerents during peacetime years. Abnormal exports obviously would be going into the war machine. No belligerent could complain against such treatment, as he might complain if all exports, normal exports included, were embargoed. No belligerent could argue that we were obliged to furnish all the materials he needed for his military manufactures. No commercial treaty would be violated if normal exports continued.

On December 28, 1935, we cabled our diplomatic representatives in London, Paris, Berlin, Rome, and Bern for their comments on whether to place an embargo on all commodities to belligerents or on essential war materials, or on such materials in excess of normal trade. Ambassador Long in Rome favored the last choice. Ambassador Straus in Paris advocated prohibiting credits only. London, Berlin, and Bern emphasized the desirability of as much Executive discretion as possible.

There was no longer too much to be hoped for from Congress on Executive discretion. The opinion of the public and of a large portion of Congress was running strongly to the view that, to permit the President to apply the Act as to one, all or none of the belligerents would push the nation into war. Many persons, duly impressed by the vigorous actions Mr. Roosevelt had taken in domestic affairs, feared lest actions of equal vigor taken in the foreign field might bring us trouble. Such opinion failed to appreciate that any President, through his function of conducting foreign relations and as Commander-in-Chief of our armed forces, could always propel the country into war if he so desired. Any President could produce war by hostile actions in the diplomatic field or by creating incidents through the deployment of military or naval units. And war could be started by another nation as well as by ourselves.

The existing Act provided that the President must apply the arms embargo "upon the outbreak or during the progress of war between or among two or more foreign states." The Senate seemed determined to retain this provision. A small measure of discretion was contained in this phraseology since the President need not apply the Act at the outbreak of the war but could do so at any time during its progress, and we decided it was useless to try to go further.

The President and I met at the White House on December 31, 1935, with Senator Pittman, chairman of the Senate Foreign Relations Committee; Representative McReynolds, chairman of the House Foreign Affairs Committee; Representative John O'Connor, chairman of the House Rules Committee, and Assistant Secretary of State R. Walton Moore to discuss the neutrality bill and the President's message to Congress. We agreed on the various items in the bill. On January 2, 1936, I met again with Pittman and McReynolds to go over details.

The following day Pittman and McReynolds introduced identical neutrality bills in the Senate and House. On that day the President delivered his message to Congress and strikingly pointed out the many dangers to peace rising abroad. Referring to his inaugural address which contained only one paragraph on foreign affairs, he said that were he to deliver a similar address now he would be compelled to devote the greater part of it to world affairs.

"Since the summer of that same year of 1933," he said, "the temper and the purposes of the rulers of many of the great populations in Europe and in Asia have not pointed the way either to peace or to good will among men. Not only have peace and good will among men grown more remote in those areas of the earth during this period, but a point has been reached where the people of the Americas must take cognizance of growing ill will, of marked trends toward aggression, of increasing armaments, of shortened tempers—a situation which has in it many of the elements that lead to the tragedy of general war."

On the question of neutrality, he said: "As a consistent part of a clear policy, the United States is following a twofold neutrality toward any and all nations which engage in wars not of immediate concern to the Americas: First, we decline to encourage the prosecution of war by permitting belligerents to obtain arms, ammunition, or implements of war from the United States; second, we seek to discourage the use by belligerent nations of any and all American products calculated to facilitate the prosecution of a war in quantities over and above our normal exports to them in time of peace." He expressed the hope that these objectives would be carried forward by cooperation between Congress and the President.

The Pittman-McReynolds Bill was based on the draft prepared in the State Department. It made no attempt to increase the President's discretion in applying the arms embargo. It restricted the export of essential war materials to normal levels, and gave the President discretion to determine when this should be applied, what items to include (food, medical supplies, and clothing were specifically excluded) and on what period to base the estimate of peacetime exports. The bill also, for the first time, prohibited loans and credits to belligerents, although the President could except commercial credits for customary current business. It also forbade American vessels to carry arms to belligerents.

At a press conference on January 3, 1936, I said that, as "we faced the probability of war abroad," we were striving to perfect a much broader set of policies than the one based on the view that munitions people got us into the last war, they might get us into another, and therefore we should embargo the export of munitions. I said we were waiving, so far as the Government was concerned, "a standing policy of one hundred and forty years relating to the right of our nationals to trade directly with the belligerents, except as to contraband." I termed this "one of the biggest developments in foreign policy within some generations."

I gave public warning, however, that even embargoing all trade with the belligerents would not necessarily keep us out of war. Trade with other neutrals, particularly in a war involving a naval power, often gave rise to as many dangerous incidents as trade with the belligerents themselves. There were other possibilities of controversy over our shipping and the arrest of Americans on the high seas. Above all, I added, we still had an interest in seeing as early a peace as possible, because "the longer a war lasts, the more danger there is of our being drawn into it and the more danger there is it will spread and correspondingly increase the danger of our being drawn in."

The Senate Foreign Relations Committee began its hearings on January 10, and I appeared before it six times in the course of two weeks. I outlined the changes in neutral rights brought about by the First World War and said that nearly all the ordinary rules of neutrality and neutral rights had been more or less set aside so that, when the war ended, there

was "virtual chaos so far as neutral rights were concerned." I added that
the collective system established for the maintenance of peace under the
League of Nations "did not undertake to preserve the old conception of
neutrality and neutral rights" and thus left this question "primarily to
the countries not members of the collective system" such as the United
States.

While, under neutrality legislation, we were waiving for the time
being certain neutral rights under international law, nevertheless we did
not renounce our right to appeal to international law when necessary. On
the other hand, I told the committee I thought "our nationals should not
go into danger zones and expect our Government to follow them with a
battleship to protect them while they are selling a few dollars' worth of
war materials. They should subordinate to a reasonable extent the privilege of demanding the protection of the Government to the far greater
undertaking by the Government to promote the safety of the American
people."

I made as strong an argument as I possibly could for the provision
prohibiting abnormal trade with the belligerents. If the arms-embargo
legislation of the 1935 Neutrality Act was wise, I said, it was "equally
necessary and equally sound as good policy, with a view of keeping the
nation out of war, to extend it to the materials which are indispensable to
the prosecution of the war." Otherwise, I said, "we would shut the front
door to belligerents as to arms, munitions, and implements of war and
then leave open not only the back door but the whole back end of the
house" for materials to be exported to a belligerent and manufactured
into arms and munitions. I pleaded for Presidential discretion in the application of restrictions on exports of essential war materials because "what
would be vital in the case of some wars would not be material in the case
of other wars."

As we fully expected, bitter opposition rose to the Pittman-Mc-
Reynolds Bill right from the moment of its introduction. Senators Nye and
Clark, among the isolationist leaders in the Senate, introduced their own
bill which, in essence, gave the President less discretion in administering
neutrality. Violent attacks were made daily against the provision prohibiting the abnormal export of products to a belligerent. One group
opposed it on the grounds that if the President had the power to select
the essential commodities that might be embargoed, he might attempt to
coordinate these with a League of Nations sanctions list against an
aggressor and thus lead the nation into war. Another group, composed

of some Italo-Americans, opposed it because they knew it would hurt Mussolini.

In the Senate Foreign Relations Committee I met deadly opposition at every turn from Hiram Johnson and Borah. It took a world of patience to deal with Johnson, an inveterate isolationist. The fight within the committee turned out to be a sleeveless controversy, with the certainty from the beginning that the opposition would win, owing to the strong isolationist sentiment in the country. During one of the hearings Johnson intimated that I was changing my policy on neutrality.

"I'm a little bit like the lawyer before the Supreme Court," I replied. "A Justice kept rapping him down. Finally he made a statement, and the Justice said: 'Mr. Jones, that is not the law.' The lawyer replied: 'It was the law until your Honor spoke.' "

If isolationist sentiment was strong prior to the enactment of the 1935 Neutrality Act, it was even stronger now. Large blocs of people were disillusioned by the failure of the League to stop Japanese aggression in China, to prevent the Italo-Ethiopian War, to promote disarmament and to curb Nazi Germany. They were disappointed over what they considered the hemming and hawing policy of Britain and France. They were appalled by the thought that Europe might be nearing another holocaust of 1914-1918.

Previously many of the peace advocates and pacifist groups believed in the League and were among the staunchest supporters of our policy of international cooperation. Now they turned away from the League and at the same time from international cooperation. They took refuge in the isolationist policies of spokesmen such as Borah, Nye, Clark, and Johnson, demanded mandatory legislation to keep us out of the neighborhood of war, and resisted the slightest effort toward cooperation with other nations for safeguarding peace. Isolationists came from both political parties.

After three or four weeks of hearings, it was obvious that our fight was lost. Although the House Committee reported out the Pittman-McReynolds Bill on January 28, it was never reported from the Senate Committee. The greatest obstacle was the question of embargoing abnormal exports of essential war materials. Resolutions were now introduced in the House and Senate extending the existing Act of August 31, 1935, until May 1, 1937. Three amendments, however, were introduced and adopted, forbidding loans and credits to belligerents, making mandatory the existing discretionary power of the President to extend the arms embargo to additional states becoming involved in a war, and exempting from the application of the Act any American Republic at war with a non-American nation, provided that Republic were not cooperating with a non-American nation in the war.

This last provision was a gesture toward the Monroe Doctrine and, as such, it helped the bill through Congress. But it had sweeping implications adverse to the basic doctrine I had supported from 1933 on—that we should do nothing to help an aggressor and everything to impede him. Under this provision an American Republic could conceivably be the aggressor in a war with a non-American state, and we would nevertheless provide arms to the aggressor and not to the victim. Also, if the League members applied military sanctions to an aggressor, in which its Latin American members took part, we would forbid the export of arms to such Latin American nations aiding other nations in a war against the aggressor.

When the question of the Latin American Republics first rose in January, 1936, the President wrote out this penciled memorandum of the provision he thought should go in the bill: "Nothing in this Act shall be construed in any way as an abandonment of the historic position of the United States in the Monroe Doctrine that no further acquisition or domination of American territory shall be effected by any non-American nation." He then crossed out the phrase "historic position of the United States in" and substituted "original purpose of." Congress desired, however, to make the exception more specific.

On February 12 I said at a press conference that the most feasible step to take at present was to support the judgment of the Senate in desiring to continue the August 31, 1935, Act because the question of peace and neutrality still required much study and clarification, and we would continue such investigation. Norman Davis having written me from London on February 3, 1936, urging that the President be given the power to distinguish between "right and wrong" so that the weight of our influence might be used to prevent wars of aggression, I wrote him on February 13 that "nothing of any consequence is possible at this time in the development of neutrality policy. The subject is so complicated that I find numerous persons of real ability changing their minds from time to time as they study the problem." I said also: "There are many groups in the country which rise up and oppose almost any proposal, upon one ground or theory, or imaginary reason or another. . . . It is problematical as to when further peace or neutrality steps will be possible."

The House adopted the new bill on February 17 and the Senate on February 18. On February 24 I recommended, in a letter to the Director of the Budget, that the President sign it. Two days later I sent the President a draft of the new arms-embargo proclamation. On February 28, at my request, Assistant Secretary Moore sent him the draft of a statement he might issue on signing the neutrality resolution. The President was strongly of opinion that the moral embargo, including our concept that all shipments of essential war materials to belligerents should be limited to peacetime levels, should continue in effect. Our draft followed this thought.

On signing the bill on February 29, the President issued the proclamation applying the new Neutrality Act to Italy and Ethiopia, and also the statement embracing, with certain changes in the wording, the suggestion on continuing the moral embargo.

"It is true," he said, "that the high moral duty I have urged on our people of restricting their exports of essential war materials to either belligerent to approximately the normal peacetime basis has not been the subject of legislation. Nevertheless, it is clear to me that greatly to exceed that basis, with the result of earning profits not possible during peace, and especially with the result of giving actual assistance to the carrying on of war, would serve to magnify the very evil of war which we seek to prevent. This being my view, I renew the appeal made last October to the American people that they so conduct their trade with belligerent nations that it cannot be said that they are seizing new opportunities for profit or that by changing their peacetime trade they give aid to the continuation of war."

The new Neutrality Act did not correspond to my basic desires—that the President be given discretion as to whom to apply the Act and when —any more than did the old Act. One slight change, however, was at least a little comforting. The phraseology in the old Act, "That upon the outbreak or during the progress of war between, or among, two or more foreign States, the President shall proclaim . . ." was changed to, "Whenever the President shall find that there exists a state of war between, or among, two or more foreign states . . ." This left it to the President to determine whether or not there was a state of war. The importance of this change became manifest the following year when Japan waged an undeclared war against China, despite which the Neutrality Act was not applied.

The Act of 1935 had been in the nature of stopgap legislation. The Act of 1936 continued it. There was no doubt in my mind that, if we had to have neutrality legislation, much more care and thought had to be given to the subject. The State Department, therefore, kept its study of the question alive, in preparation for the time when Congress would again have to consider it, prior to the expiration of the new Act on May 1, 1937.

At the close of the year we were enheartened by a decision of the Supreme Court upholding the right of Congress to delegate to the President authority to impose an arms embargo against belligerent nations. This was the case of the United States of America, appellant, *v.* Curtiss-Wright Export Corporation, Curtiss Aeroplane & Motor Company, Inc., and Barr Shipping Corporation, *et al.* The background was the arms embargo imposed during the Chaco War.

"It is quite apparent," said the Court in an opinion handed down December 21, 1936, "that if, in the maintenance of our international relations, embarrassment—perhaps serious embarrassment—is to be avoided and success for our aims achieved, congressional legislation which is to be made effective through negotiation and inquiry within the international field must often accord to the President a degree of discretion and freedom from statutory restriction which would not be admissible were domestic affairs alone involved. Moreover, he, not Congress, has the better opportunity of knowing the conditions which prevail in foreign countries, and especially is this true in time of war."

This was vitally important to us, because, had the Court held otherwise, all our machinery for the control of traffic in arms would have been wiped out.

The Neutrality Act of 1936 remained in effect as to Italy and Ethiopia until after the fighting ended. At the moment of the collapse of Ethiopian resistance, our Legation in Addis Ababa underwent a three-day siege by bandit groups from the time Emperor Haile Selassie fled from the capital on May 2, 1936, until the Italian troops arrived on May 5. Minister Engert and his staff conducted themselves admirably and bravely under fire. Finally, on the morning of May 5, the personnel in the Legation, including citizens of other countries who had taken refuge there, were evacuated, with British military help, to the British Legation which was defended by a company of Sikh troops.

The evacuation was arranged partly through one of the most roundabout systems of communication in our diplomatic history. The American Legation was only a short distance from the British Legation, but between them swarmed lawless bands of armed Ethiopians, and at times direct communication was impossible. Both Legations had their own radios, but these were attuned to communicate with their respective capitals and not with each other. Consequently, Engert radioed his message to me. I had it telephoned to the American Embassy in London, which communicated it to the British Foreign Office, which, in turn, radioed it to their Legation in Addis Ababa—all within the space of a few hours.

On May 4 we had instructed the American Chargé d'Affaires in Rome, Alexander Kirk, to ascertain what steps the Italian Government was taking to meet its responsibility to protect the lives of foreigners in Addis Ababa. He was not to make any request or much less to ask for any favors of the Italian Government. Mussolini's Government blamed the disorders in Addis Ababa on the Emperor's departure without leaving an adequate police force there, but gave assurances that all possible measures of protection would be taken.

Italian Ambassador Rosso handed me on May 12 a note from his Government stating that Ethiopia was now under the full sovereignty of Italy, and the King of Italy was also Emperor of Ethiopia. Rosso attempted a rambling explanation of what he virtually admitted was a premature proclamation. I simply indicated it was too early for my Government to make any comment on the question.

It did not seem to me either logical or moral or in our own best interests to recognize Mussolini's acquisition of Ethiopia by force and thereby condone recourse to arms and violation of treaties. Four days before Rosso's call, and the day before Mussolini proclaimed Italian empire over Ethiopia, I made an informal suggestion to Argentina that the Saavedra Lamas Pact, which all the American republics and a number of European nations had signed, might be invoked. Under this pact recognition would not be given to territory acquired by force. I remarked to the Argentine Ambassador, Don Felipe A. Espil, that great peace champions like our two nations, accustomed to proclaim the sanctity of treaties and to denounce violators of treaties, were in no position to turn and walk away from the plain letter, as well as the spirit and policy, of the peace obligation to which we were signatories, without saying or doing anything. Espil replied that this would be quite difficult because of the large Italian-born population in Argentina.

My suggestion bore some fruit, however, because the Argentine Government on June 2 requested that the League Assembly be convoked. The Argentine representative in Geneva told Prentiss Gilbert, our Consul there, that this was to obtain the widest possible support for the non-recognition policy embodied in the Saavedra Lamas Pact. But when the

Assembly met on June 30, it took no action on nonrecognition. Britain and France were already regretting the imposition of sanctions, and wondering how to regain Mussolini's friendship.

On our part, we instructed Minister Engert in Addis Ababa to be careful, in his dealings with the Italian High Commissioner, Marshal Badoglio, to refrain from any statement or action that would commit our Government in any way as to giving recognition to the Italian conquest.

We were now confronted with a delicate question on the fringes of nonrecognition. Ambassador Breckinridge Long in Rome wished to retire from his post and, also, Mussolini wanted to send a new Ambassador, Fulvio Suvich, his Under Secretary for Foreign Affairs, to the United States. We did not wish to accredit Long's successor, Under Secretary of State William Phillips, to the King of Italy and Emperor of Ethiopia, and we did not wish to receive an envoy from Italy with such credentials.

After several exchanges of telegrams with Rome, the Italian Government finally agreed to accept our new Ambassador's letters of credence addressed solely to the King of Italy, but proposed to add the title of Emperor of Ethiopia in the credentials of Italian representatives. We agreed, but with the "distinct understanding that the addition of any new title in the letters of credence does not constitute recognition of Italian sovereignty over Ethiopia." Phillips went to Rome in August. In October Ambassador Suvich presented his letters of credence which employed the two titles, "King of Italy" and "Emperor of Ethiopia," but the President in his reply referred only to the "King of Italy."

Before removing the arms embargo against the two belligerents, we waited for six weeks after the Italian occupation of Addis Ababa to determine whether all organized resistance in Ethiopia had ceased. Again we wanted to take our action independently of what the League might do. Our position was different from that of the League, as we pointed out in a telegram to our Chargé in Rome, Alexander Kirk, on May 16: "We realize that the decision of states members of the League with regard to the continuance of the measures which they have enforced would presumably be taken in the light of their obligations under the League Covenant and would entail consideration of the continued existence of Ethiopia as a sovereign state. On the other hand the revocation of the President's embargo proclamation, on the mere recognition of the fact that the conditions which caused him to issue it no longer exist, would be based on the facts of the situation and would have no relation whatever to the question of recognition of rights to sovereignty over the territory."

Accordingly, on June 20, 1936, the President, declaring that a state of war no longer existed, removed the arms embargo and withdrew the warning against Americans traveling on belligerent vessels. A statement which I sent him on that day and which he issued made it clear that both in issuing the original proclamations and now in revoking them, he was simply "passing upon a question of fact"; namely, the existence of a state of war. The League of Nations Assembly voted on July 4 to lift sanctions against Italy.

Our moral embargo also ceased. This, including oil, had remained in effect throughout. Italian protests and hints of Mussolini's resentment did not affect us. The League members, on the other hand, backed away from the oil sanctions and from a really strong front against Italy. There have been some who suggest that Britain and France might be excused for their attitude toward sanctions because, with the menace of Germany assuming portentous dimensions, they still hoped to keep Italy on their side against Hitler. If, however, the League was ever to function, two or more large nations could never be justified in stepping outside, when doing so incapacitated the League's operations, except as a last resort to protect their own safety after the League had failed. If Italy could discern hesitancy or uncertainty on the part of Britain and France, she very naturally would proceed with her war and take the minor risk of League interference. This seems to be what happened.

If total sanctions had been applied, Mussolini might have been stopped dead in his tracks. The League thereupon would have been so fortified that it might have stopped Hitler too. Instead, the western powers' temporizing with Mussolini was an added factor in encouraging Japan to prepare for another war in China and Hitler to move into the Rhineland and proceed with greater confidence toward total armament. With the League's failure and Mussolini's success, I knew that the major war against which some of us had been warning since 1933 had become all the more probable. Its chilling shadow already lay upon us.

At this time new difficulties rose between us and Germany over the Treasury's application, on June 4, 1936, of countervailing (increased) duties against certain German exports to the United States on the grounds that Germany was subsidizing them. Secretary of the Treasury Morgenthau, whose actions resulted in repeated interference in the conduct of foreign affairs, insisted on this move over the protests of the State Department that it might impair our relations with a number of other nations. Morgenthau, understandably stirred by Hitler's vile treatment of the Jews, had already declared a personal war against Germany.

The Treasury argued that Germany's manipulation of different types of marks was in effect a subsidy of her exports. I submitted the question to the Executive Committee on Commercial Policy, composed of representatives of the Departments of State, Treasury, Commerce, and Agriculture, the Tariff Commission and other agencies. This committee unanimously, with the Treasury representative abstaining from voting, stated that there was considerable doubt that currency manipulations constituted a subsidy and might not more appropriately be regarded as a special form of currency depreciation. We ourselves had depreciated the dollar in 1933.

In transmitting this report to Morgenthau on April 2, 1936, I said that the application of countervailing duties in cases arising out of currency controls could not fail to have deplorable repercussions on our foreign trade, particularly so with respect to Germany, and this at a moment when for the first time the German Government had indicated its readiness to go a long way in meeting our insistence on nondiscriminatory treatment of American commerce in Germany. Countervailing duties would run directly counter to the purpose of the trade agreements program which was designed to bring about a reopening of foreign markets for our burdensome surpluses through a reduction of trade barriers.

We further pointed out to the Treasury that currency manipulation of the general type used in Germany was employed by a number of other European countries and by several countries in South America. If countervailing duties were invoked against Germany, it was difficult to see how the Treasury could fail to invoke them against these other countries, including Argentina, Brazil, Chile, Uruguay, and Hungary. Ill feeling and probably retaliation were bound to ensue. This would be particularly unfortunate in view of the approaching Pan American Conference at Buenos Aires.

Brushing all these objections aside, the Treasury went ahead, obtained a decision from the Attorney General that, once the Treasury decided that German exports were being subsidized, the application of the countervailing duties was mandatory under the 1930 Tariff Act, and imposed them. Illogically, it did not impose them against the other nations engaging in currency manipulation similar to Germany's.

Protests and alarmed inquiries from Germany, a number of other countries, and from American importers and exporters, immediately started pouring into the State Department. The Germans then sent economic experts to the United States who gave the Treasury assurances on the basis of which the Treasury, on August 14, removed the countervailing duties.

Actually the countervailing duties could apply only to about one-seventh of the German exports to the United States, but Morgenthau had nevertheless rushed blindly ahead with a project that stood to throw a crowbar into the machinery of our foreign relations.

Following the League of Nations' failure to halt Mussolini's aggression in Africa and Hitler's violations of the Versailles Treaty, I sensed a widespread disappointment and discouragement rising in all the democratic countries. A cynical attitude was manifesting itself toward any effort involving collective action by the nations desiring peace. Opposing this trend, I delivered an address to the graduating class of Brown University, Providence, Rhode Island, on June 15, 1936. I pointed out that "the supreme care of the statesmen should be the well-being of the people. War exacts too high a price to be conducive to human welfare—a price which normal human intelligence cannot possibly accept as justified by any achievement that can be secured through a deliberate resort to arms. That is why enlightened and responsible statesmen of our day seek, in every way possible, to outlaw war as a means of national policy and to substitute for it the constructive processes of friendly conciliation and arbitration and fair adjudication of international disputes. War is sometimes described as the last resort of the statesman. I should rather say that recourse to war as a means of attaining the aims of national policy is an unmistakable symbol of bankrupt statesmanship."

I warned my audience of what was happening in the world. "The predatory instinct of national aggrandizement," I said, "is again rampant and has already set armies marching in some parts of the earth. Solemn international agreements are being violated with a light heart. Apprehension, suspicion, and confusion rule the political relations among most nations."

Finally, I appealed for public opinion to take an interest in these developments in an effort to turn their dangerous trend. "If the world," I said, "is not to be plunged into another cataclysm, friendliness and confidence, fair-dealing and good faith must triumph once more, in the relations among nations, over hostility and distrust and suspicion and greed. This cannot come to pass unless the spirit underlying national policies undergoes a rebirth—unless individuals within nations, through their personal conduct, through their influence upon others, through their exercise of responsible citizenship, devote themselves to the cause of such rebirth. For, in the final analysis, no nation is better than the individuals who compose it."

But, unfortunately for the world, too many individuals in Germany, Japan, and Italy were content to see international law shattered so that their nations might become richer, larger, or stronger. And too many individuals in other nations were indifferent or afraid to require their Governments to make a concerted effort to halt these three desperadoes before the zero hour sounded.

34: Spain Erupts

SKIRMISHING WAS still going on in Ethiopia, following the Italian occupation of Addis Ababa, when suddenly Spain erupted in civil war on July 17, 1936, and a whole new set of problems confronted us. Actually, the revolt in Spain did not surprise us. Dispatches from our Embassy in Madrid had for many months bespoken a condition of unrest and tension that could not long continue. The country was splitting into two sides, the left wing embracing the Government, and the right wing the Army and the Church. All this volcano needed to set it off was for something to happen at the crater, and that something was the assassination of several leaders of both factions.

Our first thought when the revolt broke out and rapidly assumed the character of a major civil war was not the political one of policy but the practical one of getting our citizens out of war-threatened areas. I held repeated conferences in my office with officials of the State and other departments to hasten the necessary arrangements. American consulates in Spanish ports, acting under our direction, evacuated large numbers of Americans on British, French, and Italian, as well as on American, vessels.

The war caught our Ambassador to Spain, Claude G. Bowers, at San Sebastian on the northern coast where the Spanish Government had been accustomed to set up a summer capital. The foreign embassies had gone with the Government, leaving only skeleton staffs in Madrid. Our Embassy was in charge of Third Secretary Eric C. Wendelin, who performed excellently under difficult circumstances. Bowers was never able to get back to Madrid.

On July 23 I wirelessed the President, who was cruising off the New England coast, telling him of a conference I had had with Admiral Standley, chief of Naval Operations, about evacuating Americans. "The reports which we are receiving," I communicated, "indicate that the situation is, if anything, becoming much worse and it seems like a fifty-fifty chance as to which side may come out on top, and, furthermore, with an equal chance that a completely chaotic condition may arise in Spain which may continue for some time. One of the most serious factors in this situation lies in the fact that the [Spanish] Government has distributed large quantities of arms and ammunition into the hands of Irresponsible members of left-wing political organizations."

I informed the President that Admiral Standley could have ready within a few days a heavy cruiser and four destroyers to send to Spain. The following day Mr. Roosevelt replied that, if I should decide to order naval vessels to Spain, he would "wholly approve." The dispatch of additional vessels, however, proved unnecessary. As was the case during the Italo-Ethiopian War and later in the European War, large numbers of Americans, despite our repeated warnings and urgings, remained in the war zones. They subordinated personal safety to reluctance to give up their businesses, jobs, or studies, to sentimental attachment to the country where they were living, or to the fact that they had married citizens of other countries.

Meantime we sought to formulate and state our policy with regard to the Spanish War, especially since it was evident from the start of the conflict that the major European nations had a very concrete interest in the conflict. Our cables were crowded with messages from our diplomats abroad giving the attitudes and probable actions of those Governments. Within a week after the outbreak of war, it was strongly evident that the peaceful nations of Europe, particularly Britain and France, would make a great effort to limit the conflict to Spain.

Ambassador Straus in Paris informed us that the French Government, on July 21, had received a request from the Spanish Government for help in airplanes and munitions. Straus said that the French Popular Front Government, under Premier Léon Blum, which, being of the left, was sympathetic to the Spanish Government, was at first disposed to grant the request. Britain's Prime Minister, Stanley Baldwin, however, asked Blum to go to London to discuss Spain, and there emphasized to him the British Government's view that any assistance to Spain by France might lead to an international crisis. When Blum returned to Paris on July 25, a statement was issued that the French Government had decided against supplying arms to the Madrid Government and against intervening in the domestic affairs of another nation. On July 31 Straus cabled that a French Foreign Office source told him France would probably propose to the other two principal Mediterranean powers, England and Italy, that they agree with France not to furnish arms to either side in Spain or to interfere in any way.

On August 4 the French Chargé d'Affaires came to my office to inform me that his Government had proposed to the British and Italian Governments that each should remain entirely aloof and maintain an attitude of neutrality or nonintervention during the conflict. Without mentioning names, he said his Government was very much disturbed about reports that other countries were violating neutrality and were engaging in acts of interference or intervention. After thanking him I said: "My Government is keenly interested in affairs of a threatening nature elsewhere. We anxiously hope that peace in any event might be preserved. Of course, you are aware of my Government's general attitude toward nonintervention."

Cables from various American Embassies in Europe informed us that the French Government had also made its proposal to the German, Russian, Belgian, Portuguese, and Polish Governments. Therefore, within three weeks after the outbreak of the Spanish War, two factors were evident to us. The first was that the British and French Governments believed that a European agreement strictly to abstain from intervening in Spanish affairs was the best means to prevent the spread of the conflict. The second was that the initiative in dealing with the Spanish problem lay with the European nations.

Our own policy on nonintervention, as I had stated to the French Chargé, was clear. Nonintervention in the affairs of other nations was one of the planks I helped insert in the Democratic platform of 1932. At the Montevideo Pan American Conference we had made nonintervention one of the planks of the Good Neighbor Policy. There I said: "I feel safe in undertaking to say that under our support of the general principle of nonintervention as has been suggested, no government need fear any intervention on the part of the United States under the Roosevelt Administration." Following the Montevideo Conference, we had taken one action after another in pursuance of our new policy of nonintervention, such as the treaties with Cuba and Panama, and withdrawal of our armed forces from Haiti.

I therefore felt that the time had come to state our position. On August 5 I called to my office Phillips, Moore, Welles, Legal Adviser Green H. Hackworth, and other leading officials of the Department to discuss a possible public statement of policy. After considerable conference we drafted a statement which called attention to the article of the Convention signed at Montevideo: "No state has the right to intervene in the internal or external affairs of another." We decided, however, that the time had not yet arrived to issue a formal statement, and its substance was given to the press correspondents for background purposes.

We did feel it necessary to give guidance to our diplomatic and consular officials in Spain. On August 7 we telegraphed the Embassy and

Consulates in Spain "what this Government's position thus far has been and will continue to be." The cable stated: "It is clear that our Neutrality Law with respect to embargo of arms, ammunition, and implements of war has no application in the present situation, since that applies only in the event of *war between or among nations*. On the other hand, in conformity with its well-established policy of noninterference in internal affairs in other countries, either in time of peace or in the event of civil strife, this Government will, of course, scrupulously refrain from any interference whatsoever in the unfortunate Spanish situation. We believe that American citizens, both at home and abroad, are patriotically observing this well-recognized American policy." This was made public August 11.

Thus we were again applying a moral embargo. We did not have the legal right to prohibit the export of arms to Spain, just as we had not had the legal right to prohibit the export of essential war materials, other than arms, to Italy and Ethiopia. But we could use the moral pressure of the Government to keep our citizens from involving the nation in the internal affairs of another nation and from contributing to the prolongation or spread of the war.

The question rose in more concrete form on August 6, when Spanish Ambassador Don Luis Calderón informed the State Department that his Government had inquired whether he could purchase a small amount of machine-gun cartridges in this country. Under Secretary Phillips, while pointing out that, under the Neutrality Act, we could not embargo the export of war materials to Spain, emphasized the widespread feeling in the United States against such exports to a foreign country for use in actual conflict.

Next, on August 10, the Glenn L. Martin Company asked for the Department's attitude toward the sale of eight bombing planes to the Spanish Government. I was then resting at Hot Springs, Virginia. Acting Secretary Phillips telephoned to the President and then drafted a reply which he read to me over the telephone and which I approved. Following the President's approval, Phillips dispatched the letter, which was made public on August 22. Enclosing and calling attention to our instructions to the American Embassy and Consulates in Spain, the letter concluded: "In view of the above, it seems reasonable to assume that the sale of aeroplanes, regarding which you inquire, would not follow the spirit of the Government's policy."

Similar inquiries were received from other firms, and the same answer given. Our policy toward Spain was now clear and public. Once stated, it had this added importance that it could not be changed without serious political controversy on this side and without grave embarrassment to the European nations, particularly Britain and France, to whom it was welcome as being in conformity with their own policy of nonintervention.

The American public accepted the policy at first virtually without question. For once, our position seemed acceptable to both the apparently irreconcilable isolationists and the internationalists. Isolationists approved because we were keeping aloof from the conflict. Internationalists approved because we were cooperating with Britain and France.

The Spanish War had been in progress just over a month when the President made an important foreign-policy address at Chautauqua, New York, August 14, 1936. The State Department prepared data for the address, but the speech was written at the White House. It was a strong peace appeal in which the President, describing scenes of dead and wounded he had witnessed in the First World War, passionately pleaded for peaceful relations among nations. He pointed out that, while shunning political commitments which might entangle us in foreign wars, and avoiding connection with the political activities of the League of Nations, we were cooperating wholeheartedly in the social and humanitarian work at Geneva.

"We are not isolationists," he said, "except in so far as we seek to isolate ourselves completely from war. Yet we must remember that so long as war exists on earth there will be some danger that even the nation which most ardently desires peace may be drawn into war."

As for neutrality, the President said its effectiveness depended on the wisdom and determination of whoever occupied the offices of President and Secretary of State. If war, however, should break out again on another continent, he commented, "let us not blink the fact that we would find in this country thousands of Americans who, seeking immediate riches—fools' gold—would attempt to break down or evade our neutrality." He pointed out that, no matter how well we were supported by neutrality legislation, we had to remember that no laws could be provided to cover every contingency. "With that wise and experienced man who is our Secretary of State, whose statesmanship has met with such wide approval, I have thought and worked long and hard on the problem of keeping the United States at peace," he added. "But all the wisdom of America is not to be found in the White House or in the Department of State; we need the meditation, the prayer, and the positive support of the people of America who go along with us in seeking peace."

The address met an overwhelmingly favorable response from press and public. Many sections of public opinion were too ready, however, to seize upon it to bolster their hope that our security and peace would not be affected by what happened elsewhere in the world and that we could have peace merely by wanting it and legislating for it. In later years the President's heartfelt language in favor of peace was thrown at him time and again by his opponents in accusing him of leading us toward war.

After the President had his Chautauqua speech printed and bound he sent me a copy on the fly page of which he had written:

> For Cordell Hull
> My right arm in the cause of peace
> FRANKLIN D. ROOSEVELT

Three days after the President's address we received a proposal from Uruguay that the American Republics jointly mediate the Spanish conflict. Acting Secretary Phillips replied that, although we ardently desired peace and wished to support the principle of conciliation, we could not accept in view of our commitment to the principle of nonintervention. Our belief was that an uninvited offer to mediate might be fraught with grave difficulties and possible misunderstanding, since neither the nations of Europe nor of America were united in believing that such an offer would serve any useful purpose.

On August 30 the American destroyer *Kane,* enroute from Gibraltar to Bilbao to evacuate American citizens, was repeatedly bombed by an unknown plane, without suffering damage. I cabled Wendelin in Madrid and Consul Charles A. Bay at Seville, headquarters of the insurgent forces of General Franco, to bring the incident to the attention of the Spanish Government and of Franco. I said it could only be assumed that the attack on the *Kane* was due to her identity having been mistaken for a vessel of the opposing forces, and requested that instructions be issued to prevent another such incident. Both sides denied that the plane was theirs. Our attitude was in sharp contrast to the later action of the German Government which ordered the shelling of the Loyalist port of Almería following the bombing of the German battleship *Deutschland.* On September 10 I stated at a press conference that our naval vessels in Spanish waters were withdrawing to the ports of near-by countries.

The Mexican Ambassador, Castillo Najera, called at the Department on September 14 to inform us that President Cárdenas of Mexico had telephoned him a request from the Spanish Government to take up with us the question of the shipment of arms and munitions to Spain. When his inquiry was communicated to me, I outlined this reply: "We entertain the most friendly feelings toward the Mexican Government and are always more than willing to listen to any suggestions or requests which it may desire to make. However, in the present instance this Government adopted a definite position regarding the shipment of arms and munitions to Spain long before the Mexican Government had broached the subject to it. As that position has been given much publicity, it must be presumed to be well known, and we have no intention of departing from it."

The French Government's nonintervention proposals had by now been accepted by twenty-six other nations, from Ireland to Russia. An International Nonintervention Committee was set up in London and held its first meeting on September 9.

Europe was now organized on the theory of nonintervention in Spain, however it worked out in practice. Twenty-seven nations solemnly promised not to aid one side or the other. They agreed not to send arms to the Spanish Government or the Franco forces. Later on, some of them took such positive steps as naval patrols to prevent war supplies from reaching either side.

The policy of the United States was thus in full accord with that expressed by the European nations. From the time we stated it in August, 1936, we had not varied it when the Spanish War ended in March, 1939. As time went on, this policy came more and more under attack from certain elements in this country. Some of the more extreme sections have not yet forgiven the Roosevelt Administration for its refusal to become involved in the Spanish conflict by aiding the Government there to the dangerous extent they demanded.

The President and I were in complete agreement on our policy of nonintervention in Spain throughout the war. At no time did any difference of opinion arise between us. We believed that the following factors had to be taken into consideration:

The first was that Britain and France had taken the lead in welding all Europe together into a nonintervention committee. These nations had only a few miles or a few hundred miles between them and Spain. We were three thousand miles away. They were Spain's neighbors; they were most closely informed on developments there; they were most interested in those developments. Europe had rightly taken the initiative. While twenty-seven nations of Europe had solemnly agreed not to intervene in

Spain by sending arms or men to one side or the other, it would have been unthinkable for the United States to take a contrary course.

It was as evident to us, of course, as it was to Europe that some of the nations in the Nonintervention Committee were, in fact, intervening in Spain. Germany and Italy were sending strong assistance to Franco, Soviet Russia to the Government of President Azaña. But this did not mean that the United States, as the American sympathizers of the Spanish Government desired, should do likewise.

The second consideration was that the nations of Europe formed the Nonintervention Committee in order to prevent the spread of the Spanish conflict to the whole continent. We were in sympathy with this aim. Despite many violations by Germany, Italy, and Russia, the committee continued to function until the end of the war. Britain and France saw clearly what was going on but believed that the nonintervention policy, faulty as it was in practice, would keep the war from becoming general.

On December 19, 1936, British Foreign Minister Anthony Eden said in the House of Commons: "With regard to the issue of nonintervention, I believe it to be true to say that this policy, despite its admitted short-comings, despite the blatant breaches that there have been, has on the whole reduced the risk of a European war."

Winston Churchill, then in opposition to the British Government, said on April 14, 1937: "I expect that the Nonintervention Committee is full of swindles and cheats . . . but it is a precious thing in these times of peril that five great nations should be slanging each other round a table instead of blasting and bombing each other in horrible war. Is it not an encouraging fact that German, French, Russian, Italian, and British naval officers are officially acting together, however crankily, in something which represents, albeit feebly, the concert of Europe, and affords, if it is only a pale, misshapen shadow, some idea of those conceptions of the reign of law and of collective authority which many of us regard as of vital importance? The man who mocks at the existence of the Nonintervention Committee I put on the same level as the man who mocks at the hope of Geneva and the League of Nations."

French Premier Blum said at Marseilles in October, 1937: "Call nonintervention a lie, a fiction if you like, but the fact remains that it has helped to stop a general war."

And, as late as March 24, 1938, British Prime Minister Chamberlain stated to the House of Commons: "Serious as are these infringements, they do not alter the judgment of His Majesty's Government that the policy of nonintervention, even though infractions of this policy may take place, affords the best means of avoiding a major conflagration."

Thus the leaders of Britain and France were convinced that the policy of nonintervention, though shot full of holes, was vitally necessary if general peace in Europe were to be preserved. Had the United States adopted the opposite policy and permitted a free flow of arms to Spain, we would have seriously embarrassed the very nations, Britain and France, whom we wished to encourage and bolster in their efforts toward peace. If general war were to come, those nations would have to bear the burden of fighting, without any assurance, in view of isolationist sentiment here, of assistance from us who, by intervention, might have been responsible for a widespread conflagration.

Our third consideration was our own peace and security. This, however, seemed of little importance to those vociferous groups who shouted that American arms and volunteers must go to the Spanish Government. They forgot, too, that merely authorizing the export of arms to Spain was not enough. We should have had to see to it that the arms got to Spain. Airplanes shipped to the Spanish Government in violation of our moral embargo and before the Arms Embargo Act of January 8, 1937, applying to Spain, was passed, did in fact fall into the hands of the Franco forces. This would have meant sending a cruiser or two along with our shipments. In all probability we would thereupon have become involved with Germany and Italy and been obliged a month or so later to follow the cruiser with a large naval squadron. We might well have plunged into the Spanish War before we realized it.

Had we reversed our moral embargo, had Congress later repealed the Arms Embargo Act, American arms, ammunition, and implements of war might have gone not only to the Spanish Government but also to the Franco forces, if not directly at least indirectly. In any event, shipments of arms to either side or both would have served to lengthen the war and hence conflicted with our fourth consideration, which was to prevent prolongation of the conflict. The longer the Spanish War went on the greater was the likelihood that other nations would become involved.

Our policy had nothing to do with our views on the right or the wrong in the Spanish Civil War. We were not judging between the two sides.

Looking back with keen hindsight, critics of our policy can say it was wrong because the fascist forces in Spain eventually triumphed, Hitler and Mussolini were strengthened, and Britain and France humbled. This argument would be valid only if the peace-loving nations, including the United States, had been prepared militarily and psychologically to abandon their efforts toward maintaining peace and embark on a general preventive war. Such was not the case.

These critics seek to give the impression that they were taking a broader course than the Administration. In truth they were taking a narrower course because they failed to give consideration to our own security or to the policies of the major peaceful nations of Europe. They were threatening the Roosevelt Administration with destruction for taking the broad course of working along the same lines as Britain and France in attempting to maintain peace. Our opponents also charged that the Spanish War was the beginning of the World War and that Italy and Germany were giving their armies training in Spain. That, of course, was not a controlling motive any more than it was Mussolini's intention, in invading Ethiopia, merely to train his armed forces.

A technical argument frequently raised against our policy of non-intervention was that the traditional attitude of the United States had been to favor legal governments. This argument was voiced by the new Spanish Ambassador, Señor Fernando de los Ríos, on his first visit to me, October 10, 1936. Black-bearded De los Ríos was a cultured, refined gentleman, formerly rector of the University of Madrid. He characterized the struggle in Spain as a conflict between democracy and fascism. Saying that the democracies must stand as firmly together as possible and aid each other in as practical a way as possible, he asked whether the United States would not find it possible to extend aid to the Spanish Government.

"The nations of Europe," I replied, "have agreed on a policy of noninterference in the internal affairs of Spain. This procedure seems to me to indicate a leadership among the countries most concerned. The French Government, the neighbor and special friend of the Spanish Government, has taken the very lead in this movement. Those countries have agreed that the question of noninterference is now decided."

I pointed out that the Roosevelt Administration had given great thought to the question of noninterference in the Western Hemisphere. "At times in the past," I said, "the American Government took entirely innocent steps when difficulties occurred in Latin American countries. These innocent steps often led to other complications which brought about interference and even intervention by the United States. Frequently regrettable situations rose out of such beginnings."

The Ambassador remarked that during the struggle between Calles and Huerta in Mexico the United States had lent support to the legal government.

"That," I replied, "is one of those actions to which I just referred. It led this Government to be criticized and caused those very difficulties I am now anxious to avoid in line with the Montevideo agreement." I added that it was important for the United States to adhere to the principles of the Montevideo agreement in other parts of the world as well as in Latin America.

In Spain our own Ambassador, Claude Bowers, strongly inclined toward the Loyalist, or Spanish Government, side as opposed to General Franco. I had known Bowers since the campaign of 1922 when, as chairman of the Democratic National Committee, I attended a state-wide meeting of the Democratic Party in Indiana and heard him deliver a red-hot, eloquent speech that attracted wide attention. He was one of the able, noted editors and authors of America, with a number of exceedingly valuable books to his credit. Like many persons on the ground in Spain, closely involved in its developments, Bowers, himself a liberal, promptly took sides in the Civil War. He felt that the United States should make its policies conform with the vital interests of the liberal forces prosecuting one side of the war. He buttressed this view by frequent references to the assistance rendered by Germany and Italy to Franco. At the State Department, while recognizing that what Bowers had to say about Germany and Italy was true, we had to pursue a broader course which recognized the grave danger that the Civil War in Spain might erupt into a European war.

The Presidential election of 1936 was now approaching, which would show whether the voters approved the domestic and foreign policies of the Roosevelt Administration. Some months before the 1936 Democratic National Convention in Philadelphia, I began sending various chits to the President containing suggestions for the foreign policy and international economics planks in the Democratic platform. I myself took no part in the writing of the platform, but I assumed that, in due course, I would be shown the final draft. I went to the convention and there, to my surprise, discovered that no arrangement had been made to show me the platform before it was presented to the convention. By that time it was too late to get into the platform committee where everything, during the final stages, was kept under double lock and key with guards about the door to prevent leaks of platform provisions to the press.

I attributed the fact that I did not see a final draft to persons around the President who presumed to speak for him. Still, I assumed he had passed on to the platform committee the various suggestions I had sent him. I was dumbfounded, when the platform came out, to read the planks on tariff and foreign affairs, which utterly ignored the suggestions I had submitted. I left the convention after the committee made its report and went to Atlantic City with Mrs. Hull.

The tariff plank squinted in the direction of our trade agreements policy in the first couple of sentences, but unfortunately some high-tariff advocates got in their work with the result that the remainder of the plank was Republican terminology almost word for word, such as the clause pledging adequate protection against foreign pauper labor. The foreign affairs plank was, in the main, also disappointing to me. Consisting of only one short paragraph, it seemed to be a jumble of ideas or theories in which different persons had stuck their respective notions. It lugged in the theories about bankers and munitions manufacturers which the Nye Committee had exploited to the limit, and its reference to neutrality was directly in conflict with a world organization to preserve peace.

I protested to the President about these planks, but he gave me no reply of any consequence. I do not know whether Mr. Roosevelt had given any personal attention to the tariff plank since he had shown interest in the trade agreements program only from time to time. In any event, I did not hesitate but, utterly ignoring this platform provision, redoubled my efforts to preserve the integrity of the trade agreements policy then in operation, and to develop it soundly and as rapidly as possible.

The trade agreements became a principal issue of the campaign that followed. The Old Guard Republican element, the high-tariff barons, and other supporters of embargo tariffs organized and fought stubbornly throughout the country against them. The Republicans who made this a leading issue relied on the old-time high-tariff forces to rally to their support. But the terrific effects of the panic of 1929 to 1932, which were attributed measurably to the Fordney-McCumber and the Smoot-Hawley high-tariff Acts, had alienated vast numbers of Republican farmers, laborers, and even businessmen while, on the other hand, we were beginning to show results from the Trade Agreements Act with much benefit to all and no material injury to any.

I made several speeches on foreign policy and the trade agreements during the campaign but, in keeping with my intention to keep foreign affairs out of domestic politics, they were expositions of my ideas and principles rather than campaign speeches. I delivered the most comprehensive of them, entitled "Our Foreign Relations and Our Foreign Policy," before the Good Neighbor League of New York City on September 15, 1936. I said that the foreign policy we were pursuing came close to Thomas Jefferson's expression: "peace, commerce, and honest friendship with all nations, entangling alliances with none," and to these I added settlement of disputes by peaceful means, and renunciation of war as an instrument of national policy.

"At times," I said, "there has been criticism because we would not depart from our traditional policy and join with other governments in collective arrangements carrying the obligation of employing force, if necessary, in case disputes between other countries brought them into war. That responsibility, carrying direct participation in the political relations of the whole of the world outside, we cannot accept, eager as we are to support means for the prevention of war. For current experience indicates how uncertain is the possibility that we, by our action, could vitally influence the politics or activities of other countries from which war might come. It is for the statesmen to continue their effort to effect security by new agreements which will prove more durable than those that have been broken. This Government would welcome that achievement."

Our contribution, I pointed out, must be in the spirit of our own situation and conceptions. "It lies in the willingness to be friends but not allies. We wish extensive and mutually beneficial trade relations. We have the impulse to multiply our personal contacts, as shown by the constant American travel abroad. We would share and exchange the gifts which art, the stage, the classroom, and the scientists' and thinkers' study contribute to heighten life and understanding; we have led the world in promoting this sort of interchange among students, teachers, and artists. Our wish that natural human contacts be deeply and fully realized is shown by the great number of international conferences in which we participate, both private and intergovernmental. In such ways we would have our relations grow."

Pointing out that we had increased our defense forces substantially because of the universal increase of armaments elsewhere and the disturbed conditions in the world, I said: "We must be sure that in our desire for peace, we will not appear to any other country weak and unable to resist the imposition of force or to protect our just rights." But I also said we were ready to take part in all attempts to limit armaments by mutual accord "and await the day when this may be realized."

The vote in favour of the Roosevelt Administration was overwhelming.

Immediately after the election I issued a statement on November 4 in which I said: "Not the least of our record upon which favorable judgment was pronounced were our foreign policies and foreign relations during the past four years. The central policy has been that of the Good Neighbor, the most outstanding objective of which has been the promotion of conditions of permanent peace. These high aims and purposes in time of peace and strict neutrality in time of war have been the cornerstone of American foreign policy."

I added that we had consistently acted in deep conviction that economic prosperity and world peace were closely interrelated. "Both," I said, "require normal economic relations among nations and flourishing and mutually advantageous international trade. The trade agreements program pursued by this administration has proved to be the most effective instrument for bringing about a revival of international trade, thereby stimulating general economic prosperity and affording an increasingly secure foundation for world peace."

The unequivocal endorsement by the American people of these and other foreign policies, I pointed out, was a matter of both gratification and genuine encouragement. "We shall go forward with this program," I concluded, "in the same earnest, persistent, careful, and cautious manner in which we have heretofore sought to advance this great undertaking."

Three days later I sailed from New York for Buenos Aires to attend the Inter-American Conference for the Maintenance of Peace. And exactly three weeks later, on November 25, came the announcement that Hitler and Japan had signed their Anti-Comintern Pact.

It seemed to me at once that this treaty between Nazism and Nipponism was far more than an agreement to combat Communist propaganda. For a long time and from many sources, we had been receiving indications that Germany and Japan were negotiating a basic understanding. I have already quoted, in Chapter 17, the dispatch we received in 1934 from the military attaché in our Berlin Embassy concerning a possible secret alliance between them.

Nothing could have been more logical and natural than an alliance of Berlin and Tokyo. Both Governments had the same basis of militarism, of ambitions toward conquest, of ruthlessness, and of contempt for treaties and international law. Each had already seen how well it could advance in its half of the world while the other stirred up the other half. One month before, on October 25, 1936, Hitler and Mussolini had reached an accord to work together toward the same ends, with anti-Communism as their window-dressing. This was the beginning of the Rome-Berlin "Axis." Italy formally joined the German-Japanese line-up the following year.

I was prepared from the beginning to overestimate rather than underestimate this agreement. From now on it was evident that Germany and Japan would move with equal steps along the same path toward aggrandizement. From now on they would have closer military exchanges and arrangements. This was confirmed from year to year until the Tripartite agreement of September, 1940, a brazen confession of their respective military objectives.

On December 4, 1936, Ambassador Grew in Tokyo telegraphed me that the British Ambassador there felt certain that a secret German-Japanese military agreement existed and German arms were to be shipped to Manchuria in exchange for various commodities. He quoted the Soviet Ambassador as believing that the anti-Comintern agreement, as published, was merely a façade to hide a secret agreement for joint action in the event of war with Russia and that, also aimed at Great Britain, it provided in the event of war, for a division between Germany and Japan of certain British overseas possessions as well as the Dutch East Indies.

The dictators' designs were taking solid shape.

At that moment the British and French Governments decided to invite Germany, Russia, Italy, and Portugal to join them in new and immediate renunciation of all varieties of action toward Spain that might result in foreign intervention, to institute measures through the London Nonintervention Committee to prevent the shipment of war materials to Spain, and to participate in an offer of mediation. The Acting Secretary of State, R. Walton Moore, cabled me at Buenos Aires that the two Governments had suggested we make a public statement in support of their proposals and say a word through our representatives in Berlin, Moscow, Rome, and Lisbon in favor of the mediation offer. Moore said he did not favor the latter step but thought that the President might make a statement favoring mediation. Moore cabled me the draft of such a statement.

In my reply on December 7, I pointed out that sentiment in Latin America regarding the Spanish situation was "highly combustible," and suggested that the State Department rather than the President issue the statement, in which I made a few changes. The President, who was then aboard the cruiser *Indianapolis,* returning home from Buenos Aires, agreed to this procedure. On December 10, Moore issued a statement, saying, in part:

"It is announced by the Governments of Great Britain and France that they have invited the Governments of Germany, Italy, Russia, and Portugal to join them in a mediation offer to end the Spanish Civil War. It is the very earnest hope of our Government that the six nations mentioned may find a peaceful method of accomplishing the great purpose in view."

Germany, Italy, and Portugal offered no support for the mediation proposal, and the project died.

As the Buenos Aires Conference ended and I was returning on the steamer *Southern Cross* to the United States, Acting Secretary Moore informed me by wireless that several Americans were at last seeking licenses to export airplanes and arms to Spain. Up to that time, that is, since our policy had been announced in August, American manufacturers and exporters, in addition to the virtual totality of the American public, had supported the moral embargo. Now these few Americans, who put profit above patriotism, were demanding licenses from the State Department which could not refuse them because civil war was not embraced in the 1936 Neutrality Act.

Moore kept the President, who had returned to Washington from Buenos Aires on December 15, informed of these developments. On December 28 the Department issued the first license and gave public notice of the fact. The following day the President at a press conference denounced the action of the American exporter as unpatriotic, though legal. He said he had given his approval to plans of legislative leaders to amend the Neutrality Act and cover the Spanish situation as soon as Congress convened on January 5.

Moore wirelessed me on December 31 that the President had conferred the day before with him, Senator Pittman, and Representative McReynolds on neutrality legislation. On January 5, 1937, they held another conference, and Moore wirelessed me: "President has authorized Pittman and McReynolds to introduce resolution tomorrow to ban shipments of arms, ammunition, and implements of war to Spain. It will go in as an emergency measure disconnected from general neutrality legislation."

A race now developed between the American exporter to load his airplanes aboard the Spanish steamship *Mar Cantábrico* in New York Harbor and Congress to pass an arms embargo for the Spanish conflict. On

January 5 another export license was issued for arms to Spain. On January 6 the President, in his message to Congress, asked for "an addition to the existing Neutrality Act to cover specific points raised by the unfortunate civil strife in Spain." The same day Senator Pittman and Representative McReynolds introduced their resolutions in the Senate and House respectively.

Few pieces of legislation ever passed Congress with such speed and unanimity. On the very day of their presentation, the Senate resolution was voted unanimously, 81 to 0, and the House resolution virtually unanimously, 406 to 1. A legal technicality delayed the President's signature until January 8. Meantime a portion of the airplanes licensed for export were loaded aboard the *Mar Cantábrico,* and she sailed January 7. The licenses for the remainder were revoked. The *Mar Cantábrico,* after a roundabout voyage, was captured by the Franco forces on March 8.

Several points should here be noted. This legislation received the votes of all the Democrats and Republicans present, the sole negative vote being cast by a Farmer-Laborite. It was approved by isolationists and internationalists alike. The vote was overwhelming. When vociferous groups later on bedeviled the White House and State Department to repeal the legislation, they chose to ignore this unanimous attitude and to believe that the Administration could cause Congress, almost over night, to abjure its unanimity.

Moreover, Congress did not believe that the Neutrality Act would aid the Franco forces. Senator Pittman pointed out to the Senate that suggestions made to this effect were not a fact. "The so-called insurgent forces in Spain," he said, "control a tremendous portion of that country, if not the larger portion. They control a number of the ports. They have access to imports, just the same as the Government of Spain has."

Congress recognized that the principal issues were that the democratic governments of Europe, headed by France and Britain, had decided to refrain rigidly from intervention, that American aid to Spain might conduce to the spread of the war, and that our peace and security required our keeping aloof from the struggle.

Furthermore, the President favored, without reservation, the Arms Embargo Act concerning Spain. He strongly urged its passage. When he signed it, he did so without any reluctance such as he exhibited when, on signing the Neutrality Act of August 31, 1935, he issued the statement that inflexible legislation might have the opposite effect from that intended and bring us war instead of peace. Both the Legislative and the Executive branches of the Government joined, in singular harmony, in believing that to keep aloof from the Spanish conflict was to the best interests of the United States.

35: Threat to the Hemisphere

EVENTS SWIFTLY DEVELOPING beyond the Atlantic and the Pacific in 1936 called for new decisions in our relations with the Latin American Republics. The Montevideo Conference in 1933 had established a firm foundation of friendship between us and our neighbors to the south. The next Pan American Conference would meet at Lima, Peru, toward the end of 1938, to build new floors on this foundation. But, with Europe and Asia approaching a catastrophe, could we wait that long?

Japan had won a war in China, Italy in Ethiopia; Spain, the mother country of most of the Latin American Republics, was in civil war, with Italy, Russia, and Germany intervening; Germany and Japan were linked in a virtual alliance; Hitler was violating one treaty after another; Britain and France were vacillating; the League was limping toward its end; and the United States was set in a concrete mold of isolation.

The answer was, we did not dare wait. The newborn friendship among the American Republics required solidifying. A common attitude toward the dangers rising in Europe and the Orient was essential. The existing peace agreements in the Western Hemisphere had to be strengthened.

Early in 1935 we began at the State Department to discuss the possibilities of holding a special inter-American conference in 1936. The President was among the first to embrace the idea, and he did his utmost to promote it. The negotiations to end the Chaco War were still in progress, however, and we wished to await their close. We did not want a general conference to interfere with the work of mediation between Bolivia and Paraguay being carried on at Buenos Aires, and we wanted to use the formal end of the war as a springboard from which to reach agreement to outlaw further war between American Republics.

Our initial soundings among the Latin American countries produced a welcome response. Saavedra Lamas, Argentina's Foreign Minister, agreed to the conference on the understanding that it would be held at Buenos Aires, to which we had no objection. Bolivia and Paraguay signed their final protocol of settlement on January 21, 1936, and on January 30 President Roosevelt sent letters to the Presidents of the twenty Latin American countries proposing the holding of the meeting in the Argentine capital.

The purpose of the conference, he said, would be "to determine how

493

the maintenance of peace among the American Republics may best be safeguarded—whether, perhaps, through the prompt ratification of all of the inter-American peace instruments already negotiated; whether through the amendment of existing peace instruments in such manner as experience has demonstrated to be most necessary; or perhaps through the creation by common accord of new instruments of peace additional to those already formulated."

Since the majority of the Latin American Republics were members of the League of Nations, the President was careful to make it clear that we were not trying in the Western Hemisphere to supplant the League, but rather to bolster it. "These steps," he said, "would advance the cause of world peace, inasmuch as the agreements which might be reached would supplement and reenforce the efforts of the League of Nations and of all other existing or future peace agencies in seeking to prevent war."

The Presidents of the other American Republics quickly agreed to holding the conference. At first we hoped that the meeting could be held during the summer of 1936, but the agenda required careful preparation which meant long and frequent exchanges of views among the twenty-one governments. I took part in the development of our ideas and purposes in general though not in detail, and left to Sumner Welles, the Assistant Secretary in charge of Latin American affairs, together with members of the Latin American Division, the task of formulating them in draft form. Finally, on August 20, 1936, the Argentine Government extended an official invitation to all the American Republics to take part in the conference at Buenos Aires beginning December 1.

Since a year and a half elapsed between the time the conference began to be thought of and the day it convened, few international meetings enjoyed more meticulous advance preparation. When we had sailed for Montevideo in 1933 I was obliged to evolve some of our chief projects en route on the boat. Months before I sailed for Buenos Aires on November 7, 1936, aboard the same ship, the *American Legion,* our projects had been carefully drafted and circulated among the other Republics.

The personnel of the American delegation was announced on October 31. With myself as chairman, it consisted of Sumner Welles; Alexander W. Weddell, our Ambassador to Argentina; Adolf A. Berle, Jr., chamberlain of New York City; Alexander F. Whitney, president of the Brotherhood of Railroad Trainmen; Charles G. Fenwick, professor of political science, Bryn Mawr College; Michael Francis Doyle, lawyer of Philadelphia; and Mrs. Elise F. Musser, State Senator of Utah.

The President gave me the function of choosing the delegation, as he had done in the case of the Montevideo Conference. Welles asked me to name him as a delegate, which I did gladly since he had taken a principal share in the work of preparation. He rendered efficient service at Buenos Aires, as did the other delegates, in particular Ambassador Weddell. Berle, a close friend of Welles, was selected by the President in 1938 to be Assistant Secretary of State. He possessed remarkable keenness, with literary capacity, and served with unusual efficiency.

Some time prior to my departure, the President told me he was thinking of paying a visit to Buenos Aires for the opening of the conference, and asked what I thought of it. I replied I would be delighted to have him go, and his visit would stimulate the meeting and much improve the sentiment of Latin Americans toward us.

Aboard the *American Legion* I continued the practice I had started en route to the London Conference and confirmed en route to the Montevideo Conference, of holding frequent shipboard meetings of the American delegation, along with the technical assistants who accompanied us, so that each might be familiar with the work to be achieved. We arrived at Buenos Aires November 25, and were met by Saavedra Lamas and other officials.

On that same day Hitler announced his Anti-Comintern Pact with Japan.

The Latin America I now visited differed from the Latin America I saw just three years before, because Axis penetration had made rapid, alarming headway under various guises. For many months we had received reports from our representatives in the countries to the south of us which, added together, created a picture of threatening colors. Nazi Germany, in particular, was making intensive efforts to gain an ascendancy among our neighbors, but Italy and Japan were working feverishly as well.

We began to note that many of the German ministers in Latin American countries had become figureheads in contrast to the local representatives of the German Nazi Party. These Nazi leaders, using coercion where necessary, were organizing the nearly million and a half Germans living in Latin America into segments of the Nazi Party controlled by the Auslands organization in Berlin, and were sending some of them to Germany for indoctrination in Nazi methods and beliefs. The ideas of racial superiority propagated in Germany were being spread among the Germans in the New World. They were made to understand that, despite emigration to the Americas, their loyalty was still to the Fatherland.

The German Lufthansa airlines and the German steamship companies were utilized to the utmost in spreading Nazi philosophy. German radios were beamed to Latin America, and German news services, purveying news with a strong Nazi slant, were set up. Indications began coming to us that the Germans were installing espionage agents in Latin America.

The Nazis in Germany, being themselves strongly militarized, made every effort to establish intimate contacts with the armies of the Latin American Republics. Long before Hitler came into power, unemployed German army officers, surplus from the First World War, were widely used in South America to promote German theories of war and training for war. Under Hitler this trend intensified. Latin American army officers were invited to attend German military schools, and the new might of a reawakened Reich was thoroughly impressed upon them.

The Germany of Hitler and Schacht was straining every tendon to undermine United States trade relations with Latin America. In September, 1935, Schacht launched an ambitious plan for barter trade with Latin America on a large scale. German imports from Latin America were paid for in special marks placed to the credit of the Latin American exporters, who could use them only for the purchase of German goods to be exported to Latin America. Germany's percentage of the total Latin American trade began to rise perceptibly.

I had had a conversation on this subject with the German Chargé, Herr Rudolf Leitner, on May 4, 1936, prior to his return to Germany where he was to take charge of the Division of American Nations in the German Foreign Office. Germany, I said, could, if she wanted, displace a substantial portion of United States markets in Latin America by using her present narrow, arbitrary, and artificial trade and financial methods. By continuing in this way, she could handicap the United States Government in its efforts to carry forward its present program for trade restoration.

"But Germany," I emphasized, "is not really increasing her international trade by this policy. Actually she is exporting considerable capital. Of course, we ourselves can pursue the same course if we wish. But it would be like taking opium. It would leave this Government worse off in the long run, just as it is leaving all the important nations of Europe worse off."

Herr Leitner indicated that he would convey these thoughts to his superiors in Berlin.

It was with all these developments in mind that I began my preliminary meetings with my colleagues from the other American Republics, including ten other foreign ministers. I was encouraged to find that the heritage of good will left by the Montevideo Conference was substantial.

But I soon became aware that the Saavedra Lamas of the Montevideo Conference had receded from the friendly cooperation he had shown me there. This despite the fact that on the day before my arrival at Buenos Aires he had been awarded the Nobel Peace Prize, for which I unofficially had recommended him and virtually managed the movement in his behalf. I issued a statement saying that the prize was most worthily bestowed because of his outstanding services for the cause of peace.

Unfortunately, Saavedra Lamas had just returned to Buenos Aires from Geneva, where he had presided over the League Assembly. To him the League of Nations was still a vital, powerful organization. Even before the conference met, it was apparent that he would oppose anything that seemed to him remotely to infringe on the League. His eyes would be more on the dying League than on the living Pan American idea.

President Roosevelt reached Buenos Aires on the cruiser *Indianapolis* November 30. Probably no distinguished visitor to Argentina ever received so great a welcome. I felt that both the Government and every individual citizen had made special efforts to make this an historic event. The President was met at the pier by the President of Argentina, Agustín P. Justo, the Cabinet, leading members of the legislature and courts, and thousands of outstanding individuals. The reception was all that one could have desired for enthusiastic cordiality, friendliness, and hospitality.

The following day the President addressed the opening session of the conference. Speaking of the mounting threats of war abroad and the determination of the Americas to remain at peace, he said: "We in the Americas make it at the same time clear that we stand shoulder to shoulder in our final determination that others, who, driven by war madness or land hunger, might seek to commit acts of aggression against us, will find a hemisphere wholly prepared to consult together for our mutual safety and our mutual good."

While in Buenos Aires the President promised the Argentines he would use his influence to get Congress to permit the importation of Argentine meat into the United States, previously forbidden because of the hoof-and-mouth disease in Argentina. This was an important matter to Argentina, one that could, and did, have great effect on our political relations. Unfortunately, the high-tariff members of the Senate were to insist on drastic interpretation of the sanitary law, and the President was not to be able to fulfill his and Argentina's hopes.

Three days after the President's departure on December 2, I delivered my first address to the conference, and based our Government's program for the maintenance of peace on what I called "Eight Pillars of Peace." These were:

"(1) Peoples must be educated for peace. Each nation must make itself safe for peace.

"(2) Frequent conferences between representatives of nations, and intercourse between their peoples, are essential.

"(3) The consummation of the five well-known peace agreements will provide adequate peace machinery. [These included the Kellogg Pact and the Saavedra Lamas Antiwar Pact.]

"(4) In the event of war in this hemisphere, there should be a common policy of neutrality.

"(5) The nations should adopt commercial policies to bring each that prosperity upon which enduring peace is founded.

"(6) Practical international cooperation is essential to restore many indispensable relationships between nations and prevent the demoralization with which national character and conduct are threatened.

"(7) International law should be reestablished, revitalized, and strengthened. Armies and navies are no permanent substitute for its great principles.

"(8) Faithful observance of undertakings between nations is the foundation of international order, and rests upon moral law, the highest of all law."

On December 7—five years to the day before Pearl Harbor—I introduced a resolution to bulwark peace in the Western Hemisphere. After coordinating the five peace agreements existing among the American Republics, it provided for compulsory consultation among the foreign ministers of the Republics in case of any threat to peace in the Western Hemisphere. For this purpose a permanent Inter-American Consultative Committee would be set up. It also called for the establishment of a common neutrality policy in case war broke out in the Western Hemisphere.

Although this resolution stated that it was not to conflict with the obligations of those Republics who were members of the League, Saavedra Lamas bitterly opposed it on this very point. He thought that the consultative body of American foreign ministers might cut into the League. He refused to accept the idea of a common neutrality policy embracing an arms embargo, because the League permitted the export of arms to a nation that was being attacked. My reservation in favor of the Republics that were League members was as broad as a barn door, but he could not see it.

I had several conferences alone with Saavedra Lamas and several in company with Welles and one or two other members of the delegation. These discussions became increasingly animated. Our last conference was heated, some sharp words were exchanged at least on my side, and we parted with no signs of complete agreement. I saw no more of Saavedra Lamas before leaving Buenos Aires. He did not extend the usual courtesy of seeing me off.

It would have done no good to have let Saavedra Lamas sponsor one of my proposals, as I had done at Montevideo with such good results. For one thing the proposals had been circulated long in advance and, for another, Saavedra Lamas had formulated an inflexible policy of opposition in advance of the conference.

Saavedra Lamas was backed up throughout by President Justo of Argentina. Señor Justo expressed himself as being in entire sympathy with the conference and its purposes, although he was considered to be more or less a dictator and the representative of that section of the population which favored a dictatorship. He and his Government made splendid hosts for the conference. He did not, however, participate actively and personally in its work, as President Terra of Uruguay had done at Montevideo. Justo, unlike his successor, Dr. Ortiz, sided with his Foreign Minister in his obstructive course or declined, in any event, to interfere.

The Brazilian delegation, ably headed by José Carlos de Macedo Soares and Oswaldo Aranha, gave us full cooperation, as usual.

Finally, in order to obtain complete agreement, the resolution was watered down. Consultation among the Republics was agreed to in case of a threat to peace in the Western Hemisphere, but the idea of a permanent Inter-American Consultative Committee was dropped. A common neutrality policy was retained as a general objective, but the Republics were at liberty to act under it in accordance with their treaty obligations, including those to the League, and with their domestic legislation.

I intended that this agreement should lessen the possibility of war between or among any American Republics. The Chaco War still burned in our minds. By this accord we pledged ourselves to consult and cooperate to make available effective means of pacific settlement of disputes. We promised that, while consultation was in progress, the parties to a dispute would not have recourse to hostilities of any kind for at least six months. The American Republics involved in a controversy obligated themselves to report to the other American Governments the methods of pacific settlement which they selected, as well as the progress made in adjusting the controversy. If war, despite all these precautions, should break out, the other American Republics would consult and seek to adopt a common attitude as neutrals so as to impede or prevent the spread or prolongation of the war.

The conference adopted another convention that was of more importance because it dealt with threats to the New World from the outside. By it the twenty-one Republics agreed to consult and collaborate in the event of a menace to their peace from any source, or in the event of war or virtual state of war between American Republics, or if war outside America threatened the peace of the American Republics. Thus, for the first time, the American Republics sought to lay the groundwork for meeting the threat to their peace which might come at any time as war clouds lowered over Europe. The Monroe Doctrine protected them from dangers overseas, but that doctrine had come to assume in the minds of many of their leaders a connotation of domination of the Western Hemisphere by the United States. Under the new convention, the American Republics took one step in the direction of a hemispheric Monroe Doctrine. We were to go much further at the Pan American Conference at Lima two years later, and at the Havana Conference in 1940.

The Argentines, however, were able to emasculate this resolution by inserting four words between two commas in the clause providing that the American Republics, in the event of war outside America which might menace their peace, should consult to determine the proper time and manner in which they might eventually cooperate in some action tending to preserve the peace of the American Continent. The words were, "if they so desire."

The conference implemented and somewhat strengthened the agreement we had reached at Montevideo in 1933 to refrain from intervening in the internal or external affairs of one another, by adding to it an agreement to consult among ourselves in the event of such intervention. To bolster their peace resolutions, the American Republics also approved a declaration that every act susceptible of disturbing the peace of America affected each and every one of them and justified the consultation just provided for. Under this declaration the Republics accepted the principles that territorial conquest is proscribed; that such acquisition through violence is not recognized; that intervention of one state in the internal or external affairs of another is condemned; that forcible collection of debts is illegal; and that any controversy between American nations be settled by conciliation, unrestricted arbitration, or international justice.

The conference reemphasized the economics resolution I had introduced at Montevideo to eliminate excessive obstacles to international trade. It adopted a resolution I presented providing for government assistance in the exchange of students and professors among the American Republics in order to promote their cultural relations.

The question of any action with regard to the civil war raging in Spain did not arise, despite the interest of all of us in the issues presented. The Spanish Government would have liked to see some declaration of sympathy for its cause or some measure of assistance. One of the primary objectives of the Buenos Aires Conference, however, was to keep away from the Western Hemisphere the wars in which European nations were involved, and the greater war toward which they appeared inevitably to be heading. This was in direct conflict with the desire of the Spanish Government to see the New World intervene in the affairs of the Old.

Prior to my departure from Washington, Spanish Ambassador de los Ríos had sounded me out on the possibility of having a Spanish observer at the conference. He based this on the grounds that Spain was the mother country of many of the Latin American Republics. The same question had arisen at the Montevideo Conference. Then I had said I had no objection to Spain having an observer at the conference, but I would object to his attending its secret meetings. Thereupon Spain lost interest. Now I said to the Ambassador that, although Spain was the mother country of many of the American Republics, Portugal was the mother country of Brazil, France of Haiti, and Great Britain of the United States. If we granted Spain's request, we should logically open the conference to the other nations as well. I also made the point that the Pan American Conferences were intended to deal with American affairs only, although the principles they advocated were of world application.

As the Buenos Aires Conference neared its close, I was not fully satisfied with its achievements, owing to the fact that the Argentine delegation under Saavedra Lamas had whittled down the pillars of our major agreements. Consequently, I prepared to give an address to emphasize the importance of what we had been able to achieve and to offer it as an example to the rest of the world, rushing hell-bent toward war. Owing to a cold, I was unable to deliver it, and Welles read it for me on December 23.

"The very fact of the conference itself," I said, "should offer to other quarters of the world an impressive demonstration of the value of concert and cooperation. Whenever twenty-one nations can forgather in such a spirit and for such purposes, whenever they can act together harmoniously in the cause of peace, all other nations should find profit in their example."

As powerfully as I could I tried to put into words the hatred I felt toward war. In this year of 1936 war had raged in Europe, Africa, and Asia. Even as the delegates listened to my address, soldiers undoubtedly were being killed somewhere, and civilians too. The fighting up to then appeared to me, however, to be only the prologue to a greater conflict, the script for which was already being written. Nevertheless, I never ceased to condemn the idea of war. Even if the world were to be thrown into war by the blind ambitions of a few dictators, an underlying and popular hatred of war could be built up which might shorten the conflict and, more important, incline world public opinion later on toward acceptance of an international organization to prevent war.

"Why should statesmen," I said, "looking only to the past, insist that war is inevitable? If history shows that wars have been frequent, it likewise shows that enlightened statesmanship could have prevented most of them. War is not an act of God but a crime of man. War is something that is provoked by evil passions. Hate, fear, greed, vainglory, the lust for power; these are the progenitors of war. If peoples tolerated war in the past, it has become impossible for them to do so any longer. For the instruments of destruction which have been invented are now so devastating in their effects that compromise with them is no longer possible. To attempt to humanize war is to attempt the impossible. We must destroy war or war will destroy us. I do not believe that peoples will passively accept the conclusion that because men since time immemorial have died on battlefields they have no choice but to continue to die on battlefields in the future."

The following day, Christmas Eve, I received a telegram from the President extending Christmas greetings from himself and Mrs. Roosevelt to myself, Mrs. Hull, the delegation, and their families. "In this," he said, "millions of people join, for yours has been an accomplishment in close accord with the spirit of Christmas." When I returned to Washington I found that the President had sent this message in his own handwriting to the State Department, with a request that it be cabled to me.

After my return to the United States, I summed up the Buenos Aires Conference in an address to the Council on Foreign Relations in New York City on February 25, 1937. The conference had two outstanding features, I said. "The first of these was the subject matter of the conference itself—its all-embracing concentration upon the problem of safeguarding the maintenance of peace. The second was the dismal world setting in which the representatives of the American Republics assembled for their arduous and momentous labors."

Outlining the major agreements reached at Buenos Aires, I said: "Three main premises were accepted by all. The first was that the American hemisphere has a distinct and peculiar contribution to make because no nation in it is driven by any compulsion or professes any right to threaten the peace of its neighbors. The second was that the only safety for all nations is loyal acceptance of a rule of law under which the integrity of every country, large or small, will be assured. The third was that renunciation of war and other similar declarations must be implemented by a method of action which can set into operation almost instantaneously the cooperative effort of the hemisphere in the direction of pacific settlements."

On May 15, 1937, I transmitted to the President for submission to the Senate eight agreements reached at Buenos Aires. The Senate voted its consent and the President, on July 15, 1937, ratified them.

The Good Neighbor policy was steadily expanding and strengthening.

36: "Neutrality" Made "Permanent"

FIVE DAYS AFTER the President signed the arms embargo applying to Spain, I returned to Washington from Buenos Aires. From then on, for the next two years, scarcely a day passed but that I was called upon to give consideration to the Spanish situation. We sought throughout to adhere in fact and spirit to the policy we set forth in August, 1936, a policy confirmed by the creation of the Nonintervention Committee in London and formalized by the Act of January 8, 1937. We favored neither side, but we sympathized with the Spanish people and desired an end to the war as soon as possible. In carrying out our policy, we were subjected to unrelenting pressure from both sides and had to solve innumerable delicate problems.

Ambassador Bowers, in a letter to me dated February 23, 1937, raised the question whether we should deal with the Insurgent group, especially in view of the contacts in the commercial field Britain was maintaining there. He thought Britain's contacts would give her a definite advantage after the war if the Insurgents won.

Replying on March 9, I said: "I do not see how we could escape the charge that we had abandoned our policy of neutrality and non-intervention if we were to deal with the Insurgent group, particularly for the purpose of obtaining commercial advantages, when we have not so far recognized the Insurgent movement and we are still carrying on our normal official relations with the Spanish Government. I am afraid we shall have to depend for our good will upon the recognition of the Spanish authorities that we have pursued a meticulously impartial attitude in this conflict which, if it had been followed by all the other countries of the world, might have changed the aspect of the situation as it exists today."

Even the apparently nonpolitical question of relief operations in Spain presented some delicate aspects. We emphatically encouraged relief for the thousands of civilians who were made homeless or ill or were injured by the Civil War, but we suggested that contributions and offers of assistance should be made to the American Red Cross which would work with the International Red Cross in Geneva.

"Some of the other activities being carried on for the collection of funds for relief in Spain," I wrote Ambassador Bowers on March 9, 1937, "appear to be based on the theory that humanitarian work should only be carried out for one of the political factions and distinctly not for the other."

At first we discouraged sending medical units to Spain in line with our general policy of nonintervention which included declining to issue passports for individuals to proceed to Spain. We were then still helping Americans to get out of Spain. "Many of the people who have been pressing us here for permission to send American personnel over with medical units," I wrote Bowers, "have been motivated by a strong partial feeling either for one group or the other and would presumably align themselves with the forces or authorities of one side." We were willing, however, to facilitate the travel of Americans who volunteered to work under the International Red Cross; and in March, 1937, at the President's suggestion, we agreed to issue passports to Spain for physicians, nurses, and necessary attendants of bona fide medical and relief missions.

American volunteers for the Spanish Loyalist Army presented a further difficult problem. In a dispatch on March 15, our Consul at Valencia estimated that there were 1,700 American volunteers in the Spanish Government Army. This despite the fact that the United States Penal Code made it an offense for anyone within the territory or jurisdiction of the United States to enlist himself or hire someone else to enlist in a foreign army, and that an Act of March 2, 1907, deprived of his American citizenship any national of this country taking an oath of allegiance to a foreign government. Under-cover organizations in the United States were getting around the Code by sending the volunteers to France to enlist there and cross the border into Spain.

On the day I returned from Buenos Aires, the State Department cabled our Consul General in Barcelona to call the provision of the United States Code to the attention of any American volunteers who contacted him, and point out that "the enlistment of American citizens in either of the opposing forces is unpatriotically inconsistent with the American Government's policy of the most scrupulous nonintervention in Spanish internal affairs."

One day a ringleader of the Spanish leftists in this country came to my office and referred indirectly to the work he and others were carrying on in inducing young Americans to cross the seas and join in the fighting in Spain. He was rather blunt in a remark to me, whereupon I interrupted and inquired: "Which boat are you taking to join in this fight?" He toned down immediately and said he was too occupied in the work on this side.

Countless attempts were made to evade the arms embargo. Unscrupulous persons, and sometimes innocent persons employed by those less innocent, sought licenses to export arms to France, Latvia, Poland, Turkey, Greece, Russia, Belgium, Canada, or Mexico. Upon inquiring of those Governments before issuing the licenses, we learned that neither they nor their citizens had placed orders for the arms. Further investigation developed that the arms were destined for Spain. In some cases forged requests for licenses were presented ostensibly on behalf of certain governments which, upon inquiry, knew nothing of the matter.

Joseph C. Green, chief of the Department's Office of Arms and Munitions Control, was indefatigable and successful in pursuing such requests for export licenses to their true source. The value of the legal authority given the State Department to supervise the traffic in arms was easily demonstrated.

Whenever we legitimately could, we used our influence directly to keep the Spanish War from spreading. After the German battleship *Deutschland* was bombed by a Loyalist plane and, in retaliation, shelled the Loyalist port of Almería, there was talk of open war between Germany and Spain. I called in German Ambassador Dieckhoff on May 31, 1937, and said that my Government expressed to his Government its most earnest hope that Germany would see its way clear to make a peaceful adjustment of this dispute with Spain.

As the war proceeded, both factions in Spain were supported by numerous, very vocal organizations on this side. They bombarded each other with accusations, and Congress, the White House, and the State Department with petitions. The Loyalists wanted the arms embargo lifted, the Insurgents wanted it retained. Many eminent Americans joined one group or the other, but the great mass of Americans were content to let the Government pursue its policy.

Neutrality again formed the subject of much debate in Congress from January to April, 1937, in view of the fact that the Act of February 29, 1936, was due to expire on May 1. The legislation pertaining to Spain had been a separate, emergency Act limited to an arms embargo. Now Congress had to decide what permanent, broad-scale neutrality legislation should be in effect after May 1. Prior to my departure for Buenos Aires and during my stay there, the State Department studied the question but did not prepare any legislation for submission to Congress. We felt that we would have a better chance of securing some degree of flexibility in the new neutrality legislation if we did not press our own draft on Congress. We were in frequent contact, however, with Congressional leaders.

Senator Pittman introduced a neutrality resolution on January 22 and three days later Representative McReynolds introduced one. Although both bills provided for a mandatory arms embargo, the House bill generally gave the President greater discretion. Both bills contained "cash-and-carry" provisions, meaning that American ships could not carry goods of any kind to belligerents, and the ownership of all goods shipped to belligerents had to pass into foreign hands before they could leave the United States.

To take care of cases such as the Spanish Civil War, Senator Pittman's resolution contained an amendment providing that when the President found the existence in a foreign country of a state of civil strife of such magnitude or being conducted under such conditions that the export of war products would threaten the peace of the United States, an arms embargo would apply. The resolution also made the collection of charitable funds for belligerents or factions in a civil war subject to the approval and regulations of the President. It forbade the arming of American merchant vessels trading with belligerents. The President had at first opposed this provision, believing that it applied to American vessels trading with neutrals as well, but he withdrew his objection on learning its real scope. Travel by Americans on belligerent vessels was now forbidden, whereas previously it had been declared to be at their own risk. The embargo on loans or credits to belligerents was continued, although the President could exempt short-term commercial credits used in normal peacetime transactions. The President was given discretionary authority to prevent American ports from being used as supply bases for belligerent vessels.

The President also wanted a provision inserted in the resolution providing that, if American property destined to a neutral country were seized on the high seas and transferred to a belligerent ship, he be authorized to impound in the United States a like amount of property belonging to the belligerent country or its citizens, to be held as security pending an adjustment of the seizure. I handed him a memorandum prepared by Assistant Secretary Moore and Legal Adviser Hackworth to the effect that retaliatory measures of this type might lead us into difficulties and possibly war, which it was the purpose of neutrality legislation to avoid.

The President, in a memorandum to me on February 8, 1937, replied that his suggestion would give "the Secretary of State and the President another weapon with which to protect American ships or American goods bound to neutral ports." He admitted that this might lead to objection on the part of the belligerent, but said: "Nevertheless, it goes along with the common law and statutes which provide that if one individual's property is seized by some other person who may at the same time dissipate his own means of paying damage, the original owner can get an order to impound the assets of the individual who has taken his property." The President, however, did not press the point further.

The resolution was a composite of mandatory and permissive features, with the emphasis on the mandatory side. It retained the phrasing of the February 29, 1936, Act in leaving it to the President to find whether a state of war existed. The House resolution gave him some discretion in applying the "cash" feature of the "cash-and-carry" amendment. It was permanent legislation in that it did not, as was the case with previous neutrality Acts, expire on any set date.

I did not appear before the Senate Foreign Relations Committee during their hearings on Pittman's resolution, but several officials of the Department did so and emphasized that the Department was not sponsoring any one of the neutrality bills before Congress. I felt that Congress was determined on neutrality legislation of an inflexible nature, and our arguments in favor of flexible neutrality legislation that would leave the widest possible discretion to the Executive would have little effect. Where we could, we obtained slight modifications more in conformity with our ideas.

"Cash-and-carry," for instance, was highly popular with the public. The phrase had caught the people's fancy. From my viewpoint of doing what we could to back the efforts of Britain and France toward peace, it was not wholly objectionable. If war should come between Britain and France on one side and Germany and Italy on the other, it was obvious that this provision would operate in favor of the democracies, who had the cash to buy and the ships to carry.

Pittman's resolution passed the Senate on March 3 by a vote of 63 to 6. McReynolds's resolution passed the House by a vote of 376 to 12. These overwhelming votes confirmed the determination of Congress, as expressed virtually unanimously in January, to prevent the shipment of arms to Spain. American supporters of the Spanish Government who then and later sought to get American arms to Spain could scarcely argue that Congress was divided on the issue.

A Conference Committee spent some weeks ironing out differences between the Senate and House resolutions. The State Department maintained a neutral attitude toward the two resolutions, although my opinion continued to be, as I stated it in a press conference on February 18: "Generally speaking, the attitude of the Department the last two or three years has been more in the direction of permissive legislation as a policy than Congress has been disposed to follow. In those circumstances it is natural that the Department would not send over a bill of its own, but would be disposed to look with more favor on proposed legislation in either House that might contain the smallest amount of purely mandatory and inflexible legislation."

The Conference Committee's report, retaining the House provision leaving the application of the "cash" portion of "cash-and-carry" to the discretion of the President, received the approval of both Houses of Congress on April 29. The following day I received from the President a letter asking whether I saw any objection to his signing the joint resolution. On the same day I sent the President a letter recommending he sign, and attaching drafts of two proclamations to be issued on signing. The President affixed his signature on May 1 and issued the two proclamations, one defining arms, ammunition, and implements of war and the other placing an embargo on the shipment of arms to Spain. In conformity with the new law, the State Department began on May 5 to require persons or organizations collecting funds to relieve suffering in Spain to register with the Department and to submit monthly sworn statements of the amounts received and the disposition made of them.

In this month of May, 1937, the President appointed Sumner Welles Under Secretary of State. For some months I had been carrying more than my normal share of duties because of the fact that I had no Under Secretary of State, owing to the departure of William Phillips in September, 1936, to be Ambassador to Italy. I had cheerfully—but very reluctantly—yielded to Phillips's earnest request to be made Ambassador to Rome.

My reluctance had a twofold cause. Phillips had proven thoroughly capable, loyal, and cooperative. Furthermore, I knew that creating the vacancy in the office of Under Secretary would be worse than lifting the lid of a new Pandora's box, because two Assistant Secretaries of State, Welles and Moore, were strong candidates for the position. I was told that Welles sought the post at the beginning of the Administration, but that the President preferred Phillips. I now preferred Moore for the vacancy.

Welles and Moore waged a bitter controversy for many months in

their rivalry for the appointment. The President, who had the responsibility for filling the vacancy, kept clear out of sight of this competition,
although ordinarily he seemed to enjoy making appointments. I thought
that, in his own mind, he slightly preferred Welles, with whom he had
been longer on friendly terms, although he and Moore had also been
close personal friends for several years.

I myself did not become an open partisan by making a recommendation to the President. I felt that the President intended, in any event, to
appoint Welles, and, if I recommended Moore, my friend of many years,
I would be left in a serious predicament following Welles's appointment.

Finally, after more than a half year of vying for the nomination,
Welles and Moore agreed to compromise. Previously there had existed
another position in the Department, that of Counselor, which virtually
ranked with that of Under Secretary and was above that of Assistant
Secretary. This position had not been filled for some years, for reasons
of mistaken economy. Unfortunately, before I entered the State Department, an agreement had been entered into between the Department and
the Appropriations Committee of the House of Representatives that this
office would not be filled until a new understanding was reached between
the Department and the committee.

Under the compromise accepted by Welles and Moore and submitted
to the President and me, Welles would become Under Secretary and
Moore would be named Counselor, this position to be revived through
agreement with the House committee and its functions to be given increased strength and prestige. The President and I immediately approved
the arrangement, which came into effect on May 20, 1937. So far as I was
aware, there arose out of this situation no serious disturbance of my
agreeable working relations with either Welles or Moore.

In the spring and summer of 1937, as German and Italian aid to the
Franco forces increased, a movement rose in this country demanding that
the arms embargo be extended to Germany and Italy. Senator Nye introduced a resolution pointed in this direction. I held a conference with
State Department officers on March 25 to discuss this development. We
agreed that there was no existing state of war between nations, that the
presence of volunteers did not create a state of war, and that it would be
illogical for the United States to find a state of war between Spain on the
one hand and Italy and Germany on the other when the Spanish Government itself had not taken that position.

It seemed to me that Nye's resolution was part of an effort to get the

United States to take sides in the conflict. The Office of Arms and Munitions Control studied the possible effects of such an embargo on Germany and reported they would be very small. Germany and Italy were importing only an insignificant quantity of war products from the United States, chiefly airplane engines to be installed in planes manufactured for other countries. Prohibition of credits to Germany and Italy would be of no effect because they were already prohibited under the Johnson Act of 1934.

Our conclusion was that imposing an arms embargo and other restrictions of the Neutrality Act on Italy and Germany was not likely to have a sobering effect on those countries and might, on the contrary, seriously endanger the success of the conciliatory efforts being made by Britain and France and thus increase the likelihood of a general war.

The President was now being daily besieged by visitors and bombarded by telegrams, letters, and petitions requesting him to apply the Neutrality Act to Germany and Italy. The savage bombing of the Basque city of Guernica by the Franco forces employing German and Italian planes lent fuel to the campaign. On June 29 the President sent me a note in which he said: "For many reasons I think that if Mussolini or the Italian Government or Hitler or the German Government have made any official admissions or statements that their Government armed forces are actually taking part in the fighting in Spain on the side of Franco, or are engaging in the Spanish War, then in such case we shall have to act under the Neutrality Act. I am thinking about precedents and the future. It has been our contention that war exists if the government armed forces of any nation upon the territory of another nation are engaged in fighting."

The President added he did not think we could "compound a ridiculous situation if, after the fight is established, Great Britain and France continue to assert solemnly that they 'have no proof' of Italian or German participation in the Spanish War."

He asked if I did not think we should cable Ambassadors Phillips in Rome and Dodd in Berlin and ask for categorical answers. "According to some of the newspapers," he commented, "Mussolini has personally directed participation by the regular Italian armed forces—and Hitler has also made the same kind of statement." He asked me to check all the above and telephone him at Hyde Park within the next several days.

I accordingly sent out cables asking for information and comment. I requested Ambassador Bingham in London also to ascertain, as if on his own initiative, whether the British Government considered that a state of war existed between the German and Italian Governments and the Spanish Government, and what would be the effect òn the British and Continental Governments if we declared an arms embargo against Germany and Italy.

Bingham went to see Eden, who told him that a state of war could technically not be considered to exist between the Spanish Government on the one hand and Germany and Italy on the other, or between Franco and any other nation, so long as the Nonintervention Committee continued to function under the authorization of the member governments. Eden commented that an arms embargo against Germany and Italy was, "to say the least, premature," and would complicate his task.

Bingham commented to me that intervention in the Spanish conflict had not been confined to Italy and Germany but was equally true of Russia and was likewise true of France in the first few days of the war and might be again. Any application of an arms embargo to Germany and Italy might therefore have to be extended to other nations as well. Furthermore, any departure from the spirit of the neutrality legislation, which was one of strict neutrality, would be regarded by Europe as a gratuitous interference in continental affairs.

In my cable to Rome I made it a special point to say to Ambassador Phillips that the recent series of overt acts, meaning Italian and German help to Franco, had intensified the pressure on the President to extend the arms embargo. Therefore, I was strongly disposed to call in the Italian Chargé (Ambassador Suvich was away) and German Ambassador Dieckhoff and tell them frankly, in a spirit of friendly advice, that it would be a mistake for them to assume that the President's understandable reluctance up to this point to take action precluded in any way the possibility that, if further overt acts should occur, the President might be forced by public opinion to extend the arms embargo to Germany and Italy. This was an indirect move to induce Mussolini to halt Italian intervention in Spain.

In reply Ambassador Phillips cabled the Italian attitude that Russia, France, and England had given assistance to the Spanish Government, and that this justified Italy's aid to the Franco Government, which Italy had formally recognized as the established Government of Spain. Italy would keenly resent any step directed solely against her unless similar action was taken with regard to all countries believed to have rendered notable assistance to the Loyalist Government. Furthermore, if the President declared that a state of war did exist between Italy and Spain, it might force other countries to do the very thing which they had jointly sought to avoid, that is, to spread the conflict beyond the Spanish frontier.

In the State Department we recognized, moreover, that no state of war had been declared by Spain, by Germany, or by Italy; that Germany and Italy had recognized the Insurgents as the Government of Spain, and their acts might be viewed accordingly; that citizens of many countries, including the United States, were fighting on both sides in Spain; and that the Spanish Government and the Insurgents had each received material assistance from other European countries.

I telephoned the President and placed before him all these facts and comments. After I finished, he readily agreed to continue our position unchanged. We were both decided that an arms embargo against Germany and Italy should not be applied unless general war broke out in Europe.

Significantly, the Spanish Government did not formally protest our nonintervention policy until sixteen months after the Civil War broke out. Spanish Ambassador de los Ríos had several times asked personally if arms could not be sent to Spain, but it was not until November 19, 1937, that he addressed a note to me protesting against the Acts of January 8 and May 1 on the grounds that they were contrary to the 1902 Treaty of Friendship between the United States and Spain and to a provision of international law recognizing the right of a legitimate government to acquire the means to defend itself.

Verbal discussions took place with the Ambassador on these points, and then, on December 31 I sent him a formal note in reply. I said that the legal points concerning the 1902 treaty had been fully discussed with him by Assistant Secretary of State Hugh R. Wilson, but that I would be glad to discuss them further if he wished.

With regard to the point of international law, I first recalled that, "due to the troubled state of the world and to the well known desire of this Government to keep this country out of war, this Government has in the past two years, under specific provisions of law enacted by the Congress, pursued a policy of refusing to permit the export of arms, ammunition, and implements of war to warring nations." I then said: "I must most definitely state my conviction that the question of the control of the export of arms, ammunition, and implements of war from the United States to foreign countries is a domestic question to be decided by this Government alone on the basis of the probable effect of such control upon the fundamental policies of the Government; to wit, by

every legitimate means to keep this country out of war and to avoid interference of any kind in the internal affairs of other nations. This Government does not concur in the thesis that it is obligatory under international
law to provide arms to either or both of the parties to a war or a civil
conflict."

The legal argument was frequently advanced during 1937 and 1938
by personal sympathizers of the Loyalist Government. They saw only one
question involved, which was for other nations to hurl themselves at once
into the Spanish conflict and aid the side these sympathizers favored. The
theory such elements entertained was that, under a precept of international law, a government facing an insurrection had a right to purchase
from other countries any needed military supplies; therefore there was
no excuse for other nations to prohibit the export of such supplies to the
Spanish Government. What these persons overlooked was a brand-new
and broader condition which the United States Government did not dare
overlook; namely, that the extreme danger of the Spanish conflagration
spreading over Europe imperatively called for nonintervention or the with-
holding of exports to Spain.

The possibility of our being drawn into the conflict and thereby
prejudicing our security and peace brought into play the principle of self-
defense. There are often occasions when some principle of international
law must be reconciled with another, for example, the rights and duties
of neutrals versus those of belligerents. The principle of self-defense was
over and above any isolated clause of such law. The same principle had
been threshed out at great length by more than a score of peaceful European nations. They unanimously agreed that the danger of the Spanish
War being spread over Europe by a policy of intervention was serious,
and they did not hesitate to embargo exports of arms to Spain and to go
even further and try to prevent such exports from countries that did not
have peace at heart. They had agreed on this policy months before the
United States took definite action through Congress.

Hence the United States, while supporting the general European
policy of nonintervention, based its course on the law of self-defense. The
question was not which side in Spain was right and which wrong, but
the necessity to keep ourselves from being drawn into the war. If we were
to follow the theory of the Loyalist supporters, the United States would
be kept busy traveling up and down the earth, giving support to struggling states and groups on the theory that they were in the right and
that, therefore, we had to help them regardless of any consideration for

our own security and peace. Had we been a member of an effective system of international security, the situation might have been different.

Three years later, when German U-boats were approaching our shores, sinking our ships and destroying American lives, this Government announced that the danger had become so serious it could no longer sit still and rely on policies of neutrality under international law. It decided it must adopt a broader and more compelling policy of self-defense, such as rendering the shipping lanes secure and offering Lend-Lease supplies to the democracies at war, thereby superseding all laws pertaining to neutrality that might conflict with such acts of self-defense. Then, again, many shouters and clackers demanded that we forget the imminent danger that imperatively required us to invoke the law of self-defense, and cling, with eyes shut, to the laws of neutrality.

Throughout 1937 and 1938 numerous bills were introduced in Congress to amend or repeal the Neutrality Act. Senator King, on February 7, 1938, introduced a bill to repeal and Senator Pittman sent it to me for comment. Replying on February 24, I said: "I think it is generally agreed that our law should authorize the Government in the case of war between nations or civil strife in some other nation, to take such action as will promote the preservation of the peace and welfare of this country, and it is certain that this is the purpose which the statute in question was intended to serve. Therefore, whatever changes may be made in legislative enactments, this purpose should in my opinion be preserved, but with greater discretion in the President, with whom rests responsibility for the conduct of our foreign relations."

I added that, in certain contingencies, there should be authority to apply an arms embargo. Also, that the licensing system operated under the National Munitions Control Board was an entirely sound policy because it was most important that we at all times should have a record of arms shipments. Moreover, "while differences of opinion may exist as to the wisdom of legislation authorizing the control of the export of articles other than arms, ammunition, and implements of war, that authority might in many cases be found extremely useful." I added that other provisions, such as those relating to financial transactions with belligerents, American vessels carrying arms, and prohibiting travel by American citizens on belligerent vessels, filled gaps in previous neutrality legislation.

This synthesized my attitude toward neutrality legislation, following the passage, within two years, of four separate Acts of Congress on the subject. I felt that authority should be given the President to perform certain functions, such as imposing an arms embargo or setting up a system for the supervision of the traffic in arms. Such authority could be vitally important and should be on the statute books in case of emergency. But, since the carrying out of neutrality legislation and its very presence on our statute books had a sharp effect on our foreign relations, and since the President was responsible for the conduct of those relations, I felt he should have the utmost discretion as to the time, place, and manner of applying the neutrality provisions.

And I never ceased to believe that the President should have the right to impose an embargo against an aggressor and not against a victim. Legal minds might argue that it was difficult, or impossible, to define aggression or the aggressor; but it was not really hard, in actual practice, to determine which nation began a war. When Italy invaded Ethiopia, when Japan marched into China, when Germany crossed the Polish frontier, it was easy enough to see which was the aggressor, which the victim. At no time, I was convinced, should other nations, particularly those with aggressive tendencies, be given to understand that our course of action was bound in advance, no matter what steps they took.

I gave a written opinion to Senator Pittman on May 12, 1938, in answer to his request for my comment on a Senate joint resolution introduced by Senator Nye to repeal the Act of January 8, 1937, applying to Spain, and conditionally raise the embargo against the Spanish Government. Pointing out that this legislation would lift the embargo against one party to the Spanish conflict while leaving it in effect against the other, I said: "Even if the legislation applied to both parties, its enactment would still subject us to unnecessary risks we have so far avoided. We do not know what lies ahead in the Spanish situation. The original danger still exists. In view of the continued danger of international conflict arising from the circumstances of the struggle, any proposal which at this juncture contemplates a reversal of our policy of strict noninterference which we have thus far so scrupulously followed, and under the operation of which we have kept out of involvements, would offer a real possibility of complications."

I therefore, "from the standpoint of the best interests of the United States," advised against the resolution, saying: "Our first solicitude should be the peace and welfare of this country, and the real test of the advisability of making any changes in the statutes now in effect should be whether such changes would further tend to keep us from becoming involved directly or indirectly in a dangerous European situation."

Later in the year the President, beset by pressures from all sides and by informal legal opinions from interested parties, began to wonder whether he had authority to lift the embargo on Spain. After he had asked my opinion, I sent him a memorandum on November 18, enclosing the Act of Congress of 1937 specifically imposing an embargo on shipments of arms, ammunition, and implements of war to Spain. "This makes it clear, I think, that only Congress can change our embargo policy as continued in this Act," I said.

The Spanish Civil War raged bitterly for nearly three years. But, as a result of our nonintervention policy, and the nonintervention policy of Britain, France, and a score of other nations, the war did not lead to a general conflict. True, the fascist forces won out, but Spain was not the cause of the European War when that conflict came. General Franco aided Hitler and Mussolini to some extent, but Spain herself did not enter the war. Meantime our relations with Britain and France were bettered because of our cooperation during the Spanish War. They would have been seriously impaired, and the Axis countries thereby much encouraged, had we acted otherwise.

In the absence of a general system of international security in which we participated, and in view of the dangers that would clearly confront us if we embarked on a policy independently of the European nations— in other words, given all the circumstances of the time—it was difficult for me then, as it is now, to see how we could have followed any other course.

37: Crusade for Economic Sanity

WHILE STRIVING TO PREVENT the political fabric of the world from being rent completely to bits, I kept hammering home the economic side of international relations as the major possibility for averting the catastrophe, and advocating rearmament for our defense in case the catastrophe came to pass. When 1937 arrived, the Trade Agreements Act had been in effect nearly three years. It had demonstrated its capacity to augment trade by lowering our own tariff barriers and inducing other nations to do likewise and by lessening discrimination in commerce. Our trade with the fourteen countries with whom we had negotiated agreements was markedly increasing. International groups such as the Pan American Conferences and the League of Nations recognized the reciprocal trade agreements on the most-favored-nation basis as the most practical method of curing the world's economic illness.

The Trade Agreements Act, about to expire June 12, 1937, now faced a major struggle as we sought legislation to renew it. The Act had formed one of the most controversial points of the Presidential campaign in 1936, and I could foresee that strong opposition would rise against it during the debate in Congress. Many Members would be for killing it entirely, others would seek to emasculate it.

Before I left for Buenos Aires we had begun at the State Department to prepare for the struggle. In talking it over with the President I found he favored making the bill permanent, instead of limiting it to three years as in the present Act. I also preferred the permanent idea, but seriously doubted our ability to pass it; hence I stood for the three-year limit, because I felt the bill thus would have a better chance to pass the House and Senate. The bill went up to the House as the President wanted it, but the House Ways and Means Committee inserted the three-year limitation, and it was introduced in that form.

I appeared before the House Committee on January 21, and presented a statement to the Senate Finance Committee on February 10, arguing for renewal of the Trade Agreements Act. To both committees I stressed the role that bettered economic conditions throughout the world could play in alleviating the political tension. "There is not the slightest doubt," I said to the Senate committee, "that our abandonment of the trade agreements program at this juncture would mean a resumption of international economic warfare which is now showing such marked signs of abatement. Renewed economic warfare would inevitably mean an intensification of the present-day political tension which is already pushing many nations in the direction of military conflict."

I pointed out that, if such a war came, even if we were not drawn into it, "we cannot avoid being hurt by the profound economic upheaval which must inevitably accompany a widespread military conflict anywhere in the world. There is, of course, only one sure way for us to be spared the damage wrought by war, and that is for war not to occur. There is no more dangerous cause of war than economic distress, and no more potent factor in creating such distress than stagnation and paralysis in the field of international commerce. In the years which lie immediately ahead, an adequate revival of international trade will be the most powerful single force for easing political tensions and averting the danger of war."

To the House committee I said: "No peace machinery, however perfectly constructed, can operate among nations which are economically at war rather than at peace with each other. . . . No nation is more ready to seek relief by the forcible acquisition of territory or is more easily stampeded into the hysteria of war than one whose population finds itself hopelessly mired in economic poverty and widespread privation."

The fight in both Houses was bitter. The Republicans generally united against the bill, and some Democrats, particularly from the cattle, wool, and copper states, joined them. Our opponents claimed that the trade agreements had let in a "flood" of imports, that it bound the hands of Congress, that nations with whom we did not have agreements got benefits without giving us any in return, and that we employed a "star chamber" system of negotiation. When the vote came, however, we obtained a considerable majority, 285 to 101 in the House and 58 to 24 in the Senate.

We now had three more years in which to spread the idea of freer trade throughout the world. But, with one war raging in Europe and a greater one preparing, there was every reason to doubt that we should have a fair trial.

With the greatest commercial nation of the world, Great Britain, we had as yet no trade agreement. I had been striving from the time of the London Economic Conference to convince the British Government that it should give up its ideas of preferential tariffs, which meant discrimination, and its policy of bilateral balancing agreements, which had the effect of causing discrimination and restricting trade. In numerous conversations with British Ambassador Sir Ronald Lindsay I sought to state and restate my economic principles so that he would convey them to his Government. It seemed to me that our trade agreements program could not be considered complete until the United Kingdom was inserted as the apex of the arch.

It seemed ironic to me that we should have so much difficulty getting Britain into our trade agreements system, because I had drawn heavily on the former policy of Britain herself in formulating our program. I had gone back to the British procedure before the Civil War, which was bilateral treatment coupled with the unconditional most-favored-nation policy. Once they had got it started, it spread like the waves of the ocean, two or three states coming in at a time. I had observed with interest that the British had built their great world structure of trade on this system, even though they abandoned it after the First World War.

I held a basic discussion of the whole trade question with Lindsay on January 22, 1936. Because of the importance of the conversation, I cabled a comprehensive memorandum on it to our diplomatic missions abroad. I said to the Ambassador I was not prepared to say what might happen to the world if this movement should break down through lack of support from important commercial nations, especially those greatly interested in international trade, as was Great Britain. I contrasted the broad policy of the United States in entering into trade agreements on the most-favored-nation basis with certain methods and policies in trade on the part of the British Government which I felt were seriously handicapping the prosecution of our international trade recovery program.

As an example of what I had in mind, I cited to Lindsay our trade agreement with Brazil. When it was signed, Brazil had a trade balance of $50,000,000 to her credit in this country. If we had adopted a narrow balancing agreement such as Britain, Germany, and other countries were negotiating, we would have insisted that this credit be applied to the purchase of American goods only, or toward the payment of Brazilian bonds owned by Americans. We did not take advantage of Brazil's credit, however, because we wanted to promote trade among all nations. Britain and other countries had benefited by this policy, because Brazil was thereby able to use the $50,000,000 credit to purchase goods from them as well as, or instead of, from us. I also pointed out that we had forgone sales of vast quantities of cotton to Germany rather than adopt a temporary, shortsighted trade practice.

I put it bluntly to Lindsay that a number of clearing arrangements reached by Britain with Argentina, Germany, Italy, and other countries were handicapping the efforts of this Government to carry forward its broad program with the favored-nation policy underlying it. ·

Lindsay argued that his Government's action was more or less natural because of the unfavorable balance of trade it had with some other countries.

The whole tendency in most of these clearinghouse cases, I replied, was to drive straight toward bilateral trading and to restrict and obstruct the sum total of world trade.

I then said his Government had suddenly had its attention attracted to an astonishing development in world affairs—Italy's ambitious military campaign in East Africa. It had to be admitted that if Italy's exports had approximated the pre-crisis volume, there was every likelihood that her armies would not today be involved in a campaign. Of course, Lindsay's Government could continue 'to proceed leisurely. But there was a real probability that other military forces would be on the march before this leisurely policy of restoring trade and employment had come to a head.

"The experience of Italy," I went on, "should be a warning to all our Governments alike. The most incomprehensible circumstance in the whole modern world is the dominating ability of individuals or one man to arouse the mental processes of the entire population of a country, as in Germany and Italy, to the point where overnight they insist upon being sent into the frontline trenches without delay. When people are employed and they and their families are reasonably comfortable and hence contented, they have no disposition to follow agitators and to enthrone dictators."

But the world, I pointed out, was producing and consuming substantially less than six, eight, or ten years ago, and there was ample room for a $20,000,000,000 increase in international trade and for immense investments that a hardheaded businessman would consider sound, both of which could provide employment for twelve to fourteen million persons. This action, I concluded, would probably mark the difference between war and peace in Europe in the not distant future.

I sent the President a copy of my memorandum on this conversation. On February 6 he sent me this note:

You are splendid in what you said to the British Ambassador. Incidentally, I got it from a number of sources in England and Europe that your policy and mine, working toward the long-view program of general increase in trade, is beginning to get under their skins and that they are getting heartily sick of mere bilateral agreements. Keep up the good work.   F. D. R.

In the spring of 1936, I communicated frequently to the British Government my earnest request that they should issue a public statement that their commercial policy would follow the lines of our trade agreements. Those in authority in London, however, were not willing.

The British Ambassador went to Britain in the summer of 1936. While he was gone an event occurred that had prospects of assisting economic negotiations between Britain and the United States. In September and October, 1936, agreements were reached principally among the United States, Britain, and France, to stabilize the dollar, pound, and franc and base them externally on gold. The French franc was simultaneously devalued. These accords, we hoped, would remove one of the arguments so strenuously advanced at the London Economic Conference, that certain countries could not begin to consider eliminating trade barriers until they could take action on the basis of stabilized currencies.

British Ambassador Lindsay came back to see me October 22, 1936, for another basic talk, after having spent two and a half months in his own country. I said to Lindsay that a noted Britisher had recently told me that Great Britain had no particular objective in foreign policy just now except to arm heavily for defensive purposes and await a possible military explosion in central Europe within another year or two. I myself favored necessary rearmament of the democracies in view of the rearmament of the dictatorships; but I felt that we should also offer a positive program for cooperation—namely, our trade agreements.

Lindsay admitted that his Government did not have any alternative policy, at least deeply in mind.

I replied that the United States for some time had had a very definite policy in mind—namely, our program for world economic and peace rehabilitation.

Two things, I said, were as inevitable as fate within another two or three years. One was that if a great trading country like Great Britain and another great trading country like the United States became inert and undertook further self-containment alone, such countries as Japan, Germany, and Italy with their armies and navies would in two or three years dominate nearly every square foot of trade territory other than that under the immediate control of Great Britain and the United States. That would leave our two countries in an amazingly disadvantageous situation.

The second certainty, I continued, was that, if this course of further isolation of our two countries was pursued, the food and raw-material-producing countries would be driven to establish their own crude manufacturing plants to produce their manufactured necessities at double and treble prices. And the industrial countries would be desperately attempting to do their own farming at five to ten times the present cost of production. The world would then find itself in the most uneconomic condition it had been in within two hundred years.

I expressed my belief that people of both our countries were in the same boat as far as the dangerous future was concerned, and that we could not avoid leadership. I thought, however, that Britain should take the lead in Europe because the opposition sentiment in this country was far greater than it could possibly be in Britain.

I said I was keenly disappointed that the dominant statesmanship of Britain was only disposed to pursue the one course that contemplated a military explosion. We had to keep in mind that this static attitude of statesmen in Europe as to economic policy existed while Japanese militarism moved deeper into eastern Asia, Mussolini marched his armies into Ethiopia, and Germany marched into the Rhineland. And still worse experiences were ahead for inert governments like that of Britain.

If British statesmen declined to move forward at all in support of an alternative program of peace and trade restoration, I added, this fact would inevitably become known to every other country. This alternative movement, I concluded, must either go forward or perish.

At my request, James Clement Dunn, Chief of the Western European Division, summed up my views in a letter to Ambassador Bingham in London on October 27, 1936. Dunn, beginning at the bottom in the State Department, had attracted favorable attention constantly as he moved steadily upward. He was of particular aid to me and to the Department generally.

"The Secretary," he wrote, "has a very deep feeling that the responsible heads of the British Government, while initiating and organizing their rearmament program as a means of protecting England in case of an attack from the Continent, are definitely losing an opportunity to set forces in motion which would have a most helpful effect in preventing war through the adoption of a more liberal trade policy along the lines of that now advocated by this Government.

"He feels that it may be that war will come. It may be that war will come no matter what line of action is taken by the important nations of

Europe within the near future, but the Secretary also feels, and feels very strongly, that a mere preparation for war is no way to prevent it, and no time should be lost in pressing forward the one possibility, even though it may be only a possibility, of avoiding war, that is, to reestablish sound and substantial trade upon a firm basis of equality of treatment and exchange of opportunities for trade to the greatest extent each nation can possibly contribute. In other words, the question which comes to the Secretary's mind, if he were to be told by British officials that they are rearming preparing to protect themselves for war would be, 'And what else are you doing with a view to working out an alternative program of international relations which will try to avert a war?' "

In January, 1937, Walter Runciman, president of the British Board of Trade, visited Washington, and had a long talk with me. While he tended to agree with my principles, he emphasized the difficulties Britain would have in extricating herself from the Empire preferences agreements reached at Ottawa in 1932.

Runciman made a remark on the political situation which stuck out like an old stump in a field. He said Britain was waiting to see what Germany was going to do.

I jumped him. Apparently, I said, different groups were waiting to see what each was going to do. The result was that no movements along peaceful lines were now being even undertaken. Instead, most nations were arming to the teeth, ostensibly for self-defense.

I said I realized fully that the problems facing the nations of Europe were vastly more complicated than any immediately facing the nations of the Western Hemisphere. But until three years ago the twenty nations to the south of the United States were not speaking to us except as a matter of strained courtesy. If we had sat still as some of our good friends were now doing in different countries in Europe, waiting to see what the other nations might say or do, the nations of this hemisphere would not have been on speaking terms today.

Then I outlined a program to Runciman. My idea was that some important country in Europe—Great Britain, for instance—should take the lead in proclaiming a program of liberal economic relations, on a basis of world order under law. If a country like Britain did so, the Scandinavian countries would at once get behind it, as would the countries from Holland to Switzerland, some of the Balkans, possibly Poland, and certainly the twenty-two American nations.

"As a result," I went on, "nearly forty nations would be marching across the Western World proclaiming a broad, concrete basic program to restore international order and promote and preserve peace and the economic well-being of people everywhere. The tremendous economic and moral influence of all those nations would be exerted upon any country not disposed to join with them. Such a country could no longer question the good faith of any of the nations pursuing this peaceful program or its evident desire to establish fair and friendly relations.

"Consequently, all the important nations would, in all probability, join in such a broad, wholesome movement. If, for the time being, some nations should refuse to join, the nearly forty nations formulating and supporting such a program would, in any event, be doing the wisest and most profitable thing for themselves and the world."

My point was that the economic approach should be the spear point of the approach to peace. First, get all the commercial nations in agreement on liberalizing and increasing trade, removing trade restrictions and eliminating discrimination. And then, with nearly forty nations banded together on economic grounds, show recalcitrant nations like Germany and Italy the undoubted benefits of joining in the same movement.

If the Axis nations came in, the gate would be wide open for a discussion of political problems.

The United States had taken the lead in the trade agreements program, but I felt that Britain should take the lead in this concerted economic movement. This because she had been moving in the opposite direction, toward economic nationalism, and because her commercial relations with most of the nations of Europe were closer than those of other countries.

"If Great Britain," I said, "were to proclaim tomorrow her support and leadership in this program—as she could—it would literally thrill the world and especially the peace forces and the forces of law, order, morals, and religion everywhere."

Runciman listened attentively to my exposition, and occasionally nodded in the affirmative; but I was quite sure he was not with me as fully as I should have liked.

I informed him that, while I was in South America, I had talked with various Latin American statesmen about a possible leadership by Britain in such a movement. In various talks with Latin American and British representatives I had, in fact, sought to help Britain expand her trade by indicating to her and the Latin American countries opportunities for increasing commerce between them.

"In each instance, however," I commented, "the Latin American representatives said they did not know which way Britain was moving. To be entirely candid, I myself am convinced, on viewing the entire series of British acts and utterances, that the British Government is moving backward toward the extremes of economic nationalism, instead of forward toward economic recovery."

At the end of the same month—January, 1937—British Ambassador Lindsay brought me a memorandum from his Government. This asserted that British tariff rates had been maintained at a lower level than those of almost any other country, that Britain's balance of visible trade was becoming more unfavorable to her each year, and that the Ottawa Empire tariff preference agreements did not bar the rehabilitation of world trade, or have any prejudicial effects on armaments or world peace. The memorandum did not, however, go into the question of the bilateral balancing agreements Britain had been making with other countries. It expressed a desire to cooperate with us in eliminating restrictions on world trade and indicated that they were approaching the question of trade agreement negotiations with us.

My earnest, comprehensive discussions with the British seemingly were beginning to bear some fruit. Britain could see, moreover, that a broad movement of commercial restoration would assist rather than impede all rearmament necessary for the protection of her security.

It was against this background that I held a long conversation with Canadian Prime Minister Mackenzie King when he visited Washington on March 5, 1937. I already thought a great deal of the Canadian Prime Minister from what I knew of his work, and I was to think even more of him as succeeding years brought us into close cooperation and friendship. In later years he used to make it a point, whenever in Washington, to come to my apartment for a quiet, informal luncheon or dinner with Mrs. Hull and myself alone, so that we could have long, uninterrupted conversations.

I found him a very serious-minded person, thoroughly agreeable in his relations with others, philosophical, unpretentious, and sanely liberal. He possessed great vision and constructive ability. Not an impassioned orator, he was nevertheless a fluent, forceful, and captivating speaker. I never knew a more unselfish patriot or a man who loved humanity more. These many-sided qualities had enabled him to oust a strong man, former Prime Minister Bennett, along with the Conservative Party, and to continue for many years as the foremost leader of thought and of the liberal political forces in Canada.

Mackenzie King was not too dogmatic or clannish in his attitude toward Great Britain when dealing with important relations among our three countries. While naturally basing his position at all times on the primary interests of Canada, he recognized that the best promotion of those interests called for mutually desirable, profitable relations with Canada's next-door neighbor, the United States, as well as with Great Britain. I do not recall a single instance where he went out of his way to side with Great Britain at the expense of such a policy between the United States and Canada. He was, of course, wholeheartedly friendly toward Great Britain, and conducted relations between her and Canada accordingly.

He was discouraged when he came to see me in March, 1937. He remarked that conditions in Europe continued to be very confused, were improving but little in some ways and becoming worse in others. Germany, of course, was at the heart of these difficulties.

As he made this comment I handed him, to read in confidence, an interesting cable that had just come in from Ambassador Dodd in Berlin. Dodd recounted a conference he had had with Foreign Minister von Neurath and with Hjalmar Schacht. Von Neurath said that nothing could be accomplished by a peace and disarmament conference because arms manufacturers would control their governments as they had done since 1920. Also Germany would never allow the Loyalist Government in Spain to rule that country. He blamed Britain's rearmament policy for Europe's troubles, thereby putting the caisson before the horse. Schacht said he agreed entirely with the United States about freer international trade, and that this was the basic way to avoid war.

As Mackenzie King finished reading it he exclaimed that it was absolutely amazing.

I went over with him what I had told Walter Runciman in January. I said it seemed clear to me that as matters stood in Europe, with each country arming on a huge scale professedly for self-defense, with no serious talk or movement in the direction of peace or the restoration of normal international relationships, two angles were omitted in appraising future developments.

"One," I said, "is the inevitability of an economic collapse within another two years in the light of Europe's wholly unsound economic structure, rendered even more unsound by its immense program of armaments. The second is that, if all nations simply arm and sit back awaiting future developments in international affairs, with the channels of international trade relatively dried up and with no opportunity for many nations to procure their actual necessities, seventy million Germans will some day become sufficiently hungry and ill clothed to get desperate. As a result, one to two million Germans, well trained and fairly well armed, will start on the march, probably to the south. Then what will Great Britain and other countries do who have been sitting back arming, merely for self-defense?"

Mackenzie King commented that he was in agreement with my economic theories, and that Canada was practicing the same policy.

Knowing that he was going soon to London, where he had considererable influence with the British Government, I made an earnest plea with him which I felt might have some effect in the United Kingdom. I wanted action rather than a policy of waiting.

"Some of my British friends back yonder," I said, "in discussing economic programs with me, remarked that they preferred first to see what Italy was going to do. Then they discovered what she was going to do and they proceeded to prepare a great program of armaments, which is still being steadily enlarged. Now some of my British friends say they are waiting to see what the Germans are going to do."

I said that the broad course I had outlined to Runciman, and again to the Canadian Prime Minister, was the only alternative to the present helpless, hopeless drift of uncontrolled conditions in Europe. So long as neither an individual nor a concerted effort toward this end was attempted or seriously contemplated by the countries, particularly of Europe, each month would hear more distinctly the roar of the military Niagara.

"There's not a moment to lose," I warned. "Even now it may be too late."

My conversation with Mackenzie King was one of the most comprehensive I engaged in with any visiting statesman or ambassador. It did not end until word came from the White House that the President was waiting to see my visitor. My notes are among the fullest of the hundreds on conversations I had with other representatives. The talk was basic in that it sought to hit at the roots of the problems facing the world. And I knew that Mackenzie King would faithfully interpret to the British Government what I had said.

Undoubtedly Mackenzie King did have some effect in London. The British Imperial Conference met there in May, 1937. One of its conclusions was that every practicable step should be taken to stimulate international trade. The previous month the British and French Governments induced Belgian Prime Minister Paul van Zeeland to confer with other nations, on their behalf, to see what action could be taken toward more liberal trade. Van Zeeland came to the United States and conferred with the President and me. I went into my trade principles with him in great detail. In August, Sir Frederick Leith-Ross, economic adviser to the British Government, came over. Throughout these months quiet conversations went on between the British and ourselves to see if sufficient possibilities existed to warrant the negotiation of a trade agreement. Finally, on November 18, 1937, the State Department gave formal notice that a trade agreement between the two countries was contemplated.

The world reaction to this announcement confirmed my belief that the world's political tension could be eased if a new economic basis were created. Berlin was keenly interested, and officials there tended to evaluate what effect it might have in stimulating a flow of our raw materials to Britain in case of war. Italy expressed renewed interest in negotiating a most-favored-nation treaty with us. The British Dominions were generally favorable. On this side we had to minimize the political nuances of the prospective agreement, in deference to the widespread isolationist sentiment here. We could stress our belief that liberal commercial policy, epitomized by the trade agreements, tended to promote peace, but we had to be careful to emphasize that an agreement with Britain on trade comported no agreement whatever in the nature of a mutual political or defense policy.

Our negotiations with the British proved the most difficult of any we had yet conducted. They dragged out nearly a year. Because Britain was our major customer, the variety of products to be considered was wide. Because Britain was a large exporter of manufactured products, many of which competed with ours, we had to be doubly careful in granting concessions on such items. The mere announcement of our intention to negotiate an agreement with Britain had provoked a violent response from some American manufacturers. And because Britain was still tied in with Imperial tariff preferences, she had to keep the Empire in mind in concessions she offered.

Simultaneously with the British negotiations we conducted negotiations for a new trade agreement with Canada. The negotiations became, in many respects, triangular, because concessions granted between the United States and Britain had to take into account the trade between

Canada and the United States and between Canada and Britain. Several times the negotiations seemed on the verge of breaking down, and I did not hesitate to appeal directly to Prime Minister Chamberlain through American Ambassador Joseph P. Kennedy in London.

Finally, both the British and the new Canadian agreement were signed at the White House on November 17, 1938, in the presence of President Roosevelt—Mackenzie King signing for Canada, Lindsay for Britain, and I for the United States. The agreement with Britain reversed the protectionist trend that had developed there in the previous eight years, and made major breaches in the preferential tariff wall erected around the British Empire in 1932. (In 1930 only 15 per cent of imports into the United Kingdom had been dutiable, whereas after 1932 this figure rose to 58 per cent.) The agreement was of marked benefit to American agriculture, removing duties entirely on wheat, lard, and flour and reducing them materially on rice, apples, pears, and some canned fruits.

Again, the political effect of the accord was weighed throughout the world as much as its economic effect. But unfortunately it had come too late. Europe was already living in turmoil and fear. Had the British agreement been among our first instead of among our last, had it been negotiated in 1934, 1935, or 1936, its results would have been far greater. As it was, the agreement scarcely had a chance to operate. It came into effect when war had been raging in Spain nearly two years and a half, in China nearly a year and a half; and only eight months after it began to operate Hitler marched into Poland.

38: Japan Would Swallow China

ONE MONTH PRIOR TO the outbreak of war between Japan and China in July, 1937, we had an informal but fundamental exchange of ideas on foreign policy with Great Britain. This began with a series of observations in a memorandum by Neville Chamberlain, who had become Prime Minister on May 28. Chamberlain set forth that the basis of Europe's trouble was fear of German aggression. Germany was not likely to agree to disarmament, therefore British rearmament was essential. While armaments programs were the cause of much of Europe's economic ailments, they stemmed from the political situation. The greatest single contribution the United States could offer would be amendment of neutrality legislation to make possible a distinction between aggressor and victim. Some form of collaboration between the United States and Britain would go far toward restoring confidence to the world and averting the current menace.

With regard to the Far East, Chamberlain said that anything tending to stabilize it would ease Britain's position, since otherwise she might find herself engaged in hostilities in Europe and the Far East simultaneously. Britain would therefore welcome an exchange of views on the possibility of putting Anglo-American-Japanese relations on a harmonious footing.

I had become very well acquainted with the new Prime Minister at the London Economic Conference in 1933, where we worked together almost daily for six weeks. He was unassuming, agreeable, and frank, and I enjoyed the conversations and conferences in which he took part. I learned quite a little of his personality, political leanings, and record. This knowledge stood me well in hand in dealing with the British Government when Chamberlain became Prime Minister. The Chamberlain Government was always accessible to us and was disposed to consider seriously any matters we presented to it and to give us frank replies.

Knowing that Chamberlain's father, Joseph Chamberlain, had initiated the movement for high-tariff policy in Britain and conducted a strenuous campaign for it, I feared that Chamberlain himself would oppose a trade agreement with us; but even there he was eventually willing to listen to our views. Chamberlain terribly misconceived the purposes and capacities of the Axis Powers; but it was his passionate devotion to peace that obscured his judgment. Moreover, he was keenly mindful of the state of public opinion in Great Britain, which clung to isolation almost as devotedly as did public opinion in the United States. He saw that his people were still too tired and too violently opposed to another war to consider with much patience any national defense undertakings unless they were sugar-coated with great efforts for peace, even when peace was not possible.

We at the State Department gave considerable attention to drafting an informal memorandum in reply to Chamberlain's observations. The President approved it, and, on June 1, 1937, I called in British Ambassador Sir Ronald Lindsay and handed him the note.

"Deeply concerned over the absence of a trustworthy basis in international relations and the presence of a constant menace to peace," we said, "this Government has been doing its utmost to formulate and to bring about effective application of a program which might serve to bring countries together on a more satisfactory basis than that which now obtains. If this Government emphasizes somewhat more than does Mr. Chamberlain the economic aspect of the matters which he discusses, it does so because it genuinely believes that if trade relations between nations can be broadened on lines and under conditions where it serves to advance economic welfare, existing political tensions would be thereby eased."

As for amending the Neutrality Act—which had been signed just one month before, after having passed Congress by an overwhelming majority—we could only point out that the Act gave the President some discretion because he could determine whether its provisions should be invoked and he could make exceptions as to commerce to bordering countries, meaning Canada.

With regard to the Far East, we noted the British Government's opinion that there were signs that Japan might realize that the recent trend of her policy had not been to her advantage, and that she was contemplating a change toward better cooperation with her neighbors in the Far East and with the powers that had great interests there. We, too, felt that there were forces within and between Japan and China working toward peace.

If, however, aggression should come in the Far East, we should expect to try to afford appropriate protection to our legitimate interests there, although we could not state in advance what methods of protection we would employ. "It is the traditional policy of this country," we pointed out, "not to enter into those types of agreement which constitute or which suggest alliance. We feel that the governments principally interested in the Far East should endeavor constantly to exercise a wholesome and restraining influence toward conserving and safeguarding the rights and interests of all concerned, and toward preventing friction and development of tensions. We believe that consultation between and among the powers most interested, followed by procedure on parallel lines and concurrently, tends to promote the effectiveness of such efforts."

We pointed out that the principles of policy maintained by Britain and the United States were expressed in the Washington Conference treaties, and that we regarded most of these treaties as being legally still in effect. (The naval limitation treaty had ended on December 31, 1936, as a result of Japan's denunciation.) This referred to the Nine-Power Treaty especially, which pledged its signatories to respect the independence of China and equality of commercial opportunity for all nations in China. This last principle, we said, "has always had and continues to have this Government's hearty support."

Knowing that discussions were under way between Britain and Japan for a possible agreement on Far Eastern matters, we added: "We are not oblivious to the fact that developments in the Far East may in due course call for the making of new political agreements, but we are of the opinion that if and when the time comes to proceed with the negotiation of such new agreements, the principles upon which they should advantageously be based could not deviate far from those to which the interested powers are committed in treaties at present in existence."

This memorandum set forth many of the basic concepts we were to follow during the ensuing Sino-Japanese War. We had some discretion under the Neutrality Act and therefore would not apply the Act unless to do so were in the interest of general peace. We would consult with the other interested nations. We could not enter into alliances with them, but, after consultation, we would pursue parallel and simultaneous action. We believed that the Nine-Power Treaty was still in effect and should be observed. We intended to protect our legitimate interests in the Far East. We did not favor any agreement among Britain, the United States, and Japan or between any two of them. An accord between the United States and Japan or between Britain and Japan would encourage the latter, discourage China, and destroy the united front of the Western Powers with regard to the Orient. If there were to be new accords they should be basically the same as the existing Nine-Power and Four-Power Treaties.

Prime Minister Chamberlain replied to me directly on July 30, addressing me as "Dear Secretary of State." He said:

"I need not assure you that I find myself in full agreement with the general objectives which you set out in your paper. I earnestly share your hope that the policies of the nations may be directed away from ideas of national exclusiveness into channels of political and economic cooperation; and it will be the constant aim of this country, by every means in its power, to promote the realization of this hope.

"In particular, it is my sincere desire that there should be the greatest possible measure of cooperation between our two countries."

When fighting broke out between the Chinese and the Japanese at the Marco Polo Bridge, ten miles west of Peiping, on the night of July 7, 1937, it was apparent within a few days that we were face to face with something far more serious than a mere skirmish. Although the Japanese Foreign Office told Ambassador Grew, as he cabled me on July 8, that their own military people seemed to believe that the firing by Chinese troops had not been premeditated, and although the Chinese authorities in the northern Provinces signed an agreement on July 11 to punish the officers involved, oust officials who obstructed Sino-Japanese cooperation, expel Communists, and otherwise settle the incident, the Japanese high command quickly decided to make it the springboard for a further adventure in China. Japanese troops stationed in the northern Provinces already numbered many times the combined totals of all the powers that had the right, under treaties with China, to station troops there for the protection of their citizens. But on July 12 Ambassador Grew informed me that the Cabinet in Tokyo had decided to send reenforcements to North China.

On that day, Japanese Ambassador Saito called at my office. After he had assured me that his Government was trying to work out a friendly settlement, I emphasized the futility of any other course and the awful consequences of war. "A great, civilized first-class power like Japan," I said, "not only can afford to exercise general self-restraint, but in the long run it is far better that this should characterize its attitude and policy."

I commented that I had been looking forward with increasing encouragement to an early period when Japan and the United States might have an opportunity to exercise world leadership in joining together on a constructive program like the one proclaimed at the Buenos Aires Conference. I stressed the fact that, from this and other viewpoints, it meant everything that serious military operations should not be allowed to get under way.

The Counselor of the Chinese Embassy also called at the State Department the same day and was informed of our intense hope that hostilities should not develop further. The Counselor later telephoned us the substance of a cable from his Government asking whether we could do something in a mediatory capacity. It was obvious to us, however, that an attempt at mediation would only infuriate the Japanese Government and give it the chance to present to its own people the argument that the Western Powers were trying to interfere with Japan's self-defense, as they chose to call it, in China.

Japanese Ambassador Saito came to my apartment on the following night, July 13, at my request, and I again stated as emphatically as possible the awful dangers and consequences of war to every part of the world alike, and the impossibility of exaggerating the deep interest of my Government and country in peace in the Orient at this time.

Three days later, on July 16, after consultation with the President, I issued a formal statement of our position. This was based chiefly on the "Eight Pillars of Peace" program I had presented at Buenos Aires in 1936, but it contained the fundamental principles of international conduct I had inserted in the Democratic platform of 1932 and proclaimed at Montevideo in 1933 and in numerous addresses elsewhere. We communicated it to all the Governments of the world, with a request that they state their attitude by way of reply.

"Unquestionably," I said, "there are in a number of regions tensions and strains which on their face involve only countries that are near neighbors, but which in ultimate analysis are of inevitable concern to the whole world. Any situation in which armed hostilities are in progress or are threatened is a situation wherein rights and interests of all nations either are or may be seriously affected. There can be no serious hostilities anywhere in the world which will not one way or another affect interests or rights or obligations of this country."

I then stated what we advocated: national and international self-restraint; abstinence by all nations from use of force in pursuit of policy and from interference in the internal affairs of other nations; adjustment of international problems by peaceful negotiation and agreement; faithful observance of international agreements; modification of treaties, when necessary, by orderly processes in a spirit of mutual helpfulness and accommodation; respect by all nations for the rights of others and performance of established obligations; revitalizing and strengthening of international law; economic security and stability the world over; lowering or removing excessive trade barriers; effective equality of commercial opportunity and treatment; limitation and reduction of armament.

"Realizing the necessity for maintaining armed forces adequate for national security," I concluded, "we are prepared to reduce or to increase our own armed forces in proportion to reductions or increases made by other countries. We avoid entering into alliances or entangling commitments, but we believe in cooperative effort by peaceful and practicable means in support of the principles hereinbefore stated."

Sixty nations soon gave their full adherence to these principles. Ironically, they included Germany, Italy, and Japan. Portugal alone raised any point, objecting to "the habit of entrusting the solution of grave external problems to vague formulae."

Portugal's observation requires comment. In my narrative thus far I have given frequent statement to principles of international conduct which some persons might say come under the category "vague formulae." I never lost an opportunity, in fact, to state and restate these principles in public speeches, statements, diplomatic notes, and conversations with foreign diplomats and visiting statesmen. To me there was nothing vague about them. They were solid, living, all-essential rules. If the world followed them, the world could live at peace forever. If the world ignored them, war would be eternal.

I had several purposes in mind in constantly reiterating these principles. One was to edge our own people gradually away from the slough of isolation into which so many had sunk. Another was to induce other nations to adopt them and make them the cornerstone of their foreign policies. Still another was to get peoples everywhere to believe in them so that, if aggressor governments sought war, their peoples might object or resist; and, if war did come, such peoples, having these principles at heart, would eventually swing back to the right international road.

To me these doctrines were as vital in international relations as the Ten Commandments in personal relations. One can argue that the Ten Commandments, too, are "vague formulae." But day after day millions of ministers of God throughout the world are preaching these formulae, and I believe there is untold value in this preaching. Society would lapse into chaos if the Ten Commandments were universally broken, just as international society lapses into chaos when the principles of right conduct among nations are widely disregarded.

I have also heard it said that the President and I confined our foreign policy to pious statements and no action. This is wholly untrue. We took action after action in living up to each of the principles I stated on July 16. This was of value in showing other nations that we not only preached but practiced what we preached. We observed self-restraint in our dealings with other nations, repeatedly when Japan violated our rights in the Orient. We abstained from interference in the internal affairs of other nations, as when we withdrew our armed forces from Haiti. We faithfully observed our international agreements. We modified treaties, when necessary, by orderly processes, as when we wrote new treaties with Cuba and Panama. We sought again and again to revitalize international law. We lowered or removed excessive trade barriers by means of the trade agreements, and applied the principle of equality of treatment. We attended several conferences on disarmament, and were willing to make our contribution thereto. We cooperated repeatedly with other nations in support of all these basic principles.

Furthermore, we took repeated actions whose effect would be to bolster the peaceful nations of the world and the League of Nations, such as our cooperation with League Committees for the Far East, the Chaco, and Leticia and the League committees on humanitarian and economic undertakings, our moral embargo in the Italo-Ethiopian War, our offer not to impede League sanctions against an aggressor, and our nonintervention policy in Spain. In addition, we sought further actions whose effect would have been similar but which were defeated by the isolationist elements' pressure on Congress, such as the resolution to empower the President to place an arms embargo against an aggressor, and our proposed entrance into the World Court.

If a person violates some of the "vague formulae" of the Ten Commandments included in man-made laws, the police go after him and he ends up in jail. To him, to the police, and to society there is nothing vague in these formulae. Unfortunately, if a nation violated some of the commonly accepted rules of international conduct, there was no police to ensure punishment. All the more reason, therefore, for some of us never to relax our efforts to convince the people of the world, even if some of the political leaders sneered, that international morality was as essential as individual morality.

Not until all peoples cling to the rules of international conduct as strongly as they do to the commandments of personal conduct can there be as much stability among nations as there is among persons.

The very fact that Germany, Italy, and Japan adhered to the principles I set before them on July 16, however hypocritical was their attitude, showed they dared not permit their own peoples to believe that they were willing to throw such rules of conduct overboard. The Japanese Government while concurring in these principles added this cryptic sentence: "It is the belief of the Japanese Government that the objectives of those principles will only be attained, in their application to the Far Eastern situation, by a full recognition and practical consideration of the actual particular circumstances of that region." What this meant was that, if we were willing to agree to Japan's having all she wanted in the Orient, she was willing to admit the validity of our principles.

Any doubt as to Japan's hypocrisy was quickly removed as she broadened her march into China. Within a few weeks she had occupied the two largest cities of North China, Peiping and Tientsin, seized railroad lines running south, and set up a new government in Hopei. By the second week in August the Shanghai area became another theater of operations, thereby imperiling the lives and property of thousands of foreigners as well as Chinese.

On July 20 the British Government, through Ambassador Lindsay, offered to make a joint approach with us and the French to the Japanese and Chinese Governments asking them to agree that all further movements of troops be suspended and that the British and American Governments should put forward proposals in an attempt to end the conflict.

To joint action I had three real objections. One was that it would create the impression in Tokyo that the major Western nations were bringing pressure to bear on Japan. This would only accentuate the crisis; the Japanese military could use it to strengthen their own position and to inflame the populace against us. The second was that, if there was to be any joint action, it should be by all the nations having an interest in the Far East, or, better still, by all the peaceful nations of the world, and not merely by two or three. The third was that anything resembling joint action with Britain inevitably aroused the fears and animosity of the isolationist elements in the United States.

Moreover, I seriously doubted whether any joint action, unless it embraced a real show of force, backed by an intention to use force if necessary, would be of any avail. And I was certain that neither Great Britain, distracted by developments in Europe, nor the United States, unprepared psychologically and militarily, had any thought of employing force.

Our note of June 1 to Prime Minister Chamberlain had already made clear our preference for parallel, concurrent action rather than joint action. On the day following Eden's proposal, I replied to Ambassador Lindsay that we felt that the courses of action thus far pursued by our two Governments on parallel lines had been truly cooperative and should be continued. I showed him various cables I had received containing publicity his Government had given to statements implying that, with the British and French Governments already in accord for joint action, proceeding with the British proposal would depend on whether we joined in. I said my Government trusted that henceforth there would be no charge or any publicity attributing to the American Government responsibility for failure of the British project or a noncooperative attitude because we did not support it.

In August Generalissimo Chiang Kai-shek granted an interview to a United States Treasury official, in which he said that China and the world would long remember Sir John Simon's failure to cooperate with the United States in 1931 regarding Manchuria, and now Britain would long remember the failure of the United States to cooperate. This attitude seemed to us erroneous. There was no parallel between 1931 and 1937. Now the United States was taking repeated action and bringing all the pressure it possessed to bear to stop the fighting.

I cabled Ambassador Nelson T. Johnson at Nanking to say to Chiang Kai-shek that we had repeatedly urged upon both the Japanese and the Chinese Governments, through their ambassadors here and our ambassadors there, that hostilities be avoided and peace be maintained. He should call to Chiang Kai-shek's attention my various statements and say that, from the beginning of the present conflict, the American and British Governments had been in constant consultation; they had each made efforts along parallel lines; and these efforts had the same fundamental objective—namely, the preservation of peace.

On August 10, Ambassador Grew saw Foreign Minister Hirota and on our behalf made an offer to be helpful in bringing the fighting to an end. This was an offer of good offices, but Grew emphasized that we wished to avoid any semblance of interference. Hirota replied that the most effective action we could take would be to persuade General Chiang Kai-shek to make Japan an offer promptly.

The following day we joined with the British, German, French, and Italian diplomats at Tokyo and Nanking in seeking to eliminate hostilities in the Shanghai area. Shanghai was a city of 3,000,000 people and had largely been built by foreigners. Major military operations there would be most destructive, and we did not see any occasion for them.

On August 16, 1937, Admiral Yarnell, in command of the United States Asiatic Fleet, requested that 1,200 marines at San Diego be sent to Shanghai, and the President and I agreed they should go. Simultaneously, we began receiving widespread demands from American citizens and organizations to withdraw all armed forces and all Americans from China. We had about 2,500 marines and infantrymen in China by virtue of our treaties with China giving us the right to station them there to protect Americans. For the same purpose we also had a small fleet of gunboats on the Yangtze River by virtue of a treaty with China signed in 1858.

I outlined our attitude at a press conference on August 17, saying that we found ourselves in between two extreme views: "One is the view of extreme internationalism, which rests upon the idea of political commitments. We keep entirely away from that in our thoughts and views and policies, just as we seek, on the other hand, to keep entirely away from the extreme nationalists who would tell all Americans that they must stay here at home and that, if they went abroad anywhere for any purpose—tourist, urgent business, or otherwise—and trouble overtook them and violence threatened, they must not expect any protection from their government."

I pointed out there were more than 3,000 Americans in Shanghai. If we ordered our guards away from Shanghai, these Americans might be left at the mercy of a mob that was actually reported as threatening danger there on that day. Further, if we moved out lock, stock, and barrel and hastened back to the water's edge of this country, we could very easily create the definite impression in the mind of every other Government in the world that we would get out gradually, from then on, completely and everywhere; and then Americans left behind in Shanghai, as well as Americans in every part of the world, would probably be insulted with impunity by any and every nation.

I admitted that apprehension was rising that Americans in China might get hurt if they did not get out immediately. In fact, some had already been hurt. An American sailor was killed and eighteen injured when the United States cruiser *Augusta* was struck by a bomb or shell from an unknown source. Two weeks after I made my statement, an American was killed and eight injured when the liner *President Hoover* was bombed by mistake by Chinese planes. We were facilitating the orderly and safe removal of Americans from areas where there was special danger, and Congress had been asked to appropriate $500,000 for the expenses of evacuation and emergency relief.

I pointed out, however, that we were "a nation of 130,000,000 people. We have nationals in every part of the world, living their lives abroad and at the same time proud of their home country and their contacts with it. We in no sense contemplate any belligerent attitude toward anybody . . . but we frankly do not feel disposed, by leaning back too far the other way, to give other countries a chance to suppose or to suggest that we are cowardly. If we want to be insulted fifty times a week, we only need to let the impression be gained that we did not protect our nationals and that in no circumstances would we be disposed to protect them."

At that time I was rereading a history of our war with the Barbary pirates at the end of the eighteenth century. There, it seemed to me, was a pointed example of how failure by our Government to protect the rights of our citizens could expose Americans to the worst indignities and dangers.

Six days later I issued a statement reemphasizing the points I had made on August 17. I submitted this in advance to the President, who wrote on it: "O.K. Very good." In it I stated: "The issues and problems which are of concern to this Government in the present situation in the Pacific area go far beyond merely the immediate question of protection of the nationals and interests of the United States" and related to the basic principles I set forth on July 16.

As Japan continued to pour troops into China and enlarge the area of conflict, I sent a strong cable on September 2 to Ambassador Grew so that he could communicate its substance to the Japanese Foreign Office. I said that, in view of the methods employed by the Japanese military, "it may be doubted that the elements actually controlling Japan's policies and actions value appreciably the friendship of other nations or efforts made by the United States and other Governments to cultivate good will, confidence, and stability in general."

We realized, I said, that hostilities were "not likely to be brought to an end by manifestations of disapprobation on moral or legal grounds." The Japanese having indicated their feeling that we were being fair and impartial, I commented: "The first solicitude of the United States, however, will have to be, not for the maintenance of unqualified good will by either or both of the combatants toward the United States, but for the welfare of the American people and for the general policies and broad interests of the United States."

I continued that we denied any desire to injure China or Japan, we favored being a good neighbor to both, but we did not intend to permit the United States to be hampered in making its decisions by especial solicitude lest its actions displease one or the other, or both, of the combatants. American public opinion, I informed Grew, had been outraged by the methods and strategy employed by the combatants, particularly by the Japanese, and had become gradually more critical of Japan. I thought it desirable for Grew "to suggest to Japanese officials that Japan, by the course it is pursuing, is destroying the good will of the world and is laying up for itself among the peoples of the world a liability of distrust, suspicion, popular antipathy, and potential ostracism, the liquidation of which would take many, many years of benevolent endeavor by Japan."

As for possible mediation, I said I was by no means certain that the United States wished to assume the responsibilities and role of a mediator, and I would not desire, at least for the present, "to encourage either side to believe or to expect that, after currently rejecting many American suggestions to exercise restraint, they may rely upon the United States Government serving them as a friendly broker whenever it suits their convenience."

Prince Konoye, whom I had entertained in Washington in 1933, had recently become Premier of Japan. On September 5 he delivered an address to the Diet, or Parliament, in which he said: "The sole measure for the Japanese Empire to adopt is to administer a thoroughgoing blow to the Chinese Army so that it may lose completely its will to fight." Foreign Minister Hirota told the Diet on the same day: "We firmly believe that it is in accordance with the right of self-defense as well as with the cause of righteousness that our country is determined to deal a decisive blow to such a country [China], so that it may reflect upon the error of its ways." Japan was now committed to all-out war.

The League of Nations meantime had begun to evince concern over the Sino-Japanese conflict. China was appealing to the League for action. Simultaneously Britain, France, and China began to approach us to learn our attitude toward cooperating with the League. At this point I felt it necessary to guard against a repetition of an effort made in the past by several League states to get us committed to a certain course and then use our commitment as a lever to move other League states into position. I cabled Ambassador Bullitt in Paris on September 3, 1937:

"In talking with Delbos [French Foreign Minister], I should like you to be guided by the recollection that the League states have repeatedly asked this Government to commit itself to a course of action or type of representation before they have carried through or even embarked upon the necessary campaign in the Assembly to make such a course of action possible. In other words, the tendency of the League states has often been to shove the United States to the fore and to base their campaign for action on the fact that the United States is already pledged. In this instance, we do not know under what conditions we might be asked to participate and, therefore, prefer to leave our hands free to deal with the fact when it arises. This does not indicate that we will not give sympathetic consideration to the possibility of cooperation with any serious effort of the states of the League to deal with this problem."

On September 11 I cabled Leland Harrison, our Minister to Switzerland: "It appears to us an eminently tenable position that some fifty states [the members of the League] should make up their minds and express themselves on a given problem before any one state, outside of their organization, is asked to commit itself."

Harrison cabled me on September 23 that the League was appointing a subcommittee to deal with the Far Eastern crisis. I replied on the following day authorizing him, if he should be invited, to sit with the subcommittee. This was the second time since I entered the State Department, that, with the President's concurrence, I authorized American representatives to sit with League of Nations committees dealing with Japan. Having gathered the impression from the Minister's telegrams that the subcommittee would be limited to nations having interests in the Far East, I suggested, instead, that it should embrace all other nations as well so as not to detract "from the broad effect and universal character of the attention merited by the presently occurring Far Eastern developments which concern, quite obviously, not only the nations interested in the Pacific area but also all other nations as well."

On September 28 we sent further instructions to Minister Harrison. We outlined the steps we had already taken: direct appeals to Japan and China to stop fighting; offer of good offices; repeated protests to Japan against aerial bombing of noncombatants. I said we had been approached on several occasions by certain other governments with suggestions for "joint action." "In general," I commented, "it is felt that spontaneous separate action on parallel lines, should two or more governments feel moved thereto anywhere, indicates more strongly serious feeling regarding matters under consideration and is more likely effectively to serve to attain the objectives sought than would inspired joint action."

"It is felt," I concluded, "that the United States Government, in action taken thus far, has gone further in making efforts calculated to strengthen general principles of world peace and world security and in indicating toward disregard of them disapprobation and disapproval than any other government or group of nations has gone. Therefore, it is felt that other nations might now well direct their efforts to go as far as or farther than the United States thus far has gone along these lines."

The League of Nations Assembly adopted and published two reports on October 6, 1937, concluding "that the military operations carried on by Japan against China by land, sea and air are out of all proportion to the incident that occasioned the conflict; that such action cannot possibly facilitate or promote the friendly cooperation between the two nations that Japanese statesmen have affirmed to be the aim of their policy; that it can be justified neither on the basis of existing legal instruments nor on that of the right of self-defense, and that it is in contravention of Japan's obligations under the Nine-Power Treaty of February 6, 1922, and under the Pact of Paris of August 27, 1928."

On the same day, we issued a statement at the State Department that the United States Government was in general accord with the League's conclusions.

The day preceding this announcement, President Roosevelt delivered his famous "quarantine speech" at Chicago. Ever since his inauguration, Mr. Roosevelt had been struggling desperately to restore normal conditions at home, with the result that he was at times hampered in giving full attention to our foreign affairs. For my part, I was becoming increasingly worried over the growth of the isolationist sentiment in the United States, as evidenced by the activities of many peace organizations, by letters, petitions, and public opinion polls. I was also worried over the effect this fact would have on nations abroad.

In September, knowing that the President contemplated an early trip across the Continent to the Pacific, I conferred with Norman Davis and expressed the strong opinion that the President should make a speech on international cooperation in the course of his journey, particularly in a large city where isolation was entrenched. Davis agreed with me. I then took Davis with me to call on the President, and we suggested this idea to him. He readily concurred. He said that, if we would prepare the necessary data for his speech, he would deliver it during his trip.

We returned to the State Department and prepared the address in the form of a first draft. We did not have the celebrated "quarantine" clause in our draft. The President himself was responsible for this insertion as he was perfecting the speech shortly before delivering it. I did not know the phrase was there until he uttered it.

"The peace, the freedom, and the security of 90 per cent of the population of the world," said Mr. Roosevelt, "is being jeopardized by the remaining 10 per cent, who are threatening a breakdown of international order and law. Surely the 90 per cent who want to live in peace under law and in accordance with moral standards that have received almost universal acceptance through the centuries, can and must find a way to make their will prevail. . . .

"It seems to be unfortunately true that the epidemic of world lawlessness is spreading. When an epidemic of physical disease starts to spread, the community approves and joins in a quarantine of the patients in order to protect the health of the community against the spread of the disease."

The reaction against the quarantine idea was quick and violent. As I saw it, this had the effect of setting back for at least six months our constant educational campaign intended to create and strengthen public opinion toward international cooperation. Those of us who had been carrying on this campaign, through speeches, statements, and actions wherever possible, had been working as actively as we could; but we were always careful not to go too far lest a serious attack by the isolationist element throw us farther back than we were before. If we proceeded gradually and did not excite undue opposition, our words and actions, although not so dynamic or far-reaching as we might wish, had more effect on the world at large than if we made startling statements or took precipitate action and then, because of the bitter reaction we aroused, presented the world with the spectacle of a nation divided against itself.

Six of the major pacifist organizations issued a declaration that the President "points the American people down the road that led to the World War." The American Federation of Labor resolved: "American labor does not wish to be involved in European or Asiatic wars." Two Representatives, Fish and Tinkham, threatened to have the President impeached. A Philadelphia *Inquirer* telegraphic poll of Congress showed more than two to one against common action with the League toward the Far East. A campaign was launched to secure 25,000,000 signatures to a "Keep America Out of War" petition.

All this reaction, of course, received wide publicity and was dulcet to the ears of Hitler, Mussolini, and the Japanese war lords. It undoubtedly emboldened the aggressor countries, and caused the democracies of Europe to wonder if we could ever be with them in more than words. It was certainly followed by the bolder actions of Japan, culminating in the sinking of the United States gunboat *Panay* by Japanese planes two months later.

In this month of October, 1937, Under Secretary Welles evolved an idea for a world peace plan. He drew up a long memorandum and took it across the street to the President. He wanted the President to convoke a spectacular White House meeting of all the diplomatic representatives in Washington on Armistice Day, November 11. There the President would make a dramatic appeal to the nations to sit down at a conference table and work out bases for peace. The President would outline these bases. One was agreement on principles of international conduct; another was disarmament; a third was economic stability. He would conclude that, unless a peace policy were turned to, peace could not much longer be maintained.

Almost before I knew it, I found the President completely embracing this project. The colorful drama to be staged in the White House appealed to him. For several years he had pondered the idea of inviting the heads of the nations of Europe to hold a meeting with him at sea. Around a table aboard a battleship or cruiser he would work out with them a lasting peace. He had not reached the point of making a formal proposal; but he had sounded out a few persons, and word of his idea spread. The reaction, however, was none too favorable. Ambassador William Phillips, in Rome, wrote me on October 9, 1936, after his first audience with Mussolini: "It was evident that Rosso [Italian Ambassador in Washington] had spoken to him of the President's desire to meet the assembled Heads of European States. He smiled as he referred to it and, without committing himself, gave me a broad grin and shrugged his shoulders."

I myself felt that the net result of such meetings as the President was contemplating would be a loss. It was not possible to enter into complicated arrangements with governments just by sitting down around a table for a day or two and talking. For this reason other Governments were not cordial to the idea. They knew that the President could not enter into secret agreements, which were probably the only agreements that could come from such a mid-Atlantic conference.

Something similar to what Welles had in mind had been proposed to

Ambassador Joseph E. Davies by Hjalmar Schacht, head of the German Reichsbank, on January 20, 1937, while Davies was in Berlin en route to Moscow. Davies cabled me that Schacht told him he had been authorized by Hitler to submit proposals to France and England which would guarantee European peace, secure present boundaries, reduce armaments, establish a new, workable League of Nations, abolish sanctions, and obtain colonies for Germany. France was agreeable, he said, Britain not.

Schacht then said he hoped the President would call an international conference in Washington. When Davies commented that possibly the President would not be disposed to become entangled in such a matter unless there were some assurance of success, Schacht replied that the conference should not be called unless an agreement had been practically reached in advance. The conference should not be termed an "economic conference" but a "peace congress."

When I found that the President was all for going ahead with the Armistice Day drama in the White House, I earnestly argued against the project as being illogical and impossible. I outlined the situation to Mr. Roosevelt as I saw it. At this late stage in 1937, Germany, Japan, and Italy had pushed their rearmament so far that there could be no doubt it was intended for offense, not defense, for conquest, not for peace. It would be fatal to lull the democracies into a feeling of tranquillity through a peace congress, at the very moment when their utmost efforts should actually be directed toward arming themselves for self-defense. I had seen the danger of military aggression for several years; now it seemed more immediate than ever; therefore it appeared to be wholly impractical for the peaceful nations to start a new movement for further disarmament among themselves alone, while the Axis powers continued furiously to arm. Any half-informed person knew that every effort for five years had been made to prevail upon the Axis nations to join in a disarmament agreement, and that they had deliberately refused and proceeded with rearmament on a colossal scale. The Axis would laugh at any such belated request of the peaceful nations for disarmament.

It seemed to me thoroughly unrealistic, just at the time when we needed to arouse public opinion to the dangers abroad and the necessity to rearm to meet those dangers, to turn away from thoughts of self-defense and undertake to revive a completely collapsed movement. To have pursued a theory so credulous would have played into the hands of the Axis as completely as did the later neutrality policies of Belgium and Holland. Furthermore, the peacefully minded nations would have gravitated much further than they had into a policy of appeasement probably under the leadership of our friend, Prime Minister Chamberlain.

By 1937 the United States had reached a stage where any further effective efforts to promote and preserve peace required increased military preparations for self-defense to back them up. The Axis powers were utterly intolerant of any nation that was comparatively unarmed. International lawlessness was on the rampage. By this time it was seriously questionable whether we could have any effect in our support of peace alone.

As for Welles' other points—principles of international conduct and economic stability—the former was taken care of, as much as it was possible to do so, in my statement of principles on July 16, to which sixty nations adhered; and the latter was embraced in the trade agreements program.

Even if an agreement could be reached, of what value would it be? All three members of the Axis had demonstrated repeatedly their total disregard for their pledged word and their contempt for treaties. The very word "treaty" had become a hiss and a byword with Hitler, Mussolini, and the Japanese. The President already had had an idea of Axis reaction to his appeals when Mussolini replied that, having mobilized a million men and spent two billion lire, he simply had to invade Ethiopia, or his prestige would be destroyed and he would incur the disdain of other countries. He truly echoed the sentiment of his Axis partners. They too had mobilized millions of men and spent billions of marks and yen, and they meant to take what they could.

Welles' somewhat pyrotechnical plan was to be "sprung" on Armistice Day, without any advance consultation or sounding out of the other nations. Not to ascertain in advance the opinion of Britain and France, at least, seemed unwise and unfair. They were at that moment engaged in delicate negotiations with Germany and Italy; they were trying to keep alive and functioning the Nonintervention Committee for Spain; and to "spring" so ambitious a project on them without warning might seriously embarrass them.

In June, 1937, Norman Davis, then in London, had sounded out Prime Minister Chamberlain on the prospect of a visit to Washington to see the President. Mr. Roosevelt was willing to extend the invitation, but thought it best for Chamberlain to come after Congress adjourned in September, and also thought that careful diplomatic preparations should be made in advance of the visit.

Chamberlain wrote a letter to Davis on July 8 and Davis forwarded it to the President and me, stating that he must turn down the idea of a meeting with the President in the autumn. He said he did not think the time was ripe; that nothing would be more disastrous than that a conference, which would inevitably attract the utmost publicity, should fail to produce commensurate results; and he did not see at that moment how we could expect to achieve the purposes we had in view.

As for the Orient, Japan had made it clear she did not want Occidental mediation between her and China, and there was little likelihood she would attend a peace congress with any intention of agreeing to anything substantial.

In the various conversations I had with the President on this subject, he did not take issue with the views I presented. Eventually the project was abandoned and we proceeded with our constant efforts to rearm and to arouse public opinion to the serious danger of a world conflagration.

39: Japan Plunges On

AS JAPAN'S CONFLICT with China flamed into a full-scale war and her ambition to reduce China to a vassal state unfolded, it was clear she had violated, among other treaties and obligations, the Nine-Power Treaty of 1922 which pledged respect for China's independence and integrity. The question then rose as to what actions the signatories to the Pact, including the United States, intended to take.

The League of Nations resolution of October 6, 1937, suggested that the members of the League who were signatories to the Nine-Power Treaty should initiate consultation among themselves and with other nations interested in the Far East. On the same day the British Government, after citing this passage, informed us it favored the holding of a conference. We expressed our concurrence, and suggested Brussels as its seat.

The Belgian Government sent out invitations to the interested governments on October 16, "at the request of the British Government and with the approval of the American Government." The purpose of the conference was to "examine the situation in the Far East and to study peaceable means of hastening the end of the regrettable conflict which prevails there." We accepted on the same day and acquiesced in Britain's wish to invite Germany and Russia to attend.

Three days after the invitations went out, Foreign Secretary Eden sent us a memorandum expressing his views as to three possible courses to take at the conference: deferring any action; expressing moral condemnation; or actively aiding China and bringing economic pressure on Japan. He did not think the first two would prove effective. As to the third, he did not specifically advocate it, and he did point out its difficulties and dangers. Japan, seeing aid flowing to China, would impose a blockade on neutral shipping, and we should then have to acquiesce or else keep the sea routes open by armed force.

Economic measures might be effective if generally applied, Eden thought, but probably not in time to affect the outcome of the war, unless China were simultaneously aided. There was a real danger that Japan would take violent action by warring on one or more of the sanctionist countries or by seizing territory of some other Power from which to get essential war materials. Therefore, sanctions would have to be preceded by mutual assurances of military support and guarantees of the territorial integrity of other nations. If such assurance were made, and sanctions applied, Japan might possibly be induced to make an early peace.

The dangers of imposing sanctions on Japan at that stage, with the Japanese military in the full flush of victory, were apparent to us as well. Assistant Secretary Hugh R. Wilson informed the British Embassy, on our behalf, that consideration of sanctions did not arise in a conference whose objective was to find a solution of the conflict by agreement.

A member of the Japanese Embassy informed us in conversation on October 22 that Japan would not accept the invitation to the Brussels Conference because her army in South China, jealous of the triumphs of her army in North China, had to win a compelling victory of its own. Ambassador Grew, however, cabled me on that day that Japan's excuse was that the invitation to the Brussels Conference rose out of the League resolution of October 6 and my statement of the same day, both of which condemned Japan's hostilities in China. The President, on being informed of this refusal, suggested that Japan's objections should be clarified, the conference meet, and Japan then be invited again to be present.

Almost immediately an effort began among several of the nations who had accepted Belgium's invitation, to push the United States into taking the lead at the conference. Hints came from London and Paris that Britain and France would go as far as the United States in action in the Far East, and no further. The responsibility for initiating steps was therefore being thrown upon us.

The President and I did not relish this maneuver. Throwing us into the lead would have drawn the animosity of Japan to the United States individually and would have aroused a clamor among the isolationists in this country. Moreover, the discussions preceding the calling of the conference had specifically excluded the invocation of sanctions or the application of physical pressure against Japan. As the President said in his radio address on October 12, 1937: "The purpose of this conference will be to seek by agreement a solution of the present situation in China. In efforts to find that solution, it is our purpose to cooperate with the other signatories to this Treaty, including China and Japan."

The President communicated to us a series of observations, which we sent to Ambassador Bingham to pass on to Prime Minister Chamberlain and Foreign Secretary Eden. Bingham informed Eden on October 28 that the President believed the success of the Montevideo and Buenos Aires Conferences was due to the fact that El Salvador, the smallest American Republic, was considered on the same plane not only with the

United States, the largest, but also with Brazil and Argentina. He suggested that the British should not take the lead at the Brussels Conference or push the United States into the lead, and that the smaller countries should be made to feel their own position and standing.

Eden said he hoped I would head the American delegation to Brussels; but it was impossible for me to be away for so long at such a time. The President and I agreed that Norman Davis should be the American delegate, with Stanley K. Hornbeck, Political Adviser on Far Eastern Affairs, and Jay Pierrepont Moffat, Chief of the European Division, as his advisers.

The President and I went over the conference's possibilities with Davis at the White House. The President, seeing him at Hyde Park before he sailed, expressed the view that, if we were to avoid an ultimate serious clash with Japan, some practical means would have to be found to check Japan's career of conquest and to make effective the collective will of the countries believing in peaceful settlements. He stressed the importance of mobilizing moral force in all peace-loving nations.

He suggested a strategy of repeatedly calling upon Japan to come into the conference, there to submit the issues with China to settlement by negotiation. He thought the conference should be prolonged and be an agency for educating public opinion and bringing to bear upon Japan all possible moral pressure. He advised Davis to observe closely the trend of public opinion in the United States and take full account of it. What that public opinion was, in majority, Mr. Roosevelt knew from the reaction to his "quarantine speech." He said he realized the difficulties the conference would encounter, but hoped it would none the less produce constructive results either in its influence on Japan or in mobilizing public opinion.

When Davis reached Paris he was told by Ambassador Bullitt that the French and British Governments, especially the French, were bent upon organizing an effective front of the democracies in which special responsibilities and burdens might be placed upon the United States. If this were not possible France would try to obtain a guarantee for French Indo-China, and if this too were not possible she would probably lose interest in the conference. This prospect later became a fact.

Litvinov, representing Russia, was for a strong policy toward Japan. The smaller nations, however, expressed their apprehension to Davis lest the large powers decide on measures of pressure. They recalled their unfortunate experience with sanctions in the Italo-Ethiopian War. They wanted the conference to do little and end quickly.

The day before the conference was to open on November 3, Davis cabled me a conversation he had had with Eden at Brussels. Eden, saying he was seriously worried over the Far East and believed that only by Great Britain and America standing shoulder to shoulder could the threats there be dispelled, expressed Britain's willingness to go just as far in the way of positive action as the United States, but no further. He added that Britain had been playing down her willingness to assume so strong a position, particularly because she could not judge how far America would be willing to go. Davis expressed our views that the United States had no intention of taking the lead, and that neither the United States nor Britain should follow the other but both should work along similar lines.

Davis pointed out that a large body of public opinion in the United States felt that our interests in the Far East were much smaller than Britain's, and that Britain, being unable to protect her own interests, was trying to maneuver us into "pulling her chestnuts out of the fire."

Eden said he knew this feeling existed, but greatly deplored it.

Davis commented that, if the two Powers should pursue policies which provoked retaliation from Japan, it seemed that the United States would have to bear the brunt.

Eden denied this, saying that, although the bulk of the British fleet had to remain in Europe, Britain could and would send some ships to the Orient; the base at Singapore was now completed; and the British Admiralty felt that the British and American publics greatly exaggerated the power of the Japanese navy.

Eden remarked that Britain would neither attempt to take the lead at the conference nor push the United States out in front, but he added that she would base her policy on American policy during the present crisis. If constructive efforts failed, Britain would be willing to join fully in direct pressure on Japan.

When the conference opened the following day, sixteen nations were in attendance. Germany had declined, and Italy was present obviously to represent Japan and Germany. Davis stated: "We come to this conference with no commitments except those to treaty provisions and to principles which the Government of the United States has repeatedly and emphatically affirmed. The Government of the United States is prepared to share in the common efforts to devise, within the scope of these treaty provisions and principles, a means of finding a pacific solution which will provide for terminating hostilities in the Far East and for restoring peace in that area."

With Japan absent, it was difficult if not impossible for the conference to achieve substantial results. Coercive action was not embraced within the scope of the conference. Perhaps other nations would have followed our lead if we had plumped for aggressive action, but majority public opinion in the United States would not for a moment have countenanced any such step.

Action of a positive nature would have solidified the Japanese public behind the Japanese military. It might have led to reprisals by the Japanese and possibly to war. We were not prepared in arms or mind for war. And, had it come, we should have had to bear the brunt of it in the Pacific, just as we did when it came in 1941. Our only hope was to keep on good terms with Japan so that, if the right moment came, we should have the same opportunity for stepping in to end the war as Theodore Roosevelt had had in 1904 to end the Russo-Japanese War.

The conference extended another invitation to Japan, this time in the form of an inquiry as to whether Japan would be disposed to name representatives to exchange views with the representatives of a small number of powers to be chosen by the conference. Japan again declined. She continued to insist that only direct negotiations with China could end the war.

As the conference continued its fruitless discussions, the burden for its fruitlessness was constantly being cast upon the United States. On November 17, 1937, I cabled Davis:

"The impression has been created at Brussels that the other states represented there are willing and eager to adopt methods of pressure against Japan provided the United States would do so. The tenor of these reports is that the United States is solely responsible for determining what attitude the conference will take.

"I invite your attention to the fact that some fifty nations represented at Geneva are parties to a political instrument which provides expressly for the adoption, under certain circumstances, of means of pressure, and when these nations met recently at Geneva to consider the present conflict between Japan and China, they definitely discarded the adoption of any such means and even took steps to avert public discussion of them. I invite your attention also to the purpose for which the conference at Brussels was convened and to the fact that questions of methods of pressure against Japan are outside the scope of the present conference."

After saying I was doing my utmost on this side to overcome this unfavorable publicity, I asked Davis "to do what you can to counteract what I am convinced is a general effort on the part of some of the states represented at Brussels to put the entire responsibility for action in the present situation upon this Government, in spite of their own unwillingness, made apparent to us repeatedly in private, to take definite action."

I concluded that the only countries that would benefit by evidence of disagreement among the nations at Brussels would be the very states whose action the peacefully minded states of the world were desirous of circumventing.

The Japanese Government also seemed to have gained the impression that the United States had taken the initiative in convoking the Brussels Conference. Our efforts on this side, and Ambassador Grew's in Tokyo, succeeded in surmounting this view. Foreign Minister Hirota having told Grew that he wanted to continue good relations with the United States, I cabled Grew on November 16: "Please inform Hirota that I sincerely appreciate his desire to maintain good relations with the United States; that during the past five years I have striven to that end both in season and out of season; and that in all frankness and friendliness I must express my apprehension lest the present situation in the Far East do injury to the cause of fostering and developing those mutually good relations which we both have constantly in mind."

Two days later the British Government asked us whether we would join it in a combined offer of good offices to Tokyo and Chungking. The British idea was that, in the role of intermediaries, we would pass messages regarding an armistice and peace terms from Japan to China and vice versa until a basis had been reached for direct negotiations between them. We replied that we thought this unwise because it would undoubtedly involve our transmitting from Japan to China terms of peace inconsistent with the provisions of the Nine-Power Treaty, and our doing so would lend color to the belief that we were recommending and even pressing such terms on China.

The conference came to an end on November 24 by recessing and agreeing to meet again when conditions were more favorable. The nations present—with the exception of Italy—approved a declaration that set forth, among other points: "This Conference strongly reaffirms the principles of the Nine-Power Treaty as being among the basic principles which are essential to world peace and orderly progressive development of national and international life." Not much had been accomplished, but at least the resolutions adopted showed plainly that all the nations interested in the Far East with the exception of Japan and Italy were in accord as to where lay the responsibility for the war, and that the Nine-Power Treaty was still in force and must be respected. The conference clarified a few issues, if only in a negative way.

Italy had worked hard, as was expected, to hamper the work of the conference. On November 6, three days after it convened, she formally joined the German-Japanese Anti-Comintern Pact. The Axis line-up was now complete.

While the Brussels Conference was in session, President Roosevelt received a personal letter from Japanese Premier Prince Konoye, delivered at the White House on November 9 by Konoye's son Fumitaka, a student at Princeton. It was a warm expression of friendship and of hope for cordial relations between the two countries. At the State Department we wrote the reply, which went forward November 22. In it the President complimented Prince Konoye on his son's address and bearing, and expressed his appreciation of the Premier's wish for friendship between us. He then said:

"Because I so earnestly desire to see that friendship fostered and strengthened, I feel that I must acquaint you with my concern lest the existing hostilities between Japan and China do injury to the cause which we both have so much at heart. I therefore hope that a way will speedily be found for a peaceful adjustment of the situation on a basis which is fair and just to all concerned and which will, through practical application of fundamental principles indispensable to normal healthy relations among nations, provide for enduring peace and stability."

During the course of the Brussels Conference, Norman Davis had cabled the President and me both on November 10, suggesting we recommend to Congress to repeal or suspend the existing Neutrality Act at least for the Sino-Japanese conflict. This, he believed, would aid the conference. After conferring with the President and Congressional leaders, I was obliged to reply on November 16 that "there is no present prospect of a repeal or a suspension or a modification of the existing neutrality legislation and you should proceed on the assumption that no such action will occur."

Actually, the President had not proclaimed that Act in the Sino-Japanese conflict. At this time both isolationist and pacifist organizations in the United States were pressing hard for its application. Fearing lest we become involved in the conflict as the fighting spread through larger areas of China, they demanded that the Act be invoked at once.

The President and I were in agreement not to apply the Act in the Far East unless circumstances forced us to do so. We had many valid reasons to support our stand. So far as the two parties to the conflict were concerned, invocation of the Act would have shut off supplies of arms to both Japan and China. Japan did not need them, but China did. Invoking the Act would have placed both aggressor and victim on the same footing. Its moral effect on China might have been considerable.

If "cash-and-carry" went into effect, Japan had the ships to transport our goods to herself, and the means with which to pay for them; China had not. The framers of neutrality legislation had had Europe in mind; the Orient was quiet when the various Acts were passed, whereas Europe was stirred by the Ethiopian and Spanish wars; and our warring in 1917 and 1918 had been in Europe. Those proponents of "cash-and-carry" who thought it would aid Britain and France, with their control of the Atlantic and their possession of cash, had not foreseen its effect in the Pacific.

Legally, China and Japan were not at war. Hundreds of thousands of troops were fighting and thousands were dying on each side, but neither contender had declared war. In fact, they continued to maintain diplomatic relations with each other. Chinese Ambassador Wang, seeing Assistant Secretary Wilson on September 22, 1937, explained why China had not declared war. The Japanese, he said, were marauders, and a declaration of war would, under international law, legalize their activities; you don't declare war against burglars assaulting your house. Further, the Japanese Government had no control over the military; but China hoped that at some time it could reestablish control, and it was possible that the maintenance of a Chinese Embassy in Tokyo would help the Japanese Government toward that end.

The Japanese, on their part, told us they regarded their invasion of China merely as a punitive expedition and had no desire to acquire Chinese territory.

If the President had applied the Neutrality Act, he thereby would have recognized the existence of a state of war between Japan and China, in direct contrast to the attitude of the two parties to the struggle. Thereupon Japan might have felt justified in imposing a blockade of the Chinese coast against our merchant shipping and that of other countries as well. She had already announced a blockade of Chinese shipping.

While the President and I were resisting pressure to apply the Neutrality Act, we took two steps on September 14 toward avoiding complications. The President, following a conference with Joseph P. Kennedy, chairman of the Maritime Commission, and me, announced that merchant vessels owned by our Government would not be permitted to carry arms, ammunition, or implements of war to China or Japan. Also, that privately owned American merchant vessels which carried such items to China or Japan did so at their own risk. "The question of applying the Neutrality Act," he added, "remains . . . on a twenty-four-hour basis."

I had already received from Ambassador Grew, on September 7, in answer to my request of the previous day, an estimate of probable Japanese reaction toward application of the Neutrality Act. Grew commented that, while the Government and press might regard it as a mark of American disapproval of Japanese policy, especially in view of the fact that neither Japan nor China had actually declared war, the predominant reaction would most probably be favorable because it would evince an intention on the part of the United States to make no exception in policy in the Far East as contrasted with similar cases in other parts of the world. He thought the Japanese would regard it as a further manifestation of the intention of the United States to refrain from intervention. Generally, Grew was inclined to favor application of the Act.

Had we applied the Neutrality Act, thereby expressing the American Government's conclusion that a state of war existed between China and Japan, we might have impelled those nations to declare war on each other —something we definitely wanted to avoid. There would be much less chance of composing the differences between them if they were legally at war. And there would be far greater chance of our involvement if Japan were to invoke the belligerent rights granted by international law. If American merchant ships were stopped by Japanese warships and cargoes seized, there would be no telling where recriminations would end. And if American ships should be sunk by Japanese submarines, 1917 might repeat itself exactly two decades later.

Our difficulties with Japan were already considerable enough. We were making repeated protests to Tokyo against operations of their bombing planes which resulted in the indiscriminate killing of thousands of Chinese civilians. The Japanese Government received these protests in good spirit and gave some indication of passing them on to the military authorities. But Ambassador Grew, who, on September 20, 1937, bluntly reminded Foreign Minister Hirota of what had happened in the United States following the incident of the sinking of the *Maine* at Havana, was forced to conclude his telegram of that day to me by saying: "While recent developments indicate that he [Hirota] has made and is making efforts to avoid antagonizing the United States by cautioning the military and naval forces in individual local issues, we must reluctantly face the fact that the civil government in Tokyo has very little influence with these forces where their general objectives are concerned."

The League of Nations Advisory Committee, in a resolution adopted September 27, solemnly condemned the bombing of open towns in China by Japanese planes and declared that "no excuse can be made for such acts which have aroused horror and indignation throughout the world." In a statement the following day we at the State Department supported this finding and said we held "the view that any general bombing of an extensive area wherein there resides a large populace engaged in peaceful pursuits is unwarranted and contrary to principles of law and of humanity."

Japanese indiscriminate bombings, however, continued, and we cited in our notes to Tokyo incident after incident of injury to Americans or damage to their property. The Japanese sought to shift some of the burden to us by requesting that our citizens leave certain areas or not approach others or not permit Chinese military to occupy their properties. We insisted it was not the responsibility of Americans to avoid injury or damage, and Americans could not be expected to prevent Chinese soldiers from occupying their buildings. The responsibility for avoiding injury or damage to Americans was Japan's. Americans were voluntarily painting or stretching American flags on their roofs, and the Japanese would be expected to respect such buildings.

The climax of this series of wanton acts came on December 12, when Japanese planes bombed and sank the United States gunboat *Panay* and destroyed three Standard Oil Company tankers twenty miles up the Yangtze River from Nanking. Three Americans were killed, along with an Italian journalist, and many wounded. The *Panay* flew a large American ensign and was clearly marked by two large American flags painted on her upper deck, and the Japanese bombers flew low enough to see them easily. Furthermore, Japanese authorities knew of the presence of the American ships above Nanking.

When the first accounts of the bombing arrived I felt certain that the Japanese military had acted not only recklessly but also with an entire willingness to give us warning of their power and purpose. Toward midnight of December 12 I cabled Ambassador Grew the substance of the reports we had received from Hankow, to which city the Chinese

Foreign Office had withdrawn from Nanking. I instructed him to inform Foreign Minister Hirota of them, ask for information, and request that the Japanese Government immediately take appropriate action. "Impress upon him," I said, "the gravity of the situation and the imperative need to take every precaution against further attacks on American vessels or personnel." The cable added that when we had further particulars we would give him further instructions.

As soon as I arrived at my office on the morning of December 13, I summoned officers of the Far Eastern Division of the State Department and other officials to a hurried conference. We agreed that all appearances gave Japan's outrageous act a sinister character. At the same time we were in no position to send sufficient naval forces to Japanese and Chinese waters to require the Japanese to make the fullest amends and resume something of a law-abiding course in future. Isolationists were still quarreling with the President's "quarantine speech" and demanding the withdrawal of our small forces from the Far East.

Following the conference in my office, I went straight to the White House, where I laid before the President all the information we had about the incident, our appraisal of the situation, and our suggestions that we emphatically demand an apology, indemnities, punishment of the officers involved, and assurances that similar incidents would not happen again. At the conclusion of our discussion, the President called his stenographer and dictated this memorandum to me:

"Please tell the Japanese Ambassador when you see him at one o'clock:

"(1) That the President is deeply shocked and concerned by the news of indiscriminate bombing of American and other non-Chinese vessels on the Yangtze, and that he requests [the original word, altered before signing, was "suggests"] that the Emperor be so advised.

"(2) That all the facts are being assembled and will shortly be presented to the Japanese Government.

"(3) That in the meantime it is hoped the Japanese Government will be considering definitely for presentation to this Government:

"a. Full expressions of regret and proffer of full compensation.

"b. Methods guaranteeing against a repetition of any similar attack in the future."

Ambassador Saito came to my office at one o'clock looking downcast and pretending to be humbled. He uttered all sorts of apologies and regrets at what he called "a very grave blunder," and pledged that his Government would scrupulously refrain from any such misconduct in the future. I said to him, "We here were never quite so astonished at an occurrence as at the news of this promiscuous bombing of neutral vessels." I expressed the hope that the military officials operating in that area would realize the extreme danger of their unprecedented conduct. I read to the Ambassador the President's memorandum to me and commented that its contents were, of course, "wholly reasonable."

Even prior to my conversation with Saito, we had already received apologies from Japan in the form of a personal call Foreign Minister Hirota made on Ambassador Grew. Hirota said that, although he had received no official report of the incident, he had come immediately to express "the profound apology of the Japanese Government."

On the evening of December 13, with the concurrence of the President, I sent a formal note to Tokyo. Using the President's phrase, "deeply shocked," we said that the Government and people of the United States had been deeply shocked by the bombing, sinking, or burning of the United States gunboat and the American merchant vessels. The note pointed to the repeated assurances given by the Japanese that American lives and property in China would be respected, and the repeated violations of those assurances. It concluded:

"In these circumstances, the Government of the United States requests and expects of the Japanese Government a formally recorded expression of regret, an undertaking to make complete and comprehensive indemnifications, and an assurance that definite and specific steps have been taken which will ensure that hereafter American national interests, and property in China will not be subjected to attack by Japanese armed forces or unlawful interference by any Japanese authorities or forces whatsoever."

The following day British Ambassador Lindsay came to see me to express Foreign Secretary Eden's disappointment that we had "stepped out" so far ahead of the British Government in dealing with the *Panay* incident. A British gunboat, the *Ladybird,* had also been struck by bombs, and Eden felt very strongly that there should have been joint action in so serious and critical a situation. He believed that the dangerous character of the Japanese military was such that a show of possibilities of force on a large scale was necessary to arrest their attention, their movements, and their policy of firing upon the citizens and warships of other countries in a most reckless, criminal, and deliberate manner. We did not feel, however, for the reasons I have previously stated, that joint action was the solution, or that any show of force on a large scale was possible.

Two days later, as additional details of the bombing came in, I sent a further note to Tokyo. We had now learned that Japanese planes machine-gunned the survivors of the American ships as they made for shore in small boats and after they reached shore and were in hiding. Also, that two Japanese Army motorboats machine-gunned the *Panay*, and Japanese personnel boarded the vessel, although they could plainly see the American ensign. "These reports," I said, "give very definite indication of deliberateness of intent on the part of the Japanese armed forces which made the attack." Therefore I insisted that Japan take appropriate steps against those responsible for the incident.

The Japanese Government continued to maintain that the whole incident had been an unfortunate mistake. In view of the circumstantial details that had reached us, this was the lamest of lame excuses. That some members of the Foreign Office had no hand in it may be true. Hirota himself professed to be genuinely disturbed and sincerely regretful. That the Japanese people did not like it also seemed to be true, to judge from the thousands who expressed their sympathy to the Embassy and offered contributions for the families of the victims and for the survivors. But that the Japanese military leaders, at least in China, were connected with it, there can be little or no doubt. In any case, it was their business to keep their subordinates under control. And there was ample evidence that the Government of Japan became committed to, and gave full support to, the course pursued by the Japanese military practically from the outbreak of fighting in July, 1937.

The Japanese Government undertook, in a very feeble manner, to controvert some of our statements, but in doing so it was evident it was not telling the truth. It did not, in fact, seriously deny any of our statements. On December 23 we sent Japan the official findings of the naval court of inquiry, which exposed more than ever the reckless and deliberate conduct of the Japanese military forces.

Finally, on December 23, the Japanese Government, although still asserting that the bombing had been due to mistaken identity of the ships, met our four demands: regrets, indemnities ($2,214,000 was eventually paid), assurances for the future, and punishment of the officers involved. In the afternoon of Christmas Day we sent a note to Tokyo accepting the Japanese note. On reading the note, Hirota exclaimed to Grew: "You have brought me a splendid Christmas present!"

On this side our people generally took the incident calmly. There were a few demands that the Fleet should be sent at once to the Orient. There were many more demands that we should withdraw completely from China. But the vast majority of Americans indicated their approval of our course of action. We had acted with vigor but with coolness throughout. It was a serious incident; but, unless we could have proven the complicity of the Japanese Government itself, it was not an occasion for war even if we had been prepared for war, which we certainly were not.

The state of public opinion at the time is amply proven by the episode of the Ludlow Resolution to provide for a war referendum. Representative Louis Ludlow, Democrat of Indiana, had introduced in the House in February, 1937, a resolution for a Constitutional Amendment whereby the authority of Congress to declare war would not become effective (except in case of an invasion of United States territory) until confirmed by a nation-wide popular referendum. The resolution having been referred to the Judiciary Committee, which held it without action, Ludlow sought the signatures of a majority of the House to a petition to bring it before the House as a Committee of the Whole. After months of striving, he still lacked sufficient signatures. Then came the sinking of the *Panay*, and within two days he had the requisite number.

Instantly a group of peace organizations threw their influence behind the resolution. Congressmen quickly began to feel the pressure.

To the President and me, the Ludlow Resolution seemed a disastrous move toward the most rigid form of isolationism. If the amendment envisaged by Ludlow eventually came into effect, it would hamstring the nation's foreign policy. If the resolution passed the House it would indicate to the world that the nation no longer trusted the Administration to conduct its foreign affairs. It would serve notice on the aggressor nations that they could take any action anywhere in the world in direct violation of our rights and treaties, with little if any likelihood of any concrete reaction from Washington.

Although the President and I realized that much time, perhaps years, would flow by before the Ludlow Amendment, after passing Congress by a two-thirds majority, could be approved by three-fourths of the State Legislatures, we determined to fight it at the outset. We aimed our guns at the vote that would take place on January 10, 1938, to discharge the Judiciary Committee from further consideration of the resolution.

At the State Department we prepared a letter for the President to send to Speaker Bankhead of the House, which he did on January 6. In this letter the President pointed out that the proposed amendment would be impracticable in application and incompatible with our representative form of government, that it "would cripple any President in his conduct of our foreign relations" and "would encourage other nations to believe that they could violate American rights with impunity." He concluded that, although he realized that the sponsors of the proposal sincerely believed it would help keep the United States out of war, he was "convinced it would have the opposite effect."

I wrote a letter to Representative McReynolds, chairman of the House Committee on Foreign Affairs, on January 8, in which I said: "It is my judgment that under our present form of government 'of the people, by the people, and for the people,' our foreign affairs can be conducted far more efficiently from the standpoint of keeping this country out of war than would be at all possible under the operation of any such plan as the Ludlow Resolution purposes. After the fullest consideration I am satisfied that this plan would most seriously handicap the Government in the conduct of our foreign affairs generally, and would thus impair disastrously its ability to safeguard the peace of the American people."

Postmaster General James A. Farley, who was also chairman of the Democratic National Committee, personally telephoned all the Democratic Members of the House who were available at the other end of the telephone, to enlist their support. When the measure came up for debate, which was sharp, Speaker Bankhead left his chair to speak against it. Finally, on January 10, the vote was taken, and the proposal lost by the close margin of 209 to 188.

This episode was a striking indication of the strength of isolationist sentiment in the United States, since the Administration had to exert its whole force to prevent—barely to prevent—approval of a proposal designed to take one of the most vital elements of foreign policy, the authority to declare war, out of the hands of the Government. It reveals today, as it did to us then, the difficulties the President and I had in carrying out toward the aggressor nations the stronger policies we should have liked to follow.

To me there were two types of firmness we might exercise toward the Far East as well as toward Germany and Italy. One was that of threats and demonstrations without the forces necessary to back them up, which the aggressor rulers, fully advised of our inadequate preparations and of the state of public opinion in the United States, would rightly characterize as bluff. We had no intention of using this method. The other was the procedure we did employ: to bring as much pressure on the aggressor states as we reasonably could; to support the democracies; to make ourselves strong militarily so that our words and peaceful actions carried additional weight; to fight for legislation that would give the Executive freedom of action; to apply existing legislation in such a manner as would aid the democracies and curb the aggressors, without involving the United States in war; and constantly to urge upon all nations the true principles of right international conduct. Actually, we adopted a much firmer attitude toward Japan at this time than we had the military forces on hand to back up.

The day after the sinking of the *Panay*, Senator William H. Smathers of New Jersey sent me a letter favoring the withdrawal of American ships and citizens from the area affected by the conflict. Replying on December 18, I said that "many nationals of this and other countries have, during several generations, gone to China, established themselves there in various occupations and activities, and subjected themselves both to the advantages and to the disadvantages of the conditions prevailing there; and the American Government has, along with other governments, accepted various rights and incurred various obligations. In a situation such as now prevails, many of our nationals cannot suddenly disavow or cut themselves off from the past nor can the American Government suddenly disavow its obligations and responsibilities."

After pointing out the legal basis on which we and certain other countries maintained small armed forces and gunboats in China, solely to protect Americans and not with any mission of aggression, I said: "It has long been the desire and expectation of the American Government that they shall be withdrawn when their appropriate function is no longer called for. We had thought a few months ago that the opportune moment for such a withdrawal was near at hand. The present, however, does not seem an opportune moment for effecting that withdrawal."

We had, in fact, been giving serious study at the State Department to the annulment of our extraterritorial rights in China. Although the right to maintain armed forces in China grew from the unsettled condition of China in previous decades when foreigners were often at the mercy of mobs, and although it was based on treaties and acknowledged by China herself, it was nevertheless an anomalous situation.

We, for instance, had the right to maintain a Federal District Court at Shanghai, answerable only to the Circuit Court of Appeals at San Francisco; and Americans charged with offenses in China had to be tried in our own consular courts, or in the Federal District Court. Any country granting such rights was clearly not wholly sovereign within its own boundaries, any more than we should be if we permitted Britain, France, and Italy to station troops in New York, Philadelphia, and Chicago, operate gunboats on the Mississippi and the Hudson, and establish their own courts in Boston.

In other areas of the world, where we had similar extraterritorial rights, we had already begun to withdraw. I felt that renunciation of our extraterritorial rights in China would be merely an extension of the Good Neighbor Policy as we were applying it in the Western Hemisphere. This policy embodied the principles of nonintervention, equality in law for all nations, large and small, and territorial integrity. We were taking the lead in the movement to restore to China her full sovereignty and were suggesting it to the other nations having similar rights.

We had to be sure, of course, that China was acquiring a stable government capable, by itself, of protecting the persons and properties of foreigners and of giving them adequate justice in case of difficulties or disagreements. In the spring and early summer of 1937 the moment seemed arriving for negotiations with China and exchanges of views with the other interested nations, looking toward the giving up of these special rights. There had been comparative peace for four years, and the Government of Chiang Kai-shek was acquiring strength and establishing more unity in the country. We had begun an exchange of views with the British on the subject on March 30, 1937.

The Japanese invasion, however, upset all these calculations. The presence of American armed units to protect Americans then became more necessary than before. Furthermore, the withdrawal of our marines, infantrymen, and gunboats would have taken on undesirable connotations. It would have looked like a pulling out in the face of the Japanese aggression, and an implicit acknowledgment that the Japanese were better able to protect our citizens and their property than were the Chinese. The Chinese themselves, although previously eager to have the extraterritorial rights annulled, were now anxious for us to stay, since they felt that withdrawal of our troops would appear like abandoning China to her fate. Our plan, however, was merely postponed, not abandoned. I was later to propose it to Japan as one of the bases for a general settlement prior to Pearl Harbor, and we carried it out before the end of World War II.

Positive help to China was a question we frequently had under discussion. On January 3, 1938, the President sent me a note enclosing a letter from Chiang Kai-shek, handed him by the Chinese Ambassador. The Chinese leader pleaded for help. Mr. Roosevelt wrote me: "I explained to him [the ambassador] that he would realize that it would be difficult for me to reply to it in a way which would satisfy General Chiang Kai-shek. I suppose, however, that some reply ought to be made. What do you recommend?"

We drafted a reply at the State Department, which I sent to the President on January 7. As Mr. Roosevelt realized, we could not make specific promises of direct aid. The reply informed Chiang Kai-shek that we were doing everything we could to bring about peace.

The following day I wrote Vice President John N. Garner in consequence of a Senate resolution requesting information on Americans and their property in China. After furnishing the information sought, I said: "The interest and concern of the United States in the Far Eastern situation, in the European situation, and in situations on this continent are not measured by the number of American citizens residing in a particular country at a particular moment nor by the amount of investment of American citizens there nor by the volume of trade. There is a broader and much more fundamental interest—which is that orderly processes in international relationships be maintained. Referring expressly to the situation in the Far East, an area which contains approximately half the population of the world, the United States is deeply interested in supporting by peaceful means influences contributory to preservation and encouragement of orderly processes. This interest far transcends in importance the value of American trade with China or American investments in China; it transcends even the question of safeguarding the immediate welfare of American citizens in China."

In this passage I was seeking to deal with many arguments based solely on our financial or personal interest in certain sections of the world. Some persons argued that Americans had no right to be in China and that, by remaining there, they were dragging this nation into war. Others argued that our trade with Japan was much larger than with China and therefore we should either favor Japan or do nothing to offend her.

To me the issue was far broader. It was the peace and security of the United States as a whole. It was the influence we could offer to assure peace throughout the world, knowing that the only sure way to remain out of war was to keep war from occurring. Trade with any country, and the number of our citizens and the amount of their property in any one country, were infinitesimal compared to the scores of thousands of lives and scores of billions of dollars any war would cost us.

On February 4, the State Department announced that the Fifteenth Infantry Regiment, 808 officers and men, was being withdrawn from Tientsin to be replaced by two companies of marines stationed at Peiping. The fighting had moved inland from Tientsin. We stated that the withdrawal conformed to our policy of reducing our forces in China whenever we could do so without detriment to American interests and obligations in general. The Fifteenth Infantry had been in Tientsin a quarter of a century, and had achieved an excellent record, as was attested by the honors given the regiment by British, French, Japanese, and Italian troops at its departure on March 2. The Sixth Marines, which had been sent to Shanghai in August of 1937, was also withdrawn after rendering excellent service.

For some time we had been receiving numerous reports, partly from Italian sources, that Japan was building larger battleships and cruisers than the upper limits set by the London naval limitations agreement of 1936. That treaty had fixed 35,000 tons as the maximum size of battleships and prohibited the construction of pocket battleships between 8,000 and 17,500 tons, but it contained an "escalator clause" which permitted its signatories to build ships regardless of those limits if they should find that a country not a party to the agreement—meaning Japan—were doing so. The United States, Britain, and France had agreed to keep one another informed, in advance, on their naval building programs, but no information had been received from Japan.

Finally, on February 5, 1938, Ambassador Grew, on our behalf, presented a note to the Japanese Foreign Office asking whether Japan would furnish assurances that it would not, prior to January 1, 1943, lay down any vessel not conforming to the limits of the London Treaty. If Japan did not provide such assurance, our assumption would be that Japan was constructing ships larger than those limits. In that event we would resume our full liberty of action. If Japan were willing to furnish the information requested, even if she were constructing larger ships, we would be willing to discuss with her the tonnages and gun calibers to be adhered to in future if she were prepared to agree to some limitation. Britain and France presented almost identical notes to Tokyo at about the same time.

Foreign Minister Hirota's answer, given on February 12, failed to give the assurances asked for. Consequently, after consultation with

Britain and France, we announced our intention to depart from the treaty limitations.

As Japanese bombing of crowded Chinese cities continued, with death resulting to tens of thousands of civilians, the President and I decided to take further steps to discourage it, in addition to our oral condemnation of such practices. Accordingly, on June 11, 1938, I stated publicly that I had repeatedly condemned the aerial bombing of civilian populations, and then added that I intended this especially for the manufacturers of bombing planes. On July 16 I wrote a note to the President enclosing a copy of a letter, to be signed by Joseph C. Green, chief of the Office of Arms and Munitions Control, which I wished to send to the 148 companies and persons registered with the Department as manufacturers or exporters of airplanes or aeronautical equipment.

The letter said that "it should be clear to all concerned that the Government of the United States is strongly opposed to the sale of airplanes or aeronautical equipment to any countries in any part of the world" engaged in bombing civilian populations from the air. Also, that the Department would be extremely reluctant to issue any licenses authorizing such exports to countries whose armed forces were using airplanes to attack civilian populations. The President approved, and the letter was duly sent out.

During 1938 we dispatched a series of diplomatic notes to Tokyo protesting against Japanese maltreatment of American citizens in China, the seizure of their properties, and the freezing out of American business by the setting up of Japanese monopolies. It was the old story of Manchuria all over again. Japan was clearly violating the principle of the Open Door in China confirmed by the Nine-Power Treaty, and we so charged. But on November 3, 1938, the Japanese Government brazenly proclaimed their intention to set up a "new order in East Asia," linking China and Manchuria to the Japanese system politically, economically, and culturally, and their expectation that other powers would "adapt their attitude to the new conditions prevailing in East Asia."

Finally, on the last day of the year, while I was returning from the Pan American Conference at Lima, Ambassador Grew, on instructions from the State Department, presented to the Japanese Government a basic statement of our position, which we had often discussed in previous years and agreed upon unanimously. This contested the Japanese contention that enjoyment by American citizens of nondiscriminatory treatment in China was contingent upon an admission by our Government of the validity of the Japanese new order in East Asia, and characterized this as "highly paradoxical."

The American Government, the note pointed out, "is well aware that the situation has changed. This Government is also well aware that many of the changes have been brought about by action of Japan. This Government does not admit, however, that there is need or warrant for any one power to take upon itself to prescribe what shall be the terms and conditions of a 'new order' in areas not under its sovereignty and to constitute itself the repository of authority and the agent of destiny in regard thereto."

Our note rebutted Japan's argument that the new situation rendered the basic treaties such as the Nine-Power Treaty obsolete, by saying: "These treaties were concluded in good faith for the purpose of safeguarding and promoting the interests not of one only but of all of their signatories. The people and the Government of the United States cannot assent to the abrogation of any of this country's rights or obligations by the arbitrary action of agents or authorities of any other country."

We pointed out that our Government was prepared, as always, to consider fully any proposals based on justice and reason, designed to resolve problems through free negotiation and through a new commitment by and among all the parties concerned. We invited Japan to put forward such proposals.

But Japan was not interested in presenting proposals embracing the Western Powers. She was committed to the "new order in East Asia," a euphemism covering Japanese domination of the Orient, with the thought that such dominion over half the world would eventually lead to lordship over all the world.

Reviewing our policy toward Japan as the year 1938 ended, we had assumed as constructive an attitude as possible in contrast to a restrictive attitude. A constructive attitude meant maintaining friendly relations with both Japan and China so as to facilitate their resuming friendly relations between themselves. It meant working with Britain and France as fully as was possible without unduly arousing the isolationists at home, who were horror-stricken at the thought of foreign arrangements. It meant keeping our basic principles fresh and reemphasizing them repeatedly, if need be. It meant a firm, though not a provocative or aggressive, insistence on our rights.

A restrictive attitude comported economic sanctions and possibly military sanctions. Had economic sanctions been imposed against Japan, we should have borne the heaviest burden, because our trade with Japan was almost twice as large as the trade with Japan of all the European countries combined, excluding their Asiatic possessions and India. Had economic sanctions led to war, as might well have been the case, the United States would again have borne the heaviest burden. The first objection did not greatly preoccupy us, but the second was much in our thoughts.

The policy pursued by the United States and the other democracies did not, it is true, prevent Japan from continuing her war in China. But, on the other hand, it did prevent her from imposing her own peace on China. It kept her from consolidating her domination over China even as she had solidified her hold on Manchuria. It kept her from freeing herself for the conquest of all Asia. It marshaled the opinion of the world—excepting the Governments of Germany and Italy—against the Nipponese aggressor. It gave American public opinion time to perceive the basic issues involved. It gave the American Government time to prepare for the life-and-death struggle the Japanese war lords were planning.

40: Europe in Turmoil

WITH THE ORIENT ABLAZE, our policy toward Europe in 1938 called for extreme care and close watch, as the Old World seemed driving toward destruction under the impulse of another member of the aggressor triumvirate, Hitler. Our relations with the democracies, Britain and France, grew closer, but those with Germany and Italy worsened. Trade discrimination, nonpayment of debts, persecution of the Jews, and runaway rearmament by Germany, boycott of German goods by American citizens, and bitter anti-German speeches on this side exacerbated our relations with Berlin. Hugh R. Wilson, former Assistant Secretary of State, a trained and skillful diplomat of long experience, was now our Ambassador to Berlin, replacing the sincere though impulsive and inexperienced William E. Dodd; but he could do little to divert the swift flow of events.

German Ambassador Hans Dieckhoff came in to see me on January 14 and expressed his displeasure over the way the world-wide debate between dictatorships and democracies was being carried on.

"The supreme question," I said to him, "is not dictatorship or democracy, but whether the principles underlying international law and order are to be preserved or whether the doctrine of force, militarism, aggression, and destruction of all international law and order shall prevail. No matter what a nation's form of government may happen to be, it can, with perfect consistency, join with the sixty-odd nations of the world in support of the first proposition."

Dieckhoff had come in primarily to protest against a speech by former Ambassador Dodd accusing Hitler of having killed as many people as had Charles II. He wanted our Government to state that it disapproved what Dodd had said. Dieckhoff's approach was identical with many other approaches by the German Government from 1933 on, concerning speeches made in the United States. I pointed out to him, as I had often done on similar occasions, that under our Constitution and Bill of Rights we had freedom of speech in the United States, and there was no recourse except under the law of libel and slander.

"How many men did Charles II kill?" I asked the Ambassador.

"I'm afraid I don't recall," he replied.

"Neither do I," I said. "I'm not certain that Charles II was particularly notorious in this respect."

And thus the matter rested, another sharp stone on a rough road of unfriendly relations.

President Roosevelt, although he had abandoned the idea suggested to him of an Armistice Day peace meeting in the White House, still clung to the idea that the United States might, in some way, settle Europe's difficulties, and had sought Prime Minister Chamberlain's advice. On the day I saw Dieckhoff, Mr. Chamberlain replied that the idea of the United States taking any action would conflict with Britain's efforts to "appease" Germany and Italy. He thought that those Governments might take advantage of the President's proposals to delay consideration of the specific points that had to be settled between Britain and France on the one hand and Germany and Italy on the other, if appeasement were to be achieved. He thought they would put forward demands over and above what they would make if direct negotiations between them and Britain and France were all that was in progress.

The President replied, agreeing to defer making any proposals until it could be seen what progress the British Government was making.

As he and I sought to bring all the pressure we reasonably could to keep war from engulfing all Europe, we had constantly to face a deep-rooted suspicion among the isolationists that we had already committed the country to plunge into the conflict. The President, in his message to Congress on January 28, 1938, had called for increased armament and drawn attention again to the dangers rising abroad. Although Congress backed up his request for a more powerful navy and army, some Congressmen bitterly attacked the Administration and implied that the greater armed forces were being formed to fight overseas. Their charges were echoed by some isolationist and pacifist groups. I went to the House Office Building one evening and spoke to one hundred and fifty Congressmen, giving them a comprehensive account of our foreign policy and inviting them to ask any questions they wished.

After Senator Johnson of California introduced a resolution in the Senate asking three pointed questions on alliances and the use of the Navy, I wrote to Senator Pittman on February 8, 1938: "I desire to state to you very definitely that in response to point (a), which reads 'whether or not any alliance, agreement, or understanding exists or is contemplated with Great Britain relating to war or the possibility of war,' the answer is, No; in response to point (b), which reads 'whether or not there is any understanding or agreement, express or implied, for the use of the navy of the United States in conjunction with any other nation,' the answer is, No; with regard to point (c), which reads 'whether or not there is any understanding or agreement, express or implied, with any nation, that the United States Navy, or any part of it, should police or patrol or be transferred to any particular waters or any particular ocean,' the answer is, No."

Two days later I made public reply to a letter from Representative Ludlow, author of the proposal for a popular referendum before war could be declared. Ludlow asked whether the proposed naval increases were necessary for defense of our home land and possessions, or whether any units were to be used in cooperation with any other nation in any part of the world. I answered that, in my opinion, all the ships called for were needed for the national defense of the United States and its possessions; they would contribute toward keeping us out of war, and "in our foreign policy there is not any disposition or intent to engage in warfare."

Nevertheless, I insisted we should continue to exert our influence to produce conditions of peace, order, and security in the world. I expressed the belief of the Administration that "it is a matter of simple common sense for nations which desire peace to cooperate in every satisfactory and practical way toward maintaining peace. If every peaceful nation were to insist on remaining entirely aloof from every other peaceful nation and on pursuing a policy of armament limitation without reference to relative armaments, the inevitable consequence would be that other nations inclined to play lawless roles would thereby be given great encouragement and even assistance toward so doing."

After assuring Representative Ludlow that the naval program did not contemplate the use of any units in cooperation with any other nation in any part of the world, I stated our basic lines of action: "This Government carefully avoids, on the one hand, extreme internationalism with its political entanglements, and, on the other hand, extreme isolation, with its tendency to cause other nations to believe that this nation is more or less afraid; that while avoiding any alliances or entangling commitments, it is appropriate and advisable, when this and other countries have common interests and common objectives, for this Government to exchange information with Governments of such other countries, to confer with those Governments, and, where practicable, to proceed on parallel lines, but reserving always the fullest freedom of judgment and right of independence of action."

The Johnson Resolution and the Ludlow letter were samples of the suspicion that dogged our every step toward international cooperation. In our policy toward Europe, as in our policy toward Japan, we sought to keep reasonably ahead of public opinion, even while seeking to educate public opinion to the importance of our position in the world and to the fatal fallacy of isolating ourselves. But we could not get too far ahead. To do so brought an inevitable reaction and made the situation worse than before because it caused the aggressor governments to believe that our people would not follow us in any strong action in the foreign field.

Such was the situation when Hitler invaded Austria on the night of March 11 and absorbed it into the German Reich. Dispatches pouring into the State Department from many capitals had long forecast this event, and they had also forecast that the European powers, though protesting, would do nothing to prevent it.

German Ambassador Dieckhoff came in to see me on March 12 to outline the "reasons" that had prompted Hitler's move. I asked him what was the prospect for peace in Europe following this *Anschluss*. He replied that there would be no occasion for hostilities. I tried to draw him out on the Italian reaction now that German troops were nearing the Brenner Pass. He sought to convince me that the relations between Italy and Germany were as close as they had been before the Austrian event and would continue so.

On March 19 I publicly expressed the concern of our Government over the disappearance of Austria, in these words: "The extent to which the Austrian incident, or any similar incident, is calculated to endanger the maintenance of peace and the preservation of the principles in which this Government believes is, of course, a matter of serious concern to the Government of the United States."

Ambassador Wilson, in Berlin, acting on our instructions, delivered two notes to the German Foreign Office on April 6. One announced that our Government found itself "under the necessity, as a practical measure, of closing its Legation at Vienna and establishing a Consulate General." The other stated that we would hold the German Government responsible for Austrian debts to our Government and citizens. We also, through the Treasury, applied to Austrian products exported to the United States, the same duties as for German products. Germany had been denied the lower tariffs under the Trade Agreements Act because of her discrimination against American exports.

On June 7, after Hitler had refused to assume the Austrian debts, we expressed our position in a note to Berlin: "It is believed that the weight of authority clearly supports the general doctrine of international law founded upon peaceful principles of justice that in case of absorption of a state, the substituted sovereignty assumes the debts and obligations of the absorbed state, and takes the burdens with the benefits." But Hitler wanted only the benefits.

With Hitler in possession of Austria, with Japan spreading out over China, and with the war in Spain moving toward a climax, I delivered a fundamental speech on foreign policy on March 17, 1938, before the National Press Club in Washington, to state our position. The world was racing hell-bent toward destruction, and it was essential to show the extent of our concern and to make it clear that we had to be taken into account in world developments. The address was widely broadcast in the United States and the British Isles, along with translations in five other languages. The President went over the address and approved it in advance, writing on my copy:

C. H.

Grand!

F. D. R.

I stressed the necessity for our rearmament. "No policy," I said, "would prove more disastrous than for an important nation to fail to arm adequately when international lawlessness is on the rampage. It is my considered judgment that, in the present state of world affairs, to do less than is now proposed would lay our country open to unpredictable hazards. It would, moreover, seriously restrict our nation's ability to command, without purpose or occasion for resorting to arms, proper respect for its legitimate rights and interests, the surrender of which would constitute abandonment of the fundamental principles of justice and morality and peace among nations."

We did not have the slightest intention to police the world, I said, "but we equally have not the slightest intention of reversing a tradition of a century and a half by abandoning our deep concern for, and our advocacy of, the establishment everywhere of international order under law, based upon the well-recognized principles to which I have referred. It is our profound conviction that the most effective contribution which we, as a nation sincerely devoted to the cause of peace, can make—in the tragic conditions with which our people, in common with the rest of mankind, are confronted today—is to have this country respected throughout the world for integrity, justice, good will, strength, and unswerving loyalty to principles."

If we declined our responsibility to work for law, order, morality, and justice throughout the world, and withdrew within ourselves, the consequences would be disastrous. "Our security would be menaced," I said, "in proportion as other nations came to believe that, either through fear or through unwillingness, we did not intend to afford protection to our legitimate national interests abroad, but, on the contrary, intended to abandon them at the first sign of danger. Under such conditions the sphere of our international relationships—economic, cultural, intellectual, and other—would necessarily shrink and shrivel, until we would stand practically alone among the nations, a self-constituted hermit state." Thrown back upon our own resources, we should have to reorganize our entire social and economic structure. We should have less production, at higher costs; lower living standards; regimentation in every phase of life; economic distress to workers and farmers; and the dole on an ever increasing scale.

And should we really be avoiding war by these extreme measures? "Reason and experience definitely point to the contrary," I said. "We may seek to withdraw from participation in world affairs, but we cannot thereby withdraw from the world itself. Isolation is not a means to security; it is a fruitful source of insecurity."

I outlined what we would continue to do in carrying out our foreign policy; adhere fully to the fundamental principles underlying international order; urge universal observance of these principles; cooperate with other nations actuated by the same desires and pursuing the same objectives; safeguard our legitimate rights in every part of the world; while scrupulously respecting the rights of others, insist on their respecting our rights; strive, through our reciprocal trade program and other economic policies, to expand trade among nations; promote peace through economic security and prosperity; and participate in international technical conferences.

Further than this speech we could not go. The points I made would not please an isolationist determined to confine us to our own shores. They would not please an internationalist determined to commit us to alliances. But they represented a positive foreign policy under which we could exert our influence, as well as example, for peace, increase our strength, and render ourselves a factor that no aggressor could overlook in making his plans.

We were keeping ourselves minutely informed on developments in

Europe and in Asia. I doubt if any foreign government, in those years, had prompter or ampler information. Many Foreign Offices felt it to their own best interest to pass on to us the sum of their intelligence. Our representatives abroad were alert to transmit to us the benefit of this information, along with their own deductions. At the State Department we analyzed these dispatches as rapidly as possible, passed on to the White House the most essential of them, asked our embassies and legations for additional information, conducted our conversations with the foreign ambassadors and ministers here, and made our decisions, always under the leaden feeling that no diplomacy could brake the world's skid toward chaos.

With Hitler's persecution of the Jews extended to Austria as well, the flow of semidestitute Jewish refugees from German-controlled territory was certain to increase. At the State Department we had supported the League of Nations' efforts to provide homes for these refugees in the early years of the Nazi regime. Now we believed it necessary to go further and take stronger international action lest these victims of persecution be exterminated, and lest the unsettled state of Europe be further disturbed by the wholesale wanderings of these hapless people from country to country.

With the President's approval, I therefore sent out invitations to a number of other governments to cooperate in setting up a special refugee committee. In announcing this move on March 24, 1938, we made it clear that the financing of the emergency emigration would be done by private organizations, and that no country would be expected to receive a greater number of immigrants than its existing legislation permitted. We ourselves continued the German and former Austrian immigration quotas, so that a total of 27,370 refugees could enter the United States on the German quota in one year.

Thirty-one nations responded favorably, and our representatives met at Evian, France, July 6, 1938. Myron C. Taylor, the chairman of the United States delegation, was chosen chairman. The conference laid the basis for the handling of refugees, and created a permanent Intergovernmental Committee on Political Refugees, with headquarters in London. In the months that followed, and even after the outbreak of war on September 1, 1939, this committee facilitated the emigration of scores of thousands of Jews from Germany to new and happier homes. It had to overcome innumerable obstacles, including the brutal refusal of Hitler's Government to permit Jewish emigrants to take more than an insignificant fraction of their goods or money with them, and the reluctance of many governments to receive more than a nominal number of Jews.

At about this time we had to take an important decision as to whether we would join Britain in an effort to appease Mussolini. On January 14, 1938, we had learned through a telegram to the President from Prime Minister Chamberlain that Britain considered recognizing Italy's Ethiopian Empire, and was negotiating with Mussolini toward this end.

The President, after consulting with us, immediately protested to Mr. Chamberlain against such recognition. He pointed to "the harmful effect which this step would have, especially at this time, upon the course of Japan in the Far East and upon the nature of the peace terms which Japan may demand of China." He added that it would seriously affect public opinion in the United States, and concluded: "Recognition of the conquest of Ethiopia, which at some appropriate time may have to be regarded as an accomplished fact, would seem to me to be a matter which affects all nations which are committed to the principles of nonrecognition."

The British would have liked us to take identical action, but I strenuously opposed our associating ourselves with the move. Although I recognized that Britain wanted to keep Italy on her side in case of war with Germany, my reaction to her intentions was twofold: In the first place, giving legal recognition to Mussolini's conquest meant condoning violations of treaties, resort to arms, and flouting of the League of Nations. It would further depress the nations that still believed in collective action, and would encourage other aggressively minded nations. In the second place, I did not think it would work. Mussolini had so inflamed his own mind and that of his people against Britain during the Ethiopian War that he might not be able to reverse the trend. Moreover, his ambitions were unlimited, and he could take more from rich Britain and France than from Germany, if conditions were right.

We ourselves had closed our Legation in Addis Ababa on March 31, 1937, the last of the nations represented there to do so. Marshal Graziani, the "viceroy" of Ethiopia, was insisting on exaggerated forms of courtesy toward himself and the Italian flag from foreigners as well as Ethiopians— reminiscent of the difficulties Americans had had in Germany over their refusal to give the Nazi salute—and clashes were still occurring between Ethiopians and Italians. I telegraphed our Minister Van H. Engert on February 23, 1937, that such a situation "was likely to involve us in embarrassing if not dangerous incidents which are not of any vital concern to this country," and requested his views as to his own immediate departure and the closing of the Legation as soon as possible. As the Legation was closed, I stated at a press conference that our action did not mean recognition of Italian Ethiopia.

When British Ambassador Lindsay came in to see me on another subject on January 17, 1938, I said to him there was a matter very much on my mind that I wanted first of all to talk over with him; namely, Britain's intention to recognize Italy's possession of Ethiopia. I said I realized Britain's difficulties in Europe, particularly in the Mediterranean area, and I assured him we had no desire to inject our comments into any Anglo-Italian negotiations. But I then pointed out that we were profoundly concerned about the Japanese plan to destroy the operation of the spirit and principles relating to the sanctity of international treaties and law, and that our opposition to this movement of destruction in one-half of the world rested primarily on moral concepts underlying the sanctity of agreements and the preservation of international law.

I added that the principle of nonrecognition of conquered territory had been very carefully kept alive during recent years by this and certain other governments, including the British. "If any important country like Great Britain," I said, "suddenly abandons this principle to the extent of recognizing the Italian conquest of Ethiopia, the desperado nations would capitalize it as a virtual ratification of their policy of outright treaty wrecking and the seizure of land by force of arms." I then warned Lindsay that "the repercussions in the Pacific area might be very serious," and that "it need not be surprising to see the American people let down and give way very noticeably in their present support of this Government's policies in the Pacific . . . to say nothing of the extent to which the Japanese Government would capitalize such recognition of its right to destroy solemn treaties and to make this a universal precedent." As for the League of Nations, I said that it was now understood to consist largely of Great Britain and France, and if Britain should recognize the Italian regime in Ethiopia "the precedent at this critical juncture would be very bad, not to say destructive."

I admitted that the policy of nonrecognition presented difficulties over a long period. Such a policy might eventually find large areas of the world "unrecognized," and we should be without diplomatic relations with those areas. But my point, I told Lindsay, was that "this policy is of universal importance as a factor in restoring international law and order. The question of when and how the permanency of the policy might be modified by some general arrangement entered into by all or most of the nations of the world in an orderly manner could be left to the future."

In other words, the nonrecognition policy was still a moral force. For one or two nations to throw it overboard at this time would be a confession of weakness and an incitement to the dictators. Later it could be modified by general agreement among all the nations as one factor in a world-wide settlement, if that were possible.

Lindsay did not dispute any of my points. I urged him to get them before his Government and said we should be much interested in any reply.

Prime Minister Chamberlain, however, was thoroughly committed to his policy of appeasement. The word "appeasement" appeared frequently in dispatches from London, though it had not then begun to bear the opprobrium later given it. It still meant honest, however mistaken, efforts to reach peaceful agreements with the dictators to prevent their plunging the world into war.

Mr. Chamberlain went ahead with his negotiations with Mussolini, coupling them with an attempt to get Mussolini to agree to withdraw his "volunteers" from Spain. Foreign Secretary Eden, who thought as I did on the subject of appeasement, resigned in February, and was replaced by Lord Halifax. The agreement came to a head in April, and was signed in Rome on the 16th.

I had left Washington the previous day for Pinehurst, North Carolina, for two weeks' rest. Scarcely had I gone when the Department received from Ambassador Kennedy in London a personal message from Lord Halifax, dated April 14, informing us of the Anglo-Italian agreement and saying that Chamberlain and he hoped very much that the President would agree with them in thinking that it was a definite "contribution toward world appeasement." Halifax suggested that if the President should share their views, and should consider it possible to give some public expression to his approval both of the agreement and of the principles behind it, it was hardly necessary for him to say how grateful Chamberlain and he would be.

Acting Secretary Welles took this to the President. Mr. Roosevelt agreed to back up the British Prime Minister, and prepared a statement with Welles. I was informed at Pinehurst of his intention, and reluctantly concurred. The President and Welles believed that Britain was "on the spot" and should be given moral support. On April 19 he issued this statement:

"As this Government has on frequent occasions made it clear, the United States, in advocating the maintenance of international law and order, believes in the promotion of world peace through the friendly solution by peaceful negotiation between nations of controversies which may arise between them. It has also urged the promotion of peace through the finding of means for economic appeasement. It does not attempt to pass upon the political features of accords such as that recently reached between Great Britain and Italy, but this Government has seen the conclusion of an agreement with sympathetic interest because it is proof of the value of peaceful negotiations."

After this statement came out, there was considerable press comment in the United States that I was dissatisfied with the position assumed, and even contemplated resigning. Certainly the statement, even with its reservations concerning "the political features of accords," was out of line with my remarks to Ambassador Lindsay in January. But I had no intention of following the example of Anthony Eden, and I felt that a better purpose could be served by showing the world that the Administration was unified in policy.

Following my return to Washington on May 11, I issued a statement that reports of my resignation were absurd, and that I had been consulted with regard to the President's statement and was in accord with it. The next day, to keep the record clear, I stated that our policy toward nonrecognition remained "absolutely unchanged." Referring to my July 16, 1937, statement of principles, I said: "We have not deviated and we do not intend to deviate from any of these principles and policies. The President's comment on the recent British-Italian conversations was not intended to affect or alter in any way our general position with regard to any of these principles."

The United States never recognized Mussolini's conquest of Ethiopia.

With Austria swallowed by the Reich, Hitler had partly surrounded Czechoslovakia, and could begin to work toward his next ambition, the elimination of that country. The Nazi pattern of preconquest, already blueprinted in the case of Austria, began to be applied to Czechoslovakia. A flood of propaganda issued from Germany; the Germany minority in Czechoslovakia, especially in the Sudetenland bordering the Reich, was organized; pressure, direct and indirect, was brought to bear upon Prague; and Hitler and his lieutenants spouted menaces toward the Czechs. Matters reached such a point in May that Hitler seemed on the verge of sending his troops across the border.

On May 28 I issued a public statement calling attention to the Kellogg Antiwar Pact signed nearly ten years earlier, and emphasizing that the pledge of the sixty-three signatory nations not to resort to war "is no less binding now than when it was entered into." As for our country, I said: "We cannot shut our eyes to the fact that any outbreak of hostilities anywhere in the world injects into world affairs a factor of general disturbance the ultimate consequence of which no man can foresee, and is liable to inflict upon all nations incalculable and permanent injuries."

President Beneš of Czechoslovakia resolutely mobilized his army; Britain and France were firm; and the danger passed. At the State Department, however, we knew that the peril was greater than before. It was already a question as to whether 1938, only twenty years after the Armistice, would be the war year.

I held a fundamental conversation, July 7, 1938, on German-American relations with German Ambassador Hans Dieckhoff just prior to his departure on leave for Germany. Knowing that he would see a number of high officials in the German Government, I wanted to impress our position upon him as firmly as I could. First, however, I gave him an opportunity to talk if he wished. He remarked that relations between our two countries were not very good when he came here as Ambassador, and that he had hoped to improve them. "Unfortunately," he commented, "our relations are now worse."

Herr Dieckhoff gave his reasons for this deterioration. Our press criticized his Government. High officials of our Government condemned his country's form of government and its officials. Our officials believed in a systematic war between dictatorships and democracies. Charges were made here that Germans in the United States were being organized under the direction of the German Government, whereas his Government had nothing to do with any such movements. We protested his Government's action against the Jews, and its refusal to pay the Austrian debt, whereas we had not protested to France when, after the last war, she drove 100,000 Germans out of Alsace Lorraine—including his father—and kept their property.

I waited until Ambassador Dieckhoff had run the gamut. "I thoroughly agree with you," I then said, "that relations between our two countries have become steadily worse. They are, in fact, continuing to grow worse. When I left the United States Senate in 1933 to come to the State Department and aid the President in carrying forward a broad, basic program to restore world order based on law, with a sound economic foundation, the world situation was growing more chaotic. Most of the principles governing normal, peaceful international relations and sound economics were being increasingly violated. The doctrine of force, militarism, and territorial aggression was being invoked more and more to spread violence throughout the world and to inflict unusual punishments on people both within and without countries practicing this doctrine. The world situation had become dangerous, not to say desperate.

"It was in the face of this alarming state of affairs that the President and I became consumed with a desire to furnish our country's share of leadership with a program that would, if humanly possible, check the world's momentum backward. You must appreciate the inexpressible disappointment I now feel to have to agree with you that relations between our two countries are worse than at any time within recent years."

I said to Dieckhoff that Germany had received from us all the benefits of equality with every other nation, and that I had constantly striven to prevail on her to treat us in like manner. "Greatly to our disappointment," I remarked, "Germany adopted policies and practices resulting in unjustifiable injury to my country and in corresponding benefit to Germany." I specifically called attention to her defaults on numerous debts; arbitrary discrimination against our exports to Germany and attempts to gain unfair advantage from our imports from Germany; laws making it impossible for Americans inheriting property in Germany to take one penny of it out of that country; similar restrictions against Americans owning business plants there; Germany's refusal to pay Austria's indebtedness; legislation requiring American Jews in Germany to hold their property at the disposal of the German authorities; dissemination of much Nazi propaganda; and activities of Germans in the United States, with or without the approval of their Government, which were contrary to the Constitution and our laws.

"The tide of opposition in this country to the course of the German Government," I emphasized, "has been steadily rising and continues to rise. This despite the efforts of the State Department and the President to hold it back in the hope that amicable relations between our two countries, based on a frank recognition of fair play and equality of treatment by each Government toward the other, might be brought about. It will not be possible for us to continue this course much longer in the face of Germany's seeming intention to find new methods each week or month to injure this country and correspondingly benefit Germany."

This Government, I added, had been earnestly hoping that the German Government would reach a stage where it would support our program of peace, orderly progress, and normal international relations. "There is only one alternative," I pointed out, "—the course of force, militarism, and territorial aggression which inevitably is leading the world backward instead of forward and will sooner or later bring on a more or less general war. In this event, there will scarcely be left a trace of the people who brought it on or those against whom it was waged as well."

Dieckhoff no doubt reported this conversation to his superiors in Berlin, but there was no evidence of any change in Hitler's attitude. Dieckhoff's own career in Washington was running toward its end, even as peace in Europe seemed racing toward its close.

41: Munich Settles Nothing

ALARMING DISPATCHES POURED to my desk in August, 1938, as the crisis over Czechoslovakia again seemed imminent. Feverish peace negotiations were under way principally between Britain and Germany. Walter Runciman, whom I had seen in Washington in 1937, had been sent by the British to Prague to mediate between the Czechs and the Sudeten Nazis. At the same time Hitler was seemingly preparing an invasion of Czechoslovakia.

As war veered ever closer, the European democracies became worried over the continuance of our Neutrality Act. On August 1, 1938, French Ambassador de Saint-Quentin came to see me before sailing for home on vacation, and inquired about the possibility of neutrality legislation by Congress next winter. I replied that, while we could not forecast the state of mind of Congress when it convened in January, we were making a study of every aspect of neutrality and were assembling a large mass of information on the subject.

Knowing that this might be one of the last chances I should have, and that Ambassador de Saint-Quentin would see Premier Daladier and Foreign Minister Bonnet in Paris, I stressed to him—as I had done repeatedly before—the extreme importance of thirty-five to forty nations getting behind our program of peace and economics with renewed earnestness and activity. "The moral influence of this course on countries like Germany and Italy," I said, "will be greater than any other influence short of force. There cannot be permanent stable conditions of peace or economic well-being, law, and order in Europe and elsewhere unless our broad program is subscribed to in spirit and in fact by the important nations everywhere."

I pointed out that our program did not embrace, either pro or con, any steps for temporary peace in a locality or region, or steps intended to avoid a dangerous crisis. I had in mind the negotiations being carried on between Britain and France on the one hand, and Germany on the other. These, in my opinion, could bring only a temporary peace.

Dispatches from Ambassadors Bullitt and Kennedy frequently quoted Chamberlain, Halifax, Daladier, and Bonnet as expressing the fear that Hitler was prepared and determined to take Czechoslovakia by force of arms, if necessary. Accordingly, on August 16 I made a radio address to review the fundamental principles of world law and order in which we believed. In making this speech, I had two thoughts in mind. One was to show to our own people that an isolationist position would not protect them from the effects of a major war elsewhere. The other was to state to the Axis nations as emphatically as I could, considering the isolationist sentiment in the United States, that they could not count us out in pursuing their plans for conquest.

"All nations," I said, "have a primary interest in peace with justice, in economic well-being with stability, and in conditions of order under law. These are constant objectives of this country. Each of these objectives is today seriously jeopardized in many parts of the world. All governments and all peoples should therefore be on guard against certain dangerous developments which imperil them, and be alive to the issues involved."

What were these dangerous developments? I enumerated them:

"Invasion of territory of sovereign states, destruction of lawfully constituted governments and forcible seizure of hitherto independent political entities, interference in the internal affairs of other nations, wholesale violation of established treaty obligations, growing disregard of universally accepted principles of international law, attempts to adjust international differences by armed force rather than by methods of pacific settlement, contemptuous brushing aside of rules of morality—all these appalling manifestations of disintegration seriously threaten the very foundations of our civilization."

Asserting that each day's developments "make more and more clear the fact that our own situation is profoundly affected by what happens elsewhere in the world," I said we must as a nation, "become increasingly resolute in our desire and increasingly effective in our efforts to contribute along with other peoples—always within the range of our traditional policies of nonentanglement—to the support of the only program which can turn the tide of lawlessness and place the world firmly upon the one and only roadway that can lead to enduring peace and security." I recommended this program, which I had stated over and over again since I came into office, "to all other governments and peoples for general adoption."

President Roosevelt chose this moment of crisis to deliver an important address in Canada, on August 18, in which he said: "The Dominion of Canada is part of the sisterhood of the British Empire. I give to you assurance that the people of the United States will not stand idly by if domination of Canadian soil is threatened by any other empire." Although the speech was written at the State Department, the President added that passage himself. Receiving an honorary degree from Queens University, Kingston, Ontario, he declared: "We in the Americas are no longer a far-away continent, to which the eddies of controversies beyond the seas could bring no interest or no harm. Instead, we in the Americas have become a consideration to every propaganda office and to every general staff beyond the seas. The vast amount of our resources, the vigor of our commerce, and the strength of our men have made us vital factors in world peace whether we choose or not."

This speech was warmly received by the democratic countries. Ambassador Kennedy in London cabled me Lord Halifax's appreciation of it and of my August 16 address. Halifax suggested that if the President or I could issue a further statement on the danger in Central Europe prior to the Nazi Party meeting at Nuremberg in September, it might have a restraining effect on Hitler.

On August 27, tenth anniversary of the signing of the Kellogg Pact, I gave out a statement that it was "the great tragedy of today that . . . in certain parts of the world strife and conflict are bringing untold misery to millions, and in other parts the idea of warfare is being actually glorified." Also, that "on the observance or nonobservance of the solemn pledges made ten years ago depends the preservation of all that is valuable and worth while in the life of each and every nation."

Ambassador Bullitt in Paris telegraphed on September 8 two suggestions from Foreign Minister Bonnet. The first was to continue in private conversations the positions adopted in my August 16 and the President's August 18 addresses. The second was that, in the event the Czech crisis should be settled by agreement, the President might issue a statement expressing the hope that this might constitute the beginnings of a real European peace. Bonnet also wondered whether the President would be willing to act as arbitrator in case of dire necessity—a hint he had previously made to Bullitt on July 13.

Isolationists in the United States, however, fearing the approach of catastrophe in Europe, were quick to seize upon statements or the hint of action by the President and myself to shout their alarm. On September 10 I released the text of my letter to the Peruvian Government accepting its invitation to attend the next Pan American Conference, to be held in Lima. In it I said: "The nations of the world are faced with the issue of determining whether relations shall be characterized by international anarchy and lawlessness or by the principles of fair play, justice, and order under law. No nation and no government can avoid the issue; neither can any nation avoid participation, willing or not, in the responsibility of determining which course of action shall prevail."

Pacifist organizations leaped upon the word "participation" in my letter and rang the changes with it. The approach of danger in Europe seemed to paralyze their thinking. They would have liked to deprive the Administration of virtually all power of action in foreign affairs. They were like the drowning man who, in a paroxysm of fear, convulsively grapples with his rescuer and seeks to strangle him.

Bonnet's next suggestion, on September 12, was that Ambassador Hugh R. Wilson, in Berlin, might be instructed to say to the German Foreign Office that we considered that the negotiations then in progress between the Sudeten Nazi representatives and the Czech Government offered substantial possibilities for success; also that we would deplore, as against the interests of humanity, the use of force. Two days later the French Ambassador, De Saint-Quentin, called to ask me whether we were undertaking any secret communication with Berlin or Prague to encourage peace. I replied that we were not saying anything secretly to either Berlin or Prague.

The President and I were opposed to any secret moves. Our position was clear; we had stated it repeatedly; and any restatements should be made publicly. Open approaches would have more effect than secret approaches. In addition to their influence on the governments concerned, they would marshal public opinion.

Just prior to Prime Minister Chamberlain's departure on September 15, for the first of his series of personal talks with Hitler, the British Foreign Office suggested to Ambassador Kennedy that it would appreciate any comment the President might wish to make on this development. At a press conference on that day, I said: "The historic conference today between the Prime Minister of Great Britain and the Chancellor of Germany is naturally being observed with the greatest interest by all nations which are deeply concerned in the preservation of peace."

As telegrams flowed into the Department from Europe, and tension heightened, I went repeatedly to the White House for visits with the President. I likewise frequently sent Undersecretary Welles and Assistant Secretary Berle to the White House with information and comment. Ambassadors Bullitt and Kennedy telephoned me almost daily.

One week before the Munich Conference, Canadian Minister Sir Herbert Marler and Hungarian Minister John Pelényi came separately to my office on September 21, and I said to each of them: "Since August a year ago [when Japan developed her attack on China] I have proceeded here on the theory that Japan definitely contemplates securing domination over as many hundreds of millions of people as possible in Eastern Asia and gradually extending her control through the Pacific islands to the Dutch East Indies and elsewhere, thereby dominating in practical effect that half of the world. . . . And at the same time I have gone on the theory that Germany is equally bent on becoming the dominating colossus of continental Europe."

Chamberlain went back to Germany on September 22 to see Hitler again. As it became evident that the British and French Governments were bringing strong pressure on the Czech Government to yield to Hitler's demands, criticism mounted in the American press that Czechoslovakia was being sold out to Hitler. French Ambassador de Saint-Quentin came in to see me on September 23, much perturbed over this development. I sought to reassure him by pointing out that high officials of this Government were subject to very severe criticism by the press. "The friendship of the American people for the people of France," I said, "is so sincere and deep-seated that no criticisms by a limited number of newspapers, groups, or individuals in this country would materially alienate the friendly feeling of our people for the people of France."

Kennedy telephoned me from London on September 24 about an apparent split in the British Cabinet. Chamberlain, he said, believed in "peace at any price," while some other members of the Cabinet said they did not "want to take any more back talk from Hitler" and believed they "would have to fight anyhow." He said Colonel Charles Lindbergh, who was enormously impressed by Hermann Göring's air force, had been called in by the British for consultation. Lindbergh had already reported to us that he believed Germany was easily capable of combating a combined air force of all other European countries.

That same day Bullitt telegraphed from Paris his belief that some effort should be made by us to maintain peace, even if it were unsuccessful. He suggested an appeal by the President to the British, French, Italian, German, and Polish chiefs of state to send representatives to The Hague to settle the crisis, and that we should indicate our willingness to be represented.

On the following day, the 25th, Wilbur J. Carr, our Minister to Prague, who had been Assistant Secretary of State when I entered the Department, telegraphed a plea from President Beneš that President

Roosevelt urge the British and French not to desert Czechoslovakia and allow her destruction, thereby bringing closer a great conflict embracing not only Czechoslovakia but also the world.

The President and I had already been discussing what action to take. He was prepared to make personal appeals to the heads of the European Governments concerned. My own thought was that, while I did not oppose the making of these appeals, I was not convinced that the results would justify them. I said to the President I felt that the evidence we had been receiving was overwhelming that Germany was armed to the teeth and was bent on widespread aggression at all hazards, and that nothing short of a sufficient amount of force or complete capitulation would halt Hitler in the pursuit of his plans. This meant that any steps to deal with him short of suitable force would necessarily be of an appeasement nature and purely temporary.

I feared lest too ardent steps by the President should throw us into the same appeasement camp with Chamberlain and sooner or later attract the same obloquy that Chamberlain received. I thought such steps might mislead peaceful nations into believing that we thought no other course possible. Furthermore, the very success of such efforts could be dangerous, since such nations might then believe that the danger of war had passed and hence there was no urgent need for rapid military preparations on the broad scale necessary to cope with the inevitable German danger. My view was that the hair-trigger was set so far as Hitler's plans and determination were concerned. There was the added danger that frantic appeals to him might exaggerate his already stupendous ego, convince him that no one wished to oppose him, that he was all-powerful, and that, step by step, he could achieve all he wanted. Moreover, I had no confidence whatever in any pledge by Hitler, and the thought that important strips of territory were being ceded to him to get a pledge from him seemed to me a mockery. Welles kept pushing the President on, while I kept advising him to go slow.

The President, however, believed with Bullitt that something should be done, even if it were not successful. He said to me: "It can't do any harm. It's safe to urge peace until the last moment."

With the President decided on making his appeals, we strove to choose the most telling moment to dispatch them. For some days we had been preparing text after text, with Welles and Berle doing most of the drafting and the President taking a considerable hand himself. On the night of September 25, Bullitt telephoned the Department and advised including in the appeals a "further step"; namely, the suggestion made by Bonnet that the President should offer to arbitrate. But neither the President nor I was willing to go that far. Such an offer would have aroused the wrath of the isolationists in the United States, because of the implications it would carry of involvement in European affairs.

That night, however, we put the finishing touches to the President's message. We strove desperately to make it as forceful as words could make it. Even after the final draft had been agreed to, Mr. Roosevelt made a few changes in pencil. Then at one o'clock on the morning of September 26, he sent it in identical messages direct to Hitler and Beneš, and, through me, to Chamberlain and Daladier. We also cabled it to our diplomatic missions in Warsaw and Budapest, with instructions to communicate it to the Polish and Hungarian Foreign Offices. Poland and Hungary had added their voices and menaces to the crisis by claiming sections of Czechoslovakia.

"On behalf of the one hundred thirty millions of people of the United States of America," said the President, "and for the sake of humanity everywhere I most earnestly appeal to you not to break off negotiations looking to a peaceful, fair, and constructive settlement of the questions at issue.

"I earnestly repeat that so long as negotiations continue, differences may be reconciled. Once they are broken off, reason is banished and force asserts itself.

"And force produces no solution for the future good of humanity."

We then waited almost breathlessly for the replies. We had not long to wait for three of them. That same day, September 26, Beneš, Daladier, and Chamberlain stated their complete accord with the President's views and their willingness to negotiate for peace. These were immediately published, so as to be before the public before Hitler's scheduled speech that evening. But Hitler's reply had not arrived, and this was the one we were most anxiously awaiting.

Europe was mobilizing. Kennedy telephoned me from London that the British Government had assured the French of its support in the event of war. Also, that Chamberlain had informed Hitler that his demands—they increased each time Chamberlain saw him—could not be accepted, but asked him to continue negotiations. I asked Kennedy whether the British believed the French were in very good shape to fight. Kennedy could not give me a positive answer, but he said that the British, "as they always do, feel that they can rise to the occasion," that they were alerting their fleet and had called territorial troops to arms.

Bullitt cabled me that Daladier said he hoped the time would soon come when it would be possible to hold a conference to organize a genuine European peace; he thought the call for such a conference had to come from the President.

Prime Minister Chamberlain now wanted to broadcast a message to the American people on the following night, September 27, but the President said No. He thought that a direct message from the Prime Minister to the American people might be misconstrued.

Hitler's reply arrived on the night of September 26. It was a long diatribe against the Czech Government, the Treaty of Versailles, and the League of Nations, and it concluded by placing the burden of peace or war upon Czechoslovakia, not Germany.

We now had to decide what further step to take. Bullitt cabled a suggestion that a second telegram be sent by the President to Hitler requesting him to agree to send a representative to such a conference at The Hague as Bullitt had previously suggested. Daladier, he said, was "delighted" with the idea.

A number of other Governments had already cabled their support of the President's appeal of the day before. On the afternoon of September 27 we sent instructions to our representatives accredited to other Governments, to ask those Governments to send comparable appeals to Germany and Czechoslovakia. Nineteen Governments, seventeen of them in Latin America, acted favorably on this suggestion.

We also sent a telegram to Ambassador Phillips in Rome containing a personal and confidential message from the President to Mussolini asking Mussolini to "help in the continuation of the efforts to arrive at an agreement of the questions at issue by negotiation or by other pacific means rather than by resort to force."

President Roosevelt decided to send a further appeal, this time addressed to Hitler alone. Drafted by Welles, this went forward on the evening of September 27. It suggested an immediate conference in some neutral spot in Europe, with all nations directly interested in the Czech controversy participating. It declared that "continued negotiations remain the only way by which the immediate problem can be disposed of upon any lasting basis."

While we were waiting tensely for Hitler's reply, British Ambassador Lindsay came in at my request after having given us a copy of Chamberlain's latest communications to Hitler and Mussolini. I said to the Ambassador: "I called you in to say that in the awful event of war, which looks very threatening, I want your Government to know that our Government and nation will have no policy or purpose to supplant existing, established British trade in various parts of the world. Whatever we might do in the way of securing the trade of numerous other countries I might mention, we would have no intention to displace British trade by taking advantage of its disadvantages due to the war and Great Britain's participation in it." The Ambassador seemed much moved.

German Ambassador Dieckhoff also came in to see me on that eventful day, having just returned from Berlin. He said he had laid before his Foreign Office the conversations we had had on pending problems before he went to Berlin, and he felt there was a growing interest among German high officials, from Hitler on down, in economic and trade relations. I replied that my Government, of course, had held out its trade agreement program to every nation in the world alike, but that I did not expect that a country pursuing a policy of autarchy would adopt it. "I feel sure," I said, "that if the German Government decides to change its course and adopt our liberal commercial policy, it could move in our direction more rapidly than even German officials imagine. Capital and businessmen in other countries would immediately discover your Government's basic change of policy, and your manufacturers would soon get credit with which to pay for raw materials."

I said to the Ambassador, however, that there were impressions that the head of the German Government was seeking general dominion by force.

Dieckhoff hastily denied that Hitler had world ambitions. He said Germany had a right, however, to interests in the Balkan and Danubian countries, and there was no ground on which she should be bottled up. I replied that the main question was whether Hitler wanted to acquire dominion over the territory of others, and the Ambassador again denied any such ambitions. He said he had talked with Hitler and Hitler was taking a genuine interest in the United States and realized that readjustments of trade practices by his Government and also of the Jewish situation would be important, if not vital, in restoring satisfactory relations between our two countries. I replied that I was deeply gratified to hear this. "It would be incomprehensible," I said, "for Europe to commit suicide—all alike."

Then, on the afternoon of September 28, as the world seemed to hang in the balance, Hitler invited Chamberlain, Daladier, and Mussolini to meet with him the following day at Munich to settle the Czech crisis. War was postponed.

Whether the actions taken by the President brought about this result is impossible to say. Undoubtedly they exercised considerable influence. On October 20 British Ambassador Lindsay brought me a letter for the President from King George VI of England answering the President's invitation to the King and the Queen to visit the United States during their visit to Canada in 1939. "I feel that I must say how greatly I welcomed your interventions in the recent crisis," the King wrote. "I have little doubt that they contributed largely to the preservation of peace."

But to me the Munich agreement seemed only a momentary solution. As between the alternatives of keeping peace by facing Hitler with force or by capitulating, the latter had been chosen. Hitler had not made war because he had got all he wanted without firing a single shot. Czechoslovakia now lay defenseless before him. He could bide his time and pick her off like a bird on a fodder pole. Britain and France had receded before him. There was something heroic—however misguided—in Prime Minister Chamberlain's devotion to peace and the feverish efforts and personal sacrifice he was willing to make to secure it; but to Hitler it was a manifestation of weakness. I believed, therefore, as I had said to the French Ambassador the month before, that only a "temporary peace" could come from such steps. Chamberlain called it "peace for our time," but the time was short.

On the day following the Munich Conference, I issued this statement:

"As to immediate peace results, it is unnecessary to say that they afford a universal sense of relief.

"I am not undertaking to pass upon the merits of the differences to which the Four-Power Pact signed at Munich on yesterday related.

"It is hoped that in any event the forces which stand for the principles governing peaceful and orderly international relations and their proper application should not relax, but redouble, their efforts to maintain these principles of order under law, resting on a sound economic foundation."

I did not wish to disparage the sincere efforts of Chamberlain and Daladier to obtain peace with Hitler, but I could not commit myself to more than Munich's "immediate peace results." Beyond the next few weeks I refused to go. And I felt obliged to warn the nations that, far from relaxing their efforts to maintain the basic principles of international relations, they must, in fact, redouble them.

I also paid tribute to the cooperation and efficient service rendered by State Department officials during the crisis. We had all worked night and day for several weeks. I particularly mentioned Welles, Assistant Secretaries Messersmith and Berlè, James C. Dunn, Jay Pierrepont Moffat, and Michael J. McDermott, as well as the personnel of the Code Room. I had already sent congratulations to Kennedy, Bullitt, and Carr for their able work.

Welles and I differed, however, in our interpretation of the results of the Munich Conference, he being optimistic, I skeptical. In a radio address on October 3, several days after the conference, in which he described the steps taken by the United States Government just prior to Munich, he said that today, perhaps more than at any time during the past two decades, there was presented the opportunity for the establishment by the nations of the world of a new world order based upon justice and upon law. It seemed to me that the colors in the picture were much darker.

As Poland's and Hungary's demands on Czechoslovakia for cession of territory still created a dangerous situation in Central Europe, Ambassador Anthony J. Drexel Biddle in Warsaw recommended on September 30 that the President renew his suggestion of an international conference, this time to include only Czechoslovakia, Hungary, and Poland. We replied the same day, stating that, since the Polish-Czech dispute had been discussed at Munich, we did not consider the suggestion favorably. Furthermore, the President wished Biddle to add, as a friendly, personal message from him to Polish Foreign Minister Josef Beck, that he trusted that Poland would contribute to European peace by solving its controversy through negotiations, thereby avoiding any armed conflict.

Two weeks later, Polish Ambassador Count Potocki, returning from Warsaw, called on me and expressed the opinion that his Government had come out of the situation with increased prestige, but said nothing about how this had been accomplished. Unfortunately, our conversation was interrupted before I had a chance to comment on this remark. It did not seem to me that any Government, and certainly not the Polish, had come out of the situation with increased prestige except Hitler's, and his augmented prestige, if it could be called that, was based solely on a ruthless willingness to use force.

Following Munich, I frequently mentioned to the President my fear that the conference solved nothing, except that it gave the democracies a little longer breathing spell. On October 26, 1938, the President made a radio address in which he showed that he, too, doubted that peace had really come. "It is becoming increasingly clear that peace by fear has no higher or more enduring quality than peace by the sword," he said. "There can be no peace if the reign of law is to be replaced by a recurrent sanctification of sheer force. There can be no peace if national policy adopts as a deliberate instrument the threat of war."

On November 3, Polish Ambassador Count Potocki asked me for my appraisal of Munich. I replied that we had kept entirely aloof from the questions involved, and we had not, therefore, undertaken to commend or criticize any other Government's handling of such questions. I added, however: "It's my individual view that the big fact brought out was the lack of adequate military preparations by some of the countries immediately concerned. Had there been adequate preparations there would have been less likelihood of a dangerous crisis."

Our own relations with Germany, already unhappy, were further embittered by the refusal of Secretary of the Interior Ickes to sell helium to Germany for use in a commercial dirigible, after he had approved an allotment of it to her. Following the explosion in 1937 of the German dirigible *Hindenburg* at Lakehurst, New Jersey, with many fatalities, Congress passed legislation authorizing the Secretary of the Interior to sell helium to other countries, and the National Munitions Control Board, of which I was chairman, to supervise its export. Ickes, in reply to a letter from the President, had written him a letter, which the Secretaries of War, Navy, and Commerce, and I also signed, in which he said: "With adequate safeguards against the military use of exported helium, it would appear to be the duty of this country as a good neighbor to share any unneeded surplus it may have with other countries for the promotion of commerce and science, alleviation of human suffering, and safeguarding the lives of passengers on airships, thus promoting international good will." (Helium was noninflammable, whereas the gas used in the *Hindenburg* was not.)

The War and Navy Departments having rendered their opinion that there was no effective military use to which dirigibles could be put, Secretary Ickes wrote me a letter, in answer to a query from me, recommending that the American Zeppelin Transport Company, as agent for the German Zeppelin Company, be granted an allotment for 17,900,000 cubic feet of helium for a period of one year after November 1, 1937. I granted a license for an initial export of 2,600,000 cubic feet on January 31, 1938.

As Germany became increasingly unpopular in the United States, Ickes reversed himself and began using various means to delay filling the contract. In addition, his Department began to intimate that the State Department had initiated the whole deal, thereby throwing upon the latter the onus for an act that might be construed as aiding Germany.

We at the State Department felt that a basic point of international conduct was involved in this episode. We were strongly condemning Germany for violating solemn agreements and insisting that she carry them out. In this instance, after we had made an agreement with Germany and the latter had delivered a check in payment, Ickes was proposing to repudiate the whole business, and was abusing the State Department unmercifully when we refused to join him. We felt that one effect of Ickes's position would be to give Hitler an effective talking point in support of his policy of tearing up contracts.

On March 22, 1938, I handed the President a letter which said, in part: "I see no objection on grounds of foreign policy to the proposed transaction . . . a refusal at this time to permit the transaction to take place might result in merely irritating the Germans without accomplishing any useful purpose . . . and such action would undoubtedly be given wide publicity in the press in this country and might give rise to entirely unwarranted conclusions in regard to the relations between this Government and the German Government."

Since Ickes' department continued to give the press and public the impression that the State Department had promoted the idea of selling helium to Germany over the opposition of the Interior Department, I gave to the President the letter Ickes had written requesting me to grant the export license. Mr. Roosevelt was much surprised. When the matter came up for discussion at the next Cabinet meeting, the President read this letter, and offered his comment that the State Department's position was correct. Ickes advanced no real argument. However, he continued to block the sale, and the President would not take a stand sufficiently strong to overrule him. Sometimes the President seemed to take a boyish delight in seeing two of his assistants at odds; he would say, "Settle it between yourselves," or simply let the controversy go on without taking a hand to solve it. Finally, Ickes returned to the German company the seventy-thousand-odd dollars that had been deposited with him, and the transaction was off.

In November, 1938, a savage pogrom against Jews in Germany broke out on an official scale in retaliation for the shooting of a member of the German Embassy in Paris by a German émigré Jew. Assistant Secretary Messersmith prepared a memorandum for me recommending that Ambassador Wilson be ordered home for consultation as a token of our disapproval of this wholesale inhumanity. I conferred with my assistants as to the advisability of this step. Against it was the fact that it would deprive us of an Ambassador in Berlin at a time when one was needed to keep in close contact with the aims and acts of the German Government and to give weight to any representations we needed to make. Favoring it was the fact that words seemed to have no effect on Hitler and his lieutenants; all they perceived was deeds; and, as a nation advocating certain standards of conduct, we could not let so despicable an action as that of the German Government pass unnoticed. We agreed upon Wilson's recall, and I recommended it to the President. He approved.

We also prepared a statement for the President to be given to the press. This proved a good example of the President's tendency to heighten any statement or speech we sent him, by changing words or inserting phrases and sentences. The release we sent read:

"The news of the past few days from Germany has shocked public opinion in the United States. Such news from any part of the world would inevitably produce a similar reaction among the American people. With a view to gaining a first-hand picture of the situation in Germany I asked the Secretary of State to order our Ambassador in Berlin to come home for report and consultation."

The statement, as the President gave it to the press on November 15, read:

"The news of the past few days from Germany has deeply shocked public opinion in the United States. Such news from any part of the world would inevitably produce a similar profound reaction among American people in every part of the nation.

"I myself could scarcely believe that such things could occur in a twentieth century civilization.

"With a view to gaining a first-hand picture of the situation in Germany I asked the Secretary of State to order our Ambassador in Berlin to return at once for report and consultation."

Hitler retaliated by ordering Ambassador Dieckhoff home for consultation. Germany and the United States were to be without ambassadors to each other for the remainder of their peacetime relations.

Dieckhoff came in on November 22 to say goodbye to me. I felt no spirit of cordiality and merely wished him a safe voyage. The conversation halted, and a long silence ensued. Finally, after an exchange of a few more casual expressions, Dieckhoff left rather sadly. He probably guessed, as I did, that he would not return.

Ambassador Wilson reached New York just in time for me to hold an hour's conversation with him aboard the *Santa Clara* as I was about to sail for Lima, Peru, heading the American delegation to the Eighth Pan American Conference. He gave me a graphic outline of Germany's preparations and intentions for war, but little more than he had already conveyed in his dispatches from Berlin. My opinion that Munich did not mean peace was merely confirmed. Hitler's ambitions were clearly written, as were the means with which he intended to achieve them. As I sailed for Lima at the tail end of 1938 I was sure I would return to Washington during a year that would see the decision between peace and war.

42: New World Alerted

AXIS PENETRATION of Latin America, the danger to the Western Hemisphere from the Axis nations in case of war in Europe, and the steps the American Republics could take to parry it—here was the focal point of discussion as the Pan American Conference opened at Lima, Peru, on December 9, 1938. The threat was no mere conjuring by an excited fancy; our diplomatic representatives in Latin America had given us literally hundreds of concrete instances. We had noted it when the Inter-American Conference was held at Buenos Aires in 1936, but in the next two years it had grown in size and boldness.

National Socialist parties had sprung up in various Latin American Republics, in sympathy with and apparently closely allied to the Nazi Party in Germany. Caches of German arms had been found in Brazil. A revolution was instigated there against President Getulio Vargas, and Vargas, declaring that it had been aided by help from abroad, had a number of Germans taken into custody. Berlin insisted that Germans in Latin American countries attend German schools, vote aboard German ships in Hitlerite plebiscites, refuse to marry non-Germans, become members of the Nazi Party and contribute to it, promote German business by all conceivable means, and gather information for the Fatherland. Nazi Party representatives attached to German diplomatic missions sometimes outnumbered the diplomats two or three to one.

German propaganda against the United States in Latin America was fierce and ceaseless. We were accused again and again of intervening in Latin American internal questions, of trying to monopolize trade with our neighbors to the south or to squeeze them in our financial tentacles, of favoring one side or the other in boundary disputes. Hitler's economic lieutenants, using their barter system, and blocking the credits of Latin American Republics for use only in buying German products, hoped to undermine our trade with Central and South America.

Shortly before the Lima Conference opened, the German Foreign Office sent a new diplomatic representative to Lima with an increased staff. The Germans sought in every way to cast the shadow of the Axis over the conference and to intimate to the delegations that they had better take account of the new forces in Europe and Asia. This increased my

601

determination to take these new forces into account, all right, but as they should be; namely, through a common effort to meet them. .

To me the danger to the Western Hemisphere was real and imminent. It was not limited to the possibility of a military invasion. It was more acute in its indirect form of propaganda, penetration, organizing political parties, buying some adherents, and blackmailing others. We had seen the method employed with great success in Austria and in the Sudetenland. The same technique was obvious in Latin America.

As I sailed for Lima aboard the *Santa Clara,* the only question in my mind was whether all the American Republics would see the danger sufficiently to take a common, decisive stand against it. There was some reason to doubt it. As had been the case again and again in the past, our principal doubts rose from Argentina.

Saavedra Lamas, so friendly to us at Montevideo and not nearly so friendly at Buenos Aires, was no longer Foreign Minister. His place had been taken by José María Cantilo, who had been Argentine Ambassador to Italy. As early as March 4, 1938, Cantilo, then still in Rome, suggested to us and other American Republics that the Lima Conference should be postponed one or two years.

Peru's Foreign Minister Carlos Concha, emphatically opposing any postponement of the conference to be held in his capital, informed us he believed Argentina's suggestion was influenced by certain European countries. On March 25 he said to our Ambassador in Lima, Laurence Steinhardt, that there were statesmen in Europe shrewd enough to foresee that action taken at a Pan American Conference, if held in December as planned, might accomplish more for Pan Americanism than anything heretofore achieved; it was therefore not at all unlikely that a plan had already been conceived in one or more European capitals to bring about a postponement of a conference that might have undesirable repercussions on European interests.

Two days before I sailed from New York, Cantilo, then in Buenos Aires, said to our Chargé d'Affaires, S. Pinckney Tuck, that, while Argentina believed in a policy of continental solidarity and collaboration, she could not at the same time turn her back on Europe. He thought Argentina should continue her traditional policy of assisting the sister nations of the Continent, but would find it difficult to subscribe to military pacts or engagements that might give the impression of drawing away from friendly European nations. Actually, military pacts were not on the Lima agenda, and we had no intention of suggesting them.

En route to Lima, I received a wireless message from the State Department giving the text of a declaration Cantilo intended to present to the conference. As I studied it with other members of the delegation, I felt that it did not at all meet the situation as I saw it. It was very weak and general. It did not mention the dangers to the Hemisphere from abroad. It merely provided, in a vague way, for meetings of the Foreign Ministers of the American Republics.

Our own draft of a declaration on American solidarity, which I expected to present at Lima, was far stronger. It bound the Republics to resist any threat, either direct or indirect, to their peace, safety, or territorial integrity on the part of any non-American country. In case the peace of any one of them were disturbed by direct or indirect interference on the part of one or more non-American governments in a matter pertaining to national sovereignty, the Republics proclaimed their common concern and their purpose to make their solidarity effective to resist such threat. The Republics agreed to hold meetings of their Foreign Ministers every two years, and a special consultation of these Ministers could be called by any American Government if the occasion for it arose.

I went over this draft with the strongest delegation I had yet taken to a Pan American Conference. With me, as chairman of the delegation, were: Alfred M. Landon, who had been the Republican candidate for the Presidency in 1936 (his presence was in keeping with my policy of keeping politics out of foreign affairs and was a valuable proof to the Latin Americans that both major Parties were united on the Good Neighbor policy); Assistant Secretary of State Adolf A. Berle, Jr.; Laurence A. Steinhardt, Ambassador to Peru, who would meet us at Lima; R. Henry Norweb, our Minister to the Dominican Republic; Emilio del Toro Cuevas, Chief Justice of the Supreme Court of Puerto Rico; Green H. Hackworth, legal adviser to the State Department; the Reverend John F. O'Hara, president of Notre Dame University; Charles G. Fenwick, professor of international law at Bryn Mawr College; Dan W. Tracy, representing the American Federation of Labor; Elise F. Musser, representing women's interests; and Kathryn Lewis, daughter of John L. Lewis, representing the Congress of Industrial Organizations.

At Lima I had an opportunity closely to observe the work of Ambassador Steinhardt. His record was so creditable that I later suggested to the President that he be transferred to the higher and more responsible post at Moscow, to which Mr. Roosevelt agreed. I always found Steinhardt to be alert and very efficient as a diplomatic reporter, especially during perilous periods.

On December 1, while still aboard the *Santa Clara,* I received a wireless message forwarded from Rio de Janeiro in which Brazil's Foreign Minister Aranha informed us that Cantilo planned, in his opening address at Lima, to reject the idea of any collective security pact. Aranha said Cantilo was opposed to Latin American Republics breaking away from Europe and relying exclusively on the United States for protection, because American foreign policy was unstable due to the possibility of changes in our internal politics. Aranha said his Government would seek to impress upon Cantilo that any such opening address could not fail to throw the conference into complete discord at the outset.

We spent some time aboard the *Santa Clara* in tentatively revising Cantilo's resolution to make it include the ideas we had in mind. I was quite willing for the Argentine delegation to introduce a resolution and gain all credit for it, provided it contained approximately the substance I felt we needed. I had no pride of exclusive authorship in our own draft. What I wanted was unanimous agreement. As was the case at Montevideo, I should be glad to see the Argentines take the initiative, if thereby the conference could agree on a definite, important position.

When the *Santa Clara* arrived at Callao, the port of Lima, on December 7, I saw at anchor in the harbor a new Argentine cruiser that had brought Cantilo to the conference. Cantilo, I learned, intended to spend only a couple of days in Lima and then take a vacation among the mountain lakes of Chile. He was not chairman of his delegation. Comparatively, the Argentine delegation was weak, another indication that Cantilo did not attach too much importance to the conference. It was headed by Isídoro Ruiz Moreno, legal adviser to the Buenos Aires Foreign Office. The delegations of ten Republics, including our own, were headed by Foreign Ministers.

After I arrived in Lima, Cantilo sent word he wished to call on me. I sent back word at once that, since he was spending only a couple of days in Lima and undoubtedly was very busy, I could call on him instead. I went to see him almost immediately, but our conversation was unsatisfactory. Cantilo indulging in generalities, we made no real progress. I gave him a copy of the declaration the American delegation had prepared, and he said he would take it with him.

Cantilo, even though not chairman of his delegation, addressed the first plenary session of the conference and was a good deal more cooperative than we might have expected. Pan American solidarity, he said, "is a fact that nobody can or will doubt. All and each one of us is ready to sustain and prove this solidarity, in the face of any danger which, from whatever source, might threaten the independence or sovereignty of any state of this part of the world." But he also said: "We do not require special pacts for this. The pact is already made in our history. We would act with one and the same impulse, eliminating frontiers and under one flag for everybody, the flag of liberty and justice."

My thought on this last point was that, while not requiring special pacts, we did at least require a special declaration—a strong one. This was important, not only for its effect in the Western Hemisphere in proving to each Republic that it could rely on the help of all the others, but also for its influence in the Old World in showing the Axis nations that they had to reckon, not with the easy picking off of one Republic after another, but with the combined resistance of all of us. Since the danger was real, the means to meet it must be equally real.

"Mankind," I said in my address to the first plenary session on December 10, "is tragically confronted once more by the alternatives of freedom or serfdom, of order or anarchy, of progress or retrogression, of civilization or barbarism . . . there must not be a shadow of a doubt anywhere as to the determination of the American nations not to permit the invasion of this hemisphere by the armed forces of any power or any possible combination of powers."

The next day Cantilo departed aboard his cruiser for Chile. He ordered Ruiz Moreno, chairman of the Argentine delegation, to agree to nothing without first referring it to him.

I recall the next ten days as among the most difficult of my career. Neither the Argentine delegation nor ourselves formally presented our declarations on continental solidarity. Instead we conferred informally but intensively with each other and with the other delegations in an effort to reach a common ground. But we ran into a stone wall of Argentine reluctance to agree to anything that meant anything, cemented by the fact that Ruiz Moreno was out of touch with Foreign Minister Cantilo, then incomunicado among the Chilean lakes. I felt that Cantilo had run away from the conference in order to kill it.

Finally, on December 17, I induced Dr. Afranio de Mello Franco, chief of the Brazilian delegation and former Foreign Minister of Brazil, and Dr. Concha, Peruvian Foreign Minister, to call an extraordinary meeting of the principal delegates in Mello Franco's hotel apartment that night. Both of these statesmen worked with me 100 per cent.

As the delegates arrived, Dr. Concha and I stood in the doorway and "buttonholed" them. We both emphasized as strongly as we could that the conference had been going on for more than a week, that Argentina had not yet offered anything constructive in the way of a continental declaration, and that she should be induced to take a stronger position.

After the meeting opened, the Argentine delegate insisted that any declaration should be in very general terms and not open to the interpretation that it was directed against European countries. I opposed this view with all the emphasis I could command. "This conference," I said, "must make a clear, strong statement which will satisfy the expectations of the American peoples and of the world. This declaration should have the unanimous support of all the delegations. In order to achieve this end each delegation must be prepared to make concessions. I came to this conference prepared to make concessions, and the refusal of one country, or of one or two or three countries, must not be allowed to break up American solidarity."

The Uruguayan and Chilean delegates gave partial support to the Argentines on the ground, they said, that their trade situation must take into account the German reaction to any possible conference declaration.

I put to the meeting a suggestion by President Roosevelt, cabled to me the previous day; namely, that a passage be included in the declaration whereby the American Republics stated they "shall not permit any non-American state to assist or abet in the fomenting of internal disorder in any American Republic." The President realized that the same idea was already contained in our draft, but he felt that stronger language probably would have a helpful effect on public opinion throughout the hemisphere.

Many of the delegates, however, opposed the wording as too strong.

Ruiz Moreno, the Argentine delegate, argued that there would be no harm either in referring to "non-American or any other governments," in the declaration, or in making no mention of either non-American or American governments. The first phrase, however, could have been aimed at the United States. As to the second, I said there must be a difference in attitude and in treatment where a non-American government was concerned and where an American government was concerned. The other delegates agreed.

The debate went on until well after midnight. At times it became exceedingly animated, and voices were lifted high. Finally the meeting seemed to be in general agreement, except for Argentina, that the declaration, to be known as the "Declaration of Lima," should refer principally to non-American governments. There was unanimous agreement that it should embrace activities or penetration in the Western Hemisphere other than through force or the threat of force.

Ruiz Moreno promised to telegraph his Government for instructions. I spoke to him privately and suggested he let his Government know that he was being severely criticized because he was offering nothing constructive toward an effective declaration. Following the meeting I telephoned our Embassy in Buenos Aires to contact President Ortiz directly and at once and request him from me to instruct the Argentine delegation to submit a substantial declaration on behalf of Argentina. Fortunately I had known President Ortiz as a personal friend for some years and admired him as a good financial and economic authority. In making this move I was going over the head of the Argentine delegation and of Foreign Minister Cantilo; but I felt fully justified in view of the fact that that delegation was completely hamstrung and Cantilo had deliberately placed himself beyond contact with the conference.

President Ortiz managed to get in touch with Cantilo. Several days later Cantilo, still among the Chilean lakes, sent to Ruiz Moreno the draft of a new declaration. It was in general accord with the draft of the proposal I had given him before he left Lima, except that it did not provide for the regular meetings of Foreign Ministers which I suggested, and contented itself with calling for such meetings whenever any Republic took the initiative.

We now went to work on this new Argentine draft. Late at night on December 22 all the delegations agreed to it. But just at that moment a further complication arose. The Brazilian delegate, Mello Franco, alarmed by the protracted negotiations prior to the arrival of the Argentine text, had drawn up a declaration that incorporated my views and had sent it to President Vargas of Brazil. Vargas approved it and telephoned the text to President Ortiz and got his approval. The two Presidents would thereupon have submitted the project to the conference as their joint proposal. When word of this fact reached us at Lima, I felt that any effort to force through this new declaration, after we had all agreed to the Argentine proposal submitted by Cantilo, might well break up the conference. I therefore telegraphed our Embassies at Rio and Buenos Aires explaining the situation and asking them to request Presidents Vargas and

Ortiz not to submit their formula. Fortunately, the two Presidents understood the situation and agreed without difficulty.

On Christmas Eve the Declaration of Lima was adopted unanimously by the conference. Two weeks of night-and-day work had eventually succeeded.

The declaration, though not all I had wanted, was not far from it. After calling attention to the principles on which the peoples of America had achieved spiritual unity, the American republics declared:

"First. That they reaffirm their continental solidarity and their purpose to collaborate in the maintenance of the principles upon which the said solidarity is based;

"Second. That, faithful to the above-mentioned principles and to their absolute sovereignty, they reaffirm their decision to maintain them and to defend them against all foreign intervention or activity that may threaten them;

"Third. And in case the peace, security, or territorial integrity of any American Republic is thus threatened by acts of any nature that may impair them, they proclaim their common concern and their determination to make effective their solidarity, coordinating their respective sovereign wills by means of the procedure of consultation, established by conventions in force and by declarations of the Inter-American conferences, using the measures which in each case the circumstances may make advisable. It is understood that the Governments of the American Republics will act independently in their individual capacity, recognizing fully their juridical equality as sovereign states."

Then followed a paragraph whereby meetings of the foreign ministers, when deemed desirable and at the initiative of any one of them, would be held in their several capitals by rotation.

The Declaration of Lima was a great advance over previous Pan American agreements. It affirmed the intention of the American Republics to help one another in case of a foreign attack, either direct or indirect, on any one of them. It provided for joint action not only against a military assault but also against the underground infiltration methods pursued by the Axis. While names of specific countries were not mentioned, there could be no doubt whatever what nations were meant. From now on, the responsibility of the United States to defend the hemisphere became the responsibility of all the hemisphere's Republics.

The Declaration was a triumph for no one nation, but for the New World. The Axis press, and some of our own, represented the outcome as a victory for Argentina as against the United States. Had they known the background of the presentation of the final Argentine declaration, conceived through my direct approach to President Ortiz and his instructions to Cantilo, they could not have reached that conclusion any more than I could have revealed the background at the time. Critics asserted that I had abandoned my position in order to reach an agreement. The fact is that the Declaration of Lima was far closer to my original draft than it was to the Argentine original draft.

Unanimity, as always in the Pan American Conferences, was my aim. I could have had a vote of 17 to 4 or 18 to 3 or perhaps 20 to 1 on my original draft at any time, but such was not our method of procedure. That would have shown the outside world that there was a split in the Pan American front.

The Axis press made much of the fact that the Declaration of Lima was a declaration and not a treaty. Actually, a declaration was in many ways preferable. It could contain stronger language than a treaty. It did not require ratification by the legislatures of the Republics. It entered into effect at once.

I was already deeply disappointed by Argentina's record of nonratification of the agreements entered into at previous Pan American Conferences. With the exception of Saavedra Lamas's Antiwar Pact, she had ratified not a single important agreement from the time of the Montevideo Conference on. This was part of the unfortunate policy of Argentine politicians in charge of their Government to remain aloof from any movements of leadership in the hemisphere unless they themselves were furnishing the chief leadership and policies. At Pan American conferences, impressed by the determination of almost all the Latin American Republics as well as the United States to promote a common program, they eventually coalesced their will with that of the others. But, back in Buenos Aires again, they neglected to ratify the accords entered into. A declaration that came into force immediately was better than an unratified treaty in the pigeonhole of a Foreign Office or a legislative committee.

The final attitude of the conference toward the Axis Powers and their activities was patently shown by the unanimous passage of two strong resolutions. One sweepingly condemned racial and religious bigotry and intolerance everywhere. The other condemned the collective political activity of groups of aliens in this hemisphere.

On December 24 the conference also approved unanimously a "Declaration of American Principles" prepared by Brazil. This reemphasized the principles I had stated to the Inter-American Conference at Buenos Aires two years before on the basis of which—and only on the basis of which—international relations could be conducted peacefully for the benefit of all nations.

Although the negotiations for the Declaration of Lima attracted greatest attention, the conference adopted a number of other important resolutions, ranging from the promotion of cultural relations to economics. Recognizing the importance of closer cultural relations, embracing education, literature, science, and art, I had approved the creation in the State Department of a Division of Cultural Relations a few months before the conference opened. On the score of economics, the conference reasserted my principles of freer trade. To me this was important because, during the financial recession of 1937, some of the Latin American Republics felt themselves obliged to apply temporary trade restrictions.

The question of expropriation of properties by American Governments arose at the conference, as we expected, in view of the expropriation of foreign-owned oil properties by Mexico and Bolivia. This question had furnished one of our major difficulties at the State Department in 1938. After Mexico expropriated American-owned oil companies in Mexico, a series of notes passed between us. We admitted Mexico's right to expropriate private property within its borders in furtherance of public purposes, but insisted on adequate compensation, and proposed that the dispute be submitted to arbitration. Mexico admitted liability, but in her own manner and time, and refused to arbitrate on the ground that there was no basic difference of opinion between us.

Although firm in our attitude, we sought also to be friendly, in keeping with the spirit of the Good Neighbor. Nothing could have been more unhappy for the forthcoming Lima Conference than an acrimonious diplomatic battle between our southern neighbor and ourselves. Eventually, in November, Mexico and the United States agreed to set up a commission of three persons to determine the amount of compensation, and Mexico agreed to pay at least $1,000,000 annually until this amount was liquidated. Then, on December 10, Ambassador Daniels in Mexico City cabled me that President Lázaro Cárdenas informed him that the Mexican delegation at Lima had been instructed to cooperate with me. By way of contrast, Great Britain chose a sharper course, which led to the rupture of diplomatic relations with Mexico. At Lima the conference deferred discussion of this difficult question of expropriation.

In my closing address to the conference, on Christmas Eve, I summed up our achievements, and offered them to the world. "It can be fairly said that the principles of conduct upon which the countries of this hemisphere have chosen to stand firm are so broad and essential that all the world may also stand upon them," I said. "Speaking for my country, we seek universal recognition and support for them. Were they adopted over all the world, a great fear would end. The young would see their future with more certainty and significance. The old would see their lives with more peaceful satisfaction."

As the world was preparing to celebrate its last Christmas at peace for some years to come, I said: "There are those who think the world is based on force. Here, within this continent, we can confidently deny this. And the course of history shows that noble ideas and spiritual forces in the end have a greater triumph. Tonight especially we can say this, for on this night nearly two thousand years ago there was born a Son of God who declined force and kingdoms and proclaimed the great lesson of universal love. Without force His Kingdom lives today after a lapse of nineteen centuries. It is the principality of peace; the peace which we here hope in a humble measure to help to give by His grace to the continent of the Americas."

Governor Alfred M. Landon also addressed this closing session, and stressed the importance of the conference's results. He had previously spoken to the conference and emphasized that no change of political party in the United States would alter our policy of refusing to tolerate any foreign government's gaining a foothold on this hemisphere. His was a useful effort to convince the other delegations that the United States was united in its program toward Latin America.

I was chosen by the delegations to speak on their behalf at the farewell dinner given by President Benavides of Peru. I praised the Pan American method of negotiation, the very essence of which was the quiet exchange of views among equals.

"Never before, I think, has the conference process set to work so promptly and operated with more serious determination than at this congress," I said. "We have here stated our agreements in declarations, rather than in treaties or conventions. That is wise when the matters dealt with are of general character and of political nature. The people of the American Republics have a proud history of the use of declarations. Their national life has grown in and out of the declarations of independence which mark their birth. And so in this Declaration of Lima lies the future of the solidarity of the American Republics."

43: Breath of War

ON MY WAY HOME from Lima aboard the *Santa María*, I heard over the radio President Roosevelt's "methods short of war" address to Congress on January 4, 1939. It seemed a fitting introduction to the problems that were to face us in the new year.

"The mere fact," said Mr. Roosevelt, "that we rightly decline to intervene with arms to prevent acts of aggression does not mean that we must act as if there were no aggression at all. Words may be futile, but war is not the only means of commanding a decent respect for the opinions of mankind. There are many methods short of war, but stronger and more effective than mere words, of bringing home to aggressor governments the aggregate sentiments of our own people."

"Methods short of war"! Here was a phrase that covered long hours of discussion at the State Department and many conferences I had with the President prior to my departure for Lima. To both of us the situation in Europe was as dangerous after Munich as before—in fact it was worse because Hitler now had even more confidence than before in his fateful ability to expand Germany without meeting more than protests from the democracies.

We did not intend to cease using words; we could not too often call the world's attention to basic principles of international relations without which the nations could never be long at peace. But we determined to make use of every means at our command to enforce them by action. Words were flying back and forth across Europe like birds of the equinoxes, and they were coming to have scarcely more effect. But the Axis dictators, though their ears were closed to words, still had their eyes open to deeds.

One of the "methods short of war" was to change our Neutrality Act so that the democracies might have access to the arms, ammunition, and implements of war produced in the United States. Aboard the *Santa María* I heard the President say over the radio: "At the very least, we can and should avoid any action, or any lack of action, which will encourage, assist, or build up an aggressor. We have learned that when we deliberately try to legislate neutrality, our neutrality laws may operate unevenly and unfairly—may actually give aid to an aggressor and deny it to the victim. The instinct of self-preservation should warn us that we ought not to let that happen any more."

Several weeks prior to my departure for Lima, I had begun to hold conferences of key officials in the State Department on the subject of revision of the Neutrality Act. We believed, as did the President, that the presence of this legislation on our statute books, making it impossible for Britain and France, if at war, to purchase arms or airplanes from us, was an incitement to Hitler to go to war. If Hitler, already much better armed than either or both Britain and France, knew in advance that the great industrial potential of America for armaments would be open to Britain and France in case of conflict, he might hesitate.

Immediately after my return from Lima on January 7, I made it a point to get in touch with Senator Pittman, chairman of the Senate Foreign Relations Committee. It was my thought that the State Department would prepare the necessary legislation to be introduced by him. Pittman, however, said he felt it would be more effective if he prepared, introduced, and sponsored the bill himself as head of the Foreign Relations Committee. I promptly acquiesced. There is always a certain amount of jealousy between Congress and the Executive on the subject of the drafting, and therefore the initiation, of legislation. If Pittman thought he stood a better chance with legislation of his own origin, I was willing to go along with him. The President was of the same opinion.

Pittman and I discussed what the new bill should be. We at the State Department thought that the outright repeal of the arms embargo should be sought. Failing this, we advocated an amendment to the Neutrality Act which would give the President discretionary authority to proclaim an arms embargo when he found that a state of war existed and that an arms embargo was necessary to promote the security or preserve the peace of the United States.

Pittman was not disposed to go as far as I in the direction of freeing the Executive from the restrictions of neutrality legislation. He did not believe there was the slightest prospect of any measure being adopted giving the President authority to impose an embargo against an aggressor only. Nor did he think there was any possibility of an outright repeal of the existing Neutrality Act, with nothing substituted for it.

Pittman and I finally agreed on the general terms of the new bill. Basically, its distinguishing feature was that arms, ammunition, and implements of war were made part of a cash-and-carry section. The cash-and-carry section of the existing Act of May 1, 1937, was due to expire

May 1, 1939, although the arms embargo and other sections would continue in effect. According to the new bill, there would be no distinction between arms and other exports. We believed that the raw materials employed in making or using arms, such as steel, copper, and oil, were just as important to a belligerent as the arms themselves, and any distinction between them was unnatural. Therefore, if a nation had the ships and the cash, it could come to the United States and get machine guns or airplanes just as it could steel and oil. Pittman introduced his bill on March 20, and was confident he could get it through the Senate. We relied on his confidence.

At about that time I penciled a few notes on what I had in mind by methods short of war. I listed them in part as follows:

"(1) Withdrawal of Ambassador Wilson.

"(2) Nonrecognition Doctrine.

"(3) Antidumping [application of countervailing duties to imports from Germany].

"(4) Armaments" [adequate arming of the democracies in self-defense].

Underneath these headings, I wrote:

"Aggressor & other nations know in advance all & exact plans of nation with inflexible neutrality.

"There can be no sense of safety among peaceful nations if powerful ones arm heavily & go on rampage of conquest."

Events in Europe were now rushing with ever more menacing acceleration. Speeches by Chamberlain, Hitler, and Daladier sharpened the issues. Britain and France were moving closer together toward a common policy and action, as evinced by Britain's guarantee of France made in February, 1939. But Chamberlain, though already somewhat disillusioned as to "peace for our time," was still the Chamberlain of Munich. His harsh awakening was just around the corner.

As might well have been expected, Hitler was reducing to a mockery the independence of what was left of Czechoslovakia after the lopping off of the Sudetenland by the Munich agreement and the subsequent cessions of territory to Poland and Hungary. Demand after demand from Berlin that Czech activities, political and economic, be tied into those of the Reich, coupled with the usual policy of infiltration and propaganda, rendered continuance of Czechoslovakia's independence by her own efforts impossible. The same Hitler who had said he did not wish to incorporate non-Germans into Germany was now aiming at the complete absorption of Czechoslovakia.

I was in Florida for a needed rest when Hitler's legions, in violation of the Munich agreement, marched across the borders of Czechoslovakia on March 15. On receipt of this news I telephoned my office in the State Department and dictated a statement of our position to be given Acting Secretary Welles. Welles took this to the President and together they made certain additions and changes. Welles issued it on March 17. "This Government, founded upon and dedicated to the principles of human liberty and of democracy," it said, "cannot refrain from making known this country's condemnation of the acts which have resulted in the temporary extinguishment of the liberties of a free and independent people with whom, from the day when the Republic of Czechoslovakia attained its independence, the people of the United States have maintained specially close and friendly relations."

In line with our policy of "methods short of war" to manifest our condemnation of acts of aggression, the Administration now took a series of steps following the swallowing up of Czechoslovakia. We refused to recognize the conquest and continued to receive the Czech Minister in Washington, Vladimir Hurban. We suspended the trade agreement with Czechoslovakia so that Berlin might not be able to avail itself of our tariff reductions on Czech exports, the proceeds from which would now go into German coffers. The Treasury imposed countervailing (increased) duties on imports from Germany on the ground that these imports were being subsidized by the German Government.

Dispatches from Europe were pouring to my desk in heavier volume even than before. The Britain of Chamberlain was rousing. Hitler's promises, repeatedly violated, had been broken once too often; he and his ambitions stood revealed for what they were. Chamberlain and Halifax reached with Daladier the decision that Britain's and France's policy must now drastically change. They had to convince Hitler that he could go no further with bloodless conquests. The next one would be costly.

On April 3 I outlined our policy toward German trade. "Any obstacles," I said in a public statement, "which German trade faces in the United States as compared with any and every other country are entirely the result of German policy and practices. . . . The German authorities seem to be able to trade only on their own terms as they dictate them and by their own methods as they shape them. . . . American trade cannot satisfactorily fit itself into the crevices of German need left by the barter agreements that Germany has already executed with other countries. It does not have to, nor would its interest be served by doing so."

I pointed out the basic differences between the German and American methods. "By exchanging goods and services, countries supply each other's deficiencies," I said. "Each draws upon the others for goods which it does not produce or produces at high comparative cost. This is the very essence and nature of international trade. A certain amount of similar interchange can and does, of course, take place under the so-called barter agreements, but paralyzes world markets in the process. Barter agreements involve . . . domination by the Government not only of commerce but of production; and they create arbitrary discriminations."

Another decision—recognition of the Franco Government—now faced us following the military collapse of the Spanish Loyalist Government. After nearly three years of savage fighting, the Franco side had overrun Catalonia and captured Barcelona. The Loyalists still held Madrid, but their position was hopeless. On February 18, 1939, the British Government informed us they were considering recognizing Franco's Government as the legal government of Spain, and the French Government was in accord. General Franco had made several approaches to us in 1938 seeking recognition of his regime, but we had successfully parried his efforts.

On February 23, 1939, following receipt of further communications from the British Government, I wirelessed the President, who was cruising at sea, that we had been officially advised that Britain had decided to recognize the Franco regime and that France and the Netherlands were expected to take similar action. I mentioned that some sixteen other governments had previously recognized Franco's Government. I suggested that Ambassador Bowers, our representative to the Loyalist Government, be ordered home for consultation in order to free our hands for establishment of relations with the Franco Government, if this seemed advisable. The President agreed.

I cabled Ambassador Bullitt in Paris on February 28 to see the Franco representative there informally, and tell him that our Government was naturally giving careful consideration to the problem of recognizing the Insurgents as the legal government of Spain; also, that we would be gratified to receive indications from the Franco authorities that there would be no policy of reprisal against their opponents and that the Insurgent authorities would be ready to protect Americans and their properties in Spain and otherwise to fulfill the obligations and responsibilities incumbent upon a sovereign state under international law and treaties.

On the day before, Spanish Ambassador Fernando de los Ríos came to my office. Downhearted over the approach of the end in Spain, he began to inquire what our attitude would be, when he was suddenly interrupted by an urgent call from his Embassy. He had just received instructions to inquire whether we would use our moral influence against reprisals by General Franco. I assured him we had already been giving this our attention.

Ambassador Bullitt, after seeing the Franco representative in Paris, reported that he had received absolute promises that American lives and property would be protected and that Franco would carry out the normal obligations of a government. As to promises regarding reprisals, Bullitt commented that, in the flush of victory, the Franco Government was not inclined to make any promises worth having, and he doubted, in fact, whether, under the circumstances, any promises on the subject were worth having. The Spanish representative gave Bullitt a declaration that had been sent to the British Government, containing a weasel-worded assurance.

Britain and France recognized the Franco Government on February 27. We delayed our action until it was manifest that the Loyalist Government had ceased to exist in Spain. Recognition to us centered on a question of fact—had the Franco regime gained complete control of Spain? On March 28 Madrid fell to the Insurgents. On March 31 Ambassador de los Ríos came in to say goodbye to me, and to inform me his Embassy was being closed.

The following day I telegraphed to Franco's Foreign Minister, Count Jordana, that we desired to establish diplomatic relations with Spain and that the President was prepared to nominate Alexander W. Weddell, our Ambassador to Argentina, as Ambassador to Spain. On the same day the President signed a proclamation, which I had sent him the previous day, lifting the arms embargo against Spain. Our recognition of the Franco Government was confirmed in exchanges of cables with Jordana, ending on April 3.

The following day the new Chargé d'Affaires of Franco Spain, Don Juan Francisco de Cárdenas, called on me to pay his respects. I knew him well, for he had previously been Spanish Ambassador in Washington and had gone over to the Franco side. Through him I pleaded with his Government for leniency toward their opponents.

THE MEMOIRS OF CORDELL HULL

"My own people on the border," I said, "went through all the horrors of our Civil War, and I know how to sympathize with the people of any country who find themselves in the same situation. I have been visualizing the people of Spain as a whole and without reference to the merits or demerits of the controversy, and I have thought of them with deep sympathy for all alike."

Cárdenas commented that feelings and misunderstandings existed which would have to be cleared up gradually as time went on.

"I assume as much," I replied. "I recall vividly the difficulties of the Reconstruction Period following our Civil War. Fortunately, the men who fought on both sides of that war respected each other's bravery and honesty of purpose. As a result, many of them came together from both sides and made a marvelous contribution to the work of reconstruction. Doubtless this same state of mind will exist in your country and will contribute tremendously toward a correspondingly earlier reconstruction for the benefit of your distressed people."

Cárdenas did not take issue with my comment. Soon afterwards he became the new Spanish Ambassador to the United States. I liked him personally, but later on I frequently had to use harsh words with him in referring to the highhanded attitude of his Government.

The problem of Spain had scarcely been settled when another problem arose—Mussolini's occupation of Albania. For several weeks we had been receiving cables from Rome, Belgrade, Tirana, Paris, and London relating Mussolini's sinister intentions toward Albania. Hitler's successful occupation of Czechoslovakia rendered it almost imperative that the junior member of the Axis brigand partnership do something to illuminate his own career.

Our Minister in Belgrade, Arthur Bliss Lane, cabled me on April 7 his information that Hitler was in agreement that Mussolini should seize Albania. He gave three possible reasons for Hitler's acquiescence. One was to compromise Italy in a military venture in the Balkans and thus prevent Italy's being against Germany in the event of a general war. A second was to weaken Italy's prestige in the Balkans, especially in Yugoslavia and Greece, and thus facilitate German economic and political penetration of the Balkans. The third was to give Mussolini the sop of new territory to show that he had obtained something from the Axis.

On April 7, Good Friday, Italian troops entered Albania, and next day occupied the capital, Tirana, following the flight of King Zog and the royal family. Ambassador Phillips, in Rome, replied on April 8 to a cable I sent him requesting an explanation of Mussolini's move. Phillips thought that Mussolini's intention was to secure certain points on the Adriatic coast, notably Valona, and, by maintaining troops on the Yugoslav border, to bring that country into the Axis orbit. He thought the campaign had been undertaken at the instance of Berlin as part of Hitler's resistance to what the latter considered the "encirclement" of Germany.

Albania was a very small country, but the principle of international relations involved in Mussolini's occupation by force was out of all importance to her size. On April 8, after telephoning the President at Warm Springs, Georgia, I issued a statement of our position, saying: "Any threat to peace seriously concerns all nations and violates the will of all peoples in the world that their Governments shall lead them, not toward war, but along paths of peace.

"It is scarcely necessary to add that the inevitable effect of this incident, taken with other similar incidents, is further to destroy the confidence and to undermine economic stability in every country in the world, thus affecting our own welfare."

In this statement I was reiterating two lines of thought on which the President and I were agreed. One was to assume and emphasize the belief that the peoples of the world wanted peace, even though certain governments seemed resolved on war. In view of the viselike hold the Governments of Germany, Japan, and Italy had over their peoples, it was but a forlorn hope that the peoples in those countries could have any effect on the dictatorships pressing them down. On the other hand we had had many indications that even the absolute dictatorships took account of the opinions of their peoples—otherwise they would not have gone to such lengths of propaganda and political police to sway these opinions.

The other point, which I had been careful to state on numerous occasions in these years, was that the United States could be affected by any development, even though comparatively small, which undermined the structure of peaceful international relations. This was in answer to the isolationists who continued to maintain that the affairs of Europe or Asia were of no concern to us. Albania had less than 1 per cent of our population, but the forcible swallowing up of her was another blow to international law and justice which was our only real protection against war.

We refused to recognize Italy's conquest of Albania even as we had refused to recognize her conquest of Ethiopia. We continued to receive the Albanian Minister, Faik Konitza, as the representative of his country, although we closed our legation in Tirana.

Immediately after the occupation of Albania, reports came to us that German naval maneuvers were projected off the northwest coast of Morocco and that the Spaniards were planning to occupy Tangier. At the same time we were informed that the French Mediterranean Fleet had moved out of Gibraltor to cover the eastern Mediterranean.

At this juncture the President was thinking of taking another positive step, a direct appeal to Hitler and Mussolini to guarantee the independence of all the nations that might conceivably be subject to attack by them. In addition to the appeal, he was willing to go a degree further— to act as intermediary for transmitting the replies of the dictators to the countries concerned, and to take part in discussions that might ensue on disarmament and economic questions. The idea had been suggested to him by Ambassador Bullitt in a telephone call from Paris.

In discussing this project with the President, I gave him my opinion that it would not be successful. It was another of the direct appeals to the heads of foreign Governments, in which practice I had little confidence. After some discussion he said he was of the same opinion, but he wanted to make the move anyway. He felt that, even if it failed, it would serve one good purpose: it would put Hitler and Mussolini on the spot for what they were—planners of the conquest of Europe. I agreed that this was probably true.

The President himself, with his White House advisers, wrote out a draft of the message he wanted to send, and passed it to us at the State Department for revision. We felt some doubt about certain features of the draft which made it appear that the United States would guarantee any agreement that might be reached between the Axis Powers and the major democracies. We accordingly rewrote the draft and sent it back to the White House. Thereupon the President made a new draft himself which followed his original very closely, and sent this to us for further comment. Seeing that the President was intent on retaining his first phraseology, we limited ourselves to suggesting changes of language which the Department deemed important. This draft, the fourth, proved acceptable to him.

At the same time, we completed the draft of a speech for the President to make on Pan American Day, April 14, some hours before the appeals to Hitler and Mussolini were to go out. To the Pan American Union the President made a strong address in which he reiterated the pledges of mutual support contained in the Declaration of Lima I had signed in December. "The American peace which we celebrate today has no quality of weakness in it," he said. "We are prepared to maintain it, and to defend it to the fullest extent of our strength, matching force to force if any attempt is made to subvert our institutions or to impair the independence of any one of our group. Should the method of attack be that of economic pressure, I pledge that my own country will also give support, so that no American nation need surrender any fraction of its sovereign freedom to maintain its economic welfare."

Although the speech was addressed to Latin America, we had the Axis dictators principally in mind. The President challenged Hitler's chronic complaint of "encirclement" by saying: "There is no such thing as encircling, or threatening, or imprisoning any peaceful nation by other peaceful nations." He cited his pledge of August 18, 1938, to Canada, and the Declaration of Lima, as examples of agreements among peaceful countries to defend their independence to which there could be no objection on the grounds of "encirclement."

That evening the appeals to Hitler and Mussolini went out, the former signed by the President, the latter by myself. After noting that three nations in Europe and one in Africa (Austria, Czechoslovakia, Albania, and Ethiopia) had seen their independent existence terminated, and that a vast area of China had been occupied by Japan, the appeals stated: "Reports, which we trust are not true, insist that further acts of aggression are contemplated against still other independent nations. Plainly the world is moving toward the moment when this situation must end in catastrophe unless a more rational way of guiding events is found."

After asking whether Hitler and Mussolini were willing to give assurances that their armed forces would not attack or invade thirty countries mentioned by name for a period of ten or twenty-five years, the message went on:

"If such assurance is given by your Government, I will immediately transmit it to the governments of the nations I have named and I will simultaneously inquire whether, as I am reasonably sure, each of the nations enumerated above will in turn give like assurance for transmission to you.

"Reciprocal assurances such as I have outlined will bring to the world an immediate measure of relief."

After expressing our willingness to take part in discussions on disarmament and economics, if Hitler and Mussolini should make a favorable answer, the President concluded his appeal by saying: "Heads of great governments in this hour are literally responsible for the fate of humanity in the coming years. They cannot fail to hear the prayers of their peoples to be protected from the foreseeable chaos of war. History will hold them accountable for the lives and happiness of all—even unto the least.

"I hope that your answer will make it possible for humanity to lose fear and regain security for many years to come."

Here again was the thought that the peoples of the world, and not government alone, were concerned with the maintenance of peace because it was principally they who would suffer from war.

The reaction from almost all nations of the world was excellent. But many days passed without any answer whatever from Hitler or Mussolini. Finally, on April 20, Mussolini gave the first official indication of the Axis response by making a speech ridiculing and rejecting our appeal.

With Hitler's answer still suspended in air, I delivered an address on April 25, 1939, before the Red Cross Convention in Washington, to emphasize that there was still a chance for peace, if the nations concerned saw fit to embrace it. "There is no controversy, no difference that can arise between nations," I said, "which could not be settled, with far greater benefit to all concerned, by the peaceful processes of friendly adjustment than by resort to armed force." But I also pointed out: "Terrible as are the realities and consequences of war, sooner or later conditions arise in which peaceful and peace-loving nations prefer armed defense to subjection and slavery. . . . There has never been, and there is not today, room on this earth for a political organization of mankind under which a single nation or a group of nations will enslave and dominate all the others."

I sought to dissuade the nations from the dangerous extremes of isolationism and aggrandizement, saying: "Isolation dooms a people to inescapable impoverishment; armed aggrandizement, under modern conditions of warfare, entails destruction for which no conceivable advantages secured by the conqueror can possibly provide compensation. A nation entering upon either of these ruinous courses inflicts an incalculable injury upon its own people and upon the world as a whole."

Three days later came Hitler's reply to the President's appeal. Instead of answering the President directly, Hitler sought to be dramatic and make his response in the form of a speech to the Reichstag. He derided Mr. Roosevelt's suggestions. He said he had communicated with the nations for whom the President had requested guarantees of nonaggression and they replied that they did not believe themselves threatened by Germany. He abrogated the ten-year nonaggression pact with Poland because

Poland had accepted Britain's recent guarantee of assistance. He tore up the Anglo-German naval limitation agreement of 1935 and the consultative declaration he had made with Chamberlain at Munich.

I had no doubt of Hitler's intentions before this speech, but it confirmed me in my belief that there was nothing to be expected from him but war, unless the European democracies were again willing to capitulate completely before him. I had reason to believe that such willingness on the part of Britain and France had disappeared.

As late as February Chamberlain still hoped that the peace he obtained at Munich would last. Ambassador Kennedy cabled me from London on February 17 that Chamberlain felt the European situation had improved and attributed this to our rearmament program and statements by the President as well as to the stiffening in his own attitude, which had caused Hitler to pause. Four days later I sent the President, then cruising at sea, a summary of a telegram received from Kennedy the day before concerning a long conversation Kennedy had just had with Lord Halifax. The British Foreign Secretary felt that the action of the United States Government—the recall of Ambassador Wilson from Berlin, our rearmament program, and statements by the President—had been a major influence for peace. Kennedy gave as his own opinion that the British distrusted Hitler but felt that the chances of a European explosion were small.

Hitler's occupation of Czechoslovakia in March, in violation of his solemn promises at Munich, changed Chamberlain's attitude completely. With France he thereupon agreed to guarantee Poland from German aggression, consented to the institution of conscription in Britain, and sought to make it amply clear to Hitler than an invasion of Poland meant a European war.

Such was the state of mind in Britain when King George VI and Queen Elizabeth of England visited the United States in June. The President had been keenly interested in this visit and himself followed closely the details of the plans for their reception. In accordance with custom, it fell to my lot, as Secretary of State, to go to the Canadian border at Niagara Falls, accompanied by Mrs. Hull, to meet them and welcome them officially to this country. I met them at the gaily decorated Suspension Bridge station on the Canadian border on June 7.

When the train bearing the King and Queen came to a stop, the King stepped off, closely followed by the Queen. Canadian Prime Minister Mackenzie King hurried up from an adjoining car and was present, as the King alighted, to introduce Mrs. Hull and me to the royal visitors.

The meeting went off in a thoroughly democratic manner. I expressed, for our Government, our warmest welcome.

After a short time the King and Queen reentered their car, and Mackenzie King, Mrs. Hull and I boarded the next car. Shortly after the train started the King sent for me. I went to his attractive, well furnished car and had an agreeable, interesting conversation with him lasting for some thirty to forty minutes. We did not make any attempt to discuss special questions, although we ran generally over conditions in Europe, which the King agreed were most serious.

The train reached Washington the following morning. At the station to meet the royal guests were President and Mrs. Roosevelt. I made the introductions.

The reception to the King and Queen during their stay in Washington was all that could be desired in the way of enthusiasm, cordiality, and friendliness. The King impressed favorably all whom he met. The Queen captivated everyone with the attractive gestures of greeting she frequently made to crowds. The visit of the royal couple, which was one of virtual comradeship, was very effective in improving and solidifying the already friendly relations between our two countries.

Prime Minister Mackenzie King wrote me on July 4: "In one way, the visit of the King and Queen to the United States, and the warmth of the welcome extended to Their Majesties in your country, was no surprise to me. I had said to the King several times that, so wholehearted would be the welcome, that he and the Queen would have to continue to remind each other that they were in a country other than their own, and, at that, among the oldest of their friends. High as they were, my expectations were surpassed. Nothing could have been finer or more sincere."

At the very time King George was in Washington, we were pressing his ministers in London for a final decision on a matter that I had kept much to the fore for five years—the accumulation of reserve stocks of strategic materials such as rubber and tin. If war was coming, as seemed more than likely, I felt it to our best interests to prepare in advance stockpiles of the essential materials we had to import for our own defense.

Beginning as early as 1934, I had repeatedly urged upon the President the adoption of a program toward this end. We had besought Congress to approve appropriations for the purchase of strategic materials not produced in quantity in the United States. I wrote numerous letters to key Congressmen for this purpose. I sought to induce governments in debt to us to make partial payments in the form of such materials.

On October 21, 1938, I wrote to the President that "the problem of strategic raw materials . . . becomes more and more urgent as times goes on. Events the past few weeks [the crisis in Europe at the time of the Munich Conference] have shown so clearly the wisdom of adequate handling of this problem with all possible despatch. They indicated how disturbed sources of supply would be in any general war. They made it clear that countries would undertake to control or to prohibit exports, especially of essential materials. . . . This Department has concurred in the view of the War and Navy Departments that it is highly desirable to adopt a national policy with respect to this problem and to secure early and effective action by Congress."

Legislation was eventually approved in June, 1939, authorizing purchases of reserve stocks of strategic materials, and on June 10 I wrote the President urging prompt action to put the legislation into effect.

It was clear to us at the State Department, however, that the amount of money Congress was willing to appropriate was far from sufficient to assure us an adequate reserve of strategic materials. Accordingly, in April, 1939, we began negotiations with the British, Dutch, and Belgian Governments for a direct exchange of American cotton and wheat for rubber or tin. We offered to make available to them any quantity of cotton and wheat they desired—for emergency reserve stocks—in exchange for strategic materials to be held in reserve here.

This was in no sense an interference with normal trade. We would give those Governments cotton and wheat which were just as much strategic materials to them as rubber and tin were to us; the products on both sides would be held in reserve, and would not enter into the regular market.

We told the three Governments we would like to have at least 250,000 tons of rubber and 50,000 tons of tin, but much more if possible, and we would be glad to supply up to 2,000,000 bales of cotton and much wheat. I sent instructions to our diplomatic missions to carry the matter to the highest officials in their respective capitals.

But we met with obstacles at every turn. The British and Dutch controlled rubber production, and feared that such a transaction would unbalance their market. The Belgians offered a variety of objections. Finally we were able to reach an agreement with the British on June 23, 1939, providing for the delivery by us of 600,000 bales of cotton in return for rubber. As it worked out, the agreement resulted in bringing into the United States more than 100,000 tons of rubber. Herbert Feis,

Economic Adviser of the Department, was indefatigable in promoting this program. Actually, had our efforts at the State Department been fruitful as early and as fully as we wished, the coming of war at Pearl Harbor would have found us with reserves sufficient to ease the burden of the war period.

44: Japan on the Eve

THOUGH THE AMERICAN PUBLIC turned its eyes more toward Europe than toward Asia in 1939, numerous points of conflict between ourselves and Japan rose and became important. On the day I listened, aboard the *Santa Clara*, to President Roosevelt's message to Congress on January 4, the Japanese Government changed, and Premier Prince Konoye was replaced by Baron Hiranuma. Konoye had been regarded as a liberal, although I had no illusions on this score for he had been adamant in his prosecution of the war against China. But Hiranuma was reported to us to be a Japanese counterpart of the European Fascists and Nazis. The change, therefore, could be only for the worse.

Japanese bombings of American properties in China and discriminations against American businessmen in China continued in the usual chain of incident, protest, investigation, regret, promises, then incident, protest, investigation, regret, promises, ad infinitum. But at the beginning of the year we had to deal with two still more serious manifestations of Japan's imperialist and militarist intentions.

On February 8, 1939, Ambassador Grew cabled me from Tokyo that Japan had entered into negotiations with Germany and Italy for a definite alliance, military and political. Japan, he said, wanted the alliance applied only against Russia, whereas Germany and Italy wanted it applied against other nations as well, meaning Britain and France. Grew said he had conveyed informally to Foreign Minister Arita the idea that Japan would do well to consider the possible effects of such an alliance on her relations with the United States.

Two days later I cabled Grew agreeing with him that it was desirable that Japan should not enter into the alliance. I left any further approach to Arita up to him, but suggested it should be on his own responsibility, so as not to commit us formally. "If you think best," I said, "you might emphasize the conviction that mutually beneficial and friendly relations among the nations of the world and the general adoption of policies which will serve as a basis for broadening rather than narrowing such relations will serve the best interests of all nations, including Japan." I cautioned against any implication that we might give any specific compensation to Japan for abandoning the idea of entering the proposed alliance.

On February 14 Grew cabled me that he had conveyed his personal views, in keeping with my instructions, on the negotiations between Japan and the Axis Powers. He said his conversation with Arita convinced him that Japan would fully consider all factors before reaching any decision.

On May 18 Grew cabled me Arita's statement to him that the agreement under discussion with Germany and Italy would contain no military or political commitments except as to combating communistic activities. Arita said, however, that if Russia became involved in a European war, Japan might find it impossible to avoid involvement, and that, if Britain and France concluded an alliance with Russia, Japan might be obliged to reconsider her position with regard to the Axis. Also, if war broke out in Europe and the United States became involved, the position that Russia would take might conceivably decide whether peace could be maintained between the United States and Japan.

Our representations to Arita may have had some effect. At any rate, the alliance of Japan, Germany, and Italy was not signed until September, 1940.

The other manifestation of Japan's menacing intentions came on February 10, 1939, when Japanese troops occupied the island of Hainan, lying off the coast of French Indo-China between Hong Kong and Singapore, which previously had been claimed by France. Taking parallel action, we dispatched a note to Tokyo at about the time Britain and France did likewise, requesting an explanation. Foreign Minister Arita asserted that Japan had no intention of annexing the island but wished to use it to strengthen her blockade of China. We received this with lively skepticism.

The following month Japan laid claim to sovereignty over a huge sea area within which were the Spratly Islands, about seven hundred miles southwest of Manila, and a vast number of other islands and reefs. The Spratly Islands likewise were claimed by France. The outlines of Japan's expansionist ideas were becoming ever clearer. This was the time of Europe's preoccupation over Hitler's swallowing of Czechoslovakia, and Japan, as she always did, took advantage of Europe's troubles to advance her fortunes.

Our Navy Department had made surveys in the Spratly Islands area, and reported to us that the eastern two-thirds of the area, adjacent to the Philippines, contained usable coral lagoons affording anchorage for light naval forces and aircraft. Accordingly, on May 17, I addressed a note to Japanese Ambassador Horinouchi in which I stated that our Government did not "consider that the action of Japan in blanketing within the territory of Japan islands or reefs, either known or unknown, with respect to which the Japanese Government has heretofore exercised no acts which may properly be regarded as establishing a basis for claim to sovereignty, has any international validity."

In March occurred an episode which strongly revealed that a certain percentage of the Japanese people still wanted peace with the United States, even though their Government was taking actions that heightened the friction between us. Japanese Ambassador Hirosi Saito, who had resigned in October, 1938, because of ill health and had remained in the United States, being too ill to travel to Japan, died February 26, 1939. We had had our difficulties with Saito because of his propensity for making speeches in this country which virtually attacked our policies in the Far East, but he had done what he could to improve relations between our two countries, and the President decided that his ashes should be sent to Japan aboard an American warship as a gesture of friendly courtesy. This was an extraordinary gesture inasmuch as Saito was a private citizen, no longer an ambassador, when he died.

When the cruiser *Astoria* arrived in Japan on this funeral mission, Japanese citizens by the hundreds showered the *Astoria's* crew with gifts and made every effort to extend to them favors and courtesies. Ambassador Grew wrote me that a portion of the Japanese public wished to play up the *Astoria's* visit in an effort to strengthen the hand of those in the Government who did not want Japan to enter a military alliance with Germany. This segment maintained that the public had previously been given the impression that Japan, having antagonized the democracies by her actions in China, would become isolated in the world unless she tied up closely with the totalitarian powers. The visit of the *Astoria,* they thought, indicated that this was not so because the United States was holding out a friendly hand and showing Japan where her real friendship lay. Germany and Italy would do nothing for Japan, whereas America had done and would in future do a great deal for her. This portion of the Japanese public, however, had little chance under power-mad Tokyo governments to make its opinions felt.

Japan sought to carry the gesture of good will a long step farther by suggesting that she send a naval vessel to the San Francisco or New York expositions as an expression of thanks for the visit of the *Astoria*. I cabled Ambassador Grew on April 15 to discourage the idea. I told him I felt this would react unfavorably on Japanese-American relations because our public would be apt to regard it as overplaying the principle of good will and as political capitalizing of our gesture.

In my opinion there was only one way Japan could win favor with the American public, and that was to conduct herself differently in the Orient. I made this clear on March 28, 1939, when it was reported to us that Prince Konoye, former Premier of Japan, contemplated a good-will trip to the United States. I instructed Ambassador Grew, that, if the subject came up for discussion, he should point out that Japan could accomplish more toward improving relations between the United States and herself by ceasing to violate our rights and interests in China than by mere explanations or assurances conveyed to the American Government and people through good-will missions.

On April 15 the President ordered the United States Fleet, which in January had moved into the Atlantic, partly to give color to the World's Fair at New York City, transferred back to the Pacific. The shift of the fleet to the Atlantic had been temporary, in any event, but the absence of the fleet from the Pacific began to give rise to preoccupations that Japan was thereby being stimulated to become more reckless. On March 22 Ambassador Kennedy cabled me from London a conversation he had had with Lord Halifax. The Foreign Secretary said Britain had promised Australia to send a fleet to Singapore, but she now felt unable to spare a fleet from European waters and wondered whether we would consider transferring the fleet back to the Pacific at the psychological moment.

Ambassador Bullitt in Paris sent me a cable for the President along the same lines on April 11. He said the British had intended transferring a fleet from the Mediterranean, where it was exposed to Italian attack, to Singapore, but the French informed them that France in that event would have nothing further to do with efforts to build up resistance to Hitler in Central and Eastern Europe. Bullitt therefore recommended that our fleet be moved back to the Pacific, adding " 'twere well it were done quickly."

It was done quickly.

In June serious difficulties rose between Britain and Japan which were of real concern to us. After the British at Tientsin refused to deliver to Japanese authorities four Chinese accused of killing a Chinese puppet official, the Japanese carried out insulting reprisals against British subjects, forcing them, men and women, to strip and be examined before leaving the British enclosure at Tientsin. American citizens were not molested since the Japanese sought to disrupt any common Anglo-American attitude by treating the two nations differently.

On June 17 Ambassador Nelson T. Johnson cabled me from Nanking a conversation he had had with Chiang Kai-shek. The Chinese Generalissimo said that one of Japan's main objectives was to persuade the United States that her quarrel with Britain was with Britain alone. Japan wanted to crush Britain's defense of treaty rights, and then to sweep away the treaty rights of other powers, whereupon China's position would be even more seriously damaged. Japan, he thought, was bold at this point because she felt that Britain was isolated and that she had convinced the United States and the other interested powers that they were not involved. Chiang Kai-shek believed that if the United States let it be known that American interests were involved, the Japanese position would collapse.

We had no such hopes, but on June 19 I pointed out in a public statement that, although our Government was not concerned in the original incident at Tientsin, it was concerned "with the nature and significance of subsequent developments, in their broader aspects, coupled with other past and present acts and utterances in other parts of China."

When Ambassador Grew arrived in the United States on leave in June, he brought me a letter addressed to me by Premier Hiranuma of Japan. In his letter the Premier said he thought a duty lay principally with the United States and Japan to exert every effort to prevent the outbreak of war in Europe. In this effort Hiranuma said would "be found the possibility of much closer cooperation between Japan and America as well as the foundation of a deeper mutual understanding between the two nations."

A few days after Grew left Tokyo, Hiranuma suggested to our Chargé d'Affaires, Eugene H. Dooman, that an international conference be called, and that he was prepared to consult Germany and Italy if the President would consult Britain and France toward this end.

I was more than skeptical of Hiranuma's approach. Japan was benefiting so hugely from the impending chaos in Europe that we wondered what ulterior motive lay in the Premier's mind. If we were to join with Japan in such an effort while Japan continued her attempted conquest of China, we would be manifestly condoning all Japan's actions in the last two years. The Premier's move was obviously another of the series with which I had become so familiar ever since I entered the State Department. Japan constantly sought agreements or joint action with us which would have the effect of sanctioning all her brazen expansion in the Orient up to that time.

Accordingly, I cabled Premier Hiranuma my reply on July 8. I said it would be "most gratifying to me, and I may also speak for the President, if there could be found ways for the use of your Government's influence toward discouraging among European Governments, especially those Governments with which your Government may have special relations, the taking of any action, or the pursuance of any policy, that might endanger the general peace."

But I then ventured to observe, in a spirit of frankness which I said I trusted would not be misunderstood, "that this objective is made the more remote by the existence and the continuance of armed conflict and consequent political disturbances in the Far East today. Just as the unfolding of events in the European sphere have their repercussions in the Far East, so, it appears, the prolongation of abnormal conditions in the Far East contributes to causes of unrest in Europe."

I concluded by saying that the President and I would do everything in our power to put into practice the principles and hopes to which we had frequently given expression. I added that we did not perceive any practicable steps we could usefully take at this time in addition to those we had already taken, and I asked Hiranuma to let us have any further information he could as to his idea of the steps that usefully could be taken toward moderating the situation in Europe.

Hiranuma had not advanced in writing his oral suggestion for an international conference, hence I did not reply to it in my dispatch to him.

After Ambassador Johnson in Chungking cabled me on July 6 a graphic account of a Japanese bombing that capital had just experienced, I sent this to the President. The following day I received this note from him:

"This is indiscriminate bombing, and I think it will be just as well for you to send for the Japanese Ambassador, tell him about it, and tell him that the President in person asked you to protest to him against a continuation of these actions. Further, that the President would like to have an immediate statement from the Japanese Government, without making it a matter of formal notes."

My Far Eastern advisers and I thought it best to put our protest in writing. Accordingly I asked Japanese Ambassador Horinouchi to come to my office on July 10 and handed him a written protest against the bombing of Chungking, emphasizing, among other points, that this had damaged American property.

With regard to the Tientsin incidents, I said to the Ambassador:

"Stripping citizens of other countries of all clothing in public is something abhorrent to the average citizen everywhere. While it accomplishes next to nothing for the Government engaging in such practice, it does arouse universal resentment and condemnation. If some of our American citizens in China should be thus stripped stark naked and exposed to the public view, a surprising amount of bitter denunciation will undoubtedly arise. I therefore hope your Government will see its way clear to refrain not only from depriving our citizens of their rights, interests, and businesses in China but also from other practices that create hostility between our peoples."

The Ambassador agreed with my views. In general I found that Japanese ambassadors were willing to agree to anything I said, but their agreement was not translated into favorable action in Tokyo. Horinouchi brought up the suggestion advanced by Premier Hiranuma that our two Governments should join in some effort to avoid war in Europe, and asked my opinion.

"The single test of my Government in dealing with other Governments," I replied, "relates to the question of peace. We draw the line between honest, law-abiding, peaceful countries and peoples, and those who are flouting law and order and officially threatening military conquest without limit in time or extent—without reference to their form of government.

"We will work in a friendly spirit with every peaceful nation to promote and preserve peace, without serious thought as to who they are. While we have not the slightest alliance, or secret undertakings with any nation on earth, and do not propose to have any, we will keep thoroughly armed and prepared to take care of our interests and rights. We have already made every kind of plea to the countries of Europe to indicate a willingness to adjust peacefully their economic and other relations. And we have expressed our readiness to cooperate in every feasible plan to restore international trade and finance to a normal level."

As for Hiranuma's proposal, I said: "Nations cannot but take notice that Japan herself is engaged in military operations for purposes of conquest. This situation well calls for an ending if Japan is to exercise her fullest influence, along with the United States and other countries, to compose threatened military conquest in other parts of the world."

Horinouchi asked my opinion on damage to American interests in China by reason of possible permanent Japanese control, and my Government's reported apprehension that Japan's occupation of Hainan Island was part of a plan of permanent military conquest.

"I need not remind you," I said, "that for six years I have been earnestly pleading with your Government and urging the view that there is enough room on this planet for fifteen or eighteen great nations like yours and mine. By cooperating along progressive and mutually profitable lines, great progress of the entire world population would gradually follow."

Although American interests and rights in the Far East were highly important, I said: "Our big consideration is whether all China and the Pacific islands near by are to be 'Manchuriaized' by Japan, with international law and treaties abolished and all other nations not allowed into that half of the world—the door shut and locked by Japan—except over a wall of preferences for her own citizens. If one nation is to do this in one-half of the world, some other nation in the other half of the world might follow the same example. Nothing would be more absurdly impossible. Suppose an announcement were made that this hemisphere and a part of Europe would be closed against your country in the sense of being 'Manchuriaized': I need not speculate on how your country would feel about it. Such efforts at domination, with no facilities for financing and progressive development, can only result in disaster for all concerned."

Horinouchi tried to justify his country's policy toward the European Axis by saying that Japan, because of her proximity to and difficulties with Russia, had been interested in the anti-Comintern policy of the Axis. I replied that this was primarily his country's own business and that we ourselves strongly opposed the doctrines of Bolshevism. "But," I said, "we also abstain from any entanglements with European countries. If Japan desires to tie herself up with the horribly complicated European controversies so as to become immediately involved in any European war, that is her business. My Government will keep itself in a detached position, with peace as its supreme objective, and with armaments sufficient for all purposes of security."

Ten days later Ambassador Horinouchi was again in my office discussing Bolshevism. I said to him: "With so many nations exhausting all their economic vitality by putting their entire substance into armies and navies, it's just a question of time before most nations will be utterly bankrupt. Their peoples will be destitute and, what's far worse, they'll continue, as they're doing today, to drag the entire world down toward lower levels of existence. My country fights Bolshevism as do numerous others. But the powerful nations who are steadily lowering the standards of life of their own and other peoples by militarism and conquest, are really the greatest friends Bolshevism has. They are steadily dragging the entire world unerringly in the direction of Bolshevism, even though they may imagine that they are actually fighting Bolshevism."

Britain's intensive negotiations with Japan to settle the humiliating incidents at Tientsin reached their climax in July. It was evident to us that if Britain were to obtain any settlement she would have to make concessions. On July 20 Chargé Dooman—Ambassador Grew was on leave in the United States—asked me for instructions as to expressing our view to the Tokyo Foreign Office on the negotiations.

We replied on the following day, stating our hope that formulae could be avoided in an Anglo-Japanese agreement which might be interpreted by the Japanese as British recognition of Japanese rights of a far-reaching nature in China. We did not think that any useful purpose would be accomplished by an informal approach to the Foreign Minister, but we authorized Dooman, in talks with Japanese officials, to emphasize the concern of our Government along the lines of my statement of June 19. We stated that there was no intention on our part to take any affirmative step inconsistent with the principles we had always maintained in the Far East or to waive the rights we enjoyed under treaties or international law.

Britain, hard pressed in China and anxious over Europe, signed an agreement with Japan on July 24. This noted that "the Japanese forces in China have special requirements for the purpose of safeguarding their own security and maintaining public order in the regions under their control and that they have to suppress or remove any such acts or causes as will obstruct them or benefit their enemy." Britain promised not to countenance any acts or measures prejudicial to the attainment of these objectives and to issue instructions to British authorities in China to this effect.

We were apprehensive over the effects of this agreement on our own position in China. It was disturbing in that Japan had won a victory in her never ending quest for recognition of "special rights," "special interests," or "special requirements" in China. We had experienced this as long ago as the Lansing-Ishii agreement of 1917, when our Government incautiously agreed to Japan's "special interests" in China, and then spent several uneasy years combating Japanese misrepresentation and, finally, effecting the termination of the agreement. We knew that Japan always tended to take such phrases and magnify them far beyond their context in order to influence her own people and China. Chargé Dooman in Tokyo cabled me that the Anglo-Japanese agreement was bound to affect Chinese morale.

It therefore seemed to the President and me that the time had come to take an action we had been contemplating for some time—the abrogation of our 1911 commercial treaty with Japan. Such abrogation had to be preceded by six months advance notice, and we now determined to give this notice.

In addition to the psychological factor, we had a practical consideration in mind as well. This involved embargoes on the shipment of certain materials to Japan. We already had applied a moral embargo, but without legal effect, against the shipment of airplanes to Japan. If we were in future to impose a legal embargo on airplanes and essential war materials, would this conflict with our 1911 treaty with Japan? An identical question had risen in the case of our embargoes in the Italo-Ethiopian and Spanish Civil wars, at which time protests had been made by Italy and Spain on the grounds that such embargoes were in violation of our commercial treaties with them. Eliminating our commercial treaty with Japan would therefore eliminate the possibility that Japan could protest on this ground.

Many other considerations, however, some of them more important, entered into our calculations as we discussed the abrogation of the treaty with Japan. With a lead pencil I jotted down my thoughts roughly on paper. I have those notes today, and reproduce them here:

"(1) Why keep up treaty when Japan does as she pleases with U.S. interests in China? U. S. for two yrs. has tried hard to be friendly and at same time to protect its nationals and U.S. interests in China, while all sorts of indignities, etc. have been suffered.

"(2) U.S. has approval of civilization in general.

"(3) Nation engaged in military conquest makes its own concepts & standards & ignores reason, humanity, logic and justice.

"(4) What rights & interests has U.S. in China that would get any less consideration, no matter what U.S. might do?

"(5) Soon after Jap invasion it became clear that Japan had no intention either to regard the sovereignty of China or respect the rights of others in that country.

"(6) Japan is clearly attempting the subjugation of China, despite her sworn duty to protect China against such attacks as they [Japs] are making.

"(7) If Japs think they can lick the world & that the rights of no nation in China need be respected, let them go on.

"(8) How can we treat Japan as a friendly nation when its whole policy is hostile to American interests? Why continue one treaty when another is openly violated? [This referred to Japan's violations of the Nine-Power Treaty.]

"(9) When Jap spokesmen were shouting their 'new order,' their domination of Western Pacific, etc. & that British had knuckled to them, that Japs had won 'a sweeping diplomatic victory,' etc. etc., it was high time U.S. was reproclaiming (anew) its attitude on Far Eastern affairs.

"(10) U.S. action has the effect of encouraging China, Britain & also of discouraging Japs, Germans & Italians, but it all grows out of Jap violation of 9-Power treaty. And yet it is just as plausible to criticize U.S. for seeming to favor China etc. as above, as to criticize her as to Eng. & France in case of war.

"(11) If ending treaty of 1911 by U.S. is an unfriendly act, what was Japs' action in scrapping 9-Power treaty without notice & violating most of all U.S. rights & interests in China? So, if act of U.S. is unfriendly, Japs must take the responsibility."

Senator Vandenberg of Michigan had introduced a resolution to annul the 1911 treaty. I felt, however, that we could not wait for a long, uncertain debate in Congress. The President had full authority to serve notice of abrogation of a treaty.

By agreement with the President, I addressed a note to Japanese Ambassador Horinouchi on July 26 giving Japan formal notice of our desire that the treaty of 1911 be terminated six months from that date, which would be January 26, 1940. I simply said that we had been examining treaties of commerce and navigation in force with other countries to determine what changes to make toward better serving the purposes of the treaties, and that, "toward preparing the way for such consideration and with a view to better safeguarding and promoting American interests as new developments may require," we gave the required six months' notice.

The denunciation of this treaty was a shock to Japan. It was an action that could not be concealed from the Japanese people, a step that aroused the immediate anxiety of Japanese businessmen. The Japanese Foreign Office at once made excited efforts to learn what our intentions would be

when the treaty expired. I was careful to give them no enlightenment.
I felt that our best tactic was to keep them guessing, which might bring
them to a sense of the position in which their flagrant disregard of our
rights and interests in China was placing them.

Again I jotted down in lead pencil my thoughts following my note
to the Japanese Ambassador. These jottings read:

"'New order' means for Japs to abandon intern'l law & treaty pledges,
to destroy the integrity of China and the liberties of her citizens, and by
force to require all nationals of other countries to bundle up their effects
and get out of the Western Pacific area.

"U.S. during next six months will watch to see to what extent Japan
shows signs of yielding on foregoing purposes.

"Japs for 6 mos should give calm, considered study, etc. to situation.

"U.S. interests are primary & permanent & first."

In April Senator Pittman had introduced a resolution to authorize
the President to impose embargoes on essential war materials against
any nation violating the Nine-Power Treaty. This, of course, meant
Japan. In answer to Pittman's request for an opinion, I wrote him a letter
dated July 21 in which I merely suggested that consideration of the resolution be held over until the next session of Congress.

This was in line with my desire to keep Japan guessing, which holding the Pittman Resolution over her head would do. I knew the resolution
had no chance of passing at this session of Congress, and I did not want
it defeated. At about that time I jotted down, again roughly in lead pencil,
my thoughts on what our general policy toward the Far East should be in
the following months. These notes read:

"(1) Don't want Pittman measure passed or killed. Let it keep up
present uncertainty which it and dead treaty [the commercial treaty of
1911] do very much.

"(2) Help China.

"(3) Let us not press it and consolidate Jap sentiment, nor drive
Jap. & Russia together.

"(4) Japs more and more see the necessity for U.S. finance and
cooperation.

"(5) Continue $\begin{cases} \text{to discourage credits to Japan} \\ \text{moral embargo} \\ \textit{uncertainty.''} \end{cases}$

This generally was our policy toward Japan up to and after the outbreak of war in Europe. We consistently asserted and reserved our rights

in China. We strove to make our position clear to Japan without at the same time giving her material with which to enflame her people against us. We sought to keep Japan from drawing on our war supplies and credits. We helped China as much as we reasonably could without going so far as to enable the military in Japan to use this fact to their own advantage. We kept Japan uncertain as to our next moves. We rigidly refrained from making any commitments to her which she could use to depress Chinese morale.

What were the results of this policy? In the first place we had helped prevent Japan from getting an easy peace with China which would leave her in control of a large portion of that country. That which happened in 1932 when Japan, after invading Manchuria and China, made peace with Nanking and withdrew from China but remained in possession of Manchuria, was not repeated. Japan was now increasingly feeling the strain of her two years' war in China. In 1939, her military operations having begun to bog down, she was resorting to every device of economic trickery to engulf China's business.

Secondly, Japan was left without any legal recognition of her claims in China and Manchuria, except for the doubtful support of Germany and Italy. Thirdly, our policy toward the conflict in the Orient had been so impartially handled that Japan was left with no opportunity to use it against us. When the European war broke out on September 1, 1939, Japan, instead of being free to move against other countries, having carved off a huge segment of China, was still tangled up in China after expending important quantities of men and resources.

Six days before Hitler invaded Poland, Japanese Ambassador Horinouchi came to my office and handed me a note that sought to rebut press reports that Japanese officials were instigating anti-American demonstrations in China. Knowing in advance the purpose of the Ambassador's visit, I had requested the Far Eastern Division to jot down a list of instances of injury or damage to Americans caused by the Japanese in China. It was a formidable arraignment. When I handed it to Horinouchi, he was surprised and at a loss for comment.

After a pause he informed me, speaking personally, that his Government had decided to abandon any further negotiations with Germany and Italy for closer relations under their Anti-Comintern Pact. He said the change in affairs in Europe made this course manifest and his Government would find it important to adopt a new foreign policy.

This gave me an opportunity to review with him our policy toward

Japan. "During recent years," I said to him, "Japanese authorities have been disregarding international law and treaties to which the United States and Japan are signatories. The United States has protested over and over again against such acts. The Japanese Government has given assurances over and over again that it will show its regard for the principles and provisions involved. And over and over again Japanese authorities have immediately committed other acts in disregard thereof."

I stated bluntly we had clear evidence that Japanese authorities in China were inspiring demonstrations hostile to American interests and that these actions were arousing suspicion and opposition against Japan in all countries that had interests in the Far East.

"It should be evident to Japan," I said, "that there is something wrong with policies and practices on the part of one nation which arouse antagonism on the part of almost all other nations in contact with that nation.

"The United States wishes to have amicable relations with every other country in the world. In the past we have had friendly relations with every country in the Far East, including Japan. Our policy is 'Live and let live.' We seek nowhere any special position; but we seek everywhere equality of opportunity under conditions of fair treatment and security."

Calling the Ambassador's attention to the fact that the world was being given today new object lessons in the futility of taking advantage of other nations by the use of armed force, I concluded:

"The future of American-Japanese relations lies largely in the hands of Japan. American policy is a policy of friendliness and fair dealing toward all nations. It will not change."

The decision whether there were to be amicable or unfriendly relations between us and Japan did rest, on the eve of the European War and thereafter, with Japan herself. As was the case with the European democracies in their dealings with Hitler, we could have influenced that decision effectively in only one or the other of two ways—by giving in completely or by using complete force. The former would have brought only temporary peace and for the latter the nation was prepared neither in fact nor in spirit.

45: Neutrality Disaster

DURING THESE MONTHS of difficulties in the Far East, we had been struggling with an even more important problem at home—the passage of a new Neutrality Act that would eliminate the arms embargo. Following Senator Pittman's introduction of his resolution on March 20, and his assurances that he could get it through the Senate, I expected action would be taken shortly. I personally talked to many Senators, but left the handling of the bill in Pittman's hands.

Our first reaction to the bill came from China. The Chinese Foreign Office, according to a telegram from our Embassy in Chungking on March 27, was greatly concerned lest the resolution, if passed, should obligate the President to declare a state of war between China and Japan. The cash-and-carry provision would benefit Japan. Pittman's bill would oblige the President to apply the Act within thirty days after an international armed conflict began—in contrast to the existing Act which left it to the President's discretion to find that a state of war existed. We sent Chungking's cable to the President, who wrote this comment:

"I think that before the bill gets too far it should be called to the attention of Senator Pittman that while the cash-and-carry plan works all right in the Atlantic, it works all wrong in the Pacific.

"The more I think the problem through, the more I am convinced that the existing Neutrality Act should be repealed *in toto* without any substitute.

"I do not mind if you pass this word to Senator Pittman and the leaders."

We accordingly passed the word on to Pittman. He appreciated the objection to the way the bill would work in the Pacific in that it would enable Japan to have access, on a cash-and-carry basis, to our war materials as well as other goods, while making it impossible for China to have such access because she had neither the ships nor the means for payment. A few weeks later he accordingly introduced the resolution to apply an embargo against any nation violating the Nine-Power Pact. But he objected to the President's suggestion on repeal of the whole Neutrality Act as being impossible.

Pittman's Committee on Foreign Relations began its hearings in April on a series of bills relating to neutrality, including his own. These ran the gamut from outright repeal of the Neutrality Act to mandatory legislation depriving the President of virtually any discretion in administering a Neutrality Act.

I had originally planned to appear personally before the committee and argue my views, chief of which was that the mandatory arms embargo should be removed. I had long talks, however, with Pittman and several other Senators, members of the committee, and learned from them that a dispassionate statement of our position would'neither help nor hinder our cause. They said that the opposition members of the committee, particularly the isolationists, were merely awaiting my appearance in order to ask what they hoped would be embarrassing questions. These were: whether the Administration's purpose in seeking to change the present Neutrality Act was to assist the British and French; to what extent had we been in touch with the British and French Governments; what was the position of Japan with relation to the United States and to the Axis; and a series of other leading questions that would at once get me onto controversial grounds.

I was in a dilemma. Of course one of our purposes was to assist the British and French; but even more fundamentally it was to prevent the outbreak of war in Europe. We felt that, if Hitler knew that Britain and France could have full access to our war and essential products, he would be less likely to order his troops to march. Of course we had been in constant touch with the British and French Governments, though we had no agreement whatever for any common action with them.

But to have included aid to the European democracies as one of our purposes in seeking the lifting of the arms embargo would merely have stirred up isolationist passions and misunderstandings throughout the country. On the other hand, if I declined to answer the questions, I would be accused of lack of frankness and of pursuing a policy of mystery. The committee had excluded the idea of an executive session, which meant that everything I said would be made public.

All in all, therefore, I thought it wiser, for the moment at least, not to go before the committee but to continue personal conferences with individual Senators, trying to persuade them of the logic of our views.

We were, in fact, basically hopeful. Public opinion was slowly changing in our favor. The events of 1938 and 1939 convinced most Americans that war was coming in Europe and, if it came, its perpetrator would be Hitler. They did not want to see the victims of that aggression cut off from recourse to our war supplies, provided such commerce were so conducted as not to draw us into the war. In April, 1939, the Gallup Poll reported a 57 per cent affirmative reply to the question whether the Neutrality Act should be amended to permit the sale of munitions to Britain and France.

At the beginning of May, however, Senator Pittman suddenly tossed the neutrality question into my lap. We had been supporting him in every possible way, but he said he could not get his bill out of his committee and he would be unable to secure its passage through the Senate. The embattled isolationist Senators were still too strong and stubborn. He said he left it to me to suggest a substitute course.

Our alternative, therefore, was the House of Representatives. After I had talked this possibility over with the President, he called a meeting of House leaders, including Speaker Bankhead, Majority Leader Rayburn, and Representative Bloom, in the White House on May 19, which I attended.

The President said he emphatically believed every possible effort should be made to eliminate the arms embargo from the Neutrality Act. He said he felt sure this would actually prevent the outbreak of war in Europe, or, if it did not, it would make less likely a victory for the powers unfriendly to the United States.

He said he was not seriously concerned about any other provision of neutrality legislation. He mentioned that he saw no serious objection to cash-and-carry provisions, and he inclined to the view that a war-zone provision might really be useful.

Bankhead and Rayburn warned the President that there was a real possibility of defeat of any measure providing for the repeal of the arms embargo. Even so, the President said he believed the fight should be made.

I said I had been conferring with Senators on the Foreign Relations Committee and I was ready and anxious to confer with members of the House Foreign Affairs Committee concerning neutrality legislation. I remarked that in these personal conferences I was able to discuss the situation far more frankly than I could in open hearings. We thereupon arranged that Bloom should bring to my apartment the following day the Democratic members of the House committee.

The President said he was very anxious that the House should expedite action so that the bill could be passed before the arrival of the British King and Queen. He said he had canvassed the Senate situation with Senator Pittman and they had agreed that action by the House should precede action by the Senate. If the House could pass a reasonable neutrality bill, this could be considered by the Senate after the visit of the King and Queen.

The President made clear that there was no intent on his part to send American troops to Europe in case of a general European war.

At the State Department I had been holding numerous conferences with my associates over a period of some weeks, seeking to perfect in a single document our views on what we wished in neutrality legislation. We now hastened this to completion. Few documents prepared in the State Department have ever received as minute care as this one. We had worked many weeks on it. I hoped it would be so conclusive a statement of our position that legislation based upon it might be successful. On the evening of May 26 I sent this to the President, asking him to read it and return it to me before his impending departure for Hyde Park. The President returned it with "C. H.—Excellent—F. D. R." written on my note to him. The following day I sent it to Senator Pittman and to Representative Sol Bloom, acting chairman of the House Committee on Foreign Affairs.

"We must," I said, "keep in mind that, no matter how much we may wish or may try to dissociate ourselves from world events, we cannot achieve disassociation. The simple fact of our existence as a great nation in a world of nations cannot be denied; and the substance of the legislation adopted in this country inevitably influences not only this country, but also other countries."

I argued against rigid, universal rules. I pointed out that international law did not require a neutral nation to embargo any articles destined for belligerents. "If we go in for embargoes on exports," I said, "for the purpose of keeping ourselves out of war, the logical thing to do would be to make our embargo all-inclusive. . . . A nation at war is no less anxious to keep cotton or petroleum, or, indeed, any useful product, from reaching an enemy nation than it is to keep guns and airplanes from reaching the enemy's armed forces. . . . Yet a complete embargo upon all exports would obviously be ruinous to our economic life. It therefore seems clear that we should have no general and automatic embargo inflexibly and rigidly imposed on any class or group of exports."

I emphasized that our conclusion about the undesirability of an embargo on the export of arms was not new and that experience had confirmed our belief. I cited the statement the President issued on August 31, 1935, on signing the Neutrality Act of that year, when he said that the inflexible provisions of the arms embargo might drag us into war instead of keeping us out.

My letter concluded that our involvement in controversies was more likely to arise from destruction of American lives, the risk of which could be effectively diminished by keeping our ships and citizens out of danger areas.

Finally, I set forth six points for possible legislation: prohibit American ships from entering combat areas; restrict travel by Americans in combat areas; all exports (including arms) to belligerents to be preceded by transfer of title to the foreign purchaser; continue existing legislation respecting loans and credits to belligerents; regulate the solicitation and collection in this country of funds for relief in belligerent countries; continue the National Munitions Control Board and the system of arms export and import licenses.

Since Pittman was stymied in the Senate, we placed virtually all our emphasis on the House. We hoped that, if the House could pass a Neutrality Bill dropping the arms embargo, the Senate might be induced to do likewise. On May 29 Representative Bloom introduced a bill along the general line of my recommendations given two days before. On the last day of the month the President held a conference with Administration leaders at which a decision was reached to take up the repeal of the arms embargo in Congress, even though this might delay adjournment.

I invited members of the House of Representatives to several meetings at my apartment, and discussed with them the European situation and the need to amend the Neutrality Act. I telephoned at length to other members of the House. I had one of my associates, Carlton Savage, an expert in neutrality matters, attend the hearings of the House Committee and the debate in the House. On my instructions he telephoned me every couple of hours, both day and night, to keep me abreast of developments. I gave the legislation top priority on my schedule since I considered it crucial in our foreign relations.

When my assistants in the State Department, however, asked my opinion on the prospects of getting new neutrality legislation in the House, I told them I had been in the House myself too long ever to count in advance upon the action of that body. To illustrate, I told them the story of the teacher who was showing off her bright pupils to the members of the school board. She called up Tommy to shine in arithmetic. "Tommy," said one of the board members, "if there are sixteen sheep in a field and one jumps the fence, how many are left?"

"None," replied Tommy.

"Well," said the questioner, "I'm afraid you don't know anything about arithmetic."

"The trouble is," said Tommy, "you don't know anything about sheep."

A real tragedy occurred in the House. On June 30 the House passed the bill by a vote of 201 to 187, but only after an amendment containing a modified arms embargo had been inserted. This amendment had been slipped in suddenly by a majority of two votes—159 to 157—when many Democratic members of the House were absent. Once in, it was impossible to take it out. It was confirmed by a roll-call vote of 214 to 173.

I was keenly disappointed. I knew full well that the nations of Europe were following the debate in Congress with utmost attention. I knew the effect the House vote would have upon them. I knew the impetus it would give Hitler's plans.

On May 10 Ambassador Bullitt in Paris had cabled me that the British Ambassador to France had told him three times that his Government had one real fear. This was that German Foreign Minister Ribbentrop might succeed in persuading Hitler that Germany could fight England and France without risk because there was no possibility of their obtaining military supplies from the United States. The British knew Ribbentrop was citing the neutrality debates in Congress as proof that neither England nor France would be able to buy airplanes or military supplies in the United States. The British believed it highly important that the Neutrality Act be amended in the near future and thus remove the possibility that Ribbentrop might be able to persuade Hitler to run the risk of another war.

Bullitt said that French Foreign Minister Bonnet had expressed similar views. On June 30, before the House vote on the Bloom Bill, Bullitt cabled that the French Secretary General for Foreign Affairs, Alexis Léger, believed that passage of the bill would be an important deterrent to Hitler's starting a war.

On July 1 I issued a public statement, to which the President said he gave his enthusiastic approval, expressing my thorough conviction that the six-point peace and neutrality program I had set forth in my letters to Pittman and Bloom on May 27 "would be far more effective in the interests of peace and in keeping the country out of war than the present embargo law or any equivalent." I added: "Its failure to pass the House by a narrow margin is a matter of regret and disappointment from the standpoint of peace and the best interests of this country in its international relations."

I pointed out that my proposal was "not only best calculated to keep this nation out of war in the event war comes, but also, what is all-important at this time, best calculated to make a far greater contribution than could the present law or its equivalent toward the discouragement of the outbreak of war." I therefore continued to urge its adoption.

On that same day Ambassador Bullitt cabled me that French political leaders believed the House vote had greatly increased the possibility that Hitler would attack Poland because he would feel sure that, cut off from American supplies, Poland, France, and Britain could be defeated by the Axis powers.

That evening I replied to Bullitt and referred to the press statement I had issued. I said that the neutrality question, to our amazement, had been turned into a partisan issue. I concluded that we intended to continue the fight and do all we possibly could, and that we were fully aware of the interpretation that might be given the House vote by the Axis states.

On July 2 I cabled our diplomatic missions in Rome, Berlin, The Hague, Brussels, and Bern, asking for a report on the reaction of important individuals and officials to the House vote, with an appraisal of the vote's effect on the European situation generally and on the policy of the governments to which they were accredited.

Ambassador Phillips in Rome replied that the Italian press regarded the vote as a blow to England and France and a definite rebuff to Roosevelt. Phillips said that in his opinion it was most unfortunate, and any weakening of the President's position might have disastrous consequences, since it would undoubtedly stiffen Germany and Italy in their attitude against the democracies.

Minister George A. Gordon, at the Hague, reported that the Dutch Prime Minister was dismayed by the House vote. He gave his own opinion that it would tremendously encourage the dictators and discourage the European Governments that were trying to avert a world war.

Ambassador Joseph E. Davies, in Brussels, cabled that the Belgian Premier was deeply disappointed and that the general reaction was one of disappointment, distress, and thwarted hope. Davies considered that the House vote might become a definite factor in the dictator states' decisions for the immediate future.

Our Chargé in Berlin, Alexander Kirk, cabled that the German press interpreted the vote as a severe setback to the Administration. German newspapers attacked Roosevelt as a warmonger determined on a policy of intervention and encirclement.

Minister Leland Harrison in Bern cabled that the general belief in the Swiss capital was that, if the aggressors were certain that the United States would not maintain an attitude of indifference should war break out, this would be an important factor, if not the most important, in preventing new aggression.

In the face of this reaction, significantly identical, and of our own firm beliefs, we could not abandon the fight for removal of the arms embargo. Since favorable action in the House seemed impossible at the moment, I turned again to the Senate. Pittman agreed to press the legislation before his committee, and to bring it to a vote.

On July 11, the day the committee was to vote, I restated at a press conference the recommendations I had made in my May 27 letter to Pittman and Bloom. That afternoon the President backed me up by saying that what I had said was "a very good statement." But when Pittman brought the question to a vote, the committee voted, 12 to 11, to postpone all consideration of neutrality legislation until the next session of Congress, in January, 1940.

January, 1940! What might not happen before then! In those six months the fate of the civilized world might be at stake.

The issues were so great that I still refused to accept defeat. There was yet a hope that the Senate might vote to overrule Pittman's committee. My associates and I at the State Department therefore prepared another statement to Congress, to be sent to the Capitol by the President. Mr. Roosevelt duly sent this to Congress on July 14 with a brief accompanying letter of approval in which he said: "It has been abundantly clear to me for some time that for the cause of peace and in the interests of American neutrality and security, it is highly advisable that the Congress at this session should take certain much needed action. In the light of present world conditions, I see no reason to change that opinion."

In my statement I emphasized, among other points, the peace possibilities of lifting the arms embargo. We, I said, "are convinced that the arms embargo plays into the hands of those nations which have taken the lead in building up their fighting power. It works directly against the interests of the peace-loving nations, especially those which do not possess their own munitions plants. It means that, if any country is disposed towards conquest, and devotes its energy and resources to establish itself as a superior fighting power, that country may be more tempted to try the fortunes of war if it knows that its less well prepared opponents would be shut off from those supplies which, under every rule of international law, they should be able to buy in all neutral countries, including the United States.

"It means also that some of those countries which have only limited facilities for the production of arms, ammunition, and implements of war are put in a position of increased dependence. During peacetime they would feel the compulsion of shaping their political as well as their economic policy to suit the military strength of others; and during wartime their powers of defense would be limited."

I underlined as strongly as I could my belief that "the present embargo encourages a general state of war both in Europe and Asia. Since the present embargo has this effect, its results are directly prejudicial to the highest interests and to the peace and to the security of the United States."

I intensified my discussions with the President and with leading Senators. Mr. Roosevelt agreed to call a White House meeting of the Senate leaders of both parties for the evening of July 18. At this meeting the President and I intended to make a final appeal for support of the bill, or, failing in this, to make the opposition take the responsibility for what would happen if the legislation were not passed. In view of the action already taken by the Senate and the House, it was a desperate effort. But both the President and I felt we had to make one last, supreme attempt to prevail on the Senate leaders to recognize fully and clearly the perils to our own nation that were just ahead if war should come to Europe.

As the meeting came to order in the President's upstairs study, a reasonable cordiality was apparent on the surface, but the feeling underneath was tense. Among those attending were Vice President Garner, Majority Leader Barkley, Pittman, Minority Leader McNary, Deputy Minority Leader Warren Austin, and William E. Borah, ranking minority member of the Foreign Relations Committee.

The President opened the discussion by referring to Senator Nye's extreme isolationist views which were blocking the passage of our measure in the Senate. Borah rather quickly interrupted and, with a sweeping gesture, said, "There are others, Mr. President." The President, somewhat taken back, turned to him and asked, "What did you say, Senator Borah?" Borah thereupon repeated, "There are others, Mr. President." A dialogue followed between the President and Borah, during which Borah emphasized his opposition to repeal of the arms embargo and stated emphatically his view that no war would occur at least in the near future.

The President thereupon turned to me and said, "Cordell, what do you think about the possibility of danger ahead?"

I replied earnestly, restraining myself as much as I could: "If Senator Borah could only see some of the cables coming to the State Department about the extremely dangerous outlook in the international situation, I feel satisfied he would modify his views."

Thereupon Borah, in a tone of emphasis and absolute finality, said he had access to information from abroad which satisfied him in his judgment. This information was that there would be no war in Europe in the near future. He implied that it was more reliable information than that received at the State Department.

More recently I have noticed publication of what purported to be Senator Borah's written memorandum of this conversation. I shall not enter into a discussion of the precise verbiage of the conversation, but I must say that Borah's language created the definite, fixed understanding in my mind as to what occurred, as I have just related it. President Roosevelt made clear on more than one occasion that he had derived the same understanding as I had from Borah's utterances.

Never in my experience had I found it nearly so difficult to restrain myself and refrain from a spontaneous explosion. I knew from masses of official facts piled high on one another at the State Department that Borah was everlastingly wrong, and that we were looking squarely at a state of imminent danger of a general outbreak of war before the end of summer—and I said so. Borah's statement, giving more credit to his private sources of information than to the official State Department dispatches, was a disparagement of our whole diplomatic service.

After other leaders of both parties had unanimously expressed their view that it was impossible to secure the passage of our embargo repeal through Congress, the President turned to me and asked, "Cordell, what do you think about the situation?"

I had been on the verge of an explosion during the minutes that followed Borah's reflection on myself and the State Department. My agitation was probably not concealed as I replied to the President: "I scarcely know what to think about anything in the light of the complacent way Senator Borah has brushed aside the whole mass of facts we have at the State Department, which completely disprove his theory that there will be no war." I could scarcely proceed further without losing my self-control, so deeply was I convinced of the dangers just ahead and so greatly did I feel outraged at the brusque manner in which all these facts and considerations were ignored.

At midnight, as the meeting ended on this tone, the White House issued two communiqués. One stated the consensus of the Senators present, Democrat and Republican, that no action on neutrality legislation could be obtained at this session of Congress, but that it would be considered at the next session. The other stated: "The President and the Secretary of State maintained the definite position that failure by the Senate to take action now would weaken the leadership of the United States in exercising its potent influence in the cause of preserving peace among other nations in the event of a new crisis in Europe between now and next January."

Only five weeks later we had to exert that influence in a final effort to prevent a European war. Our influence, so far as Hitler was concerned, was undoubtedly weakened by his realization that Congress had refused to follow the lead of the Administration, and by his belief that Britain and France could not obtain arms, ammunition, or airplanes in the United States.

Immediately after the meeting Senator Borah, followed by Senator McNary, disclaimed to me the least idea of reflecting on me or on my official position in any way. But it was not possible to apologize for reflecting on the State Department, which I headed. I received these disclaimers coldly. I give Borah credit for the best of intentions, but I am forced to conclude that he was so terribly wrought up as not to think clearly.

I had frequently invited Borah to come to the State Department where I could show him dispatches from our diplomatic missions in Europe and Asia and talk over the general foreign situation with him, but he never did me this courtesy. What could I have shown if he had come to the department during the discussions on neutrality? Among dozens of other references, there were these:

Our Chargé in Berlin, Alexander Kirk, cabled me on May 13 that the diplomatic representatives of many other nations, although not expecting immediate German action against Poland, were very pessimistic about the chances of avoiding a conflict. The prevailing impression in Berlin foreign military circles was that Germany was militarily able to move against Poland at any time. On June 24 Kirk reported that rumors of unusual troop movements and continued military activity in Germany had created the general impression that preparations were being made for some eventuality.

Ambassador Bullitt cabled from Paris on May 16 that Premier Daladier had expressed the opinion that peace would probably continue through June but he was not, on the whole, optimistic. One month later Bullitt cabled that Foreign Minister Bonnet had told him that, while he did not expect any immediate aggression by Germany, he was certain of a major crisis before the end of the summer. On June 28 Bullitt cabled the opinion of the Polish Ambassador to France that the chances were eighty out of a hundred that war would come between Poland and Germany by the middle of August. On June 30 Bullitt cabled the belief of Alexis Léger, of the French Foreign Office, that a crisis of the gravest character was inevitable before the middle of August.

Polish Ambassador Count Potocki said to me on May 31 that Hitler would be obliged to make a move in some direction during the coming months. On June 26 Potocki informed me that his country was preparing increasingly to fight in case Germany should start a war. I commented to him that conditions in Europe were not favorable. Increasing signs and circumstances of an ominous nature were appearing. Sooner or later—no one could say when—with Europe so highly geared to a war basis, something very serious was likely to occur unless in the meantime steps were taken to avoid it.

From London Ambassador Kennedy cabled me on June 27 Lord Halifax's thought that the German situation was very uneasy and that there was ample opportunity for trouble before the end of the next month. On July 5 Kennedy cabled that Halifax had told him the British were calling up their reserves of ships and Navy personnel, ostensibly for maneuvers in August, but actually in order to have the Navy ready a month before trouble might come, on the assumption that this would be in September.

Our Chargé at the Hague, J. Webb Benton, reported to me on June 3 the opinion of Admiral Furstner, Chief of the Netherlands Naval Staff, that Hitler might resort to war between the middle and end of August, after the harvest, and Furstner referred to known German efforts to harvest the crops as rapidly as possible.

Moreover, we were receiving from our diplomatic missions abroad constant reports on developments in Europe indicating continued German pressure on Poland and maneuvers to get possession of Danzig, and on difficulties in the way of any immediate conclusion of an Anglo-Soviet agreement toward which British diplomacy had been working for several months.

All these dispatches Borah and his associates could have seen if they had wanted to. But Borah chose instead to rely for his information on what was later reported to be a minor press service in London.

Here was the last effective stand of the powerful isolation movement in the United States. The movement continued its fight by every means at hand and it remained a danger, but after war came in Europe it was never again able to thwart an Administration proposal.

No one can say definitely that the failure of our efforts to lift the arms embargo was a final, or even an important, factor in Hitler's ultimate decision to go to war. I am certain, however, that if the arms embargo had been lifted in May, June, or even July, 1939, he would inevitably have had to take this factor into his calculations. I am equally certain that the failure to lift the embargo encouraged him to go ahead, stimulated by Ribbentrop's assurances that Britain and France would not really come to the assistance of Poland and that, if they did, they would be unable to do so effectively because American material help would be withheld from them. On July 20 Bullitt, in a cable from Paris for the President, said the opinion in both London and Paris was that the probability of Hitler's deciding to make war in August had been increased by Congress's decision to postpone action on neutrality legislation, and that British Foreign Undersecretary Vansittart was betting two to one that war would come in August.

46: Europe's Lights Go Out

WHEN AUGUST CAME the end was in sight. I had every reason to believe that Europe's great trial was at hand. For nearly seven years Hitler had been building up military forces and tearing down treaty observance and respect for international law. The moment had arrived to make a shambles of Europe and bring death to tens of millions of men, women, and children.

Feeling that war would not break out before the end of August, and being in need of a rest, I decided to take a three weeks vacation and thus be in condition when the crisis came. I left Washington on August 1 for White Sulphur Springs, West Virginia. The day before my departure I was asked at a press conference whether my taking a rest meant that I expected things to be quiet for a few days. I replied, "I never take anything for granted."

At White Sulphur Springs I followed the routine I had observed when I left Washington for rest on previous occasions. Each day my office sent me a special pouch containing paraphrases of the latest dispatches from our diplomatic missions abroad and memoranda from the leading officials of the Department. Sometimes these came to me by special messenger, at other times by registered mail. My office had a schedule of hours at which the central post office would receive registered mail for immediate dispatch by train to White Sulphur Springs. In addition, I had a special telephone line installed at my hotel. Each morning, at my request, the Under Secretary telephoned me an account of the important foreign affairs matters under discussion. Thus I was able to follow the rapid development of events abroad and to keep in daily touch with the conduct of our own policy.

Many weeks prior to my departure from Washington we had already begun at the State Department to prepare for war in Europe. There were numerous steps we would be required to take. I, who had been stating over and over again that a major war anywhere in the world would inevitably affect us, knew how many and how difficult would be our points of contact with any conflict. We created an Interdepartmental Neutrality Committee to study the probable impact of the war upon us and prepare for all necessary executive action. This was to meet in the State Department and embrace representatives of the State, Treasury, War, and Navy Departments and the Attorney General.

On August 15 I began to receive a series of ominous cables from Europe. Ambassador Bullitt cabled from Paris the substance of reports received that morning by the French Foreign Office from Berlin and Rome indicating that Hitler was insistent on war with Poland. On August 17 Ambassador Phillips reported from Rome his belief that Europe was then approaching a crisis. That same day, Chargé d'Affaires Kirk in Berlin informed me that foreign military observers in Berlin believed German mobilization measures had been going on for the past two days and that troop concentrations might be expected shortly for offensive purposes, with Poland as the primary objective.

On August 21 Welles wrote me from the State Department that the President had suggested sending a personal message to the King of Italy urging him to do what he could to prevent the outbreak of war—this in the event that war seemed imminent and that we then believed that both public opinion and the Government in Italy were opposed to going to war over the Polish issue. Welles prepared the draft of a message, which he sent me.

I had not the slightest expectation that any such message from anybody on earth would influence Hitler's plans one way or the other. The only beneficial effect it could have would be to place Italy in the role of asking for peace which Hitler would reject. It might be a means of showing up Hitler—especially in the eyes of the Italian people—for what he was, a fanatic for war. I said I had no objection to its being sent.

On the same day, August 21, Kirk cabled from Berlin the opinion of foreign military attachés there that troop concentrations had started the day before, which in three to five days would attain sufficient magnitude to make possible an attack on Poland. Later the same day Kirk sent a message through Bullitt informing us of a report that Hitler had decided to attack on the 24th or 25th and that orders to this effect had been issued to the German War Office the previous night. Bullitt added to this a confirmation from the French Foreign Office for the date of the 25th.

And then, on that same fateful day, Berlin announced that Germany and the Soviet Union had agreed to sign a ten-year nonaggression pact. The way was now cleared for Hitler to go to war without having to fight on two major fronts.

The prospect of a German-Russian pact had long been in our minds. As early as November 30, 1938, our legation in Bucharest had informed us that Germany had offered secretly a nonaggression pact to Russia. We gave due significance to the replacement, on May 3, 1939, of Foreign Commissar Maxim Litvinov by Vyacheslav Molotov. The former was known as an apostle of cooperation with the Western democracies, and as anti-Hitler; the latter was believed much less favorably disposed toward the democracies. We also knew of the many difficulties the British and French were experiencing in their negotiations for an alliance with the Soviet Union, which had been going on for several months.

Ambassador Bullitt on July 5, 1939, cabled me the substance of a conversation with Premier Daladier who said that, although he had no specific information with regard to negotiations between the Germans and the Russians, he feared they might be most serious. Bullitt commented that when he was recently in Washington on leave he found that our information was better than that of either the French or British Governments and he would be greatly obliged if we could inform him of any negotiations between Russia and Germany. I replied on July 7 that no development of any importance had yet been made known to the Department.

In July and August, 1939, Ambassador Laurence Steinhardt in Moscow sent us a series of cables concerning the negotiations between Berlin and Moscow. On August 16 he reported that steady progress could be noted. He also said he had every reason to believe that the Soviet Union had not informed the French and British of these conversations. British and French representatives were even then in Moscow seeking an alliance with Russia.

At the beginning of August, President Roosevelt sought to use his influence to bring Russia together with Britain and France. Seeing Soviet Ambassador Oumansky just before the latter left Washington for Moscow, he emphasized that if war were to break out in Europe and in the Far East and if the Axis Powers were to win, the position of both the United States and the Soviet Union would inevitably be affected thereby immediately and materially. The position of the Soviet Union, he said, would be affected more rapidly than the position of the United States. For these reasons, the President concluded that, while he was not in a position, of course, to accept any responsibility or to give any assurances as to the course Britain and France might undertake in their negotiations with the Soviet Union, he could not help but feel that if a satisfactory agreement against aggression on the part of other European powers were reached, it would prove to have a decidedly stabilizing effect in the interest of world peace. And in the maintenance of world peace the United States, as well as the Soviet Union, had a fundamental concern.

In order to emphasize this approach still further, the President asked the Department to send a memorandum of this conversation to Ambassador Steinhardt in Moscow. This was cabled to Ambassador Bullitt in Paris to be sent on immediately by courier to Steinhardt, and on August 16 reached the latter, who communicated it to the Soviet Government.

Berlin's announcement five days later that the German-Russian accord had been reached did not surprise us. Nevertheless, it was alarming, because it made the German attack on Poland all the more inevitable. The pact, according to the text cabled us by the Embassy in Berlin on August 24, was a nonaggression agreement whereby Russia and Germany agreed not to attack each other or to participate in any grouping of Powers aimed against the other. We were convinced that a further agreement had also been reached concerning territorial questions, including the Baltic countries and Poland. Russia had now been removed from the anti-Nazi front and it remained to be seen how thoroughly she had thrown in her lot with Hitler.

Our own contacts with the Soviet Union, during almost the whole of the nearly six years since our establishment of diplomatic relations, had been disappointing. Despite all our efforts, an infinity of small as well as major points of difference rose to plague what should have been a close friendship. One of my early hopes, even before we agreed to diplomatic ties with Russia in November, 1933, had been that a close working relationship between Russia and the Western democracies would prove a stabilizing influence in the Far East with reference to Japan and in Europe with reference to Germany and Italy. In numerous talks with Russian ambassadors, I hammered home again and again the point that, if only the United States, Russia, Britain, and France could work together along the same lines, they could prevent the war that otherwise I saw inevitably approaching.

On January 13 and March 26, 1939, I had had two basic discussions with Soviet Ambassador Alexander A. Troyanovsky concerning our points of tension. During the first conversation I handed him a memorandum outlining our complaints. These embraced the nonsettlement of Soviet debts and our claims; refusal to give us sufficient currency for the use of our Embassy in Moscow; cutting down our Moscow consular district; failure to provide the necessary currency exchange with which to build an Embassy in Moscow; inspection of the effects of American diplomats and restrictions on their movements; and detention for some days of drawings and papers of American engineers. I also objected strongly to the arrest of Americans in Russia and their being held incomunicado without notification to American authorities, and to spying on our diplomatic representatives.

I was forced to say, in fact: "The American Government has been constrained, in view of the conditions under which the American Embassy in Moscow has functioned ever since it was established, to consider whether the value to it of that mission is sufficient to warrant the maintenance of the Embassy on the present scale."

In my conversation with Troyanovsky on March 26 I said: "If, after we recognized Soviet Russia, your country and my country, Great Britain and France had gone forward in exercising normal relations and in developing their combined moral influence for peace, the unpleasant experience in both the Far East and in Europe would have been reduced at least 50 per cent. The present policies of Russia in these small ways, however, are seriously handicapping such supremely important efforts."

In some general instances we received gratifying support from Russia. The Soviet Government, for example, sent us a cordial note of approval following the President's peace appeal to Hitler on April 14, 1939. But concrete cooperation between our two Governments was intermittent and incomplete.

The Soviet Government also gave many indications of being willing to work along political lines with Britain and France, but the actual measure of cooperation was small. The Soviet Union was disappointed in the failure of the League of Nations during the Ethiopian and Sino-Japanese Wars, quarreled with Britain and France over the Spanish Civil War, and felt isolated by being left out of the Munich Conference. Poland, Rumania, and the Baltic countries offered difficult obstacles to a real agreement between Britain and France on the one hand and Russia on the other.

On March 17, 1938, Ambassador Troyanovsky came to see me to give me the authentic text of a press statement made that day by Foreign Commissar Litvinov. Litvinov said the Soviet Government was ready to participate in collective action, either within the League or outside it, aimed at "checking the further development of aggression and at eliminating the aggravated danger of a new world massacre."

For several weeks we debated at the State Department whether to reply to this statement. I decided, however, that, in view of the fact that no formal reply was called for, and that our response, under the limitations of our policy against entanglements, must be negative and might therefore discourage Russia, we would not send an answer.

Only in trade relations did we make any appreciable progress with Russia. In 1937, we signed a commercial agreement with her, whereby she agreed to continue to purchase $40,000,000 worth of goods from us annually and we agreed to continue to accord her the tariff reductions under the trade agreements program.

Three months prior to this agreement, I had an extensive conversation on May 12, 1937, with Ambassador Troyanovsky, who had come in to complain about a discrimination against imports of Russian coal under the operation of our excise tax on anthracite. After telling him I had been fighting desperately for many years against this and all other discriminations in international trade, I said: "The cause of economic improvement, and of peace as well, could be tremendously advanced by friendly cooperation between our two countries, especially in carrying forward our trade agreements program. Unfortunately a wholly minor incident or two has been allowed to hinder any real cooperation between us. As a result, the United States has fought largely by itself for sound, stable, and full economic recovery. The Soviet Government, instead, has really withheld the great aid it could have furnished, and now finds itself complaining about a minor phase of trade. The big objective is so much more vital that, if I could enlist the broad efforts of the Soviet Government in its support, I'd be glad to pay your Government out of my own pocket the tax involved on coal, if I were financially able to do so."

I reminded Troyanovsky that my Government was keeping up the price of gold purchased from the Soviet Union to $35 an ounce, and was making sacrifices to avoid shortsighted bartering transactions. I then said: "There are only two or three relatively small things our two Governments need to do so as to leave our two great nations perfectly free to cooperate and thus produce beneficial results which within a few years will prove absolutely astonishing. Yet all these great opportunities are being permitted to drift and drift and drift while nations are arming, both economically and militarily, with decreasing hope for the future."

Two months after we signed the commercial agreement of 1937, I held another basic conversation with Ambassador Troyanovsky, who had just returned to this country from Moscow. Troyanovsky commented that the international situation was bad, and I agreed. "The nations inclined to be lawless," I said, "are still going forward on the assumption, and even belief, that they will not be interfered with in any way by peacefully disposed nations. As you know, this Government has been striving for nearly four years to prevail upon other governments, especially those standing for peace, to organize and unify themselves behind a basic program to restore peaceful, normal international relationships and world order generally. But it has been virtually impossible thus far to induce many of them to cooperate actively. Each government seems to devote its time to looking about with a microscope for penny advantages in cutthroat, bilateral trading, utterly oblivious to the world situation, present or prospective. This state of affairs is all a lawless nation desires, and we can accordingly visualize a steady expansion of international lawlessness."

The situation, I pointed out to Troyanovsky, was well illustrated by the relations of his country and mine. "We have been standing apart," I said, "partly on account of a trivial, measly, insignificant item of indebtedness. When desperado-inclined nations see two great countries, like yours and mine, floating along for years on account of that sort of trifling difference, while burying their great combined moral influence for peace and order, it's not surprising that international lawlessness is rapidly growing."

Troyanovsky commented that if Russia knew what Great Britain had in mind to do she would be in a better position to take active steps or adopt concrete policies.

"That," I replied, "is exactly what each peaceful country is saying about the other. No country seems disposed to do anything. And that again is just the assurance desperado nations want. I'm not referring to any policy involving military force or economic coercion. I'm referring to the creation of a combination of all possible moral and other influences calculated to outlaw war, make war utterly abhorrent and exalt peace."

The commercial agreement of 1937 was renewed for one year in 1938 and again for one year on August 4, 1939, four weeks before Hitler marched into Poland. Our commercial exchanges with the Soviets continued to grow. When war came in Europe, however, our trade with Russia, although improving, was still not so extensive or on so broad a basis as we should have liked, and our political relations left much to be desired.

Events in Europe now moved toward disaster with doubled acceleration following the announcement of the Soviet-German pact. On August 22 Bullitt cabled me from Paris that Premier Daladier believed Hitler planned to attack Poland within the next eight days and most likely that week end. Daladier asked Bullitt to transmit a message to the President that a general war in Europe, which Japan would enter, was imminent; he said that, while he did not know whether any appeal by the President would have any effect, he profoundly hoped Mr. Roosevelt would declare that war appeared imminent and call upon all nations to send representatives to Washington immediately to attempt to arrive at a pacific settlement.

On the same day, the President, who was cruising aboard the cruiser *Tuscaloosa,* wirelessed Welles to know whether Welles and I thought he ought to return to Washington at once. Welles telephoned me and then replied that we saw no present reason why he should change his plan of arriving in Washington Friday morning August 25.

I myself returned to Washington on August 23, and at once plunged into conferences with my associates. A few hours before my arrival, the President's message to the King of Italy was cabled from the State Department. Ambassador Phillips gave the message to the King at Turin the following afternoon. Victor Emmanuel said to Phillips that not a single person in Italy wanted war and that he would immediately communicate the President's message to his Government—as a constitutional monarch he could not say more.

At about the time the message to the King went out, Ambassador Bullitt cabled me from Paris an account of a significant conversation with Foreign Minister Bonnet. Bonnet said he wanted to express an opinion he had never expressed during the Munich crisis, which was that he did not think there was the slightest chance any longer of maintaining peace. He believed Hitler had made up his mind to attack Poland the following Friday evening, and there was nothing that would dissuade him. Bonnet nevertheless expressed the hope that President Roosevelt would try by some means to prevent war. He said he had no suggestion to offer, but it would be of enormous benefit if the President pointed out publicly that there was nothing in the present dispute that could conceivably justify the devastation of all Europe and the sacrifice of 30,000,000 men.

Early in the afternoon of August 24, the President returned to Washington. I went to the station to meet him and rode with him to the White House. Only the gloomiest of pictures could I give him. The days of peace could now be numbered on the fingers of both hands. Just before I left the Department to go to the station a telegram had come in from Bullitt. The British Ambassador to France, who had just returned from London,

THE MEMOIRS OF CORDELL HULL

said to Bullitt that both Chamberlain and Halifax considered war inevitable and that all efforts to prevent it, while they should be continued, would prove futile.

An earlier cable from Kennedy in London reported a conversation with Sir Horace Wilson of the British Foreign Office. Wilson told Kennedy he saw no way to escape war except for the Poles to express their willingness to negotiate, and that this was where pressure should be applied. The British, however, he said, were not in a position to apply such pressure strongly, but if anything were to be done it must be at once, because Chamberlain thought the attack was fairly close.

Neither the President nor I felt any disposition to bring any pressure to bear on Poland. The President did feel that he should send appeals for peace to Hitler and to President Mościcki of Poland. I had no hope whatever that these appeals would produce peace, but, realizing that the President's maneuver was largely to place the onus for war, if it came, where it lay—on Adolf Hitler—I concurred. In his message Mr. Roosevelt urged that the German-Polish dispute be settled by one of three methods—direct negotiation, arbitration, or conciliation. He reiterated our Government's willingness to contribute its share to the solution of the problems which were endangering world peace as he had set forth in his message to Hitler on April 14, 1939.

I also cabled Ambassador Phillips in Rome to communicate to the Italian Foreign Office copies of the President's messages to Hitler and Mościcki and state that the President regarded these messages as supplementing his earlier message to the King of Italy, who, he hoped, might find them of assistance if he decided to make a move for peace.

A cooperative reply arrived from President Mościcki next day, agreeing to direct negotiations or the method of conciliation through a third party. No answer came from Hitler. Bullitt cabled the President at this point, expressing Premier Daladier's gratitude for the President's messages. Bullitt, referring to information from Ambassador Anthony J. Drexel Biddle in Warsaw that Hitler would either not reply to the President's appeal or would flatly reject it, suggested that the President send a second message informing him of the favorable reply received from Mościcki and requesting him to remember the devastations of war. The President, Bullitt thought, would have a great opportunity to place the onus for future developments squarely on Hitler.

I carried Mościcki's reply to the White House, taking Welles and Assistant Secretary Berle with me. With the President we agreed to send another message to Hitler, but I had not the slightest belief it would be of any avail, nor did the President. Mr. Roosevelt simply held to his previous thought that at least it would serve to make clear Hitler's responsibility for the war. We discussed another message, this being to King Leopold of Belgium, who had appealed for peace in the name of his country, Holland, Luxembourg, and the Scandinavian countries. The President sent his message to Leopold in the afternoon of the 25th, joining his wishes for peace to those of the nations for whom Leopold spoke. In the evening he sent his second message to Hitler. This quoted Mościcki's reply textually and concluded:

"Countless human lives can be yet saved and hope may still be restored that the nations of the modern world may even now construct a foundation for a peaceful and a happier relationship if you and the Government of the German Reich will agree to the pacific means of settlement accepted by the Government of Poland.

"All the world prays that Germany, too, will accept."

Cables from all the major capitals of Europe were now streaming to my desk. Ambassadors Kennedy and Bullitt were frequently on the transatlantic telephone to the White House and the State Department. We followed with minute care and tenseness each development, the communications passing back and forth between the British, German, and Polish Governments, Hitler's successive ultimata, and the desperate efforts of Britain and France to reach a settlement.

I now instituted a twenty-four hours-per-day duty in my office, assigning an average of three Foreign Service and Departmental officers there at night. I gave them broad authority to take appropriate action on matters before the regular staff came to the Department in the morning. This night staff was composed for a long time of two Foreign Service officers—William D. Moreland, Jr., and Aaron S. Brown—and a Department officer, Henry Allen. The night watch continued to function at least throughout the remainder of my tenure at the Department. After the war came in Europe they kept in close touch during the night with the War and Navy Departments and answered queries at all hours from press and radio representatives and others. My office was never closed, night or day or Sundays and holidays.

On August 26 we announced at the Department the creation of a special unit to handle the repatriation and protection of Americans in the disturbed areas of Europe. This being the end of the summer tourist season, scores of thousands of Americans were in danger of being trapped in Europe by the advent of war. We had already worked out, in conjunction with the Navy and with American shipping lines, a detailed system for getting Americans out of Europe. We were prepared to advance money, on a promissory note basis, for steamship fares to those who required it. We also sought to discourage Americans from going to Europe.

On August 28 Bullitt cabled the President from Paris that President Mościcki of Poland was somewhat hurt that the President had not replied to his message. Bullitt suggested another message to Mościcki applauding the Polish President's attitude and saying Mr. Roosevelt had not previously replied because he had hoped to hear from Hitler. Thus, Bullitt thought, we should be killing two birds with a single stone in a way that would prove most valuable to Europe at that moment. Shortly thereafter I cabled Bullitt and also Ambassador Biddle in Warsaw that the President had that day sent a personal message, through the Polish Ambassador in Washington, Count Potocki, to Mościcki expressing deep gratification over the latter's reply, and stating that no reply had been received from Hitler and if one were received it would be immediately communicated to the Polish President. In my cable to Bullitt I said the President did not think the release of this message would be wise at this particular time.

Ambassador Bullitt cabled again from Paris on August 30 a suggestion from Alexis Léger of the French Foreign Office. Léger wanted the President to propose to Queen Wilhelmina of Holland, King Leopold of Belgium, or the Pope that one of them at once issue an appeal to Germany and Poland to agree to the special mediation provided for by the 1907 Hague Convention. Léger felt that no appeal by the President himself to Hitler would be answered because Hitler had not replied to his two earlier messages.

I cabled Bullitt the President's opinion that, since Hitler had agreed with the British to direct negotiations with Poland, such mediation as Léger suggested did not appear practicable to him at this particular moment. The President felt that the present issue was whether such direct negotiations could be carried through and especially whether they could be carried through on a strictly equal basis as between Germany and Poland.

On that same day, August 30, King Victor Emmanuel of Italy replied to the President's appeal of August 23, saying, "There has been done and there is being done by us whatever is possible to bring about a peace with justice." The following day, August 31, which Hitler had set as his zero hour for Poland's agreement to all his demands, Mussolini proposed to

Hitler the summoning of a five-power conference (the Munich four plus Poland).

The cables now coming in to my desk contained an ever larger percentage of information on military preparations. Parliament gave the British Government emergency powers. The evacuation of London was prepared. The British Fleet was in movement. The French raised their army to 3,000,000 men. The French Government requisitioned motor vehicles to evacuate children from Paris. And "blackouts" were in readiness, a significant tribute to the new terror to come from the air. The stage was set for the greatest tragedy of all times.

Still there was no answer from Hitler to the President's two messages; nor could we hope that any answer would come except the firing of the first shot. We had only a few more anxious, fatalistic hours to wait.

Shortly after midnight on September 1, the telephone rang beside the President's bed. Bullitt was on the phone from Paris. German troops had crossed the borders of Poland.

*   *   *

Six years and six months after I came to the State Department war came to Europe. In all this period the President and I deviated not a whit from the foreign policy that we had undertaken to follow in 1933 and 1934, when we began to size up the fixed purpose of Germany, Italy, and Japan to enter on a course of unlimited world aggression. Our policy was consistent in its aims and methods.

Right from the beginning I had never ceased to point out the dangers rising abroad. In innumerable statements, speeches, and conversations with ambassadors and visiting statesmen I made it clear that, if Europe and Asia took the courses which the Axis nations were charting for them, war was certain to engulf the world.

During those six and a half years the President and I never halted our efforts to prevent the war from coming. We took numerous steps to bolster and encourage the European and Asiatic nations still devoted to peace, and the League of Nations. We took many other steps to discourage the aggressor nations from their plans of conquest, and to lay before them an alternative program for peace.

When I entered the office of Secretary of State I had a definite set of guiding principles on which foreign affairs should be conducted. We never varied from these principles, but sought by every means possible to induce other nations to embrace and follow them.

We had labored without halting to persuade other nations to join a broad, liberal economic program that would serve as a basis for a political settlement. Although the difficulties—on the part of some peacefully minded nations as well as on the part of the potential aggressors—at times seemed unsurmountable, we had made great progress when the war arrived. It was the only program consistently put forward by any nation in the thirties which had any real chance of preventing war.

The President and I had certainly made the position of the United States limpidly clear to the Axis Powers. They could have had no doubt as to where our sympathies lay. They may have doubted whether Congress would support the Administration or whether we could effectively aid the democracies, but they could have had no uncertainty that our hearts were with the victims of their aggression.

By the time the war broke out, the Western Hemisphere had been welded into a cohesive unit of twenty-one Republics resolved to aid one another. The successive conferences at Montevideo, Buenos Aires, and Lima had consolidated the Good Neighbor Policy. To the rest of the world here was both an example to be followed, and an admonition to be respected. We gathered the fruits of this policy soon after the conflict broke.

As to our own people, the President and I left no doubt in their minds about the dangers arising abroad. We repeatedly pointed out to them that, if war came, they could not repose behind the Atlantic and the Pacific, untouched by the conflict. We made it clear over and over again that a major conflict anywhere on the globe would stir up waves that would sweep over our shores. We worked hard to convince them that the United States was as indispensable to the world as the world was to us.

Week in and week out the President and I had fought to prove to them that isolation was not merely a faulty policy, it was actually a dangerous policy. I on my part had long since developed a set of principles, one of which was that the United States had to assume her full share of responsibilities in the world. I was early aware that in a general sense the President and I had the same philosophy and basic ideas in regard to international relations, especially as they related to peace, order, and human welfare everywhere. We faced adamant opposition on the part of the isolationist element in Congress and in the country at large, although during the second term more Americans seemed to appreciate the fundamental factors involved in the world situation than during the first term. Trying to win over the isolationists was for me a nerve-racking and back-breaking experience. As I looked at the isolationists in this and other countries, they reminded me of the somnambulist who walks within an inch of a thousand-foot precipice without batting an eye. Nevertheless, we were as resolved as they were to keep the United States out of war if we possibly could; and though we had repeatedly sought to encourage the democracies of Europe, the arrival of war found us with no entangling agreements that would drag us in.

We had also striven without cease to make the United States militarily strong. Although mine was the Department of Peace, I had gone out of my way again and again to stress the importance of adequate arming for our own security. When the fateful September 1, 1939, dawned, our preparations were still far from adequate, but we were appreciably stronger than in 1933.

During the period up to September 1, 1939, the United States therefore had taken her full share in world affairs, within her limits of law and of national sentiment, and had exercised her influence, in every way possible, to secure lasting peace and to improve the economic well-being of the world.

Part Four

NEUTRALITY AND SELF-DEFENSE

(1939–1940)

47: After the First Shot

THE TELEPHONE rang stridently beside my bed. Tense from days of preparing and waiting, I wakened and turned on the light. It was almost three o'clock in the morning of Friday September 1, 1939. I picked up the receiver.

"Cordell," came the President's voice, "Bullitt has just been on the phone. The Germans have invaded Poland."

The moment I recognized the President's voice I guessed the rest. But the news, though expected, was none the less a shock. In the pause that followed Mr. Roosevelt's announcement there flashed through my mind the thought that here perhaps was the end of civilization as we knew it. Here was untold death, suffering, destruction.

I said to the President I intended going to my office at once. After hastily dressing and telling Mrs. Hull what had happened, I drove to the State Department and walked through the deserted corridors to my office at about 3:30.

I asked that my principal assistants come to my office immediately. Soon I was joined by Welles, whom the President had telephoned directly. One by one the others came in, their faces alert and anxious, and sat around my desk—Assistant Secretaries of State Berle and Messersmith, Legal Adviser Hackworth, our Ambassador to Germany Hugh Wilson, Political Advisers Dunn and Hornbeck, Economic Adviser Feis, Chief of the European Division Moffat, Far Eastern expert Ballantine, and Carlton Savage, assistant to the Counselor. There was much to do, but I called them in also because I knew they would not wish to be left out of this first conference after the outbreak of war in Europe.

From my office I telephoned to Bullitt in Paris and Kennedy in London, asking for their news and appraisal. I wanted to be sure that the reported invasion was not another incident such as Hitler had been stirring up along the German-Polish border to excuse his aggression. Kennedy said the British Government had not yet been advised of the German invasion, and that we had furnished the first news the British received of Hitler's fateful move.

As reports came in later of German bombing of Warsaw and other Polish cities, I also sought confirmation.

Exactly one week before, Ambassador Bullitt had sent the President through me a personal message suggesting that immediately after the first shot the President should issue to all nations concerned an appeal to refrain from bombing civilian populations. Bullitt thought England, France, and Poland would agree, Germany probably would not, and this would make the moral position clear. The President and I agreed that the appeal should be made, and Welles drafted it and had it ready.

Bullitt now telephoned me, confirmed reports of the bombing of Warsaw and urged that the appeal be sent at once. We accordingly dispatched it immediately to Britain, Germany, France, Poland, and Italy. We followed this with a second telegram to London, Paris, Rome, and Warsaw, saying it was of the utmost importance that the reply be favorable and received as soon as possible so that it might be released to the public. Our thought was that publication of these favorable replies would either bring pressure on Hitler to agree as well, or place the full burden upon him if he refused.

In my second conversation with Kennedy the Ambassador gave me the latest information available in London, saying it was "all over" and the "party is on." When I asked him whether there was any question but that the British would act, he replied, "Oh, unquestionably none."

Between these transatlantic telephone calls the little group of State Department officers sitting around me discussed the problems that would confront the United States. Their faces were solemn, as they realized full well the enormity of the disaster facing the world. How many millions of men, how many cities, how many billions of money would have to be wiped out before the plague unleashed by Hitler could be stopped! How many dangers and difficulties would now face the United States!

At six o'clock I adjourned our conference so that we could get breakfast. We had taken no definite decisions except the dispatch of the appeal to refrain from bombing open cities, for the information we had thus far received was too meager to warrant other actions.

At 9:05 I called key officers of the Department again to my office for a further discussion of war problems. Shortly thereafter Polish Ambassador Count Potocki came in to ask anxiously for whatever news I could give him. He realized the terrible fate facing his country. I gave him what information we had.

I had been on the telephone to the President several times, passing him the news we were receiving; now he requested me to attend his press conference at 10:30. At the White House I heard the President say to the press he thought we could and would stay out of the war. Before and after the press conference I talked privately with Mr. Roosevelt. I found him calm, though of course deeply concerned. We agreed that a special session of Congress should be summoned shortly to revise the Neutrality Act. We discussed the responsibility of the United States' keeping alive our basic principles for the time when the war might end and nations would again be in position to embrace them.

Returning to the State Department, I held another meeting of my associates and told them what the President had said. I emphasized that we should make a very careful study to determine how far we could go under international law in protecting American commerce and in asserting the principle of the freedom of the seas.

We went over the preparations we had made to evacuate Americans from Europe. These had begun exactly three years before. On August 31, 1936, the Department had sent to our diplomatic and consular officers abroad an outline of a plan to be put into effect in any emergency endangering the lives and property of American citizens, and had suggested they provide the Department with a plan for each individual area and keep it up to date by revising it from time to time. As a result, we had in the Department an analysis of location and capacity of ports, steamship lines, railroads, and housing in port cities, together with an estimate of the average number of Americans to be found in any area.

In the spring and summer of 1938 we had worked intensively in the Department perfecting our plans. We then outlined the establishment of a new division in the Department to handle welfare, whereabouts, relief, and transportation cases in the event of war, and were ready to inaugurate it at the time of the Munich crisis. During the winter of 1938–1939 we held a series of interdepartmental conferences, including the Maritime Commission, the Navy Department, and the Department of Commerce, and on March 21, 1939, we sent revised instructions to our diplomatic missions in Europe and the Near East covering the evacuation of Americans caught in war zones. I placed this special work under the direction of Assistant Secretary of State Messersmith.

When many ship sailings were canceled late in August, the situation of scores of thousands of Americans in Europe became critical. Many Americans were arriving at ports without steamship tickets or funds. Hundreds of others with tickets found that these were not being honored for lack of ships. On August 25 we cabled London, Paris, and Bern—the last was to serve as our European clearinghouse for instructions and information on repatriation of Americans—informing them of our complete policy on repatriation. This set forth our plans for using merchant ships flying the American flag, and for advancing money, on promissory notes, to Americans without funds.

Now, on September 1, we issued a press release summarizing our efforts to bring Americans back to the United States and announcing the establishment, on August 23, of a special committee for this purpose, consisting of representatives of the State and Navy Departments and the Maritime Commission. This press release also urged Americans who had no impelling reason to remain in Europe to return to the United States.

The following day we announced the creation of a special division in the State Department to handle problems arising out of the war, such as the repatriation of Americans and the representation of the interests of other Governments taken over by the United States Government. I appointed Breckinridge Long, former Ambassador to Italy, to head it, assisted by Hugh R. Wilson, with George L. Brandt, a Foreign Service officer, as administrative officer. A flood of telegrams was already pouring into the State Department, asking us to locate Americans stranded in Europe and to help them get home.

Our efforts to get Americans out of Europe were hastened by the ever present fear that Hitler would use his air superiority to bomb London, Paris, and other large cities. During the day of September 1, however, favorable replies arrived from Britain, France, and Poland to the President's appeal against bombing, and these we immediately published. The German reply, also favorable, arrived during the night, and was released the following day. Italy stated that, since she was not a belligerent, our appeal did not apply.

At noon on September 1 British Ambassador Lord Lothian came in to see me. Few ambassadors have ever assumed their posts at so tense a moment. Just two days before, he had presented his letters of credence to the President. Lothian to my mind was unexcelled as an ambassador by anyone of my acquaintance. His great abilities, intensity of purpose, and strong though charming personality made him virtually a perfect diplomatic representative. Lothian and I went over the situation as we knew it twelve hours after Hitler invaded Poland.

At two o'clock I went to the White House to attend a Cabinet meeting. The President was grave, and in opening the session omitted his usual bantering or joking. We threshed over the manifold problems, both foreign and domestic, with which the war would face us. The President drew a distinction between our preparing for war and our preparing to meet the war problems, saying he wanted us to pay attention only to the latter, because we were not going to get into the war. He said he would soon call a special session of Congress to repeal the arms embargo; he planned to make a radio address to the nation after Britain and France declared war; and he requested us to remain in Washington over the week end.

After I returned to the Department I had numerous appointments with my associates to work out solutions to additional problems brought up by the war. Then during the afternoon, many hours after German troops had begun plunging into Poland, arrived Hitler's answer to the President's two peace appeals to him of August 25 and 26. This took the form of a note to me from the German Chargé d'Affaires, Hans Thomsen. It was a short, caviling statement attempting to throw the blame for everything onto Poland.

The following day, September 2, it was clear that Britain and France would go to war. I talked on the telephone to Ambassador Kennedy, who said the British were "set to go"; they did not expect the Germans to comply with their demand to evacuate Poland as a prelude to discussions, and the final decision would probably be made in London and Paris within twenty-four hours.

The President now asked me to have the Department prepare a draft for the radio address he intended to make to the nation. We set to work on it, with Assistant Secretary Berle doing most of the drafting, and sent it to the President during the afternoon.

Late that Saturday afternoon, to get a little relaxation in preparation for what I knew lay ahead in the following week, I took three of my associates with me for a game of croquet on the lawn of "Woodley," Henry L. Stimson's home.

The following morning, Sunday September 3, I was awakened at 4:45 by a telephone call from the President. Kennedy had telephoned that Britain and France had decided to declare war on Germany. I dressed, had a brief breakfast, and went to the State Department.

There I gathered around me my principal associates. We agreed that the neutrality proclamations and regulations prepared during preceding weeks should not be issued that day, but probably the next day. We sought to determine whether the British declaration of war would automatically include the Dominions, and decided to wait until we received the official text of the declaration. We decided that new regulations should be issued preventing Americans from going to Europe, with some legitimate exceptions. I wanted to know whether many current shipments of arms to Europe—France and Britain had placed large orders in the United States—would be affected by immediate application of the Neutrality Act, but was told that comparatively few shipments would be involved. We debated the question of armed merchantmen, and agreed that we should treat merchant vessels armed for defense as regular merchant vessels and not bar our ports to them. We discussed ways to avoid difficulties with the British over the detention or deviation of American ships.

The President having asked me to meet with him in the afternoon and hear him rehearse the address he was to make over the radio that evening, I went to the White House in the middle of the afternoon, taking Welles and Berle with me. The President's address was forceful and direct. He had taken our draft, as he frequently did, and rewritten it. He had great skill in taking a draft prepared by others and heightening it by the change of certain phrases or the addition of new paragraphs.

When the President asked my opinion, I emphasized to him the need for great caution and for giving the American people to understand that the Administration would maintain strict neutrality. I said I opposed retaining the sentences: "This nation will remain a neutral nation, but I cannot ask that every American remain neutral in thought as well. Even a neutral has a right to take account of facts. Even a neutral cannot be asked to close his mind or his conscience." I myself was not neutral in thought, for I emphatically favored the Allies; but I questioned the wisdom of officially proclaiming anything but a neutral attitude, because I could visualize the fight that faced us in Congress to get the Neutrality Act revised. Any hint of unneutrality on the part of the President would strengthen the hands of those who would argue that, under a new Neutrality Act, he would get us into war. That our sympathies were with Britain and France was already evident, and did not require restatement. The President decided otherwise on this point, although he accepted several other modifications I suggested.

That night I listened to the President's address. Commenting that the unfortunate events of recent years had been based on force or the threat of force, he said that we should seek a final peace that would eliminate, as far as possible, the continued use of force between nations. He warned that, although it was easy to say that conflicts thousands of miles away did not seriously affect the Americas, "every word that comes through the air, every ship that sails the seas, every battle that is fought does affect the American future." We would seek, he said, to keep war from coming to the Americas, and he pledged, in so far as it was in his power to prevent it, that there would be "no black-out of peace in the United States."

Almost simultaneously with the President's address, I received a cable from Ambassador Kennedy notifying us of the sinking of the liner *Athenia,* with scores of American passengers aboard. It was an ominous portent of the destruction on the high seas that was to follow for nearly six years. In the days and weeks ensuing, many officers of the State Department here and abroad were occupied with the aftermath of the *Athenia* disaster, taking care of the American survivors, notifying the relatives of those who were lost, or investigating the cause of the sinking.

On September 4, the German Foreign Office denied that any German submarine had been responsible for the sinking. Later it accused the British of having sunk the ship in order to arouse American hostility to Germany. We therefore instructed our officers abroad to obtain from American survivors eyewitness accounts in the form of affidavits, and we secured similar affidavits from those arriving in this country. Our investigation strongly supported the theory that the *Athenia* had been torpedoed, but we could not ascertain the nationality of the submarine. (Admiral Raeder, head of the German Navy, testified at the Nuremberg war crimes trial in 1946 that an inexperienced commander of the German submarine U-30 had sunk the *Athenia* by mistake, that this was not known until several weeks after the German denial, and that Hitler directed that no retraction of the denial be made.)

This German outrage on the high seas was paralleled by other outrages inflicted from the air. From the first day of the German invasion of Poland, reports kept coming to us that German planes, despite Hitler's promise to refrain from bombing civilian populations, were bombing Polish cities.

At the President's request, we sent instructions on September 4 to our diplomatic missions in Paris, London, Berlin, and Warsaw to insist upon the privilege of using their military attachés to inspect promptly by personal visit the scene of any bombing of a nonmilitary objective which might constitute a controversial case of disregard of the humane principle agreed to by the belligerents. We requested prompt, factual reports of such bombings.

In the two following weeks we received a number of telegrams from Ambassadors Biddle in Poland and Bullitt in Paris reporting various bombings of Polish cities without military objectives. On September 14

Biddle cabled me: "In view of what the members of my staff and my family and I have experienced and witnessed I find it difficult in many cases to ascribe the wanton barbaric aerial bombardment by German planes to anything short of deliberate intention to terrorize the civilian population and to reduce the number of child-producing Poles irrespective of category." Two days later President Mościcki of Poland sent to the President a telegram informing us of deliberate and methodical bombing of Polish open towns by German aircraft. The President sent this to me with a note:

C. H.
        Should we give this out? Should we take any further steps? (See Herbert Hoover's idea of a neutral commission.)   F. D. R.

Hoover had proposed a neutral commission to investigate bombings.

We prepared a reply to Mościcki and advised the President to publish the exchange, which was done on September 18. The President said in his cable:

"It had been my hope following the receipt from the several belligerent powers of the replies to my appeal of September 1, in which they stated their intentions to limit the operations of their air forces to military objectives, that the world would be spared the horror of witnessing during this war the bombing of open towns and villages and the slaughtering of thousands of innocent and defenseless men, women, and children.

"I have been deeply shocked, therefore, by the statements contained in your telegram as well as by reports received from other sources including officials of this Government in Poland at the scene of hostilities."

Over and above all the questions that confronted us with the outbreak of war hung the predominant one—how were we to conduct ourselves as a neutral, and what were we to do with the neutrality legislation on our books, embracing the arms embargo?

On September 5 the President issued two neutrality proclamations which we had prepared. One came under international law and the other under the Neutrality Act. The first related to the prohibitions generally accepted by a neutral under international law, such as enlisting in the belligerent armies and fitting out warships for the belligerents. The second applied the arms embargo of the Neutrality Act.

I opposed the inclusion of Canada in the proclamations until Canada herself declared war. Most of my associates, however, argued that when the United Kingdom went to war, the Dominions went to war also unless they formally seceded from the British Commonwealth. Finally I permitted the Dominions to be included, and took the drafts to the President. I informed him of our discussion concerning Canada. He decided to telephone Prime Minister Mackenzie King in Ottawa and ask his opinion. Mackenzie King said he did not regard Canada as at war until the Canadian Parliament had so voted. The President thereupon made the necessary changes with a fountain pen, and the proclamations were issued in this form. Canada was later included on September 10.

The State Department also issued an explanatory statement pointing out that the general neutrality proclamation had "to do with our activities as a neutral under the rules and procedure of international law and those of our domestic statutes in harmony therewith" and would have been issued "according to customary usage" regardless of whether the Neutrality Act of 1937 had been on the statute books. The other neutrality proclamation, we said, was based solely on the Neutrality Act. We recalled that several proposals for modifying that Act were still pending, and that "it was generally understood in Congress at the close of the last session that final action on these proposed modifications would be taken at the next session of Congress." Our purpose was to emphasize that, under international law, we did not have to impose an arms embargo, and that Congressional leaders had promised to consider the repeal of the embargo at the next session of Congress.

In subsequent days we issued other regulations under the Neutrality Act, dealing with travel on belligerent ships, credits to belligerents, contributions for relief in belligerent countries, and the traffic in arms. Then on September 8 the President proclaimed a national emergency and issued orders increasing the strength of the Army, Navy, Marine Corps, and the Federal Bureau of Investigation.

From the day war broke out it was obvious to me that in enforcing our position as a neutral we were very likely to run into the same difficulties with the Allies, chiefly Britain, as we had encountered on the high seas during the First World War. Britain would seek to examine American ships to determine whether they were carrying cargoes to her enemies, and might divert them to British ports for such examination. I believed it would be extremely bad for the world at large if serious quarrels should arise between Britain and us in this connection, and that steps should be taken in advance to remove the possibilities for trouble.

A few hours after Britain declared war, on September 3, I telephoned Ambassador Kennedy and asked him for information on Britain's detailed plans for shipping and contraband policies. The following day I called British Ambassador Lord Lothian to my office to raise the question with him.

After outlining to him the potential seriousness of the situation, I suggested: "Each of our two Governments should designate experts to confer toward adopting something like the certificate system in operation during the last part of the World War. Let's simplify in every possible way the relations between our two countries as they may be affected by British interference with American commerce."

The certificate system I had in mind was simply that British authorities would check an American ship before it left our harbors and, if the cargo were found to be genuinely destined to a neutral, would issue a certificate, also called a navicert, which would prevent the ship from being diverted to a British port for examination. Such a system, I said to the Ambassador, would reduce the occasion for halting or taking our ships into British ports or otherwise interfering with American commerce destined for small countries in Europe, such as Holland, Belgium, and the Scandinavian countries. It would also help handle and simplify the problem of rationing. Rationing in this sense meant sending to countries bordering on Germany only the amount of products they had imported before the war, so that surpluses could not go on to Germany.

After I emphasized that the steps I proposed would avoid most of the serious controversies that had raged between our two Governments during the first two years and more of the First World War, Lothian, who seemed interested in the proposal, said he would communicate at once with his Government.

Two days later Lothian sent me a note giving us the official British contraband list. On September 10 he sent me an announcement of the establishment of certain contraband control bases by the British. The note said that Britain, while forced to make full use of its belligerent rights, would give sympathetic consideration to any suggestions by the neutrals that would "facilitate their bona fide trade." The following day, Lothian called on me to give me his Government's reply to my suggestion of September 4. Britain was ready for a conference with our experts immediately. I set the next day, September 12, for the first meeting and named Herbert Feis, the Department's Economic Adviser, to take charge for us.

As a result of a series of such meetings, we worked out with the British an arrangement for quickly taking up with them the many problems that inevitably arose between us. We had our difficulties, of course, some of them sharp, but generally we kept the controversies with Great Britain from becoming as acute as those that had sprung up during the First World War. Quiet, informal discussions took the place of many of the strong diplomatic protests that had gone from Washington to London between 1914 and 1917. This procedure was of real service to the cause of the Allies, and to ourselves as well. The sympathies of the great majority of the American public toward Britain and France never weakened as a result of minor disputes between us and the western democracies.

This did not mean that we bowed to all of Britain's assertions of her belligerent rights. On the contrary, we upheld our right to normal trade with other neutrals. On September 14 I issued a public statement in which I said: "The Government of the United States has not abandoned any of its rights as a neutral under international law. It has, however, for the time being prescribed, by domestic legislation, certain restrictions for its nationals which have the effect of requiring them to refrain from the exercise of privileges which but for such legislation they would have the right to exercise under international law, such as the right to travel on belligerent vessels, to make loans and extend credits to belligerent governments, et cetera. . . .

"This Government, adhering as it does to these principles [of international law], reserves all rights of the United States and its nationals under international law and will adopt such measures as may seem most practical and prudent when those rights are violated by any of the belligerents."

Four days later I authorized the European Division of the Department to convey orally to the British Embassy and the legations of the northern neutral countries—Scandinavia, Holland, and Belgium—this thought: "This Government . . . desires that its trade with neutral countries proceed with the least possible disturbance due to the existence of a state of war in Europe. As regards trade of neutral countries (in particular the so-called northern neutrals) with the United States, it should be fully understood, as has already been publicly announced, that this Government reserves all rights of the United States and its nationals under international law and is not to be understood as endorsing any principle of interference with trade of genuine neutral character."

The obvious danger to American shipping in European waters was one of my most serious preoccupations. On September 20 an interdepartmental committee we had appointed to consider various questions affecting our merchant marine met with me for the first time. It embraced repre-

sentatives of the State, Treasury, War, and Navy Departments and the
Maritime Commission. I expressed to the committee my apprehension
that Congress was likely to be swayed by the isolationists, and I said that
the Administration was trying to devise some means to keep American
ships at sea which would meet with Congressional approval. The means
I had in mind were embraced in the creation of the combat zones, into
which American ships were forbidden to go, leaving them free, however,
to go anywhere else on the seven seas.

I received a protest on September 30 from the German Chargé, Hans
Thomsen, against attempts of neutral shipping in the area about France
and Britain to evade stoppage and search by German naval forces. His
note warned American merchant vessels to avoid, in their own interests,
any suspicious behavior.

I replied to the German note by emphasizing a warning we had already issued to our merchant ships to avoid suspicious conduct and the
fact that American merchant ships were forbidden by law to carry armament, and then by stating: "The Government of the United States feels
entitled to expect that special care will be used by the belligerent governments to respect the neutral rights of its vessels and nationals, and will
maintain all such rights in the event of violation."

The fight to modify the Neutrality Act was now at hand. The President and I had had this uppermost in mind since the outbreak of war,
recalling the promise of Congressional leaders of both parties that, if war
came, they would consider neutrality legislation at their first session.

The President, having summoned Congress to meet in special session
beginning September 21, asked me to have a draft of his message prepared
for him. In addition to working at this task, we began, at the President's
request, to assemble arguments to be used in the forthcoming neutrality
debate in Congress. I held a long meeting with my associates in my office
on Sunday September 17, to outline the attitude we would advise the
President to take toward neutrality legislation during the special session.

Basically, our position had not changed since my letter of May 27,
1939, to Senator Pittman and Representative Bloom. We believed that
the arms embargo should go, that arms, ammunition, and implements of
war should be on the same footing as other materials equally essential to
the conduct of war, such as petroleum, steel, copper, and cotton, and be
embraced in a new cash-and-carry provision; that Americans should not
travel on belligerent vessels, and that American ships should keep out of
combat areas.

The day before the opening of Congress I spent most of my time working with the President on his message. I was at the White House three different times, and also spoke to Mr. Roosevelt several times on the telephone. In the afternoon I attended a White House meeting of both Democratic and Republican leaders called to endeavor to obtain a nonpartisan approach to the neutrality question, now that war had come in Europe. The result was quite different from that of the dramatic meeting of July 18, only two months before, when Senator Borah prevented favorable action. This time the gathering agreed to deal in a wholly nonpartisan spirit with the problem of keeping the United States neutral and at peace. We emphasized that the most important subject was the repeal of the arms embargo and a return to the processes of international law, and we agreed that the Senate Committee on Foreign Relations should take up the legislation as soon as possible after Congress convened.

That night I returned to the White House to go over the President's message with him for the last time. With us was Judge Samuel Rosenman of New York, who frequently helped the President in writing a speech or message. We made a few last-minute changes. The following morning I went to the Capitol to hear the President deliver his message.

"The executive branch of the Government," he said, "did its utmost, within our traditional policy of noninvolvement, to aid in averting the present appalling war. Having thus striven and failed, this Government must lose no time or effort to keep the nation from being drawn into the war.

"In my candid judgment we shall succeed in these efforts."

Regretting that Congress had passed the Neutrality Act of August 31, 1935, precursor of the Acts that followed, and that he had signed it, the President called for the repeal of the embargo provisions and a return to international law. "I give to you my deep and unalterable conviction," he added, "based on years of experience as a worker in the field of international peace, that by the repeal of the embargo the United States will more probably remain at peace than if the law remains as it stands today. I say this because with the repeal of the embargo this Government clearly and definitely will insist that American citizens and American ships keep away from the immediate perils of the actual zones of conflict."

Nowhere in his message did the President mention the thought that had been in the minds of all of us, that lifting the arms embargo would assist Britain and France. When the Neutrality Act was proclaimed on September 5, the large armaments orders that Britain and France had placed in the United States, especially for airplanes, were frozen. Lifting the arms embargo would permit them to be filled, although the application of cash-and-carry would require Britain and France to do all the transporting of the materials they imported from the United States and to pay for them in cash.

The President and I, long before the outbreak of war, saw clearly that it would be to our own national interest to assist Britain and France, first in the effort to keep the war from coming, and second, to win the war if it came. We knew that a German victory over Britain and France would place us in direct contact with the ruthless leaders of Germany riding a powerful military machine. With Japan on a rampage in the Orient, our position in that event would be of the utmost danger.

But, with isolationism still powerful and militant in the United States, it would have been the peak of folly to make aid to the democracies an issue in connection with neutrality legislation. We were sincere in our belief that the new legislation would afford us a better chance of keeping out of the war than the old legislation because, if Britain and France won the war, we could remain at peace, whereas if Germany won there was every likelihood that we should soon have to fight.

On September 21, the day the President delivered his message to Congress, I issued a public statement to combat the argument that changing our neutrality legislation after the outbreak of war in Europe would be an unneutral act. "This nation," I said, "or any neutral nation, has a right during a war to change its national policies whenever experience shows the necessity for such change for the protection of its interests and safety. . . . In advocating repeal of the embargo provisions . . . we are endeavoring to return to a more rational position and one that is more in keeping with real neutrality under international law. The question whether such proposed action is unneutral should not, in my judgment, be a matter of serious debate. There has never in our time been more widespread publicity and notice in advance of the outbreak of war of a change in our policy than there has in this instance. This Government has given notice for well-nigh a year . . . that such a change of policy was in contemplation."

The lines for the neutrality battle in Congress were now laid. Both sides had their men and arguments marshaled. It looked as if the debate would be bitter, but this time I was confident we could win. The conflict of arguments was opening even as the conflict of cannon in Europe was dwindling to its first halt.

As the President spoke to Congress, Germany and Russia were setting up their new borders in Poland. The Battle of Poland was virtually over. For some days we had suspected that the Soviet Union would invade Poland so as to obtain a share of that country, and to keep Hitler's legions from approaching too close to Russia. On September 7 Ambassador Bullitt cabled me from Paris that the French Foreign Office had warned him of an impending Soviet attack on Poland. Ten days later, Ambassador Steinhardt cabled me from Moscow the text of a note from Foreign Commissar Molotov announcing that Soviet troops had entered East Poland to protect the lives and property of the populations of the western Ukraine and western White Russia in the absence of any Polish Government, and that both Poland and the Polish Government had ceased to exist. It added that the Soviet Union would pursue a policy of neutrality in its relations with the United States.

Although Russia's invasion of Poland could be considered an act of war, the President and I decided not to include Russia in our application of the Neutrality Act. We did not wish to place her on the same belligerent footing as Germany, since to do so might thrust her further into Hitler's arms. We had the feeling that Russia and Germany would not become full allies, and that Hitler had not abandoned his ambitions with regard to Russia.

On September 21 I sent to the President information brought in to the Department by Chinese Ambassador Hu Shih. This came from an official Chinese source in Moscow and was to the effect that the Soviet invasion of Poland did not mean Soviet participation in the European war but was solely to secure the frontier and protect the Russian minorities in eastern Poland.

Our Embassy and consular staff in Poland, headed by Ambassador Biddle, had been scattered by the German and Russian invasions. Biddle made his way to Rumania, and then to Paris, where I sent him a telegram commending the work of himself and his staff "under conditions of great emergency." I sent a similar telegram to Consul General John K. Davis, who had arrived in Berlin from Poland, commending him and all the Foreign Service officers and clerks of his staff.

I talked to Biddle in Paris on the telephone September 29, discussing with him a statement we intended to issue on the overrunning of Poland. The following day, President Mościcki of Poland having resigned, Wladyslaw Raczkiewicz, former President of the Polish Senate, who had been designated as Mościcki's successor, took the oath of office as head of the new Polish Government in Paris.

Two days later I issued a statement, after consulting with the President, declaring that this Government continued to regard the Government of Poland as in existence and to recognize Count Jerzy Potocki as its Ambassador in Washington, while Biddle would continue as our Ambassador to the Polish Government. "Poland," I said, "is now the victim of force used as an instrument of national policy. Its territory has been taken over, and its Government has had to seek refuge abroad. Mere seizure of territory, however, does not extinguish the legal existence of a Government."

The President and I wished to offer former President Mościcki a refuge in the United States.

I had telegraphed our Minister to Rumania, Franklin Mott Gunther, on September 28, authorizing him to inform the Rumanian Government that the Rumanian treatment of President Mościcki of Poland and other members of his Government who had sought refuge in Rumania was being anxiously watched by the American public. We knew that intense pressure by Germany on the Rumanian Government had resulted in the internment of Mościcki and his officials in Rumania. I also asked Gunther whether it would help King Carol and the Rumanian Government if the President sent a personal message to the King informing him that Mościcki would be welcome in the United States in accordance with our traditional policy toward political refugees, should he decide to seek refuge here.

Gunther replied he had followed my instructions, but he did not think the proposed message from the President would serve a useful purpose. Subsequently he cabled that Mościcki had made arrangements to go to Switzerland, but that Rumania would not release him. Ambassador Bullitt cabled from Paris on October 18 that he thought an important question of international decency was involved, which we should uphold.

The following day President Roosevelt sent me this memorandum:

"Now that a definite Polish Government has been set up in France and former President Mościcki is no longer President, I recur to the historic United States friendship for Poland and the historic fact that we have always welcomed refugees from defeated democracies.

"I wonder, therefore, whether it would not be a fine thing to do if we were to tell the Rumanian Government that the United States would be glad to receive former President Mościcki if he cares to visit this country; that we have held no communication with him and that this message is being sent without his knowledge.

"He is an old man, in poor health, and I think the moral effect of such action on our part would be good throughout the world.

"We might even make it easier for the Rumanian Government to release him if we send it in the form of an invitation to the former President to visit us."

I accordingly cabled Minister Gunther to this effect, instructing him to convey the President's thoughts directly to King Carol.

Gunther replied that he and the Polish Ambassador in Bucharest were agreed that the time was not ripe for intervention by the President on Mościcki's behalf. Also, that Rumanian Under Secretary of State for Foreign Affairs Cretzianu had told him Rumania could not afford to provide Germany or Russia or both an excuse to invade Rumania or otherwise make it difficult for her. Gunther asked for further instructions, saying he saw no harm in delivering the President's message so long as we did not object to receiving an evasive or negative reply.

I passed Gunther's telegrams on to the President, who sent me a memorandum saying that he did not see any reason for letting the matter drop, but that Gunther might present it to King Carol as a verbal message from the President, without anything in writing. "Frankly," he said, "I want for my own conscience to have made some further move in behalf of the poor old ex-President of Poland."

I cabled Gunther accordingly. He reported on November 1 that he had seen King Carol. The King was very sympathetic and said he would do his best, but he thought it would be easier to get Mościcki into the United States from Switzerland, where he particularly wished to go. Gunther continued his urgings in Bucharest, and on Christmas Day he cabled that Mościcki had been released and was leaving that day for Switzerland. Mościcki remained in Switzerland, however, not desiring to continue his journey.

The fighting in Eastern Europe having ended, the long, maddening period of the so-called "phony war" was upon us.

48: The New World Takes Its Stand

WITH EUROPE AT WAR, it became our task to weld the Republics of America into a common front to parry the effects of the conflict. What I had foreseen and prepared for at the Montevideo, Buenos Aires, and Lima Conferences had come to pass. The consultative procedure to which the twenty-one American Republics had agreed to have recourse if war came was ready at hand. After communications had passed back and forth among a number of American nations, it was agreed that a conference of Foreign Ministers should be held at Panama City, and the Government of Panama sent out invitations on September 5.

The manifold problems that confronted us in Europe prevented my heading the American delegation to the conference, as I should have liked. The President and I agreed that Under Secretary Welles should go instead.

It was already clear to us, as we had well envisaged, that the Western Hemisphere's interests were in serious jeopardy as a result of the war. Some export markets, sources of supply, and shipping services were cut off or curtailed, prices were fluctuating, and currencies were endangered. The American Republics would have to take steps to link their economies more closely together so that each could help the others fill the partial vacuum created by the war.

There was also the question of a common neutrality front by the American nations. Finally, these Republics had to decide whether to make a joint effort to keep the war away from the hemisphere. This part of the world, in fact, was already involved indirectly, because Canada had gone to war, and because two of the belligerents, Britain and France, had possessions in it.

On September 12 the Governing Board of the Pan American Union, over which I presided as chairman, approved an agenda for the conference. One of its items was: "Consideration of measures to preserve the American continent free from conflict whether on land, in the air, within territorial waters, or within the area of the primary defense of the Western Hemisphere." This last phrase was significant. It meant that nations, for the first time, would seek to prevent the approach of war to an area many miles beyond their territorial waters.

Following numerous discussions at the State Department, over some of which I presided, the American delegation, headed by Welles, sailed for

Panama City on September 15; and the conference opened eight days later.

On the eve of the inaugural session, I called attention to the significance of the Pan American movement in an address during Pan American Day at the New York World's Fair. "Today," I said, "the American Republics are supremely fortunate in that they are at peace within and without our hemisphere. Each of our Republics is ready to defend itself against any threat to its security that may come from any part of the world. At the same time, it is the unalterable desire of each and every one of our nations to remain at peace ourselves and to exercise all influence in our power toward the end that just and enduring peace may become firmly established everywhere."

Now that a major war in Europe, I added, was a grim reality, "there is greater necessity than ever before for all nations, still in a position to do so, to increase their exertions for the preservation of those fundamental principles of civilized international relations, through the application of which alone, we of the Americas are firmly convinced, the progress of the human race can be maintained."

On September 26 Welles presented six proposals to the Panama Conference. One would create a neutrality zone around the American Republics from which belligerent activities would be excluded. A second would keep belligerent submarines from the Republics' ports. A third would declare the neutral policies of the Republics. A fourth would create an advisory committee on monetary and commercial problems. A fifth would preserve liberal trade policies. A sixth would prevent unneutral and subversive activities by the belligerents within the American Republics.

As the conference proceeded, Welles kept me informed by cable, and I made a series of suggestions that were incorporated in later drafts of agreements. By October 3, the closing day of the meeting, the conference had adopted the proposals submitted by the United States delegation, along with numerous others.

As a result of the "General Declaration of Neutrality" agreed to at Panama City, the American Republics were now to enforce common rules of neutrality. These related to specific acts, such as prevention of the use of their territories by belligerents as bases for operations, enlistments, or the establishment of radio stations.

The most spectacular agreement, however, was the "Declaration of Panama." This stated that, for continental self-protection, the American Republics, so long as they were neutral, were entitled, by inherent right, to have the waters adjacent to them free from hostile acts by any non-American belligerent. This declaration outlined a zone three hundred to one thousand miles out from the coast, depending on the curvature of the shore line, and extending south from the Canadian border and completely embracing South America. The American Republics would patrol this zone to keep belligerent activities away from the hemisphere. The President of Panama, as spokesman for the Republics, would notify the belligerents of the creation of the zone, and request them to respect it.

The hemisphere neutrality zone was frankly an experiment. It was the idea of the President, seconded by Welles. I myself was skeptical of it on two grounds. It had no precedent in international law and could therefore be validly objected to by the belligerents. And in actual practice it would be difficult to enforce. But since the President had wholeheartedly embraced it I was willing to go along with him to see how it would work out. Much would depend on the spirit with which the American Republics sought to maintain it and on the good will of the belligerents. Even as the Panama Conference met, belligerent ships were operating within the safety zone, and, the day before the Declaration of Panama was signed, a British merchantman was sunk within the zone by a German raider, later identified as the pocket battleship *Graf von Spee.*

Although I acquiesced in the President's plan I had a different idea, which afterwards went into effect toward the end of 1940 and in 1941. This was that we should have a flexible zone. I maintained that we had the right to patrol out to sea whatever distance might be necessary to protect our shore line and territorial waters. That distance, I believed, might be greater or less depending on the circumstances at the moment. But it should not be stated as a definite zone demarcated by longitude and latitude, nor should we try to get the belligerents' consent to it. We should not limit ourselves to any watery boundary, but patrol out as far as our own protection required. In the year following the Panama Conference, the President agreed to this idea, when as a result of the difficulties of enforcing the zone created at Panama City it at length had been tacitly abandoned.

For many weeks following the Panama Conference, we were engaged in trying to make clear to the belligerents and to our own people what we had in mind by the Western Hemisphere neutrality zone. Germany, France, and Britain, of course, were hesitant to agree to the zone for fear of possible advantages it might give their opponents. Among our own people, many were fearful lest our attempt to preserve the neutrality zone would lead us into naval engagements with the belligerents.

On October 4 I stated to the press that the patrolling of the zone would be for the purposes of information only. Our naval vessels, therefore, would not seek to intercept a German submarine attempting to sink an Allied vessel, or a British warship attempting to overhaul a German submarine or merchantman. But we would gather information on belligerent activities within the neutrality zone so that the American Republics could take appropriate diplomatic steps toward the belligerents concerned.

The following day I received a cable from Ambassador Kennedy in London containing a memorandum on the zone from Winston Churchill, then First Lord of the Admiralty. Churchill began the memorandum with the phrase, "The following from naval person." He used this code name "naval person" in preference to his name in communications to us while he was First Lord of the Admiralty. The following year, when he became Prime Minister, he employed the code name "former naval person." The President and I, in turn, used it in our communications to him throughout the war. Later he sometimes used the signature "Prime."

Churchill said he understood the natural desire of the United States to keep belligerents out of our waters, and he liked the idea of a wide limit of, say three hundred miles, within which no belligerent submarines should act. If America requested all belligerents to comply, he said, Britain would immediately declare that she respected our wishes. More difficulty, however, would arise about surface ships, because Britain should be allowed to protect herself in case a German raider operated from or took refuge in the American zone. Churchill thought Britain would have difficulty accepting a zone that was policed only by a weak neutral, but it would be all right if the United States Navy took care of the patrolling.

We had many diplomatic exchanges with Britain, Germany, and France over the neutrality zone. Generally, each side was inclined to accept it, although with some reservations and interpretations, provided the other side accepted it. The zone, however, was never sufficiently agreed to by the belligerents to serve as a precedent. Numerous violations of it occurred, as German submarines sank Allied merchantmen, or Allied surface warships overtook German merchantmen. These were generally followed by protests dispatched to the warring powers concerned by President Juan Arosemena of Panama, acting as spokesman for the American Republics.

The most spectacular violation happened in December, when three

British cruisers battled the German pocket battleship *Graf von Spee* off the coast of Uruguay. The German warship, after inflicting and receiving damage, took refuge in the harbor of Montevideo. The following day, December 14, 1939, we cabled our Legation in Montevideo a summary of the rules we would follow in a similar case, because it was evident that the German Government would bring pressure on the Uruguayan Government to permit the battleship to repair its damage and leave port. We pointed out that, under international law, a belligerent warship was not permitted to remain in a neutral port for more than twenty-four hours unless damage or weather prevented its departure, and that damage inflicted by its enemy must not be repaired. We told the Legation they could use this information in conversation with Uruguayan authorities as an expression of the views of our Government with regard to our own policy.

Backed by ourselves, as well as by Argentina and Brazil, the Uruguayan Government ordered the *Graf von Spee* to depart or be interned. The battleship's commander thereupon steamed outside the breakwater and scuttled his ship. Subsequently, the President of Panama, on behalf of all the American Republics, addressed protests to the British and German Governments against their flagrant violation of the neutrality zone.

Of greater importance than the spectacular hemispheric neutrality zone was the quiet, constant work along economic lines which followed the conference. An Inter-American Financial and Economic Advisory Committee, consisting of an economic expert from each of the twenty-one Republics, began a series of meetings in Washington. Gradually a system of economic cooperation in the Western Hemisphere developed to increase commerce and transportation among the American Republics, and to take up the slack and dislocation caused by the war in Europe.

To the Allies and Germany, the fight in Congress during late September and throughout October for repeal of the arms embargo of the Neutrality Act was more important than the Panama Conference. It was readily apparent to them that the decision taken at the Capitol might well influence the outcome of the war.

Even before the special session of Congress convened to consider new neutrality legislation, Australia, Britain, and France had already indicated their views to us. On September 7 Australian Prime Minister R. G. Menzies sent the President a message calling his attention to the hardships inflicted on Australia by the neutrality proclamation issued under the

1937 Act. The following day Ambassador Kennedy in London cabled me Churchill's comment to him that the British were very discouraged by our neutrality legislation, which made their burden that much heavier and kept them from obtaining even the materials they had already ordered in the United States.

A week later Ambassador Kennedy cabled me a conversation he had had with British Secretary for War Hore-Belisha. The British Secretary said that, if our Neutrality Act were not modified, the Soviet Union, Italy, and Turkey would decide that Britain could not win and would hasten to side with Germany. He also said that if Britain did not obtain the right to buy war goods in America the situation was hopeless for her, and even if she did obtain it he wondered how long she would be able to pay for her requirements.

The French were equally emphatic. Bullitt cabled me from Paris on September 20 a compendium of his conversations with Premier Daladier, General Gamelin, Alexis Léger of the French Foreign Office, and others, to the effect that all Frenchmen who knew the facts agreed Germany would surely win if the embargo were continued. Bullitt also pointed out that, as reported by the French Ambassador to Italy, Mussolini was convinced that the embargo would not be repealed and therefore Britain and France could not win; consequently Congress's action would have an important bearing on his decision whether to enter the war on Hitler's side.

We did not need these urgings from the Allies to stimulate our desire that the embargo be annulled. The President and I had reached this decision nearly a year before. Our only question was as to the best method to secure the repeal.

Senator Pittman, as chairman of the Senate Foreign Relations Committee, began work on the new legislation as soon as Congress convened. He took the Bloom Bill, which had passed the House during the previous session, and wrote a substitute for it. Pittman again, as in January, insisted on being the sole guiding spirit of the legislation. At about the time Congress convened, he telephoned me and said rather arrogantly he hoped his committee would not be embarrassed by any indiscreet utterances from the Executive "end of the Avenue." He was also concerned lest anyone in the State Department give opinions to any other Senator.

The bill he produced eliminated the arms embargo, as we wished, but, in return for this concession, contained severe restrictions upon American shipping and commerce. In analyzing the bill in the State Department, my associates and I agreed that these restrictions would cause great hardship to Americans without keeping the nation from being involved in war. The bill was defective in many respects. Among other oddities, it permitted American ships to carry goods to Canada on rivers, lakes, and inland waterways, but neglected to mention railroads and trucks. It forbade American ships to carry goods to any belligerent other than Canada whether in a danger zone or not.

As soon as the provisions of Pittman's bill became known, diplomats of a number of countries hastened to the State Department to voice their protests. South African Minister Close sent me a note on September 30 pointing out that the bill would have a deleterious effect on our commerce with the Union of South Africa. The bill forbade American ships to go to the Union's ports, many thousands of miles removed from the European danger zone. Close said the Union itself did not have the ships to transport its purchases from this country and saw no prospect of obtaining ships from other sources in view of the war. Our Minister to South Africa, Leo J. Keena, cabled me on October 10 a statement of Prime Minister Smuts to him that the proposed restrictions would destroy a growing market in South Africa for commodities in no way connected with the war, for which the Dominion was dependent on the United States now that Germany was no longer available as a source of supply.

Two days later Canadian Minister Loring Christie brought in an *aide-mémoire* expressing the concern of his government that commercial relations between Canada and the United States would suffer. I sent a copy of this and of the South African note to Senator Pittman.

On Sunday October 15, I held a long meeting of my Department associates in my office, at which we discussed Pittman's sweeping restrictions on shipping. We drafted a new cash-and-carry section that would limit the ban on shipping to the European area. I took it to the President late in the afternoon, so that he might send it to Pittman and other Senators, which he did. Pittman, however, absolutely refused to use the draft. He continued to insist that he could not get the new neutrality bill, embracing the repeal of the arms embargo, through the Senate unless it also embraced rigid restrictions on American shipping. As new protests, including those from American interests came in, however, other Senators began to see the seriousness of the crisis that would confront American shipping under the Pittman Bill, and prevailed on Pittman to adopt at least some of our suggestions.

When South African Minister Close came back to see me on October

18, to express again the great concern of his Government, I told him that our desire was to retain the maximum amount of commerce on the seven seas consistent with the minimum danger of involvement of our country in the war. I said that the Senate Committee on Foreign Relations had not wanted to report out a bill repealing the arms embargo without an extreme prohibition relating to shipping, but that now there was a real chance that the prohibition would be rendered less severe. I concluded that the State Department was particularly concerned with the immediate repeal of the embargo, but was also hopeful that Congress would come back to some of our suggestions on shipping.

Despite Pittman's reluctance to have any members of the State Department take up neutrality questions with Senators, I myself saw various members of the Foreign Relations Committee and freely expressed my ideas. At a meeting in my office on Sunday October 8, I had received a report that we should win on neutrality legislation in the Senate by a two-to-one vote, but that the situation in the House was not so clear. Subsequently, I conferred also with members of the House.

On October 19, Senator Pittman introduced a series of amendments to the neutrality bill, one of which tended somewhat to liberalize the shipping restrictions. At a meeting I had with my Department associates to analyze the amendments, we agreed that although not as much freedom was given to American shipping as we desired, it would be inadvisable to take up with Pittman or other members of the Foreign Relations Committee the question of further over-all liberalization. However, I asked one of the Department officers to prepare a memorandum against a proposal that had been made to exclude armed belligerent merchant ships from our ports. This would have banned virtually all British and French ships.

Since the bill was still far from meeting the objections of Canada and South Africa, the Ministers of those countries came to the Department again to make further representations. The former thought the requirement for the transfer of title to goods would have a disastrous effect on ordinary peacetime commerce between the United States and Canada. The latter protested that Capetown would be prohibited to American shipping. I sent memoranda of these conversations to Pittman.

Then the Norwegian, Danish, Swedish, Finnish, and British Governments protested against a discrimination in the bill in favor of American shipping. The bill waived the transfer of title to cargoes carried by American ships going to belligerent ports outside combat areas, but not by ships of other nationality. This was more a matter of poor drafting than a deliberate intent to discriminate, and we called it to Pittman's attention.

Finally, the bill militated against China because it closed the belligerent ports of French Indo-China and Burma to our ships carrying arms. Since the Japanese were in possession of most of the Chinese ports, these French and British ports had been used for transshipments of supplies to China. We therefore proposed to Pittman an amendment that would permit American vessels to carry arms, ammunition, and implements of war from the United States to Haiphong, French Indo-China, and to Rangoon, Burma, for ultimate shipment to China. Pittman rejected it, saying it would cause much discussion, would delay enactment of the bill, and did not seem appropriate in a neutrality law. He planned to deal separately with the Far Eastern situation during the next session of Congress.

One question that arose again and again during the debates on the bill was whether we were being unneutral by revising the Neutrality Act after a war had broken out. I had already sought to deal with this point in my press statement of September 21. October 6 Spanish Ambassador Juan Francisco de Cárdenas came in to see me and inquired whether I thought there might be complications with Germany in the event of the passage of the Neutrality Act changing our neutrality policy during the war.

"From month to month, week to week, and day to day," I replied, "we've been giving effective and binding notice to all nations of what our neutrality policy was intended to be in case of war. This is particularly true since the first of last January; but both the President and I have, in effect, been urging the repeal of the embargo since the latter part of 1935.

"Moreover, a nation, especially after giving constant notice for nine months, is not expected or required to enact its neutrality policy either before a war or on the first day, the first week, or the first two weeks of a war. This Government has not been lacking in diligence in prosecuting its neutrality objective. During last summer, when we were urging the repeal of the embargo, no nation intimated that it expected to inaugurate war on the assurance that the embargo would not be repealed." In other words, if Hitler started the war on the assurance that Britain and France would not have access to our arms and airplanes, we were not bound by his miscalculation.

Eventually many of the objections we raised to the shipping provisions of the bill were met by amendments. The bill passed the Senate by a vote of 63 to 30 and the House by 243 to 172, and the President signed it on November 4. At the State Department we had already prepared the numerous proclamations and regulations which began to be issued that day.

I felt that we had won a great battle, but my rejoicing was bitter; I could not help feeling that our victory would have been far more effective for the cause of the peace-loving nations if it could have been gained in the spring and summer of 1939 rather than in the autumn. Nevertheless I issued a statement on November 4 saying:

"I am naturally gratified with the basic changes made in the so-called neutrality legislation. Throughout this year the executive department has urged the prompt enactment of these basic changes and, prior to the outbreak of the war, pleaded with all nations to preserve peace and refrain from war.

"I desire to repeat with emphasis what I have consistently said heretofore to the effect that our first and most sacred task is to keep our country secure and at peace, and that it is my firm belief that we shall succeed in this endeavor. I am satisfied that the new Act will greatly assist in this undertaking."

Britain and France now had access to our war goods, but on a cash-and-carry basis. Our own ships could not go to France, Britain, Germany, Ireland, Sweden, Denmark, The Netherlands, Belgium, Baltic ports, or Norway south of Bergen; but the Mediterranean and Black Seas, the Pacific and Indian Oceans, and all ports in Africa south of the Canaries were still open. The shipment of arms, ammunition, and implements of war on American ships to belligerent ports in the Pacific was prohibited.

Most of the other provisions of the Act were virtual continuations of provisions in the Act of 1937. The President still had the right to find that a state of war existed between foreign nations, but Congress by concurrent resolution now had the same right as well. The Act prohibited travel by Americans on belligerent vessels, the arming of American merchant vessels, and loans to belligerents. It regulated the solicitation and collection of contributions for the belligerents, continued the National Munitions Control Board in operation, and gave the President discretion to close our ports to submarine and armed merchant vessels.

Within two days after the enactment of the Neutrality Act, a delicate question arose as the United States Lines, controlled by the Maritime Commission, sought to transfer nine of its merchant vessels to the registry of the Republic of Panama. Under such registry they would not be subject to the Neutrality Act provisions.

Admiral Emory S. Land, chairman of the Maritime Commission, telephoned me on November 6 to ask my opinion. After he indicated that the President had given his approval, I said that this transfer was a function of the Maritime Commission; that no question of foreign policy was involved; therefore the State Department had nothing to do with the proposed transaction except to say that if any of the vessels had trouble abroad it must not call on the Department for aid.

As I received further information, however, indicating that the ships would continue to be American-owned and operated, although flying the Panamanian flag, I quickly changed my mind. I telephoned Admiral Land the next morning and said I was individually opposed to the proposed transfer in the light of the facts as I understood them. I added that I was naturally anxious to preserve the absolute integrity of every phase of the Neutrality Act. It was now clear to me that the transfer to Panamanian registry of ships which would still operate out of United States ports and be owned by an agency of the United States Government, was a subterfuge to escape the provisions of the Neutrality Act which could not but have unpleasant repercussions on the administration of the Act as a whole.

At a press conference later in the morning I said: "As more of the facts pertaining to the reported objectives of the applicants for this transfer of flag came to me, I did not feel favorably impressed with them, and I assumed an attitude of opposition to the proposal. I am extremely desirous, as I know every official is, of preserving the absolute integrity of every phase of the Neutrality Act, and especially the combat area phase of it, so that there cannot be even the appearance of any steps or any course that might negative that policy."

The President was at first disposed to let the proposed transfer go through, but as I made clear my attitude that, while the United States ships could legally be transferred to Panama, we were morally violating the Neutrality Act, he came around to my viewpoint. He said at a press conference that he did not think we ought to put any sister American Republic into a position that was different from our own position. On December 11 the United States Lines withdrew its application.

Somewhat analogous to this problem was another submitted to us— whether the Maritime Commission could sell its laid-up merchant ships to belligerents. Britain and France were interested in purchasing them. I called a meeting of my associates on December 8, and we agreed that a neutral Government could not sell ships to a belligerent Government without violating its neutrality. A neutral Government, however, could sell ships to private purchasers, who in turn could sell them to a belligerent, provided they were not outfitted for service with the belligerent's navy.

I stated my position on the sale of American ships in a letter to Senator Bailey, chairman of the Committee on Commerce, on January 22, in answer to his request for comments on a bill introduced by Senator (later President) Truman to prohibit the transfer of American vessels to foreign registry or to any foreigner during the period of application of the Neutrality Act. I pointed out that, under our program of building many new ships, shipowners would be faced with the necessity of disposing of older or slower vessels. I said I saw no objection to the sale of such vessels provided it were bona fide and not made for the purpose of evading the Neutrality Act.

"I wish to call to your attention," I said, "the possible effect of the bill on the commerce of the United States with belligerent countries and with neutrals located within the Combat Area. The withdrawal from these trades of a considerable number of American vessels has made it difficult, in many instances, for shippers to obtain space for their exports. It appears to me that bona fide sales of American vessels of the character indicated above to foreign operators would be highly desirable in instances where such sales will make additional cargo space available to American exporters."

I approved the sale of eight vessels of the United States Lines to a private corporation in Belgium, on condition that the Congressional leaders of both parties in both Houses concurred, and on the understanding that the State Department would not support any claim for damages for injury or loss of any of the ships. The ships were to fly the Belgian flag and to have majority Belgian ownership.

We likewise agreed to the sale of privately owned American ships to the British and to the French, although in each case we asked assurances from the British and French that the vessels would not be used as cruisers or to commit hostilities against another belligerent.

I had one domestic preoccupation over the sale of so many American ships; namely, that it might weaken our merchant marine. For many years, dating from my early Congressional period, I had been a proponent of a strong American merchant marine, and I had spoken to this effect in the House. I felt that, as a great exporting and importing nation, we should be less dependent than we were on the merchant marines of other countries. In response to my inquiries, officials of the Maritime Commission, which handled the sale of the ships, assured me that no vessel was being sold which was not old and slow, that replacement tonnage had been provided for, and that our position as a great mercantile marine power would not be weakened.

Now that the new Neutrality Act had opened the arsenal of the United States to Britain and France, we naturally expected that those countries soon would place large orders here—but such was not the case. France's orders remained substantial, but Britain's were comparatively negligible, averaging around $2,000,000 in exports per month. The Chamberlain Government was proceeding slowly to amass armaments, did not want to disturb British industry, and wished to conserve its dollar balances. Britain was still making geography the cornerstone of her preparedness—the existence of the English Channel between herself and the Continent; just as a large section of the American public was making geography the cornerstone of its thinking—the existence of the Atlantic Ocean between us and Hitlerism.

It was not until May, 1940, when the Western democracies were in mortal danger, that Britain began placing large orders for arms. Many precious months had been wasted.

49: New War and No Peace

OMINOUS DEVELOPMENTS in northeastern Europe were drawing our anxious attention while Congress debated the neutrality bill. Russia was engaging in a wide movement to outline new strategic borders for herself along the Baltic. She was evidently seeking to increase her protection against foreign nations; but an estimate of the military situation disproved that it could be the Allies, to whom the Baltic was forbidden by German might. Obviously Stalin was still preoccupied over Germany, placing no more trust in Hitler's word contained in the non-aggression agreement of August, 1939, than did the Allies.

While we could sympathize with Russia's efforts to protect herself against Germany, we were anxious lest her moves lead to an extension of the European conflict. We had been unsuccessful in preventing the outbreak of war in Europe, but we were still resolved to use what influence we could to keep the war from spreading to other countries and areas. Having received, on September 4, 1939, an appeal from General Franco, head of the Spanish Government, that the conflict should be localized, I quickly had a reply prepared, and published this the following day. The Government of the United States, I said, "fully shares the conviction that extension of the present conflict is bound to result in untold suffering for the innocent populations of the countries which may become involved, as well as for the people of other nations." I pledged that this Government "stands prepared to use all of its influence in the future as it has in the past for the restoration and the maintenance of peace between nations."

Far from peace coming to Europe, however, it was becoming clear that Russia's moves to set up a protective zone beyond her old frontiers were likely to spread the war farther. After her agreement with Germany she was like a catfish lying in the mud waiting for anything to come along. At the end of September and October she was able, without using military force, to bring the small Baltic states of Estonia, Latvia, and Lithuania within her orbit. Through a variety of pressures, she induced them to grant her a number of strategic bases, and stationed 20,000 troops in each of the three countries. Since nominally Estonia, Latvia, and Lithuania retained their governments and independence, there was no diplomatic step we felt called upon to take.

The same pressures, however, did not work in the case of Finland. That doughty little nation gave every evidence of fighting rather than yielding. She accepted the same type of invitation that had been extended to the other Baltic states, to send her Foreign Minister to Moscow for discussions; but her acquiescence ended there. The proverbial sympathies of Americans for the "underdog" were with little Finland, and they appreciated Finland's unique determination to pay her debts to this country; but we hesitated to inject the United States into the dispute. I felt that in doing so we might very well aggravate rather than resolve it. And I did not wish to alienate Russia, feeling that at some future time she might veer away from her apparently close relationship to Germany.

When Finnish Minister Hjalmar Procopé sought a promise from me on October 5 that we would say something to the Soviet Government in the event Russia made demands on Finland, I said to him that this would not be within the function of our Government, although we were always interested in the well-being of the people of Finland.

Procopé came back to me again on October 7 and urged that we say something to the Soviet Government to discourage any objectionable acts by the Russians against Finland.

"Regardless of our genuine friendship for your country," I replied, "we are not in position to project our Government into political controversies between two other countries. Even if we were so disposed and should undertake to send a message to Moscow, it would probably become public and then more harm would result both to Finland and to the United States than any possible good, on account of the unfavorable reaction Russia would have toward Finland in these circumstances."

The Scandinavian countries, Sweden, Denmark, and Norway, also were becoming alarmed over the Soviet advance into the Baltic. Swedish Minister Boström saw me on October 10 just before I left for New York City to deliver an address to the National Foreign Trade Convention, and said he had instructions from his Government to speak to me about the difficult situation that would arise if Russian demands seriously threatened the independence of Finland. I reiterated my belief that American intervention at Moscow might do more harm than good.

After I left for New York, Boström received a message from Crown Prince Gustav Adolf of Sweden for the President, urging Mr. Roosevelt to use his influence in Moscow to counteract any possible attempts of an aggressive nature toward Finland. When Boström presented this to the President, the latter replied that his influence in Moscow was just about zero. The Minister commented that the President's influence could not be zero anywhere in the world, and again urged him to send a message to Stalin.

The President finally agreed in principle and said he would talk it over with me as soon as I returned. Shortly thereafter, he received a similar appeal from the President of Finland. Also, Swedish Minister of Foreign Affairs Sandler expressed his hope to American Minister Frederick A. Sterling on October 11 that the United States, as the world's greatest neutral power, might see fit to influence the Soviet Government to discontinue its expansion into the Baltic. The President thereupon drafted a telegram himself to be dispatched to Moscow and sent it to the Department with the request that it be brought to my attention as soon as I got back.

When I saw it I drafted two alternate paragraphs and sent the cable back to the President with my comment that, whatever was done, I thought it very undesirable that the fact of sending such a cable be given any publicity. The President returned the telegram with this notation: "OK'd as amended by C. H. Rush triple priority. F. D. R." The telegram went out to Moscow on the evening of October 11.

As I feared, however, a "leak" occurred. Too many persons of other nationalities, in addition to the White House and State Department, knew about it. On October 12 we were forced to issue a short press release that we had expressed to Russia our "earnest hope that nothing may occur that would be calculated to affect injuriously the peaceful relations between Soviet Russia and Finland." It was essential to show to the Russians that we were not lining up with the Finns against them, since such an impression would deprive our step of any effect whatever.

Five days later we received a reply from President Kalinin of Russia. It was polite, and it said that Russia would recognize Finland's independence, but it did not enter into the question of Russian demands on Finland.

Meantime King Gustav of Sweden had invited the Kings of Norway and Denmark and the President of Finland to meet with him in Stockholm on October 18, largely to consider the rights and interests of the northern neutrals. Obviously they would also discuss the Finnish crisis. Four days before the conference was to meet, Argentine Foreign Minister Cantilo suggested that the Presidents of all the American Republics address telegrams of support to the King of Sweden in about the same terms. In conformity with this suggestion, the State Department drafted a telegram for President Roosevelt which went to King Gustav on the 18th. It said that our Government joined with the other American Republics "in expressing its support of the principles of neutrality and order for which the nations represented at the Stockholm Conference have, throughout their history, taken a consistent stand."

Our relations with Russia were now unfortunately complicated by an incident to an American freighter, *City of Flint*. The ship, carrying a mixed cargo to Britain, was captured on October 9 by the German pocket battleship *Deutschland*. The Germans put aboard a prize crew and took the ship to Tromsö, Norway, on October 21. After two hours in port to take on water, the *City of Flint* departed on order of the Norwegian Government, and entered the Russian harbor of Murmansk on October 23.

The following day I cabled Ambassador Steinhardt in Moscow that, under the rules governing maritime warfare, a prize ship could be brought into a neutral port only on account of unseaworthiness, stress of weather, or want of fuel or provisions, and must be required to leave as soon as the circumstances that justified its entry were at an end. Failure to leave obliged the neutral country to release the ship with its original crew and to intern the prize crew. I instructed Steinhardt to say to the Soviet Government that the United States Government assumed that such action would be taken at once, since failure to act would compromise the neutrality of the Soviet Government as announced in its note of September 17 to us. I wanted him also to ascertain the whereabouts and status of the American crew.

On October 25, after the Soviet authorities had failed to give us adequate information concerning the ship's status, I suggested to Steinhardt that he send a member of his staff to Murmansk. Also, if the Russians continued to withhold information from us, he should hint that there would be some connection after all between the treatment that foreign vessels might expect to receive in our ports and the treatment our ships were given in a foreign port.

Steinhardt was unable to make contact with the American crew by telephone or to get permission to charter a plane to send a member of the Embassy to Murmansk. The Soviet Government on October 26 issued a statement that the *City of Flint* was being released on condition that she leave Murmansk immediately.

I cabled Steinhardt on October 27, communicating to him a report from Berlin that the German prize crew would sail the *City of Flint* to Germany. I instructed the Ambassador, if he found this report to be true, to inform the Soviet Foreign Office that Russia's action had occasioned this Government considerable surprise.

On October 28 the *City of Flint* left Murmansk in charge of the German prize crew, with the American crew aboard. It was obvious to us that our pressure in Moscow was being counterbalanced by German pressure and that Stalin's predominant desire at the moment was to keep on friendly terms with Hitler.

Three days later I sent a cable to Steinhardt for the Soviet Foreign Office, in which I said that the Soviet Government's attitude toward the American Government and its representatives in the Soviet Union had been "the cause of astonishment to both the American Government and the American people." I requested an explanation.

The Soviet Government replied on November 4 with a series of somewhat specious explanations. Ambassador Steinhardt commented that, while the Soviet memorandum contained distortions and inaccuracies, it was probably the best that could be obtained in writing, and recommended that no reply be made. We had good reason to believe that the real explanation of the Soviet course of action was that it was collusion with Germany. We made no reply.

Meantime the *City of Flint* had put into the Norwegian port of Haugesund on a false pretext. This time the Norwegian authorities, on December 3, interned the German crew and freed the vessel in charge of her American crew.

The incident, occurring during the neutrality debate in Congress, was important in that it helped the supporters of new legislation which would repeal the arms embargo and set up combat zones into which American ships could not go. And it was also important in emphasizing the lack of cooperation to be expected from the Soviet Government at that delicate period of its relations with Germany.

The negotiations between Russia and Finland were proceeding during the course of the *City of Flint* incident, but they were going badly. The Soviet demands for frontier changes and for the cession of island bases in the Gulf of Finland were regarded by Finland as likely to impair her independence. The negotiations broke down on November 13, and relations between the two countries rapidly worsened. On the afternoon of November 28 Ambassador Bullitt telephoned me from Paris that the Soviet Union had just denounced its nonaggression treaty with Finland and would attack Finland in the immediate future. He suggested that if our Government could do anything in the circumstances we had better do it quickly.

I took this up at once with the President, and we decided to extend our good offices to Finland and Russia to compose the dispute, if they were willing. I accordingly dispatched a message to Moscow and Helsinski in which I said our Government was following with serious concern the intensification of the Finnish-Soviet dispute, and added: "It would view with extreme regret any extension of the present area of war and the consequent further deterioration of international relations. Without in any way becoming involved in the merits of the dispute, and limiting its interests to the solution of the dispute by peaceful processes only, this Government would, if agreeable to both parties, gladly extend its good offices."

Finland welcomed our offer, but Russia felt there was no occasion for good offices. On the following day, Stalin unleashed his attack on Finland, including the bombing of several cities.

We were bitterly disappointed at this further outbreak of hostilities. The President, after we had talked it over, made a strong press statement the day after war began, in which he said: "All peace-loving peoples in those nations that are still hoping for the continuance of relations throughout the world on the basis of law and order will unanimously condemn this new resort to military force as the arbiter of international differences." He also addressed appeals to Finland and Russia to refrain from bombing civilian populations.

Ambassador Steinhardt in Moscow cabled me that, when he presented this appeal to Foreign Commissar Molotov, the latter categorically denied that Soviet air forces had bombed civilian populations or unfortified cities or had any intention of doing so. (Our Legation in Helsinki had cabled us a number of instances of Soviet bombings of open cities.) Steinhardt said he received the impression, during his conversation with Molotov, that the Foreign Commissar did not want third-party mediation, and that Russia began the war in order to liquidate the Finnish question at the earliest possible moment and be free for developments in the Balkans and Black Sea area or from the direction of Germany.

We now decided to extend to Russia our moral embargo on the export of airplanes, already in effect with regard to Japan. The President, on December 2, issued a statement in which he recalled the policy of our Government and people of wholeheartedly condemning the unprovoked bombing and machine-gunning of civilian populations from the air, and added: "This Government hopes . . . that American manufacturers and exporters of airplanes, aeronautical equipment, and materials essential to airplane manufacture will bear this fact in mind before negotiating contracts for the exportation of these articles to nations obviously guilty of such unprovoked bombing." This moral embargo went beyond the one in effect against Japan in that it applied also to materials essential to airplane manufacture, obviously embracing a wide range of products. I cabled the President's statement to our Embassy in Moscow and our Legation in Helsinki.

We also asked American companies that had engineers in Russia having anything to do with the Soviet airplane industry to bring them back to the United States. The Soviets at first tried to impede the departure of these men, but vigorous representations made by Ambassador Steinhardt, on my instructions, facilitated their exit.

Subsequently, on December 15, the State Department, at the request of the President, extended the moral embargo to include aluminum and molybdenum.

The President and I early decided not to apply the Neutrality Act to the Russo-Finnish conflict. As a Government we could not send arms to Finland; but we did not wish to prevent the sale of arms by private exporters, if they desired. Furthermore, our shipping was already prevented from entering the Baltic by the combat zone proclaimed for the European war. Finally, we still wanted to refrain from making Russia a legal belligerent. I could not but feel that the basic antagonisms between Communist Russia and Nazi Germany were so deep, and Hitler's ambitions so boundless, that eventually Russia would come over to the side of the Allies. We had to be careful not to push her in the other direction.

We did, however, take a few modest steps in aid of Finland. The Treasury, on the President's instructions, placed Finland's last payment ($234,693) on her debt to the United States in a separate account, to await Congress's approval of its restitution to Finland. The Export-Import Bank extended $10,000,000 in credits to Finland for the purchase of agricultural products in this country.

Further than that we did not feel able to go. I was opposed to the sale of arms by our neutral Government to a belligerent government, as being a violation of international law, and I also had in mind the political capital that might be made by opponents of the Administration out of such a transaction.

The unhappy state of our own relations with the Soviet Union was exemplified by an incident at the beginning of December. Ever since we had established relations with Russia in 1933, our consular officials there had been subjected to numerous restrictions which we should not have thought of applying to similar foreign officials in this country. Their movements were curtailed, they were kept under surveillance, and their baggage was searched as they arrived or departed.

Finally we decided to see whether an instance of the same treatment applied on this side might not call the attention of the Russians, more emphatically than diplomatic protests, to their neglect of the usual courtesies. When the Soviet Foreign Office requested a laissez-passer (a document that would exempt the bearer from customs examination) for a new vice consul going to New York, Ambassador Steinhardt in Moscow replied that we should be glad to issue one if we could have assurances that in future the Soviet Government would issue similar documents to American consular officers desiring to enter or leave the Soviet Union. The Soviets refused. Steinhardt then suggested that when the vice consul arrived in New York, his baggage should be searched by custom officials.

This was accordingly done. Thereupon, on December 7, Ambassador Oumansky telephoned Assistant Secretary Messersmith and protested vigorously. He was informed that the baggage of the vice consul had been examined because the baggage of American consuls entering or leaving Russia was examined, and it was our practice to apply the principle of reciprocity.

Oumansky contended that questions of this kind should be handled on the most-favored-nation principle. This meant that the Soviets would treat our consuls as well as they treated the consuls of any other country, and we should treat their consuls as well as we treated the consuls of any other country.

The Ambassador was informed, however, that this Government had handled such matters for many years on the basis of reciprocity, meaning that we would treat Soviet consuls as well as the Soviets treated our consuls.

Oumansky thereupon asked us to ascertain, on his behalf, whether it was the custom of his Government to examine the baggage of our consuls entering the Soviet Union. In response to our request, Ambassador Steinhardt sent us a list of such instances.

Since the President was interested in this exchange, I sent him a memorandum prepared by Messersmith. On December 22 he replied:

"Your memorandum of December sixteenth in regard to Soviet restrictions against American citizens connected with the Diplomatic Corps is excellent, and I think we should match every Soviet annoyance by a similar annoyance here against them.

"When it comes to the larger questions of downright rudeness on the part of Stalin, Kalinin, or Molotov we cannot afford to repay such rudeness with equivalent rudeness over here. But I am inclined to think that the day may come soon when it will be advisable to bring the situation to the direct attention of Oumansky. He can well be told that the failure of his Government to answer my telegram regarding bombardment of citizens and the failure of his Government to let our Ambassador communicate with the *City of Flint* tend to show such a complete disregard for the ordinary politeness and amenities between civilized governments that the President honestly wonders whether the Soviet Government considers it worth while to continue diplomatic relations. We need go no further than this, but it would put a certain burden on the Soviet Government itself."

We got this idea across to the Russians, but there was no swerving them from the attitude of suspicion toward all foreigners they had inherited from many generations of Russian officials.

These minor irritations from Russia continued to rankle in the President's mind. After I had sent him a cable from Ambassador Steinhardt informing us that long-distance calls could no longer be made from the Embassy in Moscow except by personal appearance at the central telephone station, he wrote me this memorandum on January 10, 1940:

"I am wondering whether we might apply the same rule to the Russian Embassy here—or at least tell Oumansky we are thinking of doing it. What is sauce for the goose might well be sauce for him too!"

A later cable from Steinhardt, however, indicated that this difficulty had been straightened out.

Although we did not hesitate to speak up to Russia when the occasion required, I still made it a basic policy to retain as good relations with the Soviet Union as possible, and never to give her the slightest impression that we were either a present or a potential enemy. The door was always wide open to friendship, and I was willing to meet Russia at least halfway.

As the Russo-Finnish War was about to come before the League of Nations, Ambassador Bullitt in Paris, on December 1, asked the President and me to urge Britain and France to take a strong stand against Russia at Geneva. I replied to Bullitt on December 4 that the President and I shared to the full his indignation at the Soviet attack on Finland and had not hesitated to express this feeling both in public statements and more concretely by such measures as the moral embargo on the sale of airplanes to Russia. But, in fairness to others, I said, we could not assume the responsibility of urging Britain and France to pursue a given course of action in their capacity as members of the League. We were not members of the League, and we could not urge Britain and France to take an action we could not take ourselves. In fact, I concluded, the President and I both felt that at the present moment we had to be especially careful (in view of strong isolationist sentiment in the United States) to avoid connection with any political developments either within the League or contemplating the use of the League. After I had drafted this telegram, I sent it to the White House for approval or disapproval, and it came back with the President's "O.K., F. D. R." On December 14 the League Assembly expelled the Soviet Union.

The Russo-Finnish War went on amid the snows of the North, with Finnish heroism converting the Soviet's expected walk-over into a desperate three months' battle.

Even though the conflict added two more to the list of warring nations, Europe throughout the waning months of 1939 was replete with rumors of peace moves. The period of stalemate following the collapse of Poland offered tilled ground for both rumors and gestures toward peace. These were of interest to me because invariably they linked the United States with the movements supposedly in course.

As early as October 2, 1939, American Minister Gunther in Bucharest cabled me an expression of deep interest by the Rumanian Foreign Minister in the possibility that the President might be considering a peace initiative. I cabled him the next day that no such move was being contemplated, and that we had received no indications that any of the belligerents desired us to make one.

Hitler, in an address on October 6, made vague proposals in the direction of peace—naturally a peace that would leave him in possession of most of his gains in the war, as well as Czechoslovakia and Austria. Following this speech, Ambassador Joseph E. Davies in Belgium cabled the President and me that he had been asked by a high source—later revealed to be King Leopold—to say that only the President could avert a German assault on Western Europe, and Belgium hoped that the President might make another effort like those he had made during previous crises.

The same day, October 7, Alexander Kirk, our Chargé in Berlin, cabled that someone close to Hitler had conveyed the thought that the

President might use Hitler's speech as the occasion to send a confidential message to him endorsing his "efforts toward peace" and seeking clarification of his bases for establishing peace. Two days later Kirk cabled that a German press spokesman said that Germany would certainly accept from the President a suggestion for a truce and negotiations toward peace and intimated that Germany might take part in a conference somewhere far removed from the war theater—which some interpreted to mean Washington.

Then the following day came a dispatch from American Minister Schoenfeld in Helsinki, conveying a suggestion from the Finnish Foreign Minister that the United States might take the initiative in exploring the possibilities of peace.

As a result of this influx of cables, all along the same line, I called a meeting of my associates in my office on Sunday October 8. I invited Norman Davis to take part, as I not infrequently did when I had special need of his sage advice and long experience. We had already had intensive discussions among ourselves as to whether there was any reasonable move the United States could make at this time to restore peace to Europe.

During this Sunday conference we went over the draft of a possible United States proposal. In it we would ask the belligerents to state their peace terms; we would offer to act as intermediary to transmit communications on this subject to the opposing belligerents. After much exchanging of views, I said I did not believe any useful purpose would be served by a peace move by the United States at this time. With Hitler in possession of most of Poland, it was as obvious that he would not make peace by withdrawing from Poland as it was that the Allies would not make peace by agreeing to his possession of Poland. Further, would Hitler give up Czechoslovakia and Austria, or would the Allies make a peace that confirmed those acquisitions? Again, could the Allies agree to any peace that would leave Hitler and the Nazi regime intact in Germany? Could they feel any security in Hitler's guarantees, when Hitler so often had broken his word?

With Hitler the victor thus far, any move toward peace we might make could not but benefit him and discourage the Allies. We should not be warranted in pressing Britain and France to make peace on such terms. Our very suggestion of peace to Britain and France would put them on a wrong footing. If they accepted, they would have to agree in large part to Hitler's terms; if they refused, they would incur the blame for having rejected peace.

I said to the conference that we should watch our chance and perhaps later there might be an opportunity to be of service for peace. My opposition to a peace move at that time was confirmed by the adverse reception given a joint Belgian-Dutch effort a few weeks later.

Our decision not to act did not prevent the peace rumors from continuing. It seemed to us that many of these rumors emanated from Germany, and were designed partly to create the impression that Hitler was always ready for peace, and partly to confuse the Allies with alternate peace rumors and invasion rumors.

Chargé d'Affaires Kirk cabled from Berlin on November 5 that Hjalmar Schacht had indicated he would like to come to the United States, ostensibly to make a nonpolitical address, if he were assured of being received by the President so that he might present his ideas on how to settle the European conflict. Kirk also reported that other similar efforts of an entirely unofficial character had recently come to his attention; but he warned against giving them too much significance, saying that the final decision on peace and war continued to rest with Hitler.

Schacht's move appeared to us to be part of a general effort by the German Government to establish contact with other governments through unofficial agents who appeared to be acting entirely independently of the German Government and, in fact, in some ways in opposition to it. We agreed that, if we were formally approached on Schacht's proposal, we would reply that we had no more objection to Dr. Schacht's coming here to make a nonpolitical address than we should have to anyone else; but there could be no official sponsorship of his trip, and no official contacts such as he had in mind could be arranged.

When King Leopold of the Belgians suddenly went to The Hague and joined with Queen Wilhelmina of The Netherlands in offering his good offices to end the war, Ambassador Davies cabled the President and me on November 7 that their move had been prompted by information that Germany would invade the Netherlands on November 9. Dutch Minister Dr. Alexander Loudon called on me on the 9th. Very wrought up, he conveyed a message to the President and me from his Government to the effect that the neutrality of The Netherlands and of Belgium might be violated in a matter of days, even hours. The President sent King Leopold and Queen Wilhelmina messages on November 11 expressing his friendship but making no commitments.

Then on December 14 Ambassador Bullitt cabled me from Paris a statement to him by Alexis Léger, of the French Foreign Office, that Mussolini was seeking to bring about a premature peace that would preserve the Nazi regime in Germany and thereby protect his own regime in Italy. Léger believed that Mussolini wanted to return to the basic principles of the four-power pact among Britain, France, Germany, and Italy which the Italian Premier had proposed in 1933.

Meanwhile the President had been talking over with us a project to establish some kind of relations with the Vatican. In early July, nearly two months before the outbreak of the war, Welles and I had discussed the advantages that might be gained through such relations. We felt that the Vatican had many sources of information, particularly with regard to what was occurring in Germany, Italy, and Spain, which we did not possess. At my suggestion, Welles wrote a personal letter to Ambassador Phillips, in Rome, asking his opinion. Phillips replied on July 19, recommending diplomatic relations, and suggesting that a Protestant be named as the American representative. Welles sent this letter to the President.

In conversations with the President I cautioned that we could not send a regular Ambassador to the Vatican and should have to limit ourselves to a personal representative from himself to the Pope. I favored Phillips's suggestion that this representative should be a Protestant. Great Britain had followed the procedure of naming a Protestant as her Minister to the Vatican, with a Catholic as first secretary of the Legation. I also said that, if he took this step, he should simultaneously enlist the similar cooperation of the American leaders of other churches.

Ambassador Phillips in Rome had cabled me on September 25 that the Vatican newspaper *Osservatore Romano* had carried a full and objective report of the President's neutrality message to Congress. I sent this to the President for his information.

The President then sent me on October 2 a long memorandum, which began with: "This is a wholly original thought with me, and I have discussed it with no one else." He prospected the probability that when the war ended, whether "soon, next summer, or three years or five years from now," there would be a very large number of refugees, Christian as well as Jewish, coming from many countries, including even England, France, and Italy.

"I am wondering, therefore," he continued, "if you and I should not begin the consideration, *while the war is still on*, of discussing the whole subject with the Vatican and with the representatives of the Federal Council of Churches in America and some similar organizations in Europe.

The contact with the Jews has already been made through the Myron Taylor Committee.

"But a contact with the Catholic Church ought to be made directly with the Vatican itself, because this question is of infinitely more importance to European Catholics than to American Catholics.

"It is my thought, therefore, that while there is no particular reason for haste, we might give consideration to sending at a later date a special Minister or Ambassador on *Special Mission to the Vatican,* in order that we could have a direct system of communication covering the subject of European Catholic refugees."

The President said he thought his idea would put the whole refugee problem on a broad religious basis, "thereby making it possible to gain the kind of world-wide support that a mere Jewish relief set-up would not evoke."

He ended his memorandum with: "You might think this over and talk with me about it at your convenience."

In his memorandum the President based his suggestion of a diplomatic representative to the Pope solely on the refugee question. He did not mention the aspect, which later assumed great importance to him, that the Vatican would be a factor in obtaining peace.

On October 10 he sent me another memorandum in which he referred to Ambassador Phillips's communication on the *Osservatore Romano*'s reporting of the President's neutrality message to Congress: "For various reasons I think it would be a good idea for you to telegraph something along the following line to Phillips: 'Will you at your convenience intimate to the Papal Secretary of State that the President has been made very happy by the impartial printing of American news in the *Osservatore Romano?*'" I sent Phillips a cable to this effect on October 11, and on October 20 received a cable from him expressing the Pope's gratification at the President's message.

After some weeks of soundings at the Vatican, I cabled Phillips on December 23, informing him of the text of a Christmas letter to the Pope from the President which would be made public on the following day, and of the President's intention to announce the appointment of Myron C. Taylor as his representative to the Vatican. The original letter was given to the Apostolic Delegate in Washington through Archbishop (now Cardinal) Francis J. Spellman of New York. The President sent similar letters to Dr. George A. Buttrick, president of the Federal Council of the Churches of Christ in America, as a Protestant leader, and to Rabbi Cyrus

Adler, president of the Jewish Theological Seminary of America, as a Jewish leader. A more suitable selection than Mr. Taylor could not have been made. He possessed wide intelligence and unusual common sense. In addition to his work at the Vatican he became one of the moving spirits in our work of initiating and developing the outlines of a proposed world peace organization.

The President said to the Pope, in part:

"It would give me great satisfaction to send to you my personal representative in order that our parallel endeavors for peace and the alleviation of suffering may be assisted.

"When the time shall come for the reestablishment of world peace on a surer foundation, it is of the utmost importance to humanity and to religion that common ideals shall have united expression.

"Furthermore, when that happy day shall dawn, great problems of practical import will face us all. Millions of people of all races, all nationalities, and all religions may seek new lives by migration to other lands or by reestablishment of old homes. Here, too, common ideals call for parallel action."

Pope Pius expressed to the Sacred College of Cardinals on December 24 his deep gratification at the President's appointment of a representative to him, saying it was a worthy and promising contribution to his desire for a just and honorable peace and for more effective alleviation of the sufferings of the victims of war.

Myron Taylor sailed for Europe in February, 1940, and our new relations with the Vatican began. It developed that the Pope had the same realistic approach to the problem of peace in Europe as ourselves, and was determined not to put forward ideas for settlement unless a peace could be won that would last. That time was not to come until Germany lay in shambles.

As Taylor's conversations at the Vatican got under way, the President conceived the idea of sending representatives also to the Mohammedans and to the Greek Orthodox Church. He addressed a memorandum to this effect on March 27 to Assistant Secretary Berle, who had been handling the question of our relations with the churches, and asked him to talk it over with me. The President thought of appointing Lincoln MacVeagh, our Minister to Greece, to go on a special mission to visit the Patriarchs of the Greek Orthodox Church and discuss questions of peace with them. He also thought we might send another envoy for the same purpose to contact the Moslem leaders in Turkey, Saudi Arabia, Egypt, Iraq, and Iran.

In studying this proposal at the State Department, we quickly perceived that it would result in numerous difficulties. Before entering any tunnel I wanted to be sure where I was going to come out. The Greek Orthodox Church in Rumania, Bulgaria, and Greece was so closely identified with those Governments that an appeal to the Patriarchs would inevitably carry political connotations. As for the Moslems, the largest Moslem population in the world was in India, where the Hindus were in majority. An appeal to the Moslems alone could not be made without offending the Hindus, and an appeal to either or both might result in their utilizing it to force the independence issue with the British, to the embarrassment of Britain, then engaged in a death struggle.

Turkish Ambassador Ertegün, whom we consulted, informed us that sending a representative to the Mohammedan church at Istanbul would raise delicate questions for the Turkish Government, which had been trying to play down the political functions of that church, and might be made use of by other powers, particularly Italy.

Moreover, the adherents of the Greek Orthodox and Mohammedan churches in the United States were only a small fraction of the adherents of the Protestant, Roman Catholic, and Jewish religions. The Greek Orthodox and Mohammedan churches were not consolidated under single leaders, and approaches would have to be made to numerous leaders, with the possibility of offending some of them.

In view of these many considerations, the President abandoned his plan.

50: Japan Awaits Her Chance

IT WAS FORTUNATE for the United States, Britain, and France that the outbreak of war in Europe coincided with a government crisis in Japan. Four days before Hitler plunged his forces into Poland, the Japanese Government of Premier Hiranuma fell, and on August 30 the Emperor approved a new cabinet headed by General Nobuyuki Abe. The Hiranuma cabinet had fallen as a result of the German-Russian nonaggression pact, which Hitler concluded without consulting the Japanese Government. The latter was sufficiently annoyed to protest to Berlin against what it regarded as a violation of the Anti-Comintern Pact, aimed at Russia. Japanese surprise and indignation were acute at the fact that Russia was now freer than before to act in the Orient, if she wished. The cabinet fell because it had not prevented this situation from arising.

Japan, accustomed for decades to taking advantage of every European crisis, was therefore engrossed with domestic difficulties at the moment when another golden opportunity unfolded. Furthermore, it was possible that the anger felt in Japan toward Hitler might incline General Abe, the new Premier, to adopt a more conciliatory attitude toward the Western democracies.

I cabled Grew on August 30 that we should, for the present at least, refrain from any direct attempt to influence Japanese foreign policy. Efforts to influence the Japanese at that juncture of events in Europe and in Tokyo might be misunderstood by them, I pointed out, and there was greater likelihood of Japan's attitude toward the United States and other powers improving if Japan were left to her own deliberations and not subjected to any suggestion of advice, threats, or blandishments by this country.

As the European War broke out, Great Britain was intensely alarmed lest war soon follow between herself and Japan. On August 29 the British Embassy sent us an *aide-mémoire* informing us that instructions had been sent to the British garrisons in China to avoid any possibility of conflict with the Japanese. Britain rightly believed that the comparatively small forces she had in China could offer no effective resistance to the far larger Japanese forces and that any attempt to do so would bring on a major conflict. The *aide-mémoire* asked us whether, in the event of war between Britain and Japan, we would approach the Japanese Government to arrange for the welfare of British civilians in China and, if British troops laid down their arms, to obtain their internment under United States auspices. It also asked what our plans in China would be in that event.

We replied on September 4 that we could not say in advance what would be our general attitude. We shared Britain's view that small Occidental armed forces could not effectively resist the Japanese, and that any effort at resistance would lead to a full-scale war. We expressed our willingness, in case war between Britain and Japan came, to approach the Japanese Government for the welfare of British civilians in China and the internment or safe evacuation of British troops in China under our auspices. We would suggest to our own civilians that they withdraw to places of less danger; but we felt that in such a war the need for American troops in China to protect Americans would not be diminished, and these troops would continue to protect Americans unable or unwilling to withdraw.

The following day Japan asked Britain and France, in effect, to get out of China. The Japanese Foreign Office handed notes to the British, French, Polish, and German Ambassadors stating Japan's belief that the presence in China of naval vessels and troops of the European belligerents "might result in unfortunate incidents and in a condition of affairs ill adapted to Japan's noninvolvement policy." The Japanese Government therefore proffered its "friendly advice" that these powers withdraw their naval vessels and troops from China "as a voluntary act" and offered to assume the protection of the lives and properties of their citizens.

Since Britain and France were the only belligerents that had troops in China, the notes were obviously intended to apply to them. Handing identical notes to Germany and Poland was mere camouflage. The same note was also given to our Embassy in Tokyo with the request that it be communicated to the United States Government for "its information."

Here was Japan's first act in taking advantage of the war in Europe. We had had every reason to expect such an act. It inaugurated a long series, which eventually culminated in the attack on Pearl Harbor.

I believed it essential to make our attitude clear to Japan at once in view of her message. It was obvious that Japan, in communicating to us her note to the belligerents, hoped we would follow the "friendly advice" given to the European powers. Less than twenty-four hours later I cabled Eugene H. Dooman, our Chargé in Tokyo (Ambassador Grew was on leave) suggesting he point out to Foreign Minister Arita "that it is your opinion that any action on the part of the Government of Japan to force the withdrawal of armed forces of France and Great Britain in China from that country would be interpreted in the United States as a direct step toward the elimination of Western influence from China; and that in the United States the consequent reaction as regards Japanese-American relations would certainly be seriously prejudicial."

The following day, September 7, I called Japanese Ambassador Horinouchi to my office and said I was genuinely surprised to receive a copy of the notice given by Japan to Britain and France. "The advice given," I said, "directly affects rights and interests of the United States." I made it clear that at Shanghai the various powers stationing troops there had common responsibilities for the protection of the lives of their citizens and for the maintenance of order. "The fact that some of these powers have become belligerents in other parts of the world," I continued, "affords no more sound a basis for advice by Japan that they withdraw their forces from Shanghai than would the fact that Japan is engaged in hostilities afford a basis for advice by some other powers to Japan that Japan withdraw her forces from the same area. Withdrawal of the British and French forces would create a situation fraught with extreme difficulties both for Japan and for the United States." I mentioned that no such demands had been made by any power in 1914, at which time Japan was a belligerent.

"The purpose behind the Japanese notice to the British and French," I concluded, "is not a mere innocent, friendly one, but a purpose further to exclude first one set of nationals of another country, and then another set of nationals of still another country. Shanghai is international. For several other powers to be forced out would mean to the United States that all powers are being forced out. The American Government cannot and does not admit any right of any power to force it out. In the light of all the circumstances, how does your Government expect us to prevent the Congress and the country, if we should attempt to do so, from taking up the question of our monetary and financial and trade relations with your country and dealing with them in a way that you can well imagine?"

Horinouchi made no defense but quietly suggested that Japan through friendly motives was giving this notice to avoid possible friction in China. I replied that we could not possibly give the notice this interpretation. I asked Horinouchi to obtain the reaction of his Government to the statements I had made to him.

Naturally the British and French were in constant consultation with us to state their views and learn our position. The British were clearly disposed to follow the Japanese "advice." Being heavily involved in war in Europe, they understandably did not want to run the slightest risk of war with Japan at the same time. The French were inclined to follow their example.

We could not tell the British and French what they ought to do, but we made it clear we ourselves intended to stand firm. On September 11 we communicated to the British Embassy that it was one thing to yield positions and to submit to impairment or destruction of rights in the presence of overwhelming force, and quite another thing to capitulate to threats or to sign away rights. We said that, although we had already commented adversely to the Japanese on the "advice," we wondered whether there was really any necessity to make a specific reply. There were three possibilities: to say Yes; to say No; or to make no reply at all. Making no reply at all would leave the Japanese guessing and keep the question open.

Ambassador Bullitt cabled me from Paris on September 13 that the British Government had informed the French Government that, whatever might be the policy of the Japanese Government, the Japanese army in China desired to provoke conflict with Britain and France and wanted to reach an immediate agreement with both Germany and Russia. The British were apprehensive lest any day bring action by the Japanese army in China which would set off war between Britain and France on the one side and Japan on the other. Therefore the British desired to use the excuse of the floods which had rendered their barracks in Tientsin uninhabitable, to withdraw from that area, and likewise desired to get their gunboats on the Yangtze River out at once.

Bullitt also quoted information of the French Foreign Office that the Germans were working with some success to bring the Soviet Union and Japan together. Those powers, having engaged in a bitter undeclared war along the Outer Mongolian border during the spring and summer of 1939, did sign an armistice on September 16 to end the fighting.

We at the State Department did not believe, however, that Japan would be able to reach a sufficiently strong agreement with Russia to enable her to turn her full force against Britain and France. On the contrary, it seemed to us that the German-Russian nonaggression agreement, by freeing Russia from preoccupation on her western borders at least for the time being, would enable her to give more attention to her eastern frontier and thereby render her a greater danger to Japan than before. This was one reason for Japan's resentment over that agreement. Even if

Germany launched an attack in the West against Britain and France, Japan would still not be ready to move against those democracies, because Russia would then be freer than before to act. Japan was also heavily engaged in China and likewise had to bear in mind the effect that war against Britain and France would have on the United States. We knew that the Japanese previously had intended to blockade Shanghai and Hong Kong just as they had blockaded Tientsin, but had abandoned these plans. This abandonment, we believed, owed much to Japan's fear of Russia and to the very frank talks I was having with Japanese Ambassador Horinouchi.

I had my second long talk with Horinouchi on September 15. I reminded him that we had publicly stated that our policy had been to remove our guards from China as soon as Chinese authorities could preserve order. Also that we had been about to take this step when Japan invaded China. While the armed forces that the United States and other Governments maintained in China were there primarily for guard purposes, I added, any undue insistence on their removal bordering on duress would make them a symbol of their respective nations. The psychological effect of this would be much more important than any small benefits Japan might acquire by forcing the moving of the guards.

I informed Horinouchi that on the previous day, when Under Secretary Welles was leaving for the Panama Conference, the President and I had given him special instructions that in any resolutions we presented, absolute equality of industrial rights and opportunities should be preserved and kept open as heretofore to Japan, Germany, Great Britain, France, and all other nations of the world alike. "Why is it," I asked, "that your Government does not pursue this spirit as well as this policy and make it known to all so there can be no misunderstanding?"

At this the Ambassador straightened up in his chair. But he offered no particular reply except that he understood my idea.

"My Government," I concluded, "cannot bring out its guards on the basis of an unwarranted suggestion or threat by another Government."

The Ambassador agreed to take up my observations with his Government.

British Ambassador Lothian came to my office on September 19 to communicate his Government's views, as contained in an *aide-mémoire* he handed me. Britain, confronted with a grave situation in Europe, wanted to avoid friction elsewhere, and was therefore disposed to withdraw her garrisons, at least that at Tientsin, in the near future. If, how-

ever, we would adopt an attitude which would contribute to the common
interests of our Governments, and we felt that the withdrawal of the
British garrisons would weaken that position, Britain would reconsider.

I gave Lothian the substance of my last conversation with Horinouchi. I said we had promptly made earnest representations to the Japanese Government at every stage of its invasion of China touching all
violations of our rights and interests and those of our citizens. "We have
not yielded one inch in asserting our rights or in controverting the opposing contentions of the Japanese," I said.

We handed the British Embassy an answering *aide-mémoire* on
September 27, stating that we had concluded that the armed forces we
now maintained in China should remain there and we therefore did not
expect to withdraw our forces from the points where they were now
stationed.

Lothian came to see me on October 20 and gave me an *aide-mémoire*
informing us that Britain had decided to remove her guards from Tientsin and Peiping, but had no intention of withdrawing from Shanghai.
When he asked me how we felt about Britain's decision, I said it was not
remotely the function of my Government to offer advice to his Government, especially in view of the very unusual circumstances both in Europe
and in Asia.

I reiterated our own intention to keep our troops in Tientsin, Peiping, and Shanghai regardless of whether other governments removed their
guards. "If we remove our guards," I said, "it will have a depressing effect
on China, an encouraging effect on Japan, and to some extent a depressing
effect on Britain and France, likewise on other parties to the Nine-Power
treaties having interests in the Far East."

I informed Lothian that the United States might endeavor further
to bolster China's economic position by making additional purchases of
commodities from her and by establishing credits through the Export-
Import Bank, and that we were discouraging private capital from cooperating with Japanese interests. I said I hoped the British Government was doing likewise. The Ambassador said that the Burma Road
into China would be kept open by his Government.

In November Britain and France announced the withdrawal of their
troops from North China, leaving only skeleton forces at Tientsin and
Peiping. We continued the strength and location of our troops unchanged.

To convey our general views on the Far East to Japan with as much
resonance as possible, we made use of the return of Ambassador Grew to

Tokyo in October. During his visit to Washington, Grew had gone over the whole situation with the President and me at great length. We agreed that after his arrival in Tokyo he should deliver an address to the America-Japan Society, whose membership embraced important Japanese. At the State Department we gave considerable study to the text of the address, for it is always a delicate matter for an Ambassador to make a frank public speech in the country to which he is accredited. We wanted it to be a straightforward exposition of Grew's sampling of American public opinion, without being so direct that it would boomerang.

Grew delivered his address on October 19. "American public opinion," he said, "strongly resents some of the things that Japan's armed forces are doing in China today, including actions against American rights and legitimate interests in China. On that subject public opinion in the United States is unanimous." He pointed out the difference between what the Japanese public understood by the "new order in East Asia," and what Japan's actions in China were showing it to be to the American public. Finally he said: "The many things injurious to the United States which have been done and are being done by Japanese agencies are *wholly needless*. We believe that real security and stability in the Far East could be attained without running counter to any American rights whatsoever."

Grew's address had generally a good reception. Shortly thereafter the new Foreign Minister, Admiral Kichisaburo Nomura, who was to be the Japanese Ambassador in Washington at the time of Pearl Harbor, opened a series of discussions with Grew to settle American-Japanese differences. Simultaneously there was a letting up of Japanese bombings in China and incidents involving Americans, and Japan indicated that the Yangtze River would be reopened to foreign traffic. Nevertheless, a troublesome old question still confronted us: To what extent could the Japanese Government control the Japanese military? And to what extent was the Japanese Government itself sincere?

At about this time we received a proposal from Chiang Kai-shek that a conference be called to bring about a settlement of the Far Eastern situation, or to be a preliminary to taking economic measures against Japan if Japan refused to agree. The proposal was in a letter written by the Chinese Generalissimo before the outbreak of the European War and brought to the President by W. W. Yen, former Chinese Minister to the United States. Chiang said China relied on the United States to offset Japan in case of a European war.

Having received a copy of Chiang's letter in advance, the State Department prepared a memorandum for the President to use when he received Yen on November 2. We stated our belief that until Japan's military leadership became convinced of the necessity of modifying its objectives and altering its methods, action by our Government toward bringing about an adjustment of the Sino-Japanese conflict through diplomatic processes would be inopportune. Such an adjustment could be achieved only through assisting Japan to acquire legal title to some portion of what the Japanese armies had seized by force and were by no means sure of holding. We also believed that a conference called as a preliminary to economic measures against Japan would serve little or no useful purpose, especially in view of the preoccupation of other Powers with military operations in Europe and prevailing uncertainties over current diplomatic moves and developments.

At that very moment the Japanese Government was striving to set up a puppet Chinese Government in Nanking, under Wang Ching-wei, formerly an important associate of Chiang Kai-shek. The Japanese Embassy informed us on November 7 that Japan expected the new regime would become "stable and independent like Manchukuo." Japan did not expect us to give it legal recognition, but hoped that, as a solution to many difficulties, we would cooperate with it. The implication was that, if we wanted to carry on business in China, we had better deal with Wang Ching-wei.

I thereupon cabled our position to Grew on November 13. I said that the proposed regime would be a purely artificial creation. Its existence would depend upon Japanese armed support. It would lack any spontaneous or genuine broad support by the Chinese public. It would be designed primarily to serve the special purposes of Japan. This, as in the case of the regimes established by Japan in Manchuria, Inner Mongolia, Peiping, and Nanking, would deprive Americans and others of long-established rights of equal opportunity and fair treatment in China.

As Japan continued to mull over the idea of the Wang Ching-wei regime, I cabled Grew again on January 8, 1940, that, if Foreign Minister Nomura brought the question up with him, he should say: "The proposed new regime would seem to be designed primarily to serve the special purposes of Japan and would operate toward depriving the people and the Government of the United States, and the peoples and Governments of other third countries, of enjoyment of—or even opportunity to enjoy—various long-established rights in China which are legally and justly theirs."

When Japanese Ambassador Horinouchi saw me on January 31, 1940, I brought up the question myself. "It is currently believed," I said, "that this Nanking regime is being organized by Japanese military forces with the result that it will be conducted, as in Manchuria, altogether for and in the interests of Japan and at the expense of other nations."

The Ambassador rather mildly denied this would be the case, but he did not seem to me to be convinced of his own denial. I replied that the Japanese Government could in short order, if it wished, make clear to the world its position—but so far it appeared to have no real disposition, of course, to do so.

After months of hesitation, Japan finally installed the Wang Ching-wei regime at Nanking in March. I issued a public statement on March 30 that we would continue to recognize the National Government of Chiang Kai-shek at Chungking, which we believed still had the allegiance and support of the great majority of the Chinese people. "In the light of what has happened in various parts of China since 1931," I said, "the setting up of a new regime at Nanking has the appearance of a further step in a program of one country by armed force to impose its will upon a neighboring country and to block off a large area of the world from normal political and economic relationships with the rest of the world."

The installation of the Wang Ching-wei regime had all the results we expected. Japan used it as a cover to freeze out American and other national interests in China. She also used it as a buffer to counter the merited protests made against such discrimination. She argued that such matters should be taken up directly with the Wang Ching-wei regime, and that difficulties would be smoothed out if we recognized that regime as the Government of China. The Axis powers found no difficulty in recognizing Wang Ching-wei, but the puppet regime gained no headway with the Chinese people, and at the time of Pearl Harbor was still an effigy of straw and Japanese bayonets.

Because our 1911 treaty of commerce with Japan was to expire on January 26, 1940, a large portion of our conversations with Japan toward the end of 1939 dealt with the situation that would follow the end of the treaty. Foreign Minister Nomura suggested the negotiation of a new treaty or the signing of a modus vivendi to take the place of the old treaty until a new one could be negotiated. Japan was worried as to what action we would take when the 1911 treaty ended.

We obviously could not agree to negotiate a new treaty unless Japan completely changed her attitude and practice toward our rights and interests in China. To do so would be to condone what Japan had done, and would prevent our having the freedom of action toward Japan we needed in the event Tokyo continued its policy of discrimination and hostile actions against Occidentals in China. It would encourage Japan to proceed still further in China, convinced that we intended to take no action against her.

We had reached our decision at the State Department by December 11, on which day I sent the President a memorandum. I pointed out that, when the treaty with Japan expired, discriminatory tonnage duties on Japanese ships and discriminatory import duties on goods brought to the United States in Japanese ships could be levied. The President, however, had authority to suspend such duties by proclamation as to a country that did not impose similar discriminatory duties on our vessels or their cargoes. The absence of such a proclamation would result in imposing the duties.

I said further that, since Japan did not at present discriminate against our shipping to Japan, we believed that imposition of discriminatory duties should continue to be suspended. "However," I said, "it does not seem wise under present conditions to issue a proclamation declaring such suspension. Such action would quite probably be interpreted as a formal and significant declaration by this Government that Japan is in general not discriminating against our trade, and that we have in contemplation no action against Japanese trade when the treaty terminates."

Our solution, therefore, lay in the fact that a similar proclamation with respect to Japan, issued by President Grant in 1872, was still in effect. We recommended that this proclamation be allowed to stand and no new proclamation be issued. The Treasury Department and other Government agencies could treat the matter as one of routine, pointing out that only one phase of our commercial relations with Japan was involved, and that the mere termination of the treaty did not change existing practices.

The President approved this recommendation.

I laid down a basic statement of our position in a cable to Ambassador Grew on December 18, 1939. I pointed out that our Government regarded as an essential prerequisite to any new commercial treaty negotiations the advance understanding that nondiscriminatory treatment be made the basis for our commercial intercourse. Furthermore, our Government examined not only the policies and practices of a country within its own territory, but also its policies and practices as they affected American trade with other countries. Substantial and continuing discrimination against our commercial interests brought about by that country in some third country were obviously injurious to the United States.

Ambassador Grew, on the same day, cabled a suggestion that we should offer a modus vivendi or an approach to negotiations as a means of supporting the Japanese Government against the Japanese Army. We could make ratification of the treaty depend on Japan's carrying out her promises. Grew argued that the Japanese Government was endeavoring to meet our protests regarding China and needed support. If we rebuffed the Government we would not discredit the Japanese Army but rather would furnish the Army with powerful arguments it could use in its own support. He thought a favorable reply from us would be far more likely to bring further Japanese steps toward meeting our protests on China than would result from a rebuff.

Three days prior to Grew's telegram, British Ambassador Lothian had come in to see me. He said his Government was very much concerned about the Japanese and Far Eastern situation. Japan might make terms with Russia, or she might do injury to British interests and rights. Consequently his Government felt that no opportunity should be overlooked to compose the situation in Asia by making terms with Japan.

"Japan," I replied, "might be a little slow to go in with Russia at a time when all the nations of the world except Germany are so embittered against Russia on account of her attack on Finland. While there is always a possibility that Japan and Russia might enter into a temporary alliance for each other's mutual advantage in Europe and Asia—agreeing to a truce as to their long-view differences—yet it is very doubtful if such a temporary alliance will be reached."

I said that the United States had striven in every possible way by word and act to induce Japan to agree to a reasonable settlement in the Far East and to adhere to the basic policy of equality of industrial and commercial rights and opportunities. "But Japan," I concluded, "has no serious disposition to enter into a settlement based on the fundamentals of American rights and interests in the Far East, but is intent only on a policy of 'Manchukuoizing' China. Japan is willing only to make a victor's or strict Japanese peace, from the standpoint of the military group. My Government could not consider such a policy."

Lothian did not press the matter further.

We ourselves were willing to give the Japanese Government every opportunity, as Grew suggested, to increase its strength in contrast to that of the Army. We were not convinced, however, that the Tokyo Government was any less interested than the Army in building up a greater Japan ruling the eastern half of the world. Previous Japanese Governments had not lagged many steps behind the Army in staking out claims to an overlordship of the Orient. The Tokyo Government appreciated more keenly than the Army the difficulties it was getting into with the Occidental nations, because it, rather than the Army, had to try to negotiate away those difficulties. But some of the strongest statements of Japanese ambitions had come straight from the Tokyo Government itself.

Moreover, Japanese Governments were fragile affairs. Just about the time we got to understand a Japanese Government, it would fall and be replaced by another. The Army was almost always too strong for the Government, and if the Government's policies, domestic and foreign, did not suit the Army the Government got into trouble. From the time I entered the State Department until Pearl Harbor, Japan had no fewer than twelve Foreign Ministers and ten Premiers. These included, of course, some returns of the same men to office, following periods of retirement. The Government of Premier General Abe which we were trying to encourage fell on January 14, 1940, and was succeeded by a government formed by Admiral Mitsumasa Yonai, itself destined to last only six months.

I cabled Grew on December 20, after showing the message to the President and getting his "C. H.—O.K.—F. D. R.," that we concurred in his view that it would not be advisable to return a categorical negative to Foreign Minister Nomura which would close the door to further discussions and discourage the efforts of the Japanese Government. But at the same time we were not in position to commit ourselves now to entering upon negotiations. As to Grew's suggestion that a treaty be negotiated, and that ratification be held up until Japan carried out certain assurances, we felt this would be likely to produce more potentialities of misunderstanding and disadvantage than would a treatyless condition. As to a modus vivendi, we preferred to leave our attitude open for the time being.

On the immediately practical side—what would happen to Japanese exports to the United States after January 26, 1940—I pointed out we had received numerous queries on this point. We were replying that the absence of a commercial treaty did not of itself cause an interruption in commercial relations. The expiration of the treaty would not in itself produce any changes in the general customs duties or treatment applicable to Japanese exports to the United States. Similarly, there should be no marked changes in the general customs duties or treatment applied in Japan to imports from the United States. Grew should communicate this to the Japanese Foreign Office.

In conformity with our view, the Treasury two days later issued instructions to collectors of customs advising them that the 10 per cent discriminating duties under the Tariff Act of 1913 would not be collected on Japanese imports.

When January 26, 1940, arrived, therefore, commerce with Japan continued as before. We were thus able to accomplish the various purposes we had in mind. We did not apply discriminating duties against Japan, and we thereby gave the Japanese Government opportunity to strengthen itself, if it could, as against the Army. We did not affect adversely the trade of our importers and exporters. At the same time we put our trade relations with Japan on a twenty-four hour basis, and Tokyo knew that we now had legal freedom to impose any commercial restrictions we wished in the event of further Japanese violations of our rights. Tokyo was still kept guessing.

We took one action, however, which directly affected Japan when on December 20, 1939, we applied a moral embargo to the export of plans, plants, manufacturing rights, or technical information required to produce high-quality aviation gasoline. No specific country was mentioned, but the embargo was applied because Japanese interests had negotiated with an American oil company for the purchase of plans and specifications for a high-octane gasoline plant to be erected in Japan. This embargo was in line with the embargo announced by the President on December 2 against the export of any materials used in airplane manufacturing to countries engaged in bombing civilian populations.

Japanese Ambassador Horinouchi brought in to me on January 6 a written protest against this embargo. I asked him if he wanted a written reply. He said, Yes. I remarked that he no doubt knew that the embargo on all items entering into airplane manufacture and use originated in the Japanese bombing of civilian populations in China. I said I would probably list a great number of these bombings as reported to my Government and allow them to be published with the contents of my note of reply.

Horinouchi appeared startled. He brought up Japan's contention that the embargo violated the 1911 treaty. I replied, without going into the

merits of Japan's argument: "I trust your Government will not forget
how many times American commercial rights and interests have suffered
injury in China contrary to all treaties and all law. Notwithstanding this
fact, my Government and others perhaps are expected to be perfectly
quiescent while being deprived of their right to participate in economic
and other undertakings in China, although the Japanese Government expects to enjoy the benefits of the rule of equality in its economic dealings
with all the Western world."

I sent a formal answer to Ambassador Horinouchi on January 27.
As I had indicated to him, we included in the note a long list of Japanese
bombings in China. "The Government of the United States," I said, "concerned as it is with the increase and spread of war and the use or threat
of force in so many parts of the world, has recently felt constrained to
conserve vital interests which this Government has in certain commodities and technical processes relating to the national defense." I rejected the
contention that our moral embargo had been a violation of the 1911
treaty.

Six months after the outbreak of war in Europe, Japan was still
waiting to see where her best advantage lay. She was heavily engaged in
China, fearful of Russia, and uncertain of what our next action might be.
We had hedged on none of our principles and had resisted every pressure
stoutly. Yet we had left the door open to Japan if she wished to enter into
honest negotiations. The bridges to war or to peace were still intact.

51: Trouble with Britain

ON THE DAY 1940 began I made public statement of my outlook for the year, in response to numerous requests for my views as to what the twelve months would bring. I did not pretend to know the future, but said I was sure there were few men and women in the world in whose hearts and minds fear and apprehension did not mingle with hope.

In this statement issued four and a half months before Hitler's invasion of the Low Countries and France and three and a half months before his invasion of Norway and Denmark, I said: "The fear and apprehension derive from the possibility that the black shadow of violent warfare, under which the world enters upon the year 1940, may grow blacker yet in the months to come. . . . Along hundreds of miles of frontier there now stand embattled, forces that may be unleashed at any moment and make a shambles of great civilized areas."

The hope, I said, sprang from the profound conviction, common to millions of men and women everywhere, that there was no inevitability about war; also that, "in the onward march of civilized man, the forces of freedom and progress in the end do triumph." But, I warned, "in the grave crisis through which mankind is passing now, this may not happen until after a period of ruthless and unnecessary destruction of life and treasure."

I pointed out to our own people that, "if the warfare now in progress on other continents becomes intensified, its effects will fall more and more upon us, as well as upon those directly engaged."

At that point I gave expression to a program that was to form one of the pillars of our foreign policy throughout the war. "If peace should come," I said, "we shall be confronted, in our own best interest, with the vital need of throwing the weight of our country's moral and material influence in the direction of creating a stable and enduring world order under law, lest the relations among nations again assume such a character as to make of them a breeding ground of economic conflict, social insecurity, and, again, war."

In other words, while trying to keep out of the war, we would insist on being in the peace. Thus, exactly four months after Hitler invaded Poland, I made clear my belief that, when the war ended, the United States must take her full share in the responsibilities of a new world

731

order—"a stable and enduring world order under law." This goal obviously meant a world organization.

I had already been giving deep thought to the nature of the world when the fighting should be over. I recalled that, during the First World War, I had sought to forecast the economic effects of the conflict and had suggested an international conference to establish a new system of liberal world trade. Now my thoughts were both political and economic.

I realized that one of the most essential requisites for United States participation in a world organization was to prepare our people for it well in advance. It would not do to wait until the war was over and then suggest that we enter such an organization. Moreover, we had to take our share in the formation of such a society; we could not simply wait until other nations had founded it and invited us to enter. In my statement I had emphasized the vital need to use our influence toward "creating" a world order under law, not just joining in.

From that time forward I never ceased to stress to our people as strongly as I could the necessity for assuming our full responsibility as a great nation in working toward a new world order.

Exactly one week after issuing this statement I announced the establishment of a committee in the State Department to study and analyze the measures and policies issuing from both belligerents and neutrals during the war "which may have consequences of an enduring nature upon our country's foreign relations once peace is established." We had begun preliminary work on this committee as early as September, 1939. I appointed Welles chairman, Hugh Wilson, former Ambassador to Germany, vice chairman; Counselor R. Walton Moore as chairman of the Subcommittee on Disarmament, and my special assistant, Leo Pasvolsky, as chairman of the Subcommittee on Economic Problems.

The work of the committee quickly expanded until it embraced active planning for a postwar organization. Because of the importance of our postwar policies and planning, leading up to the creation of the United Nations organization, I am giving to them a separate section (Part Eight) of these memoirs. It is important at this point only to show how early we realized at the State Department the necessity for postwar planning and the equal necessity for the United States to take her full share in the peace and after.

Two days after my New Year's statement I went to the Capitol to hear the President deliver his message to Congress. We had worked with him on its foreign affairs section. He earnestly strove to show to isolationists in particular and the nation at large that the war had already deeply affected us, again proving that we could not live happily and prosperously, as a self-contained unit, inside a high wall of isolation. As for the future he said: "We do not have to go to war with other nations, but at least we can strive with other nations to encourage the kind of peace that will lighten the troubles of the world, and by so doing help our own nation as well."

The war was, in fact, providing us with numerous problems and, unfortunately, many involved disagreements with Great Britain over our neutral rights on the high seas. I had sought, beginning with my conversation with British Ambassador Lothian the day after Britain declared war, to lessen the impact of such differences on our general relations with Britain. Inevitably, however, some points of friction were bound to arise as belligerent Britain and neutral United States gave diverging interpretations to points of international law.

This diplomatic conflict soared to a climax in December, 1939, and in the first months of 1940, when I handed the British Government a series of notes of protest. These dealt with the examination of American mails, the diversion of American ships to British ports for search, the blockade of German exports, and the detention of American shipping in the Mediterranean area. Our shippers were rightly objecting that our ships were being detained as much as three weeks in British ports while being examined to see if they contained contraband articles ultimately destined for Germany.

We stated our belief that cargoes moving from one neutral to another were presumed to be legitimate, whereas the British seemed to follow the theory that all such commerce was obliged to prove its innocence to British authorities before being allowed to proceed to its neutral destination.

Our establishment of combat areas into which American ships could not go was in direct conflict with the fact that the British took our ships into these very areas for examination.

Our public opinion soon became keenly stirred. It was particularly aroused when the British took an American ship, the *Moormacsun,* to Kirkwall, Scotland (within the combat zone), for examination in January, 1940. This reaction prompted Winston Churchill, as First Lord of the Admiralty, to send a message to the President that he had given orders that no American ships were to be diverted into the combat zone thereafter.

British censorship of American mails proved a lively focus of contention. We admitted Britain's right to censor mails normally passing through the United Kingdom for transmission to their final destination, but refused to admit her right to interfere with American mails on American or other neutral ships on the high seas or to censor mail on ships that were forced by British warships to enter their ports.

Britain contended that both parcel and letter post were being used to convey contraband and military intelligence to Germany, and that the only way to uncover them was to examine the mails.

In some instances we paralleled our protests to Britain with similar protests to France growing out of like violations of our rights.

While insisting on what we regarded as our rights, we still were careful not to exacerbate relations with Britain. I felt that Britain's great trial of strength lay within the coming months. I knew that Hitler, not Britain, had started the war, and that a German victory would be dangerous to the best interests of the United States. Hence it would be poor policy to arouse public opinion in the United States against Britain at the very time when Hitler was obviously preparing his mighty armada for an assault against her. On the other hand, in justice to our own self-respect, I could not let some of Britain's practices pass without protest and without making a strong effort to get them changed lest they inflict undue damage on American citizens and arouse a real wave of anti-British sentiment.

As an accumulation of irritating incidents between ourselves and Britain began to stir our public, I frequently talked to Ambassador Lothian most earnestly on this point. In a conversation on February 14, 1940, I emphasized these three points: "First, whatever regulations, restrictions, or new methods or policies your Government adopts during the war, my Government is particularly concerned to know that these will not be hurtful to the United States after the war; second, no blacklisting practices in this country should be carried on by your Government; third, your Government should not apply the slogan—'This is necessary to win the war'—to a great variety of minor practices that affect the United States."

Lothian came back to see me on February 23, saying that his Government and he were becoming concerned by what he said was the increasingly acrimonious state of mind in this country growing out of what were mainly minor circumstances, such as the search of mails. He seemed to have the impression that there was some kind of concerted movement here to arouse public opinion against Britain, and that this might prove very damaging, especially at a later, more serious stage of the war.

I assured him that there was no concerted effort on the part of officials in Washington to array public opinion against Britain, but I said: "Many of these small occurrences are more responsible for irritating expressions in this country, and they influence public opinion more than major considerations." I made a number of specific suggestions for changes in his Government's methods, and added: "Since you have brought up the effects of adverse opinion here on the British war situation at this stage, I'm reminded to bring to your attention the real possibilities of bad relations between our two countries some time later when the war situation may be much more serious than it is at present."

Through a process of striving to work out each point amicably, we gradually induced Britain to modify many of her practices. She gave up the censorship of mail en route from the United States to South America which touched in ships or planes at the British West Indies. She speeded up the examination of our ships at Gibraltar so as to lessen the period of their detention. She refrained from taking our ships into United Kingdom ports. She made certain exceptions in her blockade of German exports which our business people had already contracted for or vitally needed in their manufacturing.

The British and French Governments sent two blockade experts in March to work out these problems with us—respectively F. Ashton-Gwatkin and Professor Charles Rist. Our conversations lasted seven weeks, and ended in a better understanding of our difficulties. The Allied representatives promised that the restrictive measures imposed by their Governments because of the war would be entirely temporary, and that at the earliest possible moment Britain and France would return to the liberal trade principles embodied in our trade agreements program.

During these discussions we also arrived at an understanding on the difficult question of navicerts. In my conversation with British Ambassador Lothian on September 4, 1939, I had suggested this system, whereby British representatives would examine cargoes prior to their departure from the United States and issue certificates that would prevent the ships from being stopped on the high seas or taken into British ports for examination. However, I also stated my wish that the details of the system be worked out by experts of the two Governments. Moreover, we had laid down four basic conditions. These were that the navicert system should not interfere with the normal volume of our genuinely neutral exports to another neutral; it should not discriminate against the United States or our exporters; the granting or rejection of a navicert should relate solely to the character of the exports and conditions in the country of importation and not to American exporters or the United States; and a clear, concise statement of the reason for rejection should be given to the applicant for a navicert.

We also told the British that we reserved all our rights under international law, despite the navicert system, and that we regarded the system as a matter between the British Government and American exporters rather than between the two Governments.

To our surprise, however, the British put the system into effect on December 1, without our having arrived at a mutual agreement on the details of its operation. In consequence we had frequent occasion to call Britain's attention to practices contrary to our conception of what the navicert system should be—for example, when the British Embassy refused to give any explanation to an American exporter as to why it had rejected his application for a navicert.

Our discussions with the visiting British and French experts made our position clear, and on April 16 Ambassador Lothian handed us a verbal note which represented an agreement between our two Governments and adequately met our four conditions.

We had discussions with the British lasting several months over Britain's proposal that she set up a contraband control port in Newfoundland or Nova Scotia at which American ships could be examined, thus obviating their being taken into the combat zone. They proposed Halifax, but the President said he could not even tacitly acquiesce in this selection because Halifax was within the hemisphere neutrality zone proclaimed at the Panama Conference. Discussions were still in course concerning Halifax and other ports when Hitler's forces rendered the whole question academic by invading Norway on April 9, 1940. Since we immediately enlarged the combat zone, American ships were now excluded from all northern Europe, and the need for a contraband control port for them no longer existed.

By degrees, therefore, our difficulties with Britain smoothed out. Only a few months later they were blacked out by the horrifying spectacle of Britain standing desperately alone against Hitler's all-conquering legions.

52: No Peace, but a War Ends

EARLY IN FEBRUARY, 1940, the President said to me at the White House that he had been thinking of sending Sumner Welles on a trip to the major capitals of Europe to see whether there were any prospects for peace. He asked whether this would be agreeable to me.

(Some time later the President expressly stated to me that Welles had come to him secretly on several occasions and pleaded to be sent abroad on special missions. For this reason I feel satisfied that Welles had requested the President to send him on the trip in 1940, and also for the reason that the President merely inquired of me whether I had any objection to Welles's going on the mission.)

I promptly replied that I offered no objection if he really wished Welles to make the trip. However, I said I had a few observations to make.

I reiterated a view I had expressed to the President several times in recent weeks. "The critical period of the war is practically at hand," I said. "The three Axis powers have built up unprecedented armaments. Hitler, Mussolini, and Japanese spokesmen have brazenly proclaimed they are bent on unlimited conquest. They are steadily and unerringly moving in that direction, as straight as a rifle shot. And this after we, from 1933 to this year, exerted all possible efforts, within the limits of isolationist opposition, to promote peace."

In these circumstances, I continued, with the world already on fire and with the Axis powers ready and virtually in the act of leaping forward with their all-powerful military forces, further talk about peace, accompanied by a trip to the warring countries, was calculated to hold out false hopes. Such false hopes would be especially fatal to nations and peoples who should right then be feverishly preparing to defend themselves instead of sitting back in the fancied security of geographical safety or neutrality.

The deadly effect of a people being lulled into false security by continued harping on a speedy peace was well illustrated at that very time by the fact that British soldiers were singing a popular melody, "We're Going to Hang Out the Washing on the Siegfried Line." I felt certain that something ominous was working up.

I said also that five hundred different rumors would inevitably arise

737

as to the purpose and results of Welles's trip. These would create confusion in Europe and here at home.

I myself would not have considered sending Welles or anyone else of his official position to Europe on such a mission at that stage in the war. Welles's thought was that, while the "phony war" continued, some basis might be found for peace. But it was evident that Hitler was madly preparing to end the "phony war" in only one way—full-scale, violent battles—and the only way to stop his preparations was to give him everything he asked. But this meant Nazi domination of Europe and another war within a few years.

The President himself announced Welles's mission on February 9, saying that, at the President's request, Welles would visit Italy, France, Germany, and Great Britain solely to advise the President and me as to present conditions in Europe. Mr. Roosevelt, having in mind the comments I had made to him, emphasized that Welles was not authorized to make proposals or commitments in the name of the United States Government, and that statements made to him by officials of governments would be kept in strictest confidence and communicated by Welles solely to him and to me.

On the same day I announced that we had begun informal conversations with other neutral Governments. I explained that these were "preliminary inquiries relating to a sound international economic system and, at the same time, world-wide reduction of armaments." Present war conditions were not involved, but belligerent nations could be included in so far as the discussions involved these two common problems of future peace.

These conversations were part of the surveying and studying we had initiated to outline, as far as we could, the type of postwar world we desired to recommend to other nations and our own people.

The announcement of Welles's mission gave birth, as I knew it would, to scores of rumors. Despite the President's disclaimer that the mission involved no commitments on our part, many isolationists seized upon it to make the welkin ring and proclaim that we were about to involve ourselves in Europe's quarrels. Others were equally certain that Welles had a definite mission to effect a peace in Europe at any cost to the Allies or ourselves. Still others conjured up dissension between the President and me and between Welles and me. To quiet these rumors I issued a statement on February 14, saying:

"I think the President and I have agreed on policies and methods pertaining to our foreign affairs as nearly uniformly as any other two persons who have occupied our respective positions. Nothing out of the ordinary occurred in the discussions and conferences between us leading to the announcements made by the President of the special mission to Europe, and later by myself relating to the problems of economic restoration and of disarmament after the war."

I followed with a compliment to Welles.

Welles, accompanied by Jay Pierrepont Moffat, chief of the Department's European Division, visited Rome, Berlin, Paris, and London. He was able to see the leaders of each Government and Pope Pius XII and to have exhaustive conversations with them. He handed them memoranda on our economic policy, centered in our trade agreements program, which we should have liked to see adopted after the war. He received from them long exposés of their own contentions regarding the war.

Although he religiously followed the President's instructions that whatever was told him be kept in strictest confidence, a flood of rumors boiled in his wake. The rumors filled the Allies and small neutrals with dismay lest the President, on Welles's return, should make a move for peace which, at this juncture of the war, would confirm Hitler in most of his gains and render another war inevitable. Consequently the President and I agreed that he should make a speech to dispel these fears. Accordingly, on March 16, Mr. Roosevelt broadcast from the White House to the Christian Foreign Service Convocation, saying:

"Today we seek a moral basis for peace. It cannot be a real peace if it fails to recognize brotherhood. It cannot be a lasting peace if the fruit of it is oppression, or starvation, or cruelty, or human life dominated by armed camps. It cannot be a sound peace if small nations must live in fear of powerful neighbors. It cannot be a moral peace if freedom from invasion is sold for tribute. It cannot be an intelligent peace if it denies free passage to the knowledge of those ideals which permit man to find common ground. It cannot be a righteous peace if worship of God is denied."

As a further step in squelching these dangerous rumors, I sent the President a memorandum on March 18, attaching the draft of a cable I intended sending Welles, then in Rome, "as a matter of special precaution." The President wrote his O.K. in pencil on the memorandum. On the same day I cabled Welles saying that I had made clear to the press that his mission was purely a fact-finding one, that he was in no way acting as go-between from one belligerent to another, or taking part in any negotiations, that it could hardly be conceived that he would be given, either for comment or for action, any peace proposal based on threat of force or an ultimatum with a time limit, and that it was my assumption that no peace terms would be given him for any purpose other than our information. Before leaving Rome, Welles issued a press statement that he had not received or conveyed any peace proposals, and that his mission had been solely one of gathering information.

British Ambassador Lothian came to see me on March 22 to thank the President and me for what he called the prompt way in which our Government had acted to check and dispel the spread of the "peace at any price" sentiment based on all sorts of rumors about what Welles might do in Europe to bring about a negotiated peace, which would be the equivalent of a German victory. He said that efforts directed toward bringing about a negotiated peace might injure the British and French war situation. I made it clear that we had not overlooked the slightest phase of the whole question during recent weeks and had been ready to make our position clear as emphatically as we could at the proper moment.

When Welles returned to Washington at the end of March, he gave the President and me a superb report of his conversations with Mussolini, Hitler, Daladier, Chamberlain, and the Pope, and their foreign ministers. No one could have gleaned more information from them than he, but nothing he learned gave us any basis for action. The leaders he talked to offered no real hope for peace. The President issued a statement on March 29 that, even though there might be scant immediate prospects for any just peace, the information gathered by Welles would undoubtedly be of the greatest value when the time came for the establishment of such a peace. Even this statement was too optimistic, as events later proved. The time for peace did not come for five more years, and when it did come the men who in 1940 headed the Governments of Britain, Germany, and Italy were dead, and the then head of the French Government was no longer in office.

Though there seemed to be no chance for peace in Europe. one of Europe's wars—the Russo-Finnish—now reached its tragic end. A gallant little nation bowed, after incredible fighting, to the overwhelming strength of a far superior opponent.

This conflict on the fringes of northern Europe had threatened to become part of the greater war between Germany and the Allies. Britain and France would have liked to send an expeditionary force through Norway and Sweden to Finland, largely with the objective of opening up a new front against Germany in the Baltic, and of hindering Soviet exports to Germany. German pressure on Sweden, and Sweden's own desire to keep all Scandinavia from becoming a battleground, prevented the project from crystalizing, for she refused to permit passage of an Anglo-French force across her frontiers.

We on our side gave some aid to Finland, although admittedly it was far too small to enable her to resist her mighty antagonist successfully. We released a variety of military equipment for purchase by Finland. On January 16, 1940, the President wrote to the President of the Senate and the Speaker of the House recommending an increase in the revolving credit fund of the Export-Import Bank so that loans could be made to Finland, limited to the purchase of agricultural surpluses and manufactured products, not including implements of war. Congress, however, did not act until the Russo-Finnish War was about to end.

We were approached several times by the Finnish Government with suggestions that we mediate in the conflict. These were at first very vague, but on January 9, 1940, Premier Ryti stated to American Minister H. F. Arthur Schoenfeld what he had in mind. This was that the United States, together with another neutral great power, Italy, should approach the Soviet Union and Finland, offering their good offices to bring about an armistice and peace negotiations, and that the United States should invite Italy and Sweden to try to bring pressure to bear on Germany at the same time for the same purpose.

Premier Ryti agreed with us, however, that his proposal did not appear likely to bear fruit. He was disillusioned about Germany and believed that Finland had been specifically dealt with in the Russo-German agreement of August, 1939. I had already asked the opinion of Ambassador Steinhardt in Moscow, who replied he did not regard the moment as propitious for suggesting negotiations to the Russians.

I wrote to Representative Sol Bloom on February 14, to comment on a House resolution asking the Executive Branch to bring about an armistice between Russia and Finland. I recalled our offer of good offices to both countries at the end of November, and the fact that no favorable reply was received from Moscow.

"Subsequently," I continued, "the Department of State, in close collaboration with the President, has been observing with the utmost care developments in Eastern Europe in the hope that some effective way may be found by which we may be able, without departing from our traditional policy of noninvolvement in European political affairs, to assist in bringing about a cessation of hostilities between the Union of Soviet Socialist Republics and Finland. Since the outbreak of hostilities, however, we have at no time found the situation such as to cause us to believe that any move on our part for the restoration of peace between these two countries would be opportune. You may rest assured that we are continuing carefully to observe the situation in Eastern Europe, and are prepared, in case we feel that such action on our part might have a likelihood of success, to extend our good offices to the Finnish and Soviet Governments."

By the beginning of March, Finland's military position was hopeless. On March 4, Finnish Foreign Minister Tanner informed us that soundings had been going on with Russia and asked whether we would lend any help at Moscow if negotiations began. As the peace talks opened in Moscow, I cabled Ambassador Steinhardt on March 7 to see Foreign Commissar Molotov and state to him that, although our Government had no desire to intervene in the negotiations, our country was deeply interested, and a deep impression would be made on our public opinion if the Soviet Union took a generous attitude. Steinhardt was further to intimate that popular demand had been increasing in the United States for measures to promote economic relations with certain areas, and that some of these movements would depend on the degree of moderation and generosity shown in the Finnish settlement. This last was a hint that the Russians, who were keenly interested in keeping the United States as a source for certain products they were now unable to get elsewhere, could expect less economic cooperation from us if they themselves showed less cooperation in laying down the Finnish peace terms.

The Russian-Finnish peace treaty signed in Moscow on March 12 contained several harsh provisions; but at least in ending the war it left Finland an independent country, in marked contrast to the results of similar campaigns by Nazi Germany.

President Roosevelt issued, on March 13, a statement that was drafted in the State Department, saying that "the people of Finland, by their unexcelled valor and strong resistance in the face of overwhelming armed forces, have won the moral right to live in everlasting peace and independence in the land they have so bravely defended. . . . The ending of this war does not yet clarify the inherent right of small nations to the maintenance of their integrity against attack by superior force." We communicated this statement formally to both the Soviet and the Finnish Governments.

Unfortunately, the new peace between Russia and Finland was to last little more than a year.

Our relations with Russia in 1940 were influenced by the desire to do nothing that would drive her further into the arms of Germany, but at the same time to keep our exports to her within such limits as not to afford her surpluses of strategic materials that could go on through to Germany.

The Soviet Union, cut off by the war from access to a variety of strategic materials, was intent on keeping open her trade channels with the United States. She could not understand, however, why we did not in all cases receive her with widespread arms. At times she wanted the impossible. For many months she had been trying to buy a complete battleship from American shipbuilders. The President and I were willing that one should be built for her. The Russians insisted, however, that the very latest American devices and inventions should be incorporated in it. The Navy was agreeable to permitting the construction of a battleship at least as modern as those we already possessed, but was rightly unwilling to give away to the Russians all the latest secrets that American research had amassed over a period of years, some of which were being embodied in our new battleships then under construction.

I wrote to Senator Pittman on January 30 outlining our relations with the Soviet Union, in answer to a Senate resolution requesting information on whether the Soviet Government had fulfilled the obligations contained in the 1933 agreements establishing diplomatic relations between us. I pointed out that on several occasions we had had ground to believe that the Soviet Government was not fully living up to its obligations. "On such occasions," I said, "this Government has made appropriate representations to the Soviet Government. In certain instances these representations have yielded constructive results; in others, they have disclosed divergencies in the interpretation of the agreements in question."

I had a comprehensive discussion of Soviet-American relations with Ambassador Oumansky on April 2, 1940. Oumansky was one of the most difficult foreign diplomats with whom we ever had to deal. He was insulting in his manner and speech, and had an infallible faculty for antagonizing those of us with whom he came in contact. Overbearing, he made demands for concessions as if they were a natural right, and protested our acts as if they were heinous offenses. In my opinion he did much harm to Russian-American relations.

Oumansky came to see me on this occasion with a large chip on his shoulder. He began the conversation by reciting a number of so-called grievances. He mentioned the refusal of certain American companies to permit Russian engineers or prospective purchasers to inspect their plants; protracted detention on Ellis Island of Russian men and women of some prominence who had come to the United States on temporary visas; and our moral embargo. He then demanded bluntly whether this Government intended to abandon or continue commercial relations with the U.S.S.R.

I was particular not to comment one way or the other.

He then sought to make the point that the moral embargo had applied only to Russia.

I made it clear that it applied alike to all nations that engaged in bombing civilian populations.

Oumansky denied that his country had engaged in bombing civilian populations.

"We have the most satisfactory evidence of Russian bombing of civilian populations," I replied. "And I cannot convince you, any more than you can convince me to the contrary in view of the tone of your discussion of this matter."

As for exports to Russia, I said: "My Government does not know what new policy or step Russia may take at any time. For example, you plunged into fighting in Finland, to the surprise of all of us. You may take a similar step with no greater advance notice than this. In these circumstances, we are naturally conserving our shipping and our strategic and other materials for the reason that we never know when fighting in the world may call for some kind of self-defense on our part. We do propose to be ready."

Oumansky wanted to know when the moral embargo would terminate. I gave him no definite answer except to say, "We do not know when your country will embark on another war."

I asked him what kind of neutrality his Government stood for, adding that there were many shades of neutrality as practiced by some countries.

He replied that it was neutrality based on the idea of keeping out of war.

"Does this mean," I asked, "being drawn into a war contrary to the desire or purpose of your Government, or a war rising out of an aggressive action by your Government?"

He simply repeated his original statement.

Each time the Ambassador attempted to state the peaceful intentions of his Government, I tried to convey an impression of doubt on my part.

The conversation lasted nearly an hour. Oumansky concluded by saying his Government had no intention to interfere with Bessarabia, the eastern province of Rumania which had belonged to Russia before the war of 1914–1918; that Russia was slow to believe that Turkey would become party to any interference by the Allies with the Baku oil area; and that she had no designs on any portion of the Near East; but he avoided the subject of Finland and Germany.

Our relations with Russia continued unsatisfactory as Hitler's armies invaded new countries. Communists in the United States formed a strange alliance with the isolationists, sought to prove that the war in Europe was simply a struggle between rival imperialisms, and inveighed against our friendly attitude toward the Allies. For my part, I continued to refuse to believe that Stalin would go on supporting Hitler, and I felt that a drastic change in their relations was almost sure to come. I was convinced Stalin would reach no real agreement with Japan. I therefore did all I could to keep our relations with Russia on an even keel in the hope that one day we could count on the Soviet Union both in Europe and in Asia.

53: Politics and Trade

IN THE MIDST of our preoccupations with the war in Europe and the prospect of war in the Orient, a major battle confronted me at home in 1940, as we fought to extend the Trade Agreements Act for another three years. The Act was to expire on June 12, 1940.

I had begun in November and December, 1939, to lay the groundwork for what I knew would be the hardest battle our trade agreements program had yet faced. The advent of the war and the dislocation of trade that naturally followed gave opponents of the program an excellent opportunity to demand its repeal or suspension. The selfish interests clamoring for tariffs so high as to serve as an embargo wall behind which they could raise the prices of their products rallied to what they hoped would be the kill.

By now we had negotiated trade agreements with twenty-one nations. Our trade with them embraced 60 per cent of our total foreign commerce. We could show convincing proof that the agreements had increased our trade with the agreement countries above that with the nonagreement nations. In the two-year period of 1938–1939 our exports to the sixteen countries with whom trade agreements had been in effect throughout that period averaged 62.8 per cent greater than in 1934–1935, when only one agreement was in force for a year or more, while our exports to all other countries increased by only 31.2 per cent. Our imports from these sixteen agreement countries averaged 21.6 per cent greater in 1938–1939 than in 1934–1935, while our imports from other countries averaged 11.1 per cent greater.

But it was a fact that the war had brought a breakdown in the pursuit by other nations of the liberal trade policies we had so earnestly preached for so many years. The Allies, particularly Britain and France, both trade agreement countries, imposed numerous restrictions to enable them to import only the materials most vitally needed for war. Neutral countries whose trade was affected by the war took similar steps for various reasons.

I believed, however, that the trade agreements program should be retained intact to serve as a cornerstone around which the nations could rebuild their commerce on liberal lines when the war ended. The trade agreements had sufficient elasticity to enable us to meet war conditions by modifying individual agreements, if necessary, without the need to suspend the program as a whole. The principles of liberal, nondiscriminatory trade under lowered tariffs should be kept alive as a goal to which all nations could look forward when the fighting ended.

I went to Chicago to open my campaign for the trade agreements on December 5, 1939, when I addressed the American Farm Bureau Federation. "If there is anything certain in this world," I said, "it is that, after present hostilities come to an end, there will be an even more desperate need than there was in recent years for vigorous action designed to restore and promote healthy and mutually beneficial trade among nations. The fact that during the past five years twenty-one nations showed their willingness, by entering into reciprocal trade agreements with us, to modify their trade policies in a more liberal direction, offers a solid basis for the hope that, with peace regained, there will be a good opportunity for completing the work of trade restoration. That precious opportunity will be lost if we, who have in the recent past taken a position of world leadership in this vital work, should now reverse our own policy and turn our face straight back toward suicidal economic nationalism, with its Hawley-Smoot embargoes."

At the next Cabinet meeting, the President complimented me on the speech and requested the other Cabinet members to study it and to get out in active support of the trade agreements program.

For the first time since 1933 I had the feeling that the President was really behind me on trade agreements. On some occasions in the past he had taken steps, as during the Peek episode, which would have maimed or killed the program. On some other occasions he had acquiesced in my going ahead, though without too much interest or enthusiasm. On the other hand, there were also numerous instances when he had backed tariff reductions I recommended, and this in the face of opposition within our own Party and from the Republicans.

The President, accepting my suggestion, devoted an important part of his message to Congress on January 3, 1940, to the trade agreements. The Act, he said, "should be extended as an indispensable part of the foundation of any stable and durable peace. . . . I emphasize the leadership which this nation can take when the time comes for a renewal of world peace. Such an influence will be greatly weakened if this Government becomes a dog in the manger of trade selfishness."

I appeared before the House Ways and Means Committee on January 11 and before the Senate Finance Committee on February 26 to argue for continuation of the program. To the House committee I said: "In the face of grave hindrances growing out of fears of war and preparations for war, the operation of the reciprocal trade agreements program had the effect of inducing many important nations to halt their runaway races in the erection of excessive economic barriers to trade and gradually to move in the opposite direction; while still other nations were induced to slow down their efforts to attain economic self-containment. Furthermore, the program was an important factor in bringing about a development of closer general relationships with and among many nations, while it was making its important contribution to income and employment in the United States."

During the hearings all the old arguments against trade agreements were brought up, and I sought to answer them. Our opponents asserted that the Trade Agreements Act gave authority to the Executive which belonged to Congress; that in reducing duties we were hurting American agriculture, labor, and industry; and that our tariff concessions to one country were granted to other countries without any return. To these they added the argument that the war rendered the operation of trade agreements impossible. Some of them pointed out that war had come in Europe and that, therefore, any contention that liberal trade was a factor toward promoting peace was ill founded.

At the same time that I strove with Congress for the trade agreements program, I was also striving with Britain and France to continue their purchases of American products. It was natural that the United Kingdom, our best customer, should try to keep her purchases as much as possible within the Empire, because she could thereby pay for them with pounds sterling and conserve her dollar exchange for war equipment. But too sweeping an abandonment of purchases of American staple products would irritate our exporters and strengthen the arguments of those who maintained that the war had so dislocated commerce that the trade agreements were useless.

Following a British announcement that they would shift their purchases of American tobacco to Turkey and Greece, I called in British Ambassador Lothian on January 22, 1940, and expressed my genuine concern. "Increasing tension and a feeling of resentment," I said, "are steadily rising in this country due to a multiplicity of what are considered here as excesses by the British Government in prescribing and carrying out war restrictions on trade and finance. There's a feeling that your Government is ceasing to show any consideration to my Government and the people of this country." I mentioned a number of such restrictions, in addition to the British announcement about tobacco.

While I said we appreciated Britain's situation as a belligerent engaged in a terrific war for its existence, I added: "There's a steadily increasing feeling in this country that American commercial and other interests are being severely injured by discriminations and unnecessary restrictions, the effect of which will extend into peacetime, perhaps permanently, to the detriment of American interests. There's a further growing feeling that in the pursuit of these policies the British Government will soon reach a stage where the advantages of these discriminations and restrictions will be decidedly less than the bad reactionary effects in this country."

The Ambassador naturally sought to defend Britain's position by pointing to her life-and-death struggle, and the necessity for doing the things she was doing.

"That," I said, "is not the question, but whether your Government is not doing itself much more harm than good—a fact in which I strongly believe."

As a result of my discussions with Lothian, the British Government agreed to modify its decision not to purchase any more American tobacco. But there was no modifying the fact that the war had drastically changed the currents of trade.

Behind all the arguments brought forth in and out of Congress against the trade agreements was a potent political factor. The year 1940 was an election year, with the Presidential elections only six or seven months away and the national conventions only three or four months distant. Since the trade agreements were a cornerstone of the Roosevelt Administration's policy, a defeat of the trade program would be a serious defeat for the Administration.

There was also a personal factor. I was generally considered as the outstanding proponent and author of the trade agreements program. I was also regarded as a Presidential prospect in 1940, although I had taken every step I could to make it clear that I was not a candidate for the Presidency. Hence opposition to renewal of the trade agreements program was based not only on economic grounds but also on political considerations aimed at me. To kill the program would be to kill the prospect.

I shall deal with the third-term situation later.

The debate over the program in Congress was bitter to the end, and the outcome in doubt until the final vote on April 5. Had I given any indication of ambition to be President, the vote might well have been unfavorable. As it was, the measure to extend the Act another three years passed the Senate by a margin of only five votes, with fifteen Democratic Senators joining the opposition. The vote in the House was somewhat less close.

Despite the narrow margin of victory, I was personally gratified at the extension of trade agreements, because I now felt we had a better chance to have a policy and method for international commerce ready to present for the world's adherence the moment the war ended. We had not been so fortunate at the end of the First World War.

When the President signed the new Act on April 12, he issued a statement in which he said: "I was very glad that, in the course of extended hearings and exhaustive debate, the Congress subjected to a most thorough examination the objectives and the underlying principles of the program, the results of its operation over nearly six years, and the procedures used to achieve these results. The facts brought out by that searching scrutiny should leave no room for doubt in the mind of any fair-minded person that the trade agreements program has brought demonstrable benefits to our nation as a whole and to every interest directly concerned, and has not inflicted injury on any group of producers."

As the war went on, it naturally affected our export trade more and more. Sales of products that the belligerents did not deem necessary to their war production suffered, but on the other hand sales of others essential for war purposes increased. We had to suspend temporarily certain provisions of many of our trade agreements, but we kept the agreements themselves valid wherever possible. I felt that their mere existence strengthened our efforts to mitigate the adverse effects of wartime measures on our trade, and constituted a basis on which we could later build.

54: Hitler Strikes Northward

NORTHERN EUROPE HAD scarcely ceased to be an arena for the conflict between Russia and Finland when it gave setting to another battle that immediately laid even more vital problems before the United States.

For some weeks early in 1940 we had been receiving intimations from several of our missions abroad that a clash was likely between Germany and the Allies over Norway. Hitler was using Norwegian territorial waters to bring down from Sweden iron ore which during winter and early spring was taken across Sweden to the ice-free Norwegian port of Narvik. The British late in March announced they intended to take over control of Norwegian waters on the ground that Norway was unable to maintain her neutrality.

Norwegian Minister Morgenstierne—a tall man with humorous eyes, calm on the outside but seething inside throughout the crisis, who had been in the United States for a number of years—expressed to the State Department on March 28, 1940, his fear that an extension of the war to Scandinavia might very well follow. Alexander Kirk, our Chargé in Berlin, cabled me on April 2 reports that German troops were being concentrated on the Danish frontier, and that other troops were being loaded with equipment on ships at Stettin. Ray Atherton, our Minister in Copenhagen, cabled us on April 6 that a German division was to be landed at Narvik on April 9. And Norwegian Minister Morgenstierne suggested to Assistant Secretary Berle that we make diplomatic representations to support Norwegian neutrality.

Any action on our part, even had we decided to take it, was precluded by the swift onrush of events. Early in the morning of April 9 my office telephoned me that German troops had entered Denmark and were landing at Norwegian ports. A few hours later, after going over the situation with my associates, I issued a press statement that we were assembling all facts so as to decide on the extension of the combat area and the application of other provisions of the neutrality law. That night the President, who had been out of town, returned to Washington, and I outlined the new situation to him.

Minister Morgenstierne called on me the following day, and spoke bitterly against Germany. Since the British and French had sown mines along the Norwegian coast on April 8, so as to force German ore ships out of Norwegian territorial waters, I sought to obtain from Morgenstierne an estimate as to when the German expeditionary force must have sailed with relation to that action. He believed that the Germans would have been obliged to organize their expeditionary force and sail at least twelve hours in advance of the Allies' action. In a later conversation the Minister informed me that the Germans must have been preparing their invasion of Denmark and Norway some months in advance, and that the invasion must have commenced at least forty-eight hours before the British and French sowed their mines. In other words, it was Hitler's ambitions of conquest and not his reaction to the British move into Norwegian territorial waters that induced him to invade both Norway and Denmark.

That same day, April 10, the President signed a proclamation we had drafted for him extending the combat area to include Norway. We also made arrangements for the transportation of Americans in Scandinavia to the United States. The President likewise ordered the freezing of Norwegian and Danish credits in the United States to prevent Germany from acquiring them.

A proclamation applying the Neutrality Act rested for the moment in abeyance. Morgenstierne asked us on April 11 not to declare a state of belligerency under the Neutrality Act between Germany and Norway if it could be avoided. We were confronted with the fact, however, that the Norwegian Foreign Minister on April 9 had informed Mrs. J. Borden Harriman, our Minister to Norway, that he deemed Norway to be at war with Germany. On April 24 Hitler signed a decree declaring a state of war to exist between Germany and Norway, and on the same day I sent the President for his approval and signature three neutrality proclamations and an executive order relative to Norway, which he signed on the 25th. To have withheld a proclamation under the Neutrality Act in the case of Norway, when we had applied it to the other countries engaged in the European War, would have exposed us to criticism. We did not apply it in the case of Denmark, which had been occupied without organized fighting and was legally not at war with Germany.

There was no doubt as to the course we would pursue with regard to continuing relations with King Haakon of Norway and his Government. Minister Morgenstierne came to inform me on April 12 that a puppet government had been set up by the Germans in Oslo and he had been notified to take orders from it alone or be held accountable. Morgenstierne doughtily said that, instead of taking such orders, he would be entirely loyal to his regular government and would be glad to stay on here, if we had no objection.

"You will be welcome here," I assured him, "as long as you are the representative of your regularly constituted government, as at present."

We also assured Henrik de Kauffmann, the Danish Minister, that we would continue to recognize him as the representative of his Government.

We prepared at the State Department a statement for the President condemning the invasion of Scandinavia, which he issued on April 13:

"Force and military aggression," he said, "are once more on the march against small nations, in this instance through the invasion of Denmark and Norway. These two nations have won and maintained during a period of many generations the respect and regard not only of the American people, but of all peoples, because of their observance of the highest standards of national and international conduct.

"The Government of the United States has on the occasion of recent invasions strongly expressed its disapprobation of such unlawful exercise of force. It here reiterates, with undiminished emphasis, its point of view as expressed on those occasions. If civilization is to survive, the rights of the smaller nations to independence, to their territorial integrity, and to the unimpeded opportunity for self-government must be respected by their more powerful neighbors."

Hitler's invasion of Denmark at once presented us with a problem at our front door, for Denmark was the mother country of Iceland and Greenland. My associates at the State Department brought me maps showing that Greenland was wholly, and Iceland largely, in the Western Hemisphere. Therefore the islands fell within the provisions of the Monroe Doctrine. Legal Adviser Green Hackworth looked into the relations between Iceland and Denmark and found that Iceland had the right to take an initiative in government and foreign affairs if the King of Denmark were unable to act in an emergency. It was clear, of course, that the King of Denmark, a prisoner of the Nazis, could not act freely.

Whether the Danish Minister could speak for the Danish King was another question. My associates and I agreed that, in the present circumstances, he could do so, whatever the Government at Copenhagen, under the domination of the Germans, might say to the contrary. We felt there was nothing to lose if he could not, and everything to gain if he could.

Danish Minister Henrik de Kauffmann—a dignified man of great courage and integrity, married to an American—sent me a note on April

10 informing me that the Icelandic Parliament had resolved on April 9 that the Icelandic Cabinet should for the time being exercise the executive authority vested under the island's Constitution in the Danish King, and take entire charge of Iceland's foreign affairs.

Five days later the Prime Minister of Iceland, Hermann Jónasson, cabled me that his Government desired to establish a Legation in Washington and a Consulate General in New York. I replied on the following day that the "establishment of direct diplomatic and consular relations between the Government of Iceland and the Government of the United States in the existing circumstances will be welcomed by my Government." I asked the Prime Minister's approval of our opening a consular office in Reykjavik, capital of Iceland.

At about the same time I induced Secretary Morgenthau to release Iceland from the application of the order freezing Danish credits.

We had begun thinking of Iceland in relation to over-all strategy some months before the European War broke out. Jay Pierrepont Moffat, Chief of the European Division, recommended to me on April 14, 1939, the establishment of a consular office in Reykjavik, Iceland. He pointed out that Iceland lay just north of the great-circle route from Oslo and North Scotland to Labrador, and it therefore seemed likely that, in the event war came, Germany would try to establish submarine and possibly air bases there. We were already aware of the recent attempt of Germany to negotiate an aviation agreement with Iceland and of German naval, scientific, and surveying activities in Icelandic waters. We decided in principle to establish the consulate if war came. Our trade with Iceland was much too small to justify a consulate before such time.

The Icelandic Foreign Minister, Stefán Jóhan Stefánsson, replied to my cable that he heartily welcomed an American consular office in Reykjavik. On April 22 I notified the Danish Government, through our Legation in Copenhagen, that, as soon as our consulate were established at Reykjavik, our official business with Iceland would be carried on through our consulate there and Iceland's representative here, and not through our representatives in Copenhagen.

British Ambassador Lothian sent me on May 10 a note informing me that the British had landed a force in Iceland that morning to prevent the island from falling into German hands. Britain assured us that her forces would be withdrawn at the end of the war and would not interfere with the administration of the island.

Since Greenland lies close to the North American Continent, it presented a definitely American problem, and we felt that that problem should be handled by the United States. I called Lothian in on April 12 to outline our position to him. I said there had already been some propaganda by anti-British or pro-German individuals and by extreme isolationists demanding some expression of our attitude, and this would probably increase to the harm of the United States and Great Britain as well.

I recalled to Lothian that the Monroe Doctrine covered the Western Hemisphere without qualification. I reminded him that in 1916, when our Government purchased the Danish West Indies, it had recognized the right of Denmark to exercise sovereignty over Greenland. Later, when called upon to do so, Britain had stated she would agree to the same proposition, provided Denmark notified Britain in case she considered disposing of Greenland. Thereupon the United States had intervened and denied the right of any non-American power to purchase or otherwise obtain sovereignty over Greenland, to which Britain agreed.

I concluded by saying: "There is an express application of the Monroe Doctrine by the United States regarding Greenland. There appears to be no serious question about Greenland forming part of this hemisphere as contradistinguished from the European side of the Atlantic."

The following day I called in Canadian Minister Christie to go over the Greenland situation with him as I had done with Lothian. "The German forces occupying Denmark," I added, "could easily cause the Government of Denmark to issue orders about Greenland, as they could about Danish shipping throughout the world. For this reason it's important that Greenland should receive our attention under the Monroe Doctrine. My Government feels disposed to see whether Greenland needs any cooperation so that, when Denmark is restored to her own independence, her sovereignty over Greenland would automatically be reinstated." I also said we would, through the Red Cross, help the Greenlanders who were now cut off from their usual supplies from Denmark.

Three days later Christie sent me an *aide-mémoire* from his Government, written before our conversation of April 13. The Canadians said they were considering whether it might not be necessary to send a small Canadian defense force to Greenland to prevent its being used as a base for German operations, to protect the cryolite mines, and to look after the needs of the Greenlanders. Before taking any action, however, Canada would like to have our views.

On my instructions, James C. Dunn, Political Advisor for European Affairs, informed Christie that we intended to move very carefully in any action toward Greenland, since we did not wish to have any such step used as a basis for action by other Powers with regard to colonial possessions of European mother countries that might be occupied by an extension of the present conflict. Specifically, what we had in mind was the necessity to avoid any precedent that might give Japan an excuse to seize the Netherlands East Indies if Holland were invaded by the Germans. Therefore we considered it essential that no action be taken with respect to Greenland by Canada or any other country which might affect a similar situation in the Pacific. Our Government itself would be prepared to consider any aspect of the situation in Greenland that might arise.

I received a visit from Danish Minister de Kauffmann on April 19, following his receipt of a cable from the Greenland authorities suggesting the possibility of applying to this Government for protection. When De Kauffmann mentioned an American protectorate over Greenland, I promptly interrupted him by saying:

"This Government has been opposing protectorates generally, chiefly because nations engaged in military conquest are seizing smaller nations under the pretext that they are merely protecting them, whereas their real purpose is permanent domination. Naturally, nations bent on conquest are looking for precedents established by those nations that criticize and condemn their course. And by precedent I don't mean a bona fide precedent for seizure and occupation by force, but any kind of precedent that could be distorted into use for this purpose."

I sent the President, then at Warm Springs, Georgia, on April 22, a long letter outlining our position on Greenland, so that he could have this before him during the visit Canadian Prime Minister Mackenzie King was about to make him. I informed him that the Danish Minister had expressed the hope that we might find it possible to send a Coast Guard ship to Greenland to reassure the population, and that Secretary of the Treasury Morgenthau, at our suggestion, was looking into this possibility.

The Danish Minister apparently apprised the Greenland authorities of my reaction, because no request for protection came from Greenland. Instead, through an exchange of letters among the Minister, myself, and the Greenland authorities, we arranged for the establishment of an American Consulate at Godthaab, and for the dispatch of a series of Coast Guard cutters to the island.

Some three months later the Danish Government, in a cable to the Danish Minister, questioned our action in opening a consular office in

Greenland without first obtaining its approval. We knew full well, however, that, had we requested permission from the Government at Copenhagen under the domination of the Germans, it would have been refused. We informed Copenhagen that we had acted in response to a request from the Greenland authorities, deprived of free communication with Copenhagen.

The Canadian Government continued apprehensive over possible German sabotage of the cryolite mines in Greenland or the appearance of an armed force from a German raider to take possession of all or a part of the island. We solved the difficulty by accepting Canada's suggestion of May 10 that, if the Greenland authorities requested, we should sell them a gun to be mounted at Ivigtut, Greenland, to defend the cryolite mines against a raiding vessel. We thought it preferable that the Greenland authorities should make their request to us rather than to the Canadian Government.

I wirelessed James K. Penfield, who was proceeding to Greenland aboard the Coast Guard cutter *Comanche*, to make the necessary arrangements and to say to the Greenland authorities that we would help them in drawing up plans for defense of the island to be carried out by the authorities themselves, and would make the necessary defense equipment available. Shortly thereafter, the Greenland authorities having made the request, the Coast Guard cutter *Campbell* carried the equipment to Ivigtut.

The Greenland authorities, however, continued to be concerned. They were apprehensive lest a British or a Canadian force be landed in Greenland, saying they considered the landing of any belligerent armed force undesirable. On June 3 the Governors of North Greenland and of South Greenland (in Greenland they were called sheriffs, but since the title of sheriff is given to a local or county officer in the United States, and we wished to augment the stature of the Greenland authorities so as to assist them in dealing with us directly, we called them governors) handed Penfield a request that the United States land a force at Ivigtut as soon as possible. I replied to the Greenland authorities on June 5 that we had received assurances from both the Canadians and the British that they would not land troops in Greenland, and that we ourselves continued to be averse, except under exceptional circumstances, to stationing American troops at Ivigtut. However, we would give the Governors' request every consideration to see what further steps might properly be taken.

It was not until the following year, when German activities became suspiciously directed toward Greenland, that we sent troops to the island.

At the very moment that Greenland, far to the north, was drawing our attention in the spring of 1940, the United States was completing a highly important project at the opposite end of the world—the United States Antarctic expedition, commanded by Rear Admiral Richard E. Byrd. The question of sovereignty over Arctic and Antarctic regions, to which numerous nations, including our own, laid claim, had occupied the attention of the President and the State Department for several years. In the spring of 1938 Mr. Roosevelt asked us to prepare a policy study to protect such territorial rights as the United States possessed in Arctic and Antarctic regions, and Hugh Cumming, Assistant Chief of the Division of European Affairs, began its preparation. On August 30, 1938, I cabled our consulate in Capetown, suggesting procedures through which the Antarctic expedition then being undertaken by Lincoln Ellsworth could assert claims, in the name of the United States, to territory he might explore which had hitherto been undiscovered and unexplored.

While I was returning from the Lima Pan American Conference in January, 1939, the Department completed Cumming's study and sent it to the President. This stated that a number of factors warranted serious consideration of measures the United States should take to assert her Arctic and Antarctic claims. These were: the development of transarctic aviation; reports of valuable mineral and fuel resources in the Antarctic; the strategic interest of our War and Navy Departments; the measures being taken by the Soviet, British, Canadian, Australian, New Zealand, French, and Norwegian Governments to establish their polar claims more firmly; and the interest expressed a short time before by the German and Japanese Embassies in Washington in newspaper reports of possible American claims in the Antarctic.

The President on January 7 approved the Department's study, and suggested we consult with other Government departments and with Admiral Byrd and Mr. Ellsworth, with a view to getting appropriations from Congress to send out two separate South Polar expeditions each autumn. I forthwith began discussions with representatives of the Treasury, War, Navy, and Interior Departments, and with Admiral Byrd. Admiral Byrd possessed a keen mind and a strong personality. Then and subsequently I had many conferences with him.

A few weeks later, on February 13, I sent the President a recommendation that scientific parties be sent to Little America and some other point of the territory recently explored by Lincoln Ellsworth, for a year-round rather than seasonal occupation. We said this would give added legal strength to United States claims and increase the contribution of scientific knowledge to be obtained from the Antarctic.

The President requested and received appropriations from Congress, and named Admiral Byrd commander of the Antarctic expedition. The State Department drafted instructions for Byrd, which were approved by the other interested Government departments.

The Byrd expedition completed its work in March and April, 1940, after discovering eight hundred miles of coast line that explorers had been trying to find for more than a hundred years, in addition to fourteen new islands and six new mountain ranges, and 150,000 square miles of hitherto unseen area. On August 1, I wrote to the President commending Byrd and pointing out the importance of his discoveries and explorations.

To return to the northern part of the world, the question of Norwegian and Danish shipping in our ports or under charter to American citizens gave us many difficulties after the Nazi invasion of those countries. In response to an inquiry I made on April 11, 1940, Britain informed us that for the time being she was treating Danish shipping as enemy shipping and, if the Germans established a puppet government in Norway, it might be necessary to treat Norwegian shipping in the same fashion. However, the British were giving full consideration to the American interest in vessels chartered by Americans.

Norwegian shipping quickly ceased to be a problem when the King of Norway decreed the requisitioning of all Norwegian-owned ships and the establishment in London of a Norwegian Shipping and Trade Mission to control them, working in close cooperation with the British. Danish shipping, however, presented a more difficult problem.

Britain, believing that Danish shipping operating under the German-controlled Government at Copenhagen would be of service to the enemy, wanted Danish ships transferred during the war to the British flag. The Danish Shipping Committee, established in New York under the sponsorship of Minister de Kauffmann, refused. On May 22 the British Embassy sent me a memorandum promising that, if the Danish Committee agreed to the transfer to the British flag of Danish ships now in neutral ports, the British Government would meet our minimum requirements, with some modifications. Britain asked us to use our influence with the Danish shipowners and with the shipping committee in New York to induce them to accept the Allied proposals. We made it clear to both sides, however, that we had no share in the dispute, other than to see that the Americans who had interests in the ships were not injured. The unfortunate dispute dragged on, and the Danish ships remained tied up in American ports for more than a year.

In June the Department, acting on the President's behalf, arranged for the Crown Princess of Norway and her children, who had taken refuge in Stockholm, to come to the United States on an American ship. We gave them passage on the Army transport *American Legion,* which, after obtaining assurances of safe conduct from the German and British Governments, we had sent to Petsamo, Finland, to bring to America those Americans in Scandinavia who wished to be evacuated.

Our Minister to Norway, Mrs. Harriman, had also found refuge in Stockholm, after a dramatic and perilous flight from Oslo. She cabled me on May 23 that it appeared impracticable for her to join the Norwegian Government, then in the extreme end of northern Norway, and that for her to return to Oslo might be interpreted by the Germans as recognition by us that Oslo remained the seat of the Norwegian Government. She suggested that she remain in Stockholm until the situation around Narvik had clarified, saying that she had access to information in Stockholm on developments in Norway. I agreed.

After Mrs. Harriman cabled on June 1 that she was planning to join the Norwegian Government the following week, I replied that we preferred her to stay for the time being in Stockholm, because it might later be necessary that she go to Oslo to contact the occupation authorities and use her good offices as our representative to alleviate the situation there. We believed that for her to have been recently at the seat of the Norwegian Government might prejudice the German authorities against such a move.

It never proved feasible to send Mrs. Harriman back to Oslo. When the Norwegian Government took up residence in London, we arranged diplomatic representation with it there.

Our problems over Norway and Denmark, however, had already been overshadowed by the German invasion of the Low Countries and France, far more momentous and far more dangerous to ourselves.

55: Cataclysm in Europe

AT 10:50 o'clock on the night of May 9, 1940, the telephone rang in my apartment, and the excited voice of Ambassador Cudahy in Brussels informed me that heavy German air forces were over Luxemburg and flying into Belgium and were reported over The Netherlands. Cudahy informed us of large concentrations of German forces on the frontiers of Belgium, Luxemburg, and The Netherlands, and of Belgium's expectation that the Germans would attack probably at dawn.

I knew then that the cataclysm foreshadowed in my New Year's message of January 1 was at hand. The Nazi hordes were ready to plunge across new borders and tear Western European civilization to bits.

I telephoned the President, informed him of Cudahy's message, then telephoned some of my Department associates, and went to my office, arriving there soon after eleven o'clock, a little in advance of the others. I immediately put in a number of telephone calls to key European capitals. When I reached Cudahy, he informed me that Luxemburg had been invaded, that German planes were bombing the airport near Brussels, and that the Germans seemed to be attacking Belgium, Holland, and Luxemburg simultaneously.

I then requested the appropriate officials to draw up the necessary proclamations and regulations applying the Neutrality Act to Belgium, Holland, and Luxemburg. At two o'clock, saddened that the fate of Poland was now being inflicted upon other countries whose only desire was to remain at peace, I returned home and to bed, though not to sleep.

For some weeks dispatches from our missions abroad had apprised us of the probability of a Nazi invasion of the Low Countries and France. As early as April 1, Ambassador Cudahy reported to me a statement to him by the Belgian Foreign Minister that Germany planned a major offensive in the west about April 15. Alexander Kirk, Chargé in Berlin, cabled that a German offensive about the same date was possible against Holland and Belgium. Minister Gordon cabled from The Hague on April 5 that an attack against Holland was possible in the near future.

Hitler's invasion of Scandinavia diminished in no way the flow of these reports. On April 9, the day of the invasion of Norway and Denmark, Minister Gordon reported to me from The Hague that the Netherlands Foreign Office had received accurate information the previous week relative to the imminent invasion of Scandinavia, and that the same source said Germany would follow this move with a major offensive in the west. The Netherlands Government was making preparations accordingly.

On April 13 Gordon cabled me that the Netherlands seemed as close to being invaded as was possible without actual invasion. He referred to the fact that his audiences with Queen Wilhelmina in November, 1939, and January, 1940, when a German invasion had seemed in the offing, had had a salutary effect, and suggested I propose to the President that he send a message which Gordon could hand the Queen. I sent this suggestion to the President.

After getting the President's reaction, I cabled Gordon on the following day that, although I would otherwise question the advisability of our taking the initiative, he was authorized to request an audience if the Netherlands Government suggested it, since that Government was in the best position to judge the effectiveness of the Minister's previous audiences with the Queen.

Ambassador Cudahy cabled the President and me on April 18 that King Leopold had requested him to inform the President he thought it only a matter of time until Belgium would be invaded. The King asked the President to draw up a statement to be published the next time a German invasion seemed imminent declaring that the United States could not be indifferent to a violation of the neutrality of Belgium, would be deeply shocked thereby, and that the British and French were not thinking of a peace designed to humiliate the German people and to destroy Germany.

I showed this message to the President prior to his departure for Warm Springs that evening. He did not feel inclined to issue such a message at that time. I cabled Cudahy accordingly the following day, adding that we wanted to be as helpful as we could, were watching the situation closely and would like the Ambassador to keep us promptly informed of developments.

Kirk in Berlin cabled me on April 17 stressing the uneasiness of all the neutral countries anywhere near Germany, Italy, or Russia, and urging the President to notify the belligerents and their associates that the United States would immediately break diplomatic relations with any one of them violating a neutral country. There was virtually no assurance, however, that any such move would have the slightest effect.

Throughout the winter of 1939–1940, Ambassador Bullitt in Paris had sent the President and me many communications in which he spoke skeptically of the ability of the French to resist a German attack. From London, Ambassador Kennedy cabled the President and me on April 26 giving a long, dismal picture of the state of unpreparedness there and the lack of efficiency of the British Government. He said that, as we knew, this bearish streak of his was not a new one, for it had started before Munich. Kennedy possessed a keen, not to say brilliant, mind and intense energy, and always spoke bluntly and courageously when necessary. He was alert and conscientious in the performance of his every duty. Nevertheless, neither the President nor I could see eye to eye with him in his extreme pessimism over Britain's future.

During that winter and spring the President and I had done what we could, in conversations with British and French officials, to emphasize the probably impending danger. We had gone out of our way, once the arms embargo was removed in November, 1939, to afford the British and French facilities for the purchase of American arms. French orders for arms became appreciable, but British orders remained comparatively negligible. Before Hitler struck at the Low Countries, the President was already appealing to Mussolini to remain out of the war.

Finally, on May 7 Minister Gordon cabled me from The Hague that the Foreign Office expected a German invasion of The Netherlands and Belgium, perhaps within twenty-four to forty-eight hours. The following day Ambassador Cudahy cabled a report that a German ultimatum was about to be presented to the Netherlands and Belgian Governments. On May 9 Gordon cabled a similar report from The Hague, but said the Dutch Foreign Office believed a German invasion of Holland might well occur without any warning.

And then Hitler struck.

At first our attention centered on the Low Countries. The crisis in France did not come until several days later. On May 10 the President froze the credits of Belgium, Holland, and Luxemburg in the United States so that the Nazis could not get possession of them. That night, in an address to the Eighth Pan American Scientific Congress, which we had drafted in the State Department, he referred to the invasion of the Low Countries and said: "We have come, therefore, to the reluctant conclusion that a continuance of these processes of arms presents a definite challenge to the continuation of the type of civilization to which all of us in the three Americas have been accustomed."

We applied the Neutrality Act on May 11 to the Low Countries. We began additional preparations for the evacuation of Americans who, lulled by the long period of "phony war," had remained in Europe. We took over the representation of the interests of Belgium and Luxemburg in Berlin, and of various Allies in Brussels and The Hague. Our diplomatic staffs at Berlin, Brussels, The Hague, Copenhagen, and Oslo now had heavier duties as they assumed the diplomatic representation of a number of governments.

King Leopold of the Belgians cabled the President on May 10, informing him of the German attack and of Belgium's determination to defend her independence, and asking for his moral support. Mr. Roosevelt sent the message to the State Department for reply, which went forward on May 11, saying: "The people of the United States hope, as do I, that policies which seek to dominate peaceful and independent peoples through force and military aggression may be arrested, and that the Government and people of Belgium may preserve their integrity and their freedom."

On the very day of the German invasion, Winston Churchill became Prime Minister of Great Britain. The President and I welcomed the change. If ever there was a moment when events required a strong, resolute man at the head of the British Government, it was now. I had followed Mr. Churchill's ideas for several years. I was particularly interested in them because they paralleled the ideas I was stating at the time. While I was warning nations to be on the alert against the Axis he was warning Britain to wake up. Then in opposition to the Chamberlain Government, his was virtually the only important voice in Britain sounding the alarm.

The Foreign Minister of Panama, Dr. Narciso Garay, cabled me on May 13 asking our reaction to a suggestion by the Uruguayan Government that all the American Republics make a joint protest over the invasion of the Low Countries. I immediately replied favorably, as did the other Republics, and a declaration of protest was made on May 19.

With the armies of the Allies staggering back under the German attack, I spoke in Washington on May 13 to the American Society of International Law, of which I was then President:

"It is no exaggeration to say that never before, in the entire history of the human race, has the problem of the preservation and development of order under law presented itself with such urgent acuteness . . .

"The specter of a new descent into the conditions of international anarchy which characterized the Dark Ages looms on the horizon today. I am profoundly convinced that it menaces the civilized existence of mankind—of every nation and of every individual. . . .

"Our own nation . . . is not secure against that menace. We cannot shut it out by attempting to isolate and insulate ourselves. We cannot be certain of safety and security when a large part of the world outside our borders is dominated by forces of international lawlessness."

Netherlands organized resistance to the German onslaught ceased on May 14, four days after the invasion. Two days later Netherlands Minister Dr. Alexander Loudon informed me that Queen Wilhelmina and the Government were being established in London, The Netherlands remained at war with Germany, fighting would continue in those parts of the country not occupied by the enemy, and the Netherlands Navy would remain in the war.

But even more catastrophic than the news of German successes in the Low Countries were the cables Ambassador Bullitt sent the President and me on May 15. The Germans, advancing with overwhelming forces of tanks and dive bombers, had broken through the French Army at Sedan. Premier Reynaud had telephoned to Prime Minister Churchill that, since the Germans had broken through, the war might be lost in the course of a few days. In Reynaud's opinion, it would be lost unless Britain sent her fighter-plane strength to France at once. Churchill promised to recommend this to the War Cabinet, insisting to Reynaud, however, that there was no chance of the war being lost. Reynaud replied that Churchill knew that as long as he, Reynaud, remained Premier, France would fight to the bitter end.

Bullitt chanced to be with the Minister of National Defense, the former Premier Daladier, when General Gamelin telephoned the news of the Sedan collapse, endangering the whole French Army. Daladier said it was obvious that, unless God granted a miracle like that of the battle of the Marne in the First World War, the French Army would be crushed utterly. The British, he said, were criticizing the French and not throwing all they had into the fight.

On the same day, May 15, Ambassador Kennedy cabled to the President and me a striking conversation he had just had with Mr. Churchill. The Prime Minister had said he was sending the President a message on the next day that he considered the chances of the Allies' winning slight if Italy entered the war. The French were asking for more troops, but he was unwilling to send men from England because he was convinced that within a month England would be vigorously attacked. He added he intended to ask for a loan of thirty or forty of our old destroyers and also whatever planes we could spare.

The Prime Minister ended with a ringing statement, a forerunner of similar battle cries in the near future which rallied around him all those not intimidated by the Nazi might. Regardless of what Germany would do to England and France, he said, England would never give up as long as he remained a power in public life, even if she were burned to the ground. The Government, he asserted, would move to Canada, take the fleet with it, and fight on.

Kennedy, however, concluded his dispatch by asking what we could do, and saying it seemed to him that if we had to fight to protect our lives we should do better fighting in our own back yard.

The President and I were asking each other the same question in those fateful days, but we reached a different conclusion from Kennedy's. It seemed to us we should do better to keep the fighting away from our own back yard. This we could do by helping Britain and France remain on their feet. Then came the question, Exactly what could we do to help them? On the political side we had to bear in mind that, although the American people were seeing ever more clearly where their interests lay in the European War, there was still a strong isolationist sentiment in and out of Congress. Many of the isolationists maintained that the United States could go peacefully on her way whoever won the war in Europe. On the material side stood the question, Exactly what war supplies could we sell Britain and France, and how quickly could we get them to the theater of war?

Of one point the President and I had not the slightest doubt; namely, that an Allied victory was essential to the security of the United States.

Hastily surveying the field, the President decided to scrape together every available war plane to ship to France. Bullitt cabled me on May 14 suggesting France be permitted to send an aircraft carrier to pick them up. After talking to the President, I replied the following day that it would be impossible to load the planes at New York because of the provisions of international law and American statutes, but they could be flown to a port on the east coast of Canada, possibly Halifax, and loaded there. This was done—but too late for them to get to France. The President was also willing to turn over to France two thousand 75-millimeter guns from our World War supply. These would have gone to France had she been able to continue fighting. After the collapse of France a large number of them went to Britain.

It was also evident to the President and me that the enormous superiority of the German Army revealed by the lightning occupation of Holland and the break-through at Sedan required the revising of all our estimates for the rearming of the United States. The President discussed with me the project of a special message to Congress requesting a virtual doubling of the military appropriations for the year, in which I fully concurred. Bullitt had sent me a cable for the President on May 13 stressing the importance of increasing our production of planes, because of the vital part planes were playing in the German advance. I thereupon suggested to the President that he tell Congress that the United States should aim for a production of 50,000 planes a year. I had already mentioned this figure to my associates. The reaction of Mr. Roosevelt was the same as that of my associates—he was literally speechless, for 50,000 planes was ten times our current annual production.

I argued, however, that it was best to aim at a high figure and take the long view. Such a production did not seem so impossible to me as it seemed to others. I felt that the mere mention of the figure, with our tremendous productive capacities known to the world, would have a good effect in stimulating our own people, in comforting the Allies, and in giving cause for worry to the Axis.

The President forthwith agreed. In his message to Congress on May 16 he said he would like to see the nation geared to a production of 50,000 planes a year. He asked for additional appropriations for all branches of the armed forces totaling $1,182,000,000. But, significantly, he asked Congress not to hamper or delay the delivery of American-made planes to foreign nations that had ordered them or might seek to purchase more planes. In other words, our own rearmament must not be at the expense of the democracies we were seeking to aid.

Now began a series of extraordinary, almost hysterical appeals to the President from Premier Reynaud. The French Premier was understandably alarmed and excited over the terrific German victories. But he asked the impossible.

Alexis Léger, Secretary General of the French Foreign Office, informed Ambassador Bullitt on May 18 that Reynaud intended that evening to send a personal appeal to the President asking if it might be possible for Mr. Roosevelt to obtain from Congress a declaration of war against Germany. Bullitt cabled the President and me his reply to Léger: that such an appeal would be worse than useless, that the President would not ask Congress to declare war on Germany, and that Congress would vote almost unanimously against a declaration of war. He pointed out bluntly to Léger that if Reynaud made such an appeal it would be purely for the record—Reynaud wished some day to be able to show he had appealed to the President of the United States and the President had rejected his appeal. Bullitt commented also that this seemed to him to be cheap, and that the moment was too serious, not only for France and England but also for the United States, to have anything but frank dealing among the three Governments.

The President and I agreed that Bullitt's response to Léger echoed our own reaction.

That evening Bullitt saw Reynaud himself, who said he had thought of sending us a formal note. Bullitt cabled the President and me that Reynaud had intended stating the following:

Reynaud was perfectly convinced that, if the French were defeated, Britain would be strangled in short order by German submarines based on French ports, and by German planes based on France and the Low Countries. Also, that Hitler would have little trouble in installing Nazi regimes in many South American countries and would threaten the United States itself in the near future as directly and completely as he was then threatening France. It would enormously encourage France and England and immensely influence Italy if we could make a public statement that, if France and England were defeated, the vital interests of the United States would be threatened, and that the United States, in defense of these interests, could not permit the fall of France and England.

Bullitt correctly pointed out to Reynaud that Congress alone could declare war, and at the present time would not declare war on Germany. A statement such as Reynaud wanted would therefore be without physical force. Bullitt added that, however much public opinion might have progressed in the United States in recent days, our people were not ready for a declaration of war. In fact, they were aroused largely because they realized our own military weakness; they were determined not to send American soldiers to Europe, and they were keenly conscious that we had virtually no planes to send to Europe, and that the fleet was properly stationed in the Pacific.

Bullitt gave us his opinion that Reynaud had not thought the matter out and had decided to send a note for the record, but was forestalled by Bullitt's conversation with Léger that afternoon.

After the President and I discussed the Reynaud conversation, the President talked to Bullitt on the telephone and informed him that anything of this nature was out of the question.

Bullitt so informed Reynaud. But on May 22 he cabled again to say that Reynaud told him he could not leave the matter in suspense. It was now more vitally important than when he last discussed it four days before. France had received information from both Italy and Sweden that, if the Germans should gain a spectacular victory in the present battle in northern France, Hitler intended to offer France a separate and generous peace. Moreover, Reynaud had said to Bullitt two days before, as the Ambassador cabled me, that French defenses against the German tanks were like walls of sand that a child puts up against waves on the seashore.

Reynaud said that, if Hitler made such a proposal at a moment of great discouragement in France, there was an enormous danger that the French public would be disposed to accept it. Reynaud himself admitted that such acceptance would be as suicidal as Czechoslovakia's giving up the Sudetenland in 1938. From that moment on, France would live under the heel of Germany and, as soon as Hitler found it convenient, he would occupy all of France just as he had occupied all of Czechoslovakia. Also, a German victory over England would follow in a few weeks. Reynaud then believed that in a matter of months German soldiers and thousands of planes would be in South America, the Panama Canal would be destroyed by air bombardment, and the American army would be able to offer little resistance.

Aid short of war from the United States, he considered inadequate to save France and Britain. If we did not give military support in addition to that, we should have to face the Germans in the United States. He did not ask for our troops; but, if we should come into the war, keep our main fleet in the Pacific but send to Europe the Atlantic fleet and all the airplanes we could get together, with pilots, and launch all American industry into war production, the tide might be turned.

Reynaud said he knew Congress would not vote for war, but suggested the President call the most influential Senators and Representatives together and convince them that a declaration of war was necessary to protect the United States. A combination of the American, British, and French fleets, he commented, was the only real guarantee that Hitler would not some day be in the White House. With such a combination we could keep the Germans out of Latin America and go on fighting for fifty years, if necessary, even though Britain and France were conquered.

The Premier finally hoped that, if a German peace offer were made to France, the President on the same day would go to Congress and ask for a declaration of war. No other course could save us Americans from the Germans. Reynaud felt certain that the President was now face to face with one of the most momentous decisions that ever confronted a human being.

The attitude of the British was calmer and more realistic, even though they were a little slow or reluctant to realize that France was rapidly being defeated. Ambassador Lothian came on May 20 to hand me a series of suggestions from his Government as to what we might do to help Britain. After talking to the President on May 12 and giving him an outline of Britain's armaments needs, he had cabled his Government to ask in what other ways we could be of assistance. The series of communications he gave me represented the Churchill Cabinet's reply.

Britain suggested that we put into operation an export control scheme similar to that operated by the Allies. This would do away with a large part of the friction inevitable in the administration of contraband control. The Allied Governments would consult with us to determine priority of distribution of all available supplies. Britain suggested that the President invite the Latin American governments to adhere to this joint control.

Pending the setting up of such a control, Britain suggested the blocking of all German balances in the United States; prevention of the sale of bearer securities obtained by the Germans in occupied territories; an extension of the navicert system; a restriction on exports to Italy; and, as "the most valuable help America can give," the sale of materials and foodstuffs to the Allies at low prices or on easy credit, especially supplies of war cut off by recent events in northern and western Europe.

I passed these suggestions on to the President. In due course some of them came to fruition.

Two days later Lothian sent me a letter enclosing a letter for the President. Mr. Roosevelt having decided to send three light warships to Lisbon, largely to assist in the evacuation of Americans, Lothian asked him to keep them there as an influence to deter Spain from entering the war, since this would make it easier to keep Gibraltar in Allied hands. He said large numbers of German "tourists" had been entering Spain, and the "fifth columns" in Spain and Portugal were actively working against the regimes of Franco and Salazar, who wished to preserve neutrality, in order to replace them by regimes that would act in concert with the Axis.

The military situation in France was now rapidly deteriorating. On May 18 Reynaud had made Marshal Pétain Vice Premier, assumed Daladier's Ministry of War himself, and made Daladier Foreign Minister. The following day he appointed General Maxime Weygand to head the supreme army command, replacing General Gamelin. Bullitt on May 27 delivered to Weygand a message from the President expressing confidence in the new commander.

With France apparently falling I held a series of conferences with my associates, and asked them to consider the possible eventualities of the war situation in Europe, with particular reference to their effects on the United States and the Western Hemisphere. We came to the general conclusion that the position of the Allied armies was desperate, and our attention centered on the necessity for preserving the British and French fleets in being, out of Hitler's hands. We realized that, if they or substantial portions of them were added to the German fleet and possibly the Italian fleet—Mussolini was certainly getting ready to plunge into the conflict—our position in the Atlantic would be dangerous in the extreme, unless we moved the Pacific fleet into the Atlantic, in which event Japan would inevitably swallow the whole of Southeast Asia.

We had no doubt of the effect a negotiated peace would have on us. It would mean complete domination by Hitler of Europe presumably and the British and French fleets probably. We and the other nations not actual participants in the war would not be allowed seats at the peace table. We would be sitting off by ourselves on our own isolated continents, blissfully imagining that we could be real factors in the exclusively Hitler peace.

The President agreed that we should make a direct appeal to the British and French Governments on the subject of their navies. We accordingly drafted telegrams which I sent out on May 26.

To Bullitt I said the President desired him to say at once to Reynaud and Daladier that, while we still hoped the invasion would be checked, nevertheless, if worse came to worst, we considered retention of the French fleet as being vital to the reconstitution of France and her colonies and to control of the oceans and to getting less harsh peace terms. We suggested that the French fleet must not be bottled up in the Mediterranean. The warships in the eastern Mediterranean should be in position to leave through the Suez Canal. Those in the western Mediterranean should be able to pass Gibraltar and, if the catastrophe came, to go to the West Indies or to safe ports in French West Africa.

We then suggested that, if the Germans held out alluring offers based on surrender of the fleet, the French Government should remember that such offers had no ultimate value, and that, if the fleet were removed to safe places, France's condition could be no worse, but actually would be far stronger.

Our message to the British Government conveyed the same thought with regard to the British fleet. On May 20 Churchill had sent the President a message emphasizing the dangers facing Britain and indicating that, if she were conquered by Hitler, the sole remaining bargaining counter with Germany would be the fleet. The President now took up this last thought in his message to the Prime Minister. He suggested that, at the worst, the British fleet could retire to Canada, and assured Mr. Churchill that the United States would not permit Germany or any other non-American Power to seize Canada or British Western Hemisphere possessions. Germany could not win the war except as concerned military operations within Europe, so long as the British and French fleets remained intact. The message asked Churchill what possible confidence any British Government could have that Germany would fulfill less harsh peace terms, and suggested that if the time came—God forbid—when a British Government found it necessary to ask for peace terms from Germany, all ships under construction in the British Isles should be destroyed and all merchant ships in British ports should leave immediately for safe Empire ports.

Mr. Roosevelt said to the Prime Minister that we were doing everything possible to cooperate with the British Purchasing Mission and to facilitate and expedite deliveries. He promised to give every possible consideration to specific requests Churchill might send him.

The reaction of both Reynaud and Churchill to these messages was stout. The fleets would not be surrendered.

Bullitt wanted to go further and tie our suggestions with regard to the fleets to active steps on our own part, particularly the sending of the Atlantic fleet to the Mediterranean. He also suggested we dispatch a cruiser to Bordeaux with 5,000 to 10,000 sub-machine guns and ammunition, since Reynaud and he feared an uprising in Paris by the Communists who, following the party line throughout the world, had hampered the defense of France. The same cruiser would bring to this side of the Atlantic a cargo of French gold. We did send, on May 29, the cruiser *Vincennes* and two destroyers to Casablanca to carry nearly $250,000,000 in gold to the United States for safe keeping.

Reynaud's appeals now became yet more frantic. Bullitt cabled us on May 28 that Reynaud suggested that the President of the French Republic and the King of England address a joint appeal to President Roosevelt. Reynaud had written out one sentence of the appeal when Bullitt saw him. It read: "The armies fighting to preserve the liberties of the world have been stabbed in the back." Reynaud said he had enough evidence to convince him that, if France and England were conquered, Hitler would move almost immediately against the United States.

Reynaud said he knew perfectly well that we could not fly an army to France in planes that did not exist, even if we were to declare war on Germany tomorrow. But there was our fleet. The Atlantic fleet should be sent at once to the Mediterranean. This act might at least prevent another stab in the back, this time from Mussolini.

On that same day King Leopold surrendered the Belgian army to the Germans. Just prior to the surrender he wrote a letter to the President setting forth his reasons for the surrender. He handed the letter to Ambassador Cudahy on June 2 for transmission to the President. Cudahy, in Brussels, had been out of communication with the State Department since May 16, the day before the German occupation of the city. He gave the message to German military authorities for transmission through Berlin, but it was never received here. It was not until Cudahy went to Berlin himself on June 7 that the Department received a duplicate and sent it to the White House.

Leopold maintained that Belgium and her army had done their "whole duty"; the last means of resistance were gone; he saw no point in continuing a conflict that would lead to "our extermination without helping the Allies"; and he himself was determined to remain on Belgian soil to share the fate of his people and army. He felt called upon to explain this to the President without delay because of "the solicitude which the United States have always shown Belgium."

We received this communication in the spirit in which it was sent. It was not up to us to judge whether the King had acted rightly or wrongly, wisely or unwisely.

The military position of the Allies was now falling to bits. The British had begun to withdraw their army from Dunkirk in one of the bravest operations in all military history, and the French were reeling back toward Paris.

Reynaud's appeals continued on a rising pitch. Bullitt cabled the President and me on May 29 that Reynaud, saying it was "now or never for the United States," suggested that the Atlantic fleet be sent to Tangier. He predicted that, if Mussolini were informed that we were doing so after the fleet started, he would not dare to strike. Otherwise he would strike, and in a very few months we should face alone a joint attack by Germany, Italy, and Japan.

After talking over this message with the President, I cabled Bullitt on May 30 Mr. Roosevelt's decision that it was absolutely impossible to consider sending the fleet to the Mediterranean. The presence of our fleet in the Pacific at this time we considered to be a very practical contribution to the maintenance of peace in that ocean. The British Government appreciated the importance of this contribution, and we assumed the French Government did too. The warships we had in the Atlantic were required for patrol duty or for special service in South and Central American waters. (We were obligated by the Declaration of Panama to conduct such patrols; moreover, removing our warships from the western Atlantic would have produced an adverse reaction in Latin America.)

The presence of an American fleet at this time in the Mediterranean, I added, would result in very serious risks. It would be impossible to base the fleet on any ports in or near the Mediterranean should Italy enter the war. And unless we sent a fleet sufficiently large to be effective, the impression created would be just the opposite of what we wanted.

When Bullitt communicated this reply, Reynaud commented that France was most grateful for the presence of our fleet in the Pacific because, without firing a shot, it was keeping the war from spreading to the French and British Empires in the Far East. He hoped that the fleet would stay there, but he thought the Atlantic fleet could play exactly the same role in the Mediterranean. Unfortunately, the Atlantic fleet was very small compared to the Pacific fleet, and it would have had little if any effect on a desperado like Mussolini.

The President now sent another message to Congress, on May 31, asking for additional military appropriations of more than one billion dollars and for authority to call the National Guard into active service.

As Britain completed the evacuation from Dunkirk, she made it clear to France that she would send no more planes to the Continent. The British Ambassador in Paris explained to Bullitt that the rate of destruction of planes in battle was so great that if Britain sent over her remaining planes, none would be left in two weeks. Since there was no longer any hope of saving Paris or even the French army, it seemed wiser to keep the planes in England for the forthcoming Battle of Britain.

In response to Reynaud's almost pitiful pleas for backing, the President urged Mr. Churchill to send planes to France; but the Prime Minister refused. Bullitt, outraged by this decision, communicated to the President and me on June 5 his fear that the British might be conserving their air force and fleet so as to use them as bargaining points in negotiations with Hitler.

The President and I, however, thought differently. France was finished, but we were convinced that Britain, under Churchill's indomitable leadership, intended to fight on. There would be no negotiations between London and Berlin. Only the day before Bullitt's telegram, Churchill had made his magnificent speech in the House of Commons which he concluded by saying: "We shall never surrender, and even if, which I do not for the moment believe, this island or a large part of it were subjugated and starving, then our empire beyond the seas, armed and guarded by the British fleet, will carry on the struggle until in God's good time the New World, with all its power and might, sets forth to the liberation and rescue of the Old."

The President and I believed Mr. Churchill meant what he said. Had we had any doubt of Britain's determination to keep on fighting, we would not have taken the steps we did to get material aid to her. There would have been no logic in sending arms to Britain if we had thought that, before they arrived there, Churchill's government would surrender to Germany.

The Administration was frantically trying to get together every available weapon for Britain. On May 29 I had amended the Neutrality Act regulations so that American pilots could deliver American planes to the Maritime Provinces of Canada, for shipment to Europe. A day or two later I informed the President of the existence of a 1917 statute, brought to light by Joseph C. Green, Chief of the Department's Division of Controls, whereby Army and Navy aircraft could be traded back to the manufacturers for immediate resale to the Allies. The President decided to send to Britain half a million rifles, eight hundred 75-millimeter field artillery guns, many hundreds of machine guns, and several hundred planes, most of which had originally been destined for France. The Department communicated to the Canadian Government the President's informal opinion that American pilots might enlist in the Canadian air force provided they were not obliged to take an oath of allegiance to Canada.

But we could not go further and declare war, however much many statesmen throughout the world wanted us to do so. When Australian Minister Casey came to see me on June 6, he emphatically expressed the joint view of himself and Australian High Commissioner S. M. Bruce in London that Germany could conquer Britain. He said that, since we were doing about all we could in every legitimate and practical way to sell equipment and supplies to the Allies, he would be extremely interested to see this Government declare war.

"That," I promptly said, "is unthinkable in the present situation."

I reviewed to him the many large steps we were taking to assist Britain, but he then said that the moral effect of a declaration of war by the United States would be very great.

I again summarily dismissed this idea, and reminded him that we were doing all possible in the circumstances, without becoming involved in a military war or making a military alliance.

Churchill's decision not to send British planes to France, however sound it later proved for the Battle of Britain, had an immediate and unfortunate psychological effect on the French Government. Vice Premier Pétain expressed this to Bullitt on June 4. He felt the British would permit the French to fight to the last and then, with quantities of troops and planes on British soil and a dominant navy, would make a compromise peace with Hitler. Unless Britain sent its air force and reserve divisions to France, he believed the French Government should come to terms with Germany immediately, whatever might happen to England.

This thought of terms with Germany now began to dominate the French Cabinet. Dispatches from Bullitt reflected ever more the likelihood that a French surrender was only a matter of days. The Germans were driving toward Paris. On June 10 the French Government left the capital for Tours.

And on that day Mussolini declared war on France and Britain.

56: Stab in the Back

NO GOVERNMENT ever made a more sincere effort to keep another Government from going to war than the United States in the case of Italy. Five months of appeal and pressure from us preceded Mussolini's entrance into the conflict.

In January, 1940, the President, receiving Italian Ambassador Prince Colonna, emphasized his satisfaction that public opinion in the United States had become markedly more friendly toward Italy because she had maintained her neutrality during the present conflict. Mr. Roosevelt also expressed the hope that she would remain neutral.

When Welles went to Rome in February, the President instructed him to present these same views on his behalf to Mussolini.

After Myron Taylor began his conversations with Pope Pius XII on February 27, he asked the Pope's opinion as to whether the President could helpfully use his influence with Mussolini to persuade him to remain nonbelligerent. The Pope said the President's influence with Mussolini would be helpful.

Hitler's rapid conquest of Norway and the complete inability of Britain and France to bring effective aid to that country obviously impressed Mussolini. Ambassador Phillips wrote from Rome on April 12:

"The political atmosphere of Rome these days is very unsettling, knowing, as we all do, that Mussolini remains intensely pro-German and anti-English, and knowing also his susceptibility to German pressure. One cannot be sure that he will preserve his balanced position between the belligerents. Presumably he will not make any new move until he is convinced that the Germans will come out victorious. But the point is that one will never know in time when he has come to that conclusion. When he does reach that point, he may act suddenly. . . . No one, whether in or out of the Government here, has the slightest idea of what this one-man Government intends to do in certain eventualities."

Then on April 20 Myron Taylor sent me two cables for the President. In one he said there was real danger of Mussolini's joining Hitler or engaging separately in aggression in new fields. He quoted the Cardinal Secretary of State, Maglione, as urging the President to take action within two or three days, preferably immediately. In the other cable he quoted the Pope as urging an immediate message from the President to Mussolini. The Pope said he would make a parallel endeavor at this time.

Upon receiving these cables I communicated with the President who was at Warm Springs, Georgia. He felt that in the two expressions he had already made to Mussolini, through the Italian Ambassador and Welles, he had said enough. In reviewing to the President the cables we had been receiving from many capitals, it did not seem to us that action by Mussolini was likely to occur in a matter of days. At Mr. Roosevelt's request I cabled Taylor on April 25 that the President did not feel that a useful purpose would be served at that particular moment by repeating again to Mussolini a message which in effect had been twice delivered.

My own faith in the value of these personal appeals had always been low, and I had said so to the President on several occasions. It was even lower now, in view of the failure of such appeals as he had made in recent years. I could not but remember the almost insolent reply Mussolini had made to his plea for peace at the time of the Italo-Abyssinian War.

On the following day, however, Taylor again cabled, saying that he had once more seen the Pope and Cardinal Maglione, who reemphasized their previous suggestions. Taylor reported the Vatican's belief that a surprise move by Mussolini was quite likely, especially since it was being said that he would need to move suddenly in order to overcome such opposition as existed in Italy against going to war.

The President returned to Washington on Sunday April 28. I met him at the station and went with him to the White House. I went over with him the cables from Taylor and informed him that the British and French Governments were also worried that Mussolini would throw his forces into the war. The President thereupon decided he should make an appeal to Mussolini, this time in the form of a written message.

We at the State Department began working with the President the following day on a draft. At about this time British Ambassador Lothian came to me with a message from his Government that the terrain in Norway was so difficult that the British and French might have some preliminary reverses. This would be the period when the greatest effort would be made by Germany to get Mussolini to enter the war. Britain wanted us to know this so that, in view of our interest in keeping the war from spreading, we might find something further to say to Mussolini to persuade him to keep out of the war, at least for the present. I promised Lothian we would give his request due attention, but I did not tell him of the decision the President had already made. If our move was to have any success—which I doubted in any event—it would have to be done entirely on our own, and with an absence of publicity.

The drafting of the message was completed that afternoon, April 29, and went forward by cable to Mussolini that evening. "A further extension of the area of hostilities," the President said, "would necessarily have far-reaching and unforeseeable consequences, not only in Europe, but also in the Near and the Far East, in Africa, and in the three Americas. No man can today predict with assurance, should such a further extension take place, what the ultimate result might be—or foretell what nations, however determined they may today be to remain at peace, might yet eventually find it imperative in their own defense to enter the war."

The following day Taylor cabled the President that the Pope had fulfilled his part of the proposed parallel action by sending a handwritten message to Mussolini direct.

Mussolini received Phillips on May 1 to have the President's message read to him. He said that Germany could not be beaten, and that peace in Europe could not be considered without recognizing the "new geography" resulting from Hitler's conquests. As for Italy, her situation as a "prisoner within the Mediterranean" was intolerable, and he inveighed against Britain's possession of the Suez Canal and Gibraltar.

Mussolini was actually more conciliatory orally to Phillips than in his written reply to the President, handed in at the White House by Ambassador Colonna on May 2. He now blamed the Allies for the invasion of Scandinavia. He said Germany and Italy opposed further extension of the conflict, but peace was not possible until "the fundamental problems of Italian liberty" had been settled. He pointedly recalled that Italy had never concerned herself with the relations of the American Republics with one another and therefore might ask for "reciprocity" with regard to European affairs.

The following day Phillips cabled me that he had seen Count Ciano, Mussolini's son-in-law and Foreign Minister, who told him Britain's decision to withdraw her merchant marine from the Mediterranean had come as a surprise to Rome, since Italy had no intention of going to war unless the Allies attacked Italy.

Immediately after the invasion of the Low Countries began, Phillips again cabled me on May 10 that he had seen Ciano, who had just come from Mussolini. Ciano assured him that no change had been decided upon or was contemplated as a result of the new invasion. While Mussolini desired to carry out his obligations under the Axis alliance, Ciano said, no situation had developed which called for Italy's going to war.

Just four days later, however, the situation had changed entirely. Phillips then cabled me Ciano's statement to him that, whereas a week before he thought chances of Italy's remaining out of the war were 50–50, they were now 90–10 in favor of participation. Ciano said Mussolini had made up his mind. The information received from Hitler on the progress of his campaigns had always been correct, and the information received that morning clearly showed complete German victories in Belgium and Holland.

There was near-consternation in London and Paris when they received this news. Ambassador Bullitt cabled me a frantic request that the President bring more pressure to bear on Mussolini. Premier Reynaud told him that, with the participation of Italy in the war, the result would be tragic not only for France and Britain but also for every country in the world, including the United States. Reynaud asked that some of our over-age destroyers be sold to Britain and France because of the Italian submarine attacks he expected in the Mediterranean.

When Phillips's cable reached the Department, I sent it to the President. He thereupon decided to make another appeal to Mussolini. Again we at the State Department worked with him on the text. It went forward at midnight that same day, May 14, in a cable from me to Phillips.

"I have sent word to Your Excellency before that I am a realist," the President said. "As a realist you also will, I know, recognize that if this war should extend throughout the world it would pass beyond the control of heads of States, would encompass the destruction of millions of lives and the best of what we call the liberty and culture of civilization. And no man, no matter how omniscient, can foretell the result either to himself or his own people."

Phillips tried to see Mussolini personally again, but Mussolini sent word that he preferred to receive the President's second message through his Foreign Office. Three days later, on May 18, Phillips cabled Mussolini's reply: "Italy is and intends to remain allied with Germany, and Italy cannot remain absent at a moment in which the fate of Europe is at stake."

On the same day Phillips cabled me that he had no doubt Italy was on the edge of a precipice, but he did doubt whether "there is a person in Italy who knows definitely what or when Mussolini's next move will be."

Meantime, during the few days preceding this reply, Bullitt in Paris, who had the closest possible contacts with the French Government and reflected their natural consternation over the catastrophic turn in the fighting, cabled numerous suggestions for action on our part toward Italy. He proposed that the President request the Pope to threaten Mussolini with excommunication if Italy should enter the war and to denounce Hitler's invasions on spiritual grounds approaching a bull of excommunication. He also suggested that our Atlantic fleet be sent on a courtesy visit to Greece, that Italian immigrant remittances be cut off if Italy went to war, and that Italian immigrants and Italo-Americans adopt resolutions opposing Italy's participating in the conflict.

On the day Mussolini's reply was received, British Ambassador Lothian came in to see me. He read me a memorandum from his Government proposing that we immediately embargo shipments of strategic materials to Italy as a means of keeping Italy out of the war.

I talked over these various suggestions with the President. If there was any step that had a reasonable chance of succeeding, we were willing to take it. But it was clear that Mussolini's mind was made up. Hitler's victories were so stupendous that Mussolini had reason to believe that the whole war would be over shortly, and that any action we saw fit to adopt would come too late.

As for sending the Atlantic fleet to Europe, we had to bear in mind that any indication that we were directing any large-scale naval attention to that continent might prove an irresistible temptation to Japan to act in the Orient. Japan was even then searching frantically for every lever with which to pry advantages for herself from the military debacle in Europe.

French Foreign Minister Daladier suggested to us, through the French Ambassador on May 20, that President Roosevelt ask the Presidents of the American Republics to join with him in an appeal to Mussolini. The President's reaction to this suggestion coincided with mine, and I asked Welles to inform the Ambassador the following day that we thought such a move would produce an effect the opposite of that desired by his Government. To use the President's phrase, it would give Mussolini the impression that the United States and the other American Republics were "ganging up" on him. Also, if the President were to make a request of this nature to the other American Republics, we should have to make known to them the texts of his previous messages to Mussolini, which would be inexpedient.

Phillips cabled me on May 21 that Mussolini was simply waiting to see how the military situation in northern France and Belgium worked out, and that, if the Germans broke through the present Allied defense positions, "Mussolini will probably consider that Italy's moment has arrived."

Then on May 25 Churchill and Reynaud invited the President to make a further démarche toward Mussolini. They suggested that he make a statement to him on these lines:

(1) The President had reason to believe that Britain and France knew Italy entertained certain territorial grievances against them.

(2) Britain and France were fully disposed to consider Italian claims now with a view to reaching an agreement that would satisfy reasonable Italian claims at the end of the war.

(3) The Allies would admit Italy to the peace conference with a status equal to that of any belligerent.

Churchill and Reynaud suggested that the President should add that the United States would do its utmost to see to it that any agreement reached would be carried out, provided Italy refrained from going to war against Britain and France.

These various suggestions were to be made by the President acting on his own behalf and not as an agent of the Allies.

The President agreed without much difficulty to this approach. He did say, however, that, rather than act at the instance of the British and the French, he preferred to pursue the next logical step in his previous correspondence with Mussolini on the same general subject, which he had begun on his own initiative, and without any request from any Government.

The President's message, which we drafted at the State Department, went forward in a cable from me to Ambassador Phillips on May 26. In it the President said that if Mussolini were willing to inform him of Italy's specific desires, he would communicate them to Britain and France. If an agreement were arrived at, he said, it would involve an assurance to him by Britain and France that they would faithfully execute it at the end of the war and would welcome Italy in the peace conference with a status equal to that of the belligerents. Also, it would involve an assurance to him by Mussolini that the execution of the agreement would satisfy the claims of Italy, and that Italy would not enter the war.

Here was something concrete and specific. It went well beyond the President's previous messages, which were limited to words of appeal together with a veiled threat that the United States herself might eventually have to enter the war. Now Mussolini had before him a definite proposal whereby he could have obtained any reasonable demands without recourse to war, with the United States guaranteeing that Britain and France would live up to their agreement.

But the following day Phillips cabled me Mussolini's "No!" Ciano said to him that Mussolini's intention was not merely to realize the legitimate aspirations of Italy but also to fulfill his obligations under the alliance with Germany. Mussolini desired to keep his "freedom of action" and was not disposed to engage in any negotiations, because these would not be "in accordance with the spirit of Fascism." Finally, "any attempt to prevent Italy from fulfilling her engagements is not well regarded."

The President, undaunted by the fact that each time Mussolini replied his tone became more hostile, wanted a still further appeal to go forward to the Italian dictator. We accordingly worked on it, and I cabled it to Phillips on May 30. This time the President said that a further extension of the war as a result of Italian participation "would at once result in an increase in the rearmament program of the United States itself and in a redoubling of the efforts of the Government of the United States to facilitate in every practical way the securing within the United States by the Allied Powers of all the supplies and matériel which they may require." The President reminded Mussolini of our historic interests in the Mediterranean, which we had upheld for nearly one hundred and fifty years.

Mussolini's reply was even more definite and hostile than before. Phillips cabled on May 31 Ciano's statement that Mussolini had made his decision to enter the war and it was now only a matter of days. When Phillips had commented that a profound change would occur in the attitude of the American public toward Italy if Italy entered the war, Ciano replied that this fact had already been taken into consideration.

The following day Phillips cabled Mussolini's own statement that he desired to fulfill his engagements with Germany and preferred not to receive "any further pressure" since this "would only stiffen his attitude." He said he did not believe that Italy's intervention would necessarily enlarge the war in the Mediterranean, and he questioned our claim to interests in the Mediterranean, saying these were the same as Italy had in the Caribbean.

Ciano wanted Phillips's opinion as to whether the United States would go to war. When Phillips replied that he could not say so certainly, but that Italy's entrance into the war would go a long way in leading the United States in the direction of war, Ciano commented that he was very definitely of the opinion that the United States would, in fact, enter the war. He said he had great admiration for the American soldier, with whom he had come in contact in China, and he realized the immense power of our nation.

At this point France made a direct offer to Mussolini to settle Italy's territorial claims. Bullitt cabled me on June 3, however, that Ciano replied to the French Ambassador in Rome that Mussolini was not interested in receiving any French territories by peaceful negotiation. He had decided to make war on France, and there would be no reply to the French note.

The President and Welles now entertained the idea of a still further appeal to Mussolini, using the French offer as a springboard. A draft of the message was prepared in the State Department. But by now I had had more than enough of such appeals to a bandit who was determined on war to satisfy his own vanity and wish for glory. I strongly opposed sending the message. I said that the French Government had not asked us to back up its offer, and that Mussolini's last communication to the President left little doubt that he had taken his decision to cast Italy into the war. Another message from the President would simply invite a sharp retort from Mussolini. We had had enough insult from that quarter already.

My objections held, and this message, which was ready on June 7, was not sent.

It was no surprise to any of us when Mussolini declared war against Britain and France on June 10. Nor were we surprised that he had waited so long. It had been obvious that he was simply calculating his chances, holding back until he was certain that France was crumbling, that Britain would fall within a few weeks, and that his own participation would gain him all and cost him nothing.

That night the President spoke at the University of Virginia. He reviewed the many efforts he had made to prevent Italy from entering the war. Then he said:

"On this 10th day of June, 1940, the hand that held the dagger has struck it into the back of its neighbor."

This phrase was contained in the draft we had worked on in the State Department. Welles suggested to the President that it come out, on the ground that it would so prejudice Mussolini that it would be impossible to obtain his cooperation when the time came to make peace. Actually the idea of the stab in the back had been expressed by Premier Reynaud as early as May 20 and occurred several times in cables from Bullitt. The President removed the phrase from his text, but changed his mind en route to Charlottesville and reinserted it.

Neither the President nor I believed, as did so many statesmen in Europe, that the entrance of Italy into the war, coupled with the sweeping German victories in France, meant the end of the war. We were more determined than ever to provide Britain, plus the remnants of the overrun democracies, with all the help we could. The President said at Charlottesville:

"In our unity, in our American unity, we will pursue two obvious and simultaneous courses; we will extend to the opponents of force the material resources of this nation; and, at the same time, we will harness and speed up the use of those resources in order that we ourselves in the Americas may have equipment and training equal to the task of any emergency and every defense."

Ironically, Italian Ambassador Prince Colonna that same day sent me a note, in reply to the usual semiannual notes I had dispatched requesting payment from governments indebted to us. While Mussolini was prepared to spend billions in going to war, his Government regretted that it was still unable "at the present moment" to submit any proposals for settling its debt to us.

At the State Department we already had drawn up all the necessary proclamations whereby the President would apply the Neutrality Act to Italy and extend the combat zone into the Mediterranean and the Red Sea, as well as the various regulations I would issue concerning travel of Americans, solicitation of funds, and the like. These were put out on June 10 and 11.

On the day after Mussolini's declaration of war the Italian Ambassador again called upon me and handed me an official announcement of the declaration. Colonna remarked that his mission that day was disagreeable.

"I must be as candid as you are," I replied, "and tell you it is my deliberate judgment that Italy's entry into the war will prove deeply disappointing to peoples everywhere. It will constitute one of the greatest human tragedies. The implications of the announcement you've handed me are broad and far-reaching."

Few episodes in history have seemed so cynical to me as Mussolini's declaration of war against Britain and France. He had virtually declared war a month before he entered it. He gave his enemies to understand he would fight them and would reject any offer they made him, but he left the date for hostilities to be filled in at his convenience. He coolly waited until German arms had almost completed the collapse of France and there seemed no danger in thrusting Italy into the conflict. He consulted none of the 40,000,000 Italians he destined to disaster.

57: Fall of France

PREMIER REYNAUD, just before leaving Paris with his Government a few hours after Mussolini declared war, cabled a dramatic appeal to President Roosevelt to state publicly that the United States would support the Allies by all means short of an expeditionary force.

"We shall fight," he said, "in front of Paris; we shall fight behind Paris; we shall close ourselves in one of our provinces to fight, and if we should be driven out of it we shall establish ourselves in North Africa to continue the fight, and if necessary in our American possessions."

The President and I knew the French could not fight in front of Paris or behind Paris, or close themselves in one of their provinces (Reynaud had Brittany in mind). But it was still possible to retain control of the fleet, withdraw to North Africa, and carry on the fight from there.

With all the best intentions and good will in the world, we also knew there were physical and political limits on what we could do to aid France. The fight for France was effectively over, there was nothing we could possibly do to keep Hitler from conquering metropolitan France. We therefore sought to make a reply that would encourage Reynaud and his Government to carry on from North Africa and to preserve the French fleet intact.

While this answer was in preparation, British Ambassador Lothian sent me on June 11 a message from Mr. Churchill for the President. The Prime Minister said he was fortified by the President's speech at Charlottesville the night before. Everything must be done, he continued, to keep France in the fight and prevent the fall of Paris from becoming the occasion for any kind of parley with the Germans. If Hitler were thus baffled of quick results, he would turn upon Britain, and the British were preparing to resist his fury. Churchill promised that, as soon as British troops were equipped on the much higher scale needed for continental service, they would be sent to France in 1941. Churchill stressed his need for airplanes and thirty or forty reconditioned old destroyers from us.

Two days later I transmitted the President's reply to Reynaud, in which he said he was particularly impressed by the Premier's declaration that France would continue to fight, even in North Africa and the Atlantic. "It is most important to remember," he said, "that the French and British fleets continue mastery of the Atlantic and other oceans; also to remember that vital materials from the outside world are necessary to maintain all armies." The President assured him that our efforts to aid the Allies were being redoubled.

Reynaud sent the President a further appeal on the following day, this time going well beyond his previous message by saying: "The only chance of saving the French nation, vanguard of democracies, and through her to save England, by whose side France could then remain with her powerful navy, is to throw into the balance, this very day, the weight of American power.

"It is the only chance also of keeping Hitler, after he has destroyed France, and then England, from attacking America, thus renewing the fight of the Horatii against the three Curiatii."

Conceding that a declaration of war did not depend on the President alone, Reynaud nevertheless concluded: "But I must tell you at this hour, so grave in our history as in yours, that if you cannot give to France in the hours to come the certainty that the United States will come into the war within a very short time, the fate of the world will change."

Reynaud had now carried out the intention he had cherished since May 18, of getting on record as appealing for an American declaration of war, without which France would fall. We had made every effort to convince him of the impossibility of such a declaration by Congress at that time, but he had determined to make the appeal just the same. His desperate situation explained his desperate action. That evening, on the radio, he asked that "clouds of war planes from across the Atlantic come to crush the evil force that dominates Europe." But Reynaud knew, just as well as he knew that the President could not declare war, that there were no "clouds of war planes" to come from across the Atlantic.

The President and I both appreciated the intensity of Reynaud's excitement; but we did not agree with his premise that England could be saved only through France, and that after France fell England would fall too.

We drafted what reply we could, which went forward on June 15. After expressing admiration for the courage of the French, the President promised ever greater material aid to the Allies, and said that so long as the French people continued to defend their liberty they could count on ever increasing war material and supplies from the United States. He stated that the United States would not recognize any attempts to infringe by force the independence and territorial integrity of France. But he had to caution Reynaud that these statements carried no implication of military commitments, which only Congress could make.

The Germans occupied Paris on June 14, the day before the President's reply. Ambassador Bullitt acted with the military governor in turning the undefended city over to the Germans without loss of life. Bullitt, at his own wish, had remained behind rather than accompany the French Government to Tours and then to Bordeaux. His thought was that he could render greater service to the Allied cause and to the people of Paris by remaining on, at least temporarily, under German occupation, than by going with the French Government in flight. He had in mind the action of American Ambassador Myron Herrick, who remained in Paris instead of accompanying the French Government to Bordeaux during the First World War.

This decision, in my opinion, was unfortunate. It deprived Bullitt of all contact with the French Government during the crucial week between June 10, when it left Paris, and June 17, when it asked for an armistice. Had Bullitt, with his unequaled contacts with the leaders of the French Government, been able to represent us during those historic days, it is possible, if not probable, that that Government would have taken the fleet, gone to North Africa, and continued the fight from there.

Bullitt's place was taken by Ambassador Biddle, who had been in Paris representing us to the Polish Government-in-exile. Biddle was a fine diplomat, but his contacts and influence with the French Government were not to be compared to those of Bullitt.

Bullitt explained to me later that, three years before this event, he had discussed this very possibility with Mr. Roosevelt, and they had agreed that Bullitt should remain in Paris if the Germans were about to occupy it. They had before them the precedent not only of Herrick but also of Gouverneur Morris, who stayed in Paris during the Terror of the French Revolution, and of Minister Washburne, who remained during the siege of Paris and the Commune in 1870–1871. The precedent of Herrick was not altogether apropos, since in 1914 there had been a good fighting chance to save Paris, whereas in 1940 the German occupation, as the French armies collapsed, was inevitable. Bullitt said that he had discussed the matter with the President again in February, 1940, when he was home on leave, and the President again had agreed with him on this point.

In any event, as the Germans approached Paris, Bullitt communicated to the President direct that he knew the State Department would oppose the proposal he was about to make, hence he was approaching him personally. He then proposed staying in Paris, instead of going with the French Government.

Bullitt had communicated directly with the President on many occasions by telephone and cable. He also employed a private code he had worked out solely with the President. Liking the dramatic side of foreign affairs, Mr. Roosevelt did not discourage the practice. This routine reached a climax in the tragic days of France's defeat. The result was that at times the State Department remained in the dark as to what Bullitt was thinking and doing, although the President informed me of many of these communications from Bullitt and always gave me full information when I asked him about any particular item.

When I became aware of Bullitt's proposal I went to see the President. I said I opposed this project and thought our Ambassador should go with the French Government. It seemed to me that his influence with the German occupation authorities in Paris would be very small, because his strong anti-Nazi sentiments were well known to the German Government. On the other hand, his influence with the French Government might be decisive.

The President himself then telephoned Bullitt and said that he and I thought the Ambassador ought to leave Paris with the Government. He made the argument that Bullitt might be murdered by either the Communists or the Nazis, since he was hated by both. Bullitt said he could not run away from danger, and argued the President out of his opposition.

Mr. Roosevelt, however, returned to the belief that Bullitt should go with the French Government. On June 11, two days after this telephone conversation, I forwarded to Bullitt a cable signed by the President, which said: "It is strongly recommended that if all foreign chiefs of mission follow French Government to its temporary Capital, you should do likewise. Because it is impossible here to know last minute developments or the wishes of the French Government, I must rely on your discretion and assume you will make your decision in the best interests of the United States and of humanity." If he remained behind, Bullitt, being on the spot, was, "as a red-blooded American," to do what he could to save life.

No one can say what would have been the precise effect of Bullitt's influence had he been able to exercise it personally on the Government at Tours and Bordeaux. Churchill himself, even by a personal visit to Tours, the dispatch of envoys and messages to Bordeaux, and the offer of a union between Britain and France, was unable to keep France in the war and to get more than paper assurances regarding the fleet. But then the French Government was angered at the Churchill Government, whereas our own influence with Reynaud and his cabinet was of the highest. I feel that, with Bullitt at Reynaud's side, we should have had a reasonable chance to induce the French Cabinet to continue the fight with the fleet and colonies.

Nevertheless, to my mind Bullitt was both capable and sincere. And, having the courage of his convictions, he naturally did not hesitate to proclaim and pursue them.

At Tours and then at Bordeaux Ambassador Biddle took up the struggle, seeing Reynaud, Pétain, Minister of the Navy Admiral Darlan, Daladier, and others, and impressing upon them again and again our view that France, with her navy intact, should continue to resist. Biddle's dispatches gave us a vivid narrative of the drama being played within the French Cabinet, with Reynaud opposing an armistice and Pétain favoring it, while from outside the Cabinet the sinister Laval began to use his influence for capitulation.

Then on the night of June 16 Reynaud resigned, and Pétain formed a new Cabinet, with Baudouin as Foreign Minister and Admiral Darlan as Minister of Marine, to seek an armistice. Biddle at midnight saw the new Foreign Minister, who assured him formally that the fleet would never be surrendered to Germany. As a guarantee thereof, he added, Admiral Darlan, whose views were well known on this subject, had been named Minister of Marine. In the early hours of June 17 the Pétain Government requested an armistice of Germany and Italy.

We immediately took a series of actions in Washington. The President issued an Executive order freezing French assets in the United States. I sent notes to the German and Italian Governments informing them we would not recognize any transfer, and would not acquiesce in any attempt to transfer, any geographic region of the Western Hemisphere from one non-American Power to another non-American Power. This had reference to French and Dutch possessions in the New World. I cabled a similar message from the President to Pétain at Bordeaux. This informed Pétain the United States would be prepared to constitute an inter-American trusteeship over French possessions here, in conjunction with the other American Republics, which would continue only until France had regained her independence. Also, I cabled the twenty other

American Republics asking their agreement to an inter-American conference at Havana as soon as possible to discuss this and other questions.

Later that day French Ambassador Count de Saint-Quentin handed the State Department a note stating that the French Government was resolved not to yield to any condition contrary to national honor, dignity, or independence. "If, in reply to the overtures made to Germany," the note said, "inacceptable demands should be returned, it is with fierce resolution that the whole country, preferring to suffer what it could not accept, would continue the struggle on bases in the French Empire until the day when the common effort of all free peoples would lead to its liberation."

All the assurances we had received regarding the fleet were, however, oral or paper ones. The major assurances sought by Churchill on his side, that the fleet be sent to British ports, or by the President on his side, that it be sent out of the Mediterranean to West African or West Indies ports, had not been met. With the exception of those warships already in British or West Indies ports, it lay within possible capturing distance of the Germans and Italians, or it could still be surrendered to the Axis under the terms of the armistice to be agreed to.

The British and American Governments therefore made desperate efforts to ensure the safety of the French Navy. Churchill sent his First Lord of the Admiralty, his First Sea Lord, and his Secretary for the Colonies to Bordeaux to represent him. After discussing the situation with the President, I sent one of the strongest cables of my career to Ambassador Biddle at Bordeaux for communication to the Pétain Government.

"The President," I said, "desires that you obtain immediately an interview with Admiral Darlan and subsequently, if possible, with the Minister for Foreign Affairs, and state that the views of this Government with regard to the disposition of the French fleet have been made very clear to the French Government on previous occasions. The President desires you to say that in the opinion of this Government, should the French Government, before concluding any armistice with the Germans, fail to see that the fleet is kept out of the hands of her opponents, the French Government will fatally impair the preservation of the French Empire and the eventual restoration of French independence and autonomy. Furthermore, should the French Government fail to take these steps and permit the French fleet to be surrendered to Germany, the French Government will permanently lose the friendship and good will of the Government of the United States."

This was almost a brutal message, but the situation was such that only a stronge message could serve any purpose.

Biddle handed this cable to Darlan as he was about to enter a Cabinet meeting on June 18. Biddle also called Baudouin from the meeting to hand him a copy. Although Baudouin seemed to Biddle keenly irritated over the vigor of the note, he and Darlan laid it before the Cabinet. The Government thereupon decided that under no circumstances should the fleet be turned over to the Germans, and that, if surrender were embraced in the German terms, the armistice should be rejected.

Biddle cabled me shortly afterwards that Baudouin assured him "in the name of his Government in the most solemn manner that the French fleet would never be surrendered to the enemy." Baudouin added that "he could not, however, say that the French fleet would join the British fleet; it might be sent overseas or it might be sunk." The French Cabinet was then discussing this last question. Biddle urged emphatically that the fleet be moved to safety rather than destroyed.

Baudouin commented that the final sentence of our message, referring to the permanent loss of the friendship of the American Government if the fleet were surrendered to Germany, had "deeply pained" his Government. Biddle stated to us, however, his belief that, in spite of this natural feeling, the effect of the message was highly salutary at that juncture.

Former Premier Reynaud, who regained something of his old drive following his narrow escape from nervous collapse just prior to his resignation, sent Ambassador de Saint-Quentin a message for President Roosevelt at the moment he left office. The Ambassador left this with the President on June 18. "I wish to say to you, Mr. President," cabled Reynaud, "that I feel that the reply which you made to my last message went to the extreme limit of what was permitted by existing circumstances. . . . France feels that, because America exists, the form of civilization which is hers will not die, and that the day will come when liberty will be reborn in old Europe."

Then passed several days of anxious waiting to see what the German armistice terms would be, and whether France would accept them. Biddle informed me on June 19 that the German reply had arrived that morning, instructing France to name delegates to an armistice meeting. Meantime a struggle continued among members of the French Government as to whether to remain in France or go to North Africa. I thereupon cabled Biddle on June 19 that I felt, in the event President Lebrun or any group of officials constituting the French Government moved to North Africa, he should accompany them and take with him such members of his staff as he required.

On the same day Biddle cabled us that the French had informed the Germans that negotiations for an armistice must be contingent on a cessation of the German advance southward. If the German advance continued, a majority of the Government would go to North Africa and continue the fight from there. The German advance halted, and with it any real desire in the French Cabinet to transfer the government to North Africa.

Our public was now more keenly conscious of the grave dangers threatening us than at any time since I had entered the State Department. But on the following day, when I went to Harvard University to receive an honorary degree, I used this occasion to drive home again the need for action.

"There are at work in the world today," I said, "powerful forces the significance of which no individual and no nation can ignore without falling into a position of the gravest danger and of the utmost jeopardy. . . . They spring today from the same source from which they have always sprung in the past—from godless and soulless lust for power which seeks to hold men in physical slavery and spiritual degradation and to displace a system of peaceful and orderly relations among nations by the anarchy of wanton violence and brute force. . . .

"No more vital test has ever confronted the American people than that which confronts it today. There are difficult and dangerous times ahead. Our national independence and our cherished institutions are not immune from the challenge of the lust for power that already stalks so much of the earth's surface. Unprecedented effort and heavy sacrifices will be required of us as the price of preserving, for ourselves and for our posterity, the kind of America that has been fostered and preserved for us by the vigilance, courage, and sacrifice of those who preceded us. We shall succeed if we retain unimpaired the most precious heritage which they bequeathed us—an unshakable faith in the everlasting worth of freedom and honor, of truth and justice, of intellectual and spiritual integrity; and an immutable determination to give our all, if need be, for the preservation of our way of life."

I returned to the State Department the following day to find a discouraging dispatch from Biddle. He reported that, as the French Government remained in ignorance of Germany's armistice terms, the atmosphere of capitulation was growing apace. Such will to resist as still remained was being sapped by stories of collapse at the front and by anti-British feeling in the Government. Shipment of war material to North Africa had stopped. Sinking rather than escape of the fleet seemed probable. The passing of time had ill served the supporters of a free government in Africa.

Then, about midnight on June 21, the German armistice terms were received at Bordeaux. Biddle cabled me the provisions: Germany to occupy the entire Atlantic and Channel coasts and leave less than one-third of the country to the French Government. Demobilization and disarmament to be immediate and complete. The entire French fleet to return to or remain in French ports and be dismantled under German supervision, with the exception of units released for the protection of the French colonies. The German Government declared to the French Government that it did not intend to use the French war fleet in harbors under German control for its purposes of war.

The Pétain Government agreed to these terms, and the armistice between Germany and France was signed on June 22.

With the armistice an accomplished fact, there were no further diplomatic steps the British or American Governments could take. Biddle cabled me a variety of assurances from Foreign Minister Baudouin that, in case of last-minute German treachery as the Germans superintended the dismantling of the fleet, the ships would be sunk; but the Ambassador commented that the value of such a last-minute safeguard seemed pitifully small.

As the President and I minutely scrutinized the wording of Article VIII of the armistice terms, relating to the fleet, we could not but be anxious. If the Germans were to superintend the dismantling of the French warships, they could also seize them. As for German promises not to use the French fleet for their own war purposes, they were worth less than an oat.

When French Ambassador de Saint-Quentin came on June 27 to complain about our freezing of French credits in the United States, I pointedly inquired about the status of the French fleet. He said he recognized our interest in its disposition.

I interrupted by saying: "France's recovery both at home and in the colonies depends primarily on the disposition of your naval and merchant fleet. If France loses control of the fleet, she will come completely and hopelessly under the domination of Hitler and his economic policies of totalitarian autarchy.

"I'll be frank to say very earnestly and definitely that my country is greatly interested in France's not permitting Germany to get control and possession of the French fleet. We have made clear to the world our interest in and our aid to France in the war. After we have incurred the ill will of Germany by reason of this fact, it is naturally a matter of very great importance to us if France hands to Germany a cocked gun to shoot at us." And I reminded De Saint-Quentin that his Government had said to us that our fleet in the Pacific was of real value to French interests in the Far East, which were very great.

The Ambassador agreed entirely with what I said, but he tried to make it appear that Germany would be more or less harmless under her promise not to use the French warships for her military purposes.

"Of course," I retorted, "nobody would trust Hitler on a promise of that sort."

De Saint-Quentin also said he wished this Government would urge upon the British the importance of agreeable relations between the British and French Governments. He had in mind the recriminations that had been passing back and forth between Britain and France since Pétain's request for an armistice; many French accused the British of not having aided them to the utmost of their ability; many British blamed the French for having failed to carry on the fight against the Nazi enemy.

"Speaking individually," I said, "I know that no harm can come—on the contrary, nothing but good can possibly come—from the preservation of friendly relations between the two Governments. I'll keep your suggestion especially in mind."

This now became one of the cardinal points of our policy, to keep Britain and France on as friendly terms as possible.

The French fleet was not our sole preoccupation. We were also preoccupied as to what might happen to the British fleet. Now that France had succumbed, Hitler was free to turn his full power against Britain. The President and I believed Britain could and would resist the Nazi attack successfully, but there were many in America and Europe who believed with Pétain and his group that Britain would be conquered or make peace within a few weeks.

When British Ambassador Lothian came to me on June 11 he said he had received from Churchill a suggestion that staff conferences be held between naval officials of our two Governments with regard to fleet movements in both the Atlantic and the Pacific. I replied that I doubted whether there would be any occasion for staff conferences, but I should be glad to pass his suggestion on to the President.

Commenting then on the fact that there was much public talk with regard to the disposition of the British fleet in the event of the defeat of Britain, I said: "Any friend of Britain, like myself, knows that she will fight to the last penny, to the last man, and to the last ship, if necessary. The people primarily interested in the British Navy are the members of the British Empire. Great Britain, of course, will not think of turning the fleet over to Germany if she expects to recover from this wholly unexpected temporary defeat due to sudden attack with new devices or weapons."

Lothian said Churchill did not remotely contemplate Germany's getting the British fleet so far as his Government was concerned. The only danger in this respect would arise in connection with some successor government of the Mosley (British Fascist) or Communist type.

I recalled to him that, in the First World War, a new peace government took charge in Germany to negotiate the peace, but sank the German fleet before peace terms were formulated.

Lothian asked if his military attaché could confer with appropriate officials in the War Department on the effect of British and French bombings inside Germany. I said I was sure our military people would be glad to give his attaché any information at all feasible, although we could not be connected with any exchange of information of that nature. Subsequently I arranged for the military attaché to confer with the War Department on this subject, and I requested our diplomatic and consular officers in Germany to keep us informed on the results of British bombings in Germany.

I talked further with Lothian on June 24 about the disposition of the British fleet. He again made the suggestion that confidential staff conferences be held between the appropriate military and naval officials of our two Governments. They would be highly important in the event the British Government had to move to Canada, taking with it what would be left of the British fleet. But this would result only from a British defeat —and neither Lothian nor I contemplated this at all.

I remarked that it might prove more desirable to have an exchange of information through diplomatic rather than army and navy officials, at least during this stage. I commented that it was all-important to avoid publicity, which might be misunderstood, even though nothing would be said in conferences that needed to be concealed from the public, if correctly interpreted and understood. What the President and I had in mind was the possibility that the holding of military staff conversations would "leak out" and opponents of the Administration, along with the isolationists, would forthwith charge that the President was planning to get the United States into the war.

A dramatic, though only partial, settlement of the question of the French fleet came on July 3. The British took over the French warships in British ports; they informed the French Admiral in command of a squadron at Alexandria that they would sink his ships if he tried to take them to France where they would fall under German control; and they delivered an ultimatum to the French Admiral in command of a large portion of the French Navy, at Mers-el-Kébir, near Oran, North Africa. The ultimatum required the French warships at Mers-el-Kébir to join the British or else proceed to British or West Indian or United States ports to be interned. When the French Admiral refused, the British opened fire and put most of the French ships out of commission, killing more than 1,000 Frenchmen.

This was an action solely between the British and the French. It did not call for comment on our part. Nevertheless, I did not think the attack had been necessary. I could not help being inexpressibly saddened by this latest manifestation of the tragic break between Britain and France. For more than seven years I had done everything I legitimately could to keep the two major democracies of Europe working closely together toward the common end of law and order throughout the world. I had supported them both on every possible occasion. We three had developed a parallel policy toward the Far East. We at last saw eye to eye on a program of liberal commerce. Now for the warships of Britain and France to fire on one another, at the very moment when the hordes of Hitler were preparing to overwhelm the last remaining bulwark of Western civilization in Europe, was to me a tragic blunder.

A year and a half later, when Mr. Churchill was visiting the President toward the end of December, 1941, I sat between the Prime Minister and a British admiral at one of the luncheons the President gave for his distinguished visitor. The admiral asked me what I had thought of the British attack on the French fleet at Oran. I parried the question because I did not want to get up a squabble between him and Mr. Churchill, for I had heard that the British Navy had been opposed to the attack, and that serious differences over it had risen within the British Government.

A few minutes later, however, I brought up the subject with Mr.

Churchill himself. He wound up with a general statement that the Vichy French were not to be trusted and would have turned the fleet over to the Germans if the attack had not been made. He also said that, since many people throughout the world believed that Britain was about ready to surrender, he had wanted by this action to show that she still meant to fight.

I was not able to go along with him in this view.

Marshal Pétain wrote to President Roosevelt to denounce what he called "this odious aggression." He said there was no excuse whatever for it in view of the assurances that had been made to the British Government concerning the fleet. He immediately broke off diplomatic relations with Britain.

Bullitt, who had left Paris after some days of German occupation, saw Pétain, Laval, Baudouin, and others at Vichy on July 4, the day after the British attack. He cabled me on the 5th that their reaction was violent in the extreme. Several Cabinet members advocated immediate acts of war against Britain, but Pétain resolutely opposed anything more than a break of diplomatic relations. The Axis was quickly trying to take advantage of the violent wave of anti-British feeling by lightly modifying the armistice clauses with regard to the French fleet and air force and by permitting the Pétain Government to make radio broadcasts. Pétain nevertheless said to Bullitt he recognized that only a defeat of Hitler by some other power could restore independence to France, and he therefore sincerely desired a British victory. He sought to minimize the breach with Britain by attributing it to what he called Churchill's personal lack of balance.

Bullitt's first impression of the group at Vichy, however, given in a cable to me on July 1 after he had talked to virtually all members of the Government, was discouraging. He said the French leaders desired to cut loose from all that France had represented during the last two generations. So as to have as many companions in misery as possible, they hoped England would be rapidly and completely defeated by Germany and the Italians would suffer the same fate. They hoped that France might become Germany's favorite province, a new *Gau* (German word for province) which would develop into a new Gaul.

Bullitt quoted Admiral Darlan to the effect that Britain would die of asphyxiation even without a German invasion. Under no conditions would Darlan send the French fleet to Britain because the British would never return a single warship. And if Britain won the war the treatment

France would receive would be no more generous than her treatment by Germany.

To us Mr. Churchill justified his attack on the French Navy on the ground of the supreme necessity of self-defense.

In any event, Britons who feared that the French Navy might be joined to the Germans in an overwhelming assault on the British Isles could now sleep of nights with a little more assurance.

58: Democracies at Bay

AS FRANCE FELL, Great Britain laid before us a frank and somber picture of her perilous position. With her back to the Atlantic wall, she was now fighting for her life, and she needed all the help we could possibly give her.

Ambassador Lothian brought me on June 27 an *aide-mémoire* from his Government which documented Britain's fears and hopes. Britain thought it was by no means improbable that the French might be compelled to hand over their fleet to the Germans. All European neutrals, with the possible exception of Turkey, might eventually fall under German or Italian domination, and Britain's position in the Mediterranean might be reduced to denying the Suez Canal to the enemy.

The British Government thought that the whole Empire, with the possible exception of Eire, would increase its efforts to support the mother country, although the attitude of India might be doubtful. The British also thought that Japan might become more active, but that Russia, probably alarmed at Hitler's success, might cease to assist him.

The undaunted British felt that Germany could still be defeated, but only by combining economic pressure, air attacks on Germany, and the creation of widespread revolt in the conquered territories. Toward this end the British Isles had to be secured as the main base for naval and airforce operations. They had to withstand the effects of large-scale air attacks on centers of industry and ports and of naval and air attacks against their sea-borne trade.

The British Government informed us that its ability to defeat Germany depended on a complete blockade of Europe. Full Pan American cooperation would be essential so that raw materials might be controlled at the source. Relief to people in occupied territories would only prolong the struggle.

As for carrying on the struggle from North America in the event the United Kingdom were overrun by the Axis, the British observed to us that, in resisting invasion, the whole of the home fleet would be thrown into the battle, and a successful invasion of the British Isles would automatically imply the loss of a large part of it. The remaining forces operating from America would be faced with considerable problems, and the combined German and Italian fleets, possibly augmented by French warships, might extend their activities well beyond Europe. Without air bases close to Germany and with Britain's ability to exert economic pressure considerably reduced, her chance of victory would be virtually gone, even with the full military and economic assistance of North America.

Britain then stated her full requirements from us. She needed aircraft, destroyers, light naval craft, military equipment and supplies; also personnel, possibly volunteers, to man ships and aircraft. She suggested stoppage at source of all supplies to enemy countries and occupied territories and full cooperation in her contraband control with reference to the remaining European neutrals, including Asiatic Russia. She requested supplies of food, munitions, and raw materials on a credit basis, if necessary, and merchant shipping to ply between the Americas and the United Kingdom. She suggested that the United States Government make a declaration that any attempt to change the status quo in the Far East would not be tolerated.

I took up these various points with the President. We were even then making every effort humanly possible to get military equipment to Britain. Large quantities had already left our ports. We were also willing to cooperate to the utmost in preventing supplies from reaching Germany. The Administration was supporting a bill before Congress to authorize the President to embargo the export of materials essential to our national defense. This went into effect less than a week after my conversation with Lothian. And we were making strenuous efforts to uphold the status quo in the Pacific, as I shall narrate later.

Lothian came back on July 3 and handed me two additional memoranda from his Government. Britain now suggested that, if we were to complete our own rearmament program and at the same time provide the much larger supplies necessary to enable the Allies to maintain the struggle, we should have to make far-reaching changes in our industrial organization. Britain confessed that her own program had suffered severely from her slowness to realize this necessity. Now production for domestic civil consumption would have to be curtailed, and priorities given to war production.

The British felt they should inform us frankly that, although they would continue to pay for their purchases here, it would be impossible to do so indefinitely because of the vast quantities they needed. They suggested an amendment of the Neutrality Act to permit American merchantmen to carry supplies to Britain, and a joint use of the mercantile fleets of the United States and the Allies.

Britain renewed her previous suggestion that we cut off all exports to Germany, Italy, and the occupied territories. We had informed Britain on June 20 that we could not agree to her previous recommendation that we freeze German and Italian financial balances in the United States, but Britain urged that we reconsider.

I discussed all these suggestions with the President. Some of them embraced possible actions in the domestic field, and were therefore beyond my jurisdiction. In making others, such as that American merchant ships should carry cargoes to the United Kingdom, Britain failed to realize that such proposals by the Administration would provoke passionate opposition from isolationists in and out of Congress. The great majority of the American public were behind our efforts to aid the Allies in all ways possible, but they were equally resolved that we should stay out of the war.

Lothian brought me a further memorandum from his Government on July 15, asking us to use our influence to induce Argentina, Brazil, Uruguay, Chile, and Venezuela to take all the measures we had already taken to prevent the assets of the conquered countries on deposit in the Western Hemisphere from falling into the hands of the Axis. I was to leave four days later for the Havana Conference, where I discussed these questions with the delegations there.

The day before my departure, Lothian brought yet another memorandum from his Government, which laid down the British opposition to the extension of relief to countries occupied by the Germans. The British argued that the Germans had it in their power to see that the inhabitants of the occupied territories were adequately fed. Britain, while appreciating to the full the humanitarian ideals inspiring the desire to supply relief to the stricken territories, was convinced it would be an entirely mistaken policy to lengthen the war by allowing Germany to be assisted in the difficulties which confronted her and were of her own creation. Britain also said she felt obliged to treat unoccupied France in the same way as occupied France.

The British stated they realized that their decision might lay them open to criticism; but their intention was to win the war in the shortest possible time and so to liberate the conquered peoples from Nazi oppression. They therefore hoped our Government would be able to see the question in this light.

I asked Lothian whether his Government did not propose to strengthen the basis of its action by stating publicly that so long as German methods and policies were in force, a relief undertaking at this time would really be for the benefit of Germany, German armed forces, and German citizens. He said he would bring this to the attention of his Government.

Our own humanitarian feelings were stirred by the plight of the occupied countries, but it was obvious to the President and me that the sending of supplies to the conquered nations would simply lighten Hitler's obligation to furnish such supplies, and would increase his economic strength. In the long run the occupied countries would benefit more from a policy that made Hitler's defeat more certain in a shorter time than one that gave them a temporary relief.

Former President Herbert Hoover, whose relief operations in Belgium during the First World War were well and warmly remembered, was now making relief plans for France, Belgium, and Holland. He came several times to enlist my support. I got along well with him, and I could appreciate his sincerity and humanitarianism; but, since his plans were in conflict with our ideas and those of Britain on winning the war, I could not encourage him. .

By the time I left for the Havana Conference on July 19, our policy toward the Pétain Government at Vichy had crystallized. There were four main facets to this policy.

The first was to see that the French fleet was not turned over to Hitler.

The second was to see that the Axis did not get possession or control of French bases in Africa or in the Western Hemisphere. In June I sent a series of telegrams to all our consular representatives in the French African possessions, requesting them to keep us closely and quickly informed of all developments in this connection. The status of the French and Dutch possessions in the Western Hemisphere was to form the center of much of my work at Havana.

The third was to see that the Vichy Government did not go beyond the terms of the armistice toward active collaboration with Hitler. The terms had dangerous possibilities, in our opinion, but if France lived up to them she would not aid Hitler directly. If they were interpreted and enlarged, as Laval and his clique wished, they could make France a virtual ally of the Nazis.

The fourth was to restore a degree of friendship between France and Britain. The British attack on the French fleet made this difficult, but I felt that with the passage of a little time it was not impossible.

The President and I had no hesitation in continuing diplomatic relations with the Pétain Government, while waiting to see what its ultimate policy would be. Diplomatic relations between Britain and France had been broken because of the naval engagement at Oran, but no such incident lay athwart Franco-American relations. The Pétain Government was a legal Government. When Bullitt came back to the United States at the end of July he expressed to the President and me his view that Marshal Pétain was respected throughout France and was trying to restore order. Our only excuse for breaking off diplomatic ties with Vichy could have been the fact that the Pétain Cabinet was leaving the democratic traditions of France for a dictatorial form of government which smacked of fascism. But at that time we still maintained relations with such completely fascist governments as those of Germany, Italy, and Spain.

It seemed to us to be the part of common sense to continue full contact with Vichy, particularly since the British had no contact at all. By maintaining our relations we could buttress the Pétain Government during a future that we knew would inevitably be marked by more extensive demands from the Germans. We could encourage the French people by convincing them that we were still behind them. We could keep in close touch with developments in French colonial possessions. We could obtain information through our diplomatic and consular representatives which otherwise would not be available. This would be of use to both ourselves and the British. Ambassador Kennedy forwarded to me from London on June 24 a request that we keep the British Government informed on developments in German-occupied France and in Italy, where it had no representatives.

On the same day Ambassador Lothian said to me he expected soon to receive instructions from his Government to ascertain our attitude toward the Pétain Government, then still at Bordeaux. I replied that we would that day announce the temporary designation of Ambassador Biddle to represent our Government to the French Government while it was absent from Paris, but that Biddle would soon return to his post with the Polish Government, now in London, by making his way through Spain. I added that Bullitt's services were ended by a German occupation or military control of France, and we should expect him to return to the United States. Relations with the French Government would go on.

The Churchill Government was not opposed to our continuance of relations with Vichy. On the contrary, we received various informal expressions from that Government of the value to Britain of our maintaining

this contact. The British Government itself enjoyed an indirect contact
with Vichy through the Canadian Legation there.

General Charles de Gaulle had now established the headquarters of a
resistance movement in London, and had been recognized by Britain as
the leader of all Free Frenchmen. This was not recognition of De Gaulle
as the head of a government, however, and Mr. Churchill carefully
avoided such recognition. Our own attitude toward De Gaulle was that
of waiting to see what he would do, and to what extent he could rally
Frenchmen to his cause. There was then no question of our "recognizing"
him. We could not accord him diplomatic recognition as a government
and at the same time maintain diplomatic relations with the Vichy Government.

As our policy toward Vichy France came into being, we noticed a
new development, one that might eventually be as important as France
or even more so in the scales of war. It seemed to me that the Soviet
Union, alarmed by the overwhelming German victories in France and the
Low Countries, was beginning to shift toward a policy of active defense
which recognized that Hitler might at some time turn his might eastward.
Ever since the Russo-German nonaggression pact of August, 1939, Moscow had relied on a long war of exhaustion in the West as her best
guarantee against Hitler's oft expressed ambitions. Almost overnight,
however, the situation had changed. Hitler, freed of any active enemy
on the continent of Europe, was now free to shift his forces to the east.
It behooved Stalin to get ready.

The *aide-mémoire* which Ambassador Lothian handed me on June 27
mentioned Britain's belief that Russia, probably becoming alarmed at
Hitler's success, might cease to assist him. We ourselves felt that, although
relations between Germany and Russia were probably started in the direction of a break, Stalin, while making his own defense moves, would do
everything he could to maintain friendship with Hitler by continuing
to send supplies to Germany, at least in normal amounts, in an effort to
gain time.

The Secretary General of the French Foreign Office, Charles Roux,
who had succeeded Alexis Léger, had suggested to Bullitt on May 21 that
our Government get in touch with the Soviet Government and suggest
that, as two great neutral peoples who might some day be menaced by
Germany, we should withhold any supplies possible from Germany. Bullitt commented to Charles Roux that he did not believe we could take this
step. I cabled Bullitt the same day that I fully approved his attitude; we

were convinced, on the basis of such information as we possessed concerning the Soviet Government's attitude, that such a move would serve no useful purpose at present.

The attitude of the Soviet Government was clearly, if bluntly, expressed when I cabled our Embassy in Moscow on May 29 to seek information concerning Soviet military movements toward Rumania. American Minister Gunther in Bucharest had cabled me there was a concentration of Russian troops along the Rumanian border and the Rumanians believed that Stalin, aghast at the extent of the German victories in the west, was seeking possession of the Rumanian province of Bessarabia in order to place himself in a better bargaining position toward Hitler.

Our Chargé at Moscow, Walter Thurston, after seeing Foreign Commissar Molotov, cabled me on May 31 that Molotov had launched into a violent complaint against the United States—specifically at the cancellation of orders placed with American firms by the Soviet Union, which he described as unfriendly and intolerable. When Thurston explained that, for reasons of national defense, we were requisitioning orders placed by other Governments also, and therefore there was no discrimination against Russia, Molotov's anger rose. He said we had no mandate to revise the normal methods of intercourse between Governments; our action was unlawful and intolerable; we must assume full responsibility for it, and it would bring us no good.

At the beginning of June, however, Thurston began to inform me of a change of attitude on the part of the Soviet Government toward the Allies. Moscow, shaken by the rapidity of the German advance, now wanted France to continue in the war. Previously Moscow had supported the movement of the French Communists to impede the Reynaud Government.

Soviet Ambassador Oumansky, a walking insult when at his worst, came to see me on June 12. I knew he wanted to protest the fact that our own Government, for purposes of national defense, was taking over machine tools previously ordered by his Government. I was aware of his numerous conferences on this subject with other officials of the State Department and of the vituperative tone he had adopted. I therefore opened the discussion myself.

I emphasized at some length the extremely dislocated, lawless state of the world resulting from policies of countries that were carrying out plans of conquest by force and of rule by force. I reviewed our relations with Russia since our recognition of the Soviet regime in 1933, and commented that Russia had urgently desired recognition because of the dangerous relations between her and Japan.

"I and some of my associates," I said, "have incurred bitter criticism during the past seven years because of our earnest efforts to cooperate with Russia. We had hoped that this cooperation not only would be for our mutual benefit but also would be a stabilizing factor in the international situation and would discourage heavy armaments and prevent war. In these efforts we have been hopelessly disappointed in many important respects."

After mentioning the numerous efforts we had made to work with every other country at all disposed to go in the direction of peace, especially Russia, I said: "It is with unspeakable disappointment and regret that we have seen all our efforts come to naught. In these circumstances my Government has proceeded on a new policy of arming and arming and arming in order to defend itself against anybody. To this end my Government has no hesitation in taking necessary materials and otherwise conserving all the commodities needed for this day-and-night program of armament. If anything unlawful is done we will take the responsibility, though I am not intimating that anything unlawful is being done. In any event, my Government has no notion of making further sacrifices or engaging in further delays that would in the slightest retard or handicap its program of armament. Here it stands, and your Government ought to be able to understand and realize that this is exactly our position."

I concluded by saying that it had been a great disappointment to us not to have the cooperation of Russia to a much fuller and broader extent in the past seven years. This especially in view of the great lengths to which we had gone to encourage such cooperation for peace and mutual welfare.

Oumansky began to speak of the "trade discriminations" by this Government. I interrupted him by saying:

"I'm surprised, in the light of existing exigencies, to see your Government engaging in such small topics of controversy. Your Government is discriminating in favor of other countries in its trade methods, and we are saying nothing. This includes immense war supplies to Germany."

Oumansky remarked that this was normal trade.

"In any event," I replied, "it comprises immense supplies urgently needed for war, which fact makes it vastly different from normal trade. Russia, of course, has a perfect right to pursue this trade so far as my Government is concerned. We followed a very different policy toward

Italy during the Italo-Ethiopian War, when we held down our trade to the prewar level by a moral embargo. My primary contention, however, rests on our present policy of conserving materials for increasing our armaments."

I said then that in our extreme desire to see Russia pursue a course that would give her a great influence for peace, the President had generously offered his good offices to Russia before she invaded Finland.

Oumansky said rather sarcastically—sarcasm poured from the Ambassador like wheat from a thresher—Yes, but his Government did not respond very well to the President's speech on a certain occasion at that time. He was referring to the President's condemnation of Russia's invasion of Finland.

"When a giant country," I replied, "has a little microscopic helpless country by the throat and is choking it to death, I must agree that the Government of the large country is not in a position to respond or to react. Naturally the deepest possible silence is about the only recourse in such circumstances."

The Ambassador looked uncomfortable, but said nothing in reply.

Having in mind the bitter and patronizing talk of Molotov to Chargé Thurston in Moscow a few days before, and the loud, insulting talk of the Ambassador here in Washington on all possible occasions, I commented:

"Mr. Molotov seems to have gotten on a high horse. I have also been hearing of the vituperative talks round and about Washington by Mr. Molotov's representative here. This seems to be my compensation for having undergone biting criticism for seven years in my efforts to keep up something like desirable relations with Soviet Russia, and the reward for my hope of their improvement."

At that point Oumansky handed me a note of protest from Molotov, citing instances of our Government's taking over machine tools and the like for which Russia had placed orders with American firms. Russia threatened to file claims for damages against us.

"I have already anticipated the contents of this paper," I said, "because I have heard nothing harped on except these comparatively small items." I again called his attention to our basic defense policy, and said that other Governments whose orders were taken over were not raving like his.

When Oumansky continued to stress his complaints, I remarked that I could list a whole ream of earnest complaints against Russia, but I did not want to say anything more than I had said. He invited—rather, challenged—me to list any I might have in mind. Fortunately, Ambassador Steinhardt, who had returned to Washington from Moscow, had written out for me a number of pages of complaints, and I had these before me. I thereupon read off the first page of Steinhardt's indictments, and added that I could read several additional pages but would not do so.

Finally, referring again to the long, earnest efforts I and others had made to get along amicably with Russia, I said: "My Government will be glad, whenever Russia sees fit, to return to a set of policies to develop more fully the relations of peace and mutually profitable cooperation in every practicable way. The amount of Russian trade with us is relatively small, and it would be a mistake to exaggerate any special importance we might attach to it. But we should be glad to see it retained and developed, provided such development can take place under mutually acceptable relations between our two countries."

At almost the hour of this conversation, I began to get dispatches from our representatives in Estonia, Latvia, and Lithuania concerning demands from Russia that Soviet troops be permitted to occupy those countries fully, and that their governments be reorganized so as to be more friendly to Russia. The Baltic countries had to accede, and the Soviet occupation began on June 15.

One reason for this move was obvious; Stalin wanted a better defensive position with regard to Germany. John C. Wiley, our Minister to Latvia, cabled me on June 19 information from a reliable informant that the Kremlin was in a state of acute anxiety and confusion over recent developments. Stalin's policy had been premised on a long war of exhaustion in the west. This policy collapsed with the collapse of France. Hitler's recent statement—made in an effort to induce a peace offer from Britain—that he did not desire the destruction of the British Empire had created panic in the Soviet mind, which now feared that the problems of western Europe would be solved at Russia's expense.

Within a fortnight after Russia occupied the Baltic countries, she took another important step in Europe by invading Rumania to occupy Bessarabia and part of Bukovina. The fears that Minister Gunther in Bucharest had expressed to me in May had turned out to be real. Russia now had a more defensible southwestern frontier. The occupation of the Baltic states and the Rumanian territory had straightened out the curve in her western border.

Dispatches from various of our representatives pointed to the conclusion that Hitler's Government had been given scarcely any advance notice of Russia's moves. A note of strain now began to appear in Russo-German relations.

Undoubtedly it was fear of what might happen in Europe that motivated Stalin to negotiate a settlement of the long-standing dispute with Japan over the border between Manchuria and Outer Mongolia, which at times had flared into open warfare. The agreement was announced in Moscow on June 9. Robert L. Smyth, our Chargé in Peiping, cabled me on June 20 that Russia had hoped that assistance from the United States to the Allies or a declaration of war by us would counterbalance Germany, even after the invasion of France began, but the fall of France upset her calculations. She had accordingly made the border settlement with Japan in order to be free to act in Europe.

Great Britain, utilizing these various signs of Soviet alarm over Germany's victories, now sought to bring about a definite shift in Russian policy. Chargé Thurston in Moscow cabled me on June 20 information from the new British Ambassador, Sir Stafford Cripps, that Cripps had taken up with Molotov a switch in Soviet policy away from Germany toward active support of the Allies. Molotov had not rejected the arguments Cripps advanced. Cripps had suggested to London that Ambassador Lothian here be instructed to say to the President or me that it would be helpful if the United States Government would intimate to the Soviet Government that we would welcome such a shift.

Lothian did come to the State Department a few days later to make this point.

It did not seem to us, however, that action such as Britain was taking or we might take would have the desired effect. Stalin did not want war with Hitler; the moves he was making to obtain a more strategic frontier were taken partly for defensive reasons; and he would resent any effort to propel him into the conflict.

On our part, we froze the credits of the Baltic countries held in the United States, and continued to recognize their diplomatic representatives.

Three months later Nevile Butler, Counselor of the British Embassy, communicated to us a suggestion Cripps made to his Government that, as a principal action toward inducing the Soviets to line up with the Allies against the Axis, the credits of the three Baltic states be released, of course to Russia. I asked James C. Dunn, our Political Adviser on European Affairs, to advise Butler that Britain was free to act as she chose.

As for ourselves, we had refused to recognize Russia's absorption of the Baltic countries, and we therefore could not release the credits to Russia.

In midsummer of 1940 I called Welles to my office and set forth a division of labor between us. I said I would assume charge of the conversations with the Japanese Ambassador, and he should assume charge of the conversations with the Soviet Ambassador. He should try, through a series of conversations with Oumansky, to see whether some real bases for agreement between our two countries could be reached. He thereupon began a succession of a score of conferences, on an average of one each fortnight. I shall comment later on the outcome.

Such was the situation in Europe—ever increasing aid going from the United States to Britain; a watchful, buttressing policy on the part of this Government toward Vichy; and Russia assuming an actively defensive role toward Hitler—as I left Washington for Havana to work with the other American Republics toward a common defense of the hemisphere.

59: Assault on the Hemisphere

HITLER'S SPECTACULAR DEFEAT of the armies of France and the Low Countries immediately deposited acute problems on our doorstep in the Western Hemisphere.

One was the fact that France and Holland possessed islands and other territory in this half of the world. The French possessions ranged from the islands of Saint-Pierre and Miquelon off Newfoundland to the islands of Martinique and Guadeloupe in the Caribbean and to French Guiana in South America. The Netherlands had Dutch Guiana in South America and a string of islands in the Caribbean, including Curaçao and Aruba with their important oil refineries. What was to become of these lands, and what was to be our attitude toward them and toward the possibility that the conquering Germans might claim them?

The other problem was the tremendous psychological springboard that victory gave the Nazis to intensify their penetration of Latin America, both politically and economically. The conquest of France and the Low Countries had scarcely begun when reports from our diplomatic missions in Latin America started coming to my desk that the Nazis were preparing to make Central and South America an economic appanage of Germany.

German businessmen, working closely with the Nazi Party, were scattered all over South America. They were developing their businesses and digging in socially, commercially, and politically. They were using every method possible in the line of subversive activities. They were invading the universities. They were insinuating themselves into every kind of official and individual activity that would give them influence or control in their respective orbits.

In May our vice consul at São Paulo, Brazil, reported that German businessmen in that area, confident that the war would soon end in Germany's favor, had begun negotiations for resumption of trade. At least one firm was guaranteeing delivery in September, only four months later. Our Embassy in Rio reported that the German commercial attaché there had instructed all German commercial firms in Brazil to place their orders in Germany, with delivery guaranteed for October. The German Ambassador in Brazil offered in mid-July to deliver war tanks during the latter part of September.

So confident of speedy victory were the German firms that they sometimes agreed to pay fines in event of nondelivery by the stipulated date.
They quoted prices lower than those on United States goods, with dis-
counts as high as 25 per cent, and offered the most liberal credit arrangements. In the face of these offers and of adverse developments in the war,
Latin American firms hesitated to place new orders with North American
companies.

The Nazis in Latin America, officials and private citizens alike, sedu-
lously spread the thought that Germany would soon control the whole
economy of Europe and therefore any country or company in Latin
America wishing to deal with any country or company anywhere in
Europe had better negotiate at once with the nearest German representative.

In general the Nazis in Latin America, according to the cables I
received from our diplomatic missions, were making no secret of their
plans and were boasting openly that Germany could easily conquer South
America. Their plans ran as follows:

(1) Use the British, French, Scandinavian, and other merchant fleets
to carry on commerce with Latin America at rates that would put American lines out of business.

(2) Blanket Latin America with German aviation lines carrying
freight and passengers at rates with which American lines could not
compete.

(3) Export German and European merchandise to Latin America
at whatever prices necessary to undersell American products.

(4) Overthrow any Latin American Government not favorable to
Germany and substitute one that would cooperate.

(5) Then take over the Latin American countries as virtual dependencies.

Had Hitler's armies and air force conquered Britain, I am convinced
Germany would have tried to pursue this program to the letter. It was
therefore evident to me that we had to take rapid and decisive steps to
prevent our neighbors to the South from succumbing to German pressure
and propaganda.

Our first diplomatic exchange with regard to territories in the Western Hemisphere, however, occurred with Britain and not with Germany.
Immediately upon the invasion of Holland, British and French troops
occupied the Dutch islands of Curaçao and Aruba respectively to protect
the valuable oil refineries there. This action was doubly important to us

and had dangerous implications because it not only concerned the Western Hemisphere but might also set a precedent for the Japanese to land troops in the Dutch East Indies.

I at once called British Ambassador Lothian to my office on May 10. I began by mentioning the real possibility that Holland would be overrun and occupied by the Germans with the result that questions would arise concerning Netherlands colonies throughout the world. Coming then to the report that the British were occupying Curaçao, I said:

"Countries throughout this hemisphere will be likely to construe this action as assumption of more or less jurisdiction over Curaçao, regardless of the real intention of the British to the contrary. I feel that the possible arousing of adverse comment among the American nations will do the British needless harm, assuming that you have no intention of violating the Monroe Doctrine."

At first Lothian seemed to resent my comment. He bluntly and with some feeling asked whether we would guarantee the oil resources on Curaçao from being sabotaged.

"That," I replied, "is not the question I'm undertaking to raise. My only question is that, whatever might be the motive of the British, they can very easily develop misunderstanding and criticism throughout the American continent and thereby do themselves more harm than good. The point I had first in mind was to suggest that there is undoubtedly a different method of approaching the whole problem in lieu of British military occupation under circumstances calculated to arouse criticism.

"This method is to confer in advance with the interested countries in this hemisphere in order to find a way to solve the matter to the satisfaction of the British while avoiding suspicion and criticism on the theory that the British had some secret intention to occupy Curaçao more or less permanently."

Lothian seemed finally to understand and appreciate what I was saying. He promised to take it up with his Government.

The dangers in this situation quickly became apparent as reports were propagated that Britain intended to occupy—or had occupied—the Dutch East Indies in addition to the Dutch West Indies. After I had gone over the problem with the President, he himself called the Ambassador's attention to the perilous complications that might arise.

Lothian thereupon telephoned Foreign Secretary Lord Halifax. On May 12 he sent me a note saying that Halifax was issuing a statement immediately that Britain had no intention whatever of intervening in the

Dutch East Indies, and that British and French forces would be withdrawn from Curaçao and Aruba as soon as the Dutch and Allied Governments were satisfied as to the situation at Curaçao and Aruba or sufficient Dutch forces were available. Also, that Britain had no intention to alter the status of the islands.

A further question with regard to Aruba rose after the fall of France, when the Vichy Government withdrew its troops from the island. Ambassador Lothian came to see me on July 8 and said that the British would need to send guards to Aruba even though French troops were there, and a clash might result. After first advising him that, according to our reports, the French had departed, I said:

"My Government, of course, cannot agree and does not agree for any British troops to be sent to Aruba."

Lothian suggested that they might send Canadian guards.

"The same objection of my Government applies," I replied, "although the situation would not be so acute in these circumstances."

After I pointed out that the French had had only seventy-five to one hundred troops on Aruba, Lothian suggested that his Government might send the same number of guards from Curaçao to Aruba that the French had withdrawn from there.

I repeated that the United States could not agree to any British guards going there, and said that ample plans would be worked out at the forthcoming Havana Conference to deal with the question. A conference of the Foreign Ministers of the American Republics had been scheduled for October 1; but, as a result of the drastic problems presented by the fall of France and the Low Countries, it had been moved up to July 21, on our initiative.

Meantime we had formally made clear to all the belligerents that we would not acquiesce in any attempt to transfer territory in the Western Hemisphere from one European nation to another. At the State Department we drew up the draft of a joint resolution to be introduced in Congress, which the President approved and I sent to Senator Pittman and Representative Bloom, chairmen respectively of the Senate Committee on Foreign Relations and the House Committee on Foreign Affairs. They introduced this in Congress on June 3. It declared that our Government would not recognize the transfer of any Western Hemisphere territory from one European nation to another, nor acquiesce in any attempt at such transfer, and, if any such action seemed likely, we would immediately consult with the other American Republics on measures necessary to safeguard our common interests. The Senate passed the resolution unanimously on June 17, and the House virtually unanimously on the following day.

On June 17, the day the new Pétain Government in France sued for an armistice, I sent a note to Germany and Italy, saying: "The Government of the United States feels it desirable, in order to avoid any possible misunderstanding, to inform Your Excellency that in accordance with its traditional policy relating to the Western Hemisphere, the United States would not recognize any transfer, and would not acquiesce in any attempt to transfer, any geographic region of the Western Hemisphere from one non-American Power to another non-American Power." I informed France, Britain, and The Netherlands in the same sense. As the armistice negotiations between France and Germany were about to open, I wanted to make it as clear as words could do so that German acquisition of French possessions in the New World must not form part of any armistice agreement.

German Foreign Minister Ribbentrop replied on July 1 that Germany had given no occasion whatever for the assumption that it intended to acquire possessions in the Western Hemisphere and, therefore, our note was "without object." He went on to argue that our interpretation of the Monroe Doctrine conferred upon some European countries, and not upon others, the right to possess territories in the Western Hemisphere. Also, that the nonintervention in the affairs of the American continents demanded by the Monroe Doctrine could be legally valid only on condition that the American nations did not interfere in the affairs of the European Continent.

Following receipt of this note, I issued a public statement that the Monroe Doctrine was solely a policy of self-defense, intended to preserve the independence and integrity of the Americas. It was designed to prevent aggression in this hemisphere on the part of any non-American Power, and likewise to make impossible any further extension to this hemisphere of any non-American system of government imposed from without. It contained within it not the slightest vestige of any implication, much less assumption, of hegemony on the part of the United States.

In view of the so-called "new orders" that Hitler was seeking to set up in Europe, and Japan in Asia, I continued: "It never has resembled, and it does not today resemble, policies which appear to be arising in other geographical areas of the world, which are alleged to be similar to the Monroe Doctrine, but which, instead of resting on the sole policies of self-defense and of respect for existing sovereignties, as does the Monroe

Doctrine, would in reality seem to be only the pretext for the carrying out of conquest by the sword, of military occupation, and of complete economic and political domination by certain powers of other free and independent peoples."

I pointed out that the Monroe Doctrine had not the remotest connection with the fact that some European powers had colonies in the Western Hemisphere and others had not, because this situation existed before the Doctrine was proclaimed. But the Doctrine did make clear that the future transfer of existing possessions to another non-American state would be regarded as inimical to the interests of this hemisphere.

As for Ribbentrop's final argument, I said: "The Government of the United States pursues a policy of nonparticipation and of noninvolvement in the purely political affairs of Europe. It will, however, continue to cooperate, as it has cooperated in the past, with all other nations whenever the policies of such nations make it possible, and whenever it believes that such efforts are practicable and in its own best interests, for the purpose of promoting economic, commercial, and social rehabilitation, and of advancing the cause of international law and order, of which the entire world stands so tragically in need today."

The French island of Martinique, in the West Indies, proved a magnet attracting much of our diplomacy in the summer of 1940. When the Vichy regime was established, the Governor of Martinque, Admiral Robert, aligned himself entirely with it, and instituted a miniature dictatorship to keep this alignment.

The problem of Martinique was not solely that of the island as such. At Martinique were several French warships including the aircraft carrier *Béarn*, with 106 American-made planes that had been en route to France at the moment of the collapse, and a few French merchant ships. On the island was stored $245,000,000 in French gold that had been transferred from Canada.

We directed our diplomacy toward several objectives, all having the same end. We sought to avoid trouble between France and Britain over Martinique. We tried to effect the release of the airplanes aboard the *Béarn* to Britain or otherwise to have American manufacturers repurchase them and sell them to Britain—the British had taken over the French war-supply orders in the United States at the time of the armistice. And we endeavored to induce Admiral Robert to send his warships to American ports, or at least immobilize them so that they could not be used against the British.

British warships began to patrol the waters off Martinique on or about July 4. In view of the open battle between British and French warships at Oran on July 3, there was reason to believe that a bitter clash might occur between them in West Indies waters.

I therefore spoke very earnestly about this possibility to British Ambassador Lothian in my office on July 5. After telling him we had reports that two British cruisers were blockading the principal harbor of Martinique, and that British warships had prevented a French merchantman from entering, I said:

"My Government is concerned over possible developments of an undesirable nature at Martinique. Our Navy thinks that the British may seize the French vessels and also occupy Martinique with military forces. If this is done, it will involve real trouble between your Government and mine."

Lothian promptly disclaimed any idea whatever of this nature. He said he did not consider that British ships were blockading the harbor but were merely observing the situation.

"I'd like to suggest," I said, "that an agreement between the British and the French be worked out so that the French vessels and their cargoes might peacefully sail to an American port and be interned here, and the airplanes on the *Béarn* be turned over to Britain."

Lothian said he would present this proposal to his Government at once. He said he thought it might be accepted, although he added that his Government was very much in need of a plane carrier.

The President and I agreeing that an American naval force should be sent to Martinique waters to make sure that no naval battle occurred there, Mr. Roosevelt promptly ordered the dispatch of a heavy cruiser and six destroyers.

I carried on a series of conversations regarding Martinique with Ambassador Count de Saint-Quentin, now representing the Vichy Government. He was well disposed toward my suggestions, but it was obvious that his hands were tied by the unwillingness or inability of his Government to cooperate with us.

De Saint-Quentin said to me on July 16 that his Government would like to get permission from the German Government for the ships at Martinique to be exempted from the requirements of the armistice agreement so as to use them in trade for the benefit of French colonies and the French Government.

I replied that of course we would be obliged to have a commission

in charge of the ships before we could have sufficient assurance ourselves
and give sufficient assurance to the British that they would not fall into
the hands of Germany.

We sent Rear Admiral John W. Greenslade to Martinque on a special
mission to discuss ships, planes, and gold with Admiral Robert, and to
make sure that the island would not serve as a base for German submarine activity. The Governor, in general, was obdurate. Like many officials at Vichy, he could not see that his country's future lay solely in
a British victory. In the next few months we were unable to do more
than obtain vague assurances. The fighter planes that could have been
used in the defense of Britain against Göring's air armada rusted away.

We also decided to reopen our consulates at Fort-de-France, Martinique, and at Saint-Pierre and Miquelon, and to establish a new consulate at Cayenne, French Guiana, so as to give us additional points from
which to observe the activities of the Vichy French in the Western Hemisphere.

Meanwhile Nazi political activities in Latin America were coming
more and more to the surface and causing us no little concern. Backed
by their impressive military victories in Europe and by a widespread impression that Britain would soon have to bow to Hitler's armies, the Nazis
were visibly reaching out for control of Latin America. Many of these
activities seemed to center in Uruguay. That country was comparatively
small, inadequately armed, adjoined the large German settlements in
southern Brazil, and was strategically located to constitute a headquarters
from which to dominate the southern Continent.

British Ambassador Lothian brought me on May 24 a series of reports from his Government which showed that the situation at Montevideo was becoming dangerous. These but confirmed our own information.
In June Uruguayan police discovered a document in the home of a local
Nazi leader indicating that Montevideo was to be the headquarters of a
movement to fuse all South America into a world-wide Germany. Subsequently the police arrested twelve Nazi leaders suspected of being involved.

The reaction from Berlin was almost violent. The German Minister
made a strong protest. He virtually threatened that Uruguay would suffer
economic retaliation after the war unless she now adopted a friendly
policy toward Germany.

Even as we had enheartened Uruguay at the time the German battleship *Graf von Spee* put into Montevideo the preceding December; so now

we decided to support her again, and to prove to her and other Latin American Republics that, however preoccupied we were with the situation in Europe and Asia, we still intended to protect the nations to the south of us. The President and I agreed that the cruiser *Quincy*, then en route to Buenos Aires on a good-will visit, should call at Montevideo, and that the cruiser *Wichita* should go there shortly thereafter.

I also authorized our Minister to Uruguay, Edwin C. Wilson, to make this statement at a luncheon for the captain of the *Quincy:* "It is the intention and avowed policy of my Government to cooperate fully, whenever such cooperation is desired, with all of the other American Governments in crushing all activities which arise from non-American sources and which imperil our political and economic freedom."

German diplomatic blows in Latin America intensified as the Inter-American Conference at Havana, scheduled for July 21, drew near. The German Minister in Central America delivered formal notes to Costa Rica, Guatemala, Honduras, and El Salvador which in essence warned them not to join in Pan American agreements at Havana aimed directly or indirectly against Germany. The note advised the American Governments not to take part in Pan American economic arrangements because these "would be against the economic interests of the majority of the American states since only European suppliers, and especially German ones, are in position to receive in payment the products of the American states."

At about the same time the German Minister to Bolivia "advised" an official of the Bolivian Foreign Office that Bolivia had no interest in the Havana Conference and should take no part in it. It was typical of Nazi methods that their diplomatic pressure was applied to the smaller nations of Latin America.

I said at a press conference on July 11 that Germany was apparently attempting to intimidate nations whose sovereignty, freedom, and integrity merited the fullest respect of all countries. The reaction of the Central America Republics was strong, and the German Minister was obliged to withdraw his note of warning.

German and Italian propaganda directed against the Havana Conference now reached a zenith. All the old charges of Yankee domination of the Western Hemisphere, distorted versions of the Monroe Doctrine, and vivid depictions of the decadence of democracies were brought out and embellished by radio, news dispatches, and leaflets. Added to them was the new argument that Germany, having virtually won the war, would soon have the whole buying and selling resources of Europe at her disposal, and that the Latin American Governments had better set their diplomatic courses accordingly.

The President concurring, I decided to head the American delegation to the Havana Conference, and to take a strong delegation with me, among them being Assistant Secretary Berle, William Dawson, Ambassador to Panama; State Department officers Green H. Hackworth, Leo Pasvolsky, and Laurence Duggan; Harry D. White of the Treasury; Grosvenor M. Jones, Department of Commerce, and Leslie A. Wheeler, Department of Agriculture. After a conference with the President, I left Washington with the delegation on July 18 and arrived at Havana by boat on July 20, in the middle of a steaming summer. It was my first visit to Cuba since I went there as a bemustached infantry captain in 1898.

The problems before the conference sifted naturally into three categories. The first related to the possible transfer to Germany and Italy of Western Hemisphere territories of France and The Netherlands, and perhaps even of Britain later on. The second concerned subversive activities directed by the Axis Powers within American Republics. We had before us the vivid examples of what Nazi "fifth columns" had accomplished during the invasions of Scandinavia, the Low Countries, and France, the full details of which were only then coming to our attention. The third comprised the extremely grave economic difficulties resulting from the war.

I became chairman of the committee to consider the first topic—the transfer of territories. At the State Department we had already done intensive work on all possible questions relating to Germany's assuming possession of French and Dutch colonies in the Western Hemisphere, and I had talked them over at length with the President. It seemed to me there were two possibilities of danger in any transfer of territory in Germany's favor. One was that Germany herself might obtain bases within striking distance of the Panama Canal. The French and Dutch possessions, with the exception of Saint-Pierre and Miquelon, were strategically near the Canal. The other was that Germany, instead of herself taking possession of these territories, might offer them or part of them to one or more Latin American countries in return for political and economic vassalage, and thereby possibly break the phalanx of Pan American solidarity.

Through numerous conferences in the State Department, we had evolved a method for handling the problem, based on these provisions:

The American Republics would refuse to recognize and acquiesce in the transfer of present European possessions in this hemisphere to other non-American nations; they would disclaim any selfish interest in them; they would recognize the interests of the inhabitants of the colonies; they would refuse any offer regarding the territories, whether made by the present possessors or by any other non-American Power; the existing claims that some Republics had long since made to part of the territories in question would not be affected one way or the other; and, finally, the Republics would agree, in case of necessity, to undertake jointly to administer and protect the colonies through a collective trusteeship for the period of the emergency, and to provide all financial and military help necessary.

In my opening address to the conference on July 22, I renounced any desire of the United States to absorb the Western Hemisphere possessions of European countries or to include them in any sphere of influence. "We could not, however," I said, "permit these regions to become a battleground for the adjustment of such differences. Either situation could only be regarded as a threat to the peace and safety of this hemisphere, as would any indication that they might be used to promote systems alien to the inter-American system. Any effort, therefore, to modify the existing status of these areas—whether by cession, by transfer, or by any impairment whatsoever in the control heretofore exercised—would be of profound and immediate concern to all the American Republics."

My Government, I continued, considered it essential that a joint approach be made to this common problem, and we therefore endorsed the establishment of a collective trusteeship. This trusteeship, I added, "must not carry with it any thought of the creation of a special interest by any American Republic. The purpose of a collective trusteeship must be to further the interests and security of all the American nations, as well as the interests of the region in question. Moreover, as soon as conditions permit, the region should be restored to its original sovereign or be declared independent when able to establish and maintain stable self-government."

The following day I introduced a resolution embodying the idea and method of a collective trusteeship. And instantly Argentina, in the person of her delegate, Dr. Leopoldo Melo, opposed it. As at so many previous inter-American conferences, Argentina preferred the role of opposing the United States. Dr. Melo said he did not favor untried experiments to solve problems that might never arise. He thought that any transfer of sovereignty was solely hypothetical because the British fleet kept the Ger-

mans away from this hemisphere. He was willing to go no further than
a declaration by the Republics along the lines of the position the United
States had already taken in the Pittman-Bloom Resolution and my notes
to the belligerents; namely, that we would not recognize or acquiesce in
the transfer of the territories. He further argued that any assumption of
sovereignty by the American Republics over territory of European powers
in the Western Hemisphere was an act of war, and war in the case of
Argentina could not be declared except by the Argentine Congress. Finally,
he felt that the people of the territories should be consulted before being
given a new administration.

I ran head on into skepticism on the part of the Argentine and other
delegations as to our ability to protect their countries. Admiral Stark,
Chief of Naval Operations, had recently pointed out our naval deficiencies
to the Naval Affairs Committee of the House of Representatives. The
Argentines came to me and said that Stark's testimony had been circulated
to every reading citizen in the Argentine, and they added, in effect: "From
what Stark said, we're convinced you can't defend yourselves, much less
come down here 6,500 miles to defend us."

Another group of delegates argued, in effect: "Your Government
sends you down here to commit us to what we've sworn we would never
agree to on account of its many abuses—and that's the Monroe Doctrine.
Yet you are here to get us to sign away all our ideas without any chance
to go back home and confer."

I had several long talks with Dr. Melo. I pointed out as earnestly as
I could that only forthright action would make any impression on Hitler.
I emphasized that machinery should be set up now in case Hitler sought
to gain possession of the European colonies, and we should not wait until
we were faced with an accomplished fact. An actual taking of possession
by Hitler was only one factor, I felt; he might also seek to use the colonies
for Nazi penetration of Latin America unless we took immediate action.

My general arguments to Melo and other delegates ran along these
lines:

"We are moving into a brand-new world with the rules and practices
of seven or eight hundred years ago steadily increasing in large portions
of Europe and Asia. We are facing not local or regional wars about local
or regional matters, but a wild runaway race by certain rulers bent on
conquest without limit. And I have never yet known one of that type to
stop voluntarily. Their very system requires increasing momentum, fur-

ther expansion of their conquests, further seizure and subjugation of peoples, further glories for their armies."

What picture did the Western Hemisphere present in this regard?

"This hemisphere has been very much like the nations were in most of Europe—entirely complacent, ready to listen to propagandists, to the subversion of peaceful governments. In Europe the nations imagined that all they had to do was to fold their arms and look pleasant when an invader approached and to cry out, 'Neutrality and peace,' and this would render them immune. They did not realize that a typical conqueror has no concern about whether a peaceful country has been neutral or otherwise. When the peaceful country comes to, it is being swallowed as a boa constrictor swallows a squirrel, without inquiry as to whether it is friend or enemy, neutral or unneutral."

The lessons had become apparent, I went on. By degrees it dawned on pe ple in this hemisphere that they were directly affected in many ways by the onward march of the conquerors, both in Europe and in Asia. Also, that there might be political and military, as well as economic repercussions.

"Some Governments in Europe and Asia," I said, "have long heard the American nations speak about solidarity and about conferences and cooperation for various problems—political, economic, social, educational, and so on. But they have seriously doubted whether they would face any danger from us, whether the American nations would be able to make good all their professions about solidarity. They felt that if our breakup did not occur automatically, they could initiate here many movements to accelerate it, subversive methods of all kinds, political penetration, and even implications of military action. They felt they could arouse some prejudice in the American Republics, create fear and misunderstandings, and ingratiate themselves with some Governments here and gradually control them for their own purposes in Europe."

I then came to the question of the European colonies in this hemisphere. "It's apparent," I said, "that overnight the conqueror in Europe could require the home Government to transfer title to these possessions to it. Then we would have an accomplished fact. Unlesss we agree on a strong program here, we will have no implemented plans or definite or concerted methods for dealing with such events."

Dr. Melo personally was most cooperative. I saw at once, however, that he had come to Havana with rigid instructions from his Government, from which he could not budge. All my arguments would be of no avail as long as this condition persisted.

I therefore felt it necessary, as I had done at the Lima Conference, to go over the heads of the Argentine delegation to the President of Argentina, Dr. Ortiz. I went to see Dr. Melo and asked him to send a telegram to Dr. Ortiz, outlining my thought on the action we should take to safeguard the European colonies and stating my suggestion that Dr. Ortiz send instructions to Melo to work with the United States and other delegations supporting decisive action.

When Dr. Melo hesitated, I said that what I had in mind was a cable in my behalf which he would transmit. He thereupon agreed. In sending his cable we were actually going over the heads of the acting Argentine Government. President Ortiz, seriously ill, had retired to a seaside resort, and Vice President Castillo was acting in his stead.

The answer was not long in arriving. It was substantially in the form of instructions such as I had sought. By the evening of July 26 my committee was in agreement. Our accord took the form of two documents. One was a resolution, known as the Act of Havana, going into effect immediately and continuing in effect until the other document, a convention, could be ratified by the various Governments.

The Act of Havana set up an emergency administrative committee authorized to assume the administration of any colony in this hemisphere attacked or threatened. It consisted of a representative from each Republic and could be called together at the request of any of the Republics. If action were so urgent that the convening of the committee could not be awaited, any American Republic, acting by itself or with other Republics, could act as required by its own defense or by that of its continent. The agreement was not to apply to territories already in dispute between European powers and the American Republics. This last provision was designed to quiet the concern of Argentina over the Falkland Islands, of Chile over Antarctica, and of Guatemala over a portion of British Honduras.

As events developed, the Act of Havana never had to be applied. Britain continued stoutly fighting, with mounting aid from the United States, and Hitler made no attempt to assume or to transfer to others sovereignty over the European colonies on this side of the Atlantic. But the Act had several highly important effects. It showed the Axis powers that the Western Hemisphere was as one in self-defense. It undoubtedly had a depressing effect on plans of the Axis to use the colonies as spear points for political penetration of Latin America. And the discussion that preceded its adoption brought home to the American Republics the common dangers that threatened them and induced them to take far-reaching steps to meet these perils.

On the score of the second important problem before the conference —Axis subversive activities—I said in my opening address to the conference:

"Looming ominously on our horizon is the danger that attempts may be made to employ against our nations, too, the same means of subordinating their destinies to control and dictation from abroad that have already been notoriously employed elsewhere against numerous other countries. We must recognize the serious possibility that no effort or method may be spared to achieve, with respect to some of us, economic domination and political penetration, and to sow, among our nations, the seeds of suspicion, dissension, and discord—the frequent prelude to even more menacing action."

The committee handling this subject, of which Dr. Melo of Argentina was chairman, reached a number of important agreements designed to curb subversive activities. These accords called for common action by the Republics to put down any subversive movements. The Republics would exchange information concerning any such activities going on within their borders. They would promptly pass to the interested Government any information concerning activities about to take place in another Republic. They agreed not to aid rebellion in any Republic. They recommended the prohibition of political activities by foreign individuals or groups and the supervision of the entry of foreigners.

The same committee agreed on a resolution to restrict the political activities of diplomatic or consular officers. This was a serious question throughout Latin America. The staffs of German and Italian Embassies and Consulates had doubled and trebled in some cities, and they were conducting propaganda and political penetration activities having no relationship to the accepted functions of such missions.

On the score of the third important subject before the conference— how to parry the economic effects of the war—I outlined in my opening address a program to expand the activities of the Inter-American Financial and Economic Advisory Committee, to create facilities for the temporary handling and orderly marketing of accumulated surpluses, to negotiate commodity agreements with a view to assuring equitable terms of trade for both producers and consumers, and to consider methods for improving the standard of living of the peoples of the Americas, including public-health measures, nutrition studies, and suitable organizations for the relief distribution of some part of any surplus commodities.

We had done much of our work on the economic side even before the Havana Conference met. At the State Department we had spent many hours during June and July, 1940, discussing measures to prevent the American Republics from falling under the economic domination of Germany. We realized that in peacetime 55 per cent of South American exports went to Europe. We knew that, unless the South American countries could sell their exports, they would face a crisis. And we knew that Germany knew it too and would utilize this fact as a lever to force the Republics into their economic system.

It was obvious, therefore, that some arrangements had to be made to buy up the export surpluses of the Republics, as well as to stimulate increased internal consumption of such surpluses and greater commercial exchanges among the American nations. After much consultation with our neighbors south of the Rio Grande, we therefore recommended to the President that he ask Congress to authorize a $1,000,000,000 increase in the credit capacity of the Reconstruction Finance Corporation. The RFC would be authorized to organize a corporation for the purpose of acquiring, holding, and distributing emergency surplus products of the Western Hemisphere.

The President, accepting this recommendation, made the appropriate request of Congress on June 22, although he reduced our suggested $1,000,000,000 to $500,000,000.

In due course Congress approved the President's recommendation of June 22, and one of the most important projects in history of international economic cooperation among neutrals went into effect. During succeeding months and years, with some modifications, it served to prevent the American Republics from succumbing to the blandishments and threats of the Axis, it kept them from virtual bankruptcy, and it helped mobilize the resources of the New World in defense of Britain and ourselves.

The Havana Conference approved the principles of this arrangement, and again asserted the belief of the American Republics in liberal trade.

Previously British Ambassador Lothian had handed me on July 5 a memorandum in which Britain asked that the plans of the British nations and their Allies for dealing with their export surpluses be concerted with those of the United States and other Western Hemisphere Republics. Such coordination later became very close.

The conference held its final plenary session on July 3, after ten days of meetings. I had done my utmost to hasten its deliberations so as to get back to Washington and the many problems that awaited me there. On July 28, while presiding over the committee of which I was chairman, I said I would like to have the conference end two days later, and requested the members to meet with me the next morning at nine-thirty. A chorus of protest arose. They were going to a reception that evening and could not possibly get up in time for a meeting at nine-thirty. "All right then, gentlemen," I said, "we'll have a session tonight at ten-thirty." Thereupon they compromised on nine-thirty next morning.

At the final session I summed up the results of the conference. After mentioning the three main topics debated—the colonies, subversive activities, and economics—I said: "With regard to all three of these sets of menacing conditions, the American Governments have manifested their full recognition of the dangers which confront them in common and have created machinery for common action. Instead of faltering and abandoning the spirit of unity and concerted steps for safety, they have demonstrated to the world their unalterable determination to preserve and strengthen the spirit and the system of continental unity and solidarity. They have thus cleared the decks for effective action whenever such action may become necessary."

The final session was a tense one for the American delegation because the ship *Oriente* which was to take us to Miami was waiting in harbor, scheduled to leave at five o'clock. The meeting began at three, and was to hear only a few speeches and the reading of certain resolutions and then adjourn. As the resolution dealing with European colonies was read, a delegate suddenly rose and called attention to the fact that a certain island had been omitted from the text. The session stopped in dismay. The resolution forthwith had to be amended and reported again for signature, all of which occupied an additional hour. Eventually the meeting ended, we hastened to our cars waiting outside the Cuban Capitol, and drove fast to the ship which was all ready to hoist anchor.

Returning to Washington on August 1, I had a long talk with the President that afternoon. I reported to him that the success of the Havana Conference would better enable the Western Hemisphere as a whole to meet the dangers still looming ominously across the Great Circle.

Tired from the heat and labors of Havana, I left Washington on August 5 for White Sulphur Springs, West Virginia, to rest. Prior to my departure I issued a public statement pointing out that at Havana we had forged new instrumentalities of continental defense, but that other immense tasks still lay before us.

"I am firmly convinced," I said, "that what is taking place today in many areas of the earth is a relentless attempt to transform the civilized world as we have known it into a world in which lawlessness, violence, and force will reign supreme, as they did a thousand years ago. . . . We must continue to arm, and to arm to such an extent that the forces of conquest and ruin will not dare make an attack on us or on any part of this hemisphere. . . . In the face of terrific problems and conditions, and until the present serious threats and dangers have disappeared, we cannot pursue complacently the course of our customary normal life."

And I strove to make the issue patent to our people by saying: "The vast forces of lawlessness, conquest, and destruction are still moving across the earth like a savage and dangerous animal at large. By their very nature, those forces will not stop unless and until they recognize that there exists unbreakable resistance."

60: "Swap" with Britain

NEW DECISIONS CONFRONTED us in the summer of 1940 as Great Britain's plight on the high seas grew acute. Contrasted with the period before we entered the First World War, it was perilous. A quarter of a century before, Britain had had the assistance of the French and Italian fleets in the Atlantic and Mediterranean, and of the Japanese fleet in the Pacific. Now the French fleet lay immobile, German submarines operated out of French ports, the Italian Navy was an enemy and the Japanese Navy a potential enemy. Britain's shipping losses were rising dangerously. If she were to survive, it was necessary for her not only to purchase huge quantities of war supplies in this country, but also to get them safely to the United Kingdom.

British Ambassador Lord Lothian came in to see me on August 4, the day before my departure for White Sulphur Springs, and expressed his Government's "urgent desire" to purchase from us a number of older type destroyers. Britain, he said, needed them to bridge over what he described as her "present emergency situation."

During my attendance at the Havana Conference, the President had been talking to Lothian and cabling Prime Minister Churchill on this subject and also on the possible cession or lease to us by Britain of some of her bases in this hemisphere. The sale or loan of the destroyers had first been broached by French Premier Reynaud on May 14, only four days after the invasion of France, and by Mr. Churchill on the following day.

At that time the President opposed the proposal. On May 16 he cabled Mr. Churchill that, as the Prime Minister knew, a step of that kind could not be taken except with the specific authorization of Congress, and he was not certain that it would be wise at this moment to make that suggestion to Congress. He said furthermore that, in view of our own defense requirements which had inevitably to be linked with the defense requirements of this hemisphere and with our obligations in the Pacific, he doubted whether we could dispose even temporarily of the destroyers. He added that, even if we were able to take the steps Mr. Churchill suggested, it would be at least six or seven weeks as a minimum before the destroyers could undertake active service under the British flag. He expressed every determination to get other equipment to Britain.

The Prime Minister having suggested a visit of United States warships to Irish ports, the President said he would give further consideration to this suggestion.

On the same day we cabled Ambassador Bullitt with reference to Reynaud's request for destroyers, saying that the question would have to go to Congress and that Congressional permission at this moment seemed unobtainable. Also, we had no excess naval tonnage, and selling or leasing the destroyers would impair our defenses by creating an actual shortage of destroyers for our own use. Furthermore, it might create complications in the Pacific.

A fortnight later, on June 1, we cabled Bullitt again at the direction of the President, as a result of further requests from the French Government. The President believed that an exchange of American destroyers would probably be inexpedient because of the enormous sea area we had to patrol. It would require Congressional action which might be difficult to get. Our old destroyers could not be sold as obsolete because they were now in commission or were being reconditioned for commissioning. He suggested that destroyers might be obtained from some of the South American Republics.

But all things are comparative. When the fall of France enormously increased our dangers, we leaned much more toward disposing of the overage destroyers, especially if their loss to our defenses could be compensated for in other ways, as by our acquiring new bases. The Navy had long wanted additional bases along the Atlantic. We also felt that, since our destroyers would increase the strength of the British fleet, which stood between the Axis desperadoes and us, this was actually an added protection to ourselves. Furthermore, Congress passed an Administration bill, the National Defense Act of June 28, 1940, which permitted the sale of naval equipment provided the Chief of Naval Operations certified that it was not essential to the national defense.

When Lothian came to my office on August 4 I could appreciate Britain's dangers as fully as he could depict them. He said Britain had lost five destroyers during the previous week alone. Destroyers, he pointed out, were vitally important in combating submarine activities and other enemy action in the English Channel where large warships could not be used to advantage.

He said he had already discussed the question with the President while I was at Havana, and now desired to lay the situation before me in the hope that something might be done within the next few weeks. He added that Britain would be willing to make available to us facilities for naval and air bases in certain British islands adjacent to Central and South America and in Bermuda, as well as for aircraft bases in Newfoundland. He said he would give us later in the day a memorandum indicating the bases and facilities Britain had in mind.

I first explained to Lothian that such facilities would, of course, be for the benefit of all the American Republics. "In keeping with the understandings reached at Havana and at prior conferences," I said, "any action taken by the United States would be in cooperation with the other American Republics."

I also pointed out the legal difficulties in the way of our selling the destroyers. The United States Code forbade the departure of vessels from American waters outfitted for cruising against a foreign nation with which we were at peace. Also, the National Defense Act, approved June 28, 1940, forbade the sale of naval equipment without the approval of the Chief of Naval Operations, and military equipment without the approval of the Chief of Staff of the Army.

"To meet the wishes of your Government," I said, "an amendment to these provisions of law may be necessary, and you well know that such procedures move slowly. Members of Congress are extremely sensitive to representations by constitutents who for one reason or another may oppose legislation of this kind."

Britain's dangers, however, were a fact, as it was also a fact that the menace from the dictator who was devouring Europe like a mad dog was ultimately a menace to us. I said to Lothian that we were giving the matter attentive consideration.

On the same day I sent the President a memorandum relating to the sale of warships and auxiliary vessels. This contained a proposed draft of a bill to be offered in Congress which would specifically authorize such sale. In discussing this draft bill with the President, however, we agreed that there might be two objections to sending it to Congress—one, that it would stir up considerable isolationist antagonism; the other, that many weeks of discussion might pass before it could be adopted.

I also informed the President that I had had a long telephone conversation with William Allen White, noted editor, who was chairman of the Committee to Defend America by Aiding the Allies. I outlined to White the bill we might send to Congress. White said that the Republican candidate for the Presidency, Wendell Willkie, agreed in principle with our methods for aiding Britain.

Such was the situation when I left Washington. While I was at White Sulphur Springs we added materially to the defense of one member of the British Empire—Canada—when the President and Prime Minister Mackenzie King signed on August 18 at Ogdensburg, New York, a joint-defense agreement and created a Permanent Joint Board of Defense. During June and July I had had diplomatic exchanges with Canada on the subject. With the President's authorization, I advised General Marshall, Chief of Staff, and Admiral Stark, Chief of Naval Operations, on July 3, that I had informed Mackenzie King we would be delighted if he would send high-ranking Army and Navy officers to Washington to discuss matters of joint defense.

During my three weeks rest at White Sulphur Springs I had a private telephone line into my apartment there and received daily pouches from the State Department, hence closely followed and participated in the destroyers-bases negotiations in the hands of the President and Welles. A few hours after I returned to Washington on August 23, I went to the White House to attend a Cabinet meeting.

There the President said to me: "Our negotiations with Britain on the bases and destroyers have bogged down. Please see what you can do."

In talking over the bases with the President, I found he had an amazing personal knowledge of almost all of them. He had either cruised, swum, or fished in those harbors. He knew how many feet deep and wide they were and how many ships they would take.

He also knew the penurious condition of the native populations of most of the islands, and consequently did not want to assume the burden of administering those populations. Therefore he had changed, during my absence from Washington, from his original idea of outright purchase of the bases to that of ninety-nine-year leases. I had originally favored outright cession, but was willing to agree to leases instead.

I thereupon undertook the negotiations, determined to push them to completion as quickly as possible. The fact of the negotiations being public property, I felt that to drag them on much longer would be to prejudice the excellent psychological reaction to be expected in Europe when the arrangement went through.

Moreover, Britain vitally needed the destroyers at that very moment, to cover a period of low strength in smaller types of warships until a number of such ships she now had on the ways could be ready in the first part of 1941. As Churchill said in a message to the President on August

15: "The worth of every destroyer that you can spare to us is measured in rubies."

On the following day, as I was reviewing the negotiations to date, the White House informed me that the British Ambassador had an appointment with the President the next evening, a Sunday, and Mr. Roosevelt would like to have me present.

Lord Lothian came in to see me at the office early Sunday afternoon so that we could go over the situation prior to his conversation with the President that evening. He brought up certain objections to the proposals delivered to him on August 19 by Welles as Acting Secretary. He said his Government did not like the American proposal that we have exclusive authority to locate and select the bases we needed, with no voice whatever on the part of Britain. His Government also objected to the proposed exchange of the destroyers for the bases, and desired to put the matter in the form of gifts back and forth.

The difficulty on this latter point was that Mr. Churchill, in a speech on August 20, had committed himself to an outright gift of leases to the bases. He had not mentioned the destroyers at all. The Prime Minister felt that a better feeling of cooperation would be created on both sides of the Atlantic by the making of reciprocal gifts instead of a *quid pro quo*. He also noted that the British public would be less likely to scrutinize gifts than an exchange and to say that Britain, in giving away leases to valuable bases, was not getting full value in the receipt of fifty old destroyers.

We had difficulties on our side as well, however. The Attorney General, Robert H. Jackson, believed there was legal authority for the President, as Commander-in-Chief of our armed forces, to sell the destroyers to Britain. But if the President were to do so without special Congressional authority, he should be able to satisfy Congress that, in return for the destroyers, we were obtaining facilities to bases which would clearly give us greater security than would the retention of the fifty destroyers. Furthermore, the Chief of Naval Operations, Admiral Stark, had to satisfy himself that the leases to the bases would so increase our security that he could certify that keeping the fifty destroyers was not essential to our national defense.

More important still was the fact that the President had no authority to make a gift of Government property. I so told Lord Lothian.

That evening I met Lothian at the White House and, while we sat together awaiting our appointment with the President, I again emphasized to him that the President had no authority to give away Government property.

When the President received us, however, Lothian to my surprise, seemingly ignoring my statement that the President legally could not make a gift of public property, proceeded to present the British proposal. He said he had prepared this himself, in the form of three draft notes, which he handed to the President and me. The first was from himself to me, the second was my reply, and the third was the British acknowledgment of my reply. Lothian said he had sent these to his Government for its approval.

Although Mr. Churchill had suggested that he should define some of the facilities he was prepared to turn over to us, Lothian proposed that a joint Anglo-American body immediately proceed to agree on what the facilities, naval and air, were to be. He thought that Churchill's suggestion would lead to delay and dispute.

In presenting his views, Lothian handed me a personal letter from himself which began: "I understand that all the papers about this awkward destroyer question have been handed over to you. It seems to me that Washington and London are in danger of getting at loggerheads, which if the fact were disclosed might have deplorable effects on public opinion in both countries, largely through a misunderstanding which it is difficult to resolve by telegraph or transatlantic telephone."

Lothian argued in his letter that, if the transaction were treated as a bargain, Mr. Churchill did not feel that he could give us, in return for fifty "oldish destroyers," the right to get whatever air and naval bases in Newfoundland, Bermuda, the Bahamas, Jamaica, St. Lucia, Trinidad, and British Guiana we might choose to ask for, "because the British Government might incur the charge of defaulting on its share of the bargain if it created difficulties about any particular thing the United States Government wanted."

"I think," he said, "Mr. Churchill feels that British public opinion would not support a bargain of this kind if it was presented as a contract and that it would in practice lead to the most dangerous controversies between the United States and Great Britain. . . . In point of fact there is and can be no parallel between the two halves of the transaction, and to try to make it a bargain is to spoil what would otherwise be a demonstration of mutual good will between our two countries in which the question of the relative consideration on each side has no place."

In general, Lothian argued to the President and me that there should not be cold commercial bargaining but a friendly interest between the two Governments. This would afford a basis for gifts back and forth which would be voluntary and apparently without definite understanding in advance.

After Lothian had finished his arguments, I said for the third time to the Ambassador, and for the first time to the President, that the latter had no authority whatever to make a gift of public property to any Government or individual. Mr. Roosevelt at once agreed with me. I said, and he agreed, that a different arrangement would be necessary to achieve our objectives.

The President thereupon left it to me to work out a solution with Lothian.

The following morning I called to my office Green H. Hackworth, Legal Adviser of the State Department, whose advice was always invaluable to me, and Judge Townsend of the Department of Justice, to try to find a way out. After some discussion, Hackworth suddenly suggested that there might be a compromise after all between Churchill's desire for reciprocal gifts and our own legal position that the President could not give away the destroyers but had to get something in return.

Since the British had not stated precisely what bases they intended to lease to us, why not divide them into two parcels? The first would comprise the bases in Newfoundland and Bermuda. These Britain could lease us as an outright gift. The second would comprise the bases around the Caribbean, strategically more valuable to us because of their nearness to the Panama Canal. These could be leased to us in consideration of the cession of the fifty destroyers.

I saw at once that here was the formula for which we had been looking.

We thereupon set to work to redraft the proposals. Leaving Hackworth and Townsend to complete the drafting, I telephoned the President, told him Hackworth had offered a solution, and asked if I could send Hackworth to outline it to him. That afternoon Hackworth and Townsend saw the President, who agreed to the compromise.

As finished, our draft began with an assurance from the British Government that, if the waters surrounding the British Isles became untenable for British warships, "the British fleet would in no event be surrendered or sunk, but would be sent to other ports of the Empire for continued defense of the Empire."

Mr. Churchill had already given such assurances in his speech to Parliament on June 4, but I wanted a formal repetition because of our transfer of the destroyers to Britain. Basically I was confident that Britain could hold out; but it was obvious that Hitler was now about to unleash a full-scale attack on Britain, first probably by air, then, if that did not bring surrender, an all-out invasion by sea and air.

If my confidence was misplaced and the British fleet were surrendered, the position of the United States would be perilous in the extreme. But if the surrendered fleet included the fifty former American destroyers, our position would be rendered yet more dangerous, and the fire of the isolationists who were opposing the Administration on selling the destroyers would be turned on the White House.

On the following day, August 27, I took the draft as prepared by Hackworth, Townsend, and myself to the White House. After a Cabinet meeting, the President held a special session with Secretaries Knox and Stimson and myself. We went over the draft carefully, made a few changes in phraseology, and then approved it.

During the late afternoon, when I intended handing the draft to the British Ambassador, Admiral Stark telephoned me and asked for two or three hours more in which to study it because he himself would be called upon to give a certificate, under the Act of June 28, 1940, that the destroyers were not essential to our national defense. I of course agreed. Knowing that Lord Lothian was going on a boat trip down the Potomac River that evening with Secretary Knox, I asked Stark to give the draft to Knox to hand to Lothian.

Meantime Lord Lothian sent me on the same day a long cable from Churchill to the President. Churchill, signing himself "Former naval person," approved the proposal previously submitted by Lothian, which, making the leases to all the British bases out to be outright gifts, had not been acceptable to us.

Churchill also was ready to give assurances that the British fleet would not be scuttled or surrendered. This would be in the form of a separate exchange of letters between Lothian and me. According to Churchill's draft he would merely refer to and confirm the statements he made on this subject in his addresses on June 4 and August 20.

With his usual indomitable spirit, he said he did not wish this latter exchange to be published because "I think it is much more likely that the German Government will be the one to surrender or scuttle its fleet or what is left of it. In this, as you are aware, they have already had some practice. You will remember that I said some months ago in one of my private cables to you that any such action on our part would be a dastardly act, and that is the opinion of everyone of us."

Churchill had already stated his objection to publicity concerning these assurances in a cable he sent the President on August 15, when he said: "You will please bear in mind the disastrous effect from our point of view, and perhaps also from yours, of allowing any impression to grow that we regard the conquest of the British Islands and its naval bases as any other than an impossible contingency. The spirit of our people is splendid."

The Prime Minister now urged immediate action on the destroyers-bases transaction, saying it had become especially urgent in view of Mussolini's menace to Greece. (The Italian invasion of Greece occurred on October 28, 1940.) "If our business," he said, "is put through on bilateral lines and in the highest spirit of good will, it might even now save that small historic country from invasion and conquest. Even the next forty-eight hours are important."

Lothian having cabled to London the location of the bases the President had in mind, Churchill agreed and himself added the island of Antigua, in the Caribbean, which he said might be useful as a base for flying boats.

That steaming night of August 27, Lothian, Knox, and Stark all appeared at my apartment at about ten-thirty. For more than an hour we four went over the draft I had given Stark. Lothian at first had a few suggestions for revision, but eventually seemed quite satisfied and said he would send the note to his Government.

The negotiations now remained in abeyance for two days, until Lothian could hear from his Government. On August 29 I handed the Ambassador an informal memorandum from myself to argue further our idea that the destroyers and bases should not be dealt with as outright gifts. I said that our proposal whereby Britain would give us leases to bases in Newfoundland and Bermuda and would exchange leases to the other bases for fifty of our destroyers "in the main speaks for itself. It would be unfortunate if the arrangement should be made to appear in any other light, such as that all the bases were to be turned over to the United States as an unqualified gift with no thought or expectation of receiving fifty destroyers. The fact is that the destroyers have been in the mind of the British Government throughout and prior to the beginning of the discussions regarding bases. If the British Government desires to drop the idea of acquiring the destroyers and to turn over the bases as an unqualified gift, a different situation would be presented."

That night at seven o'clock Lord Lothian called at my apartment and left with me his Government's counterproposal. I called Admirals Stark and Woodson and also Green Hackworth to my apartment, and we went over it carefully. We found that Lothian's draft differed in only a few details from my proposal, and added the island of Antigua, which was quite agreeable to us. We made a few changes in the text, and I then telephoned Lothian, who came back to my apartment at ten-thirty. He agreed to our changes.

The following day, August 30, I telephoned the changes to the President at Hyde Park and received his approval.

We drafted at the State Department a message for the President to send to Congress along with the exchange of notes between Lothian and myself. I sent all three documents to the President at Hyde Park on August 31. It was understood that the notes should be signed and exchanged on Monday September 2. The President gave his approval to the three documents, making only a slight change in the message, and handed them to me when I met him at the Union Station in Washington Sunday afternoon September 1.

The President also handed me a letter from himself, which said: "I have carefully read the note from the British Ambassador and your reply thereto as Secretary of State of the United States.

"I give my full and cordial approval to both of these notes." He signed his full name.

Lord Lothian, who had spent the week end in Boston, returned to Washington Monday afternoon, and came to my apartment at seven o'clock that evening. There we signed and exchanged the notes confirming the destroyers-bases transaction.

Lothian also handed me his reply to an *aide-mémoire* I had previously given him requesting assurances concerning the disposition of the British fleet. My *aide-mémoire* had referred to the June 4 speech of the Prime Minister in which he said that if the waters surrounding the British Isles became untenable for British warships, the British fleet would in no event be surrendered or sunk but would be sent overseas for the defense of other parts of the Empire. It then asked "whether the foregoing statement represents the settled policy of the British Government."

Lothian stated in his reply: "His Majesty's Ambassador is instructed by the Prime Minister to inform Mr. Secretary Hull that this statement certainly does represent the settled policy of His Majesty's Government. Mr. Churchill must however observe that these hypothetical contingencies seem more likely to concern the German fleet or what is left of it than the British fleet."

The last sentence was Churchill's own addition. The Prime Minister now agreed to having the exchange of *aides-mémoire* published on condition that the main notes regarding the bases and destroyers should be made public first.

The following morning, September 3, I sent to the White House the President's message to Congress, which he had signed and handed to me; the destroyers-bases notes, and an opinion of Attorney General Robert H. Jackson declaring the transaction legal. All these were for communication to Congress. The President was en route to the Capital, after dedicating Chickamauga Dam, when the documents were published.

Thus were concluded within a week negotiations among the most momentous in our history. As the President said in his message to Congress: "This is the most important action in the reinforcement of our national defense that has been taken since the Louisiana Purchase. Then as now, considerations of safety from overseas attack were fundamental."

Mention of the Louisiana Purchase was not without significance because it, too, had been made without authorization from Congress and, though the reaction to the destroyers-bases exchange throughout the nation was, in general, wholeheartedly favorable, some opponents objected that Congress should have given its approval.

We based our stand, however, on the necessity for defense. "Preparation for defense," said the President's message, "is an inalienable prerogative of a sovereign state. Under present circumstances this exercise of sovereign right is essential to the maintenance of our peace and safety."

The President pointed out that the exchange was not inconsistent in any sense with our status of peace. He put the value of the new bases to the Western Hemisphere as "beyond calculation." They were essential, he said, to the protection of the Panama Canal, Central America, the northern portion of South America, the Antilles, Canada, Mexico, and our Eastern and Gulf seaboards.

In conformity with the thought I had expressed to Lord Lothian when he first broached the subject of bases and destroyers with me on August 4—namely, that any bases we obtained in this hemisphere must be for the benefit of all the American Republics—I sent instructions on September 6 to our diplomatic missions in those countries. I requested them to notify those Governments that we had acquired leases to British bases not only for our own defense but also for more effective cooperation with the other American Republics in the common defense of the hemisphere. "The resulting facilities at these bases," I added, "will, of course, be made available alike to all American Republics on the fullest cooperative basis for the common defense of the hemisphere and in entire harmony with the spirit of the pronouncements made and the understandings reached at the conferences of Lima, Panama, and Havana."

A few international lawyers might have argued that we had violated the Hague Convention of 1907 in that we, a neutral, had sold warships to a belligerent. However, that convention started off with the proposition that "belligerents are bound to respect the sovereign rights of neutral Powers." Neutrals like Poland, Norway, Denmark, The Netherlands, Luxemburg, and Belgium, could testify that the principles of the Hague Convention had not protected them. The convention laid down rights and duties of neutrals and belligerents alike, and the Axis dictators, who had wrecked the convention and alone would have a motive for questioning our transaction, were estopped, by every rule of reason and law, from raising the question. It would be absurd to contend that the convention, which represented a compromise between rights and duties of belligerents on the one hand and neutrals on the other, should bind only the neutrals.

The destroyers-bases transaction went into effect with great speed. The destroyers, reconditioned and stocked with food and munitions, were turned over to Britain at once. Experts of both Governments met and agreed on the exact sites of the eight bases we had acquired, extending along four thousand miles of Atlantic seaboard.

To judge from the many cables I received from our diplomatic missions abroad in the days that followed, the effect of the destroyers-bases deal went far beyond the physical fact that Britain now had fifty more destroyers and we had eight more bases. It was a demonstration to the world that this Government believed that Britain had a real chance to hold fast against all Hitler's might. It showed that we were willing to go beyond ordinary methods and to find new means to aid the major democracy fighting Nazism.

The transaction enheartened the democracies then under the heel of the Prussian boot. The Axis dictators sought to make propaganda that, by acquiring the bases, we were seeking the break up of the British Empire, but in their calculations they had to recognize a new factor, the prospect of ever more American assistance to Britain. Hitler could no longer hope that his offer of peace to Britain, naturally on his own terms, would be accepted. Mussolini realized by now that what he thought an easy chance for booty had turned into a dangerous gamble. Japan, awaiting a British collapse before moving toward the South Sea area, paused and took stock.

61: We Are Firm with Vichy

WITHIN A WEEK after the destroyers-bases agreement was signed, Hitler began his full-scale aerial assault on the British Isles. As the largest attack from the air yet made in history burst into the headlines we literally held our breath, from the President on down. We had every reason to regard it as the prelude to all-out invasion, as records now prove that to have been Hitler's design. And we knew that if Britain went down, we would inevitably face attack, direct or indirect, from the whole armada of the victorious Axis.

Preceding weeks had been marked by the vague meanderings toward peace we had become accustomed to see emanating from German sources as well as from neutrals whose intentions were honest. These preceded and followed Hitler's speech of July 19 in which he expressed his willingness to make a Germanic peace with Britain.

Our Chargé in Berlin, Donald R. Heath, cabled on June 26 that the Italian Ambassador to Germany, Dino Alfieri, after conferring with Hitler and German officials, had called Heath in and said that Germany and Italy had no desire to destroy England, but that only a few days remained in which this catastrophe could be averted. Alfieri was confident that peace terms acceptable to England would be offered by the Axis if England requested them. Under these terms Churchill need not resign, but the British cabinet must undergo some change. He avoided a direct suggestion that the United States persuade Britain to ask for peace, but commented that responsibility for continuance of the war rested primarily on the United States.

I instructed Heath to ask Alfieri whether his remarks were made with the knowledge of the Italian and German Governments and also whether the Italian Government desired us to take any action. Alfieri replied that the views he had expressed were those of the German and Italian Governments, but he was not authorized to speak for those Governments. He added that he did not want to expose the Axis Governments to the accusation of having initiated an overture for peace since it was obvious, in view of the military situation, that the initiative must be taken by Britain.

It was clear to me that Berlin and Rome were attempting to use the United States as an agency to advise Britain to make peace. I had no intention of becoming the instrument for such a maneuver. After talking this over with the President, I asked Welles to call in British Ambassador Lothian and read him these cables from Berlin, making it entirely clear to Lothian that they were being shown him solely for his information and that of his Government and that we were making no suggestions of any kind with regard to them.

Lothian sent me on August 31 a letter containing information from his Government concerning another peace offer, which he asked me to pass on to the President. The King of Sweden had sent telegrams on August 2 to the King of England and to Hitler offering his good offices toward examining the possibilities of making peace. Britain, after consulting the Dominions, replied on August 14 that no useful purpose would be served by a meeting in Sweden between British and German representatives so long as Germany had not granted freedom to France and the other conquered countries and thereby made the British Empire secure by deeds as well as words.

President Aguirre Cerda of Chile wrote the President on September 5, proposing an initiative toward peace by all the American Republics. We in the State Department drafted the reply, which went forward October 26. The President expressed the belief that "it would be catastrophic for the future welfare of all of us were an appeal of this nature to be construed as a recognition of the ruthless conquests of aggression . . . the timing of a peace appeal becomes all-important . . . there is little likelihood of acceptance of a peace proposal on any basis that the Republics of this hemisphere would wish to support. Accordingly, I am reluctantly forced to the conclusion that the strength and prestige of the united voice of the Americas might more usefully be held in readiness for a more propitious and opportune moment."

Peace other than on Hitler's terms was impossible. And such a peace would be more dangerous to the safety of the United States than a continuance of the war.

The battle for Britain then began. Watching with the keenest anxiety, we made every effort to get all help possible to the embattled Isles. Our own efforts to rearm were colossal. The President on September 16 signed the Selective Service Bill, after having in previous weeks signed other bills authorizing appropriations for defense exceeding five billion dollars, calling the National Guard into active service, and providing for a two-ocean Navy.

The loss of the French fleet, plus the thinning out of the British fleet on convoy patrols, while our major fleet was on watchful duty in the

Pacific, reemphasized to us all again and again the need for powerful fleets in both oceans. One day when the Cabinet, presided over by the President, was discussing these difficulties, I remarked that our effort to stretch a one-ocean Navy to cover two oceans reminded me of an unusual occurrence in a lawsuit in Tennessee some years before.

"A will case," I said, "was being tried, involving three interests—the estate, the legatees, and the devisees. One lawyer represented the estate, while a second lawyer undertook to represent the more or less conflicting interests of the legatees and the devisees.

"During the trial this latter attorney sought to maintain the legal rights of the devisees, whereupon he discovered he was injuring the rights of his other clients, the legatees. He thereupon tried to present and bolster the claims of the legatees, whereupon he discovered that he was weakening the claims of his other clients, the devisees.

"At that point the attorney for the estate rose and compared the embarrassing situation of his opponent to that of a passenger who was shipwrecked when a steamboat on the Mississippi sank in a hurricane.

" 'This unfortunate man,' said the attorney, 'was able to reach the Arkansas shore with nothing on but a very flexible red flannel undershirt. He tried to conceal himself in the bushes, but the disaster had attracted all the residents of the community, who quickly spotted him.

" 'He thereupon tried to conceal his nakedness by drawing his undershirt down in front, whereupon it rose up in the back and seriously exposed him there. Then he pulled it down in the back, and it reared up in the front and exposed him there.

" 'The plight of this unlucky gentleman,' concluded the lawyer, 'reminds me of the impasse my friend here has gotten himself into.'

"And," I said to the Cabinet, "it reminds me of our difficulties in trying to apportion our fleet so as to have enough to cover the Atlantic and the Pacific at the same time."

The President joined in the hearty laugh that went round the table.

Our preoccupation over the situation in the Atlantic was inextricably tied in with the course of the Vichy Government with particular reference to the French fleet, to French bases in Africa, and to Vichy's relations with Britain.

When French Ambassador de Saint-Quentin called on me on August 30 to say goodbye before leaving for France—he was being replaced—he read me a short message from his Government criticizing Churchill for a recent speech on relations between France and Germany.

"Without entering into the merits of the British and French utterances and attitudes," I commented, "I do regret that the two countries feel constrained to engage in crimination and recrimination. The one real hope for a peaceful civilized world is for Great Britain to check the Hitler movement of world conquest. Even the French people will probably find this the only opportunity to restore France. I've discovered no signs of appreciation on Hitler's part in return for neutrality and even friendship on the part of a number of peaceful nations in Europe. On the contrary, these nations have been seized one after another by Hitler's military forces."

De Saint-Quentin had served his country well as her Ambassador, and I was sorry to see him go. His successor, Gaston Henry-Haye, a little man with ruddy cheeks and a truculent mustache, the first Ambassador to come from the Vichy Government, arrived with the taint of association with Laval and his group. When he called on me on September 11 to present his credentials, his first effort was to exonerate himself from the recently published charges that he was pro-German or anti-British.

"It is due you to know," I said, "that your Government is anti-British and pro-German when it goes beyond the requirements of the spirit of the letter of the armistice agreement. I call this to your attention merely for the reason that our Government and people, responding to the ancient friendship that has always existed and fully exists today between our two countries, will be extremely desirous to do everything practicable for the French people in their terrible misfortune. However, our people look on Mr. Hitler as the most devastating and all-pervading conqueror and destroyer within a thousand years, and we believe there is no geographical limit whatever to his infamous plans. Therefore we do not propose to say or do one single thing knowingly that would aid or encourage him and his ruthless forces of destruction in the slightest degree."

I cited to the Ambassador the fact that the United States had incurred Hitler's hostility because of our efforts to assist France in her terrible emergency.

"It is impossible for the American people," I remarked, "to understand why the French Government would hand to Mr. Hitler a loaded gun with which to shoot at their best friends. I emphasized this point to the French Government for some time before and until the last split second before they virtually signed away their navy to Germany. We in this country could not possibly have been more deeply disappointed."

Henry-Haye made a labored effort to explain that the French fleet was in African harbors where Germany could not reach it and that all plans were made to send the fleet away or scuttle it if the Germans attempted to get possession of it.

"No matter how good may have been the intentions of the French Government," I replied, "the theory that Germany could never get the French fleet is wholly fallacious. There is also this point: the German power to prevail on France to sign away her fleet for the period of the armistice will enable Germany, to an even more clinching extent, to require and, if necessary, compel France to turn over the fleet, lock, stock, and barrel, to Germany in the final peace agreement that Germany will write for herself and France."

I made it clear to Henry-Haye that the American people were observing with instant concern any reported act or utterance of other Governments, including the French, which seemed to be hostile to Great Britain in her struggle to check Hitler, or, in the case of France, favorable to Hitler beyond the requirements of the armistice terms.

"Our people," I said, "know in their own minds from past observation that there is no such thing as appeasing Mr. Hitler any more than a squirrel can appease a boa constrictor. Those poor little countries in Europe, with which you are familiar, have had that experience. My country is proposing to expend some fifteen billion dollars and to organize a vast army on account of Mr. Hitler. The French Government, of course, will realize that this is a most serious business for this country and its Government, if France has not already realized it from its own experience and that of its neighbors."

Henry-Haye remarked generally that the French had been taken unawares and thus brought to their present humiliating situation.

"A number of us connected with this Government," I said, "including the President, myself and others, have for several years pursued the fixed policy of basing all our utterances and actions on the assumption that Mr. Hitler was out to become the ruthless and utterly destructive conqueror of Europe, and that the Japanese military clique was bent on the same course in the Pacific area from Hawaii to Siam."

We had good reason to be worried over developments at Vichy. Many dispatches were coming to my desk from our Embassy there telling of the growing influence of Vice Premier Laval, of his bitterly hostile attitude toward Britain, of his conversations with the Germans, and of the plan that seemed to be forming in his mind to throw France into active cooperation with Germany.

Pétain on his part had sent a representative to London to see if some easement of the dangerous relations between Britain and France could not be arranged, but at this very moment Laval was doing his utmost to bring about a swing in the opposite direction. He saw Hitler on October 24 at Montoire, France. Meantime Hitler went on to Hendaye, on the Spanish border, to meet General Franco who made him the unwelcome statement that Spain could not and would not enter the war.

Ambassador Kennedy in London had cabled me on October 21 a message to the President, from Mr. Churchill, consistently signing himself "former naval person." The Prime Minister reported rumors that Vichy was preparing ships and colonial troops to aid the Germans against Britain. He said he himself did not believe the reports, but if the French fleet were turned over to Germany it would be a very heavy blow. He suggested that the President speak in the strongest terms to the French Ambassador because Vichy would pay great heed to such a warning.

The President was debating this suggestion when Hitler and Pétain met at Montoire on the scheduled date. We could not learn at once what decisions they reached, if any. From the elaborate groundwork laid by Laval, whose intentions were well known, and from what our diplomatic representatives could learn in conversations, we could only judge that Pétain had agreed, or been forced to agree, to a collaboration with Germany which went beyond the terms of the armistice. The official agreement, which came to light five years later in captured German documents, did contain sentences such as these: "The Axis Powers and France have an identical interest in seeing the defeat of England accomplished as soon as possible. Consequently, the French Government will support, within the limits of its ability, the measures which the Axis Powers may take to this end." However, the details were to be worked out later, and Pétain felt that this fact justified his agreeing to the general clauses.

Not knowing the precise details, and fearing the worst, our Government and the British Government agreed to take strong, parallel action toward Vichy. We transmitted on October 25, on Britain's behalf, a message from King George to Pétain in which the King pleaded with Pétain not to harm a former ally by making concessions not called for by the armistice or by taking sides against Britain.

At the same time we assisted the President in drafting a much stronger appeal, which was handed to French Ambassador Henry-Haye on October 24. "In the opinion of the United States Government," the message said, "the fact that the French Government alleges that it is under duress and consequently cannot act except to a very limited degree as a free agent is in no sense to be considered as justifying any course on the part of the French Government which would provide assistance to Germany and her allies in the war against the British Empire. The fact that a Government is a prisoner of war of another power does not justify such a prisoner in serving its conqueror in operations against a former ally."

The President recalled to Pétain the solemn assurances we had received from his Government concerning the French fleet. "If the French Government now permits the Germans to use the French fleet in hostile operations against the British fleet," he said, "such action would constitute a flagrant and deliberate breach of faith with the United States."

The President concluded with what was really a series of threats. Any such agreement, he said, would definitely wreck the traditional friendship between the French and the American peoples. It would permanently remove any chance that we would aid the French people in their distress; and in these conditions we would make no effort to exercise our influence in insuring to France the retention of her overseas possessions.

Chargé H. Freeman Matthews in Vichy cabled us the following day that officials of the French Foreign Office were deeply dejected by the message and its "painfully curt" language. They admitted, however, that Hitler and Laval had sold Pétain on a policy of straightout cooperation with Germany.

Matthews cabled again on November 3 that our message had had a really constructive effect. It had restrained the French Government from going further under Laval's persuasion and under Hitler's reported threats of reprisals against French prisoners of war. Matthews heard that even Laval had no desire to burn all his bridges across the Atlantic. There was a full if somewhat vague realization, he said, that in the future we alone might be in position to save France from great, undefined injury.

Henry-Haye delivered to me on November 4 Pétain's reply to the President, a copy of which we had already received from Matthews at Vichy. Pétain said that the French Government had always preserved its liberty of action and expressed his surprise at "an appraisement as inaccurate as it is unjust." As for the fleet, he said: "The French Government has declared that the French fleet would never be surrendered and nothing can justify questioning today that solemn undertaking."

The Marshal made a point that the British had attacked the French fleet, not vice versa, and were supporting French "rebels" and endangering the unity of the French Empire. Nevertheless France would not engage in any unjustified attack against Britain and wanted to maintain her traditional friendship with the United States.

As Henry-Haye handed me this reply, he commented that we should appreciate the desperate situation of the French Government at Vichy and not be too severe in judging it.

"The chief trouble," I commented, "seems to be that high-ranking officials in the French Government seem disposed to keep entirely away from this Government in most everything that relates to normal relations. At the same time they seem to keep extremely close to Hitler and to show every sympathetic interest in his plans and purposes. All the while they reveal the utmost antipathy toward Great Britain and the cause for which she is fighting.

"My Government has the usual normal relations with all other Governments except those at Tokyo, Berlin, Rome, and Vichy. I can always understand readily the attitude of all the other Governments and get legitimate information promptly and voluntarily from all—with the exception of the four I mentioned. But Vichy, along with Tokyo, Berlin, and Rome, is just the opposite in its disposition to be frank and friendly."

Henry-Haye said he supposed I referred to Mr. Laval in this connection.

"You know, of course," I replied, "that the definite impression created here and everywhere by Mr. Laval is that he is an extreme partisan of Hitler and Mussolini and very bitter toward Great Britain. Also, that he is reported to favor strongly a permanent rejection of the so-called 'old order' in Europe, and the embracing of Hitler's political, social, and other policies with totalitarian autarchy a basic part. Mr. Laval has the privilege of becoming an ally and associate of Hitler and the monstrous things for which he stands, but he must not imagine that this Government does not know what his attitude and purpose are. We propose to be on our guard."

Our Government, I said, had thus far retained its high regard for Marshal Pétain; we wanted to help the French people to the fullest practical extent; and we recognized the unfortunate situation of France as a captive nation. But we strongly maintained our original position that the French Government had no right to go beyond the armistice terms, or render the slightest military aid to Germany.

Henry-Haye tried to argue that Laval was merely attempting to procure the release of French prisoners and other concessions.

"There again," I said, "comes up the matter of attempted appeasement of Hitler. In the end Hitler will do what he pleases with all the captive nations regardless of whether they offer him gifts and other appeasement considerations. The French Government must understand that this Government is too much concerned about possible future attacks by Hitler to acquiesce in the slightest in acts of the French Government that would aid or encourage Hitler in still wider conquest, especially in the direction of this hemisphere."

As this conversation shows, neither the President nor I had any thought of indulgence toward the Pétain regime. We could sympathize with the plight of France, and we would continue to maintain relations with the Vichy Government. But we would insist, in the strongest possible terms, that France's misfortune offered her no excuse for working with Hitler against the Allies—and therefore against the United States.

I cabled this long conversation to Chargé Matthews at Vichy, who handed it to the French Foreign Office to be shown to Laval, who had now become Foreign Minister.

In our policy toward Vichy we began to take ever more cognizance of the importance of French North Africa and French West Africa in relation to the war and Hitler's further ambitions. France's other colonial possessions, in French Equatorial Africa, in the Pacific (except Indo-China), and in India, had now declared in favor of De Gaulle and the Free French movement; but French North and West Africa presented a problem of prime importance.

Following the fall of France we had recognized the heightened strategic position of Dakar, in French West Africa, only 1,700 miles from the bulge of Brazil. After consulting with the President, we reopened the American consulate at Dakar and to it sent Thomas C. Wasson, who arrived on September 15.

The British, too, appreciated the importance of Dakar, knowing that if a German naval force were stationed there it could interrupt their shipping route around the Cape of Good Hope to India and Australia. One week after Consul Wasson arrived at Dakar, a British and Free French naval and marine force attempted to capture the base but failed. Numerous casualties resulted on both sides. This attempt was unfortunate not only in its failure but also in its effect in exacerbating still further the already precarious British-French relations. These relations had been one of my chief concerns since the fall of France.

At about this time a new development of great importance to us occurred in French North Africa. Partly to keep North Africa loyal to Vichy and partly to get General Weygand out of the Cabinet in which he was Minister of National Defense, Marshal Pétain named him to be Delegate-General in North Africa on September 9, 1940, at the instigation of Laval.

To us it seemed that Weygand in North Africa might become a cornerstone around which to build a policy of resistance to Germany. We could have no hopes that he would declare in favor of the Free French, as French Equatorial Africa had done, but we could hope he would reorganize the French Army in North Africa, shy away from any concessions to the Axis, and bide the time when an Allied army could join him in aligning French North Africa in the battle against Hitler.

We began to maintain the closest possible contact with General Weygand on political, military, and economic subjects. When in October we received from London and other capitals an outline of the peace terms Hitler had in mind for France, including the cession of Alsace and Lorraine to Germany, and colonial naval and air bases to Germany and Italy, I cabled this to Consul General Cole at Algiers to be communicated to Weygand. Our intention, in this and later cables, was to keep Weygand informed of German demands on France and the extent of Vichy's bowing to Hitler.

We realized, however, that our best approach to Weygand would lie in the economic field. Dispatches from our consular agents in French Africa told of a disintegrating economic situation. The British blockade having partly cut off French North and West Africa from the rest of the world, those lands were in acute need of many products, including green tea, which had a political importance because the Arabs demanded it.

We felt that French North Africa would be less likely to fall into Axis hands if its economic situation were improved and if the Frenchmen there had the impression that a highway of commerce was still open between them and the Western world. Moreover, French North Africa produced certain minerals of value to us, such as manganese and cobalt.

Chargé Matthews at Vichy cabled us on November 6 a statement to him by the Secretary General of the French Residency that closer economic relations between French Morocco and the United States were important in maintaining Moroccan "independence." If Morocco could not trade with the United States, it would be compelled to deal with Germany. General Weygand, according to the Secretary General, would not accept German control in Morocco.

Thereupon we instructed Robert D. Murphy, of the Embassy at Vichy, who had been Consul General and Counselor of the Embassy at Paris for ten years, to go to French North Africa and discuss possible economic relations with the authorities there. Instructions of a similar nature went to Consul General Felix Cole at Algiers, who had been keeping us closely informed of economic conditions there. These efforts bore fruit the following year, 1941, when we laid the bases for an economic relationship with French North Africa which had a material effect on the progress of the war.

As our contact with Weygand got under way, French Ambassador Henry-Haye suddenly brought me on November 8 a joint message from Pétain and Laval, addressed to the President, expressing their sincere, hearty gratification at his reelection. Perhaps I showed my skepticism at the spectacle of Laval congratulating Mr. Roosevelt, for the Ambassador hastened to emphasize the absolute good faith of both officials in sending the message. I thanked the Ambassador and said I would deliver it to the President who, I felt sure, would be much pleased.

The President had been reelected to a third term three days before.

62: The Third Term

THE THIRD TERM WAS an immediate consequence of Hitler's conquest of France and the specter of Britain alone standing between the conqueror and ourselves. Our dangerous position induced President Roosevelt to run for a third time.

Up to that time the President, in personal conversations with me and with some Democratic Party leaders, had indicated his expectation and wish that I should be his successor. I had taken every step I could, however, to make it clear I was not a candidate for the Presidency. With Europe at war, with Japan preparing for her next move, and with the United States facing innumerable problems in foreign affairs, I felt that I should continue to guide our foreign affairs under the President, rather than strive tó be President myself. Moreover, my health at times was not all it should have been, and I had no intention of being drawn into national politics in 1940.

Various movements had been under way for several years to put my name forward for the nomination in 1940. I did everything I could to discourage them.

In June, 1937, proposals came to me from friends in Tennessee that they should begin to organize on my behalf. I told them I had no present or prospective plans in the direction of the Presidency. An old friend, Judge J. M. Gardenhire of Nashville, thereupon wrote me inquiring as to my real intentions. I replied on June 29, 1937:

"I am of course very grateful for your fine letter of June 25. The fact was that when organization proposals came to me last week from different sources in Tennessee, I had given absolutely no thought to the future, particularly the future as far off as 1940.

"Secondly, in the event I was looking definitely forward to that period, organization steps now would be inadvisable. Furthermore, you are aware that six months these days are a generation in politics. And again, I was desirous of making my statement so definite and unequivocal that others, especially critics, would not have the slightest ground to intimate that my statement was not really unambiguous and serious, or intended to mean less than it purported to mean.

"The honest truth is that, being wholly engrossed with the broad program for peace and economic well-being of peoples, I accurately said that I have no present or prospective plans in other directions."

From the end of 1938 until July, 1940, President Roosevelt expressed himself to me as definitely in favor of my being his successor in 1940. The matter first came up in October, 1938, when I went to the White House to discuss a point of foreign policy with him.

"This point," I said, "will not be settled for several years, until after this term is over."

His face lighted up, and he replied: "Why, that's fine. At that time you'll be in my chair, if my efforts succeed, and you'll be in good position to deal with it."

I might have thanked him and suggested that we proceed toward organizing my candidacy. This I did not do—just the contrary. I made clear to him that I did not intend to get into presidential politics.

"I believe the world is going straight to hell," I said, "and I think I can be of greater service in the State Department."

Several times after that the President took occasion to mention the same subject. Each time he brought it up, I, instead of proposing that we organize, said just the opposite. If we had proceeded to organize, he would have been committed.

Mr. Roosevelt also mentioned to numerous Senators and Congressmen and Democratic leaders throughout the country his interest in having me succeed him.

In March, 1940, the Washington *Post* quoted an unnamed Member of Congress as saying the President had told him he was tired, did not wish to run again, would not do so unless the Germans had conquered England and were moving in our direction by summer, and that I was his choice to succeed him. Governor Hoey of North Carolina, who had talked with the President, stated to the North Carolina State Democratic Convention on April 18, 1940: "I have very good reason to believe that President Roosevelt will indicate his preference for his Secretary of State."

At about the same time, during a Cabinet dinner, Mrs. Hull sat next to the President. There seemed some indication that I would be called upon to speak after the dinner. Mrs. Hull remarked to the President that I did not like to make speeches, to which he replied: "Well, tell him he had better get used to it. He'll have a lot of it to do soon."

Beginning in January, 1940, I made several press statements in which I said I had no ambitions whatever for the Presidency. I then began receiving numerous letters from friends protesting that I should not shut the door so sharply, and asking for definite assurances that I would accept their support for the nomination. I thereupon drew up a letter which went to all of them in more or less this form:

After mentioning my press statements on the subject, I said:

"Referring to your specific question, there are no such definite indications of personal political recognition as to furnish any serious reason for my consideration of possible eventualities. This is precisely my comment to other close friends. Furthermore, four months (or more or less depending on the date of the letter I received) are a generation in political affairs in this period of confusion and turmoil. Events are moving with such rapidity as to make the future utterly unpredictable, and accordingly it is easy to understand that a decision arrived at this moment might be subject to reversal or modification a few months hence."

Publicly my position was that I did not desire the Presidency and would not strive to secure it, and such was also my own sincere conviction. To my closest friends, however, who were anxious to work for me, I could go no further in discouraging them than the language of this letter.

In the spring of 1940 a popular-opinion poll gave me a slightly larger number of votes than the President as a candidate for the next term, and a much larger number of votes than the prospective Republican candidate paired off against me.

Within my own Party this situation aroused considerable alarm among extreme left-wing elements in the New Deal group, including some persons very close to the President. This and other groups were determined that the President should run for a third term, and they did not relish the prospect of my being a candidate.

Beginning several years before 1940, certain members of this circle, allied with a few columnists, began a series of sharp attacks against me. Each time I went away from Washington for a rest furnished them with the argument that I had run down, was worn out, would soon resign, or should resign, and that the State Department was really being run by the President. I was probably receiving more opposition from a portion of the New Deal group than I was from the Republicans. They singled out a few of my assistants, particularly Joseph C. Green, in charge of munitions export control, and James C. Dunn, Political Adviser on European Affairs, for virulent attack, hoping that, by striking at them, they would hit me. The policies of these assistants were my policies, and they carried out none to which I had not agreed. Hence they became the unfortunate victims of certain newspaper calumny and distortion which was really aimed at me.

As late as about June 20, 1940, when I saw the President at the White House, he again referred to the statement he had made at repeated intervals since October, 1938, that he wanted me to be his successor. On this occasion he still gave me no indication that he intended to run again —in fact, just the opposite.

The New Deal group close to him had been insistently urging him to run, but he had held them off. Scattered critics have said that the President, in telling a few close friends that I was his choice in 1940, was simply using me as a buffer until he himself got in, and that he was not maintaining good faith with me. I am sure, however, that he meant what he said to me. Not desiring the post, I was in better position to judge than otherwise.

It seemed to me that, although he continued to retain the views he had expressed to me in October, 1938, there may have been times when, under the terrific pleadings of some of his advisers, he felt disposed to run for a third term. He unquestionably desired my nomination as late as the spring of 1940, to judge from statements he made to me and others up to that time.

Then on July 3, 1940, I had another conversation with him. By now, France had signed the armistice with Germany, Britain was making frantic preparations against invasion, Mussolini had plunged into the war, Japan was preparing to move, and our own position was grave. This conversation made such an impression on me that, when I returned to the State Department, I wrote out some notes in longhand.

The President had invited me to luncheon. We were alone. During the eating stage, I discussed and disposed of several Department matters. Finally the President suddenly said: "Well now, let's talk some politics. You know, there are many people saying to me, 'You can't afford to let us down.' "

The President, in saying this, used a sort of impatient, incredulous tone.

I remarked that it was probably an avalanche of people.

The President said he had been reading Washington's letter to Madison in which Washington complained about criticism against his running for a second term. Mr. Roosevelt said he had in mind to address a letter to someone like Senator George Norris and end by saying that he desired to go back to Hyde Park. Thereupon, he said, the convention would nominate me. He asked me what I thought of such a letter.

I promptly replied: "Of course such a letter would not delay your nomination by a split second."

The President thereupon began to speculate on how he himself might win under certain circumstances. He spoke slightly haltingly and disconnectedly. His tone was that of deprecating the idea of running. He said he thought he could win in November, unless the war should stop. In the latter event Wendell Willkie, the Republican nominee, might defeat him; but he would not care except for the country's sake. I made no comment.

He then started to get onto my strong and weak qualities as a candidate for President. He was extremely guarded compared to his former conversations with me, when he had forthrightly said he considered me his successor.

I interrupted him to say that, in any event, I was not to be considered. My interruption was inspired by the two reasons I have mentioned for not wishing to run, and also by the fact that at that moment I was clearly of the opinion that he himself had made up his mind to become a candidate. I emphasized my state of health, and said:

"For many months my wife and I have agreed that I should go out of public service, and especially politics. In order that my situation might not in the slightest interfere with presidential talk about you, I've often made public statements to the effect that I have no desire or intention to get into presidential politics."

The President went ahead, however, to point out my weaknesses, as he saw them, after saying generally that my standing throughout the nation was good. He mentioned only one item of weakness, however—the propaganda against the trade agreements in the farm belt. He then added that I could probably take Wallace or some person in the farm belt as Vice President and win.

I repeated my disclaimer of any intention to run for the nomination. I said I had not only kept myself carefully and entirely out of his political picture and range, but I had also seen to it that he had credit for everything we had done and were doing at the State Department. He cheerfully agreed that this was the truth.

The President's whole tone and language during our conversation was a complete reversal of what it had been ten days before, when he was still advocating my candidacy.

The President at this time must have made up his mind to accept a third term. Certainly a huge movement was already in motion to urge him to do so. In view of my course from January on of issuing numerous public statements to the effect that I had no intention of getting into politics in 1940 and refusing to permit any organized effort by friends in many States who desired to make one, it was not unnatural that certain sections of the Party, especially the more extreme New Dealers and other strong partisans of the President, should start organized movements over the country in favor of a third nomination because of the emergency conditions confronting the country. This movement gradually gained momentum until members of the Democratic National Committee and Federal officials and other friendly elements fell into line. The matter was now settled.

Almost immediately the President began urging me to run with him as Vice President. He called me to the White House and pleaded with me for some two hours and forty minutes. I declined and stood firm in my declination.

To me, being Vice President meant that a man would permit himself to sit as presiding officer of the Senate with no authority to participate in the proceedings or even to vote except in the case of a tie. I recalled Jefferson's characterization of the Vice Presidency, with which I agreed. Elected Vice President in 1796, he wrote: "It will give me philosophical evenings in the winter, and rural days in the summer. The second office of the Government is honorable and easy."

Comparing this situation with my present position, I was quick and strong in saying to the President that I could render far more valuable service in the troublous days ahead by staying at the State Department.

I was not interested in an easy, soft place with the highest honor next to the Presidency.

One or two days later the President called me back to the White House and again pressed his proposal on me most earnestly. I stood firm in my original attitude. During this and the previous conversation, we discussed almost every imaginable phase of the present and prospective political situation.

A night or so later the President telephoned me at my apartment. He again pressed his offer with much emphasis. Again I refused.

He then said: "Let me talk to Frances. I'll convince her, and she can convince you."

Mrs. Hull, who was right beside me, kept shaking her head. She did not want to be drawn into the discussion.

I said to the President: "Mrs. Hull has gone to bed. I can't call her to the phone."

He then said: "If you don't take it, I'll have to get Henry Wallace to run."

I continued to refuse. "That's all right with me," I said.

This remark does not mean I supported Wallace for the Vice Presidency. The fact was, I was having a strenuous time to keep from being pressed into the office by President Roosevelt, and I was not objecting to anybody he mentioned as a substitute. It was in that sense that I said "O.K." to his mention of Wallace rather than in the sense of approving Wallace or of taking part in the selection of the Vice President.

In casual conversations with the President, and with other persons who had discussed the matter with me, I had made complimentary reference to such outstanding and exceptionally well qualified men as Senator Alben W. Barkley, James A. Farley, Jesse Jones, and others for the Vice Presidency. In fact, quite a list was mentioned. These names naturally came up when the President talked with me about the Vice Presidency. It should not be understood from this, however, that I was recommending anyone to the President. I did not do so because I had no wish to interfere in the selection of the Vice President.

I asked Assistant Secretary of State Breckinridge Long, who attended the Democratic National Convention at Chicago, to see to it that my name was not put in nomination for the Vice Presidency.

The convention on July 18 nominated President Roosevelt for a third term. I went to the White House that day and congratulated him. The following day I left for the Conference of Foreign Ministers at Havana, Cuba.

I myself was strongly opposed to the third-term idea. I feared lest it set a precedent for some future President to abuse the power entrusted to him. I felt it had only one justification. This was that we were then in the midst of a terrible international crisis, when Western civilization seemed in the greatest danger in its history; if Roosevelt did not run, another Democratic nominee might have lost; and it would have been disastrous in that event for the Government to be left without a real head during the two and a half months between the election and the inauguration, on January 20, 1941. I felt that no foreign Government would have any respect for an Administration that had been repudiated, and there was no telling what action the Axis countries might take and what results might have ensued during what would have amounted to an interregnum. What I had in mind was something like Pearl Harbor occurring during that period.

I had one major disappointment during the Democratic Convention —one of the foreign policy planks in the platform leaned toward the isolationist view. I had had several meetings with my associates in the State Department during which we drew up suggestions for the foreign policy sections of the platform, and I submitted these to the President.

I felt that the only really valid excuse for the nomination of the President for the third term was the crisis in Europe, yet Harry Hopkins, representing the President at Chicago, agreed to an isolationist plank in an endeavor to conciliate the isolationists.

On the morning of July 17, while the platform was under discussion in Chicago, I telephoned the White House to protest to the President that this plank completely misrepresented the Administration's views. I could not get through to the President, and three hours later he had not telephoned me back. I felt that his neglect to telephone me might be due to his possible irritation over my refusal to accept his offer of the nomination as Vice President. I telephoned the President again at noon, and this time he called me back.

I emphasized to him the glaring defects of the foreign policy plank. Particularly, I said, it would cause us difficulties in our relations with Japan because she might naturally take it as an invitation to ignore all our interests in the Far East.

The President replied, however, that it was too late to do anything. No matter what plank was adopted, he said, he intended to state that there would be no change in our foreign policy.

I took no part in the campaign that followed, until the last few days. I spent the last half of July at the Havana Conference, the first three weeks in August resting at White Sulphur Springs, the next ten days working on the destroyers-bases exchange, September engrossed in our difficulties with Japan, and October preparing the foundations for our policy of self-defense and Lend-Lease.

I made every effort, however, to keep foreign policy from being knocked about in the battledore and shuttlecock of politics. I talked to Republican friends who were close to Willkie to induce them to use their influence with him toward this end. Willkie was in general agreement with a policy of aiding Britain, but he made several sharp attacks on the President, accusing him of pushing us toward war.

On September 30 I telephoned the President that I had just received word that Willkie was going to make another attack on the Administration's foreign policy, holding the President and me responsible for the Munich Conference and the outbreak of the war in Europe. I said to the President that I was trying through mutual friends to get Willkie to tone down his intended speech, in the interest of an American common front toward the world, but did not know whether I would be successful.

I made the effort, but the attacks continued. Those were months when it seemed to me Western civilization hung in the balance. Night after night I tossed in bed, pondering the effect on this country if Hitler should conquer Britain. Despite Britain's magnificent resistance, I had to envisage the possibility that Hitler's superior military machine might overcome her, and that we would then be faced simultaneously in the Atlantic with the combined remaining portions of the German, French, and Italian fleets, and in the Pacific with the Japanese fleet, while Nazi and Fascist agents in Latin America undermined our neighbors to the south.

Yet many of our most prominent citizens failed to see these dangers. Some of the leading isolationists said openly that it made no difference to our future whether Britain or Germany won the war. I regretted that men so intelligent could be so blind.

Toward the end of the campaign reports were spread about that Willkie, if elected, would continue me in office as Secretary of State. The disseminators of this report were obviously seeking to win over blocs of voters who intended to support Roosevelt on the basis of the Administration's foreign policy record of which I, as Secretary of State, was the chief exponent.

The White House wanted me to issue a blunt statement that I would refuse to be Willkie's Secretary of State. Such an approach seemed to me unwise. I felt that the people around Willkie who fostered the rumor had put me on hot embers. If I ignored the rumors, it would seem that I was countenancing them. If I said I would not serve under Willkie, it would appear that I was placing Party considerations above the nation's interests. And I could not say I would serve under Willkie without appearing to indicate a belief that Roosevelt would be defeated. I therefore drew up the following formula which I stated to the press and to persons who wrote me inquiring whether the rumors were true and what my reaction was:

"I have no knowledge of the origin of such reports as you refer to. They would seem to smack of politics, and I would not countenance them for a moment. On the contrary, I most strongly disapprove of their circulation over the country."

Much of the debate between the two parties hinged on the question of which party was more likely to keep us out of war. In this respect, it seemed to me that the platform of the Democratic Party was the more realistic. The Republicans promised flatly that American soldiers would not be sent to fight abroad. The Democrats promised that they would not be sent to fight abroad except in the case of attack against us.

In line with the nonpartisan approach to foreign policy I had followed since 1933, I did not intend to make any campaign speeches in 1940. I gave one of the most important foreign policy addresses of my career on October 26—nine days prior to the elections—before the National Press Club, Washington, but it was purely a statement of our policy.

I made this address at what I considered one of the greatest crises of the war. Hitler was pounding at Britain from the air, and there was every reason to believe that he had been preparing, and perhaps still was preparing, an invasion of the United Kingdom. Mussolini was getting ready for his invasion of Greece, which began two days later. With the Nazis using France's western ports as submarine bases, Britain's shipping losses were doubling and trebling. Germany, Japan, and Italy had signed their tripartite alliance, obviously aimed at the United States. Japan had moved into French Indo-China and there was no telling what her next step would be.

Exactly two weeks before speaking to the National Press Club, I asked a group of officials of the War and Navy Departments to my office for a conference. I opened the meeting by saying we should not overlook certain possible and, in fact, probable developments in the war.

"I therefore want to suggest," I said, "that Hitler recently more than at any time in the past holds the whip hand among his outlaw associates, Japan and others. He may at any time order a general advance from London to Tokyo, in the air, on the sea, and on the land. He may announce that the bombardment of Great Britain will continue right through the winter, with no let-up until Britain is conquered from across the Channel and through the air.

"At the same time and during the coming winter, the Germans will

make every possible effort to conquer Egypt, Africa, and the Suez Canal
—which would mean possession of the Mediterranean. For this purpose
they might use any or all of three avenues: the avenue across at Gibraltar, the avenue across the Mediterranean near Sicily, and, lastly, the
route through the Balkans, Turkey, and Syria.

"Since Stalin is mortally afraid of the German Army, Hitler, by both
threats and persuasion, might well keep Russia aloof even from the Turkish and Balkan route. Hitler might well tell Russia not to bother Japan
temporarily, and not to aid Turkey either in the event of a German invasion or an Italian attack on Greece, in case Turkey should come to the
aid of Greece.

"As a fourth step, Hitler, driving toward Egypt, may leave nothing
undone to utilize the French forces in the air, on the land, and on the sea.

"Finally, Hitler, having kept Russia off of Japan and having required
the Vichy Government to admit Japan to Indo-China, might well prevail
upon Japan to take much greater risk in advancing than she otherwise
would. She is already extremely anxious to invade and occupy the South
Seas area."

This was the grim but realistic picture I placed before the representatives of War and Navy. It was my own analysis of the situation,
based on my estimate of numerous dispatches from all corners of the world
and my knowledge of the Axis leaders and their intentions. It added up
to a possible juncture of the forces of the European Axis with their Asiatic
partner somewhere in the Indian Ocean or the Middle East.

When I spoke, therefore, on October 26, an address broadcast to the
nation, it was with this menacing situation in mind. In this speech I
made the first official exposition of what became the Administration's
doctrine of self-defense. We could no longer rely on strict interpretation
of neutrality. Just as the man who is menaced by an assailant is free to
utilize any weapons at hand to defend himself, so we as a nation could
utilize all means to defend our independence.

"There can be nothing more dangerous for our nation," I said, "than
for us to assume that the avalanche of conquest could under no circumstances reach any vital portion of this hemisphere. Oceans give the
nations of this hemisphere no guarantee against the possibility of economic, political, or military attack from abroad. Oceans are barriers but
they are also highways. Barriers of distance are merely barriers of time.
Should the would-be conquerors gain control of other continents, they
would next concentrate on perfecting their control of the seas, of the air

over the seas, and of the world's economy; they might then be able with ships and with planes to strike at the communication lines, the commerce, and the life of this hemisphere; and ultimately we might find ourselves compelled to fight on our own soil, under our own skies, in defense of our independence and our very lives."

Such being the case, I argued that our inalienable right of self-defense justified our taking two main measures to defend ourselves: one, to rearm to the utmost; two, to help the Allies with supplies. "We believe," I said, "that the safety and the primary interests of the United States must be upheld with firmness and resolution—supported by the speediest and fullest possible armament for all defensive purposes. . . . We have frankly recognized the danger involved and the increasing need for defense against it. As an important means of strengthening our own defense and of preventing attack on any part of the Western Hemisphere, this country is affording all feasible facilities for the obtaining of supplies by nations which, while defending themselves against barbaric attack, are checking the spread of violence and are thus reducing the danger to us. We intend to continue doing this to the greatest practicable extent. Any contention, no matter from what source, that this country should not take such action is equivalent, in the present circumstances, to a denying of the inalienable right of self-defense."

I had expected to rest for a time on this address, which was non-political. However, two factors developed suddenly that made me alter my position. One was the fact that Willkie was sharply attacking some of the Roosevelt Administration foreign policies. The other was the probability that the election would be close, a fact Roosevelt recognized by changing his own previous intention not to campaign against Willkie. It seemed to me that, if Roosevelt were defeated, almost anything could happen during the two and a half months until Willkie would be inaugurated.

The picture of the appalling dangers I had presented to the War and Navy officials on October 12 still stood in its original colors. Japan was casting about for her next move; she was already installed in French Indo-China; the British had withdrawn from Shanghai but had reopened the Burma Road. During the confusion and uncertainty of the interregnum between election day and inauguration day if Willkie won, Japan might strike even as she struck one year later. And Hitler, aware that our aid to Britain was assuming serious proportions, might strike at the same time to cut it off.

On October 27 I met with my State Department associates in my office for one of the usual Sunday morning meetings during which we informally went over various segments of our foreign policy. I said to them I intended to make an address on November 1 supporting our foreign policy against the attacks that had been leveled against it during the election campaign. It was still my intention at that point to keep the speech out of the political arena.

In the next few days I had several additional conferences with my associates during which we went over successive drafts of the address. Then, on November 1, when we met for the last time, Willkie's latest attack on the Administration's foreign policy was brought to my attention, particularly his statement that Roosevelt's "foreign policies are leading us straight to a war for which we are totally unready." We thereupon reshaped the entire speech better to meet this charge. The address was not completed until 6:30, and I spoke at 9:45, immediately following the President.

I delivered my address from the National Broadcasting Company studio in Washington. Previously Edward J. Flynn, chairman of the Democratic National Committee, had requested me to make the speech during a political rally in Baltimore or in Philadelphia. I did not want to make a speech on foreign affairs in the midst of a political rally, however, nor did I wish to absent myself from Washington at this dangerous moment in international affairs. "The ever increasing dangers of the international situation keep me tied to my desk almost day and night," I telegraphed Flynn on October 29.

In my address I replied to two principal charges made against the Administration's foreign policy. One was that the President was "leading us into war." "This Government," I said, "has consistently and persistently proceeded in the firm belief that adequate preparedness on this country's part will greatly minimize the danger of assaults against us. We are creating the weapons and the organization needed, first, to discourage would-be assailants and, second, should we be assailed, to repel assaults. We are warning our people of danger to this country, should other countries which are under assault go down. We are making available access to the resources and the products of this country to countries under assault, whose survival is important to our own security.

"In all these ways, this country is being entrenched against war."

To the second charge, that the Administration's foreign policies had brought this country into a position of "loneliness" in world affairs, I replied:

"The nations of the Western Hemisphere are our friends. All nations fighting desperately for survival are our friends. Only the rulers of those nations which are bent on conquest are at odds with us. But surely, anyone who believes in law is unpopular with lawbreakers. And, naturally, anyone who strives wholeheartedly to keep the peace has the enmity of willful peacebreakers."

Directly on the point of the President's reelection, I said that, in the presence of such problems as confronted this country, it was necessary to weigh more carefully than usual the disadvantages that would attend a change in leadership. "It should be manifest that today the balance of advantage lies with continuity of national leadership," I emphasized. "The President's practical experience and his familiarity with the facts and problems of the international situation as they affect this country are at this moment an extraordinarily valuable asset. This is no time for the country to be making a change from experience to inexperience—a change which, furthermore, would immediately involve two and one-half months of confusion and uncertainty."

On the day I delivered this address I outlined a short talk with which to introduce the President over the nationwide radio network for his last address of the campaign on November 4, the night before the elections. I spoke from my apartment in the Carlton Hotel, while the President spoke from Hyde Park.

These addresses of November 1 and 4 were the furthest I ever went in the direction of political speeches during my twelve years in the State Department. I would not have spoken politically at all were it not for the bitter attacks made on our foreign policies by speakers of the opposing Party.

Several persons working with the President wanted me to follow his lead and put a paragraph in one or both of my speeches saying flatly that American troops would not be sent to fight abroad. Knowing the situation and dangers as I did, I refused.

Following the reelection of President Roosevelt, I issued a heartfelt appeal on November 6 for support of our foreign policies by both political Parties. It was obvious to me that Hitler, Mussolini, and the Japanese war lords had taken encouragement from some of the bitterness engendered during the campaign.

"Consciousness of the tremendous responsibility which rests upon all of us in the present crisis," I said, "should overshadow any sense of personal elation or disappointment over the election result.

"In a spirit of nonpartisanship and nonfactionalism, I want to appeal again for united effort to carry forward a program of principles and practical measures, the success of which means everything to the peace and safety and welfare of the American people."

63: Hitler Will Not Win

FOLLOWING THE ELECTION, the tempo of our aid to Britain accelerated. It was clearer now than ever that Britain would stand and that the assistance we were sending her would not fall into German hands. In the desperate days of October, the German air force had been beaten back in the skies over the British Isles, Hitler's plans for the invasion of Britain were postponed at least for the moment, and it was evident that our aid to the embattled British was having an ever greater effect both in Britain and wherever men still dared believe in an Allied victory, however long it took.

Never have I admired a people more than I admired the British in the summer and autumn of 1940. Each man and woman and even the children seemed to realize that upon their indomitable spirit depended not only their own fate but also that of the whole democratic world. They were all soldiers in one vast army. History has no more thrilling story than this, of a whole people working and fighting almost as one person against odds so great that it was better not to think of them lest to do so bring despair. In their extreme crisis they exhibited the same fortitude and love of freedom that had moved them to protect popular institutions against countless efforts to destroy them during the centuries of the past.

And no people in history had a more courageous and inspiring leader in the moment of their greatest need than had the British in Winston Churchill. As long as the history of the British people is written, his actions and speeches at the very edge of the precipice will ring through the chapters of this time.

Three days after the Presidential election, Mr. Roosevelt announced that henceforth half of all the planes and other implements of war produced in the United States would go to Britain. Soon thereafter the Army released twenty-six "Flying Fortresses" to augment the offensive that Britain was making in the air. In the daily war-situation reports from London which the British Embassy sent me and I forwarded to the President, the note of earlier desperation was changing to one of grim determination.

We were working closely with the British Government in diplomatic matters in many parts of the world—seeking to prevent the Vichy Government from falling into the arms of Hitler, to solidify our relations with French Africa, and to prevent Japan from going on a rampage.

Ambassador Kennedy cabled me on November 10 a message from Mr. Churchill to the President informing us of reports that the French Government intended to bring the new battleships *Jean Bart* and *Richelieu* from African ports to French Mediterranean bases for completion. The Prime Minister said it was difficult to exaggerate the potential danger of this move because the ships could then fall under German control. He said his Government had already warned Vichy on this score, and asked the President to deliver a like warning.

After discussing this with the President, I cabled our Embassy at Vichy on November 12 to obtain confirmation of the report given us by Churchill and to express our view that these battleships should remain in stations where they were not exposed to control or seizure by the Germans. On the following day we went further and offered to buy the battleships from France, promising that, in such event, we would not use them during the course of the war.

Pétain replied, however, that he could not sell the ships, even if he wanted to, because of the terms of the armistice. The Germans, he said, would never permit it, adding that "we are under their heel and are powerless." He again gave "most solemn assurances" that the French fleet, including the two battleships, would never fall into Germany's hands and would not be used against the British unless they were attacked by the British.

Pétain now stated to Chargé Matthews his view that the British were fighting a good fight and would never yield, but on the other hand they could not land on the Continent and invade Germany. He therefore foresaw only a drawn peace after much tragic destruction. The sooner such a peace came the better, because France would pay the price of continued war.

British Ambassador Lothian, returning to Washington on November 23 following a period of leave in Britain, said to press correspondents that Britain was nearing the end of her cash resources and would soon require some form of financial assistance from the United States.

Lothian brought up the subject of credits when he came to see me on November 25, but we did not go into it in detail. He was optimistic concerning Britain's morale and unified spirit of resistance, and said he believed she could hold out against attacks from the air and from across the Channel. But he emphasized long-range difficulties, a threatened invasion of Egypt by Germany, and Britain's growing need for ships.

Lothian said the first consideration was to secure permission to occupy Irish harbors. Undoubtedly he would have liked to have our diplomatic assistance, but I interrupted him by saying:

"In my opinion, De Valera and his associates will not agree to anything at present. Any aid from us, therefore, seems virtually impossible just now."

Although the President was annoyed at Lothian for giving an interview on finances, actually the Ambassador had stated nothing we did not know already, nothing we had not already been considering. I had had several conversations with the President and with Secretary Morgenthau on this subject. We realized that Britain was, as Morgenthau put it, beginning to "scrape the bottom of the barrel" of her liquid resources. Toward the end of 1940 she had placed with us more orders than she could possibly pay for even by converting into cash all the securities she could. If the sinews of war were to continue to flow to Britain at an increasing rate, we ourselves would have to find means to pay for them.

In November and December I held several conferences in my office on this problem, generally on Sunday mornings. We realized that there were certain legal difficulties. There was the Neutrality Act and the United States Code, as far as domestic legislation was concerned. Green Hackworth, Legal Adviser of the State Department, ruled that the Neutrality Act applied to American citizens but not to the Government, and in any event could be superseded by a new Act of Congress, as could the United States Code provisions. Some of my advisers were in favor of repealing the Neutrality Act, but I knew that any such attempt would provoke a long conflict in Congress which would merely serve to acidify the waters.

International law, as stated in the Hague Convention of 1907, forbade the supply of war materials of any kind by a neutral Government to a belligerent Government. That convention, however, was not to apply unless all the belligerents were parties to it—and Britain and Italy were not. Moreover, the convention's rules relating to the rights and duties of neutrals and belligerents complemented each other. Germany and Italy had paid no attention to the rights of neutrals, having invaded many such countries.

My associates and I soon agreed that whatever legal obstacles existed in the way of extending aid to Britain on other than a cash basis could be overcome by a new Act of Congress. We next agreed that a loan to Britain was not the best method. We were still sending Britain the semi-annual demands for payment of installments on the war debt for the previous war. More loans would probably produce eventually the same ill feeling that resulted from Britain's nonpayment of the remainder of her First World War debt. Furthermore, we believed we would have more control over prices of war materials if we did not give Britain cash with which to bid against us for supplies in the open market.

It would therefore be better to order the equipment ourselves and turn it over to Britain and the other Allies. We were against the idea of an outright gift. This might be unacceptable to British pride, and there was also the possibility that we might otherwise get certain items in exchange from the British Empire in addition to the return of the war material that was not used up or damaged.

As these ideas evolved in the Treasury and State Departments, the President was away for several weeks on a Caribbean cruise with Harry Hopkins aboard the cruiser *Tuscaloosa*, partly to think over problems such as Lend-Lease and partly to visit our new bases in that area. Meantime Secretary Morgenthau was discussing the Lend-Lease conception with Sir Frederick Phillips, Under Secretary of the British Treasury, who came to Washington to lay the financial plight of his country before our fiscal experts.

I held discussions in my office with Morgenthau and his associates, chiefly E. H. Foley, General Counsel of the Treasury, and Oscar S. Cox. I also called in some of the leaders of both Houses of Congress. One of the points we had to decide was whether to define what articles would come under the term "Lend-Lease." We agreed this should be left open to enable the President to turn over to the Allies all the articles needed. Another point was whether Lend-Lease should include facilities and labor such as our reconditioning of British ships. We agreed that it should.

When the President returned to Washington on December 16 he was ready to announce the idea. The following day he stated it at his press conference, with the homely illustration of the neighbor who loans a garden hose to another neighbor whose house is on fire.

Morgenthau and his assistants took the burden of drafting the necessary legislation, after lengthy discussions with us. The Treasury assumed this task because of the number of financial clauses required. They brought their drafts to the State and other interested Departments so that we could make suggestions, and we spent many hours in my office advising a change here or a rewording there. The text also incorporated some of the phrasing of the Pittman-Bloom Act of June 15, 1940, drafted in the State Department, which authorized the Secretaries of War and Navy to sell to Latin American Republics war materials constructed in arsenals or shipyards under War or Navy jurisdiction.

With the completion of the draft, the concept of Lend-Lease was launched. The fight for it in Congress came within a few weeks.

British Ambassador Lothian died without having had a chance to hear the President's statement on Lend-Lease. A brief illness took him four days before the President's return to Washington. I went personally to the British Embassy to express the condolence of our Government, and I attended the funeral services at the Washington Cathedral and the burial in Arlington National Cemetery. At the Department we drafted the sincere and heartfelt statements of regret issued by the President and myself. Lothian's death was an acute loss. His outstanding ability, his willingness and readiness to grasp our point of view and to represent that of his own Government, and his pleasing personality had made him an unsurpassed medium through which to carry on relations between the two Governments.

One of the last topics I had been discussing with Lothian before his death was our relations with Spain. When the European War broke out, a cardinal point of British policy was to keep Spain and Portugal out of the conflict. The reasons were obvious, including Gibraltar and communications through the Mediterranean. After France fell and German troops appeared on the Spanish border, the importance of Spain's neutrality became yet more pronounced.

General Franco was under constant pressure, both from within his own country and from the Axis, to join openly with Berlin and Rome. Our diplomacy, working parallel with that of Britain, strove to emphasize that Spain's best interests lay in refraining from war and in maintaining normal economic relations with the United States and the British Empire. In this policy there was no appeasement of Spain.

On the day Marshal Pétain sued for an armistice, the British Government, stating its great concern over the size of Spanish oil reserves, requested our assistance in limiting the number of neutral tankers available for Spanish charter, and in restricting the export of lubricating oil and aviation gasoline to Spain to her normal peacetime requirements, lest excessive oil stocks in Spain either serve that country as a war reserve or pass into Axis hands. Working in conjunction with the Maritime Commission, we took a series of steps toward this end.

Capable and long-experienced Alexander W. Weddell, our Ambassador to Spain, cabled us from Madrid on September 7, 1940, that Spain was approaching a crisis with respect to foodstuffs and raw materials, particularly wheat, cotton, and gasoline, and that the Spanish Government had suggested an American credit of $100,000,000 to permit the purchase of these supplies in the United States. Weddell said he had replied by referring to earlier conversations he had had with Franco in which they discussed the provision of surplus American commodities to Spain on condition that Spain continued to remain neutral and really desired to maintain friendly relations with us.

In requesting the Department's instructions, Weddell recommended we give sympathetic consideration to the Spanish proposal. He said it was becoming increasingly evident that the Spanish Government was trying to resist Axis pressure to enter the war, but that unless some relief were obtained the resulting international chaos might either force the Government to accept complete Axis domination or supplant it by another Government willing to join the Axis.

I authorized Weddell on September 19 to indicate to the Spanish Government that while we were aware of Spain's economic difficulties and wished to foster all mutually beneficial economic relationships between our two countries, such action on our part could be justified only if we had sufficient assurance that it would have a lasting and genuine economic result and would conform to the general international political principles for which we stood. We would likewise have to receive assurances against the reexport of commodities obtained through credits.

Ambassador Weddell accordingly saw the Spanish Foreign Minister, Juan Beigbeder y Atienza, and the Ministers of Finance and of Industry and Commerce, on September 30. He quoted the Foreign Minister as saying that, while for political reasons his Government could not issue a public declaration or sign an agreement defining the Spanish Government's attitude in advance, he was able officially in his Government's name to assure us that unless Spain were attacked she would not enter the war. All three Ministers stressed their belief that assistance to Spain by the United States would strengthen the Spanish Government's intention to remain out of the war.

After a further conversation with the Foreign Minister, Weddell cabled on October 3 that Beigbeder had told him that an announcement by

President Roosevelt that Spain would be supplied with wheat could change Spanish and European policy, that the psychological moment had come, and that the arrival of a cargo of wheat in an American ship would have a very deep effect.

After I had called a special meeting of my associates on October 4 to discuss this question, and after talking it over with the President, we cabled Weddell that the President was prepared to ask the American Red Cross to act on behalf of our Government in shipping a quantity of wheat to Spain at once, provided we received advance assurances from Franco himself on three points. These were that there would be no exportation from Spain of wheat from any source; that the American Red Cross would supervise the distribution of the wheat to the needy population of Spain in cooperation with the Spanish Red Cross or another Spanish organization designated by the American Red Cross; and that full information would be given through the Spanish press concerning these shipments.

The British Government was in full accord with this initiative. British Ambassador Lord Lothian said to me on October 7 that his Government was in harmony with our views and that this was the psychological time for such action.

Weddell cabled us the following day that he had been received that day by Franco, who gave his personal assurances with respect to the three conditions, and asked him to transmit his thanks to the President. I therefore informed Weddell on October 12 that the President had asked the American Red Cross to arrange immediately for a wheat or, if preferable, flour shipment. I authorized the Ambassador to inform Franco that we were ready to discuss the bases for making credits available to Spain, keeping in mind the conditions set forth in my previous cables.

At this moment, however, Spanish Foreign Minister Beigbeder was supplanted by Franco's brother-in-law, Serrano Suñer, a Falangist or Fascist leader and an avowed friend of the Axis. Reports reached us that Franco would shortly meet Hitler on the Spanish frontier. We accordingly held up the Red Cross shipment to await the development of this new situation.

Ambassador Weddell was unable to see the new Foreign Minister until October 31. He cabled on that day that Suñer, following Weddell's question as to whether the change in Foreign Ministers meant a shift in Spanish foreign policy, replied that the change was small in substance but indicated a closer rapprochement between Spain and the Axis. Suñer said he was able to assure Weddell of the political solidarity of Spain with Italy and Germany, but that neither Mussolini nor Hitler had suggested that Spain enter the war. When Suñer raised the question of food shipments, Weddell pointed out that the delay had been occasioned by the Spanish Foreign Office, and that naturally we would wish to be fully informed of the Spanish Government's policy before going more deeply into Spain's needs. He informed Suñer of this Government's desire that the Ambassador see General Franco again to obtain his further personal assurances, following the change of Foreign Ministers.

We cabled Weddell on November 5, however, that we did not consider any further efforts to obtain an interview with Franco desirable in view of Suñer's objectionable statements relative to Spanish solidarity with Italy and Germany. Nevertheless, if the Ambassador were given an interview on the basis of his previous requests, he was to make clear the following four points: First, United States Government, and not Red Cross, funds would be used to purchase any food supplies for Spanish civilian relief. Second, our policy, as the Spanish Government knew, was to provide all assistance possible to the British in their fight against aggression. Third, if the Spanish political solidarity with Italy and Germany referred to by Suñer meant Spanish assistance to them in their fight against Britain in the form of facilities, naval bases, or any other types of direct or indirect aid, it would obviously not be possible for this Government to expend Government funds in assisting Spain. Fourth, the premise upon which this Government was considering relief in Spain was Spain's maintenance of an absolute neutrality, and we regretfully concluded that Suñer's statements very clearly indicated that it was not the Spanish Government's intention to maintain such neutrality.

On the same day Weddell cabled us that the Spanish Government had accepted our conditions relative to the distribution of wheat through the American Red Cross and our text of a proposed press release. Suñer also said Weddell would be received within the next few days by General Franco, who would reiterate the personal assurances he had previously given the Ambassador. Weddell followed this cable by another, on November 6, repeating his earlier recommendations in support of relief for Spain.

We cabled Weddell on November 8, however, instructing him to say to Franco that this Government must postpone any final decision on the question of food shipments and of credits to Spain, in view of the recent developments there which seemed to involve a change in Spanish policy. We instructed him to say also that we naturally hoped and expected that a policy of mercy would be adopted by the Spanish Government toward Spanish political refugees and prisoners within the jurisdiction of Spain.

We added for the Ambassador's information that public opinion in the United States was greatly exercised over the possibility of American help to Spain so long as it seemed likely that Spain would give active assistance to Italy and Germany and while the Spanish Government was carrying out political executions that deeply shocked public opinion here. Although we fully recognized the need of the Spanish people, we would be unable to justify relief of that need if Spain gave direct or indirect practical assistance to Germany and Italy. This situation could be remedied only by the Spanish Government's making a clear-cut, public-policy declaration that not only did it plan to stay neutral but also it would not assist Italy or Germany in any way in their struggle with Britain.

Subsequently, on November 20, Acting Secretary Welles, while I was absent from Washington for a few days, cabled Weddell, at the President's direction, authorizing him to modify our position to the extent of withdrawing our demand for a public statement. At the same time, however, he was to make it clear that public opinion here would be greatly benefited and relief measures by this Government greatly facilitated by an indication publicly of the Spanish Government's intention of remaining neutral. This authorization was based on a recommendation made by Weddell after he had discussed with Suñer and other members of the Spanish Government our position as set forth in my cable of the 8th.

The British Government pressed us to go ahead with relief and credit measures for Spain. Ambassador Lothian came in to see me for this purpose on November 25. Two weeks before, his Government had given us an *aide-mémoire,* dated November 9, urging that we immediately ship wheat to Spain in view of the imminence of famine there and of the possibility that famine might cause Spain to veer more to the Axis. The British requested our cooperation in the question of relief to Spain, saying they planned to open discussions witih the Spanish Government on providing supplies and credits for Spain.

I said to Lothian that this Government would have a difficult situation to contend with because of unfavorable public sentiment which recently had been accentuated by attacks in the Spanish press over our negotiations with Latin American countries for the use of certain bases in the event war came to us. I suggested that, if Britain was of the opinion that the sending of foodstuffs would keep Spain out of the war, wheat might be sent there from Canada. Lothian thought this idea good and said he would cable it to London.

Lothian came back to me on the same subject on November 29, saying that Britain intended going ahead with relief shipments to Spain. He wondered whether this would be agreeable to us since it might appear that the policies of our two Governments were diverging. I replied that I saw no reason to raise any question about divergence in the circumstances.

"We're struggling with the Spanish food-relief problem very sympathetically," I said. "As you well know, however, the Spanish Government seems to do almost everything it can to antagonize popular opinion in this country, thereby making it practically impossible for this Government to give the relief desired."

I mentioned the inflammatory criticism frequently indulged in by the Spanish press; Suñer's widely advertised trip to Berlin, presumably to bring the two countries closer together; and Franco's refusal for two weeks to see Ambassador Weddell on this very subject of relief.

I added that we were also considering very sympathetically the sending of condensed milk and vitamin concentrates to French children, and that, when we had done so, we would have a much better chance to take part in relief to Spain. Since we were then having difficulty with Britain over the question of our sending relief to the children of unoccupied France, I emphasized that the British Government could well consider this point in determining whether to allow milk and concentrates to go to France through their blockade.

Ambassador Weddell reported on November 29 that at last he had been received that day by General Franco. When Weddell asked directly whether he might inform his Government that Spain did not envisage any departure from her present international attitude nor did she contemplate any aid to the Axis powers, Franco gave his assent, but immediately said that Spain could not help the Axis powers even if she wished, and that no one could foresee what the future might bring forth.

After giving much consideration to the exact wording of Franco's assurances, my associates and I prepared a memorandum which I took to the President on December 16. He approved it.

In this memorandum we stated that the British had informed us they were prepared to make credit arrangements to send shipments of wheat to Spain from Canada and Argentina. As soon as public announce-

ment of this action was made, we were ready to go ahead with the first of
two or three shipments of foodstuffs to Spain through the American Red
Cross, to be paid for out of the $50,000,000 appropriation granted for
foreign civilian relief.

We added that negotiations for credits with which Spain could purchase American surplus commodities would have to embrace the Spanish
Government's attitude on four points. The first was that Spain intended
to remain outside the war and did not contemplate aiding the Axis. The
second was formal recognition by the Spanish Government of the validity
of the claims of private American creditors for payment of blocked accounts owing them in Spain. The third was equality of opportunity and
fair treatment of American citizens and firms doing business in Spain.
The fourth was cessation of press attacks and other manifestations of
hostility toward the United States in Spain and, through Spanish sources,
in the Spanish-speaking countries in this hemisphere.

Further delay ensued, however, by reason of developments in the
international zone of Tangier, North Africa. Spain had moved troops into
the zone in June, 1940, and in November she took over its administration.
I thereupon sent a note to Suñer, stating we assumed there would be no
departure from the declaration Spain made in June that the occupation
was undertaken to guarantee Tangier's neutrality and normal functioning.
ing. We concluded that we could not recognize any unilateral act of the
Spanish Government affecting the Tangier zone.

The British postponed their announcement of credit arrangements
for Spain until the Tangier situation clarified. Ambassador Weddell cabled
us on December 20, urging that the United States proceed with relief
operations without waiting for the British. I replied on December 27
that any assistance by us to Spain must primarily be governed by the
Spanish Government's actions and attitude in the war since the whole
question of relief for Spain from the United States was based on our policy
of giving Great Britain all assistance possible short of war in her struggle
against aggression. I said it would be hard for us to justify in this country the use of Government funds to help Spain unless it were perfectly
clear that the Spanish Government desired to follow a course of peaceful
reconstruction.

I then referred to indications of increasing collaboration between
Spain and the Axis and of growing unfriendliness toward us, saying that
this had caused us to stop plans for food shipments to Spain. We had

subsequently revived these plans at the request of the British when the British considered themselves justified in providing Spain with credits.

Mentioning the fact that the whole question of food shipments to European countries not in the war, particularly milk shipments for French children in unoccupied France, was being urged upon us for consideration at the same time, I said we had been trying to arrive at a solution of both the French and Spanish relief problems. However, while the British attitude toward food shipments to Spain had been made quite clear, their attitude toward food shipments to unoccupied areas elsewhere had not been clarified. I pointed to the terrific criticism occasioned by our planning to send food to Spain and not planning at the same time to send milk to the children of unoccupied France. We therefore thought that our announcement of relief for Spain must follow the British announcement unless the whole prospect of shipments of food from the United States as well as the future discussion of possible credits for Spain were to be jeopardized. If, because of Spanish acts which the British considered unfriendly or calculated to aid the Axis, the British Government no longer found itself able to make foodstuffs available to Spain, it would certainly not be possible for us to justify assistance by the United States to Spain.

My associates at the State Department, with my approval, prepared a message that the President might send to Prime Minister Churchill to resolve this double problem of relief for unoccupied France and for Spain. The President approving, we sent the message to London on December 31. In it the President proposed to the Prime Minister a plan for the shipment, through the American Red Cross, of milk, vitamin concentrates, and certain other supplies for the children of unoccupied France, as well as flour and milk for the Spanish civilian population.

The message concluded: "As you know, our desire to afford relief to the civilian population in Spain is in part due to the desire expressed by your Government that we should take such action. I feel that it is of the utmost importance to make every practical effort to keep Spain out of the war or from aiding the Axis Powers. If the policy of affording relief is to be undertaken, I am convinced that it should be undertaken now without further delay. Furthermore, if Spain is given assistance and this Government is not able to send even milk for the relief of the children in unoccupied France, the distinction made between the two countries by this Government would, in my judgment, help to weaken the resistance of the Vichy Government to the pressure now being exercised upon that Government by Germany."

The Prime Minister concurred in the President's recommendations. I cabled Ambassador Weddell on January 7, 1941, that, following consultation with the President and agreement with the British Government, the American Red Cross was prepared to proceed with the shipment of flour and milk products to Spain in conjunction with shipments of foods and medicines for the children of unoccupied France.

Although the question of relief supplies was now resolved, the further question of credits remained unsettled.

Our difficulties with Spain continued until almost the end of the war. Our disappointments were many, but they were not so acute as Hitler's disappointment at Franco's refusal to enter the war. German troops were not to march through Spain against Gibraltar and across to North Africa. Franco lent aid to Hitler in many ways, but his aid would have been far greater had it not been for the parallel policy pursued by Britain and the United States.

Meantime our difficulties with Vichy France seemed suddenly and somewhat alleviated by the dramatic dismissal of Laval from the Government on December 13. Laval had been spending ever more time in Paris conferring with Hitler's representatives there. He returned to Vichy on December 13 and proudly informed Pétain that Hitler had graciously agreed to return to France the ashes of Napoleon's son, the Duke of Reichstadt, and Pétain would have to be present at the ceremonies on December 16.

This seems to have added the final straw to the bale of Pétain's suspicions of Laval. That night he forced Laval to resign, and had him arrested. Cables from our Embassy in Vichy informed us that Pétain believed Laval and the Germans were working to reduce him to a figurehead, with Laval becoming the actual ruler of France. Although pressure from Hitler soon obtained Laval's release, it did not obtain his return to the Government for some time to come.

The reaction that Laval's actions and utterances had aroused abroad, particularly in the United States, might also have had its effect. I had stated as bluntly as I could to French Ambassador Henry-Haye our opposition to everything Laval stood for, and I had cabled this conversation to Vichy for presentation to the Government there. Pétain certainly knew that, as long as Laval remained Vice Premier and Foreign Minister, the United States would look with suspicion on every act of his Government. Pétain named Pierre Étienne Flandin as the new Minister. We were convinced we had not heard the last of Laval, but at least his star had temporarily declined in magnitude.

Meantime the President had announced his appointment of Admiral William D. Leahy, Governor of Puerto Rico, to be our new Ambassador to France. The President at first had thought of General Pershing for this post. Mr. Roosevelt and I agreed that the appointee should be one who could talk to Pétain on the highest and the most personal level. Preferably he should have high military or naval rank and thus be better able to approach the Marshal. Either Pershing or Leahy could have fulfilled these requirements, but Pershing's doctors refused to let him accept. I said to the President that Leahy was ideal in that he could command Pétain's respect; he was forthright, a very straightforward and excellent man all around. The President agreed.

Leahy was, in fact, highly competent by reason of experience, intelligence, and judgment, and his services were correspondingly useful. Later I had occasion to confer with him fairly often during the war while he functioned, with exceptional ability, as head of the Joint Chiefs of Staff.

I had several conferences with Leahy before he left for his new post. Leahy asked me if he could not be given written instructions from the President laying down the basic policy he should follow as Ambassador. I agreed. I had them drafted in the Department, principally by Ray Atherton, our capable Chief of the European Division, and sent them to the President for his approval along with a note telling him of Leahy's request. They came back on December 20 with an O.K., and I handed them to Leahy.

The instructions outlined the policy we were following and would continue to follow toward the Vichy Government until our invasion of North Africa. In them the President pointed out to Leahy the unique position occupied by Pétain "both in the hearts of the French people and in the Government." Leahy should therefore cultivate the closest possible relations with him. We believed that Pétain had not been cognizant of all the acts of Laval, and the same might be true with Flandin. Leahy was therefore to bring to Pétain's attention any actions taken or contemplated in the name of France which he deemed inimical to the United States.

Leahy should also give Pétain and his Government concrete information on the American program of supporting the Allies. He should keep himself informed of any French resources being placed at the disposal of Germany beyond the requirements of the armistice. He should try to persuade Pétain and others of our Government's conviction that "a German victory would inevitably result in the dismemberment of the French Empire and the maintenance of most of France as a vassal state."

The President listed the many assurances we had received from the French Government on the score of their fleet. Leahy was to convince officials of the French Government and high officers of the Navy that "to permit the use of the French fleet or naval bases by Germany or to attain German aims, would most certainly forfeit the friendship and good will of the United States and result in the destruction of the French fleet to the irreparable injury of France."

As for relief to France, the President pointed to our efforts to forward through the Red Cross medical supplies and milk for children in unoccupied France. Nevertheless, "before the American people would be willing to have influence exerted upon the British Government to permit the shipment of food through the British blockade to France, it would be necessary that the American people be convinced beyond peradventure that such action would not in the slightest assist Germany."

Leahy was to point out our desire to maintain the status quo in the West Indies, and our desire that the naval vessels in the French Western Hemisphere possessions be immobilized and adequate guarantees given that the gold at Martinique be not used to the benefit of Germany.

Finally, the President noted sympathetically the efforts of France to maintain her authority in her North African possessions and to improve their economic status, and offered our assistance in this regard.

Leahy reached Vichy in January, 1941.

I had talked to French Ambassador Henry-Haye on December 7 concerning the antagonistic attitude of British and French officials and press toward each other. I made an attempt, as I had been doing for several months, to calm down the extreme expressions passing from time to time between British and French officials.

"We are always pleading," I said, "for self-restraint among Governments and peoples. We are striving to soften the tone of their utterances whenever possible, and this is especially true now in view of our lasting friendship for the French. I particularly object to the fact that fairly often someone makes a threat in the press against someone else."

Henry-Haye did not seem to relish my comment, and remarked that there had been all sorts of false publicity in the United States during the past six months about the purpose of the French Government.

"This may be true in part only," I rejoined, "but I think it is chiefly due to the often careless and surprising utterances of Laval. These have led our people to believe he was determined to deliver France over to Hitler and Hitlerism. Naturally much suspicion and bitterness has arisen. And we in this country feel great concern over it because of the traditional friendship between our two peoples and our deep desire to see the people of France restored to their former greatness."

Henry-Haye very earnestly and almost vociferously set forth the extreme need of foodstuffs for children in unoccupied France. He admitted, however, that the Germans had taken over immense quantities of food in occupied France. I assured him that we had been giving this project every consideration, and that British Ambassador Lothian, at our request, had emphatically urged this upon his Government. I said we hoped Britain could be prevailed upon to relax her blockade—which not long thereafter was done.

Three weeks later, on December 29, the President delivered an outstanding "fireside" address to the nation, passionately stating our national interest in a British victory. We at the State Department presented material for the speech, but it was written at the White House. "If Great Britain goes down," said the President, "the Axis Powers will control the continents of Europe, Asia, Africa, Australasia, and the high seas—and they will be in a position to bring enormous military and naval resources against this hemisphere. It is no exaggeration to say that all of us, in all the Americas, would be living at the point of a gun—a gun loaded with explosive bullets, economic as well as military."

The President assured his nation-wide audience that there was no intention on the part of any member of the Government to send an expeditionary force outside our own borders. But he called for the most strenuous rearmament and said: "We must be the great arsenal of democracy."

He closed his address on a note of optimism by saying: "I believe that the Axis powers are not going to win this war. I base that belief on the latest and best information."

This information included such items as the growing power of the Royal Air Force in fighting off German air attacks, the successful arrival in Britain of increasing quantities of American equipment, the dismissal of Laval, a resurgence of spirit in French North Africa, the growing friction between Hitler and Stalin, and the miserable showing of the Italians in their invasion of Greece.

Mussolini had thrown his troops into Greece on October 28, and they were now bogged down in the mountain fastnesses of the Greek-Albanian border. This attack came as no surprise to us. Ambassador Phillips in Rome had cabled me on October 21 a report that the invasion of Greece was planned for the early morning of October 25.

We applied the provisions of the Neutrality Act to Greece on November 15, but our sympathies were with the Greeks in their heroic struggle, and we so informed the Greek Government. The Department encouraged the formation of the Greek War Relief Association to which Americans contributed at the rate of more than $5,000,000 a year, and stimulated the American Red Cross to give quick help.

I received a cable from our Legation in Athens containing a message from King George of Greece to the President, and sent this to the President, then aboard the cruiser *Tuscaloosa*, along with the draft of a possible reply. King George said that, as his country was engaged in a hard and unequal struggle, he was deeply moved by the warm sympathy and keen interest of the United States. The President approved our reply, dated December 5, which stated: "It is the settled policy of the United States Government to extend aid to those Governments and peoples who defend themselves against aggression. I assure Your Majesty that steps are being taken to extend such aid to Greece which is defending itself so valiantly."

We made war supplies and medicines available for shipment to Greece and declared Greece eligible for Lend-Lease aid as soon as enabling legislation should be passed. The Germans, however, coming to the help of the humiliated Italians, overran Greece before our Lend-Lease help could get there. Some of it then went to equip the Greek armed forces being reorganized in the Near East and to assist Greek refugees.

On the final day of the year 1940 (our last full year at peace) which had brought us so many dangers and problems but had also seen a stupendous rising of the nation to meet its perils, I expressed to Brazilian Ambassador Carlos Martins some of the reasons I had for being optimistic that Hitler could not win in the end. Martins had just returned from Brazil, and hastened to tell me that the Brazilians were more and more recognizing the relationship of the wars abroad to their part of this Hemisphere, and the real danger involved. I expressed my satisfaction and my hope that they would continue to keep thoroughly alert.

I then emphasized some of the strong points in the President's speech of December 29 and said that South America would be the first to be affected by a German victory because she lacked adequate defenses and because she was a producer of foodstuffs and raw materials coveted by the Axis.

Martins said some people in Brazil thought Germany might win the war, others thought Britain would win, and still others thought either side could win, and therefore this generally resulted in a confuse outlook.

I then recalled to the Ambassador the President's carefully worded opinion that Great Britain could win.

"Even if there should be a stalemate," I said, "Britain and the United States would retain control of the high seas. Hitler could not rest on his oars any great length of time because he would not be supported for very long even at home unless he continued to gain new victories.

"On the other hand, all the tens of millions of conquered peoples in Europe still have the same patriotism and the same spirit of liberty they have always had. They are waiting with extreme concern and anxiety for news of movements that might give them an opportunity for liberation. They are watching for the smallest opportunity to contribute to the success of such movements by sabotage or in any way at all within their power. This might well start a successful movement that would terminate Hitler's invasion of the world."

64: Japan's Golden Chance

WHEN HITLER THREW his legions at northern and western Europe, there was no spectator more interested than Japan. Each time Europe had fallen into turmoil in the past, Japan had seized her advantage. And now, as the pillars of Western civilization seemed crumbling, her greatest opportunity of all appeared to her to be drawing nigh.

As I surveyed the chaos in Europe and tried to calculate the dangers that threatened us from that quarter, I could never for an instant relax the attention I had concentrated on the Far East. In addresses and statements in previous years, I had pointed out again and again the interrelation of the various areas of the world, emphasizing that war in one was certain to have disruptive effects in all the others. But never had this fact become so evident as now.

Less than one week after Hitler invaded Norway, Japanese Foreign Minister Arita issued a statement on April 15, 1940, contending that Japan was economically bound in an intimate relationship with the South Seas regions, especially the Netherlands East Indies. At that moment many statesmen in Europe regarded a German invasion of The Netherlands as a certainty for the very near future. If hostilities in Europe, Arita went on, were extended to The Netherlands, with repercussions in the Netherlands East Indies, "it would not only interfere with the maintenance and furtherance of the above-mentioned relations of economic interdependence and of co-existence and co-prosperity, but would also give rise to an undesirable situation from the standpoint of the peace and stability of East Asia." He therefore stated the deep concern of his Government over any development that might affect the status quo of the Netherlands East Indies.

On its face this statement was not too objectionable, provided that what Arita really had in mind was the preservation of the status quo of the East Indies. But the emphasis he placed on Japan's special and intimate economic relationship with the islands raised the question whether Japan intended to take some action in the direction of the East Indies to assure her supply of materials from that area. Some of the Japanese press at once seized on his statement to restate Japan's claims to dominance in the South Seas area.

Ambassador Bullitt cabled me from Paris the following day a suggestion from the French Foreign Office that the British, French, and American Ambassadors in Tokyo call on Arita and bring to his attention the Four-Power Treaty of 1921 in connection with which Britain, Japan, France, and the United States promised to respect the rights of The Netherlands in relation to their Pacific possessions.

I did not believe, however, that a joint *démarche* would be as effective as individual action by the separate Governments. The next day, April 17, by agreement with the President, I stated our position emphatically and publicly.

Noting the statement made by Arita, I said: "Any change in the status of the Netherlands Indies would directly affect the interests of many countries."

I pointed out the great importance of the islands in the international relationships of the whole Pacific Ocean, and in the commerce of the whole world. Extending a distance of about thirty-two hundred miles, they produced considerable portions of the world's rubber, tin, quinine, copra, and the like; and many countries, including the United States, depended substantially upon them for some of these products.

"Intervention in the domestic affairs of the Netherlands Indies or any alteration of their status quo by other than peaceful processes," I went on, "would be prejudicial to the cause of stability, peace, and security not only in the region of the Netherlands Indies but in the entire Pacific area."

After calling attention to a 1908 exchange of notes between Japan and the United States and to the Four-Power Treaty of 1921, I expressed the hope of my Government that the principles of respect by every nation for the rights of other nations, nonintervention in their domestic affairs, equality of fair treatment, and the faithful observance of treaty pledges, would be applied not only in every part of the Pacific area but also in every part of the world.

Three days later Japanese Ambassador Horinouchi called upon me and said he thought the American press had misinterpreted Arita's statement and had been more or less critical.

I interrupted him by saying that our press could well have taken the lead given by the Japanese press which seemed to imply a limitless assumption of leadership and special influence in the South Seas. "Possibly," I commented, "it was the Japanese press which misinterpreted Arita."

Horinouchi remarked that Arita and I were agreed about not disturbing the status quo of the Dutch East Indies.

"Yes," I replied, "the difference between us is that I placed the matter on a far broader ground than one primarily affecting the interests of Japan in the economics of the Dutch East Indies."

Since a portion of the Japanese press had sought to interpret Japan's interest in the Netherlands East Indies in the light of a Japanese Monroe Doctrine, I said to Horinouchi:

"I wish I could get over to you and to your Government the fact that there is no more resemblance between our Monroe Doctrine and the so-called Monroe Doctrine of Japan than there is between black and white. Our Monroe Doctrine only contemplates steps for our physical safety. Japan's Monroe Doctrine is seemingly applicable to all other purposes and all objectives, including economic, social, political, and the like. Thus far the question of a Monroe Doctrine for physical protection has not been needed or invoked by Japan."

Horinouchi sought to play down this description of Japan's application of the Monroe Doctrine, but I reminded him of how Japan had employed it in Manchuria and then, to our great surprise, in China, and now believed that it applied economically to the Dutch East Indies.

Extending the conversation to include Europe as well as Asia, I concluded: "If conditions go on as they are, Europe will go bankrupt and will not get back on its feet until after a long period. Japan and China will also find themselves bankrupt, while the United States will be greatly handicapped in its normal progress by wholesale bankruptcy in both Europe and Asia."

The question of the Netherlands East Indies now lay in abeyance for three weeks. Arita seemed taken aback by the flurry his statement had raised. Then suddenly, with Hitler's invasion of Holland, the issue rose with new vigor.

On May 10, the day of the invasion, I suggested to British Ambassador Lothian that the United States Government might approach Japan and say that the British Government had advised me it stood unequivocally for the maintenance of the status quo of the Dutch East Indies just as it did before the invasion of Holland, and that our Government likewise stood unequivocally for the maintenance of the status quo of the Indies just as we, and Japan too, had announced some days ago. I would thereupon inquire of Japan if she were disposed to continue her position as previously announced. Lothian seemed favorably disposed, and said he would convey the suggestion to his Government.

It was important to me that Britain should immediately declare a hands-off attitude on her part toward the Dutch East Indies, since the dispatch of British or other Allied troops to the Indies might furnish Japan with an excuse to send her troops there.

On the same day the Department expressed its view to Australian Minister Casey that the status quo of the Indies should be preserved, and for this reason we were anxious to see no Allied landings made there unless at the definite request of the Dutch authorities, under Dutch command, and solely for the purpose of temporary assistance to the Dutch Government.

Foreign Minister Arita called in the German, British, and French Ambassadors on May 11 and, handing them copies of his statement of April 15, said that events in Europe had accentuated the concern of the Japanese Government over the status of the Indies.

Since expressions of "concern" had been an introductory phase in the ominous pattern of many Axis military movements, I issued a further statement on May 11. Recalling that official utterances of a number of Governments, including Great Britain, Japan, and the United States, had made clear their attitude of continued respect for the status quo of the Netherlands East Indies, I repeated a phrase from my April 17 statement that alteration of the status quo in the Indies would be prejudicial to the cause of stability, peace, and security in the entire Pacific area. "Commitments and expressions of intent to respect the status quo of the Netherlands East Indies," I concluded, "cannot be too often reiterated."

During the next few days, after Britain and France suddenly sent troops to Curaçao and Aruba in the Dutch West Indies, we were acutely worried lest this furnish the Japanese an excuse to dispatch troops to the Dutch East Indies. When Japanese Ambassador Horinouchi came in to see me on May 16, I saw how keenly Japan was studying this new development to see whether it would justify similar action by her in the Dutch East Indies. He proceeded at great length to question and cross-examine me about the Netherlands West Indies.

I outlined the situation there according to the facts we had assembled. I said it was my understanding that the British and French patrols were in no sense interfering with the islands' Governments. They were recognizing the authority of those Governments during the brief time necessary to aid in safeguarding the islands.

None of my explanations seemed to satisfy Horinouchi. He continued with an increasingly minute cross-examination.

Suddenly I interrupted him emphatically by saying: "If your Government sent you to go into this almost interminable examination, I want to know now what your Government's motive was for doing so."

Before Horinouchi could resume his questioning, I said my Government would never produce friction with any other government by doing anything unlawful or unfair, and that, if friction arose, it would be due to something unlawful done by another government. I had devoted most of the past seven years, I said, to efforts at understanding and peaceful relations between our two Governments.

I then picked up several pages of press reports from Tokyo in which members of the Japanese Government discussed Japan's supposed special rights in the Netherlands East Indies, and showed them to Horinouchi. "Japan, the United States, Britain, and France have each and all repeated recently their prior commitment that each was obligated to respect the status quo in the Netherlands East Indies," I said. "I had thought that settled the matter. But, notwithstanding our efforts to maintain a thorough understanding with your Government, additional discussions of the Netherlands East Indies are continually coming out of Tokyo as if the commitment to respect the status quo had not been made. My Government strives for peace year in and year out, and it desires at all times to avoid controversy. Therefore, if controversy arises, the fault will not lie at the door of this Government."

Horinouchi said his Government had no purpose to send him to me and subject me to a long examination. Tokyo was entirely satisfied with the situation in the Dutch East Indies following the statements of the four Governments interested. He added that his Government did not intend to raise any further controversy in that connection unless the British or French should land troops in the Indies.

I said I had made appropriate inquiries of the British and French Governments and gathered the unequivocal understanding that they had no idea whatever of intervening in the Netherlands East Indies in any way.

Horinouchi, in connection with the Dutch West Indies, raised the question of the Monroe Doctrine.

"I've sought to point out to your Government, seemingly in vain," I replied, "that, under the Monroe Doctrine, your merchant ships have equal access to every harbor in the Western Hemisphere—excepting a special arrangement between the United States and Cuba. But under the policy your Government is seeking to impose in the Pacific, the United States and other countries are to be denied equality of trade and industrial opportunity in every Chinese port. And yet your Government seems to look with complacency on this conflicting situation."

Returning to the Netherlands East Indies, I said:

"It seems very surprising that, after the Japanese Government has undertaken to spread itself out over the huge Republic of China, news reports from Tokyo intimate that it will not be content unless it extends itself three thousand miles beyond and modestly takes in the great archipelago comprising the East Indies. Presumably this would be with a view to shutting out all equality of trade opportunities among nations, while Japan continues to demand equality of trade opportunities in every other part of the world."

Horinouchi, seeing that his cross-examination had aroused me, sought to smooth matters by again expressing his Government's satisfaction with the Netherlands East Indies situation. The interview eventually ended in a friendly spirit.

I remained convinced, however, that Horinouchi had come to see me on instructions from his Government to develop a pretext in connection with the Dutch West Indies on the basis of which Tokyo could act toward the Dutch East Indies. If we had not adopted a firm attitude from the very outset, and if we had not brought immediate pressure on Britain and France to explain their actions in the Dutch West Indies and deny any intention to move into the Dutch East Indies, Japan might well have made a decisive move toward the East Indies in the summer of 1940.

The Netherlands East Indies formed one topic in an important series of conversations initiated in Tokyo at the beginning of June between Foreign Minister Arita and Ambassador Grew and designed, if possible, to improve Japanese-American relations. As we saw that the stupendous German victories in western Europe would require us to channel more of our military supplies to Britain and concentrate yet more attention on Europe, the President and I wished, if at all possible, to prevent the Orient from falling further into chaos at the same time. Accordingly Arita and Grew began elaborate but quiet discussions to review all points of conflict between our two countries and seek to find some bases on which relations could be improved.

There still remained between us these points:

Japan was factually at war with China, whatever the legal situation.

She was seeking to establish the puppet Wang Ching-wei regime at Nanking, whereas we continued to recognize and to assist the Government of Chiang Kai-shek.

Japan, by means of innumerable restrictions and discriminations, was driving us out of business in the area of China she occupied. Bombing incidents involving Americans had greatly diminished but still continued. There was no doubt of Japan's intention to control all China even as she controlled all Manchuria.

Japan was obviously preparing other moves, this time southward, toward French Indo-China, British Malaya, or the Dutch East Indies, possibly even the Philippines.

Our commerce with Japan was now on a treatyless basis, the treaty of 1911 having been abrogated on January 25, 1940.

As the Arita-Grew conversations developed, Japan posed three questions on the basis of which we could reach agreement:

(1) Since the treatyless situation was "the greatest cause of uneasiness in the relations between our two countries," could not at least a commercial modus vivendi be concluded as a temporary measure?

(2) Could we not find it possible to cease aiding Chiang Kai-shek and cooperate with Japan in the "reconstruction of China"?

(3) Could we not recognize the "new conditions in East Asia"? Could not our two countries, each preserving its sphere of influence in the Pacific Ocean, contribute to the peace of the world by acting in concert?

These were unpropitious bases for any agreement. Agreeing to them would have resulted in complete Japanese conquest of China, discouragement of the Western powers having possessions in the Orient, and Japanese overlordship of the Eastern half of the world. It would have meant initialing a blueprint under which Japan, in the course of a few years, could make herself the mistress of the Orient.

Nevertheless we did not wish to say "No" bluntly and terminate the discussions. We sought to lift the conversations from the material level whereby Japan was willing to "give" us one-half of the Pacific and herself take the other and far richer half, up to a level of basic principles. If we could get Japan to agree to acknowledge and practice the principles of national sovereignty, justice, and law and order which we had stated and restated over and over, then the specific details could be worked out much more easily.

At about that time I called my three ranking Far Eastern experts—

Stanley K. Hornbeck, Maxwell M. Hamilton, and Joseph W. Ballantine—
to my office. I said to them: "I can't think of anything we have overlooked in trying to arrive at working relations with Japan. But I want
you to take a fine-tooth comb and a microscope and go back over our
relations with Japan and see if it is humanly possible to find something
additional with which to approach them and prevail upon them not to
gallop off on a wild horse."

We did make one specific proposal, relating to the Pacific Ocean possessions of the European belligerents. I cabled Grew on June 22 to propose
a formal exchange of notes with Japan guaranteeing the status quo of
such possessions. I further proposed that our two Governments should
consult should any question arise concerning the status quo of these
territories.

Arita looked on the proposal with disfavor. He raised many difficulties, the outstanding one being the absence of a commercial treaty.
Behind all his reasons, however, lay the obvious one that Japan did not
want to tie her hands through such an exchange of notes at the very moment when the door appeared to be swinging wide open to numerous
possibilities for expansion.

Japan had begun negotiations with the Netherlands East Indies Government to increase exports to Japan of strategic materials, including
rubber, to expand the number of Japanese business concerns in the Indies,
and to facilitate the entry of Japanese into the Indies. I sent instructions
to our various diplomatic missions concerned to keep us closely informed
of the conversations. The manner in which Japan was carrying on the
discussions, plus the official statements coming from Tokyo, suggested
that she might be seeking to obtain economic control or predominance in
the Netherlands Indies while avoiding the risk of direct conflict with the
Western Powers through sending troops there.

Diplomatically, our action took two forms. We encouraged the Netherlands East Indies Government, bewildered and disheartened by Hitler's
conquest of the mother country, to make no concessions that impaired
either the Indies' independence or their freedom of commerce with other
nations. And we pointed out to Tokyo that the products of the Netherlands Indies were important to the economy of many countries, including
the United States. On my instructions, Ambassador Grew gave Foreign
Minister Arita on July 11 statistics showing that 15.8 per cent of the total
foreign trade of the Netherlands East Indies in a normal year—1937—
was with the United States, compared with 11.6 per cent with Japan.

Grew emphasized that the United States therefore had an important interest in the continuance in the Netherlands East Indies, as well as in other countries, of the principle and observance of equality of trade opportunity and enterprise.

As Japan developed her conversations in Batavia, capital of the Netherlands East Indies, it was apparent that she had much more in mind than an increase in commerce. She was aiming at the economic inclusion of the islands in her "co-prosperity sphere," the result of which would be complete Japanese economic control of the Indies, with other nations doing business with them only under regulations established by Tokyo. The Indies Government agreed to increased exports of petroleum products to Japan but, gathering courage as it saw the struggle against Hitler continuing in Europe and the United States gaining strength in the Pacific, successfully resisted strong Japanese pressure to make concessions that would have undermined its independence.

Japan's pressure, however, was not limited to The Netherlands. As soon as she saw the apparently boundless extent of Hitler's victories in Western Europe, she made it clear to Britain and France that the moment had now come to accede to a series of demands. On June 17, 1940, as the French Government of Marshal Pétain was suing for an armistice, Japan demanded that the French cease shipping materials through French Indo-China to China. Within three days the French gave in and also agreed to the stationing of Japanese inspectors along the French Indo-China railroad to see to the carrying out of the agreement. France also signed an agreement with Japan recognizing that Japan had special rights in China to safeguard the security of her army and to maintain order.

At almost the same time, on June 19, British and French banks at Tientsin turned over to Japanese authorities a portion of the silver in their vaults belonging to the Chinese Government, and agreed to the circulation of Japanese occupation currency in the British and French concession areas at Tientsin.

British Ambassador Lothian, accompanied by Australian Minister Casey, came in to see me on June 27 and handed me an important *aide-mémoire* from his Government relating to the whole Far Eastern situation. The collapse of French resistance was compelling Britain to reconsider the policy she had pursued in the Far East during the last year—namely, to try to agree with Japan on minor issues such as Tientsin but to parallel the United States in rejecting Japanese plans for a "new order" in China.

The *aide-mémoire* informed me that Japan had just demanded of Britain that she withdraw her troops from Shanghai and close the Hong Kong frontier and the Burma Road to keep supplies from reaching Chiang Kai-shek.

Britain recognized that yielding to these demands would bring further demands, that French Indo-China might be occupied at any moment, and that this process would finally compromise not only the security of the British Commonwealth but also the interests of the United States. Nevertheless, having the whole responsibility for resisting the Axis in Europe, Britain felt it was impossible for her to oppose aggression in both Europe and the Far East.

Britain therefore believed there were only two courses open. One was for the United States to increase pressure on Japan either by imposing a full embargo on exports to Japan or by sending warships to Singapore, fully realizing that these steps might result in war. The second was to negotiate a full settlement with Japan.

Britain wanted to know if we would adopt the first course, saying she would cooperate. If not, would we join with Britain in making proposals for a Far Eastern settlement? Such proposals might embrace: joint assistance in bringing about a peace with China that would leave China independent; Japan to remain neutral in the European War and to respect the integrity of Occidental possessions in the Orient; the United States and Britain to give Japan financial and economic assistance; the Allied Governments to be guaranteed against reexports to enemy countries; status of foreign settlements and concessions in China to be settled after restoration of peace in Europe and China.

After I had listened to Lothian's reading of this *aide-mémoire*, I said that my Government for manifest reasons would not be in position to send the Navy as far away as Singapore, even assuming that it might desire to do so, which I was not assuming. I promised to let him know later my reaction to his second proposal.

The following day, after discussing Britain's proposals with the President and with my associates at the State Department, I called Lothian and Casey back to my office. I confirmed what I had said the day before about the fleet.

"Sending the fleet to Singapore," I remarked, "would leave the entire Atlantic seaboard, north and south, exposed to possible European threats. Our main fleet is already well out in the Pacific, near Hawaii.

"As to the embargo proposal, we have been progressively bringing economic pressure on Japan since last summer, now a year ago." I enumerated the list of steps we had taken in this regard. I also reminded them that on several occasions the British Government had suggested we not go too far in using this method lest we worsen rather than better the situation.

"We've been doing and are doing everything possible short of a serious risk of actual military hostilities," I continued, "to keep the Japanese situation stabilized. This course during the past year is the best evidence of our intentions and activities in the future."

As to Britain's second proposal—a joint effort to bring about peace between Japan and China—I outlined to Lothian and Casey the conversations between Arita and Grew in Tokyo during the past several weeks.

"Until the French surrender," I said, "the developments from these conversations were increasingly encouraging. But since the surrender the military group is moving in the direction of Hitler and Hitlerism, with all that this means in aggravating their application of the 'new order' in Eastern Asia.

"Japan's leaders feel that an extraordinary opportunity lies before them to impose their political will in the Far East. They intend to pursue that objective wherever they are not confronted with material opposition. I see little to warrant the hope that the Japanese can be weaned away from this objective by offers of intangible concessions or of future material assistance. The United States possesses nothing tangible in the Far East which it might offer and we are not willing to offer Japan concessions or assistance at the expense of third Powers."

Lothian then inquired whether there would be an objection to the British and Australians trying to bring peace between Japan and China.

"We should have no occasion to object," I replied, recalling again that we had been exploring the situation with the Japanese for some weeks. If Britain and Australia could make concessions—Casey had mentioned iron-ore privileges in Australia—and then call on Japan and China to see what concessions they were willing to make, on the theory that all the countries concerned must make some concessions if peace were to be brought about, this would be in line with our own desires.

"My Government, however, makes only two points in this connection," I continued. "First, the principles underlying Japan's application of her 'new order in East Asia' would need negativing or at least serious modifying. Second, no properties or interests of China should be offered to Japan by Britain or the United States. In other words, we do not make peace with Japan at the expense of China or of the principles I set forth in July, 1937, when Japan invaded China."

Finally I suggested that, in addition to the two courses of action proposed by Britain, there might be a third choice. "Many impairments of the rights and interests of Britain and the United States have occurred in the Far East," I said. "In combating them, however, the various Governments concerned have not resorted to either of the methods you suggest. We all have had to acquiesce in various of them. Acquiescence may be a matter of necessity. Giving of assent, however, is quite another matter. If a process of bargaining is engaged in, that which may be conceded or given by those powers now on the defensive will become irrevocable. And the future performance of Japan, in return for them, still remains problematical."

In other words, neither should we make concessions so sweeping that Japan would accept them as a basis for agreement and then bide her time to make further demands or take further steps, nor should we embark upon military or economic action so drastic as to provoke immediate war with Japan. I did not believe Japan was yet ready to make war on Britain and the United States. She would make her moves toward further expansion but, as long as Britain stoutly resisted Germany and at the same time the American fleet remained in the Pacific, she would try to nibble off what she could without engaging in a major conflict.

65: Japan Advances

THE PARALLEL LINES along which Britain and the United States had been acting toward the Far East since Japan's invasion of China in July, 1937, tended to diverge in the summer of 1940. Britain, understandably alarmed by the threat of the German hordes that had overwhelmed France, and believing that war with Japan might be imminent, sought to appease Tokyo by various concessions. We, on the other hand, increased our economic pressure on Japan, though being careful not to push the excitable military element to the verge of conflict.

British Ambassador Lothian came to me on July 12 and said that Japan would declare war on Britain at any time unless Britain should close the Burma Road, especially to arms, ammunition, and implements of war, including gasoline and trucks, going into China. He said his Government was proposing to adopt one of two alternatives. One was to close the road for three months to any larger volume of freight than existed the previous year. This period was during the rainy season when the flow of goods to China over the highway was very limited. The other was to suspend the transport of all war materials for three months, and devote this period to an effort at a general settlement of the Sino-Japanese War.

After hearing Lothian through, I commented:

"I must express my real regret and disappointment at any such course. This because it will deal China a blow in her conflict with Japan, and because my Government, engaged as it is in international commerce, has an interest in seeing all arteries and channels of trade kept open."

The British announced their agreement with Japan on July 14. They had chosen the second alternative, and they also prohibited the shipment of war materials to China from Hong Kong.

Lothian came back to me on the following day and asked me whether this Government, in connection with Britain's Burma Road agreement with Japan, would be disposed to help out by making some statement about the difficult situation the British were in and their purpose to develop some permanent understanding with Japan of a generally useful nature.

"I must promptly discourage any such idea," I replied. "I can only refer you to my other talk with you three days ago about the Burma Road."

With reference to Britain's hope of improving relations between Japan and China, I remarked:

"As I've often said to you, my Government has kept entirely separate and apart from other governments in dealing with such matters. It maintains its entire freedom of action. In taking steps of a collaborative nature it acts along parallel lines, and not jointly with other governments."

The following day I made a public statement of our reaction.

"This Government," I said, "has a legitimate interest in the keeping open of arteries of commerce in every part of the world. It considers that action such as this, if taken, and such as the action taken recently in relation to the Indo-China railway, would constitute unwarranted interpositions of obstacles to world trade."

My statement drew keen appreciation from Chungking, but it created a flurry in London. When Lothian saw me again on July 18, I remarked to him that, in recording our opposition to the closing of the Burma Road at the instance of Japan, I did not quite expect a furor in Great Britain. "Our chief purpose," I said, "was, of course, to direct attention to the lawless conduct of Japan." Lothian seemed perfectly satisfied.

About a fortnight later Britain announced she was withdrawing her troops from Shanghai. Local authorities agreed that American troops should take over one sector of the vacated area and Japanese troops the other; but, the Japanese disagreeing, negotiations on the subject began in Tokyo.

On our part the Administration now had at hand a new weapon with which to bring economic pressure on Japan—an Act of Congress approved by the President July 2, 1940, authorizing him to prohibit or curtail the export of military equipment or munitions, or parts thereof, or machinery or materials used in making such products. Hitherto we had relied on moral embargoes to accomplish our purpose—namely, to bring home to Japan our indignation at her indiscriminate bombing of Chinese cities and to avoid adding unduly to Japan's military strength. Now this Act of Congress, primarily designed to keep strategic materials and tools in the United States to increase our own defense, gave us an additional instrument for use in our relations with Japan.

The President issued a proclamation on the same day he approved the Act, making the export of a long list of raw materials and machine tools subject to export licenses to be issued by the Secretary of State. The export of these items to the belligerents was already governed by the cash-and-carry provisions of the Neutrality Act, but there were no restrictions regarding Japan with the exception of the moral embargoes, which were confined to comparatively few articles. At the same time the President set up a new office, that of the Administrator of Export Control, to administer the provisions of the Act of Congress under his direction as Commander-in-Chief of the Army and Navy. He appointed Lieutenant Colonel Russell L. Maxwell, United States Army, to this post.

With this appointment the President ended a long struggle initiated by Secretary of the Treasury Morgenthau to wrest from the State Department control over exports and imports of arms, ammunition, and implements of war. The struggle had been going on for about three years, and at times had led to much confusion. Morgenthau's determination to bring the Office of Arms and Munitions Control under his Department stemmed from the period of the Spanish Civil War when he would have liked to ship military equipment to the Spanish loyalists. Morgenthau himself had a personal leaning toward getting into foreign relations, and we not infrequently found him engaging in discussions with ambassadors or carrying on correspondence with statesmen of other countries, properly the function of the State Department. Morgenthau's personal relations with the President being very close, he occasionally induced the President to grant him jurisdiction which infringed on that of the State, War, or Navy Departments.

Neither the United States' effort to bring more economic pressure upon Japan nor Britain's attempt to conciliate her availed to prevent new and alarming developments in Tokyo. The day after the Havana Conference opened, the Government of Premier Admiral Mitsumasa Yonai fell, on July 22, and was succeeded by that of Prince Fumimaro Konoye. The new Foreign Minister was Yosuke Matsuoka.

The change was certainly not for the better so far as Japanese-American relations were concerned. Konoye, though regarded by some as leaning toward the liberal or civilian as opposed to the military sect, had been Premier at the time of the Japanese invasion of China in July, 1937. He believed in one-party government and seemed likely to play along with the militarists' desires for yet closer rapport with the European Axis. As for Matsuoka, I had long considered him to be as crooked as a basket of fishhooks. He had led the Japanese delegation out of the League of Nations in 1933. He was committed, by statements and actions, to the support of an aggressive imperialism.

We had not long to wait for evidence of the intentions of the new Government. Early in August informal reports came in of new demands by Japan on French Indo-China, and the Department called these to the attention of the Japanese Foreign Office, through Ambassador Grew, on August 7. I instructed our Embassy in Vichy on August 26 to state to Marshal Pétain's Foreign Office that we hesitated to believe that the French Government actually had made the concessions to the Japanese which were being reported to us. The making of such concessions, I said, would react unfavorably on American public opinion.

The French Foreign Office replied that no agreement had yet been reached with Japan, that Japan had not demanded the use of military bases but solely the passage of Japanese military forces through Indo-China, and that the French Government had taken the position there should be no military occupation of their colony.

At the beginning of September, reports from several of our diplomatic missions came to us that Japan had presented an ultimatum to the French Indo-Chinese authorities, demanding that Japanese troops be permitted to pass through French Indo-China into China and to use certain of the colony's ports and air bases.

I therefore cabled Ambassador Grew in Tokyo on September 3 to call these reports to the attention of the Japanese Foreign Minister and to point out the unfortunate effect they, if proven correct, would have on American public opinion from the point of view of Japanese-American relations. The Japanese Foreign Office admitted to Grew that their military forces did intend to pass through French Indo-China, but said there would be no permanent occupation.

The following day I made a public statement, recalling that several Governments, including ours and the Japanese, had recently expressed their desire that the status quo be preserved in the Pacific, with special reference to the Netherlands East Indies and French Indo-China. Saying we were reluctant to believe the reports that Japanese military authorities had delivered an ultimatum to French Indo-China, I added: "The situation and the subject to which these reports relate is, however, a matter to which this Government attaches importance, and it stands to reason that, should events prove these reports to have been well founded, the effect upon public opinion in the United States would be unfortunate."

The very next day, however, the Vichy Foreign Office informed us that on August 30 Japan and France had signed an agreement whereby France not only gave Japan right of passage through French Indo-China and the use of bases in the colony, but recognized the predominant interest of Japan in the Far East in both the economic and the political domain.

The new French Ambassador, Henry-Haye, came to see me on September 11 to discuss this subject.

"The French Government," I commented, "cannot imagine our surprise and disappointment when it took this step without any notice whatever to us."

The Vichy Foreign Office informed us that Japan had given assurances that the stationing of Japanese troops in Indo-China would be merely temporary, and suggested we seek the same assurances from Japan. I thereupon cabled our Embassy at Vichy on September 11 to say to the Foreign Minister that we were very surprised to learn of the extent of the French assent to the Japanese demands. I pointed out that there was little warrant for entering into agreements which assented to a derogation of principles. We deprecated France's recognition of Japan's claim to a preponderance of interests and a preferred economic position in Indo-China and of Japan's violation of French and other rights and interests. As for asking Japan for assurances similar to those given to France, I said we perceived no reason to associate ourselves with an assent to an unlawful procedure by asking for such assurances. Moreover, what value could anyone give such assurances?

On the following night I received a long cable from Grew in Tokyo in which he argued that the time had come to discontinue "restraint and patience" toward Japan and adopt a policy of firmness. He narrated that the military and some other elements in Japan saw in the present world situation a "golden opportunity" to carry their dreams of expansion into effect, and that they had discounted effective opposition on our part. Their initial belief in a quick German victory had now changed, however, and they saw Britain and the United States drawing closer together in mutual defense, as evidenced by the destroyers-bases exchange.

Grew believed, as did the President and I, that we should strive to preserve the status quo in the Pacific while bending every effort to assist Great Britain. He thought this could not be done merely by expressing disapproval of Japan's actions, but we must follow a policy of firmness. If by firmness we could preserve the status quo in the Pacific until and if Britain won in Europe, the present opportunist policy in Japan could not keep the upper hand, and the time might then come for a readjustment of the whole problem of the Pacific on a basis of lasting benefit to both Japan and America.

Actually, the policy followed by the President and me had long since traveled well beyond the use of words to express disapproval of Japan's actions. The abrogation of the 1911 commercial treaty, the imposition of moral embargoes, followed by extensive legal embargoes, a vast program of rearmament, the maintenance of the fleet at Pearl Harbor, and various forms of assistance to China, were all part of our policy of firmness.

The Japanese Army's original intentions toward French Indo-China had involved a wholesale invasion of the colony. Grew indicated in his cable that the Japanese Government had been able, at least temporarily, to restrain the military from these plans, and attributed this "degree of caution" at least partly to the position of the United States.

A good indication of the attitude of the Konoye Government toward us came two days later when the Foreign Office handed Grew a reply to the representations we had made concerning French Indo-China on August 7. The reply was written in pencil. It admitted that negotiations had been carried on with the French Indo-Chinese authorities, but gave no details. It asserted that Japan had been making efforts not to bring about undesirable changes in the status quo in the Pacific, in so far as the status quo did not interfere with "the firm preservation of a minimum right to existence." The reply then said:

"Despite the fact that in the Western Hemisphere epoch-making changes are actually being made in the status quo, Japan has as yet expressed no opinion for or against those changes. It has to be pointed out that intrusion by the United States in an area which is so remote from that country as in this case brings about the same effect upon Japan's public opinion as the meddlesome attitude of a third country toward the policy of the United States concerning third-Power territories in the Western Hemisphere would bring about upon public opinion in the United States."

It was impossible not to perceive the obvious tone of insult in this communication. I replied to the note in a statement Grew handed Foreign Minister Matsuoka on September 20. We contended that the status quo of a third country was seriously affected when a nation, in order to attack another nation, insisted on the right to use the third country's airports and to send troops through its territory. "The American Government," I said, "urges upon all governments the employment of peaceful means only in their relations with all other governments and with all other regions." And this attitude "toward the unwarranted use of pressure in international relations is global."

At the same time, Grew, on our instructions, protested against a further Japanese ultimatum to the effect that Japan would invade Indo-China on September 22 unless France accepted Japan's demands for the occupation of Hanoï, Haiphong, and five airports.

Four days prior to this protest I had a basic discussion of the Indo-Chinese situation with British Ambassador Lothian and Australian Minister Casey. Lothian stressed the need for some steps that would deter Japan from occupying Indo-China, and indicated that the British Government was undertaking to render some substantial military aid to the Indo-Chinese Government.

I commented that there were real difficulties in attempting to aid provinces to resist Japan seriously by military efforts when the mother countries, as in the case of France, The Netherlands, and even Great Britain herself, were known not to be in position to render any material aid to their dependencies. In these circumstances, I said, my Government had gone almost to the limit in resisting Japanese aggression step by step without running the very serious danger of a military clash. We had encouraged countries like Indo-China, just as we did the British, to delay and parley and hold out to the last minute against Japanese demands. In all probability, I ventured, Japan would not dare make a military attack at this time.

I added that my Government expected to continue its protests and opposition to Japanese aggression. To this end we planned to render further financial aid to China and to impose more and more reprisals of a commercial and economic nature on Japan.

I next stated a point that governed the reasoning of the President and myself toward the Far East until the attack at Pearl Harbor. "It will not be wise," I said, "even from the British standpoint, for two wars to be raging at the same time, one in the East and the other in the West. If this country should enter any war, this would immediately result in greatly cutting off military supplies to Great Britain which she can ill afford to do without. Furthermore, most of us are of the opinion that the fate of both the Eastern and Western worlds will be tremendously affected by the success or failure of the resistance of Great Britain to the threatened or attempted German invasion of the British Isles."

We discussed the possibility of holding conferences in regard to bases and a more or less unified defense in the Pacific from Singapore to Australia and then toward the United States. "Japan," I remarked, "is assuming that all these steps are probable on short notice, regardless of whether they have actually been consummated." I let the matter rest there for the present.

The Vichy Government succumbed to Japanese pressure. They handed us the text of their agreement on September 22, and on the following day issued a statement alleging that the United States Government had approved their agreement of August 30 with Japan.

Accordingly, on the same day, September 23, I made a public denial that our Government had at any time or in any way approved the French concessions to Japan. I said it seemed obvious that the status quo in Indo-China was being upset and that this was being achieved under duress. "The position of the United States in disapproval and in deprecation of such procedures," I concluded, "has repeatedly been stated."

A more concrete response than words came two days later when the Administration announced the loan of $25,000,000 to China, to be liquidated through the sale of tungsten. And, on the following day, the President brought the export of iron and steel scrap under the licensing system, effective October 16, with licenses to be issued only for shipments to countries in the Western Hemisphere and Great Britain.

In the following months the Vichy Government made repeated attempts to purchase airplanes and munitions in the United States for Indo-China. We on our part saw no reason to sell planes to Vichy when at that very moment about one hundred American planes originally destined for France were rusting away at Martinique. I so informed the Pétain Government, offering to get British clearance for the planes at Martinique to go to Indo-China. Vichy replied that the German Armistice Commission would not permit it, but on October 14 the French Foreign Office informed our Embassy at Vichy that the Germans were willing for arms from the United States to go to Indo-China. The French Foreign Office thought this was because the Germans did not wish to see complete Japanese domination in Asia, but another reason might well have been that Hitler wished to see us embroiled with Japan and therefore less able to aid Britain. With Japan in control of key points in Indo-China, we were reluctant to sell any additional military equipment to Indo-China, knowing full well that it would shortly fall into Japanese hands.

Even so, the Vichy Government appreciated the fact that our policy in the Orient was preventing further Japanese encroachments. On November 7 Jean Chauvel, Chief of the Far Eastern Section of the French

Foreign Office, stated to our Chargé in Vichy, H. Freeman Matthews, that Japan had made preparations for a large-scale invasion of Indo-China which would proceed on through to Malaya to capture Singapore, but that these plans had been abandoned as a result of our strong attitude. Even Pierre Laval remarked to our new Chargé, Robert D. Murphy, on December 9, that he was aware that the United States was the bulwark that was giving protection to French Indo-China against Japan.

I instructed Murphy on December 16 to suggest informally to Chauvel that steps be taken with the appropriate German authorities to request that a restraining influence be exerted by Germany upon the Japanese Government to preserve French interests in the Orient. The Germans could not refuse without thereby showing that they had abandoned France to Japan, nor could they comply without irritating Japan.

We were, of course, interested to know what role the German Government had played in the negotiations between Vichy and Tokyo. It was obvious that our pressure at Vichy was being countered by German pressure and that the latter was supreme in view of the military stranglehold the Nazis maintained over the Pétain Government. On September 20 French Ambassador Henry-Haye gave us his opinion that Hitler, in the first flush of his conquest of France, had hoped to take over France's colonial possessions in the Far East and objected strongly to any indication from Japan that Japan herself would like to absorb them. Later, however, as it became apparent that Britain would not fall at once, Hitler wanted the Japanese to immobilize our Navy in the Pacific; in return for an agreement by Japan to pursue a policy that would bring this about, he was obliged to give Japan the go-ahead signal to occupy French, Dutch, and British possessions in the Pacific.

We had known for some time of discussions going on among Tokyo, Berlin, and Rome to implement their Anti-Comintern Pact with a military alliance. These discussions came to a head a few days after Vichy bowed to Tokyo, when, on September 27, 1940, the Axis capitals announced the signing of their tripartite alliance. Japan had held off her signature until German pressure succeeded in forcing the Vichy Government to accede to Tokyo's demands.

The tripartite pact, of course, was aimed at the United States. Article 3 provided that the three powers would assist one another with all political, economic, and military means when one of the three was attacked by a power at present not involved in the European War or in the Sino-Japanese conflict. Under the tripartite pact Japan recognized and respected the leadership of Germany and Italy in establishing a "new order" in Europe, and Germany and Italy did likewise for Japan in "Greater East Asia."

After discussing the pact with the President, I issued a public statement of our reaction on the same day the treaty was announced. "The reported agreement of alliance," I said, "does not, in the view of the Government of the United States, substantially alter a situation which has existed for several years. Announcement of the alliance merely makes clear to all a relationship which has long existed in effect and to which this Government has repeatedly called attention. That such an agreement has been in process of conclusion has been well known for some time, and that fact has been fully taken into account by the Government of the United States in the determining of this country's policies."

Three days later I said to British Ambassador Lothian that the alliance had come about primarily because of Hitler's effort to divert attention from his failure to invade Great Britain. Hitler had wished to preserve his prestige by a sensational announcement of something that already existed.

"As an ordinary precaution," I commented, "Japan has had to assume that, whether or not the United States and Great Britain have express agreements in regard to naval and air bases across the Pacific to and including Singapore, the special relations between our two countries are such that overnight we could easily establish cooperative relations for the mutual use of all these bases. Therefore, the relations among Germany, Italy, and Japan, each country having a common objective to conquer certain areas of the world and each pursuing identical policies of force, devastation, and seizure, have been on a basis of complete understanding and of mutual cooperation during recent years. The recent announcement was simply part and parcel of this chain of related events."

Lothian said this coincided with his view and that of his Government.

I then said I would like to address an inquiry to the Ambassador as to whether and to what extent the British and Dutch Governments, especially in the South Pacific area, had conferred on pooling their defense forces in case of threatened danger. If so, what were the facts as to the size of their pooled forces and what size fleet would be necessary to overcome them and capture the territories they defended? Lothian promised to take this up with his Government.

With the Axis tripartite pact still revolving in my mind, I went to the

White House on Saturday October 5, to take up with the President a number of urgent matters. Bringing up the Axis alliance, I suggested to Mr. Roosevelt that he answer the challenge by announcing a further stepping up of the program of preparedness and national defense, including the urgently needed aid to Britain. This program, I said, should include four points. The first was a further increase in the Army. The second was the designation of some person with the authority and ability to step up the production of war planes. I cited the reported success of Lord Beaverbrook in Britain, who was understood to have increased production 20 to 30 per cent above what was supposed to be Britain's maximum possible production. All kinds of Gordian knots and red tape should be slashed toward this end. The third was that we should secure the services of some man who filled the description of what I called "the ablest two-fisted slave-driving person in the country" as director of war production in all other lines. This man should be instructed to let nothing stand in the way of bringing all production up to 100 per cent, and of shortening the time of deliveries as part of this 100 per cent efficiency. I urged that Britain be supplied with the very maximum of airplanes and other most needed supplies by March rather than by June. The fourth point was that, while I opposed the centralization of power as much as any living person, the President should not hesitate to assume enough emergency powers under existing statutes as would make these achievements possible.

I had, in fact, become considerably wrought up over what I thought was insufficient activity in our defense program. Since the fall of France we had been making noteworthy progress, but it did not seem to be as all out as was necessary.

Mr. Roosevelt seemed in hearty agreement with my suggestions. After leaving his office I dictated a memorandum of our conversation so as to circulate my suggestions more widely. I then got hold of Secretaries Stimson and Knox and one or two others, and emphasized to them the ideas I had expressed to the President. Stimson immediately invited me to luncheon and got together a few Government production experts to listen to my views.

In succeeding weeks, and especially after the election, President Roosevelt took positive steps along the lines of several of my suggestions. On December 20 he appointed a four-man council, known as the Office of Production Management for Defense, with William S. Knudsen as Director.

Britain was now moving back to her policy of parallel action with the United States in the Far East. She had seen that Japan was not using the period of three months during which the Burma Road was closed to negotiate peace with China, but on the contrary was aiming more directly at the heart of China by sending troops through French Indo-China. Britain's and France's attitude had not appeased Japan but had rendered her yet more demanding.

As early as August 26 Ambassador Lothian spoke to me about the possible reopening of the Burma Road when the three months period expired on October 15. On September 5 he asked me to what extent my Government might cooperate in discouraging or deterring Japan from blocking the reopening. His suggestion was that we might again protest against the closing of an international commercial highway. Finally, on September 30, he said his Government would be interested to know our views about a British announcement now to the effect that the Burma Road would be reopened on October 17.

I replied that, although I could not express an opinion as to the effect an advance British announcement would have, I doubted if it would change any of Japan's plans except that the Japanese might say something or do something they had already decided to say or do.

As for my own Government, I said we had pursued a definite and somewhat progressive line of acts and utterances in resisting Japanese aggression and treaty violations during recent years. I added that I would not undertake to predict, much less to make commitments, as to how fast and how far my Government would go in following up our various acts and utterances. But I emphasized this:

"The special desire of this Government is to see Great Britain succeed in the war. Our acts and utterances with respect to the Pacific area will be more or less affected as to time and extent by the question of what course will most effectively and legitimately aid Great Britain in winning the war."

As Lothian was leaving my office he said that I knew, of course, that Singapore was available for use by our fleet at any time. I merely said I had already heard a report to this effect.

Britain reopened the Burma Road beginning October 18.

As the President and I, in various discussions following the announcement of the Axis alliance, developed American policy in the Far East, we fixed on these points:

(1) Avoid an open struggle in the Pacific so as to bend all efforts to aiding Britain and strengthening ourselves.

(2) Maintain as to Japan all our rights and principles, continue our economic pressure, and aid China, but not push Japan to the point where her military elements would demand war.

(3) Let Japan realize that we were strong in the Pacific, and gaining in general strength.

(4) Never let her gain the impression that we would not use our strength, if required, but at the same time refrain from quarreling with her and leave the door open for discussion and agreement, always in conformity with our basic principles.

In talking to my associates in the Department about our conversations with Japan, I used to remind them of a man I knew in Tennessee who had agreed to talk things over with a highwayman. Having a very chivalrous nature, he unstrapped two revolvers that he had attached to his belt and laid them on a stump seventy-five yards from the meeting place, proceeding unarmed to the interview. "I leave it to you," I commented, "to guess how that conversation ended."

With this analogy in mind, I held several conversations with Lothian and Australian Minister Casey at the beginning of October to lay the basis for exchanges of information among the United States, Britain, Australia, New Zealand, and the Dutch East Indies concerning the forces available in the Far East to resist a Japanese attack.

Japanese Ambassador Horinouchi handed me on October 8 a written protest against our having placed iron and steel scrap under the licensing system. This stated that, if our economic restrictions against Japan continued and expanded, future relations between the two countries would be "unpredictable."

I said to Horinouchi that this Government at all times had to determine for itself such internal questions as those material to our national defense program. It would be impossible for us when seriously engaged in a program of national defense to allow every other nation to come in and pass upon the question of our need for given commodities. I reminded the Ambassador that for some years the Administration had been criticized for not imposing numerous embargoes.

"It is really amazing," I continued, "for the Government of Japan, which has been violating in the most aggravating manner valuable American rights and interests throughout most of China, to question the fullest privilege of this Government from every standpoint to impose the proposed iron and steel scrap embargo. It is still more amazing for Japan to call it an unfriendly act in view of the conduct of the Japanese Government in disregarding all law, treaty obligations, and other rights and privileges and the safety of Americans while it proceeds at the same time to seize ever more territory by force."

The Government of Japan, I said to Horinouchi, had the least occasion of all the countries with which I had had to deal during the last eight years to accuse the United States of an unfriendly act. "Apparently," I concluded, "your Government entertains the theory that all other nations must acquiesce cheerfully in all injuries inflicted upon their citizens by the Japanese policy of force and conquest, unless they are to run the risk of being guilty of an unfriendly act."

Horinouchi repeated a remark with which he had begun our conversation; namely, that he regretted very much the serious differences between our two countries. He said he naturally hoped that trouble might yet be avoided since strife between us would be extremely tragic for both alike.

"It would be extremely unfortunate for such an occurrence to take place," I replied. "But my Government has been patient, extremely patient. You yourself can bear witness to the long, earnest efforts you and I have made, and that I made prior to your coming here, to promote and preserve friendly, satisfactory relations with Japan."

I said bluntly to the Ambassador that the men now controlling the external policies of Japan were bent on the conquest by force of all worthwhile territory in the South Pacific. "And we and all other nations are expected," I remarked, "to sit perfectly quiet and be cheerful and agreeable, but static, while most of Asia is 'Manchuriaized.' Satisfactory relations between Asia and outside nations would then become impossible, and lower levels of existence would be the ultimate lot of the people of most of Asia. The least taking of issue with Japan over these questions would be called an unfriendly act." And here I called the Ambassador's attention to a statement by Premier Konoye to the press that it would be the occasion for war so far as Japan was concerned. "Of course, if any one country sufficiently desires trouble it can always find occasion to start it. It is not left to the other country to participate in that decision."

Horinouchi repeated the old line of talk about how fair Japan proposed to be to foreign nations within its conquered territory.

"It is unheard of," I rejoined, "for one country engaged in seizing another country to insist that a third nation is guilty of an unfriendly act if it does not cheerfully provide the necessary implements of war to aid the aggressor nation in carrying out its invasion. Two nations, one in Europe and one in Asia, are undertaking to subjugate their respective areas of the world and to place them on an international order and social basis resembling that of seven hundred and fifty years ago. In the face of this growing world movement, peaceful nations are denounced and threatened if they dare to engage in any lawful acts or utterances in opposition to such movements of world conquest."

At almost the hour of my talk with Horinouchi, we took action that strikingly called to Tokyo's attention the seriousness with which we regarded the tension existing in the Orient. At the State Department we announced that we had sent instructions to our consuls in the Orient to advise Americans to withdraw immediately from that area, including Japan, China, Indo-China, and Manchuria, and that we had sent three passenger liners to the Orient to hasten their evacuation. Since this looked to the Japanese Foreign Office as if we were preparing for the worst of eventualities in the Far East, that Government paused temporarily in its headlong course.

When Australian Minister Casey called on me on November 12 to ask whether we intended sending a good-will naval mission to Australia, I said we had other plans in mind than a good-will mission. I informed him we had assembled at Manila all our warships in the Far East (the Asiatic Fleet), including a number of submarines, as well as planes. I inquired of Casey whether his Government would not consider it very important to send further planes to Singapore, and I more than once emphasized the importance of a substantial number of planes being stationed there.

British Ambassador Lothian went to London on leave and, following his return to Washington, came to see me on November 23 and said he believed the Japanese were likely soon to attack Singapore. He gave me the opinion of some naval experts that, if the American Navy should largely make its base at Singapore, this would safeguard the entire situation in the Orient. He expressed the view that our fleet, if stationed at Singapore, could reach Japan much sooner than a Japanese fleet could reach the South Pacific, and therefore there would be no risk involved. I merely remarked that this was a matter for experts to pass upon.

Throughout the remainder of the year, our attitude toward Japan became one of increasing firmness. Our export controls were extended. When Tokyo, after a year of wavering, finally announced the establishment of the puppet Chinese Government of Wang Ching-wei at Nanking on November 30, our Export-Import Bank on the same day extended a new credit of $50,000,000 to the National Government at Chungking to stabilize Chinese currency.

Prior to his departure on a Caribbean inspection cruise, the President had signed the proclamation and regulations placing restrictions on the export of iron and steel products. He and I had agreed that these should be issued some days after the announcement of the loan to China and the sending of additional naval vessels to Manila, but that I would check again with him before releasing them through the White House.

I wirelessed the President on December 9, saying I believed the time had come to issue the proclamation and regulations. I pointed out that while this meant increased irritation in Japan as a result of the way the news would be handled by the extreme elements in that country, Japan would still be permitted to obtain quantities of iron and steel products approximating her usual prewar imports from the United States. The main effect would be to shut off immense increases which we knew Japan was about to purchase.

The President approving, the announcement was made the following day. Japan duly protested.

I also wirelessed the President again concerning the public announcement that he and the Navy Department had had in mind about the sending of reinforcements to the Philippines. I said to the President that we at the Department felt that a formal announcement giving numbers and types of ships would be susceptible of misconstruction both in Japan and in some quarters here. It might be misrepresented as a deliberate waving of a big stick and might easily be sensationalized by the press.

The Japanese higher authorities, I pointed out, would obtain knowledge of our moves by their own methods. By letting the public obtain information piecemeal and gradually, there would be public knowledge of the moves we made, but several possible varieties of agitation might be avoided. Doing it quietly would facilitate the present movement of forces and possible similar operations in the future. We had already convinced the Navy Department of the wisdom of this course. The President agreed.

This was in line with my theory that, in dealing with lawless governments, it was important to lead them to do a bit of guessing, without making any threats. I believed in letting them guess as to when and in what set of circumstances we would fight. While Japan continued to guess, we continued to get ready for anything she might do.

Partly or largely as a result of our firm policy, the Japanese Government decided to wait awhile before proceeding further. Despite the threats emanating from Tokyo that reopening of the Burma Road would bring the European War to the Orient, Japan did nothing when the road resumed traffic. Having occupied a few bases in French Indo-China and dispatched troops into China through the French colony, she refrained from the full-scale military occupation that the Nipponese Army had had in mind. She tried to obtain sweeping economic concessions in the Netherlands East Indies, but postponed any project of occupying them militarily.

If our policy had shown any signs of weakness or wavering, Japan would not have hesitated to take over all Indo-China and the Netherlands Indies, and perhaps Malaya as well.

Our Far Eastern policy in the months following the fall of France gave us another year and a half in which to get ready, while denying to Japan many of the materials needed for a greater military machine. It enabled us to extend invaluable help to Britain so that, when Pearl Harbor came, Britain was stronger than in the summer of 1940.

Had war broken out in the Far East in the summer of 1940, our assistance to Britain might have dwindled rather than increased, our aid to Russia in 1941 would have been hampered, and we ourselves would have faced the Axis alliance relatively much less prepared than when the ordeal of fire burst upon us. As our last year of peace ended, we still had nearly one full year before us in which to gird for the battle if our opponents chose the hazard.